East Asia in a New Legal Landscape:

FTAs and Dispute Settlement

SNUAC SERIES in Asian Studies ❽

East Asia in a New Legal Landscape:
FTAs and Dispute Settlement

First edition published by Seoul National University Press in 2022

Seoul National University Press
1 Gwanak-ro, Gwanak-gu, Seoul 08826, Republic of Korea
Tel: +82-2-880-5252
Fax: +82-2-889-0785
Homepage: http://www.snupress.com
Facebook: @snupress1947
Instagram: @snupress
E-mail: snubook@snu.ac.kr

ISBN 978-89-521-2993-2 (94360)
ISBN 978-89-521-1125-8 (set)

East Asia in a New Legal Landscape:

FTAs and Dispute Settlement

Jaemin Lee

Seoul National University Press

Contents

Chapter IV

Chapter V

Chapter VI

Chapter VII

Preface

The global trading regime is in a chaotic situation in 2020. The US-China confrontation has consumed the entire global community and the spread of the COVID-19 has effectively suspended much of the global trade. The faltering World Trade Organization (WTO) continues to lose its relevance as the architect and coordinator of the multilateralism. States, embarrassed and embittered, are struggling to survive the unprecedented threats from many different fronts. States are currently engaged in discussions to reform the WTO and re-formulate the global trading regime.

East Asia is directly exposed to the latest development in the global trading regime. As China, Japan and Korea take up a significant portion of the global trade and as China itself is the party in the US-China dispute, the current development is causing significant impact on these three countries. Any change to the existing trading regime stands to carry enormous consequences to the three countries. In that regard, the three states are currently standing at a doorstep for a new era — for better or worse — of the global trading regime. Needless to say, the three states' situations are all different and their respective challenges are all distinct. And yet, there are also commonalities among the three states' situations and challenges with respect to their participation in the global trading regime.

One specific area that falls into such a category is the dispute settlement proceedings contained in trade agreements of the three countries. While dispute settlement proceedings constitute a major portion of their trade agreements and the three countries are actively participating in these proceedings one way or another, few studies have been undertaken so far on this particular topic. Studies on dispute settlement proceedings have usually addressed the proceedings of the WTO or Free Trade Agreements (FTAs) in general, but not on those adopted and implemented by the three coutries specifically.

This book covers this issue. It aims to discuss various aspects of dispute settlement mechanisms contained in the FTAs concluded by the three East Asian countries. The dispute settlement proceedings contained in the three countries' FTAs largely follow, in their form, the basic features of such proceedings found in FTAs concluded in other parts of the world such as those concluded by the United States and the European Union. But, at the same time, specific contents and operating mechanisms of these East Asian countries' FTAs show distinctiveness from those in other regions. Likewise, the practice surrounding the operation of dispute settlement proceedings in East Asian FTAs also indicate their own share of uniqueness.

These characteristics embedded and found in the East Asian FTAs' dispute settlement proceedings sometimes exert positive impact on the implementation of the FTA obligations. But they sometimes invite negative consequences on the implementation of the obligations as well. Over the years, many FTAs have been negotiated and concluded in East Asia, but few attempts have been made to ascertain the uniqueness of East Asian FTAs' dispute settlement proceedings including both their strengths and weaknesses. Each individual FTA has been simply negotiated and concluded and it has been then presented for implementation. Generally speaking, this trend is being observed in all three countries.

An individualized and fragmented approach of the three countries' FTAs in terms of dispute settlement proceedings has arguably failed to offer a bird's-eye view analysis of those proceedings of various FTAs in a comparative and horizontal manner, so as to help their governments understand why and how those proceedings in the their FTAs are the same with and at the same time different from FTAs of other countries.

This realization will be able to help the three countries design and introduce dispute settlement proceedings for their bilateral or trilateral trade agreements, which suit their unique characteristics and circumstances. It may also help states in other regions contemplate their own, custom-tailored dispute settlement proceedings in their own FTAs, breaking away from copying the mechanisms that are simply presented to them during FTA negotiations. If one believes that the most important objective of any dispute settlement mechanism is to ensure effective and prompt resolution of a dispute, such a mechanism should be formulated to reflect the unique characteristics of the countries concerned.

The purpose of this book is to provide an overview and then identify the unique characteristics of dispute settlement mechanisms of the FTAs concluded by the three East Asian countries. It attempts to elicit unique elements contained in these mechanisms, and explain the practical consequences of these unique elements on actual dispute settlement settings. It also attempts to provide analyses of how and in what respects the East Asian FTAs' dispute settlement proceedings are distinct from those of other regions, notably the US and the EU. Finally, based on these discussions, this research will provide a new framework to be adopted in dispute settlement mechanisms of prospective East Asian countries' FTAs — either their new FTAs with other countries or their FTAs between or among themsevles. It is hoped that such discussions will be able to facilitate the development of "East Asia-tailored" FTAs and dispute settlement mechanisms as opposed to mere repetition of those adopted by other countries in other regions.

With this in mind, this book discusses key principles and jurisprudence that are invoked and applied as regards dispute settlement proceedings of the WTO, FTAs, and Investor-State Dispute Settlement (ISDS). To the extent that issues of FTAs are also examined by domestic courts of the East Asian countries, relevant proceedings and jurisprudence of these domestic courts are discussed from time to time.

Most importantly, this book purports to offer basic elements of a prospective framework for dispute settlement proceedings of FTAs in East Asia, tailored to address specific cultural backgrounds, historical underpinnings, and diplomatic surroundings in this region. The three countries have also seen the rise of disputes among themselves in many different sectors. The current system of dispute settlement have been largely futile when it comes to disputes between or among the three countries. Bearing this in mind, the new framework for future East Asian FTAs should focus on exploring practical and realistic mechanisms to resolve disputes. Future FTAs should explore both binding and non-binding dispute settlement proceedings and more easily accessible ones. East Asia provides a viable test-bed for these new mechanisms. If successful, these experiments can be transplanted to other countries and regions as well.

Finally, while the discussion in this book is focused on trade and investment disputes, implications from the discussion could be equally applied to other areas of dispute settlement under other treaties. East Asia has been faced with a series disputes among themselves and with other neighboring countries spanning over diplomatic, territorial and historical issues. What has been elicited from this book may apply, *mutatis mutandis*, to these other non-trade, non-investment areas so as to find the best and most suitable dispute settlement mechanism in the region and other parts of the world.

I would like to thank the Seoul National University Asia Center for its generous support (2015-2017) for the research and publication of this book. Ms. Hyein Kim, Who is a Ph.D. candidate at Seoul National University School of Law, has assisted me in conducting research and writing this book. I stand grateful to her for the thorough review and research.

Introduction

This book aims to provide basic information and knowledge about trade disputes and dispute settlement mechanisms in East Asia while bringing to light the salient features of trade disputes in East Asia. In this context, it also discusses various issues from the WTO and FTA dispute settlement proceedings related to East Asian countries. As such, it will mainly discuss various legal issues arising from the current WTO/FTA dispute settlement proceedings applicable to East Asia. The book is intended to serve as a platform for future discussions of Trade Dispute Settlements in East Asia.

This book is designed to assist readers in achieving the basic objective of the course. It thus discusses key principles and jurisprudence that are invoked in and applied to the dispute settlement proceedings conducted at the WTO, FTAs and Investor-State Arbitrations. To the extent issues of international law are examined by domestic courts, relevant proceedings and jurisprudence of domestic courts are also discussed from time to time.

Any discussion of the dispute settlement proceedings at the WTO and FTAs should first be based on a clear understanding of the basic principles of international law applicable to dispute settlement proceedings. It is not an appropriate approach to believe that each dispute settlement proceeding can operate separate from and independent of the basic rules and jurisprudence of international law. It is true that sometimes a dispute settlement proceeding is governed by a particular enabling treaty at issue, under a system called "self-contained regime." But even in this instance, other basic rules and jurisprudence of international law can still find a place through their penetration into these proceedings. For instance, international trade law has traditionally been considered a legal norm that is independent of or separate from the principles and jurisprudence of public international law. This has probably been caused by the fact that international trade law is administered by the WTO Agreements and FTAs. In fact, the WTO Agreements and FTAs contain very detailed provisions to regulate members' actions in almost all economic areas. As such, most of the time it has not been necessary to go outside the WTO or FTA regime to discuss international trade law issues and solve disputes among states. Most disputes could be solved through the application of the relevant provisions of the WTO Agreements and FTAs.

This traditional notion and practice are now rapidly changing. Recently at the WTO dispute settlement proceedings, there have been disputes that involve both trade aspects and other governmental policy aspects at the same time, such as trade and environment, trade and natural resources, trade and culture, to name a few. These new disputes sometimes require the WTO panels and Appellate Body to look at principles and jurisprudence of international law which are not related to trade issues specifically. As such, recent reports from the panels and the Appellate Body contain interesting discussions of international law. It seems almost impossible to settle these new disputes without adequately considering international law jurisprudence in addition to WTO Agreements. Similar situations are also arising in investment arbitrations as well.

This new trend indicates that international trade law and international investment law also require continued interactions with public international law to become a viable norm in the international community. This is hardly surprising because international trade law and international investment law are also respective branches of international law. At the same time, the precedence in WTO Agreements and investment agreements, particularly with regard to dispute settlement proceedings, may in turn provide guidelines for other areas of international law as well. As such, the exchanges and interactions between international trade law and international investment law on the one hand, and interactions with international law on the other, should be further expanded in the future. The two-way interactions and exchanges are crucial for the advancement of international trade law, international investment law and public international law.

Most notably, the WTO's Dispute Settlement Mechanism (DSM) has been widely hailed as one of the most significant successes of the WTO system since its inception in 1995. It introduced the first legally binding state-to-state dispute settlement proceedings into the universe of trade disputes. It broke away from the previous DSM of the *General Agreement on Tariffs and Trade 1947* (*i.e.*, GATT 1947), which was legally non-binding. Most experts agree that the WTO's DSM has been the hallmark of the multilateralism enshrined in the WTO and fostered rule of law in the global trade. Its popularity explains the trust 164 WTO Members place in the WTO's DSM. As of this writing, the number of cases at the WTO DSM docket has reached 611 in just 27 years.[1] Its success is also evidenced by the development in other areas of international law where states purport to borrow the WTO DSM's experience for other international dispute settlement mechanisms. The current discussion of the reform of the ISDS provides a vivid example in this regard. States and experts look to the WTO's DSM to reform ISDS in a way that can multilateralize it as seen in the WTO. While the WTO has been struggling since May 2016 when the United States officially made clear its dissatisfaction with the international organization in Geneva by blocking appointment of the WTO's Appellate Body members, its DSM's experiments and contribution to the global rule of law in the trade sector still remain meaningful and significant.

While these disputes at the DSM are often raised by members — that are states — on their own accord based on their belief that the measures of other members at issue are in violation of covered agreements, WTO disputes are also initiated because of the request from specific domestic interest groups. Although the government of a complaining member makes all decisions in the course of the proceedings, it does so with close consultation and cooperation with a corporation behind the scenes. In this process, sometimes the interest of the government of a complaining member and that of the corporation does not necessarily converge. On the surface, they share the same objective — *i.e.*, prevailing in the dispute at the end of the day — but what they have in mind is not always identical: while a government's fundamental objective is to preserve "systemic" interest as a party to the WTO Agreements, business interests are more geared toward gaining "immediate" relief for the damage that has been done.

Put differently, a government's real interest in participating in the WTO DSM is to bring the allegedly distorted situation back to a state of equilibrium. Hence, the WTO DSM only permits a prospective remedy, and any sanction at the end of the day is simply a suspension of concessions by the prevailing member. In contrast, from the perspective of the corporation that has prompted the underlying dispute, such a "systemic" remedy may seem quite remote and distinct from a "specific" remedy that it would otherwise gain from a domestic litigation. At an initial consultation meeting with government officials discussing the initiation of a WTO dispute, officials of corporations are usually surprised and disappointed on realizing that a remedy they will ultimately receive does not cover the damage done. Perhaps this situation may explain a recent trend in which business interests sometimes lean toward an investment dispute proceeding in which monetary compensation is available.

A further layer of complexity will be added to the present situation should the WTO DSM be amended in a way that enhances transparency of the proceedings and facilitates (indirect) participation of non-state actors (most notably, corporations) in the proceedings. Increased interface between non-state actors and the WTO DSM may further expose the divergent views between the governments and corporations, as well as the gap between a systemic remedy and a specific, individual remedy.

In this respect, one of the important tasks of the WTO in the future seems to be helping corporations to be more precisely aware of the unique aspects and fundamental objectives of the WTO DSM. It may be understood that the real beneficiaries of this systemic remedy are the corporations themselves in the long run. At the same time, members might want to contemplate whether there are certain ways to address corporations' desires for effective remedies within the current framework of the WTO DSM.

As a matter of fact, in essence, the FTA's DSM basically follows the WTO model. Its jurisdictional structure, composition, timeframe, decision and implementation look quite similar to the WTO's panels. Most importantly, the final objectives of the two DSMs are the same: to bring a challenged measure into compliance with the agreement at issue, be it WTO Agreements or FTAs. In other words, this means that any remedy from the WTO DSM or FTA DSM is only prospective in nature. Any remedy from them does not cover past violation; it only aims to rectify the situation *for the future*. In that respect, the two DSMs share basic feature. The only difference is that (i) it is the contracting parties of the FTA, compared to the WTO's Dispute Settlement Body (DSB) that establishes a panel in the FTA DSM, (ii) the overall timeframe for the FTA DSM is relatively shorter compared to its WTO counterpart, and (iii) an appellate mechanism is usually (with some exceptions) non-existent at the FTA DSM. To the extent the basic features of the WTO DSM are incorporated into the FTA DSM, the strengths and weaknesses of the WTO DSM are equally reflected in the FTA DSM as well. At the same time, there are also notable developments in the FTA DSM as contracting parties are freer in experimenting new methods and schemes to settle disputes in an innovative manner. This is not necessarily the case with the WTO DSM which operates under a separate WTO Agreeement called the *Understanding on Rules and Procedures Governing the Settlements of*

Disputes (DSU). As with covered agreements, WTO Members and Secretariat are all bound by this agreement (DSU) and deviation from it is not permitted. On the other hand, FTA partners are more liberal in experimenting new dispute settlement schemes. Consider a new dispute settlement mechanism for non-tariff barriers (NTBs) disputes adopted in the Korea-China FTA and Korea-EU FTA. These two FTAs introduced 'mediation' mechanisms to settle NTB disputes. Mediation is a legally non-binding proceeding where amicable solution is sought as opposed to a legally binding, adversarial solution from the ordinary panel proceedings of the WTO or the FTA. This new experiment reflects the increasing recognition that non-binding dispute settlement is also quite useful to settle state-to-state disputes as with commercial disputes. The new experiment realizes that disputes involving amorphous and ambiguous issues like NTBs may be better solved through candid discussions between states with the support of a third party facilitator — the mediator. It remains to be seen how this new experiment will fare in settling bilateral trade disputes between FTA contracting parties.

On the other hand, investment arbitration (ISDS proceedings), another major dispute settlement proceeding in international economic law, is fundamentally different from the WTO DSM or FTA DSM, in that it aims to offer *retrospective* remedy, something that does not exist in trade dispute settlement proceedings. As such, monetary compensation is the focal point of investment arbitration, because rectifying the past wrongdoing is only possible through monetary compensation for it. At the same time, the ISDS proceedings provide standing to individual investors — as opposed to governments of contracting parties — to initiate legal action against another government at an international tribunal. The unique aspect of allowing monetary compensation and providing standing to individual investors have made investment arbitration appealing to claimant-investors. The increasing popularity has also raised concern over the proceeding on the part of the states.

This book aims to provide an overview of the basic features

of all of these dispute settlement proceedings of the WTO and FTAs so that readers can be apprised of the contributions of these proceedings together with their shortcomings. The readers may also understand how to improve these dispute settlement system in the WTO and FTAs for ther future. Granted, the global trading regime is now in a perilous situation as of March 2020. Nonetheless, accurate evaluation and careful contemplation of dispute settlement mechanisms will help the international community devise and administer more efficient and reliable dispute settlement proceeding in the future.

Endnotes

1. As of March 19, 2022, 611 disputes have been initiated by WTO Members against other Members since the inception of the WTO in January 1995, see https://www.wto.org/english/tratop_e/dispu_e/dispu_status_e.htm (last visited March 19, 2022).

Chapter I

An Overview: Public International Law in the Domestic Plane

1. The New Institutional Framework: Globalization and Legal Disputes

Globalization expedites the movement of goods and services across international borders. It expands world trade and investment both in terms of diversity as well as coverage. This phenomenon creates room for many disputes resulting from multiple interactions within the international community. This possibility of multiple disputes in turn requires a complex dispute settlement mechanism. In the context of globalization and the expanded sphere of trade, traditional dispute settlement set-ups are insufficient to handle various kinds of disputes. The multidimensional nature of both the sources of disputes and the law requires a responsive dispute settlement mechanism for it to be effective. Multiple sources of law for the regulation of international transactions in turn multiplies the number of dispute settlement mechanisms and forums. This in itself is a serious concern that needs to be addressed properly. Unless it is managed through appropriate mechanisms, forum shopping and other related problems may arise.

2. Legal Norms That Affect Sovereign States, Transnational Corporations and Individuals

For a better understanding of the pertinent dispute settlement mechanism, understanding the legal norms that regulate the conducts of states, transnational corporations and individuals is necessary. International norms and municipal rules can affect transactions involving individuals, transnational corporations as well as sovereign states. The traditional notion of international law that limits its subject to sovereign states is now waning; instead, the notion that transnational corporations as well as individuals can be subjects under international law is on the rise. Meanwhile, the defense of sovereign immunity which is a hindrance to the exercise of jurisdiction over a sovereign state before the domestic courts of other states is now facing various challenges from some jurisdictions. Thus, it can be safely concluded that both international law and domestic law are the sources of law that regulate the conduct of sovereign states, transnational corporations and individuals. This does not mean, however, that both sets of rules are equally applicable to individuals, states and transnational corporations, nor that both sets of rules are relevant to address disputes involving individuals, states and transnational corporations. What matters here is the transaction effected by the actors.

3. Relationship between International Law and Domestic Law

By ratifying a trade agreement, parties commit themselves to respect the obligations of the agreement and to implement the rules in their jurisdiction. However, the agreement itself or international law in general does not provide the manner in which the agreement is integrated into the parties' domestic legal structure. This matter is to be decided by each party in accordance with its own constitutional system.

The issue of how a country accepts the trade agreement is important for its own domestic preparation and also for ensuring the other party's implementation. This has become one of the most contentious issues in Korea's ratification process of the Korea-US FTA. Some opponents of the Agreement have argued that the difference between the two countries in accepting the agreement makes the relationship fundamentally unfair, and that it must be redressed.

Theoretically in international law, there are two contrasting views on the relationship between international law and national law, called monism and dualism. In monism, international law does not need to be transformed to be applied under national jurisdiction because international law and domestic law are part of the same universal legal order. Yet in dualism, international law should be transformed to be applicable in national jurisdiction because they operate separately. No economy in the world would take a purely monistic or dualistic approach; most of them are partly monist and partly dualist. Some economies have more monistic elements than dualistic elements, others vice versa.

1) Monism: Instant Incorporation of Treaties into Domestic Law

The monistic approach originated from continental Europe, and it influenced Japan in the modern ages and later Korea as well. In countries that take a monistic approach, international agreements can be directly applied in their territory (direct applicability), and the rights specified in international agreements can be directly claimed by individuals (direct effect). However, these are only possibilities and are not always the case, because no economy applies international agreements as if they were national law.

As a practical example of monism, Article 6 of the Constitution of Korea states: "[t]reaties duly concluded and promulgated under the Constitution and the generally recognized rules of international law shall have the same effect as the domestic laws of the Republic of Korea." Under the Korean system, an international agreement is incorporated into domestic law, and customary international law is also treated as part of domestic law.

There are other provisions in the Constitution that are relevant to the interpretation of "treaties duly concluded and promulgated". They are, for instance, "Article 73: [t]he President shall conclude and ratify treaties," and "Article 60: [t]he National Assembly shall have the right to consent to the conclusion and ratification of treaties pertaining to mutual assistance or mutual security; treaties concerning important international organizations; treaties of friendship, trade, and navigation; treaties pertaining to any restriction in sovereignty; peace treaties; treaties which will burden the State or people with an important financial obligation; or treaties related to legislative matters." Like many other countries, it is not the National Assembly that ratifies the treaty in Korea. When it gives its consent, the President, acting as the head of the state, ratifies the treaty. Once this procedure is carried out, the treaty is considered to have the same effect as domestic laws.

With regard to the meaning of "shall have the same effect as the domestic laws," the hierarchy of the Korean legal system must be taken into account. The order of hierarchy, from the highest to the lowest, is as follows: Constitution — Acts — Presidential Decrees — Prime Minister's Ordinances — Ministerial Ordinances — Ministerial Regulations — Local governments' rules. The prevailing view of the interpretation of "shall have the same effect as the domestic laws" is that international agreements shall have the same effect as Acts, as both the treaties and Acts are reviewed and approved by the National Assembly. There are other types of international agreements that are not concluded and promulgated under the Constitution but are initiated by the government on its own without following the procedure of the legislative body. In this case, the agreements do not have the same effect as Acts but still have the same effect as other domestic regulations at the lower level.

Korea has always handled trade agreements in accordance with Articles 6, 60, and 73 of the Constitution. Therefore, the trade agreements have the same effect as domestic Acts, which is high up the hierarchy, second only to the Constitution.

To further understand the meaning of "shall have the same effect as the domestic laws", two features of monism should be reviewed — direct applicability and direct effect. In fact, these concepts were developed through the European integration process. The Europeans wanted to establish the supremacy of the Union law over the domestic law of individual members. Therefore, the Union law needed to be directly applicable and effective and had to become part of national law. In a practical sense, Union law was regarded as domestic rather than as international law.

Direct applicability is set out in Article 288 of the Treaty on the Functioning of the European Union: "(EC) regulations shall be binding in its entirety and directly applicable in all Member States." Direct applicability refers to the fact that international law — EC regulations in this case — does not require the implementation of legislation to be applied within individual member states. On the other hand, direct effect is not explicitly stated, although implied, in the EU's constitutional treaties. It is instead developed through the case law of the European Court of Justice (ECJ), and refers to the principle that the Union law may confer rights on individuals which the courts of member states are bound to recognize and enforce. In other words, the Union law can be invoked and relied on in an individual's lawsuit.

To establish supremacy, it would be ideal if the provisions of a treaty were both directly effective and directly applicable. However, the two concepts are not always inter-connected. For instance, some provisions are directly effective but not directly applicable, and others are directly applicable but not directly effective.

It appears that monism has been accepted by a majority of states globally. For instance, states such as Korea, Japan, China and continental European countries follow this system. With respect to Korea, through the operation of monism, treaties duly concluded by the Korean government are binding on Korea, are directly applicable in Korea and have the same effects as the domestic law of Korea.[1] As such, the Korean government does not need to enact an implementation act to enforce a treaty, because the treaty is automatically enforceable domestically. It is increasingly common these days that much legislation is passed before or at the time of its ratification by the Korean National Assembly with the operation of Article 60 of the Korean Constitution,[2] but this is because these recent treaties include provisions that specifically require adopting and/or amending legislation even if the treaties at issue become part of Korean law instantly. In other words, these implementing statutes are the outcome of the provisions of the treaties, not the operation of the monism system. Again, the monism system does not require any enactment of the implementing legislation.

Not surprisingly, the recent phenomenon is incredibly visible in trade agreements where agreed terms expect to create massive changes in domestic laws and regulations of contracting parties. As such, Korea along with other countries have introduced new legislation and amended that which exists right before new trade agreements enter into force. FTAs with major trading partners offer the best examples. Each FTA in Korea has meant a significant legislative undertaking before and sometimes after its entry into force. This is not something that is usually expected of a state that subscribes to the idea of monism.

As Korea is a monism state, treaties have the same effect in Korea as the domestic laws of Korea. Consequently, it is sometimes possible for there to be a conflict between the two, which then raises the issue of which one prevails. The status ultimately granted to a treaty within the domestic legal hierarchy differs from country to country. Some countries, such as the Netherlands and Belgium, place treaties above domestic law, and the court can even declare a national law invalid when it contradicts applicable international law.[3] In these monism states, international law is placed at the top of the domestic legal echelon. Other countries, on the other hand, are not bold enough and so provide duly concluded treaties with the same status granted to domestic statutes.[4] Yet others confer a lower status on treaties than on domestic statutes. Between treaties and domestic statutes falling under the same category and in the same echelon, these states including Korea determine the prevailing status based on the general principles of law such as *lex posterior* and *lex speciali*. The same rules set forth above also apply to trade agreements.

Whether trade agreements have the effect of direct application to domestic court proceedings is a question that is separate from whether a country follows monism or dualism. Even in monism states, where treaties automatically become part of domestic law, some agreements by nature do not have the effect of direct application. In other words, treaties in these states become part of domestic law, but being part of domestic law does not necessarily mean that these treaties become directly invokable by individual complainants and become directly applicable to court proceedings. The contracting parties to treaties sometimes stipulate that the treaties at issue only create rights and obligation for the states and governments but not to individual persons and corporations. One of the most common examples of such agreements is found in trade agreements. In these cases, trade agreements are not supposed to be directly enforceable by aggrieved individuals and corporations. What they can invoke instead are the domestic laws and regulations implementing these trade agreements domestically. Most of the time, these domestic laws and regulations contain same provisions or more elaborated provisions. Individuals and corporations can rely upon these provisions and invoke them before domestic courts. They are directly enforceable only by states who are the holders of the rights and obligations for these trade agreements.

As such, in these states, the courts tend to deny the direct effect of WTO Agreements or FTAs.[5] The basic intention of trade agreements is to regulate government measures such as the imposition of tariffs and regulation of NTBs, not to create rights and obligations for individuals. It presents a clear contrast to, for example, human rights treaties where the intention of contracting parties are clearly stipulated to provide individuals with the option and possibility of resorting to international agreements. On the other hand, the school of thought that favors the denial of direct effect of trade agreements argues that unclear matters about trade agreements are better resolved through consultations between governments or through DSM between them, and that local judges should refrain from interpreting and applying the technical provisions of trade agreements.

The practical problem in this respect is that the victims of the violation of trade agreements are not accorded a remedy from the trade agreements themselves. Only the individual's state can initiate dispute settlement proceedings under the trade agreement, either the WTO Agreement or an FTA, to seek relief. The fact that victims of the violation of the trade agreements cannot resort to trade agreements by themselves arguably imposes significant limitations in terms of the effectiveness of any remedy. But this limitation should be put into perspective: the aggrieved individuals may still refer the matter to domestic courts by invoking a violation of domestic laws and regulations where often companion provisions are found. Such being the case, it is not necessarily accurate to say that the absence of direct effect forces the individuals into a legal limbo. The Korean court has taken the position that trade agreements are not directly enforceable unless parties' intentions are clearly stipulated otherwise.[6] The courts of Japan and China also take a similar view in this respect.

At any rate, regarding all treaties it is important for the government of a contracting party to keep monitoring its domestic legislation process to ensure the legislation's compliance with international obligations and to apply preemptive control over a potential violation of the agreement before legislation is enacted. If domestic legislation that is inconsistent with the obligations under trade agreements is found to exist, the government may actively use its executive and administrative authority to rectify the situation. As necessary, it may also consider resorting to judicial proceedings to remedy the alleged violation. Again, it should be noted that the government, unlike individuals, is not barred from invoking the provisions of trade agreements in a domestic lawsuit. This process may be called an ongoing flow of efforts to ensure the rule of law.

2) Dualism: Transformation of Treaties into Domestic Law through Special Procedure

The dualism states are relatively small in number. Most notably, the United Kingdom and Commonwealth States lean toward dualism. These states emphasize the difference between national and international law. In its purest form, international law does not domestically exist as law, and only national laws that are implemented are effective. Therefore, international law must be "transformed" into national law, and existing national law that contradicts international law must be abolished or amended beforehand to be in compliance with international law. In a dualism country, implementing legislation is mandatory and always necessary in order to implement the obligations under the treaty at issue or to avoid any breach of the obligations of the treaty. However, the state has full discretion over how to implement the treaty as long as it is transformed into a national law. Trade agreements in these states are implemented domestically through the same mechanism. So, implementing legislation should be adopted before the trade agreements enter into force. If the implemented legislation in monism countries are not mandatory and simply reflect the demand of specific provisions of the treaty in question, implementing legislation in dualism countries is mandatory and is a constitutional requirement: it does not matter what is demanded from the text of the treaty.

A simple method of dualistic approach would be to use a "blanket" transformation language that changes the entire treaty into a new web of domestic law. In this situation, the legislature may enact legislation with a title that indicates the implementation of a certain treaty at the request of the government. Only a few provisions are inserted under the title, one of which is to generally state that the provisions of a specific treaty is hereby transformed into the domestic law of the country. This would then turn the whole provision of the treaty in question into a municipal law, which would then render the treaty domestically enforceable. The objective of the treaty is hereby achieved, so to speak.

A more common practice is to repeat individual provisions of the treaty with modifications *mutatis mutandis* in newly introduced domestic law. Through this process, the entire body of the treaty is now transformed into domestic law. Only this domestic law is applicable and enforceable domestically within a dualist state. Again, the dualist states note the distinction between international law and domestic law, and to them it is only domestic law that is applicable to the domestic plane. Korea, Japan and China are monist countries, so to them this transformation mechanism is rather new and unique.

The United States is one of the countries that have a mixed monist-dualist system. Article 6 of the Constitution of the United States has a monistic element and provides that "all Treaties made, or which shall be made, under the Authority of the United States, shall be the supreme Law of the Land; and the Judges in every State shall be bound thereby, any Thing in the Constitution or Laws of any State to the Contrary notwithstanding."[7] With regard to treaties, Article 2 of the said Constitution provides that "[the President] shall have power, by and with the advice and consent of the Senate, to make treaties, provided two-thirds of the Senators present concur."[8]

As such, the term "treaty" has a special and restricted meaning in the United States compared to its rather general use in international law. In international law, a treaty is a generic term, and any written document which aims to create legal rights and obligations for states is regarded as a treaty regardless of titles.[9] In the US constitution and the domestic legal system of the United States, a "treaty" is distinguished from other types of international agreements such as executive agreements. Treaties only refer to those international documents concluded with the advice and consent (that is, ratification) of the Senate. These treaties become part of the US law, which is the trait of the monist states. Other international agreements such as executive agreements are not considered to be treaties per se; they are negotiated and concluded based on the authority given to the executive branch under the constitution. They are not regarded as statutes; they are treated as executive orders or presidential decrees domestically in the United States. They of course carry equally binding force abroad. The specific status of an internationally legal binding document within the domestic legal system of a state does not affect the status of the document under international law. Any such document is regarded as a treaty whether it is are called a treaty or not in a country's domestic constitutional system, or whether a somewhat different legal status is accorded to different sets of documents.[10] Treaties made under the Constitution can be directly applicable and effective.

The United States also adopts the concept of "self-executing" treaties and "non-self-executing treaties." The former refers to treaties which are designed to be applied domestically without specifically implementing legislation. The provisions are detailed and specific enough so as to permit such application. The latter, on the other hand, refers to treaties which are not specific enough, so that implementing legislation needs to be adopted for elaboration and specification. This concept is different from the existence or absence of the direct effect of a treaty that is discussed above. The issue of direct effect is whether an individual may invoke the provisions of the treaty before a domestic court. Self-executing or non-self-executing refers to the level of elaboration and specification. They therefore address different situations. In other words, a self-executing treaty can either be one with direct effect or one without such an effect. It should be noted, however, that the division between self-executing and non-self-executing treaties is sometimes unclear. An international agreement may be considered self-executing in the United States and not so by other contracting parties to the agreement. Also, some provisions in an agreement may be self-executing while other provisions in the same agreement may not be. While this lack of clarity seems to cause confusion sometimes, the canon of Article 27 of the Vienna Convention on the Law of Treaties renders this issue generally unimportant or moot.[11]

3) Two Legal Systems in the World: Anglo-American Legal System and Continental Legal System

The Anglo-American Legal System and the Continental Legal System are the two major legal systems in the world featuring their own particular aspects in the administration of justice. Dispute settlement mechanisms in the domestic courts reflect these particular characteristics depending on which legal system the jurisdiction belongs to. They have their own litigation procedures akin to the system the country follows. This does not mean, however, that there is no transposition or influence from one to another. Nevertheless, the fact that a given country follows one or the other can dictate the nature of a legal proceeding and how litigations are administered. When we come to international dispute settlements at international tribunals it is difficult to talk in terms of the Anglo-American or Continental Legal System as a dominant or governing tradition. However, it is natural for judges and arbitrators to be influenced by the legal tradition that they are practicing. Hence, it is often the case that certain legal traditions have an impact on the consequences of international legal proceedings. Thus, understanding these legal traditions also helps us understand their impact in international legal proceedings as well. Anyone who has an interest in international dispute settlement proceedings should understand the impact these legal traditions have on dispute settlement mechanisms.

4) Overlapping Application of International Law and Domestic Law

As international transactions developed and inter-state relations intensified, states have been increasingly required to deal with various issues involving multiple sources of law. These days it is common for domestic tribunals to be called upon to deal with international issues and for international tribunals to interpret domestic legislation. It is no longer the case that such conflicts can be resolved with a simple rule of conflict of laws as well. It requires a deeper understanding of the nexus between international law and municipal law and their potential overlap in administering international disputes. It is important to understand the boundary between a purely domestic and a purely international issue as well, even though it might be hard to distinguish them in this complex world where transactions change hands quickly and repeatedly requires judges and arbitrators to consider all the relevant rules. Thus, it is possible for international tribunals to interpret municipal legal rules while resolving international disputes.

4. Distinction between International Law and Domestic Law

As already discussed, it is not a simple task to identify a case as a purely international dispute or domestic dispute. It is common for international tribunals to consult municipal legal rules in resolving international disputes. Nevertheless, it is important to distinguish domestic law and international law. Traditionally, international law is defined as the law that governs the relationship between sovereign states. It also governs the relations of international organizations as well as states and international organizations and individuals to some extent. On the other hand, domestic law governs the relationship between the state and its citizens as well as the relationship of individuals within a given state. However, one should note that the distinction is not as clear in practice. Specific legal developments by subject areas create instances where international law can be applicable within the domestic jurisdiction and thereby be applicable in the determination of rights to individuals.

Endnotes

1. *See* Korean Consitution, Article 6 which states: Treaties duly concluded and promulgated under the Constitution and the generally recognized rules of international law shall have the same effect as the domestic laws of the Republic of Korea.

2. *See Ibid.*, which states: The National Assembly shall have the right to consent to the conclusion and ratification of treaties pertaining to mutual assistance or mutual security; treaties concerning important international organizations; treaties of friendship, trade and navigation; treaties pertaining to any restriction in sovereignty; peace treaties; treaties which will burden the State or people with an important financial obligation; or treaties related to legislative matters.

3. *See* for instance, H.F. van Panhuys, W.P. Heere, J.W. Josephus Jitta Ko Swan Sik and A.M. Stuyt, *International Law in the Netherlands*, Vol. III (Alphen aan den Rijn: Sijthoff & Noordhoff, 1980), p. 416.

4. The majority view of the Korean constitutional jurisprudence is that treaties concluded with the ratification of the Korean National Assembly in accordance with Article 60 of the Constitution is given the same status with domestic statutes. Treaties concluded otherwise, such as executive agreements, are provided the status of an enforcement decree, a lower rank than a statute.

5. It is worth noting that European courts also deny the direct effect of WTO Agreements.

6. *See Case Concerning Revocation of Limitation of Operating Hours for Certain Retailers*, Supreme Court of the Republic of Korea, 2015DU295, Nov. 10, 2015, available at http://www.scourt.go.kr/supreme/news/NewsViewAction2.work?currentPage=5&searchWord=&searchOption=&seqnum=5035&gubun=4 (last visited Jan. 10, 2019) (in Korean) (hereinafter "Judgment"), p. 18.

7. *See* art. 6 of the Constitution of the United States, *available at* https://www.senate.gov/civics/constitution_item/constitution.htm (last visited Apr. 29, 2020).

8. *See* art. 6 of the Constitution of the United States, *available at* https://www.senate.gov/civics/constitution_item/constitution.htm (last visited Apr. 29, 2020).

9. *See* Vienna Convention on the Law of Treaties, May 23, 1969, entered into force Jan. 27, 1980, 1155 U.N.T.S. 331, art. 2.

10. *See* Vienna Convention on the Law of Treaties, art. 27.

11. *See* Vienna Convention on the Law of Treaties, art. 27.

Chapter II

International Economic Disputes and Their Settlement

1. Legal Disputes and Remedies

The definition of a dispute may seem simple and straightforward. However, "dispute" could refer to a large bundle of possible conflicts which all require different sets of rules and procedures for resolutions. Legally, it is important at least to identify what constitutes a dispute that requires formal procedures. In addition, it is also necessary to understand the nature and sources of disputes in order to address them properly in the proceedings. The nature of a dispute determines the nature of a given proceeding while the sources of a dispute determine remedies that can be sought by the contesting parties. The following sections will discuss the various dispute resolution mechanisms together with their implication in order to help readers understand the various factors that need to be taken in to account in deciding to utilize one or the other available dispute resolution mechanism.

1) Legal Disputes Arising from International Activities

Before discussing the mechanisms by which legal disputes can be resolved, it is important to understand the essence of legal disputes and a dispute itself. An authoritative definition of a dispute is provided by the Permanent Court of International

Justice (PCIJ) in the *Mavrommattis Palestine Concessions (Jurisdiction)* case as a "disagreement over a point of law or fact, a conflict of legal views or of interests between two persons."[1] Again the ICJ discussed the issue in a dispute before the court in relation to the interpretation of a treaty, and referred to it as "a situation in which the two sides held clearly opposite views concerning the question of the performance or non-performance of certain treaty obligations."[2] This definition does not make a distinction between legal disputes and other disputes. Thus, it is imperative to try to find a distinguishing feature for a legal dispute. Even though it is difficult to treat legal disputes in isolation from other disputes or factors, attempts have been made to qualify legal disputes from other disputes. In this regard it is informative to cite the definition supplied by the International Court of Justice (ICJ) in the *Nicaragua (Nicaragua v. Honduras)* case as a dispute capable of being resolved by the application of principles and rules of international law.[3]

2) International Economic Law Related Disputes

Among legal disputes arising from international activities, the bulk of the disputes are now related to international economic activities. This is a natural reflection of the increasing trend of globalization coupled with faster and deeper integration of the global community. These legal disputes are then divided into two categories. The first category is domestic legal disputes that are lodged in the dockets of domestic courts. The second category is international legal disputes that are brought to the dockets of international courts.

(1) International Economic Law Disputes in Domestic Proceedings

It is a common misconception that international economic law disputes are brought to international courts or tribunals only. As a matter of fact, many such disputes are brought to domestic administrative and judicial proceedings. This is because aggrieved exporters and importers are only permitted to proceed to domestic proceedings and are not eligible to bring a claim to international administrative or judicial proceedings. This is the outcome of the application of the concept of sovereign immunity.[4] The only exception to this cardinal rule are the investor-state dispute settlement proceedings under an International Investment Agreements (IIAs). As exporters and importers are those who stand in the front line of international trade, disputes arising from these entities and individuals are naturally destined to be heard by domestic procedures of the state at issue — most commonly the domestic proceedings of an importing country. As such, the WTO Agreements and FTAs pay significant attention to how to regulate and discipline these domestic proceedings. As a matter of fact, the entire Anti-Dumping Agreement and Safeguards Agreement and a significant portion of the SCM agreement are about this issue. They set forth the basic rules to be applied in domestic adminsitrative proceedings related to trade remedy measures. They also stipulate the right of interested parties to bring their claims to domestic judicial proceedings.[5]

Korea, China and Japan have also established and are now administering administrative proceedings to deal with trade remedy issues and customs issues as mandated by the WTO Agreements and FTAs. All in all, they seem to be rather faithful implementers of the norms of the agreements. Decisions taken by these agencies are sometimes challenged at the WTO dispute settlement proceedings. When the WTO's panels or the Appellate Body find violations of the decisions of these agencies, Korea, China and Japan have been relatively prompt in adjusting or changing their laws and regulations.

(2) International Economic Law Disputes in International Courts

Some of the legal disputes of international economic activities are brought to international courts. Considering the voluntary nature of the jurisdiction of an international court in international law,[6] it is indeed remarkable that treaties in international economic law area have adopted a system of mandatory jurisdiction for their dispute settlement proceedings. The accession to the WTO and conclusion of an FTA require concurrent acceptance of the blanket jurisdiction of the dispute settlement proceedings arising from these treaties.[7] Consequently, it is much easier for international economic disputes to be brought to international court proceedings. As of March 2022, there have been 611 disputes at the WTO and 1,023 instances of investment arbitration globally.

Contracting parties of the trade agreements and IIAs can bring their claims to the WTO or FTA dispute settlement proceedings as the holders of rights and obligations of the treaties. Individuals or corporations cannot: as explained above, they can only proceed to domestic courts that can hear their disputes. The only exception at present is investment arbitration where an individual investor can initiate an international legal proceeding *vis-à-vis* another state — namely the government of the host state.

Korea, China and Japan have been active users of the WTO dispute settlement proceedings. Since 1995, as of March 2022, these three countries have participated in these proceedings 40, 71 and 44 times respectively as direct parties. They have also participated in 139, 192, 225 disputes as third parties, respectively. Regarding investment disputes, none of these three countries have been traditionally active participants. But in recent years, Korea and China have been brought to investment arbitration proceedings by foreign investors, signaling that investment disputes are becoming an increasingly common phenomenon for these countries. Japan has yet to see its first invesment arbitration dispute brought by a foreign investor. Investors from these three nations operating in foreign countries such as in Europe have also started to resort to this mechanism to address their own problems in those countries.

3) Means to Resolve International Legal Disputes

Basically, states are not obliged to settle their differences no matter how serious they are.[8] This does not include disputes which may lead to a threat of international peace and security, in which case states are obliged to settle their disputes peacefully under the direction of the Security Council. In addition to choosing whether to settle their dispute or not, states are free to choose the mechanisms by which they settle their disputes. There are various mechanisms utilized by states to resolve their international disputes. These mechanisms can be broadly categorized as diplomatic methods and binding methods of dispute settlement mechanisms. Regarding the diplomatic mechanisms, negotiation, mediation and good offices can be cited as examples. On the other hand, judicial settlement and arbitration are categorized under binding dispute settlement mechanisms. This does not, however, mean that there is a water-tight distinction between these two categories of dispute settlement mechanisms. Binding dispute settlements are often preceded by diplomatic settlements.

(1) Legal Disputes at Internatioanl Tribunals

Some of the international legal disputes are presented to international courts with proper jurisdiction. While international courts provide neutral and objective adjudicators for international legal disputes involving competing interest of states and entities with diverse nationalities, it is not necessairly the case that a court with jurisdiction exists. One of the peculiar aspects of international courts is that consent to the jurisdiction needs to be established independently. In other words, consent is needed to establish substantive norms such as treaties or customary international law, and another consent is required for an international court to hear a case where a violation of the substantive norms — be it treaty or customary international law — is alleged. This is indeed a unique trait of an international court and arguably one of the weakest links in the enhancement of the rule of law in the global community.

Interestingly and notably, this situation is changing fast. In particular, in the area of economic relations treaties the change is quite palpable. In these treaties, jurisdiction is automatically provided to a court adopted in the treaties at issue. Acceptance of the jurisdiction has become a condition precedent to the accession to the said treaties. WTO Agreements and FTAs are the most common examples. BITs are are also another example. Mandatory jurisdiction is provided to the courts established by these treaties.

(2) Legal Disputes at Domestic Tribunals

Sometimes, international legal disputes are lodged at the domestic courts of a state. States and entities sometimes feel pressure or face burdens in proceeding to international courts even if there are those with mandatory jurisdiction, and so they instead find alternatives through domestic judicial proceedings. Diplomatic, logistical and financial burdens arising from international litigation are the main hindrances that are taken into consideration by states. As such, they sometimes prefer to resort to domestic legal systems. In addition, at least in the trade sector, the domestic legal procedures have a clear incentive. If a party prevails then a remedy will be quite effective. The remedy may include a refund of erroneously collected duties with interest or the impositon of injunctive relief. Such refunds and injunctions are not available in international litigation. At the WTO or FTA disputes settlement proceedings, in principle the remedies are to bring the measure into conformity with the agreements, in other words, the remedies are prospective in nature. There will be no refund or compensation. Compensation is mentioned as a possibility in the WTO Agreements and FTAs but they are virtually always impractical because it requires consent from the losing party. Recent FTAs have tried to adopt a different system, but still the majority of the dispute settlement systems only provide remedies prospectively.

At the same time, these domestic procedures are only available at the domestic courts where the govermental measure have been adopted. Domestic courts of other countries such as the entities' home countries or third countries will be unable to hear these cases because of the jurisprudence of sovereign immunity. A governmental action issued with a regulatory authority can only be challenged at the court of the same country.

(3) Non-Binding Dispute Settlement Mechanism

It is increasingly the case that a non-binding dispute settlement mechanism is sometimes as effective as those that are binding. States are more willing to accommodate the views of the other party or the compromise of a third party if a decision is taken from a non-judicial, non-binding proceeding. Sometimes legal proceedings are indispensable and inevitable. But some disputes are more prone to discussion and resolution through non-binding mechanism. As such, recent treaties pay attention to how to establish and galvanize these non-binding proceedings. They have different names and procedures. Some of them are called mediation or conciliation. Some of them are called joint committee proceedings. Whatever the titles are, these non-binding proceedings are becoming more important and effective as the number of disputes increase and their contents become more complex.

4) Dispute Settlement Mechanism Available to Key Entities

Different dispute settlement mechanisms are suitable for different disputes and different parties. Thus, dispute settlement mechanisms available to states may not necessarily be available to corporations or individuals. By the same token, dispute settlement mechanisms available to corporations or individuals may not necessarily be suitable for disputes involving states. Parties to a dispute choose a given dispute settlement mechanism taking various factors in to account. Some dispute settlement mechanisms may prescribe stringent procedures while others may lack the necessary apparatus to enforce the decisions of the tribunals. Therefore, the choice of a given dispute settlement mechanism takes into account all the factors that have a bearing on the dispute and its outcome.

Keeping this point in mind, domestic courts, State to State arbitration, investor-state arbitrations and international courts for inter-state disputes can be cited as examples of binding dispute settlement mechanisms. As indicated above, these dispute settlement mechanisms have their own particular features that would make them better candidates for each category of parties.

2. International Investment Law and Investment Dispute Settlement

As foreign investment expands both in terms of volume and direction the need grows to develop dispute settlement mechanisms that can provide effective and timely solutions. The expansion of international investment also brings to the forefront various issues that need to be addressed adequately. It is unthinkable to envisage an expansion of investment without an effective dispute resolution mechanism being in place. At the same time the investment disputes are giving raise to various rules and principles in the investment area. As the need for an effective dispute settlement that can handle complex investment disputes becomes pressing various stakeholders are coming up with different modalities of dispute settlements. A case in point, in this regard, is the attempt by the European Union (EU) to come up with an investment court system to handle investment disputes that might arise from the investment clauses negotiated by the EU with other states. In this regard an investment court system is incorporated in trade agreements signed by the EU with its partners.[9] Therefore, the effort to introduce an appeal system in an investor-state arbitration to the introduction of an investment court indicates the ongoing struggle to reform the system and come up with an effective dispute resolution mechanism.

1) Overview of Domestic Regulation Affecting Foreign Investment: Korea's Example

Traditionally and until recently, Korea's approach to foreign investment has been relatively simple: the focus has been on how to invite foreign investment which will provide the necessary financial capital for Korea's economic activities. The government has been able to mobilize the necessary administrative and regulatory measures to accommodate the needs of foreign investors, and more often than not, foreign investors have apparently been able to achieve reasonable returns from their investment. This may explain the absence of any investor-state dispute for Korea despite its status as the world's 13th largest economy.[10] The legal regimes under these circumstances have not had to be overly detailed or complex.

Only recently Korea has been exposed to and been made fully aware of the interaction between investment and trade, the role of investment issues in a trade agreement and the complexity of implementing investor protection measures within the parameters of domestic jurisprudence. Korea has made significant strides in addressing these issues over the past couple of years. However, it will take more time to align itself across every dimension without further final touches. In the meantime, it is most likely that Korea will struggle to deal with investment issues in general, and the close interaction between investments and trade in particular. This prediction is based on the realization that some of the investment-related issues are not susceptible to immediate correction or changes.[11]

For instance, some of the key topics of dispute in the investment area these days are about how to balance the sovereign right of the host state and the protection of investors. In the Organisation for Economic Co-operation and Development (OECD), there have been discussions about how to carve out a "national security" exception and how to define the term.[12]

These discussions do show that there is a wide spectrum of difference among states in evaluating what kind of situation falls under the "national security" category for the purpose of foreign investment regulation. As the failure of the international community to adopt a multilateral investment agreement both in the OECD context and the Uruguay Round context shows, different opinions on these touchy, yet fundamental issues operate as a key dragging force in the regulation of international investment. The continuing work in the Doha Development Agenda (DDA) has also failed to produce any tangible results.[13] Korea is monitoring all these developments on the international level and is generally ready to adjust its policy to any new situation or consensus.

The real problem for Korea at this point seems to be that Korea is forced to close its trade/investment deals with trading partners and initiate adjustment of the domestic regime and policy while many loopholes in specific provisions are still to be filled by international negotiations and discussions.[14] It would be much easier if everything was crystal clear for Korea at this juncture. Unless and until there is a reliable guideline for key outstanding issues in this area, managing the mounting tension in the investment sector and its continuing burden on the trade sector could turn out to be a daunting task for Korea.

(1) Advent of Investment Arbitration in Korea

The four decades of silence ended in 2012 when Korea faced its first investment arbitration filed by a US equity fund. Since then, two more cases were filed against Korea by different foreign investors under different Bilateral Investment Treaties (BITs). As of December 31, 2016, Korea has undergone three investment arbitration proceedings in four years: one of them is still pending as of this writing, and one has been decided against Korea and one has been settled. This recent development is noteworthy, considering the four previous decades of silence on this front.

More importantly, these arbitration cases touch upon key

national economic policies and legislation. Arguably, they are anything but clear instances of mistreatment of foreign investors that would entail easy disposition of the matters at issue under the respective BITs. Rather, these disputes ask arbitral tribunals to decide whether the Korean government's economic regulatory regime and exercise of regulatory authority may somehow lead to the violation of certain provisions of the relevant BITs. Thus, the outcome of these disputes stands to affect the future economic policies of Korea in many respects. In addition, these disputes involve multiple governmental agencies, so the defense has turned out to be substantial and challenging, both logistically and legally. Such being the case, these investment arbitration cases have been handled by an inter-governmental task force.

Government officials, scholars and practitioners in Korea are currently closely monitoring the development of these disputes. When awards are released in these proceedings, the consequences could be monumental if Korea is found to be in violation of BITs and required to provide a sizable amount of financial compensation to the allegedly aggrieved foreign investors. The general direction of Korea's policy relating to foreign investment may also be affected by the outcome of these disputes.

(2) Investment Arbitration Proceedings Involving Korea

The first investment arbitration proceeding was filed by Lone Star, a US equity fund, on November 22, 2012 under the 2011 Korea-Belgium BIT.[15] This case is still pending at the International Centre for the Settlement of Investment Disputes (ICSID). The US equity fund claims that certain actions and omissions by Korean tax authorities and financial regulatory bodies violated various provisions of the said BIT.

While Lone Star itself is a US equity fund, it established a company in Belgium, and it was the Belgian company that purchased shares of the Korea Exchange Bank (KEB) in 2000. The KEB is one of the major commercial banks operating in

Korea. Thus, this Belgian company is the foreign investor under the Korea-Belgium BIT that resorted to arbitration against the Korean government in 2012.

Around mid-2000s, the Belgian company attempted to sell its shares in KEB to domestic and foreign banks and withdraw from the Korean market. The attempted sale, however, did not fare well because the Belgian company failed to comply with the regulatory requirements under the applicable laws and regulations at that time. The sale of KEB, a financial institution, was subject to a variety of regulatory oversights by the government's financial regulatory watchdogs — the Financial Supervisory Commission (FSC). According to the Belgian Company, the company has suffered financial losses due to the failed sales plan. As the FSC's restriction of the sales was inappropriate and discriminatory, Korea breached its obligation under the BIT. In addition, taxes imposed by the Korean tax authorities — National Tax Service (NTS) — on certain proceeds of the Belgian company that was accrued from its operation in Korea was also challenged as a violation of certain provisions of the BIT. The erroneous taxation is claimed to constitute expropri-ation of the Belgian company's assets by the Korean government. Main provisions of the BIT cited in this arbitration include indirect expropriation and fair and equitable treatment. Hearings took place in 2015 and 2016, and the final award has not been released as of March 2022. Not surprisingly, the final award will draw a great deal of attention from the general public as well as from the experts in this field since this is the first case of investment arbitration involving the Korean government. The political sector of Korea including the National Assembly is keenly anticipating the outcome of the proceedings, in view of the Korea-US FTA revision that ended on September 24, 2018.

The Korea-Belgium BIT was originally concluded in 1976 before being amended in 2011. This case was brought almost immediately after the amendment. The timing of the initiation of this arbitration has since alerted Korea: amendments of old BITs can sometimes facilitate filing investment arbitration proceedings through the inclusion of new provisions or the exclusion of old ones. At the same time, the fact that this case was brought by a US investor under the Korea-Belgium BIT rather than Korea-US FTA's Investment Chapter where various defense schemes are available for a respondent government has also caught the attention in Korea: multinational foreign investors can easily "shop" for the BITs and FTAs that best suit their position.

The second investment arbitration involves Dutch investors. On May 20, 2015, a Dutch company called Hanocal, owned by Abu Dhabi-based International Petroleum Investment Company, brought an investment arbitration against Korea under the 2003 Korea-Netherlands BIT. In *Hanocal Holding B.V. and IPIC International B.V. v. Republic of Korea* (ICSID Case No. ARB/15/17),[16] the claimants challenged the alleged tax levied by the NTS on the 2010 sale of the claimants' controlling stake in Hyundai Oil bank, a Korean petroleum and refinery company based in Seosan, Korea. The claimants argued that the taxation measure constituted a violation of the said BIT because it deviated from the general rule of taxation and thus was tantamount to illegal expropriation of the property of the foreign investor. The Korean government countered that its taxation followed the general rules of international taxation and was thus consistent with provisions of the relevant tax conventions. The main provisions of the relevant BIT cited in this dispute also included indirect expropriation as well as fair and equitable treatment.

While the two sides were preparing their legal submissions, they succeeded in settling the dispute on October 5, 2016. The specific terms of the settlement have not been revealed yet. It is also not clear whether the whole dispute has been settled once and for all, or whether the claimants still reserve the right to re-initiate the proceedings.

The third investment dispute involves an Iranian investor. In *Mohammad Reza Dayyani and Others v. Republic of Korea*,[17] an Iranian electronics company, Entekhab Group, filed a notice of arbitration against Korea on September 14, 2015 based on the 1998 Korea-Iran BIT. The claimants challenged the creditors' termination of an agreement for the sale of a majority stake in Daewoo Electronics to the claimants and their refusal to return the claimants' USD 50 million deposit.

Daewoo Electronics, a Korean corporation, has been in a workout program as a result of the creditors' decision to restructure the outstanding debts of the corporation. As such, the creditors were authorized to make decisions on key business matters under the relevant law of Korea, *the Corporate Restructuring Promotion Act*. Thus, the creditors had aimed to sell their shares of Daewoo Electronics to the Iranian investor, and had signed a sales contract subject to a condition that the contract would be cancelled with the forfeiture of the deposit if the investor as a purchaser failed to meet the deadline for the payment of the purchase money. When the Iranian investor failed to meet the deadline for that payment, the creditors exercised their right to cancel the contract and forfeited the deposit. The claimants allege that the cancellation of the contract and forfeiture of the deposit were illegal as they were in violation of the Korea-Iran BIT, most notably its provisions relating to indirect expropriation and non-discrimination.

One interesting aspect of this dispute is that, as a matter of fact, the alleged non-return at issue does not involve any governmental agency *per se*. So, the non-return, in and of itself, does not constitute a governmental measure in the first place, a precondition to invoke the BIT. Nonetheless, the claimants argue that one of the major creditors of Daewoo Electronics, the Korea Asset Management Corporation, is in fact controlled by the Korean government, and thus the decision of the creditors reflects the government's decision. As such, the claimants argue that the non-payment should be attributable to the government and satisfy the requirement of the BIT. The outcome of this dispute, therefore, will shed light on the role of a state-owned enterprise and its implications for international investment law.

When an adverse ruling was rendered in 2018, the Korean government initiated a set aside proceeding in the court of the United Kingdom challenging the error of the arbitration panel regarding its jurisdictional discussions. The UK court, however, dismissed Korea's claim and sustained the original argument. Unlike the previous two cases, UNCITRAL rules are applied to this dispute.

(3) Implications of Recent Developments

The advent of investment arbitration has startled Korea in many aspects and the situation has been further complicated by rather fluid circumstances surrounding IIAs in the international community where various reform proposals are being floated at the moment. Most notably, the European Union (EU) proposed in September 2015 a new scheme that would change the framework of the current IIAs and investment arbitration in a significant manner. The EU's proposal presents new ideas to amend the current investment arbitration, through the creation of a new standing court to resolve investment disputes. A proposal to introduce an appellate mechanism also entails fundamental changes in the current investment arbitration. There have been robust discussions in the international community on these issues recently. Korea is actively following these recent international developments.

The apparently changing paradigm of IIAs has put Korea in a more difficult situation, as it is participating in the negotiation of new IIAs at the moment and struggling to implement the existing IIAs, based on its experience from recent investment disputes. Korea is making efforts to keep abreast with the fast developments in IIAs and to fathom the resulting consequences for Korea and its investors.

In any event, the nine pending investment arbitration cases indicate that Korea is likely to see more investment disputes in the future, concerning various governmental regulations and policies. Likewise, any investment arbitration in the future will continue to draw keen attention from government agencies, professionals and the general public.

2) Situations in China

China is also realizing the importance of international investment arbitration. Recently some disputes have been lodged against the Chinese government by foreign investors and Chinese investors have raised disputes against foreign governments. These disputes are all raised under respective BITs as follows:

Table 1. Status of Investment Arbitration Relating to China (as of April 2020)

A. Foreign Investor against China

China	Case name	forum	The other party
1	Ekran Berhad v. People's Republic of China (ICSID Case No. ARB/11/15)	ICSID	Erkan Berhad (Malaysian)
2	Ansung Housing Co., Ltd. v. People's Republic of China (ICSID Case No. ARB/14/25)	ICSID	Ansung Housing Co., Ltd. (Korean)

B. Chinese Investor against Foreign Governments

	Chinese Investor	Case Name	Forum	The Other Party
1	Tza Yap Shum	Tza Yap Shum v. Republic of Peru (ICSID Case No. ARB/07/6)	ICSID	Republic of Peru
2	Standard Chartered Bank (Hong Kong) Limited	Standard Chartered Bank (Hong Kong) Limited v. Tanzania Electric Supply Company Limited (ICSID Case No. ARB/10/20)	ICSID	Tanzania Electric Supply Company Limited
3	Ping An Life Insurance Company of China, Limited and Ping An Insurance (Group) Company of China, Limited	Ping An Life Insurance Company of China, Limited and Ping An Insurance (Group) Company of China, Limited v. Kingdom of Belgium (ICSID Case No. ARB/12/29)	ICSID	Kingdom of Belgium
4	Beijing Urban Construction Group Co. Ltd.	Beijing Urban Construction Group Co. Ltd. v. Republic of Yemen (ICSID Case No. ARB/14/30)	ICSID	Republic of Yemen
5	Standard Chartered Bank (Hong Kong) Limited	Standard Chartered Bank (Hong Kong) Limited v. United Republic of Tanzania (ICSID Case No. ARB/15/41)	ICSID	United Republic of Tanzania

6	Sanum Investments Limited	Sanum Investments Limited v. Lao People's Democratic Republic (ICSID Case No. ADHOC/17/1)	ICSID	Lao People's Democratic Republic

See ICSID Cases: Advanced Search, *available* at https://icsid.worldbank.org/en/Pages/cases/searchcases.aspx (last visited Apr. 29, 2020).

In particular, China's sensitivity to these investment disputes have increased because Chinese regulatory authorities afford a wide discretion in terms of formulating domestic policies due to its socialist economic system. Some of the decisions taken by China, while perfectly justifiable domestically and under even trade agreements, may be in contravention of IIAs. China has become more cautious and conservative when it comes to investment arbitration and BITs. As of now, China is the country with the largest number of BITs: its total BITs have reached 145 in total. This means that China will have to see more and more investment disputes in the future.

3) Situation in Japan

Japan has not experienced any investment disputes yet, although Japanese corporations have raised two investment arbitrations against foreign governments under respective BITs. Japan's investment disputes as of now are as follows:

Table 2. Status of Investment Arbitration Relating to Japan (as of April 2020)

A. Foreign Investor against Japan: No cases
B. Japanese Investor against Foreign Governments

	Japanese investor	Case name	forum	The Other Party
1	JGC Corporation	JGC Corporation v. Kingdom of Spain (ICSID Case No. ARB/15/27)	ICSID	Kingdom of Spain
2	Eurus Energy Holdings Corporation and Eurus Energy Europe B.V.	Eurus Energy Holdings Corporation and Eurus Energy Europe B.V. v. Kingdom of Spain (ICSID Case No. ARB/16/4)	ICSID	Kingdom of Spain

See ICSID Cases: Advanced Search, *available at* https://icsid.worldbank.org/en/Pages/cases/searchcases.aspx (last visited Apr. 29, 2020).

Nonetheless, Japan is also becoming more concerned about the possible reach of investment arbitration having seen the development in other countries, including Korea and Japan. In particular, its participation in the negotiations of the TPP has brought national attention to the investment issue, as the investment chapter was one of the contentious chapters of the TPP deal. Japan is also rather cautious in terms of concluding BITs. Japan has concluded only 34 BITs so far, the lowest number by far compared to amount by Korea and China.

4) Evaluation and Assessment: Claims on Infringement of Domestic Regularatory Authority

In all three countries, investment arbiration is receiving increased domestic attention these days because of its potential to infringe upon domestic regulatory authority. Such infringement has also been found in trade agreements, but the reach and scope of such possibilities is more urgent and acute in the area of interantional investment law where the norms are more loose and coverage is much wider. As such, the current focal point of the three countries in investment arbitration is how to ensure the protection of their respective governments' authority to exercise and implement legitimate governmental authorty and policies without triggering claims under relevant IIAs.

3. International Trade Law and Trade Dispute Settlement

International trade law regulates international trade through various bilateral and multilateral trade agreements. As international trade expands, the rules that regulate it have also expanded and diversified. As trade expands it is also common to encounter multiple and multifaceted trade disputes. To facilitate international trade it is imperative to not only have sufficient rules but also a well organized dispute settlement mechanism. Thus, international trade law deals with both the substantive rules as well as the procedures for dispute settlements arising from international trade. The sources of the rights and obligations of trading partners and the means to resolve any dispute arising therefrom are regulated by international trade law. Technically speaking, international trade law is a legal regime in its own right within the general family of international law. It sets out the rules that govern the bilateral as well as multilateral relation of states including the dispute settlement mechanism. It contains both customary and conventional rules developed over the years as international trade has developed.

As international trade evolves, so do the rules and institutions regulating international trade. These days we have diverse rules, from the WTO to various bilateral and multilateral FTAs, all predicated on the general rules and principles of international trade law. All these regimes contain their own peculiar features both in terms of substantive rules as well as dispute settlement mechanisms. As such, any discussion of the various international trade regimes needs to take in to account the basic rules and principles underlying international trade law.

1) Overview of WTO/FTA Agreements

Understanding the nature of a legal obligation under a given legal regime helps one understand the dispute settlement mechanism of that regime. Thus, it is imperative to have a brief look at the main international instruments regulating international trade. The bulk of the rules governing international trade are found under the WTO Agreements and the various FTAs. WTO and FTA agreements are the typical interstate agreements meant to liberalize international trade. WTO Agreements stipulate the basic rules for trade liberalization, including well-organized rules on dispute settlement mechanisms.

On the other hand, FTAs are meant to further liberalize trade among member states. While WTO Agreements regulate trade relations almost throughout the entire world, FTA agreements cover few member states and most of them are bilateral agreements. In addition, while the WTO serves as a multilateral trading organization governing trade liberalization, FTAs are meant to further trade liberalization beyond what is secured under the WTO rules. In other words, FTAs are extensions of the trade liberalization started by the rules of WTO. However, this does not mean that FTAs are supposed to be concluded within the auspices of the multilateral trading system. It is possible for states which are not members of the WTO to conclude FTAs.

2) Nature of Rights and Obligations under the WTO/FTA Agreements

By nature, foreign investment could be affected by a broad range of issues and elements. It is probably the case that anything that affects foreigners' activity in one country could also affect foreign investment. Therefore, when it comes to the legal regimes that affect the investment sector, one could easily think of multiple legal regimes, both international and domestic, that may directly or indirectly be implicated in the investment sector. Given the close relationship between investment and trade, these legal regimes governing the foreign investment per se could also implicate the trade sector as well. Among these, the following are the key legal regimes that apply to foreign investment and trade in Korea.

Since 2003, Korea has been aggressively engaged in expanding its FTAs in an effort to complement the multilateral trading regime of the WTO. Korea first concluded FTAs with Chile and Singapore on April 1, 2004 and March 2, 2006, respectively. Korea also signed FTAs with the United States on June 30, 2007, and with India on August 7, 2009. As multiple FTA negotiations with many other trading partners are currently in progress, in the near future Korea is expected to stand in the middle of a complex web of FTA arrangements.[18] One of the key negotiating topics in these FTA negotiations has been investment, particularly how to effectively protect foreign investors' rights in the host states. Most of the time, FTA negotiations turn out to be the first occasion for the Korean government to examine the entire spectrum of investment-related issues with that particular trading partner, in addition to the conventional trade aspect, in the context of discussing and adjusting the overall bilateral economic structure. While Korea's BITs have mainly focused on the promotion and liberalization of investment between the contracting parties, the FTAs have put more emphasis on how to protect foreign investors in the respective territories. When it comes to foreign investor protection, novel issues, both substantive and procedural, have been raised and discussed, including how to reconcile different legal systems and judicial structures between the negotiating parties. As of 2020, Korea is connected to 55 countries through a network of 16 FTAs.[19]

Discussions about these structural issues have alerted Korea to the difficulty and complexity of attracting and managing foreign investment in the global economy. They have also clearly indicated that investment issues are indeed one of the key topics of Korean trading partners in establishing trade rules with Korea. In summary, through FTAs, Korea has realized that investment and trade are closely intertwined, and that they represent two sides of the same coin.

3) WTO/FTA Dispute Settlement Proceedings

As mentioned above, the DSM has been regarded as one of the most important and noteworhty achievements of the WTO. After the entry into force of the WTO Agreements as of January 1, 1995, many Members refer to the WTO Agreements whenever their trade interest is adversely affected by meausres of other Members. Most importantly, when their concern are not addressed appropriately, these Members are quick to bring their claims to the WTO's DSM. The frequency with which WTO

Members utilize the DSM is almost sixteen times higher than states' utilization of the ICJ. Even today, while the WTO itself is struggling due to the surge of protectionism, regionalism, and unilateralism, its DSM still operates robustly. It is quite telling that even the United States is still proceeding to the WTO's DSM to settle its disputes even if Washington is continuously criticizing it. This apparently shows that there is unique benefit flowing from the WTO's DSM.

The WTO's DSM is not static. Rather it evolves over time. As a matter of fact, the WTO Members have been discussing amendment of the DSU since as early as 1997. The negotiation has gone through ups and downs. As a result of the United States' complaint over the Appellate Body jurisprudence and practice and ensuing blocking of the appointment of new members of the Appellate Body starting from May 2016, the negotiation to amend the DSU has picked up pace to find a compromise, if not the best, solution to avert a total collapse. The Appellate Body ceased to function as of December 11, 2019 since the retirement of two members on December 10, 2019 left the Appellate Body with only one member. Three members constitute a Division to hear an appeal, so a one-member situation means that no appeal is taking place at the moment. So, efforts are being mobilized through various channels to revive the Appellate Body and to find a breakthrough solution. Watchers say that the amendment of DSU is one of the low-hanging fruits at the multilateral negotiation process of the WTO, so it may not be long that the DSU is amended and a new DSM is put into place. A significant change is expected, at any rate, because the United States, the driving force behind the proposed change, tables a variety of deviations from the current system. It remains to be seen as of this writing.

In addition, even before the current discussion of the DSU amendment that started from 2016, ideas for systemic changes had been presented through various fora and occasions. Examples include enhancement of transparency and participation of non-state actors (NCAs) in the DSM. If adopted and implemented, these changes will usher in a further layer of complexity. Transparency will change the way WTO litigation is conducted as reliance on the outside counsel will be practically restricted. Likewise, participation of NSAs (most notably, corporations) in the proceedings will also begin ensuing discussions of how to reflect the interests and views of the non-governmental entities and corporations. Increased interface between NSAs and the WTO DSM may further expose divergent views between the governments and corporations, and the gap between a systemic remedy (usually for the governments) and a specific, individual remedy (usually for corporations). As such, there are other potential issues than the current "WTO reform options" that may change the DSM for the future. Again, it is still too early to tell.

Even if NSA's participation in the DSM is permitted, however, this does not mean that the fundamental tenet of the trade dispute settlement system is changed. The fundamental objective of trade dispute settlement proceedings is not to provide remedy to victims in situations to be covered by domestic court proceedings. Rather, it is the restoration of balance in accordance with the schemes and designs of the trade agreement at issue. So, the question here is how to restore the once lost balance. Such being the case, compensation for the victim companies is not feasible in the first place. Here, a remedy should be prospective in nature, inevitably. Companies should find another forum with jurisdiction to seek individual remedy or monetary compensation, be it domestic court proceedings or ISDS proceeidngs. By all accounts, this basic feature will remain the same in the amended DSU and changed DSM.

Individuals and corporations usually have difficulty in understanding this basic feature. They are frustrated to realize that WTO DSM does not provide specific remedy for their specific damage as a result of a trade measure. They should realize, however, that trade dispute settlement proceedings under trade agreements are not designed to address individual concerns. They aim to restore the overall trade interest of contracting parties. Once balance is restored, those entities making trade in the system will enjoy restored benefit in the future. So, the remedy is for the system, and individuals stand to benefit from the system. In other words, the benefit is indirect and trickling down from the top. Many individuals and companies are not fully apprised of this feature of trade agreements' DSM. It may be the case, therefore, that one of the important tasks for the WTO in the future seems to be in helping corporations become more precisely aware of the unique aspects and fundamental objectives of the WTO DSM. It may be understood that the real beneficiaries of this systemic remedy are the individuals and corporations themselves in the long run.

The same feature equally applies to FTA DSM as well. Here also, the basic objective is to identify the breach of balance of interest between the contracting parties, if any, and to restore the balance. Any remedy, therefore, is also for the system, not for the corporations and individuals suffering from the impugned measures directly, and it only applies toward the future. Here also, the rule of "let bygones be bygones" continues to hold.

To seek an individual relief for the past damage done, corporations and individuals should resort to domestic court proceedings of the states imposing the trade measure at issue. It is the obligation of the WTO Members to administer judicial processes to hear these disputes.[20] One thing to note, however, domestic courts apply their own domestic laws and regulations, not trade agreements *per se*, in deliberating and deciding these disputes. In many countries, Korea, Japan and China included, international agreements and treaties are automatically incorporated into respective domestic legal systems through the operation of monism.[21] In these countries, therefore, treaties become domestic law, and it is the domestic law (originating from treaties) that apply to specific disputes as governing law. So, still it is the domestic law, not treaties, that applies. To sum up, it is domestic laws and regulations that apply in domestic court proceedings involving trade measures.

(1) State-to-State Dispute Settlement Mechanisms in FTAs

From the texts, FTAs look grandiose when it comes to dispute settlement proceedings. First of all, there are many types of them. Not only a bilateral DSM to settle disputes arising from the applicaton of the FTA, which follows the basic feature of the WTO DSM minus appellate mechanism, a typical FTA includes chapter-specific bilateral committees to deal with outstanding issues arising from the chapter, treaty-wide Joint Committees (or Commission as the case may be) composed of high ranking officials of the contracting parties where all outstanding issues are to be taken up, and mediation or conciliation proceedings for specific topics such as NTBs. Furthermore, an FTA DSM is also applicable to the investment chapter: that is, it offers a forum to resolve state-to-state disputes arising from the investent chapter in addition to the ISDS proceedings. In short, diverse options are available to the contracting parties.

Among various options, chapter-specific committees and treaty-wide committees are regularly convened and utilized. Mediation is a new mechanism and stands at a doorstep for more usage. What is peculiar, however, is the relatively low utilization rate of the FTA DSM, either for trade issue or for investment issue. According to recent statistics, only five panel reports for US-Canada FTA (Chapter 18) and only three for North American Free Trade Agreement (NAFTA) (Chapter 20) have been recorded for the past 27 years.[22] While the number of the global FTAs has surpassed 300, almost all of which are equipped with respective DSMs, this low number draws our attention. The number presents a stark comparison with WTO DSM's 595 cases during the almost the same time period and 1023-plus ISDS disputes with many of them arsing from FTAs. So, one would wonder why the utilization rate is so low on this front.

Perhaps there are a couple of reasons. By way of example, the absence of the appellate mechanism in the FTA's DSM may have prompted states to prefer the WTO's counterpart as the latter provides more room for comfort and stability. This factor makes sense given the recent negotiation at the United Nations Commission on International Trade Law (UNCITRAL) to reform ISDS proceedings where introduction of an appellate mechanism is one of the key issues. Secondly, the insufficiency of textual guidance may prove to be another reason. The FTA DSM usually possesses only skeletal provisions for dispute settlement. On the other hand, the WTO has a full agreement to regulate dispute settlement — the DSU. As a result, the operation of the FTA DSM is pretty much subject to the discretion of the contracting parties on an *ad hoc* basis, a situation that may increase uncertainty and unpredictability. Finally and most importantly, the lack of logistical support is pivotal as well. FTA DSM lacks secretariat or standing staff who can handle a dispute. The entire administrative structure and human resoucres should be created from scratch. It is not only costly and time-consuming, but also difficult to be completed within a short timeframe. All in all, these reasons are considered to have contributed to the low utilization rate of the FTA DSM. These are obstacles to be overcome for a robust FTA DSM.

The FTAs concluded by Korea, Japan and China follow the conventional formats of the FTA DSM. Thus, they have chapter-specific committees, treaty-wide committees, mediation procedure (in the case of Korea-China FTA, Korea-EU FTA), and bilateral DSM. The DSM adopted in the three countries' FTAs. They hardly contain surprises and follow the general contour of the global trade rules and WTO's DSM. Their commonalities can be summarized as follows.

First, they all adopt a prospective remedy system: bilateral DSM panels provide rulings or recommendations that are only applicable prospectively.[23] The traditional concept of balance restoration still lives on in the three countries' FTAs. Second, the three countries' FTA DSMs are all formulated as a "self-contained regime."[24] Stated differently, panels composed under the bilateral DSMs are not permitted to look to other treaties or customary international law for governing law: instead, they have to look to the specific FTA at issue for legal guidance. As for the three countries, what happens in an FTA should stay in the FTA and should be resolved through the texts of the FTA. The well-known problem of a self-contained regime due to the limitation of inward-looking legal analyses remain equally relevant to the three countries' FTAs.

Third, FTAs of the three countries do not have an appellate mechanism.[25] The three countries have placed importance on appellate mechanism in the WTO DSM, so FTA's absence of appellate system may turn out to be unpopular at least to the three countries in the long run. This issue has not presented itself yet because of the low utilization rate of FTA DSM for the three countries. One good aspect of the absence of the appellate mechanism is the shortened timeframe of the dispute settlement proceeding: the total time required for the three countries' FTA DSMs is almost halved compared to that of the WTO's DSM. As the WTO DSM takes usually 3-5 years from consultation to implementation when intermediary steps proceed smoothly,[26] the FTA DSMs for the three countries take roughly about 2-3 years in total. Fourth, unlike the WTO DSM where the Secretariat and the DSB take care of various legal, logistical and procedural matters, the three countries' FTA DSMs hardly possess such supportive entities. The three countries' FTAs do have consultative bodies in the name of "Joint Committees".[27] But in the context of dispute settlement proceedings, the Joint Committees' capacity and wherewithals are far below the WTO benchmark. Fifth, the objective of the DSMs of the three countries' FTAs is to bring the measure at issue into conformity with the FTAs.[28] This is a mirror image of the first element above, which is about a prospective remedy. It follows then that a losing party in a FTA DSM will have the benefit of a "reasonable period of time (RPT)" within which to bring the challenged measure into compliance. This is the same system as the WTO, in accordance with Articles 21.3 and 21.5 of the DSU.[29] It means that practically speaking a losing party can cure the problem if it withdraws or modifies the challenged measure during the RPT.[30] In other words, the losing party may maintain the challenged measure until the expiration of the RPT. Possibility of foot-dragging is a chronic problem of the WTO DSM at the moment and it also lives on in the FTA DSMs of the three countries as well.

At the same time, the three countries also explore in their FTAs a new terrain in the dispute settlement. An example is the possibility of paying out of the implementation obligation. According to the Korea-US FTA, a losing party may offer to pay monetary compensation to the prevailing party in lieu of the implementation of the rulings or recommendation of an FTA DSM panel.[31] Monetary compensation is technically available in the WTO DSM, but it is hardly used because implementing the rulings and recommendations of a panel is much easier and more straightforward under the DSU.[32] In the Korea-US FTA, the pursuit of monetary compensation is more practical and readily available. The Korea-US FTA also adopts a fund system. In this scheme, a fund is established and receives contribution from a losing party. The fund may then be used to cover financial expenses required in the implementation of panel's rulings and recommendations.[33] These examples show that the three countries are cautiously experimenting new schemes in dispute settlement proceedings, while they largely follow the general formats and contours of the WTO DSM.

The bilateral DSMs of FTAs are more meaningful than WTO's DSM in that they have wider areas for application. Labor, environment, State-Owned Enterprises (SOEs), competition are examples. After the signing of the Korea-US FTA in May 2007,[34] the US Congress began to demand inclusion of new issues to protect interest of the US businesses and industries using the Trade Promotion Authority as a leverage against the adminstration.[35] What the US Congress demanded to include is labor and environment.[36] The two countries re-opened negotiations and included these two issues in the agreement. Consequently, the FTA DSM then applies to these newly added issues as well.[37] They are not covered by the WTO DSM. The *Comprehensive and Progressive Trans-Pacific Partnership* (CPTPP)[38] also presents a similar example. Japan is a contracting party to this 11-state mega FTA entered into force on December 30, 2018. The environmental chapter[39] and SOE chapter[40] of the CPTPP introduce new norms (fisheries subsidies and SOE regulation) that have never existed in other trade agreements including the WTO Agreements. These new norms, once added to the mega-FTA, are subject to DSM. Japan apparently feels the pressure of implementing the new norms domestically as they pose politically sensitive and legally complex issues.

As with the WTO DSM, the prevailing party in the three countries' FTAs has the authority to retaliate by imposing trade sanction once the losing party fails to implement the rulings and recommendations of a DSM panel.[41] As the three countries are highly inter-dependent and intertwined, any trade sanction in this regard may turn out to be practically difficult and politically sensitive. This is more so considering diplomatic confrontation among the three countries where trade is frequently used as a leverage or a bargaining chip. Recent trade friction between Korea and China regarding the deployment of the Terminal High Altitude Area Defense (THAAD) missile system of the United States,[42] and between Korea and Japan concerning Tokyo's export control as a result of the Korean Supreme Court's judgment on forced labor during World War II on October 30, 2018 indicates the precarious nature of the diplomatic relations of the three countries and the easy spill-over effect to the trade sector. In the long run, such trade implications raise the possibility of FTA DSMs being invoked. At this time, there is only one FTA among the three — that is, Korea-China FTA. So, trade disputes between the two countries of the three or among the three countries are mainly brought to the WTO DSM.

So, all in all, it can be said that the DSMs of the three states largely follow the basic contours of the DSMs of the WTO and FTAs of other countries. At the same time, the three states are mindful of the need to update their DSMs to better deal with their bilateral disputes. In that spirit, they sometimes purport to introduce new schemes to settle disputes. Applying the DSMs of FTAs and WTO to the three countries in the East

Asia is sometimes rather delicate because of the historic and geopolitical implications of the three countries. From time to time, diplomatic confrontation leads to trade restrictions. This may indicate that resolution of trade disputes among the three may not be easy.

(2) Investor-State Arbitration Mechanism

Investment arbitration proceedings — the ISDS — is another type of dispute settlement mechanism that simultaneously appears in the FTAs of these three countries in East Asia. The three countries have largely incorporated existing dispute settlement proceedings in various sectors of international law, and that general tendency has continued in their negotiation and conclusion of FTAs. As a matter of fact, this unique DSM (to the extent it provides standing to individual investors of another country) also appears in the bilateral Investment Treaties (BITs) concluded by these three countries as well. China is the country that has concluded the most BITs in the world with 145 of them.[43] Korea is also one of the major BIT countries with its 105 BITs.[44] Japan is relatively different from the two countries: it has concluded just 34 BITs so far.[45] As a developed country with the status of capital exporting nation, Tokyo may have felt little incentive in promoting conclusuion of BITs. Nonetheless, the absolute majority of the the BITs of the three countries all share one commonality — the ISDS proceedings. The tendency also appears in the investment chapters of the FTAs of these three countries. Investment chapters of FTAs are basically the same as the BITs except some general provisions such as state-to-state DSM or security exceptions. Substantive provisions and ISDS proceedings, the core elements of BITs, remain the same in the investment chapters of FTAs. Investment chapters of the FTAs and the BITs collectively constiutute IIAs. Thus, it can be said that the ISDS mechanism has become a fixture of the IIAs concluded by these three countries.

In many respects, this is a unique mechanism. It introduces international arbitration between investors and host states' governments at an international tribunal applying international law — that is the IIA at issue. All the other DSMs are basically state-to-state dispute settlement mechanism (SSDS), be it WTO or FTA, or be it binding or non-binding. And yet, this investment arbitration is formulated as ISDS, and not surprisingly has attracted a great deal of attention and increasing concern from the international community. The situation is not that different in three countries. The three countries have expressed concern over the ISDS mechanism generally. As a matter of fact, the sensitivity has further flared up commensurate with the increasing number of ISDS proceedings involving the three countries. Specific reaction, however, varies. While China has faced three ISDS proceedings so far[46] and Japan none,[47] Korea has faced as many as ten cases.[48] As a result, the issue has become more sensitive in Korea compared to the other two countries. And yet, the three countries share the consensus that the current regime of ISDS affects regulatory authority of the host state governments and that reform is needed one way or another.

Admittedly, this development is not solely found in the three states. Anxieties and concerns over the ISDS have become one of the hot potato issues at the global fora in this field. Not only developed states but also developing states agree that the current regime needs fixing. The question is, and the difference is, how to fix it. Since 2017, the ICSID, UNCITRAL and OECD have all placed this topic in the priority lists of their agendas, and discussions and negotiations in these international fora are going on as of this writing. Up until now, the IIAs of the three states have incorporated standard ISDS proceedings. Indeed, there are differences among three states' IIAs, but they are relatively minor and insignificant. Perhaps, the only exception is the amended Korea-US FTA of 2018, which revised the original investment chapter (Chapter 11) of the FTA. The amended investment chapter incorporated some of the new elements of reform proposals such as dealing with frivolous claims and guarding against duplicative ISDS proceedings. When new IIAs of three countries emerge, they will probably attempt to include new suggestions and proposals.

It should be noted that ISDS does not proceed to arbitration directly. There are procedural steps to be taken prior to the initiation of ISDS. There must be consultation and negotiation between the claimant and the respondent government. All the FTAs of the three East Asian states require the notice of the intent to commence arbitration proceedings submitted to the respondent at least a certain period of time, for instance, 90 days prior to submitting any claim to arbitration.[49] Only if the consultation and negotiation fail, may the claimant proceed to ISDS. The claimant can initiate ISDS either on its own behalf or on behalf of an enterprise that he or she owns or controls. Pure derivative action by a shareholder(s) are not intended to be covered by ISDS of the three countries, but it is not clear yet whether the current text ensures such a firewall.

An arbitration tribunal consists of three arbitrators is then established. The disputing parties — the investor-claimant and foreign government-respondent — nominate the arbitrators and/or presiding arbitrators.[50] Most of the time, each disputing party appoints one arbitrator, and the third, selected by their mutual agreement, becomes the presiding arbitrator.[51] The monopolized pool of renowned arbitrators in the global ISDS practices has been a source of concern for the three countries, particularly Korea and China facing an increasing number of ISDS cases, because only few arbitrators are from East Asia or from the Asian region generally. It is a delicate issue because ISDS cases are heavily loaded with cultures and contexts which may require expertise in understanding regulatory environment of host states as well as legal expertise. At this point, among the three states only two Korean arbitrators have been appointed as arbitrators in ISDS proceedings in the global community.

With respect to the specific conduct of international litigation, the three countries arguably take a conservative approach. They seemed to favor state-centric litigation at international courts with only limited participation by private experts and professionals. They also seemed to appear to treat international litigation between states as heavily implicated by political and diplomatic considerations. The same also appears in ISDS proceedings. The tendency can be evidenced by the three countries' rather conservative stance when it comes to transparency provisions of the ISDS proceedings. They accept transparency provisions in principle, but they are cautious to preserve governments' right to protect confidentiality when they deem necessary. The transparency provisions in some of the recent IIAs require public disclosure of all documents submitted in the course of the ISDS proceedings, except confidential information to be designated by disputing parties.[52] Hearings are also supposed to be made public, again except for those portions dealing with confidential information, to be designated by disputing parties.[53] While the parties can determine which is confidential and which is not, the rule is not clear when there is a dispute over the designation itself.[54] It is another procedural legal issue to be determined by the ISDS tribunal. This reality then raises concern as governments might want to designate confidentiality wider than other entities. The three countries' governments may have realized such a possibility and have taken a conservative or cautious approach to the transparency issue.

The three countries agree to the basic principle of transparency. As such, they have agreed to the adoption of the UNCITRAL Transparency Rules[55] and Transparency Convention.[56] Much, however, remains to be seen depending on how the Rules and Convention are actually interpreted and implemented. As regards transparency, Korea has been the most active among the three, but this is not necessarily the reflection of the different approach of Korea. Rather, it largely reflects Korea's acceptance of transparency provisions in the Korea-US FTA's investment chapter by dint of prodding from the United States.[57] The Korea-US FTA has been perceived as a default rule, as with many other areas, in this regard as well. That said, as of December 31, 2021 going through as many as 10 ISDS cases in less then 8 years since 2012,[58] the government of Korea has presumably become more cautious in disclosing the hearings and documents to the general public in ISDS cases.

In terms of arbitration awards, the ISDS mechanism of the three states' IIAs do not recognize punitive damages to a claimant, again in line with the general jurisprudence and IIA texts globally.[59] Requiring specific action from the respondent government is not an option.[60] This is in contrast with the trade dispute settelement proceedings as seen in WTO DSM and FTA DSM where "specific caution" such as withdrawal or modification of the measure at issue is the whole point. Exclusion of specific action, in any event, is also in line with the general trend of IIAs (BITs and FTA investment chapters). All ISDS mechanisms of the three states' FTAs require the enforcement of the award in the domestic territory of each party.[61] They are all parties to the New York Convention of 1958[62] and the ICSID Convention of 1966.[63]

Recent IIAs of the three states also underscore the role of the Joint Committees. This is a phenomenon observed in recent IIAs in an effort to expand the authority of contracting parties in interpreting the texts of IIAs. These provisions allow a responding party or the party of a claimant (investor)'s nationality to refer the issue to the Joint Committee of the IIA.[64] Interpretation from the Joint Committee is binding on the investment arbitration tribunal.[65] In other words, contracting parties have a wherewithal to control breakaway interpretation by investment tribunal for issues they deem important. It is regarded as an important tool and has taken an important place in the current ISDS reform discussion at multiple fora. The problem, however, is a rather practical one. Decision making in a Joint Committee is through consensus.[66] A party's adamant opposition may defeat the creation of consensus and will render the interpretation issuance impossible. For some issues, the two parties may have the same view on a particular interpretation but for other issues, they may have different views. When the latter is the situation, the reference to the Joint Committee and the divisive position so exposed would only undermine the legitimacy of the award from the tribunal at the end of the day.

So, it may be the case that a binding interpretation is elusive in practice and that the procedure may carry its own consequence. At any rate, with all the pluses and minuses, the three states are apparently paying a great deal of attention to this function of the Joint Committee in future ISDS proceedings.

Concerning the manner by which investment arbitration is conducted, the Korea-US FTA includes unique provisions regarding official languages and location of arbitration. Unlike the other FTAs that Korea has concluded or those China and Japan concluded that do not specifically mention official languages of arbitration, the Korea-US FTA's investment chapter includes a provision on official languages of ISDS proceedings wherein both both English and Korean are listed as such.[67] This provision is rather unique, because almost all ISDS proceedings are conducted in English. Other IIAs' and Japan/China IIAs' absence of such a language provision is reflective of this reality. As a matter of fact, Korea's ISDS cases conducted under the Korea-US FTA are conducted in English at least until this point. This is so because using English as official language could increase the time and cost for simultaneous translation even for Korea. At the same time, even if Korean is used as an official language, the Korean government should translate the original Korean documents anyway because arbitrators do not comprehend the Korean language — so the translation burden will remain the same. Originally, it was thought that with Korean as as an official language, the Korean government could submit documents in Korean if Korea became a respondent state. But it turned out that it is not the case. Korea's sensitivity to ISDS proceedings is also reflected in the fact that arbitrations involving Korean measures are supposed to take place in Korea where there is proximity to witnesses and evidence.[68] It has also turned out that an ISDS proceeding in a third country may be more reasonable even for Korea as well due to political sensitivity and the appearance of neutrality. These two unique provisions have remained intact even after the amendment of the Korea-US FTA in September 2018. These instances show that textual provisions and actual reality are two different things in ISDS proceedings. In any event, these provisions are showcase examples of three states' efforts to deal with the sensitivities and challenges of ISDS proceedings in a creative way.

As regards possible introduction of an appellate mechanism, the three countries are generally enthusiastic about it. China is supportive of the idea even as much as to submit its own proposal for an appellate mechanism in the UNCITRAL Working Group III discussions. Korea is in pursuance of the idea ever since it was first introduced to the Korea-US FTA as early as May 2007. Japan is also receptive of the appellate mechanism even if it is generally opposed to the structural reform of ISDS proceedings. The global consensus for an appellate mechanism is quite palpable as seen most notably in the CPTPP.[69] It is not surprising, therefore, to see provisions in the three states' FTAs anticipating future adoption of an appellate mechanism once one is made available internationally.[70] An appellate mechanism can come either in a multilateral, regional or bilateral fashion.[71] Any of them may be welcomed by the three states under the circumstances. The three states are also hopeful that an appellate mechanism can handle the inconsistency and incoherence problem of the awards of the ISDS proceedings which are by nature *ad hoc* process. As active participants in the WTO DSM where the Appellate Body plays such an important role, the three states in East Asia may think that a similar entity in the increasinginly important ISDS will evolve into a comparable contributor for the global rule of law. There are of course other related issues that may negatively affect the ISDS such as additional cost and duration. That said, a properly constituted appellate mechanism may find a new balance in the proceeding so that the benefit can outweigh any associated burden going forward. This is the basic underpinning of the relevant provisions of the IIAs of Korea, China and Japan.

Other than basic preference for an appellate mechanism, few details are available, however. IIAs of the three countries are also basically silent on the details. They express their positions as being watchful of the development in the international community and ready to join the majority view on this issue. China has elaborated its ideas recently by submitting a proposal for an appellate mechanism. Its idea is to establish a multilateral appellate mechanism that can hear appeals from ISDS awards rendered by IIAs. China does not use the term "court." Nor does it indicate its preference for a standing entity called "court." And yet, it makes clear that a standing entity with whatever appellation should handle appeals through a multilateral instrument such as a new convention. As Korea and Japan do not seem to possess an assertive position in this regard, the two states may follow China's lead at least for this issue.

(3) Joint Committees

The third type of DSM contained in the FTAs of the three countries in East Asia is the Joint Committees. As explained above regarding ISDS proceedings, the Joint Committees are consultative bodies composed of high ranking officials of the contracting parties for FTAs. This body is supposed to deal with disputes arising from the contracting parties whether they are trade, investment or any other dispute. So, its jurisdiction is wide and broad. The expectation is that disputes can be resolved amicably before it proceeds to the official DSMs of the FTAs. Direct negotiation between disputing contracting parties is always an option. But direct negotiation has difficulty in breaking away from the subjective points of view. On the other hand, a Joint Committee at least attempts to make an issue a task of common undertaking between the contracting parties. Reviews from a Joint Committee could put the issue into an (at least ostensibly) objective perspective. A new landscape may change the way states present their positions. The objectivity element becomes further expanded when there are multiple parties for an FTA. Consider the CPTPP where 11 states are parties.[72] Consider also the Korea-Japan-China Trilateral Investment Treaty of 2012.[73] 11-state committee or three-state committee provide circumstances where representatives of the states view the issue from a more objective and systematic point of view.

At the same time, the Joint Committees in the FTAs are tasked with the role of monitoring and supervising the function of the entire spectrum of the FTAs. In a sense, this is going to play the role of a gatekeeper for the FTA and more importantly for the DSMs of the FTAs as well because the committees can play the role of filtering disputes. At the same time, from time to time, Joint Committees are empowered to issue "binding interpretations" of provision of FTAs. It can be directed at investment chapters of FTAs and it can be geared toward other chapters of FTAs as well such as taxation or financial issues. The point is, binding nature of such interpretation compels contracting parties and even arbitration tribunals to accept and apply it in pending and future cases. It is an effective way of placing the FTAs under the ongoing surveillance of the contracting parties. It can also guard against FTAs going out of the grips of the contracting parties by future decision makers that may or may not be fully cognizant of the provisons at issue.

So, it can be said that a Joint Committee of an FTA composed of the contracting parties is now mandated with the task of dealing with difficult issues arising from the implementation and interpretation of an FTA;[74] that is, (i) mobilizing collective efforts of the contracting parties to strike a balance in key provisions of FTAs, and (ii) interpreting the provisions of the FTAs at issue to make sure that the parties' intention is adequately reflected. If properly operated, Joint Committees can be a pivotal tool to deal with many issues of the FTAs. It is a pity that the WTO does not have a comparable mechanism. It does have a Ministerial Conference that can issue binding interpretation. But its aloof status meeting in two years with 164 Members has made the fuction elusive.[75] The fact that the Ministerial Conference has yet to adopt its first interpretative decision is quite telling in this regard. FTAs' Joint Committees are better positioned to carry out their functions.

i) Roles of Joint Committees: Recent Examples

Against this backdrop, the roles of Joint Committees have been expanding over the years. Various roles have been explored. Conspicuous examples of the new roles assigned to the committee are the authority (i) to make a decision on critical issues arising in arbitral proceedings, and (ii) issue a 'binding interpretation' that will dictate the interpretation to be issued by investment tribunals. By way of example, recent investment agreements contain the following provisions regarding Joint Committees.

① Korea-Australia FTA[76]

Chapter 21 of Korea-Australia FTA outlines institutional provisions of the Agreement and establishes a Joint Committee to oversee the implementation and operation of the Agreement. More specifically, pursuant to Article 21.3.2, a Joint Committee, comprised of officials of each Party, is under an obligation to supervise the implementation of the Agreement; supervise the work of committees and working groups; explore ways to enhance further trade and investment; seek to resolve disputes, and consider any other matter that may affect the operation of the Agreement.[77] The use of the word "shall" in this particular Article, which presumably imposes strict obligatory requirements on the Joint Committee, can be manifestly contrasted with the subsequent Article that appears to broaden the scope of the Joint Committee's role. According to Article 21.3.3, the Joint Committee "may" consider and decide any amendment or other modification to the Agreement subject to ratification by each Party, issue interpretations of the provisions of the Agreement, and take such other action in the exercise of its functions as the Parties may agree.[78] While the two provisions contain different levels of obligations, they collectively provide the Joint Committee with a broad authority and discretion that may fundamentally affect the operation and implementation of the Agreement, either through the linkage of "resolving disputes" or that of "issuing interpretation."

The role of the Joint Committee, as stipulated in Chapter 21, extends to the involvement chapter in ensuring the transparency of arbitral proceedings. For instance, with regards to the disclosure of information, Article 11.21.4(e) states that "on request of a disputing Party, the Joint Committee shall consider issuing a decision in writing regarding a determination by the tribunal that information claimed to be protected was not properly designated."[79] In addition, this provision goes even further to equip the Joint Committee with the significant power that can be exercised over the tribunal. Thus, the second part of the same provision elaborates that the Joint Committee's decision issued within 60 days of such a request shall be *binding on the tribunal*, and the tribunal's decision or award must be consistent with the Joint Committee's decision.[80]

The binding interpretation authority of the Joint Committee extends to other aspects of the investment chapter as well to the extent to which interpretation of substantive provisions is involved. As anticipated above, the Joint Committee is empowered, under Article 21.3.3(c), to issue interpretations of the provisions in the Agreement. Such an authority is reflected in Article 11.22.3 in the context of arbitral proceedings where the tribunal is obliged to be *bound* by the Joint Committee's interpretation of a provision.[81] In the same vein, Article 11.23.1 provides that the Joint Committee's interpretations of Annexes I and II are also *binding on the tribunal* and hence the tribunal's award must be consistent with the Joint Committee's decision.[82] In other words, the Joint Committee can issue its own interpretation of various key provisions in Chapter 11 that will bind reviewing investment tribunals.

② Japan-Australia EPA

Similar to Chapter 21 of Korea-Australia FTA, a Joint Committee is also established under Article 1.13 of Japan-Australia Economic Partnership Agreement (EPA) where its mandatory functions are manifestly stipulated. Pursuant to Article 1.13.2,[83] the Joint Committee, composed of representatives of the governments of the Parties, is under obligations to: review and monitor the implementation and operation of the Agreement; consider and recommend any amendments to the Agreement; supervise the work of all Sub-Committees, and adopt any necessary decisions. One of the most distinctive features that distinguish the Joint Committee of Japan-Australia EPA from that of Korea-Australia FTA is the existence of the "Sub-Committees."[84] Although there are 12 Sub-Committees in charge of different subject matters in the Agreement, a close analysis of each Article indicates that they all share a common root in terms of obligatory functions. Take the "Sub-Committee on Investment" as an example. Its roles are dictated in Article 14.18.2 where it is obliged to exchange information on any matters related to the Investment Chapter; review and monitor the implementation and operation of the Investment Chapter; consider any issues concerning the imposition or enforcement of performance requirements; consider any issues concerning investment agreements; report the outcome of discussions to the Joint Committee; and carry out other functions delegated by the Joint Committee.[85]

Unlike Korea-Australia FTA where the Joint Committee itself is given a wide scope of discretionary power, the Joint Committee in Japan-Australia EPA, as indicated above, appears to have a much narrower range of power. The Joint Committee's role is further diminished by the fact that some of its functions may be delegated to the Sub-Committees. Moreover, the Joint Committee's involvement in arbitral proceedings is relatively minimal in comparison to Korea-Australia FTA where the Joint Committee plays a significant role in arbitral proceedings. Article 19.16.2 merely provides that the "arbitral tribunal shall follow the Rules of Procedure adopted by the Joint Committee."[86] Apart from this, the rest of Chapter 19 (Dispute Settlement) is silent on the role of the Joint Committee in relation to arbitral proceedings.

③ China-Canada BIT

The recent China-Canada BIT also follows this new trend. This BIT also establishes a Joint Committee that can issue a binding interpretation to an ISDS trubinal. In particular, it can issue a bindind interpretation regarding a bona fide prudential measures.[87] A prudential measure of a contracting party's financial regulatory authorities is treated as an exception to some of the substantive provisions of the BIT. So, it is likely that a respondent government may invokve this exception to defend its otherwise problematic measure under the BIT. In this case, it will be important for a tribunal to determine whether a particular measure at issue falls under this category. In this situation, the Joint Committee can make a binding decision on this, when asked by a contracting party. A reviewing ISDS tribunal must follow the determination so rendered.[88]

This scheme shows that the binding interpretation authority can be exercised toward the entire BIT text generally or toward a specific issue in the BIT such as prudential regulation. The specific areas so identified for Joint Committee's binding interpretation issuance are mostly related to policy-oriented ones where expertise of the government is highly valued. The underlying idea is that it may not be appropriate to leave these areas and issues to the discretion of the arbitrators. It is an important counterweight againt a possible abuse of authority of an ISDS tribunal.

It is not entirely clear whether a decision from a state-to-state dispute settlement proceedings of the BIT on the validity or invalidity of an alleged prudential measure can be directly applicable (or binding) to an ISDS tribunal reviewing the same measure. If the decision of the state-to-state dispute settlement proceeding is conveyed to the Joint Committee, which then adopts it as its own decision so as to issue a binding decision, then such decision will compel the ISDS tribunal.

④ Korea-China-Japan TIT[89]

Basically the same mechanism above (regarding the

China-Canada BIT) also appears in the 2012 Korea-China-Japan Trilateral Investment Treaty (TIT). Although an explicit provision referring to a parituclar type of measure such as prudential measures in the context of the Joint Committee deliberaton is absent, the basic format of the TIT still permits a similar outcome. Contracting parties of the TIT have the option of resorting to the state-to-state dispute settlement proceeding[90] in order to elicit a ruling on prudential measures or to the Joint Committee[91] to reach consensus on this issue, either of which should carry significant weight for the analysis by an ISDS tribunal. This is so, because any governmental measure is challengeable through the state-to-state dispute settlement proceeding and Joint Committee deliberations. A prudential measure, also as a governmental measure, should be treated the same way as with any other measure.

Now, any decision from the state-to-state proceeding or Joint Committee deliberation is critical because the TIT explicitly carves out prudential measures from the ISDS proceedings, and because any decision from either of the proceedings stands to exert important influence on the ISDS tribunal, even if specific reference to issuance of binding interpretation is missing in the BIT. In other words, the parties' joint agreement on a particular interpretation cannot be ignored or taken lightly in normal circumstances. So, the absence of a specific reference to "binding interpretation" does not necessarily bring about a fundamental difference in practice. This is yet another reason that the role of a Joint Committee should be underscored.

⑤ Korea-US FTA[92]

The Korea-US FTA establishes a Joint Committee in Article 22.2 of the Agreement. The provision also sets forth two categories of authority of the Joint Committee: the one of a stringent nature using the term "shall," and the other one of a permissive nature using the term "may." The provision stipulates in pertinent part that:

> 1. The Parties hereby establish a Joint Committee comprising officials of each Party, which shall be co-chaired by the United States Trade Representative and the Minister for Trade of Korea, or their respective designees.
> 2. The Joint Committee shall:
> . . .
> (d) seek to resolve disputes that may arise regarding the interpretation or application of this Agreement;. . . .
> 3. The Joint Committee may:
> . . .
> (d) *issue interpretations of the provisions of this Agreement*, including as provided in Articles 11.22 (Governing Law) and 11.23 (Interpretation of Annexes). . . .

So, the role of the Joint Committee in the Korea-US FTA is equally critical. It has the status of entity endeavoring to resolve disputes between the two countries,[93] and of issuing interpretation for the agreement. In other words, the authority to issue interpretation covers the entire sector of the FTA. It indicates the broad nature of the Joint Committee's jurisdictional coverage. In particular, interpretations so prononunced will be binding on ISDS tribunals.[94] So, it can be said that the force of interpretation has peculiar meaning for ISDS cases. The legal force of interpretation of Joint Committee on state-to-state dispute settlement proceedings is not entirely clear: there is no specific reference mentioning binding force of interpretation on SSDS. It seems thus debatable. However, one could presume that if the parties can issue interpretation, the tribunal hearing SSDS would have to defer to and accept interpretation of the parties (through Joint Committee) thus pronounced. This is a question to be explored in future administration of the Joint Committee.

The Joint Committee of the Korea-US FTA is also tasked to play an important role for the transparency purposes. It can make a binding decision on whether a party's designation of information as protected information is appropriate. Disputing parties in ISDS proceedings may have different view as to whether a particular piece of information from the respondent government is protected (confidential) information. When this issue arises, it can be referred to the Joint Committee by either disputing party for a binding decision. Once decision is rendered, it is then transmitted to the ISDS tribunal. The consequence is that once designated as confidential, that information does not have to be disclosed. In this respect, Article 11.21 of the FTA (Transparency of Arbitral Proceedings) provides in pertinent part that:

> 4. Any protected information that is submitted to the tribunal shall be protected from disclosure in accordance with the following procedures:
>
> (e) At the request of a disputing Party, the Joint Committee shall consider issuing a decision in writing regarding a determination by the tribunal that information claimed to be protected was not properly designated. If the Joint Committee issues a decision within 60 days of such a request, it shall be binding on the tribunal, and any decision or award issued by the tribunal must be consistent with that decision. If the Joint Committee does not issue a decision within 60 days, the tribunal's determination shall remain in effect only if the non-disputing Party submits a written statement to the Joint Committee within that period that it agrees with the tribunal's determination.

With respect to the governing law provision, Article 11.22 of the FTA provides:

> 3. A decision of the Joint Committee declaring its interpretation of a provision of this Agreement under Article 22.2.3(d) (Joint Committee) shall be binding on a tribunal, and any decision or award issued by a tribunal must be consistent with that decision.

This provision should be read in conjuction with Article 22.2.3(d) above. Joint Committee's decision on governing law is binding on an ISDS tribunal. A governing law raises a critical question in terms of a tribunal's jurisdiction. It is one of the core legal issues in jurisdiction. And yet, the authority for a final say for this important issue is given to the Joint Committee. This is an important insertion. Normally, a Joint Committee handles a policy-related issues. The most legalistic decision to be made by it, as a result of recent IIAs, is the issuance of an interpretation. Interpretation is of course a legal question, but that can be understood as providing the contracting parties with the authority to their treaty text in case there is ambiguity. Examples already exist in trade agreements.[95] That said, a decision on a governing law is a different breed: it directly relates to the tribunal's authority to determine its own scope of jurisdiction. And yet, the authority is given to the contracting parties through Joint Committee. It evidences that the role of Joint Committee is expanding over the years and more advanced IIAs such as the Korea-US FTA is leading such drive for expansion. This trend offers a good reason to spend more time and resources to develop and improve Joint Committee proceedings in future IIAs.

⑥ Korea-Peru FTA[96]

Likewise, the Korea-Peru FTA introduces a similar mechanism but the entity in the Agreement is termed as "Joint Commission." The term is used interchangeably with Joint Committee. Article 22.1 of the Agreement thus provides as follows:

Article 22.1: Joint Commission

> 1. The Parties hereby establish a Joint Commission comprising the Minister of Foreign Trade and Tourism of Peru and the Minister for Trade of Korea, or their respective successors or designees.
> 2. The Joint Commission shall:
> . . .
> (d) seek to resolve disputes that may arise regarding the in-

> terpretation or application of this Agreement in accordance with Chapter Twenty-Three (Dispute Settlement).
> 3. The Joint Commission may:
> . . .
> (d) *issue interpretations of the provisions of this Agreement.*

As can be seen from above, the substantive contents are basically quite similar to the text of the Korea-US FTA. Except for the use of a different name of for the entity, basically the same role is expected of the Joint Commission so that it can issue an interpretation of the provisions of the entire agreement including the investment chapter. The authority of interpretation does not simply stop at investment chapter but includes the whole FTA. Assessment of the Korea-US FTA in this area applies to Korea-Peru FTA with equal force.

⑦ Korea-Turkey FTA[97]

Not surprisingly, a Joint Committee is also established in the Korea-Turkey FTA. Interestingly, however, this Agreement arguably contains provisions which envisage a more assertive role for the Joint Committee of the two countries. Article 7.1 of the Agreement provides the following under the title of "Joint Committee":

> 1. The Parties hereby establish a Joint Committee comprising representatives of Turkey, on the one hand, and representatives of Korea, on the other.
> . . .
> 3. The Joint Committee shall
> . . .
> (e) without prejudice to the rights conferred in Chapter 6 (Dispute Settlement), seek appropriate ways and methods of forestalling problems which might arise in areas covered by the Korea-Turkey FTA, or of resolving disputes that may arise regarding the interpretation or application of the Korea-Turkey FTA. . .

4. The Joint Committee may:

. . .

(d) *adopt interpretations of the provisions of the Korea-Turkey FTA. . .*

The above provision seems more detailed than that of the Korea-US FTA. The Joint Committee is thus expected to play a role in addressing contracting parties' disputes and resolving them to the extent that it does not infringe upon the rights of contracting parties to resort to official FTA DSM. Stated differently, as long as the contracting parties' rights to initiate FTA DSM and to defend themselves in the proceedings are ensured, the Joint Committee possesses a leeway to discuss and address bilateral issues and disputes. Further stated differently, it also means that Joint Committee should not function to intervene or hamper the operation of the FTA DSM. This is an important provision because other FTAs do not have a similar provision: they seem to state basic principles only by simply stating that their Joint Committees shall seek to resolve disputes. On second thought, they should have said that the role of the Joint Committees should not forfeit the role of the official DSM, if that is the intention of the contracting parties (which by the way appear to be the intention of the parties). By not setting forth hierarchy or sequence between the DSM and Joint Committees, these texts of other FTAs invite possible conflicts between the two entities in the future. In that respect, the Korea-Turkey FTA offers a more advanced version on this issue.

On a different note, the term "adopt" in paragraph 4 also draws attention. Other FTAs use instead the term "issue" here. The term "adopt" apparently conveys a stronger meaning than "issue." Adoption as the term is used in the trade agreements carries more official flavour and authentic nature compared to the mere issuance.[98] As for correct description of the role of the Joint Committee, the term "adopt" seems to be more appropriate.

⑧ Korea-Canada FTA[99]

On the other hand, the Korea-Canada FTA, another important FTA for the two countries, goes one step further regarding the role of the Joint Committee — the FTA uses the term Joint Commission, though. Article 20.1 of the Agreement provides the following under the title of "Joint Commission":

> 1. The Parties hereby establish a Joint Commission, composed of representatives of the Parties. The Commission shall be co-chaired by representatives of the Parties at the Ministerial level, or their designees.
> 2. The Commission shall
> . . .
> (f) without prejudice to the rights conferred in Chapter Twenty-One (Dispute Settlement), endeavour to resolve disputes that may arise regarding the interpretation or application of this Agreement. . .
> 3. The Commission may:
> (a) *adopt interpretive decisions* concerning this Agreement, which *shall be binding on dispute settlement panels* established under Article 21.6 (Establishment of a Panel) and on *Tribunals* established under Section B of Chapter Eight (Investor-State Dispute Settlement). . . (emphasis added).

As with the Korea-Turkey FTA, the Joint Commission will have to strive to resolve disputes arising from the interpretation and application of the Agreement as long as it does not infringe upon the contracting parties' right under the official FTA DSM. Again, as much as the parties' rights to initiate the FTA DSM and defend themselves in the proceedings are guaranteed, the Joint Commission can play a wide variety of roles in terms of addressing disputes arising from the interpretation and application of the Agreement including the investment chapter (Chapter 8). The hierarchy or sequence wording here also seems appropriate as seen in the Korea-Turkey FTA. Joint Commission should not hamper, delay or defeat a party's plan to proceed to the FTA DSM, if it wishes to.

Furthermore, the Joint Commission is provided with a much broader and clearer authority with respect to *all* dispute settlement proceedings of the FTA: that is, with respect to *both* the investment arbitration tribunals as well as to state-to-state dispute settlement panels. At the same time, the Joint Commission does not simply "issue interpretation" but "adopt interpretative decisions". The meaning of adoption has been discussed above in the Korea-Canada FTA. The wording "interpretative decision" can also be regarded as a stronger term than mere "interpretation". By inserting the term decision after "interpretative", the intention of the drafters is clear in that the Joint Commission is issuing 'decisions' and thereby playing the role of a dispute settlement entity. These wordings do not appear in other FTAs that Korea has concluded. In short, without any qualification, the Joint Commission for this FTA can "adopt interpretative decisions" that bind *all* types of dispute settlement tribunals including investment arbitration tribunals. Not only is the term "adopt" used (as in the Korea-Turkey FTA), but the term "interpretive decision" is chosen to stand for the more expanded role of the Joint Commission. The phrase of the FTA offers by far the strongest statement of the authority to the Joint Commission compared with other comparable FTAs and BITs.

In addition, the Korea-Canada FTA introduces yet another committee that can issue a binding decision on a particular topic of investment arbitration. Article 10.16 of the Agreement establishes the Financial Services Committee and it is expected to play a vital role in investment arbitrations. One of the roles for the committee to play is to issue a *binding decision* on whether the critical exception of "prudential measures" under Article 10.10 satisfies the requirement of the provision. This decision on the prudential measures exception will then bind the investment arbitration tribunal. According to the relevant two provisions of the Agreement:

Article 10.16: Financial Services Committee

> 1. The Parties hereby establish a Financial Services Committee. The principal representative of each Party shall be an official of the Party's authority responsible for financial services set out in Annex 10-C.
> 2. The Committee shall:
> . . .
> (c) *participate in dispute settlement procedures* pursuant to Article 10.19.

Article 10.19: Investor-State Dispute Settlement in Financial Services

> 1. If an investor of a Party submits a claim under Article 8.18 (Claim by an Investor of a Party on Its Own Behalf) or 8.19 (Claim by an Investor of a Party on Behalf of an Enterprise) to arbitration under Section B of Chapter Eight (Investor-State Dispute Settlement) and the disputing Party invokes an exception pursuant to Article 10.10, *the Tribunal shall, at the request of the disputing Party, refer the matter in writing to the Committee for a decision.* The Tribunal shall not proceed until it receives the decision or report under this Article.
> 2. In a referral pursuant to paragraph 1, the Committee *shall decide* whether and to what extent Article 10.10 is a valid defence to the claim of the investor. The Committee shall transmit a copy of its decision to the Tribunal and to the Commission. The decision shall be *binding on the Tribunal*. . . (emphasis added).

The Joint Commission and the Financial Services Committee in the Korea-Canada FTA thus stand to play a critical role in the decision-making process of ISDS tribunals. The Joint Commission and the Financial Services Committee can exercise overlapping jurisdiction in this regard. The Joint Commission can exercise its role for adoption of general interpretative decisions which may also include financial regulatory bodies' prudential measures while the Financial Services Committee can exercise its own role to issue binding interpretation for prudential measures specifically. It can be called a belt-and-suspender approach for prudential measures. The situation also shows that not only treaty-wide Joint Committee but also chapter-specific committees can play an important role in settling disputes under the FTAs. Again, this Agreement between Korea and Canada envisages one of the most important roles of the contracting parties' committees as reining in the decision-making process of ISDS tribunals.

ii) New Roles: Decision on Specific Issues

In short, one of the new functions assigned to Joint Committees is to make a decision on some of the key issues raised in specific ISDS proceedings. For instance, Joint Committees are eligible to make a decision on the status of confidential information as claimed by a party submitting such information. Joint Committees also possess the authority to determine whether a particular governmental measure falls under the prudential measure exceptions, which basically carves out governmental measures that aim to ensure the capital soundness of a financial institution from the reach of the FTAs or BITs. These issues are closely related to general policy objectives of the government at issue and are not necessarily amenable to a purely legal inquiry. It is therefore believed that having Joint Committees make decisions on these issues may better serve the interest of the parties and perhaps even free the ISDS tribunals of SSDS panels from the onerous task of making decisions on a highly political and professional topics. These decisions of the Joint Committees then bind the tribunals with respect to the issues posed. Some FTAs or BITs do not have the specific term "binding" from time to time. But in practice the absence would not make much difference because parties' common voice for a particular phrase for a bilateral treaty should exert immense influence on the tribunals and panels' deliberation no matter what. In practice, therefore, there does not seem to be any meaningful difference.

It should be noted, however, that the decisions of the Joint Committees do not necessarily dictate the outcome of the ISDS or SSDS proceedings. Nonetheless, decisions on the key intermediary issues stand to affect the fate of the disputes significantly. What is being observed now is the increasing tendency to favor insertion of new procedural and substantive elements into the texts of FTAs and BITs, so that the contracting parties can have more leeway and authority to dictate what they want for the treaty to mean. For this purpose, Joint Committees and similar chapter-specific or function-specific committee are set to play a pivotal role.

iii) New Roles: Issuance of 'Binding' Interpretation

Another important role increasingly being assigned to treaty-based Joint Committees is an issuance of an interpretation of treaty provisions that will then *bind* reviewing ISDS tribunals and/or SSDS panels. Since ISDS and SSDS proceedings are arguably all about treaty interpretation in accordance with Article 31 of the Vienna Convention, Joint Committees' issuance of binding interpretations is both meaningful and critical in reaching a conclusion in a particular proceeding. This is particularly the case given that disputes arising from FTAs and BITs have been suffering from the ambiguities and loopholes of treaty provisions due to the gap between the conventional texts and fast-changing business realities in the global community. In the case of Korea, Japan and China, BITs concluded as early as 1970s still continue to apply in 2020. Reflecting a half-century gap in disputes while not overstepping the textual parameters is anything but easy, and always prone to controversies.

Commentators have contended that the binding interpretation mechanism is an important tool for the contracting parties to preserve their original intention as drafters of the FTAs and BITs.[100] It is still important wherewithal for the contracting parties to provide proper evolutionary interpretation — if such interpretation is not prohibitied in the FTA or BIT — to reviewing tribunals and panels. Contracting parties may be able to avoid the situation where they are caught off guard by overly broad or unreasonably creative interpretation by decision makers. At the same time, this is an important departure from the principle of judicial independence and rule of law. In a sense, the parties dictate how their judges should decide on a particular issue. As with anything, the robust Joint Committees is also a double-edged sword. The question is how to find and maintain proper balance.

While some FTAs and BITs stipulate the Joint Committees' authority to issue binding interpretations in an open-ended manner,[101] others simply set forth the authority of Joint Committees to issue interpretation.[102] As such, Joint Committees of the second category may not issue a "binding" interpretation because a specific stipulation to that effect is absent. Nonetheless, as discussed above the practical difference may be minimal: any interpretation issued by a Joint Committee, composed of ministerial level officials of all contracting parties, should carry significant weight in the course of analyses and reviews by a reviewing tribunals and panels, as such joint declarations of interpretation by the contracting parties indicate the true intention of the parties and is eligible to be accorded significant legal weight in the course of interpreting the relevant terms.[103] Few, if any, tribunals or panels could easily disregard such joint pronouncement. Thus, even if an interpretation is not specifically termed as "binding," the fact that the contracting parties have agreed to jointly issue such an interpretation itself still carries significant weight in the tribunal's and panel's decision on the issue. So, one could assume that even the 'simple' interpretation model may carry a similar legal weight with the 'binding' interpretation model.

As the three countries in East Asia have seen relatively lower representation of their experts in the international tribunals and panels, they seem to have higher likelihood of resorting to the usefulness of Joint Committees when critical treaty terms are on the balance. Arguably, the governments of these three countries may have stronger sympathy for such party-controlling mechanisms as Joint Committees.

iv) Prospective Consequences of Expanded Roles of Joint Committees

Most notably, the newly found roles of Joint Committees arguably stand to address the complex and controversial issues of investment arbitral proceedings, most notably balancing the conflicting interests between a host state and a foreign investor. Consider a recently released EU guideline for BIT negotiations that shows the intensity of efforts by states (even developed countries such as the EU) to strike a balance between the two conflicting interests:

> - Significant clarification of the substantive protection provisions to ensure that the state's right to regulate to pursue legitimate public policy objectives is protected;
> - Clarification and precise definition of the content of FET;
> - Detailed language on indirect expropriation (step-by-step guidance to arbitral tribunals in finding indirect expropriation and definition of regulatory takings);
> - Narrow definitions of investment (characteristics) and investor (shell companies are not to be protected);
> - Detailed provisions on ISDS including transparency, procedural provisions to deal with time limits, concurrent proceedings, frivolous cases, unfounded claims by shifting costs;
> - Novel features such as encouragement of ADR with a detailed mediation annex, the introduction of an appellate mechanism and a code of conduct for arbitrators.[104]

The above guideline showcases the EU's sensitivity in protecting its regulatory authority in the increasing number of investment arbitration. The same level of sensitivity is being observed in Korea, Japan and China. In fact, Chapter 11 (investment chapter) of the Korea-US FTA was one of the most controversial chapters during the negotiation and ratification of the agreement between 2006 and 2011.[105] The sensitivity arose again during the amendment negotiations in 2018. Mainly, the focus of the domestic debates was about the erosion or usurpation of Korea's national sovereignty in favor of the foreign investors' expanded rights. As a matter of fact, investment agreements and investment chapters are different because the interface between agreements and municipal law is more direct and closer than other agreements and other chapters.[106] Furthermore, the decision of investment arbitration — an award — entails monetary compensation, something that is not seen in other FTA and WTO DSMs.

Political sensitivities surrounding the ISDS proceedings have also changed how hearings are conducted. Open hearings in investment arbitrations have become an increasingly new phenomenon these days. Protecting confidential information has become an important issue in the open hearing formula.[107] As such, specific ways to protect confidential information have been developed and inserted into IIAs (that is, FTA investment chapters and BITs), such as having two different sessions (comprising a public session and a confidential session),[108] and using closed circuit transmission with a time lag.[109] These safeguards would certainly help alleviate the concern of the information-submitting governments. And yet the governments would continue to face the inherent dilemma of whether, when and how to open up its internal decision-making process and attendant documentation to foreign and domestic observers.

In light of all these political sensitivities associated with investment arbitration and legal difficulties in finding an equilibrium between host governments and foreign investors, as well as the legal principle that investment arbitral tribunals should operate under the strict bounds of stipulated texts of IIAs replete with ambiguities and vagueness,[110] states are destined to find Joint Committees useful. Joint Committees may arguably offer a route through which parties can present their intentions and views. The open hearings have made this possibility more meaningful because what their governments have argued and not argued are directly disseminated to the general public. Such being the case, the governments have more incentives to present their views and have them reflected correctly in the process of ISDS proceedings. Governments of both or all contracting parties may have similar incentives. If so, Joint Committees is a useful tool to register governments' intention and reflect it in ISDS proceedings. So, the 'transparency' drive has arguably made the governments exposed to the outside viewing including their domestic constituents. One way to avoid domestic criticism is to mobilize Joint Committee deliberations so that governments can try to reflect their view in the ISDS proceedings properly and show the domestic constituents that the governments have made their best efforts. FTA and WTO DSMs also pursue enhanced transparency. Joint Committees' or similar entities' role in those state-to-state proceedings will be equally important.

Joint Committees also have the potential to become an avenue to reflect the fast-changing business and investment environment of the global community more appropriately. They are freed from the legal straitjackets that tie the hands of a tribunal or panel's hands: basically a tribunal or panel should only apply the text as it is written. As the gap between the text and the business reality grows over the years, tribunal's and panel's tasks become more and more difficult. The governments may try to bridge the gap by finding consensus in their Joint Committees. The Joint Committees can then issue interpretations that officially bind a tribunal and panel. So, the consequence is the same, the only difference being that the Joint Committee option does not require sometimes onerous a treaty amendment process.

Joint Committees have another important potential. They offer a forum where the contracting parties can consider not only a particular treaty but also other related and similar treaties and/or disputes pending between the two parties, and then try to come up with a solution that can resolve these related disputes in a *comprehensive* manner. This is not possible in other FTA or WTO DSMs or in ISDS proceedings, because they are presumed to operate within a respective self-contained regime. A comprehensive approach is not feasible.

More importantly, a Joint Committee may more properly be able to take into account the policy dimension of the measure at issue. This is not something that a tribunal or a panel is able or permitted to carry out. The policy expertise of governments may ensure interpretation that accurately captures underlying intention of the governments.

The combination of all these various aspects would certainly help guarantee an appropriate interpretation of the terms of the IIAs. Granted, investment tribunals and state-to-state dispute settlement panels may also take into account all these elements in their scrutiny. But their acclaimed expertise in legal matters may not necessarily ensure the ability to see through the plethora of these non-legal, practical and policy prisms.

Such being the case, an argument can be made that Joint Committees, when an appropriate division of labor is achieved vis-à-vis investment arbitral tribunals and state-to-state dispute settlement panels, would offer the most readily available alternative route to deal with political sensitivities and legal complexities associated with investment disputes. It is not to argue that Joint Committees should take the supreme or monopolized position; rather it means that Joint Committees and ISDS and SSDS proceedings can complement each other. Where a fundamental overhaul of the existing regime and an introduction of an innovative scheme are either too elusive or ambitious at least for the time being, contemplating an enhanced role of Joint Committees or their equivalents may offer a reliable, though not perfect, alternative. This is a particularly intriguing option for East Asian countries who presumably have more confidence in government-to-government discussions on treaty interpretations than in dispute settlement settings.[111] They seem to welcome the recent development in the ISDS front. They will probably welcome similar development in other dispute settlement proceedings.

Joint Committees of the three states' FTAs also deal with administrative issues relating to dispute settlement proceedings. For instance, the Korea-US-FTA obliges the Joint Committee to manage the remuneration and expenses to be paid to panelists.[112] It also monitors the implementation of the rulings and recommendations of the panel. In addition, it authorizes trade sanctions in the case of non-implementation.[113] It can be said therefore that Joint Committees of the three states' FTAs are designed to perform function comparable to that of the DSB of the WTO. Joint Committees in the BITs have not been elevated to the status of dispute settlement administrator yet.

As with any other Joint Committees, those in the FTAs and BITs of three countries are also structured to operate in accordance with consensus of contracting parties.[114] Consensus between or among contracting parties can sometimes be easy to achieve but sometimes quite difficult. Needless to say, if the two parties have a polarized view, consensus would be elusive. Also, consensus in a bilateral setting would mean full agreement between the two states. If so, Joint Committees sometimes may not be able to carry out its intended function. So, despite treaty provisions, Joint Committees cannot issue a binding interpretation because of the absence of consensus. Likewise, in the case of conflicting views between the parties, the Joint Committee may reach a compromised deal, which could make the treaty provision more ambiguous and murky. These situations, if materialized, would defeat the very objective of Joint Committees. So, while the role of Joint Committees should be underscored and expanded, it should not be forgotten that their successful operation is premised upon the building of consensus. As the three states in East Asia have more commonality in the understanding of the proper role of the government — as opposed to their western counterparts — consensus finding and building may be relatively easier in Joint Committee deliberations of the three states. One could predict a higher likelihoold of success of Joint Committee in the context of FTAs and BITs concluded between or among the three countries. At this point, there is only 2012 TIT among the three states. They are engaged in the negotiation of the trilateral FTA, but finalization of the deal does not seem likely in the near future.

4) Evaluation and Assessment: Surge of Protectionism and Ensuing Disputes

The various types of DSMs contained in the FTAs of the three states are about to be mobilized for a variety of disputes arising from the three states. The three states have regularly met each other at the WTO's dispute settlement body. Their disputes at the WTO will continue to take their own paths. At the same time, new disputes are to be assessed by and resolved through DSMs contained in the FTAs. The utility of these DSMs of the FTAs is further underscored due to the surge of protectionism in this part of the globe.

(1) Overall Assessment of the DSMs of the FTAs of Korea, China and Japan

A review of the dispute settlement mechanism of the three countries in East Asia highlights the importance of the dispute resolution mechanism in the overall architecture and scheme of the FTAs. It is supposed to operate as a main pillar for the implementation of the respective trade agreements. The SSDS proceedings of the FTAs of the three countries have adopted the basic template of the WTO's DSM, except for the appellate proceedings. The timeframe for the entire proceeding has been reduced almost by half compared to that of the WTO's DSM, which may incentivize the utilization of the proceeding in the long run. It is particularly the expectation because the three countries are one of the most frequent users of the WTO's DSM, with China placed at fourth, Japan at ninth and Korea at tenth places among 164 Members as of December 31, 2021. While in the initial stage the SSDS of FTAs has shown a low level of utilization as with other regions in the world, it however seems to be the case that over time the case numbers will go up under the circumstances, at least with respect to the three East Asian countries. By way of example, Korea has already had multiple disputes with the United States as the United States is not fully satisfied with Korea's implementation of the Korea-US FTA. As such, it can be said that there is a higher chance for the SSDS proceeding in the US-Korea FTA to be invoked in the future.[115] The EU has already taken the first step *vis-à-vis* Korea based on its FTA with Korea. In July 2019, the EU has initiated the first official dispute settlement proceeding under Chapter 13 of the FTA claiming that Korea had not fulfilled its obligation under the Chapter regarding implementation of the core conventions of the International Labor Organization (ILO).[116] While the dispute is a chapter-specific dispute proceeding as opposed to an FTA DSM, it speaks volumes about the imminent advent of the FTA dispute settlement proceedings for Korea. By all accounts, a similar situation may also flare up as regards other DSMs of FTAs concluded by Korea, and DSMs of FTAs concluded by China and Japan as well.

In short, the FTAs concluded by the three countries so far indicate that a series of new dispute settlement proceedings are being put into place. They range a wide spectrum. Some of binding DSMs while other non-binding ones. Some cover the entire FTA texts while others cover specific chapters. As the three countries are one of the most frequent users of these mechanisms due to their robust trade and investment activities, their performance and evaluation from these various proceedings of the FTAs are expected to provide a benchmark for the future development of these proceedings internationally. In fact, the recent surge of protectionism and mounting trade frictions among the three states and/or involving three states offer a recipe for wider utilization of the system in the near future.

(2) Particular Challenges for the FTAs of Korea, China and Japan

In the fast-changing landscape of the global trading regime, the three states face the same challenges the larger global community face. This is natural and inevitable given the fact that the three countries constitute major components of the global trading regime. Likewise, the problems associated with dispute settlement proceedings on a global scale apply to these three states with equal force. The three states, therefore, are struggling with the multiplication of DSMs as a result of surge of FTAs, insufficient enforcement mechanism of DSMs, increasing political sensitivity of ISDS proceedings, and increasing demand of human and financial resources for these DSMs. As time passes by, the problems seem to be getting more acute in proportion to the number of FTAs and number of DSMs contained therein.

The marked discrepancy between developed states and developing states in terms of capacity building in dispute settlement proceedings, which is arguably evident on a global scale and which is a fixture topic for any negotiation of dispute settlement proceeding, also appears in East Asia as well. Japan has been an active player in WTO DSM for a long time with its strong legal and expertise infrastructure. Korea has also made important strides over the years. Its dispute settlement infrastructure has been established and solidified over the years, particularly after 2005 with its initiation of the Korea-US FTA negotiations. Largely, Korea is still training Japan in terms of the overall capacity and infrastructure of handling dispute settlement proceedings. China started late — presumably around 2006 when WTO disputes started to flare up with the United States — but has overtaken the two countries fast. As of 2020, China seems to be better situated than Korea or Japan to the extent WTO DSM is concerned. Its human resources and expert pools have skyrocketed in a short time frame. As only China is regarded as developing Member in the WTO jargon, this situation indicates the possible inappropriateness of looking at dispute settlement capacities only through the prism of developed-developing binary perspective.

With respect to the three countries of Korea, China and Japan, while they have been doing relatively well compared to other countries in other parts of the world, their capacity problem will continue to remain. This is so because of the multiplication and fragmentation of DSMs through as many FTAs. All three countries will soon face a shortage of infrastructure and human resources to deal with all these different dispute settlement proceedings. To avert the worsening situation, they will have to make doubled effort to build up their infrastructure and resources. Frankly speaking, still there seems to be obvious gaps between the capacities and resources of three countries on the one hand, and those of the United Statees, the EU, on the other hand. The three countries are lagging behind these other countries in the overall capacity of DSM participation and management. Many issues are involved here, indeed. Language, culture and education have all affected the current situation. As much as these issues are hard to change in a short period of time, the three countries will have to deal with the thinly stretched workforce and experts in handling an increasing number of DSMs of various kinds either simultaneously or consecutively.

A similar problem is also raised regarding DSMs adopted among or between the three states. The discrepancy in capacities among the three states in the region may trigger disproportionate burdens and complex dynamics for the three states when they resort to DSMs of FTAs between or among themselves. Also, the three states' disputes are usually laden with historical or political issues, which again make their resolution more challenging. It will be interesting to see how the three countries approach DSMs and how they use them for the resolution of their disputes in the long run.

i) Burden from Legal Aspects

While the three states are active in negotiating and concluding FTAs, they are also struggling to deal with a wide range of sensitive issues contained in FTAs. The difficulties stem from the reality that FTAs tend to cover many different issues. Some of the issues are arguably conventional trade topics, so their inclusion in trade agreements is natural. Other issues, on the other hand, are not conventional trade issues, and yet, contracting parties agree to include these non-trade issues in their trade agreements because trade agreements nowadays provide a framework for bilateral relationship between the two states. So, FTAs have expanded their jurisdiction to different sectors, such as labor, health, human rights, environment, SMEs, competition regime, investment, SOEs to name a few.[117] Arguably, these issues span over almost the entire spectrum of national economic activities. If anything, the FTAs of these days could be better termed as "Bilateral Relationship Framework Agreement". The term "Free Trade Agreement" seems misleading in this regard. As such, negotiations of an FTA have become more time-consuming and politically sensitive — interest groups collide as if they did in the national legislature. Implementation of an FTA has become equally challenging — various segments of national sovereignty are implicated. All these aspects of new FTAs have caused the three states to deal with an increasing amount of burden. The burden is not merely burden from practical perspectives; it also means burden from legal perspectives. Negotiations of the new norms, incorporation of the new norms into domestic laws and regulations, implementation of the new norms, and management of disputes all constitute different faucets of legal burden.

All three states apparently face difficulties. Among the three, Japan seems to face a relatively less burden in this regard. As the country that was the main gate of importing modern law and legal culture in East Asia in mid-19th century, Japan presumably has deeper legal infrastructure and more sophisticated legal environment, which would make acceptance and implementation of new norms relatively easier than the other two countries. Japan's leaderhip in the CPTPP since 2016 and the WTO reform discussion since 2018 provide good examples in this regard. On the other hand, China seems to face the highest burden. Its economic regime, still containing socialist elements at its core, shows a wide margin and gap with new norms being contemplated in the global community at the moment. As such, China has been a conservative negotiator, to put it mildly, in many FTA negotiations currently pending, most notably the RCEP. It may believe that the introduction of new rules and norms in FTAs would pose a disproportionate challenge to them. Korea seems to be in the middle. It is ready to incorporate new norms when necessary. But at the same time it still maintains conservative positions when the new norms spark domestic controversy.

In short, *de facto* disparity among the three states in FTAs' incorporations and implementation of new norms needs to be taken into consideration. This disparity affects and sometimes determines specific policy position of these three states in individual topics of new norms. So, the three states are in a unique position: culturally they have many things in common including Chinese characters in their languages. Economically, they are distinct as the two (Korea and Japan) follows liberal capitalism while the other one adopts market socialism. Legally, they are distinct as the same two adopt western legal culture and education, the other one has its own legal culture and education.

ii) Burden from Logistical Aspects

At the same time, FTA's burden from logistical perspectives is equally important. Negotiations for multiple FTAs cause critical burden. Implementation of the FTAs equally invites similar burden. All FTAs have different provisions and non-identical contents. Government agencies have to apply their laws and regulations differently to other trading partners depending upon the specific contents of FTAs with them. It has not been the case at the WTO because all rules are the same and all applications are the same, except for minor differences such as those stemming from S&D treatments. In FTAs, the traditional singular approach does not exist anymore, thereby driving up the level of logistical burden for all contracting parties. The three states seem to face an increasing level of challenges on this front.

One of the areas where such logistical burden is sorely felt is none other than dispute settlement proceeding. Preparation for and participation in dispute settlement proceeding require budgetary support and human resources. When there are only a handful of cases under the WTO, the burden does not stand out. Countries like Korea, Japan and China have dealt with the task relatively efficiently. The situation, however, changes drastically in the FTA regime where multiple disputes settlement schemes of various sorts exist in an FTA and where multiple FTAs coexist at the same time. Even these three states have difficulty in handling all these diverse dispute settlement schemes. As for Korea, it has now 18 FTAs. Because each FTA usually has state-to-state bilateral DSM, Joint Committee, non-binding dispute settlement proceedings as well as ISDS proceedings, one FTA means extra 3-5 new schemes. In other words, 16 FTAs means almost 50-plus new proceedings for Korea. And this change is all happening while the number of government officials remain the same and financial support shows only a minimal increase.

One might raise the point of dormant FTA's DSMs in the FTA era. That is true, but the situation is now changing fast. As FTAs assume more jurisdictions and WTO falters, the pendulum of dispute settlement starts to swing in the FTA's direction. The recent experience of Korea and China is indicative of this situation. Once the situation suddenly leaps into another dimension, the three states are likely to find themselves in a dire situation to cope with multiple disputes at multiple dispute settlement proceedings under multiple legal norms. It is doable, but only if sufficient financial, human and systematic support is guaranteed. The three states, while economically vibrant, have still a long way to go in this area.

The FTAs of the three countries adopt a conventional definition of a "measure" to be challenged at the dispute settlement mechanisms. The definition of a "measure" is so broad that it may capture a wide range of governmental action and inaction of a state.[118] As long as there is a "measure" falling under the FTA at issue, a dispute settlement proceeding can be initiated.[119] Consequently, it is not surprising that it is merely a matter of time before a governmental measure is brought to an FTA's DSM. Once the initial stage is over and the FTAs of the three states are brought to a full implementation mode, dispute settlement mechanisms are expected to be fully mobilized. WTO's DSM will be utilized continuously, but in addition, FTAs'

DSMs will have to be invoked as well so as to address new issues that do not appear in the WTO Agreements and can only be treated in FTAs' DSMs.

In other words, in the near future, Korea, China and Japan will have to deal with multiple dispute settlement mechanisms — both WTO's DSM and various mechanisms in their respective FTAs with many other countries: in the case of Korea, there are already 18 FTAs that Korea has to deal with at the moment. China and Japan have similar numbers of FTAs and DSMs. Going forward, the three states will have difficulty in dealing with all these disputes in a short time frame. Burdens can be acute because the three states are one of the most frequent parties of global trade disputes. So, their exposure will be much higher than average trading nation.

iii) Interaction of Multiple DSMs in a Single FTA

Korea, China and Japan concluded FTAs with many of their trading partners starting from the middle of 2000s. These FTAs have largely turned out to be successful, as evidenced by their continuingly strong activities in the trade sector. Diverse reasons spanning over economic rationale and geopolitical considerations have prompted the governments of the three countries to push ahead with the FTA drive with other countries. Since these FTAs have been negotiated and concluded almost contemporaneously in a short time period, key traits and characteristics of the agreements are similarly formulated. The dispute settlement mechanisms of their FTAs are no different. While they contain state-specific variations, they the variations seem to be mostly minor adjustments rather than fundamental differences. The DSMs of these FTA generally share more commonalities. What stands out in this regard is the fact that these three countries have shown the tendency of following the development of DSMs in FTAs concluded by other countries, mainly their western counterparts such as the United States and the EU. Considering the unique cultural, legal and historical backgrounds surrounding the three countries, it may be the case that DSMs could also be experimented and engineered rather creatively and distinctively. That, however, has not been the case so far.

How the three countries will respond to the burgeoning DSMs in their FTAs is now a critical question. FTA conclusion has been the main task for the three countries for the past decade and now their implementation is coming to front and center, which inevitably brings up the issue of trade disputes. Recent development is already indicating the changing direction of wind on this front. A great deal of homework lying ahead waiting for the attention of the three states' governments. In particular, the marked disparity in human and financial resources concerning the three East Asian states *vis-à-vis* their trading partners in other parts of the world may impose disproportionate burdens on contracting parties in implementing their obligations under FTAs and utilizing the FTAs' DSMs. Granted, they have experience similar problems in their participation in the WTO DSM, but the new challenge on the FTA front is not comparable to the WTO front, both in terms of quantity and quality. New norms not seen in the WTO are flooding the FTAs these days. All these FTAs have a variety of their own DSMs. Combining the two, the three states are supposed to face challenges on their dispute settlement front in a way that has not been seen or experienced before. The three countries' status as trade dispute-prone countries may further foster the tendency. At the same time, how the three countries deal with FTA DSMs will provide meaningful and insightful guidelines to other countries in other parts of the world, because at present the three countries each represent different groups of economic development. China represents the group of developing states, Japan the group of developed states together with United States and EU, and Korea in the middle of developed and developing states. This is a very useful mixture of groups that is particularly useful in contemplating new norms in trade.

4. International Economic Law Disputes at Domestic Courts

International economic law disputes are also frequently lodged at the domestic courts of contracting parties. This situation reflects the point of view of the interested parties that domestic courts are the easiest avenue to use. They can also control the entire procedure as they themselves are the parties in disputes. Still, there are unique aspects to be considered in this process.

1) Sovereign Immunity; Absolute Sovereign Immunity; Restrictive Sovereign Immunity; Act of State Doctrine

Sovereign immunity has become "customary international law" which is "solidly rooted in the current practice of States."[120] The ICJ opined that this concept "occupies an important place in international law and international relations."[121] This sovereign equality-based jurisprudence basically dictates that the judicial branch of one state does not have jurisdiction over another state.[122] Due to the lack of jurisdiction, any case falling under this category would have to be dismissed by the reviewing court once it is determined that sovereign immunity indeed applies.[123] Such being the case, when an individual plaintiff, either a natural person or a juridical one, brings a legal action against a foreign government at a domestic court other than the court of the foreign government's state, this concept is invoked to prompt a possible dismissal of the case at issue. Although the scope of the jurisprudence has been narrowed over the years, since the introduction of the concept of "restrictive sovereign immunity" in 1952, instead of the traditional "absolute sovereign immunity,"[124] this rule nonetheless poses a significant legal hurdle when an individual initiates a legal action against a foreign government at a court other than the foreign government's own.[125]

As a matter of fact, sovereign immunity deserves particular attention in the context of investment disputes. Both practical and legal aspects can be contemplated in this regard. With respect to the practical aspect, it should be noted that investment disputes, by nature, constitute classic instances of invoking sovereign immunity even under the restrictive sovereign immunity concept. This is because investment disputes presuppose "governmental action" on the part of a host government toward a "foreign individual." Any legal dispute between the two, therefore, is unable to proceed to a court of another state other than the host state. Courts of other states including the aggrieved foreign individual's own would have to dismiss the case, as the underlying claim arguably relates to the governmental function (*i.e.*, acts *jure imperii*) of a foreign government. Stated differently, in the absence of an international tribunal with proper jurisdiction,[126] sovereign immunity basically means that more often than not an aggrieved foreign investor would have to proceed to the court of the host state to have his or her day in court. This reality should then be put into perspective by considering that a judicial branch is also considered to be part of the government of a state along with the executive and legislative branches.[127] The inevitable outcome would then be an awkward situation where investment disputes are now supposed to be reviewed and decided by a direct party in a dispute — the disputing foreign government. This is certainly not an ideal environment to deal with such volatile issues as investment disputes.

Next, an obstacle can also be found in the legal aspect. Again, the nature of investment disputes is premised upon the regulatory authority of a host government toward a foreign individual. A challenge by a foreign individual against a regulatory decision of an agency would usually be susceptible to a deferential standard by a court vis-à-vis the executive branch. By way of example, in the case of the United States, this jurisprudence has been called the *Chevron* standard after the US Supreme Court decision in *Chevron U.S.A., Inc. v. Natural Resources Defense Council*,[128] where the court issued a highly deferential standard for an agency determination when based on the agency's statutory interpretation authority. The court in *Chevron* thus stated that it "[has] long recognized that considerable weight should be accorded to an executive department's construction of a statutory scheme it is entrusted to administer."[129] Arguably the *Chevron* standard or any other variation for that matter also applies to an investment dispute as the dispute basically takes the form in which an agency determination based on an enabling statute is challenged by a foreign investor. The reviewing court would then approve a wide latitude of discretion for the defendant governmental agency at issue.[130] Under these circumstances, from the domestic legal perspective a foreign investor is likely to face a strong legal obstacle in prevailing in domestic court proceedings of the host state, the only available domestic court under the concept of sovereign immunity.

The prevalence of FTAs is directly relevant to this issue of sovereign immunity. The increase in trade disputes as a result of the application of FTAs has also triggered a commensurate surge of domestic court disputes. The interested parties can only proceed to the domestic courts of the party taking a measure in an FTA. The problem here is that interested parties end up in domestic courts of the state whose measures are the subjcts of the disputes. An outcome of the domestic court proceedings therefore sometimes tends to raise the issue of neutrality.

In light of this, the conclusion of IIAs and the introduction of ISDS proceedings are designed to address these practical and legal problems arising from the conventional concept of sovereign immunity. ISDS proceedings offer a new avenue to interested parties so that they can avoid proceeding to the domestic courts of a disputing party. So, the concept of sovereign immunity arguably warrants careful attention in the discussion of investment issues and disputes, including, most notably, the umbrella clause.

Sovereign immunity has undergone a significant change over time. It has now evolved into a concept called "restrictive concept of sovereign immunity" which basically does not accord the protection of sovereign immunity to actions of state if those actions not regulatory but commercial.[131] This means that a contract between a host state government and a foreign corporation may not be subject to sovereign immunity, and the dispute can be brought to the courts of foreign countries as well as those of the host state.[132] Arguably many contracts that a government enters into with foreign corporations can be categorized as commercial in nature. Without the protection of sovereign immunity, the government of a host state basically takes the same status as other private entities.

That said, an umbrella clause in an IIA raises a peculiar problem. It may trigger an internal contradiction whereby the government, on the one hand, is treated as if it were a private entity under the restrictive concept of sovereign immunity, while the same government is treated, on the other hand, as if no different from the regulatory authority wielding governmental authority in substantive provisions of an IIA. In short, umbrella clauses in IIAs view the government in commercial contracts as a party to be brought to ISDS. IIAs note the 'public' element of contract violation even if contracts are commercial and the transactions are commercial. Restrictive sovereign immunity under public international law, however, views governments in this context as the same as private entities, by negating 'public' element even if government is a party to the contract at issue. This internal contradiction is the outcome of the lack of coordination between the concept developed in public international law and that evolved in international investment law. Closer coordination of concepts and jurisprudence is certainly in order.

In any event, the direction of the development of jurisprudence in international law is to ensure the availability of a dispute settlement mechanism for aggrieved private interested parties. As such, there are wider possibilities of overcoming the traditional walls of sovereign immunity, and even a new dispute settlement mechanism has been introduced for private entities in lieu of domestic court proceedings. Nonetheless, the core elements of internatioal law is still preserved in essence. Consequently, private entities are forced to pursue their claims in domestic courts of the states that have adopted the measures at issue in the first place. The advent of FTAs have made this issue more acute and complex. Increasingly, Korea, China and Japan are now experiencing related problems in their domestic court proceedings. The courts of the three countries are producing new jurisprudence or confirming existing ones through the FTA related disputes that have been brought to their case lists.

2) Right of Diplomatic Protection

The jurisprudence for the right to diplomatic protection is yet another cardinal rule of public international law that is said to have a "fundamental character."[133] As such, this rule should also be taken into account in the discussion of DSMs of FTAs to the extent these proceedings are relied upon to protect the basic human rights of their nationals abroad. With respect to trade agreements such as FTAs, the services chapters directly involve the minimum level of treatment of nationals as service providers in foreign markets. This issue is raised more directly in investment disputes and ISDS proceedings in accordance with investment chapters of the FTAs. As is widely known, this right to diplomatic protection is the right of the state and not of an individual investor, and the claim is thus legally distinct from the individual's own claim.[134] The state may or may not raise the right of diplomatic protection in a particlar instance. This uncertainty has led to the creation of ISDS proceedings wherein an aggrieved foreign investor himself or herself has standing to pursue an international legal action.[135]

This claim of diplomatic protection under international law is rather unique: it does not require violation of a treaty or customary international law in the first place. The claim starts from an alleged violation by a state of the basic human rights of a national of a foreign state. If the harm caused to the national is not remedied through domestic procedure of the state where such harm occurred (called exhaustion of local remedies), then the foreign state can take up the situation as its own claim and then proceed to the international law plane. As this concept is anchored in customary international law, one can say that the legal basis can be found from customary international law. But the initial harm has nothing to do with the state, and the harm to the state (foreign state) is rather fictional, in that non-remedied situation for its national abroad has now caused harm to the sovereign interest of the national state. Stated differently, conceptually the right to diplomatic protection presupposes the existence of a violation of the rights of a private person first, which is distinct from any violation of a treaty or ordinary violation of customary international law.[136]

The right of diplomatic protection is usually given up in exchange for an IIA. Since the IIA now provides a special dispute resolution mechanism for individual investors called ISDS proceedings, the need for the investor's home state's intervention through the right of diplomatic protection is not pressing any more, so goes the rationale. The validity of such rationale is now being revisted in the context of the reform of the ISDS proceedings at UNCITRAL, ICSID and OECD. That said, elimination of the right of diplomatic protection has been widely understood to be a general feature of an IIA, because a *quid pro quo* was obvious.

Now, the situation becomes rather murky in the context of an umbrella clause. Unlike other claims of ISDS where violation of substantive provisions of IIAs are raised, umbrella clauses in fact do not have direct relevance to substantive provisions of IIAs. Instead, the claim centers on violation of a contract a party of which happens to be a governmental agency of the IIA at issue. Furthermore, in this context, the foreign investor has the option of pursuing a conventional proceeding such as domestic court litigation or commercial arbitration or now pursuing an ISDS proceeding. If the foreign investor chooses the ISDS option, then the choice will now negate the right of diplomatic protection. The choice is unpredictable by any account. It is not clear which part of the contract is violated and why it is violated. Worse yet, why the investor decided to go ahead with the ISDS is more unclear. And yet, an unpredictable choice made by a foreign investor eliminates the right of diplomatic protection, which, under international law, is the right belonging to the state. Indeed, the same situation can also happen in ordinary ISDS proceedings wherein substantive provisions of IIAs are implicated. But those claims are based on clearly stipulated provisions of IIAs of which the contracting parties are cognizant and about which they made an informed decision. That does not apply to claims and ISDS proceedings arising from umbrella clauses. If the existence of the right to diplomatic protection is determined by the choice of an investor, one would view this as amounting to a foreign investor's unauthorized usurpation of the right to diplomatic protection of his national state.[137] Again, an argument can be made that an important right of a state is somehow given up by an investor's decision at a particular point in time in the future. This also reflects the lack of coordination between public international law and international investment law.

Korea, China and Japan have arguably cherished a paternalistic view of the government. Such tendency has largely paid off, so to speak. They are more prone to the concept of protecting their nationals abroad, and thus naturally those trading with or in foreign countries. The right to diplomatic protection is the concept that has been developed and raised in this context. So, the three states still remain to keen the circumstances that have triggered the invocation of the right of diplomatic protection. While IIAs have generally blocked this avenue, the continuing tendency may still preserve the potential to thrive in other contexts of FTAs. The FTAs and their DSMs have the potential that the three states' continuing desire to emerge, albeit in different names, through various DSMs of

FTAs. In particular, they may use the SSDS or Joint Committees to cater for their desire. In that respect, the three countries of East Asia could turn out to be more active subscribers of SSDS and Joint Committee proceedings as time passes by.

Endnotes

1. Permanent Court of International Justice, *The Mavrommatis Palestine Concessions*, Collection of Judgments, Series A, No. 2 (Aug. 30, 1924), p. 11.

2. *Interpretation of the Peace Treaties with Bulgaria, Hungary and Romania, Advisory Opinion: I.C.J. Reports 1950*, p. 74.

3. *Border and Transborder Armed Actions (Nicaragua v. Honduras), Jurisdiction and Admissibility, Judgment, I.C.J. Reports 1988*, pp. 16, 91; 84 ILR, pp. 218, 246.

4. *See Schooner Exchange Case.*

5. *See* Anti-Dumping Agreement, art. 13.

6. *See* Statute of the International Court of Justice, art. 36.

7. *See* Dispute Settlement Understanding, art. 23.

8. Malcolm N. Shaw, *International Law* (Cambridge University Press, 2008), p. 1012.

9. *See* for instance, the Comprehensive Economic and Trade Agreement between the EU and Canada (CETA).

10. *See* the ICSID website listing all the cases so far available at http://icsid.worldbank.org/ICSID/FrontServlet?requestType=GenCaseDtlsRH&actionVal=ListConcluded. (last visited on Apr. 29, 2020); In 1984, there was a case filed by an American company against the Korean government but it was promptly settled afterwards without producing any procedural or substantive implication. *See Colt Industries Operating Corporation v. Republic of Korea* (ICSID Case No. ARB/84/2).

11. The change in the regulatory regime for foreign investment sometimes requires an overhaul of the existing Korean judicial or administrative regime applicable to the area. This task is obviously quite daunting. One scholar once commented that "Law is a form of cultural expression and is not readily transplantable from one culture to another without going through some process of indigenization. French law is as much a reflection of the French culture as Russian law is a reflection of Russian culture." *See* Mary Ann Glendon, Michael Wallace Gordon and Christopher Osakwe, *Comparative Legal Traditions in a Nutshell* (St. Paul, Minn.: West, 1982), p. 10.

12. *See* Organization for Economic Co-operation and Development, Build-

ing Trust and Confidence in International Investment (Draft report to the OECD Ministerial on the "Freedom of Investment, National Security and 'Strategic Industries'" Project), DAF/INV(2008)11 (Dec. 17, 2008). In the report, there are discussions among OECD members about the appropriate legal definition of the term "national security." But it is not clear whether the term should mean (i) the national security exception as appearing in the WTO Agreements, (ii) some other similar concepts appearing in public international law such as "*ordre public*," or (iii) an entirely new concept such as "essential national security interest."

13. Progress in this area has been slowly made at the WTO Working Group on the Relationship between Trade and Investment. *See* the WTO website, *available at* http://www.wto.org/english/tratop_e/invest_e/invest_e.htm(last visited Apr. 29, 2020).

14. *See* e.g., *supra* note 12, concerning still continuing discussions in the international community regarding the definition of the national security in the context of the foreign investment.

15. *LSF-KEB Holdings SCA and others v. Republic of Korea* (ICSID Case No. ARB/12/37), *available at* https://icsid.worldbank.org/en/pages/cases/pending-Cases.aspx?status=p (last visited Jan. 14, 2017).

16. *Hanocal Holding B.V. and IPIC International B.V. v. Republic of Korea* (ICSID Case No. ARB/15/17), *available at* https://icsid.worldbank.org/en/Pages/cases/casedetail.aspx?CaseNo=ARB/15/17 (last visited Jan. 14, 2017).

17. *Mohammad Reza Dayyani and others v. Republic of Korea, available at* http://investmentpolicyhub.unctad.org/ISDS/Details/679 (last visited Jan. 14, 2017).

18. As of this writing, Korea has completed negotiations for FTAs with 58 countries. *See* The Ministry of Foreign Affairs and Trade, Current Status of FTA Negotiations, *available at* http://www.fta.go.kr/main/situation/kfta/ov/ (last visited Mar. 20, 2022).

19. *Ibid.*

20. *See, e.g.*, Antidumping Agreement, art. 13.

21. *See, e.g.*, Constitution of the Republic of Korea, art. 6, para. 1.

22. *See* NAFTA Secretariat website, *available at* http://www.nafta-sec-alena.org/en/DecisionsAndReports.aspx?x=312 (last visited Apr. 29, 2020).

23. *See* Free Trade Agreement between the Republic of Korea and the United States of America [hereinafter "Korea-US FTA"], art. 22.4, *available at* http://www.fta.go.kr/webmodule/_PSD_FTA/us/doc/us_Fulltext_eng.pdf (last visited on Apr. 29, 2020); Free Trade Agreement between the Government of the People's Republic of China and the Government of The Republic of Korea [hereinafter "China-Korea FTA"], art. 20.2, *available at* http://fta.mofcom.gov.cn/korea/annex/xdzw_en.pdf (last visited on Apr. 29, 2020); Agreement between Japan and the Republic of Peru for an Economic Partnership [hereinafter "Japan-Peru FTA"], art. 204, *available at* http://www.mofa.go.jp/region/latin/peru/

epa201105/pdfs/jpepa_ba_e.pdf (last visited on Apr. 29, 2020).

24. *See* Korea-US FTA, *supra* note 23, art. 22.10.2; China-Korea FTA, *supra* note 23, art. 20.9; Japan-Peru FTA, *supra* note 23, art. 214.

25. *See* Korea-US FTA, *supra* note 23, art. 22.12.1; China-Korea FTA, *supra* note 23, art. 20.12; Japan-Peru FTA, *supra* note 23, art. 218.

26. *See* Korea-US FTA, *supra* note 23, arts. 22.8, 22.9.1, 22.9.2, 22.11.1, 22.11.4, and 22.12.1; China-Korea FTA, *supra* note 23, arts. 20.6, 20.7, 20.11.1, 20.11.5, 20.12; Japan-Peru FTA, *supra* note 23, arts. 209, 210, 216.1, 216.2, 218.

27. *See* Korea-US FTA, *supra* note 37, art. 22.2.2(d).

28. *See* Korea-US FTA, *supra* note 23, art. 22.12.2; China-Korea FTA, *supra* note 23, art. 20.12.2; Japan-Peru FTA, *supra* note 23, art. 218.

29. *See* Korea-US FTA, *supra* note 37, art. 22.13.1; China-Korea FTA, *supra* note 23, art. 20.13.4; Japan-Peru FTA, *supra* note 23, art. 218.2.

30. *See* Korea-US FTA, *supra* note 23, art. 22.13.2; China-Korea FTA, *supra* note 23, art. 20.15; Japan-Peru FTA, *supra* note 23, art. 219.1.

31. *See* Korea-US FTA, *supra* note 23, art. 22.13.5; China-Korea FTA, *supra* note 23, art. 20.15.7; Japan-Peru FTA, *supra* note 23, art. 219.3.

32. *See* Dispute Settlement Understanding, art. 21.1.

33. *See* Korea-US FTA, *supra* note 23, art. 22.13.6.

34. *See* US Congress House Ways & Means Committee, *Summary of the May 10 Agreement, available at* http://waysandmeans.house.gov/Media/pdf/110/05%2014%2007/05%2014%2007.pdf (last visited Apr. 29, 2020); Jeanne G. Grimmett, *Dispute Settlement Under the US-Peru Trade Promotion Agreement: An Overview*, Congressional Research Service (Aug. 12, 2011).

35. *See* Bipartisan Congressional Trade Priorities and Accountability Act of 2015 (TPA-2015) P.L. 114-26; Ian F. Fergusson and Richard S. Beth, *Trade Promotion Authority (TPA): Frequently Asked Questions*, CRS Report (Jul. 2, 2015).

36. *See* Ian F. Fergusson and Richard S. Beth, *Trade Promotion Authority (TPA): Frequently Asked Questions*, CRS Report RL 33743, pp. 12-13; Mary Jane Bolle and Ian F. Fergusson, *Worker Rights Provisions in Free Trade Agreements (FTAs)*, CRS Report IF10046 (June 18, 2015); ILO Declaration on Fundamental Principles and Rights at Work and its Follow-up, *available at* http://www.ilo.org/declaration/thedeclaration/textdeclaration/lang--en/index.htm (last visited Jul. 8, 2016); Richard K. Lattanzio and Ian F. Fergusson, *Environmental Provisions in Free Trade Agreements (FTAs)*, CRS Report IF10166 (Jun. 18, 2015).

37. *See* Fergusson and Beth, *supra* note 36, p. 13; Bolle and Fergusson, *supra* note 36, p. 2; Lattanzio and Fergusson, *supra* note 36, p. 2; M. Angeles Villarreal, *Proposed US-Colombia Free Trade Agreement: Background and Issues*, CRS Report RL34470; William H. Cooper, *The Proposed US-South Korea Free Trade Agreement (Korea-US FTA): Provisions and Implications*, CRS Report RL34330; J. F.

Hornbeck, *The Proposed US-Panama Free Trade Agreement*, CRS Report RL32540.

38. Comprehensive and Progressive Agreement for Trans-Pacific Partnership (hereinafter "CPTPP"), Entered into force on December 30, 2018, *available at* https://www.iilj.org/wp-content/uploads/2018/03/CPTPP-consolidated.pdf (last visited Apr. 29, 2020).

39. *See Ibid.*, Chapter 16.

40. *Ibid.*, Chapter 17.

41. *See* CPTPP, Chapter 17.

42. US-China Economic and Security Review Commission, China's Response to US-South Korean Missile Defense system Deployment and its Implications, Jul. 26, 2017, *available at* https://www.uscc.gov/sites/default/files/Research/Report_China's%20Response%20to%20THAAD%20Deployment%20and%20its%20Implications.pdf (last visited Apr. 29, 2020); Florence Wen-Ting Yang, Asymmetrical Interdependence and Sanction: China's Economic Retaliation over South Korea's THADD Deployment, 55 Issues and Studies (2019).

43. UNCTAD, International Invesment Agreements Navigator: China, *available at* https://investmentpolicy.unctad.org/international-investment-agreements/countries/42/china (last visited Apr. 29, 2020).

44. UNCTAD, International Invesment Agreements Navigator: Korea, Republic of, *available at* https://investmentpolicy.unctad.org/international-investment-agreements/countries/111/korea-republic-of (last visited Apr. 29, 2020).

45. UNCTAD, International Invesment Agreements Navigator: Japan, *available at* https://investmentpolicy.unctad.org/international-investment-agreements/countries/105/japan (last visited Apr. 29, 2020).

46. UNCTAD, Investment Dispute Settlement Navigator: China, *available at* https://investmentpolicy.unctad.org/investment-dispute-settlement/country/42/china (last visited Apr. 29, 2020).

47. UNCTAD, Investment Dispute Settlement Navigator: Japan, *available at* https://investmentpolicy.unctad.org/investment-dispute-settlement/country/105/japan(last visited Apr. 29, 2020).

48. There are ten ICSID cases as of Apr. 29, 2020. UNCTAD, Investment Dispute Settlement Navigator: Korea, Republic of, *available at* https://investmentpolicy.unctad.org/investment-dispute-settlement/country/111/korea-republic-of(last visited Apr. 29, 2020).

49. *See* Korea-US FTA, *supra* note 23, art. 11.16.2; China-Korea FTA, *supra* note 23, art. 12.12; Agreement between Japan and the United Mexican States for the Strengthening of the Economic Partnership [hereinafter "Japan-Mexico FTA"], art. 76, *available at* http://www.mofa.go.jp/region/latin/mexico/agreement/agreement.pdf (last visited Apr. 29, 2020).

50. *See* Korea-US FTA, *supra* note 23, art. 11.19.1; China-Korea FTA, *supra* note 23, art. 12.12.8; Japan-Mexico FTA, *supra* note 49, art. 82.

51. *See Ibid.*

52. *See* Korea-US FTA, *supra* note 23, arts. 11.21.1 and 11.21.3.

53. *See* Korea-US FTA, *supra* note 23, art. 11.21.2.

54. *See* Korea-US FTA, *supra* note 23, art. 11.21.4.

55. *See* UNCITRAL Rules on Transparency in Treaty-based Investor-State Arbitration, *available at* http://www.uncitral.org/uncitral/en/uncitral_texts/arbitration/2014Transparency.html (last visited Jul. 8, 2016).

56. *See* UN Convention on Transparency in Treaty-based Investor-State Arbitration, *available at* https://www.uncitral.org/pdf/english/texts/arbitration/transparency-convention/Transparency-Convention-e.pdf (last visited Jul. 8, 2016).

57. Shayerah Ilias Akhtar & Martin A. Weiss, US International Investment Agreements: Issues for Congress, CRS Report R43052 (Apr. 29, 2013), pp. 11-15.

58. UNCTAD, Investment Dispute Settlement Navigator: Korea, Republic of, *available at* https://investmentpolicy.unctad.org/investment-dispute-settlement/country/111/korea-republic-of (last visited Apr. 29, 2020).

59. *See* Korea-US FTA, *supra* note 23, art. 11.26.4; Japan-Mexico FTA, *supra* note 49, art. 92.3.

60. *See* Korea-US FTA, *supra* note 23, art. 11.26.1; Japan-Mexico FTA, *supra* note 49, art. 92.1.

61. *See* Korea-US FTA, *supra* note 23, art. 11.26.8.

62. The accession dates for the New York Convention are as follows: Japan (Jun. 20, 1961), Korea (Feb. 8, 1973), and China (Jan. 22, 1987), *available at* http://www.newyorkconvention.org/countries (last visited Apr. 29, 2020).

63. The dates of entry into force of ICSID Convention are as follows: Korea (Mar. 23, 1967), Japan (Sep. 16, 1967), China (Feb. 6, 1993), *available at* https://icsid.worldbank.org/en/Documents/icsiddocs/List%20of%20Contracting%20States%20and%20Other%20Signatories%20of%20the%20Convention%20-%20Latest.pdf (last visited Apr. 29, 2020).

64. *See* Korea-US FTA, *supra* note 23, art. 22.2.3 (d); Japan-Mexico FTA, *supra* note 49, art. 165.3.

65. *See* Korea-US FTA, *supra* note 23, art. 11.22.3; Japan-Mexico FTA, *supra* note 49, art. 84.2.

66. *See* Korea-US FTA, *supra* note 23, art. 22.2.7.

67. *See* Korea-US FTA, *supra* note 23, art. 11.20.3.

68. *See* Korea-US FTA, *supra* note 23, art. 11.20.2.

69. *See* CPTPP, art. 9.23.11.

70. *See* Korea-US FTA, *supra* note 23, art. 11.20.12.

71. *See* Korea-US FTA, *supra* note 23, art. 11.20.11 (b).

72. The relevant provision in the Comprehensive and Progressive Agreement for Trans-Pacific Partnership is as follows:

CHAPTER 27 ADMINISTRATIVE AND INSTITUTIONAL PROVISIONS

Article 27.1: Establishment of the Trans-Pacific Partnership Commission

The Parties hereby establish a Trans-Pacific Partnership Commission (Commission), composed of government representatives of each Party at the level of Ministers or senior officials. Each Party shall be responsible for the composition of its delegation.

73. The relevant provision in the Agreement Among the Government of Republic of Korea, the Government of the People's Republic of China and the Government of Japan for the Promotion, Facilitation and Protection of Investment is as follows:

Article 24 Joint Committee

1. The Contracting Parties shall establish a Joint Committee (hereinafter referred to in this Article as the "Committee") with a view to accomplishing the objectives of this Agreement. The functions of the Committee shall be:

(a) to discuss and review the implementation and operation of this Agreement; and

(b) to discuss other investment-related matters concerning this Agreement, including the scope of the existing non-conforming measures referred to in paragraphs 2 and 3 of Article 3.

2. The Committee may, as necessary, decide to make appropriate recommendations to the Contracting Parties for the more effective functioning or the attainment of the objectives of this Agreement.

3. The Committee shall be composed of representatives of the Governments of the Contracting Parties and may decide to invite representatives of relevant entities other than the Governments of the Contracting Parties with the necessary expertise relevant to the issues to be discussed. The Committee shall decide on the modalities of its operation as necessary.

4. Any decision of the Committee shall be made by consensus.

5. Unless otherwise decided by the Contracting Parties, the Committee shall convene once a year.

74. *See Vattenfall AB and others v Federal Republic of Germany*, ICSID Case No ARB/12/12, Notice of Arbitration (May 31, 2012), *available at* http://www.italaw.com/cases/documents/1655 (last visited Apr. 29, 2020), *See Philip Morris Asia Ltd v The Commonwealth of Australia,* UNCITRAL, PCA No 2012-12 , *available at* http://italaw.com/851 (last visited Apr. 29, 2020).

75. *See* the Marrakesh Agreement Establishing the WTO, art. IX, para. 2.

76. Free Trade Agreement between the Government of the Republic of Korea and the Government of Australia (hereinafter "Korea-Australia FTA"), Apr.

8, 2014, entered into force Dec. 12, 2014.

77. *Ibid.*, art. 21.3.2.

78. *See*, *Ibid.*, art. 21.3.3.

79. *Ibid.*, art. 11.21.4(e).

80. *Ibid.*

81. *Ibid.*, art. 11.22.3.

82. *Ibid.*, art. 11.23.1.

83. Japan-Australia Economic Partnership Agreement (hereinafter "Japan-Australia EPA"), Jul. 8, 2014, entered into force Jan. 15, 2015, art. 1.13.2.

84. Currently there are twelve Sub-Committees: on Trade in Goods (art 2.21); on Rules of Origin (art 3.28); on Customs Procedures (art 4.9); on Sanitary and Phytosanitary Cooperation (art 5.4); on Technical Regulations, Standards and Conformity Assessment Procedures (art 6.8); on Energy and Mineral Resources (art 8.8); on Trade in Services (Article 9.15); on Telecommunications (art 10.22); on Financial Services (art 11.10); on Investment (art 14.18); on Intellectual Property (art 16.21) and; on Promotion of a Closer Economic Relationship (art 18.2).

85. *See* Japan-Australia EPA, *supra* note 83, art. 14.18.2.

86. *Ibid.*, art. 19.16.2.

87. *See* Agreement Between the Government of Canada and the Government of the People's Republic of China for the Promotion and Reciprocal Protection of Investments (hereinafter "China-Canada BIT"), Sept. 9, 2012, arts. 20 and 33, para 3.

88. *See* China-Canada BIT, *supra* note 87, art. 20, para 2.

89. The Agreement among the Government of Japan, the Government of the Republic of Korea and the Government of the People's Republic of China for the Promotion, Facilitation and Protection of Investment (hereinafter "Korea-China-Japan TIT"), May 13, 2012.

90. *See*, *Ibid.*, art. 17.

91. *See*, *Ibid.*, art. 24.

92. *See* Korea-US FTA, *supra* note 23.

93. *See* Korea-US FTA, *supra* note 23, art. 22.2, 2 (d).

94. *See* Korea-US FTA, *supra* note 23, art. 22.2, 3 (d).

95. *See* Marrakesh Agreement Establishing the WTO, art. IX, para. 2.

96. Free Trade Agreement between the Republic of Korea and the Republic of Peru (Korea-Peru FTA), Nov. 14, 2010, entered into force Aug. 1, 2011.

97. Framework Agreement Establishing a Free Trade Area between the Republic of Korea and the Republic of Turkey (hereinafter "Korea-Turkey FTA"), Aug. 1, 2012, entered into force May 1, 2013.

98. The WTO's Ministerial Conference also uses the term "adoption" of interpretation by the Minsterial Conference. *See* Marrakesh Agreement Establishing the WTO, art. IX, para. 2. Such interpretation is regarded as official interpretation of the Members for the particular provision at issue. Likewise, the WTO's DSB also uses the term "adoption" of panel and Appellate Body reports, which accord legally binding force for these reports.

99. Free Trade Agreement between the Government of the Republic of Korea and the Government of Canada (hereinafter "Korea-Canada FTA"), Sept. 22, 2014, entered into force Jan. 1, 2015.

100. The Parliament of the Commonwealth of Australia, 'Report 142: Treaty Tabled on ay 13, 2014 — Free Trade Agreement Between the Government of Australia and the Government of the Republic of Korea' (Commonwealth of Australia, Sept. 2014), p. 27.

101. *See eg*, Korea-Canada FTA, art. 20.1, para 3; Korea-US FTA, *supra* note 23, art. 11.22, para 3.

102. *See eg*, Korea-Peru FTA, art. 22.1, para 3.

103. *See* Vienna Convention on the Law of Treaties, art. 31, para 3, subpara (a).

104. European Commission, Investment Protection and Investor-to-State Dispute Settlement in EU Agreements — Fact Sheet (Nov., 2013), *available at* http://trade.ec.europa.eu/doclib/docs/2013/november/tradoc_151916.pdf (last visited Apr. 29, 2020); European Commission, Investment Protection and Investor-to-State Dispute Settlement (ISDS) in EU Agreements — Fact Sheet, Mar. 2014, *available at* http://trade.ec.europa.eu/doclib/docs/2014/march/tradoc_152273.pdf (last visited Apr. 29, 2020).

105. *See*, Ministry of Trade, Industry and Energy, Press Release: ISD is not a poison pill but is an equality clause (Apr. 30, 2007), *available at* http://www.fta.go.kr/main/info/news/paper/doc/ (last visited Apr. 29, 2020); Hankyoreh, FTA clash looms (Oct. 31, 2011), *available at* http://english.hani.co.kr/arti/english_edition/e_entertainment/503237.html (last visited Apr. 29, 2020).

106. *See,* Catherine Yannaca-Smal, 'Improving the System of Investor-State Dispute Settlement: An Overview' in OECD, *International Investment Perspectives* (OECD Publishing, 2006), ch. 7, p.189.

107. *See* discussions on members of the UNCITRAL Working Group regarding UNCITRAL Transparency Rules in Treaty-based Investor-State Arbitration (Apr. 1, 2014), art. 7, *available at* http://www.uncitral.org/pdf/english/texts/arbitration/rules-on-transparency/Rules-on-Transparency-E.pdf (last visited Apr. 29, 2020).

108. *See* Muthucumaraswamy Sornarajah, 'The Case against a Regime on

International Investment Law' in Leon Trakman and Nick Ranieri (eds.), *Regionalism in International Investment Law* (Oxford University Press, 2013), ch. 16.

109. *Ibid.*

110. *See* Vienna Convention on Law of Treaties, art. 31.

111. *See* Korea-US Free Trade Agreement, *supra* note 23, arts. 11.23.1 and 22.4; Japan-Mexico FTA, *supra* note 63, art. 89.1, art. 165.2(e).

112. *See* Korea-US Free Trade Agreement, *supra* note 23, art. 22.2.2 (e).

113. *See* Korea-US Free Trade Agreement, *supra* note 23, art. 22.2.3 (f); Japan-Mexico FTA, *supra* note 63, art. 165.3 (b).

114. *See* Korea-US Free Trade Agreement, *supra* note 23, art. 22.2.7.

115. USTR, 'USTR to Request First-Ever Environment Consultations Under the US-Korea Free Trade Agreement (KORUS) in Effort to Combat Illegal Fishing', *available at* https://ustr.gov/about-us/policy-offices/press-office/press-releases/2019/september/ustr-request-first-ever (last visited Apr. 29, 2020).

116. Ministry of Employment and Labor, 'Announcement on Ratification of the ILO Fundamental Conventions', *available at* https://www.moel.go.kr/english/poli/poliNewsnews_view.jsp?idx=1513 (last visited Apr. 29, 2020).

117. *See* Korea-US FTA, *supra* note 23, chs. 20 (Environment), 19 (Labor), and 11 (Investment); Japan-Mexico FTA, *supra* note 49, chs. 7 (Investment), art. 74 (Environment).

118. The term "measure" is defined by the WTO Appellate Body in *US - Corrosion-Resistant Steel Sunset Review* where it stated that:

In principle, *any* act or omission attributable to a WTO Member can be a measure of that Member for purposes of dispute settlement proceedings. Measures that can be subject to WTO dispute settlement can include, not only acts applying a law in a specific situation, but also "acts setting forth rules or norms that are intended to have general and prospective application. Instruments of a Member containing rules or norms could constitute a 'measure', irrespective of how or whether those rules or norms are applied in a particular instance.

This definition is also accepted by the four free trade agreements being discussed in this chapter.

119. *See* art. 1.1 of the WTO's Dispute Settlement Understanding. For a free trade agreement, *see, e.g.*, art. 22.4 of the Korea-US FTA, *supra* note 37.

120. United Nations, *Yearbook of the International Law Commission, Report of the Commission to the General Assembly on the workof its thirty-second session,* Volume II, Part Two, A/CN.4/SER.A/1980/Add.l (Part 2), New York (1981), *available at* http://legal.un.org/ilc/publications/yearbooks/Ybkvolumes(e)/ILC_1980_v2_p2_e.pdf (last visited Apr. 29, 2020).

121. *Jurisdictional Immunities of the State (Germany v. Italy: Greece intervening), Judgment, I.C. J. Reports 2012,* p. 28, para. 57.

122. The rule of sovereign immunity is basically procedural in nature and does not indicate or determine whether or not a conduct at issue is either lawful or unlawful. *See Arrest Warrant of 11 April 2000 (Democratic Republic of the Congo* v. *Belgium), Judgment, I.C.J. Reports 2002,* p. 25, para. 60.

123. *See* Antonio Cassese, *International Law* (2nd ed.) (Oxford University Press, 2005), pp. 99-101.

124. *See* Tae Hyun Choi, *Reception of the Restrictive Theory of Sovereign Immunity in Korea, in* Choong Hyun Paik (ed.), *International Law in Korean Perspective* (Seoul National University Press, 2004), p. 383. ("[T]he restrictive theory of sovereign immunity has been recognized and accepted by almost all countries in the world except a few remaining communist countries and developing countries"); *See* also *Jurisdictional Immunities of the State (Germany v. Italy: Greece intervening), supra* note 135, p. 30, para. 61; By way of example, as for the United States, a federal statute, called Foreign Sovereign Immunities Act (FSIA) of 1976 incorporates the restrictive concept of sovereign immunity. *See General exceptions to the jurisdictional immunity of a foreign state* (28 US Code § 1605); *Republic of Austria v. Altmann* (541 US 677 (2004)), Supreme Court of the United States (Jun. 7, 2004); *Hwang GeumJoo v. Japan* (542 US 901 (2004)), Supreme Court of United States (Jun. 14, 2004).

125. *See Ibid., Republic of Austria v.Altmann*; *Hwang GeumJoo v. Japan*.The former case is about applicability of sovereign immunity for the Government of Austria for its expropriation of personal property of Jewish nationals during World War II, and the latter case is about the applicability of sovereign immunity for the Government of Japan for its mobilization of comfort women during World War II. Although specific factual background and contested legal principles are different, in both of the cases, the US Supreme Court confirms that it applies sovereign immunity (restrictive sovereign immunity) when foreign sovereign government is brought to the US court for its governmental action. Although the United States Supreme Court in *Hwang GeumJoo v. Japan*, vacated the appeals court judgment in *Hwang GeumJoo v. Japan* (332 F.3d 679, 685 (D.C. Cir. 2003)), it nonetheless reaffirmed the principle of sovereign immunity. The US Supreme Court only remanded the case to the D.C. Circuit on the issue whether the Foreign Sovereign Immunities Act (FSIA) of 1976 could apply to incidents that occurred before 1952 when the United States decided to incorporate the restrictive concept of sovereign immunity. Subsequently, the D.C. Circuit affirmed the original decision on yet another ground, *i.e.* political question doctrine, *Hwang GeumJoo v. Japan* (413 F.3d 45 (D.C. Cir. 2005)), followed by the Supreme Court's virtual affirmation by denying certiorari for the case in *Hwang GeumJoo v. Japan* (126 S. Ct. 1418 (2006)). In this case, the judge in the appeals court (*i.e.*, the D.C. Circuit) expresses his pain at having to dismiss the case because of the sovereign immunity principle although ample evidence supports for a remedy under the law ("Much as we may feel for the plight of the appellants [comfort women], the courts of the United States simply are not authorized to hear their case [against Government of Japan]").

126. This is so because the concept of sovereign immunity does not apply

to proceedings before international tribunals.

127. *See Difference Relating to Immunity from Legal Process of a Special Rapporteur of the Commission on Human Rights, Advisory Opinion, I.C.J. Reports 1999,* p. 62, para. 62.

128. *Chevron U.S.A., Inc. v. NRDC* (467 US 837 (1984)), (Jun. 25, 1984), p. 842.

129. *Ibid.*, p. 844.

130. *See* Adam Hoffman, "Corralling Constitutional Fact: De Novo Fact Review in Federal Appeals Court," 50 *Duke Law Journal* (2001), p. 1448.

131. *See, e.g., Republic of Austria v. Altmann*; *Hwang GeumJoo v. Japan.*

132. Stephen M. Schwebel, *On Whether the Breach by a State of a Contract with an Alien Is a Breach of International Law*, in *International Law at the Time of Its Codification: Essays In Honour of Robert Ago* (Giuffrè Editore, 1987), pp. 408-409.

133. *United States Diplomatic and Consular Staff in Tehran, Judgment, I.C.J. Reports 1980*, p. 3.

134. *See Nottebohm case (Liechtenstein v. Guatemala) (Second phase), Judgment of April 6th, 1955: I.C.J. Reports 1955*, p. 4l; Eritrea Ethiopia Claims Commission, Partial Award (Diplomatic Claim: Ethiopia's Claim 8), between the Federal Democratic Republic of Ethiopia and the State of Eritrea (The Hague, December 19, 2005), para. 24.

135. Thomas W. Walde, *The "Umbrella" Clause in Investment Arbitration - A Comment on Original Intentions and Recent Cases*, 6 The Journal of World Investment & Trade, (2005), p. 195.

136. *See* Susan D. Franck, "Foreign Direct Investment, Investment Treaty Arbitration, and the Rule of Law," 19 *Global Business & Development Law Journal* (2007), *available at* http://www.mcgeorge.edu/Documents/Conferences/JUDIND_FRANK_MASTER.pdf (last visited May 10, 2014), p. 342.

137. *See, Nottebohm Case, supra* note 154, para. 4.

Chapter III

An Anatomy of Trade Disputes in East Asia

1. Key Issues in Regional Trade Relations

Despite the fact that trade liberalization has a positive effect on the overall welfare of the states involved, it is hard to achieve trade liberalization among states. The endeavor to bring about trade liberalization is not driven by economic rationale alone. Rather, other non-economic considerations also play a significant role in achieving trade liberalization. Access to the domestic markets of states can be secured through bilateral trade arrangements, regional integration process or a multilateral undertaking. The East Asian countries such as China, Japan and Korea are active participants in the multilateral trade arrangements as well as bilateral and regional economic integration endeavors. If we go back to past multilateral trade negotiations, East Asian countries were active participants in the various trade negotiations. Currently, as the momentum decreases for trade negotiations in the multilateral forum, East Asian countries are turning their attention to bilateral trade negotiations and other smaller trade arrangements. As such these moves coupled with increasing membership of East Asian countries in the WTO and other regional FTAs will alleviate the problem of access to domestic markets among East Asian states.

2. Various Fora of Trade Disputes

1) Emergence of FTA Era and AD/CVD Investigations

The international trade order has recently undergone significant changes, from its traditional conduct under the GATT/WTO system. At the center of these changes is the system of FTAs. On top of the existing obligations under WTO membership such as the Anti-Dumping and SCM Agreements, WTO member countries have been forced to assume additional obligations resulting from the conclusion of multiple FTAs. If South Korea eventually signs an FTA with 30 different trade partners in the future, the country has to comply with 30 extra obligations in addition to the existing WTO obligations. FTAs ostensibly continue to follow existing WTO obligations within a broad framework, and yet there is a difference in the detailed requirements and procedures for each FTA. Thus, the authorities responsible for investigations in each country must inevitably bear a growing practical burden of understanding and applying different requirements and procedures to each investigation. Considering such matters, this section deals with new challenges and issues of AD/CVD investigations raised by the introduction of the FTA system.

2) Overview of Anti-Dumping Investigations

An AD investigation is a trade remedy measure, and the most frequently applied instrument for maintaining fair competition in international trade. When a foreign company exports a product at a price lower than the normal value (which refers to the sales price in the domestic market), thereby inflicting severe harm on domestic companies and the industry manufacturing the same kind of products, the importing country must verify the damage incurred and impose tariffs on the imported product. AD investigations do not target a certain country's government but a certain company, but it should be stated that once an investigation is launched against dumping by a certain company, the scope of investigation extends to apply to all companies in the targeted country that manufacture and export the same kind of products to the importing country in question. Since dumping is an unfair trade practice that distorts international trade, the confirmation of dumping must be followed by the imposition of additional tariffs and efforts to recover the trade balance, which is the basic purpose of AD investigations.

Each of the 164 WTO members, including Korea, conducts Anti-Dumping investigations in their own characteristic way. This is because the WTO Anti-Dumping Agreement provides only a general frame for investigation against dumping, while granting each member discretion with regard to the specific means to implement it. The common trait identified in each nation's Anti-Dumping investigation procedure is generally conducted with the aim of protecting domestic industries. While advanced countries strive to achieve this aim with a variety of grounds and procedures without exposing their intention, developing countries directly express their aim or reflect it in the process of investigation. This difference makes it more difficult for developing countries to make an objection with regard to judicial review on the final resolution and the WTO panel.

3) Increasing Awareness of Procedural Issues

Another noteworthy development in recent years in the Korean Anti-Dumping investigations is the increasing awareness of the importance of the procedural issues. Traditionally, the decision-making process at an agency level in Korea has not adhered to the stringent procedural requirements observed in western counterparts. The government's paternalistic perspective used to permeate policy formulation and implementation. Administrative investigations and decision-making processes also followed a similar path. It was not uncommon in a practical, result-oriented investigation approach, that insufficient emphasis was not put on the satisfaction of procedural requirements. On the other hand, WTO jurisprudence has become ever firmer with respect to fundamental due process as codified in Article 6 of the Anti-Dumping Agreement.[1]

This traditional atmosphere has changed dramatically in recent years. Two developments have triggered this change. One is the *Korea-Paper* dispute at the WTO dispute settlement proceeding and the other is the surge of FTAs.

First, the *Korea-Paper* dispute is the first (and only) dispute brought against Korea for the Korea Trade Commission (KTC)'s Anti-Dumping investigation. This is a dispute brought by Indonesia against Korea claiming that the KTC's 2002 Anti-Dumping investigation against coated free sheets from Indonesia was inconsistent with Korea's obligation under the Anti-Dumping Agreement. The *Korea-Paper* dispute[2] was initiated by Indonesia in June 2004 in response to Korea's imposition of definitive Anti-Dumping duties against imports of "business information paper and wood-free printing paper" from Indonesia as a result of an Anti-Dumping investigation initiated by the KTC in November 2002.[3] After questionnaire responses, on-the-spot verification, preliminary determination, and final determination, Anti-Dumping duty was imposed as of September 24, 2003.[4] In many respects, this dispute was a turning point for the KTC. The fact that most of the substantive parts of its final determination were upheld by a WTO panel gave confidence to the KTC. In fact, despite the fact that the panel found a violation of the Anti-Dumping Agreement in two minor procedural deficiencies, the KTC considered the dispute a successful defense.[5]

The problem arose in the implementation stage. During the reasonable period of time granted by the panel, the KTC did not pay sufficient attention to fulfill the rulings and recommendation of the DSB, due in part to the fact that the findings of the panel concerned only minor procedural issues. In a subsequent compliance panel proceeding, the panel determined that the KTC failed to bring the Anti-Dumping measure into compliance in accordance with the rulings and recommendations of the DSB, which ultimately led to Indonesia's request for and DSB's approval of suspension of the concession against Korea. Although this dispute was later settled when the KTC revoked the order through a statutory review, it made the KTC aware of the importance of satisfying all the procedural requirements in an Anti-Dumping investigation. The *Korea-Paper* dispute has forced the KTC to change its traditional view and pay more attention to the procedural elements ever since. Thus, the agency has come to realize the importance of maintaining various due process requirements, such as providing equal opportunities to both parties at all times, responding to comments from interested parties, explaining fully all small decisions the KTC makes, avoiding *ex parte* contacts, etc.

Second, the advent of the FTA era has also confirmed yet another reason to be more sensitive to the procedural aspects of all administrative decision-making process including Anti-Dumping investigations. One of the major topics at the negotiating tables in the Korea-EU and the Korea-US FTAs was to enhance transparency and procedural due process in the administrative decision-making process. These agreements have caused Korean agencies to be more alert to the procedural requirements. This post-FTA environment has prompted the KTC to solidify its procedural hurdles in Anti-Dumping investigations.

4) Inevitable Increase in the Number of AD/CVD Investigations

It is a predictable trend that the spread of FTAs would lead to an increase in the frequency of AD/CVD investigations.[6] After signing a FTA, every government will strive to prevent the products of an FTA partner country from entering its domestic market by actively initiating AD/CVD investigations. For example, in 2011, the US Department of Commerce undertook both AD and CVD investigations against Korean refrigerator exports, while in the following year it investigated washing machines manufactured in Korea.

This is in some respects a natural phenomenon. As more traffic on the road brings about more traffic accidents, an increase in the trade volume between trade partners due to the conclusion of a FTA inevitably leads to growing cases of AD/CVD disputes. This is particularly understandable given the fact that AD/CVD investigations are the last resort available to each government to protect domestic markets. As such, the focus should be on the domestic measures required by Korea to effectively overcome this trend, while expressing excessive concern over the trend itself is counterproductive.

3. Overview of Regional Disputes Pending at the WTO Dispute Settlement Procedure

The East Asian Countries and in particular, China, Japan and Korea are frequent users of the dispute settlement mechanisms of the multilateral trading system. Of the total of disputes considered by the WTO dispute settlement mechanism, these states participated in 194, 209 and 146 disputes respectively in a capacity as complainant, respondent or as a third party.[7] These figures are significant when seen in terms of the whole case distribution among WTO members.

1) Perceptions of the Private Sector

While these disputes at the DSM are raised by members on their own accord based on their belief that measures at issue are in violation of covered agreements, often times WTO disputes are initiated because of the request from specific domestic interest groups. Although the government of a complaining member makes all decisions in the course of the proceedings, it does so with close consultation and cooperation with a corporation behind the scene. In this process, sometimes the interest of the government of a complaining member and that of the corporation do not necessarily converge. On the surface, they share the same objective — i.e., prevailing in the dispute — but what they have in mind is not always identical: while a government's fundamental objective is to preserve "systemic" interest as a party to the WTO Agreements, business interest is more geared toward an "immediate" relief for the past damage done.

A government's real interest in participating in the WTO DSM is to bring the allegedly distorted situation by a measure back to equilibrium. Hence, the WTO DSM only permits a prospective remedy and any sanction at the end of the day is simply suspension of concession by the prevailing member. From the perspective of the corporation who has prompted the underlying dispute, such a "systemic" remedy may seem quite remote and distinct from a "specific" remedy that it would otherwise get from a domestic litigation. At an initial consultation meeting with government officials discussing initiation of a WTO dispute, officials of corporations are usually surprised and disappointed when they realize that a remedy they will ultimately get does not cover past damage done. Perhaps, this situation may explain a recent trend in which business interests sometimes lean toward an investment dispute proceeding where monetary compensation is available. Increased interface between NSAs and the WTO DSM may further expose the divergent views between the governments and corporations, and the gap between a systemic remedy and a specific, individual remedy.

2) Judicial Reviews

Judicial review plays an important role in the administration of the WTO's agreements on trade remedies. It is one of the key features designed to ensure the fairness and integrity of the investigative process. In addition to the WTO's dispute settlement mechanism which allows affected members to challenge trade remedy measures at the multilateral level, a domestic judicial review is an important legal tool which ensures that such measures are imposed as a result of investigations conducted in accordance with the relevant procedural and substantive rules.

Like other WTO members that use trade remedies, the three states have had a judicial review system in place for trade remedy measures as required under the WTO Agreement since they joined the WTO in 1995, for Korea and Japan, and in 2001 for China. It should be underlined, however, that judicial review of trade remedy measures has not received the attention it deserved from stakeholders, such as the domestic industries, or from academia for a long time. Trade remedy measures have long been seen as technical issues within the competence of the IA, and not amenable to judicial review.

As a matter of fact, the main reason why a judicial review has not been used frequently in the three countries is because those countries have not been among the very active users of trade remedies in the world. The level of three countries' activity in the field of trade remedies stands out when this is compared with its share of international trade. Whereas the three countries, particularly Korea and China, have become one of the most frequent targets of Anti-Dumping investigations globally, they rank low in the category of users of trade remedy measures. This is mainly because the three countries have been export-oriented countries and have been more interested in the Anti-Dumping investigations initiated against them rather than ensuing judicial review in foreign jurisdictions. Consequently, inbound trade remedy investigations and judicial reviews in the three countries have been relatively slow in coming and few in number. This traditional atmosphere, however, is fast changing now with the advent of increasing foreign penetration into the the domestic markets of the three countries as a result of the growth of domestic demand and continuing market openings in all sectors.

By way of example, in Korea, starting from 2005, the judicial review has been receiving attention from Korean and foreign producers. Since 2005, several judicial review cases have been handled by Korean courts, including one which made it to the Supreme Court. This new trend indicates that the judicial review will become an important issue for Korea in the aftermath of the Doha negotiations and the conclusion of FTAs.

In response to the likely surge in imports in the near future, Korea is likely to strengthen the KTC's infrastructure and start initiating more trade remedy investigations. Consequently, more judicial review cases should also be expected in the future in Korea.

Article 13 of the Anti-Dumping Agreement provides for a requirement that each WTO member offer an independent and meaningful administrative and judicial review process with respect to definitive Anti-Dumping measures.[8] Provisions have been included in the relevant Korean laws and regulations to implement this obligation.[9] A judicial review of KTC determinations, however, used to be relatively dormant in Korea. Several reasons may be cited to explain such dormancy. One of the reasons may have been the adoption of the perspective of an aggrieved interested party, whether correctly or incorrectly, that an appeal is not always effective in the trade remedy sector where technical issues are abundant and the agency enjoys wide latitude of discretion.[10] Over the years, however, the permeation of the rule of law principle in society in general and the increasing number of trade remedy measures (mostly anti-dumping determinations) have slowly changed this traditional trend. Since 2005, five judicial review cases have been handled by Korean courts, including one which made it to the Supreme Court.[11] As it is predicted that more Anti-Dumping determinations will be issued by the KTC in response to the surge of foreign penetration into the Korean market, most notably due to the conclusion of the FTAs, the number of judicial review cases is likely to increase as well. Through judicial review proceedings, relevant laws and regulations will be adjusted or amended accordingly, and the jurisprudence will be further elaborated and fine-tuned in Anti-Dumping proceedings.

Judicial review of trade remedy determinations in Korea is

conducted by the Administrative Court pursuant to the general procedures for the judicial review of the actions of government agencies.[12] The Administrative Court, located in Seoul with roughly 50 judges, was first established in March 1998.[13] The Administrative Court does not have a chamber specializing in trade remedy issues, which may turn out to pose a problem given the increasing complexity of Anti-Dumping investigation related disputes.

Unlike the judicial review systems of some countries, such as the United States, and the European Union, judicial review in Korea, the 12th largest trading member of the WTO, is hardly known by outsiders. The lack of research and published information with regard to Korea's judicial review system often leads to questions being raised and inquiries made in various fora. Against this backdrop, in this chapter, we will attempt to fill in this important gap by providing an overview of the judicial review of trade remedy determinations in Korea, with particular emphasis on Anti-Dumping.

Although judicial review of trade remedy determinations has been provided for in the Korean statutes for a long time, it is a relatively new phenomenon that interested parties are starting to consider as a way to remedy agency determinations alleged to be erroneous. Recent Anti-Dumping investigations and determinations of the KTC have presented opportunities to test the judicial review mechanism in Korea. Recent judicial reviews have also presented more structural issues as well, relating to the hierarchy of the WTO Agreements within the Korean legal system, and how they are applied by the Korean court to the specific cases. As more and more cases are reviewed by the Korean court, the relevant statutes and decrees will be adjusted or amended accordingly, and the relevant jurisprudence will be further elaborated and fine-tuned.[14]

As the number of the Anti-Dumping investigations by Korea has increased recently, various issues relating to the investigations have emerged for Korea. These issues are sometimes resolved at the agency level in the course of the investigation, but they sometimes lead to WTO litigation or a domestic judicial review. WTO disputes and domestic judicial review have all provided opportunities to weigh the KTC's investigation practice and methodology in a more objective manner and to improve them gradually. In that regard, the judicial review system also plays an important role in preserving the rule of law in the trade remedy sector.

In any event, judicial review of Anti-Dumping determinations by Korean courts should be further improved so as to ensure that the interests of foreign exporters and their importers are adequately protected. As much as Korean exporters have suffered from sometimes dubious trade remedy determinations by foreign investigating authorities, foreign exporters who similarly may have suffered from investigations initiated by Korea should be given full access to an effective tool for the review of the investigating authorities' determinations. Obviously, judicial review is one of the most effective mechanisms to achieve this objective. Korea is also learning this fact quickly through recent experience.

(1) Applicable Law in Judicial Review

i) Treaties

The applicable law for the judicial review is quite complex. This complexity mainly stems from the fact that the three countries adopt so-called monism regarding the incorporation of international law into domestic law. While the three countries' constitutions adopt different provisions with respect to how to incorporate treaties and international agreements, the essence of their system indicate that they follow the system of monism.

For instance, regarding Korea, Article 6, paragraph 1 of the Korean constitution stipulates that:

> (1) Treaties duly concluded and promulgated under the Constitution and the generally recognized rule of international law shall have the same effect as the domestic laws of the

Republic of Korea

This provision has been interpreted as pronouncing the adoption of monism by Korea. As such, all international treaties and agreements, upon their conclusion or accession by Korea, are automatically incorporated into the domestic legal system and become binding. These treaties and agreements have the same status of Korean statutes, below the constitution. In fact, this is quite a convenient provision because it allows the government to go through the enactment of implementing legislation each time. Of course, despite the monist nature, sometimes it is necessary to adopt implementing legislation, such as when a treaty requires the adoption of implementing legislation or contains provisions contrary to existing Korean law.

It should also be noted that the issue of a self-executing or non-self-executing treaty is an issue which is distinct from the issue of the adoption of a monism or dualism system. Even if an international agreement is incorporated into Korean law based on Article 6 of the constitution, if the law is considered to be non-self-executing, the judge will have difficulty in applying the agreement in a given case in the absence of an implementing legislation. This will also be the case for the judge when the agreement itself states that private right is not accorded by the agreement. The Korean court has been quite meticulous regarding these points.[15]

This basically means that international agreements such as the WTO Agreements become part of the law of Korea that judges will apply in reviewing a case before them. In a judicial review case, the reviewing judge will apply WTO Agreements, FTAs (if there are any) and the Korean municipal law in making a decision. In the case of conflict among them, a special law will prevail over a general one and a new law will prevail over an old one.

① WTO Agreements

Despite Article 6 of the constitution and monism, the

GATT and the WTO Agreements have not received that much of attention as an applicable law in judicial review. That mainly stems from the fact that judicial review of trade remedy action has only been a recent phenomenon in Korea. As an export-oriented economy with a relatively small domestic market, a judicial review has usually meant a review conducted by foreign courts against Korean exporters in their countries. This traditional trend, however, is slowly changing. In one recent case, the judge directly applied the GATT to render a judgment involving the imposition of Anti-Dumping duties.

The Seoul Administrative Court, in its judgment of December 2007,[16] held that the Anti-Dumping determination of the KTC was appropriate because it was consistent with the *Customs Act*, *Enforcement Decree of the Customs Act* and the WTO's Anti-Dumping Agreement. Thus, the court explicitly refers to the Anti-Dumping Agreement for the disposition of the judicial review of an Anti-Dumping determination. The court also took the same position in October 2009 regarding yet another judicial review of an Anti-Dumping determination of the KTC.[17] The Korean Supreme Court, however, indicated that the WTO Agreements may not directly apply to the judicial review by the Korean court in its January 2009 decision.[18] It is not entirely clear whether the court opinion should be read as negating the applicability of the WTO Agreements to the domestic judicial review in their entirety, or if the decision is simply the reflection of the facts and issue of the case. In any event, if the decision is regarded as negating the applicability of the WTO Agreements in judicial review, it seems contrary to its position in another recent case where the court did recognize the GATT as an applicable law. In a case where a government of a local government brought an action against the local congress when the latter enacted an ordinance arguably in violation of the WTO Agreements, the Supreme Court applied the GATT 1994 as an applicable law.[19]

The Korean Constitutional Court also took a similar position. For instance, a defendant of a case claimed that the punishment that the defendant received for the criminal violation of tariff rate rules was introduced as a result of the Marrakesh Agreement, and the court stated, while rejecting the defendant's argument, that because the Marrakesh Agreement does constitute part of the Korean law, punishment for the criminal violation of tariff was in accordance with law.[20]

In any event, it is still not entirely clear whether the Korean court accepts the notion that the WTO Agreements provide private entities with the right to present their claims in a Korean court. The situation is still somewhat fluid. Nonetheless, the fact that the Seoul Administrative Court, which is the court of first instance for the judicial review of a trade remedy determination, tends to continuously find the WTO Agreements to be an applicable law, along with the position of the Supreme Court in certain instances, may indicate the general direction of the development of this issue.

② Free Trade Agreements

What makes the situation more complex for the future is the introduction of FTAs with many countries. All the FTAs have provisions relating to trade remedy measures. Although most of the FTAs include trade remedy provisions that are quite similar to those appearing in the Anti-Dumping Agreement, different FTAs do have different provisions regulating trade remedy measures. So, an Anti-Dumping measure could constitute a violation of a particular FTA while it is consistent with another FTA or the WTO's Anti-Dumping Agreement.

As the FTA is also an international agreement that is automatically incorporated into the Korean domestic judicial system with the application of Article 6 of the Constitution, a reviewing court will have to apply the FTA in addition to or in lieu of the Anti-Dumping Agreement or municipal law.

③ WTO Precedents

The precedents of the international courts are not accorded binding force, nor do the Korean courts treat them as sources of legally binding obligations. Thus, the jurisprudence of WTO panels and the Appellate Body, in and of itself, are not treated by a reviewing judge as a source of legal norms.

Nonetheless, to the extent the jurisprudence explains how a particular provision of the WTO Agreement should be interpreted, it may be referred to by the reviewing judge of the Korean court as a guideline for the proper interpretation of the Agreement. It may be argued, therefore, that the WTO jurisprudence (decisions of panels and the Appellate Body) will have a de facto precedential value in the judicial review proceedings in Korea. It would not be surprising if the attorneys representing interested parties present their arguments based on recent Appellate Body decisions in the Korean court.

An interesting question would arise when the Korean court ruled in favor of an Anti-Dumping measure finding for the domestic industry in a judicial review but Korea subsequently receives an adverse ruling from the panel or the Appellate Body and faces an implementing obligation to bring the aggrieved measure into compliance with the Anti-Dumping Agreement or the GATT 1994. In this case, there will be two conflicting decisions, one from the court and one from the WTO. Of course, Korea should fulfill its implementation obligation to avoid retaliation. Domestically, however, the domestic industry may argue that the decision from the court should be controlling because it has already received a final judgment from the court and the WTO rulings do not carry binding force vis-à-vis the Korean court directly. This situation arises from the fact that Korea has not put in place the legal framework to implement the adverse ruling of the WTO, as found in Section 129 of the Uruguay Round Agreements Act (URAA) of the United States. As more cases are reviewed by the Korean court and Korea faces adverse rulings from time to time, legislative amendments will soon follow.

ii) Municipal Law

The judge applies municipal law in the judicial review of

Anti-Dumping determinations. Municipal law includes statutes, enforcement decrees and regulations regulating trade remedy investigations by the KTC. They are the *Customs Act*, the *Enforcement Decree of the Customs Act*, the *Act on Unfair Trade Practice Investigation and Remedy for Industrial Injury*, and the Enforcement Decree of the Act. These statutes and regulations provide the procedures to be applied in an Anti-Dumping investigation.

Specific details of the Anti-Dumping investigations can be found in Articles 51 to 56 of the *Customs Act* and Articles 58 to 71 of the *Enforcement Decree of the Customs Act.* These provisions mainly follow the comparable provisions of the WTO Anti-Dumping Agreement, but there are still some issues missing from the municipal law. An example is the absence of detailed provision requiring the existence of causation between the dumped imports and material injury. Ideally, in these instances, the court may resort to the WTO Agreements to make a decision in a case of judicial review. As a matter of fact, this is the very rationale that many countries use to adopt monism to the extent the international agreement provides for the right of private claims.

(2) Enforcement of Court Decisions

Enforcement of the court decisions in a judicial review of an administrative action is usually prompt. If a judge finds for the complainant, the judge will direct the KTC to revoke the trade remedy determination or will remand the case back to the KTC for further proceedings, as the case may be. In the case of revocation, if duties have been paid, they will be returned to the foreign respondent with applicable interest. In the case of a remand, the KTC will re-investigate the issue for re-determination. If the judgment is not enforced as stipulated in the judgment, the KTC will be further punished for contempt of court.

4. Dealing with NTBs

NTBs have become key issues in the trade regime of Korea, China and Japan. Other trading countries regard the three countries as those prone to introducing NTBs of various types for the benefit of their respective domestic industries. The three countries also regard NTBs as key issues in trade deals between and among each other.

NTBs entail complexities at various levels. The term has become one of the most commonly referred to terms in international trade and trade disputes. At the same time, it has not been always clear what the outer parameters of the term are.

1) Absence of Consensus on the Definition of NTBs

It is difficult to have a consensus on the nature of a particular government measure alleged to be an NTB by one country. Generally, NTBs or NTMs are those policy related trade costs imposed on international trade from production to final destination, excluding tariffs.[21] Thus NTBs include wide-ranging measures that can affect the flow of international trade. As international negotiations in the trade sector are aimed at ensuring the free flow of international trade, NTBs are serious concerns for trade liberalization. Past international trade negotiations were mainly centered around the reduction of tariffs. However, as trade liberalization continues and significant reductions in tariff rates are secured, the attention is shifting to tackling NTBs. Despite the attention on the eradication of NTBs, the NTBs are still serious concerns for trade liberalization. These emanate from different angles, from their nature to the willingness of negotiating states to address them expeditiously. In this part, therefore, an attempt will be made to discuss the salient issues involved with regard to NTBs as applied in the context of South East Asian countries.

Furthermore, we are witnessing the emergence and advent of new norms in trade in various sectors. They target issues that have not been covered by the existing trade agreements. As these new norms are still in the initial stage, it is still too early to pinpoint the general contour of consensus among states. Likewise, predicting a future direction or course of action still remains rather elusive. Confirmation of principles is not sufficient to come up with specific rules and norms in the provisions of FTAs. So, consensus on principles does not necessarily mean consensus on provisions elaborating the principles. If the above clarification is about those issues that are already contained in the covered agreements of the WTO, these issues without consensus relate to issues that have been traditionally discussed in other international fora and documents, but somehow are being dragged into the trade agreements' jurisdiction because of the impact on trade. The issues that extend beyond the purview of the WTO Agreements or that concern other international agreements are not covered by the jurisdiction of the WTO's dispute settlement proceeding.[22] The current DSU rather clearly stipulates that WTO panels and the Appellate Body cannot look to other instruments beyond the WTO Agreements. In this regard, Article 3.2 of the DSU provides that "recommendations and rulings of the DSB cannot add to or diminish the rights and obligations provided in the covered agreements." In other words, only those stipulated in covered agreements should apply as they are written down. Other international instruments cannot be applied to disputes if they add or reduce the rights and obligations — in other words, if they bring about any substantive impact on WTO Agreements. Article 19.2 of the DSU echos the same principle. These two provisions mean that there is a fundamental legal obstacle in addressing new trade norms and new issues that do not appear in the texts of WTO Agreements.

A vivid example in this regard is offered by the intensifying disputes between the United States and China. One country looks at new norms by finding fault with old norms. The other country looks at existing norms by repeating the principles set forth in Article 3.2 of the DSU. An answer is not to be found easily. Renewable energy raises another example. On the one hand, governmental support for private entities for whatever purpose is proscribed by the GATT 1994 and the Agreement on Subsidies and Countervailing Measures (SCM Agreement).[23] On the other hand, the international community has committed itself to the attainment of green growth mandating respective governments to consider various support measures.[24] The Paris Agreement of December 2015 mandates states to take specific actions to achieve the specific goals of the agreement. States are torn between the two competing legal norms. A controversial topic of currency undervaluation and countermeasures is arguably a more recent example. Some countries argue that currency undervaluation is a hidden trade measure and constitutes an indirect subsidy. Others argue that monetary policy and foreign exchange policy are not within reach of the WTO. If anything these issues must be raised at the IMF, not at the WTO or through trade agreements.[25] While providing financial support — even those in the form of a monetary policy or foreign exchange policy — is regulated by the GATT and the SCM Agreemnets, the arrangement with the International Monetary Fund (IMF), constituting yet another important international legal instrument, may still require and permit such a policy. Again, a government may well be torn between the two systems of international community. Protection of cultural identity in the trade liberalization context is another example of such division of systems.[26] Treaties in other sectors say one thing and WTO Agreements say another. Coordiantion is required. The WTO is not able to provide such coordination, because of the absence of consensus for such a role and because of the legal obstacles in Article 3.2 of the DSU.

Such being the case, the Sino-US disputes may be used as a platform to address these issues through WTO negotiations or other international venues. Within the WTO, multilateral negotiations such as DDA or post-DDA may address these issues. Other international fora, such as G-20 summit meeting, may address these issues outside the WTO context. The Sino-US disputes showcase important issues to be dealt with in these negotiation settings and the juxtaposed views on such issues.

2) Facilitating Legitimate Government Objectives

Ever since the 2008 Global Financial Crisis, the tendency of protectionism has been apparent in many countries as an immediate alternative to reviving a sagging national economy. Having been alerted by this development, the G-20 summit meeting held in Washington D.C. in November 2008 agreed upon a "standstill" of any trade barriers. Since then, the WTO has been issuing monitoring reports on import restriction measures adopted by the WTO members on a regular basis.[27] The monitoring reports still record a continuing trend of global protectionism which presents itself in many different and creative forms.

Over the years, various forms of NTBs have emerged, igniting an increasing number of international trade disputes.[28] NTBs now constitute a bulk of trade disputes globally. The difficulty in dealing with NTBs and the controversy surrounding NTBs arguably stem from the fact that most NTBs are anchored in legitimate government objectives. Few, if any, pronounce their objective as protectionist desire. Most of them refer to environment, labor, national security, public welfare, human rights, consumer safety, fair competition, and what not. These legitimate public objectives offer a façade but true intentions are deeply hidden at the back stage. So, it is indeed difficult, if not entirely impossible, to discern the true intent of a particular measure of a foreign country. A suspicion emerges to be only confirmed after the accumulation of a long record of repeated cases. In the interim, disputes are destined to boil. To the contrary, it may well be the case that a challenged measure is indeed a bona fide legitimate public objective measure, and the other state is simply raising a political claim or making an erroneous claim because of wrong information.

This reality shows how far away two countries can be when it comes to a particular (alleged) NTB. Different perceptions and viewpoints heavily paint different observation toward an NTB. For instance, the United States claims that Korea maintains certain standards, technical regulations, and conformity assessment procedures that are burdensome and appear to have a disproportionate effect on imports.[29] Korea, however, has disagreed with the US characterization. As the Korea-US FTA[30] generally imposes tighter rules in a wide range of sectors than the WTO-based multilateral rules, including NTBs, related disputes seem bound to surge in the near future, although both Korea and the United States make efforts to implement various provisions domestically by enacting and amending laws and regulations.[31] A similar situation is also observed between the United States and Japan, another two close trade partners.[32] The two countries have not always been on the same page when it comes to the NTB issue. Stated differently, the protectionism-infected global trading environment had induced an environment in which different views and perspectives of many governments over the legitimate governmental regulatory are juxtaposed. Again, the currency depreciation controversy and disputes unfolding at present offer a good example in this regard.

5. East Asia's FTAs and NTBs

As NTBs become one of the focal points of trade relations, provisions have been introduced to address NTBs in the FTAs of Korea, China and Japan. Some of them have been introduced at the initiative of other trading countries *vis-à-vis* the three countries. Others have found their way to FTAs between and among the three countries on the initiative of one of the three countries.

1) Provisions to Identify NTBs

Parties to the FTAs have started to strengthen the function of the Joint Committee, a bilateral consultative body of an

FTA, in a way that can issue a "binding" interpretation of the text of the FTA.[33] Once issued, this binding interpretation then constrains a dispute settlement entity — such as a panel or arbitration tribunal — that hears the dispute. Through the Joint Committee, therefore, the parties specifically control the decision-making process of the international dispute settlement body established under the FTA at issue.[34] In a sense, the Joint Committee almost exercises the function of a de facto appellate mechanism. Similarly, various new experiments are also taking place in the FTAs in the field of dispute settlement. More new rules are thus coming up and being put to the test through the operation of FTAs.

2) Special Dispute Settlement Mechanism in Korea-China FTA

Dispute settlement mechanisms offer yet another example of experiments with new rules in the FTAs. New schemes of resolving disputes are created and introduced. E.g., Korea-EU FTA and Korea-China FTA adopted a non-binding mediation mechanism to deal with disputes of NTBs.[35] This new dispute settlement mechanism is a reflection of the fact that NTBs have become one of the most controversial and complex issues in recent FTAs. Navigating through the web of laws and regulations, both written and unwritten, of the FTA partners is sometimes like walking down the labyrinthine streets of an old city. Unpredictable exercise of discretion and invisible regulatory restriction couched in vague terms unfortunately neutralize the benefits from the tariff elimination of the FTAs.

NTB detection and elimination has thus become critical. After realizing the inherent limitations of the existing dispute settlement mechanism in dealing with disputes of NTBs, this new scheme of mediation has been introduced as a flexible alternative wherein parties expect and are willing to accept and implement decisions by third party mediators. Here again, depending upon how these new schemes fare in the future, perhaps other countries will also follow suit.

Endnotes

1. Appellate Body Report, *United States-Sunset Reviews of Anti-Dumping Measures on Oil Country Tubular Goods from Argentina*, WT/DS268/AB/R (adopted Nov. 29, 2004), para. 241; Appellate Body Report, *Guatemala — Definitive Anti-Dumping Measures on Grey Portland Cement from Mexico*, WT/DS156/R (adopted Nov. 17, 2000), para. 8.119; Appellate Body Report, *United States — Sunset Review of Anti-Dumping Duties on Corrosion-Resistant Carbon Steel Flat Products from Japan*, WT/DS244/R (adopted Jan. 9, 2004), para. 7.255.

2. Panel Report, *Korea - Anti-Dumping Duties on Imports of Certain Paper from Indonesia,* WT/DS312/R (adopted Nov. 28, 2005).

3. *See Ibid.*, paras. 1.l, 2.1 (explaining the background of Indonesia'a challenge of the KTC's definitive Anti-Dumping duties against uncoated wood-free papers from Korea).

4. *See Ibid.*, paras, 2.1, 2.2, 2.3.

5. *See* the Press Release of the KTC (Oct. 23, 2005), *available at* http://www.ktc.go.kr/kboard/view.jsp?bm=5&pg=15&bd=999999972 (last visited Apr. 29, 2020).

6. On this subject, Park Soo Chan (2008) conducted an empirical investigation and concluded that FTAs tend to increase the number of Anti-Dumping investigations. As policy implications, the paper insisted that regulations on abolishment of Anti-Dumping investigation should be included in FTAs.

7. As of March 19, 2022, the total number of disputes considered by the Dispute Settlement Body of the WTO is 611.

8. Jaemin Lee, *A Brief Comparison of Antidumping Investigation in Korea and China*, 18 Trade Remedy 11, p. 14.

9. *See* arts. 119 and 120 of the *Tariff Act.*

10. *See*, Lee, *supra* note 8, p. 14.

11. Jeonju District Court 2007gahap3553 decision on the SOFA (Agreement on The Status of US Forces in The Republic of Korea); Seoul Administrative Court 2007guhap37650 and Seoul High Court 2009nu8016 decision on Transfer Income Tax; Seoul Administrative Court 2007guhap37285 decision on Corporate Tax; Seoul Administrative Court 2007guhap16875 decision on Resident Tax; and Seoul Administrative Court 2008guhap17110 decision on Corporate Tax.

12. *Ibid.*

13. *Ibid.*

14. The Korean judiciary has been exploring various reform measures to

keep up with changing environment of the society. For instance, on October 28, 2003, the Judicial Reform Committee was composed inside the Korean Supreme Court with experts participating from various sectors of the society. As a result of the discussions, the Committee produced specific reform proposals on the following issues at the end of December 2004, which are being implemented by degrees.

Judge Appointment System: to institute a system of appointing judges from attorneys with substantial practical work experiences, in order to meet the public request of being tried by judges with broad understanding of the society and diverse experiences.

Legal Education and Qualification of Lawyer: to establish an efficient system for legal education with specialization and international competitiveness and set up a new qualification system for lawyers.

Public Participation in the Judicial Process: to study methods in which the public may participate in the trial process, such as the jury system or the lay judge system.

Legal Services and the Criminal Procedure System: to create an efficient and fair legal system which can be easily accessed by the public and research methods which can better protect the rights of the accused and the victim during criminal proceedings.

See the website of Supreme Court of Korea, *available at* http://eng.scourt.go.kr/eng/judiciary/judicial_reform.jsp#05 (last visited Apr. 29, 2020).

15. *See* the Compatibility of Ordinance of Jeollabukdo-province with GATT 1994, 2004 Do 2432, Decisions of the Korean Supreme Court (Sept. 14, 2005).

16. Seoul Administrative Court, Case No. 2006 Guhab 29782.

17. Seoul Administrative Court, Case No. 2008 Guha 40363.

18. Supreme Court of Korea, Case No. 2008 Du 17936 (Jan. 30, 2009).

19. *See* the Compatibility of Ordinance of Jeollabukdo-province with GATT 1994, 2004 Do 2432, Decisions of the Korean Supreme Court (Sept. 14, 2005).

20. Korean Constitutional Court, Case No. 97 Hunba 65 (Nov. 26, 1998).

21. *See* UNCTAD, Non-Tariff Measures to Trade: Economic and Policy Issues for Developing Countries (2013), p. 1.

22. *See* DSU, arts. 3.2 and 19.2.

23. *See* SCM Agreement, arts. 1 and 2.

24. Request for Consultations by China, *United States-Countervailing Duty Measures on Certain Products from China*, WT/DS437/1, G/L/988, G/SCM/D90/1 (May 30, 2012), p. 8; The green growth issue remains at the top of the agenda of the G-20 meeting. *See* White House Office of the Press Secretary, *G-20 Leaders Declaration*, summarizing the discussion at the latest G-20 meeting held in Los Cabos on June 18-19, 2012, *available at* http://www.whitehouse.gov/the-press-office/2012/06/19/g20-leaders-declaration (last visited Mar. 1, 2013).

25. See GATT 1994, Article XV, para. 1.

26. *See* Appellate Body Report, *China-Measures Affecting Trading Rights and Distribution Services for Certain Publications and Audiovisual Entertainment Products,* WT/DS363/AB/R (Dec. 21, 2009), para. 25.

27. Since a monitoring report was published on Feb. 9, 2009 for the first time, seven more reports were published with the lasted one released on Dec. 5, 2012. In the latest report, WTO Director General Pascal Lamy stated "[t]he world needs a renewed and stronger commitment from all Governments to revitalize the multilateral trading system that can restore economic certainty at a time when it is badly needed. The policy determination to resist inward-looking policies seems to be faltering in some countries, even as the world economy needs more trade to stave off recession."; *See* World Trade Organization, *Reports on Recent Trade Developments, available at* http://www.wto.org/english/news_e/news12_e/trdev_28nov12_e.htm (last visited Mar. 1, 2013).

28. Asia Development Bank, *How to Design, Negotiate and Implement a Free Trade Agreement in Asia* (Manila: Asia Development Bank, Office of Regional Economic Cooperation, 2008), p. 12.

29. Office of the United States Trade Representative, *2012 National Trade Estimate Report on Foreign Trade Barriers*, pp. 241, 246.

30. Korea-US FTA, art. 23.2.

31. Song Jung-a, "South Korea to Tighten Foreign Investment Rules," *Financial Times* (Dec. 28, 2007).

32. Scott Bradford, *An Analysis of a Possible Japan-US Free Trade Agreement*, Petersen Institute of International Economics, powerpoint presentation material *available at* http://www.jef.or.jp/PDF/S2-1-2bradfordppt1107.pdf 22 (last visited Mar. 1, 2013), slide nos. 16, 17, 20, 21.

33. Korea-Australia FTA, art. 11.21.4 (e).

34. *Ibid.*, art. 11.23.1.

35. Free Trade Agreement between the Republic of Korea and EU (hereinafter "Korea-EU FTA"), entered into force on Dec. 13, 2015, *available at* http://www.fta.go.kr/eu/info/2/ (last visited May 7, 2020), Annex 14-A; Free Trade Agreement between the Republic of Korea and People's Republic of China (hereinafter "Korea-China FTA"), signed in Seoul on Jun. 1, 2015, art. 20.5, para. 4.

Chapter IV

An Anatomy of East Asia Investment Disputes

1. Increasing Investment and Increasing Sensitivities

Despite this seemingly drastic improvement, it is also true that some foreign governments and investors still harbor suspicions when it comes to the investment environment of the three countries. Their main complaint is not that the three countries' markets are open but that there are still invisible barriers that hinder the activities of foreign investors there. In fact, the foreign investors mainly criticize that the governments of the three countries introduce and maintain various policies that tend to favor domestic investors and companies over foreign ones.

1) Sources of Concern

Some of the foreign trading partners of the three countries allege that state-sponsored, export-driven tendencies also appear in the investment regulations. They thus argue that the governments of the three states maintain investment regulation to artificially inflate their companies' competitive edge in international transactions: *i.e.*, to protect their domestic market from foreign competition and to help their companies penetrate foreign markets. Such criticism originally targeted the goods sector but has become increasingly applicable to the services sector as well, due to the services sector's increasing share of the total amount of foreign investment.

One of the concerns of foreign trading partners is the restriction on foreign ownership in key public corporations that provide social infrastructure, such as telecommunications.[1] Foreign investors explore possibilities to expand their investment and participation in these lucrative corporations. Likewise, they also demand acceleration of the privatization process of these corporations, which may release them from any alleged governmental intervention.[2] The vivid experience of the 1997 financial crisis and the foreign investors' continued attempts to take over their crown jewel companies, however, still make the governments of the three countries cautious about fully eliminating restrictions.

Although various reform measures, significant both in quantity and quality, have been taken over the years so as to boost foreign investment, there still remain areas in which foreign investors request further changes to guarantee stable in-flow and stay of foreign investment. It may be the case that despite reform measures, many foreign investors still view the three countries as regulation-prone states in which their investment could be exposed to uncertain vulnerabilities of various sorts. For instance, mergers and acquisitions are sometimes claimed by foreign watchers to be hindered by insufficient transparency in corporate governance and nuanced signals from the government delivered through certain senior government policy makers, possibly affecting the final disposition of pending cases.[3]

Foreign investors also claim that a few business conglomerates in the three countries maintain a relatively close relationship with the governments and attempt to preserve a dominant position in the respective market in a way that would negatively affect the interest of foreign competitors entering the market.[4] In the aftermath of the 1997 financial crisis and at the recommendation of the IMF, the Korean government, contemplated measures to alleviate over-investment and capacity expansion among large Korean conglomerates. At that time, the large conglomerates themselves also acknowledged the necessity of restructuring and realigning their business areas to overcome the economic crisis. The excess-capacity industrial sectors which were identified at the time were related to, for instance, semiconductors, oil refineries, aerospace assembly and maintenance, shipbuilding, consumer electronics, petrochemicals, and automobiles, all of which are main business areas of big Korean conglomerates.[5] One of the suggestions contemplated by the Korean government was to explore the possibility of swapping overlapping business sectors among large conglomerates to alleviate redundant and excess investments nationwide.[6] Although any decision of a conglomerate was voluntary, and discussions and recommendations took place in the context of stabilizing the Korean economy in general, foreign governments have viewed this coordination as another showcasing of the Korean government's favoritism for certain Korean conglomerates.[7]

Against this backdrop, foreign investors have continued to claim that even if the governments of the three countries have initiated various programs to introduce more transparency and accountability in governmental regulation relating to investment and trade, there still remains a lot to be done. Although there is no conclusive evidence, it is suspected that the continuing concern on the part of the foreign investors functions in some way as a dragging force against greater expanded foreign investment in the three countries. Unfortunately, for instance, Korea is ranked only 21st in terms of net Foreign Direct Investment (FDI) inflows in 2005 and Korea's accumulated FDI share to the GDP was a mere 8.0% in 2005 compared to the 21.7% global average.

2) Addressing the Concern

Clearly, there still remain areas where the governments of the three countries should adopt more aggressive and expansive reform measures to address the concerns of foreign investors, if they want to become hubs for foreign investment in the far eastern region. Although the governments of the three states have implemented various measures to address foreign governments' and foreign investors' concerns, some of the concerns apparently still remain. As for these concerns, the governments will have to continue to adjust their policies to meet international standards and to compete with other foreign investment destinations in the region.

But it also seems true that some of the complaints by foreign investors are based on a misunderstanding or misperception of the economy of the three countries and the role of the respective governments. Foreign investors tend to believe that the governments are orchestrating almost all business decisions of almost all of their companies and that through such orchestration they attempt to drive their governmental policy objectives. Apparently, this does not appear to be an accurate description of the current situation, for instance, in Korea: due to the regulatory changes and increased public oversight both in Korea and abroad, the Korean government does not seem to possess the wherewithal to carry this out. Rather, this may have been caused by lingering memories of the role of the Korean government in the early stages of Korea's economic development. Influenced by these former associations, foreign governments and companies have a strong perception (or misperception) that the Korean government maintains disguised measures for the purpose of protecting its domestic market while assisting penetration into foreign markets. So, under this line of approach, an argument could be made that investment policy is also a governmental tool to achieve trade goals. This perception (or misperception) is mainly based on the long history of government-sponsored, export-driven economy in Korea. Therefore, to continue to implement the liberalization measures on the one hand and to dispel such misunderstandings or misperceptions on the other, the Korean government has adopted various initiatives.[8]

One could fairly argue that, for instance, Korea still maintains regulatory barriers to foreign goods and services

Table 1. Total number of BITs of Korea, China and Japan, with information on the most recent BITs (as of May 2020)

A. Korea*

	Partners	Status	Date of Signature
1	Kenya	Signed (not in force)	08/07/2014
2	Myanmar	Signed (not in force)	05/06/2014
3	Camerron	Signed (not in force)	24/12/2013
4	Colombia	Signed (not in force)	06/07/2010
5	Zimbabwe	Signed (not in force)	24/05/2010

B. China**

	Partners	Status	Date of Signature
1	Turkey	Signed (not in force)	29/07/2015
2	Tanzania, United Republic of	In force	24/03/2013
3	Canada	In force	09/09/2012
4	Congo, Democratic Republic of	Signed (not in force)	11/08/2011
5	Uzbekistan	In force	19/04/2011

C. Japan***

	Partners	Status	Date of Signature
1	Israel	Signed (not in force)	01/02/2017
2	Kenya	Signed (not in force)	28/08/2016
3	Iran, Islamic Republic of	Signed (not in force)	05/02/2016
4	Oman	Signed (not in force)	19/06/2015

* Korea has a total of 105 BITs including those that are not yet in force. *See* UNCTAD, International Investment Agreements Navigator: Korea, Republic of, *available* at https://investmentpolicy.unctad.org/international-investment-agreements/countries/111/korea-republic-of (last visited May 4, 2020).

** China has 145 BITs including those that are not yet in force. *See* UNCTAD, International Investment Agreements Navigator: China, *available* at https://investmentpolicy.unctad.org/international-investment-agreements/countries/42/china (last visited May 4, 2020).

*** Japan has 34 BITs including those that are not yet in force. *See* UNCTAD, International Investment Agreements Navigator:Japan, *available* at https://investmentpolicy.unctad.org/international-investment-agreements/countries/105/japan (last visited May 4, 2020).

providers, and to related foreign investment. However, whether a particular measure constitutes a barrier to these international transactions and whether that measure is indeed WTO-inconsistent or an FTA-inconsistent are two different questions. It may appear to be a barrier in the opinion of the foreign investors, but it is nonetheless consistent with Korea's obligation under the relevant international agreements. So, it may be considered to be a legitimate measure after all. The fact that Korea has never been challenged by another member at the WTO dispute settlement procedure for an investment-related or service-related issue, nor has it been brought to an international investment arbitration by a foreign investor may prove that investment regulation, though not optimal, has been reasonably managed and improved over the years. But Korea has not gone through a real test yet in this regard and that real test will be looming on the horizon once Korea enters into the full implementation mode of the FTAs.

2. Status of Outstanding Investment Arbitrations

Korea has been one of the active participants in the regime of international investment agreements (IIA). Since 1971, Korea has concluded as many as 123 IIAs, 105 BITs and 18 FTAs with investment chapters as of March 19, 2022. While having established a web of IIAs, Korea managed to remain an investment arbitration-free country for four decades. As a consequence, IIAs and investment arbitration had not drawn that much attention domestically, which stood in sharp contrast to the level of attention directed at trade agreements and trade disputes dealt with by the WTO dispute settlement mechanism. This traditional calmness ended in 2012 when Korea faced its first investment arbitration filed by a US equity fund. Since then, nine more cases were filed against Korea by different foreign investors under different BITs and FTAs as of December 31, 2021. This recent development is noteworthy, considering the four decades of silence in Korea on this front.

As indicated before, the first investment arbitration proceeding was filed by Lone Star, a US equity fund, on

November 22, 2012 under the 2011 Korea-Belgium BIT.[9]

After the hearings in 2015 and 2016, the final award has not been released as of March 2022. Not surprisingly, the final award will draw a great deal of attention from the general public as well as from the experts in this field since this is the first case of investment arbitration involving the Korean government with a unprecedently sizable amount of compensation around 5 trillion KRW (4 billion USD) being requested.

The Korea-Belgium BIT was originally concluded in 1976. The BIT was then amended in 2011. This case was brought almost immediately after the amendment. The timing of the initiation of this arbitration has since alerted Korea: amendments of old BITs can sometimes facilitate filing of investment arbitration proceedings through inclusion of new provisions or exclusion of old ones. At the same time, the fact that this case was brought by a US investor under the Korea-Belgium BIT rather than Korea-US FTA's Investment Chapter where various defense schemes are available for a respondent government has also raised attention in Korea: multinational foreign investors can easily "shop" the BITs and FTAs that best suit their position.

As explained before, the second investment arbitration involves Dutch investors. On May 20, 2015, a Dutch company called Hanocal, owned by Abu Dhabi-based International Petroleum Investment Company, brought an investment arbitration against Korea under the 2003 Korea-Netherlands BIT. In *Hanocal Holding B.V. and IPIC International B.V. v. Republic of Korea* (ICSID Case No. ARB/15/17),[10] the claimants challenged the alleged tax levied by the NTS on the 2010 sale of the claimants' controlling stake in Hyundai Oilbank, a Korean petroleum and refinery company based in Seosan, Korea. They settled the dispute on October 5, 2016. The specific terms of the settlement have not been revealed yet. It is also not clear whether the whole dispute has been settled once and for all, or whether the claimants still reserve the right to re-initiate the proceeding.

The third investment dispute involving Korea is *Mohammad*

Table 2. Status of Investment Arbitration Relating to Korea **(as of May 2020)**

A. Foreign Investor against Korea

Korea	Case Name	Forum	The Other Party
1	Colt Industries Operating Company v. the Korean Government (ICSID Case No. ARB/84/2)	ICSID	Colt Industries Operating Company(United States)
2	LSF-KEB Holdings SCA and others v. Republic of Korea (ICSID Case No. ARB/12/37)	ICSID	HL Holdings SCA (Belgian), Kukdong Holdings I SCA (Belgian), Kukdong Holdings II SCA (Belgian), LSF SLF Holdings SCA (Belgian), LSF-KEB Holdings SCA (Belgian), Lone Star Capital Investments S.ár. l. (Luxembourg), Lone Star Capital Management SPRL (Belgian), Star Holdings SCA (Belgian)
3	Hanocal Holding B.V. and IPIC International B.V. v. Republic of Korea (ICSID Case No. ARB/15/17)	ICSID	Hanocal Holding B.V (Dutch), IPIC International BV(Dutch)

B. Korean Investor against Foreign Governments

	Korea investor	Case Name	Forum	The Other Party
1	Ansung Housing Co., Ltd.	Ansung Housing Co., Ltd. v. People's Republic of China (ICSID Case No. ARB/14/25)	ICSID	People's Republic of China
2	Samsung Engineering Co., Ltd.	Samsung Engineering Co., Ltd. v. Sultanate of Oman (ICSID Case No. ARB/15/30)	ICSID	Sultanate of Oman

See ICSID Cases: Advanced Search, *available at* https://icsid.worldbank.org/en/Pages/cases/searchcases.aspx (last visited May 7, 2020).

Reza Dayyani and Others v. Republic of Korea,[11] an Iranian electronics company, Entekhab Group, filed a notice of arbitration against Korea on September 14, 2015 based on the 1998 Korea-Iran BIT. The claimants now challenge the creditors' termination of an agreement for the sale of a majority stake in Daewoo Electronics to the claimants and their refusal to return the claimants' USD 50 million deposit. Hearings took place in May 2017 and the decision in favour of investor was rendered on 6 June 2018. Unlike the previous two cases, this dispute took place under the rules of UNCITRAL.

3. Implications of Recent Development

The sudden advent of investment arbitration has startled Korea in many respects. The four decades of silence on the investment arbitration front had made Korea passive with regard to the negotiation and the drafting of the provisions of IIAs. Korea had also been rather receptive of new proposals raised by IIA counterparts. Having seen the fast development of investment arbitration proceedings brought against it, and the scope of the claims presented in those proceedings, however, the government of Korea has now become more cautious in terms of formulating provisions in the new IIAs and discussing these issues through negotiations.

Furthermore, recently the situation has been further complicated by rather fluid circumstances surrounding IIAs in the international community where various reform proposals are being floated at the moment. Most notably, the EU proposed in September 2015 a new scheme that would change the framework of the current IIAs and investment arbitration in a significant manner. The EU's proposal presents new ideas to amend the current investment arbitration, including creation of a new standing court to resolve investment disputes. A proposal to introduce an appellate mechanism as part of this standing court also entails fundamental changes in the current investment arbitration. There have been robust discussions in the international community on these issues recently. Korea is actively following these recent international developments.

The apparently changing paradigm of IIAs has put Korea in a more difficult situation as Korea is participating in the negotiation of new IIAs at the moment and struggling to implement the existing IIAs, based on its experience from recent investment disputes. Korea is making efforts to keep abreast with the fast development in IIAs and to fathom resulting consequences for Korea and its investors.

In any event, the three pending investment arbitration cases indicate that Korea is likely to see more investment disputes in the future concerning various governmental regulations and policies. Likewise, any investment arbitration in the future will continue to draw keen attention from the government agencies, professionals and the general public.

Endnotes

1. *See* Office of the United States Trade Representative, *2007 National Trade Estimate Report on Foreign Trade Barriers*, pp. 367-368.

2. *See Ibid.*, p. 368.

3. *See* generally the arguments raised by the governments of the United States, European Union and Japan in the WTO disputes of US-DRAMs, EC-DRAMs, and Japan-DRAMs, respectively. The underlying thinking of these countries arguments is basically the same.

4. *See Ibid.*

5. *Ibid.*

6. *Ibid.*

7. *Ibid.*

8. As recently as October 2006, the Korean government identified 151 FDI improvement tasks in total to make Korea an attractive destination for foreign investment. Furthermore, the Korean Trade Ministers have mentioned making policy efforts to liberalize trade and investment. *See* Invest Korea, "Trade Minister Strives for Trade and Investment Liberalization" (May 30, 2014), *available at* http://www.investkorea.org/en/news/ivest.do?mode=view&articleNo=38376 (last visited May 11, 2020). In this regard, Korea has been loweing barriers and easing regulations for investment entries. *See* Invest Korea, "Seoul to Ease Regulations for New PEF Entries, Investment," *available at* http://www.investkorea.org/en/news/ivest.do?mode=view&articleNo=473484 (last visited May 11, 2020).

9. *LSF-KEB Holdings SCA and others v. Republic of Korea* (ICSID Case No. ARB/12/37), *available at* https://icsid.worldbank.org/en/pages/cases/pendingCases.aspx?status=p (last visited Jan. 14, 2017).

10. *Hanocal Holding B.V. and IPIC International B.V. v. Republic of Korea* (ICSID Case No. ARB/15/17), *available at* https://icsid.worldbank.org/en/Pages/cases/casedetail.aspx?CaseNo=ARB/15/17 (last visited Jan. 14, 2017).

11. *Mohammad Reza Dayyani and others v. Republic of Korea* (PCA Case No. 2015-38), *available at* http://investmentpolicyhub.unctad.org/ISDS/Details/679 (last visited Jan. 14, 2017).

Chapter V

Key Elements and Basic Structure of Dispute Settlement Proceedings in FTAs

1. Emergence of FTAs in the Multilateral Trading Regime

1) Current Status of Multilateral Trading Regime under the WTO

The multilateral trading system is considered to be the major forum for negotiating multilateral rules for international trade and investment. Unfortunately, however, it is not living up to its promises with regards to delivering multilaterally agreed rules following its establishment. Trade negotiation rounds are taking far longer without producing meaningful agreements or deals. Currently there are outstanding trade negotiations initiated almost immediately after the establishment of the WTO without having delivered commendable results. A case in point is the DDA negotiation and the amendment for the Dispute Settlement Understanding (DSU). Although negotiations have been in place for 20 years, none of these projects have so far come to fruition, except some package deals at the Bali and Nairobi Ministerial Conferences from the agendas in the DDA negotiations.

2) Current Status of Doha Round Negotiation

The word "implementation" is not as frequently mentioned in FTAs as it has been in the context of WTO. In particular, difficulties in implementing trade agreements are a major discussion topic at the WTO where special and differential (S&D) treatment is one of the established principles, though probably not so much at the FTA level where the parties to the agreement are regarded as equals. The Uruguay Round Agreement which launched the WTO in 1995 is a set of highly complex agreements. Many developing country members signed such a broad agreement for the first time, although many developed countries had experience from the plurilateral codes of the Tokyo Round. Although much flexibility is provided under the S&D treatment, developing countries still lack the financial, human, and institutional resources and experience, in particular with respect to such agreements as Trade Related Aspects of Intellectual Property Rights (TRIPs), Trade-related Investment Measures (TRIMs), Sanitary and Phytosanitary (SPS), and Technical Barriers to Trade (TBT) Agreements.

Many developing countries did not have a proper system for protection of IPRs and had difficulties in creating or refurbishing the system to fulfill the obligations in the WTO Agreement. They further argue that the WTO Agreement did not deliver the benefits it promised to the developing countries, for instance, in exporting agriculture and textiles and clothing products. Some developing countries officials even expressed their frustration by saying that they had been deceived in the Uruguay Round negotiations. Their voices were strongest when the WTO attempted to launch another round of negotiations, generally called "a new round." The implementation issue became one of the most contentious issues at the Seattle Ministerial Conference of 1999, which failed to launch a new round, and again at the Doha Ministerial of 2001, which eventually succeeded in launching the DDA negotiations. Developing countries wanted to redress the unfair situation that resulted from the previous round before they could agree to the launch of a new round.

The implementation issues from the point of developing countries are two-fold. First, the obligations are too harsh for developing countries, and the S&D provisions in the current agreement are considered insufficient. Therefore, they claim for more and enhanced S&D treatment, for example, a longer implementation period and softer commitments regarding market access and rules. The other issue is about assistance from developed countries. There are a number of provisions in WTO Agreements regarding the obligations of developed countries, for example, technology transfer. Developing countries argue that most of these provisions are vague and rhetorical, and thus must be further strengthened to ensure that specific obligations are placed on developed countries.

Developed countries were generally reluctant to address these issues on their own. They have argued that the attempt to rebalance the past agreements required new negotiations. The compromise made around the Doha Ministerial was that some issues were immediately decided at the ministerial meeting and others were to be discussed and settled later in the broader negotiations by including S&D issues in the Doha work program.[1] It was recognized that the implementation issues could be agreed on a so-called early harvest basis, despite the overall single undertaking principle. So far, no early harvest decision has been made to date in the DDA negotiations, with regard not only to the developing country issues but also other sectors. However, at the Bali Ministerial Conference as well as the Nairobi Ministerial Conference held in 2013 and 2015 some progress has been made. The upcoming Ministerial Conference in June 2022 to be held in Geneva will provide a further barometer for future developments.

3) Reasons Behind the Recent Surge of FTAs in East Asia

Korea, China and Japan started their FTA drive beginning from the middle of the 2000s. Of the three, Japan was the last in order. The recent surge in FTA use has been mainly caused by the realization of the countries that FTAs will form the trading norms of the future as the negotitions at the WTO have either faltered or dragged on. In order for the three states to participate in the global trading regime as robustly as before, they inevitably have to resort to FTAs as a new compass for their future. The three countries have also realized that the FTA negotiations and conclusion are the most efficient ways to globalize their domestic regulation system and invite more investors from abroad. Realizing this, Korea was the quickest among the three, followed by China and then Japan. At present, the FTA policy takes center stage of the trade policy of the three states.

In the case of Korea, the drive was initiated in 2003 when Korea concluded the FTA with Chile. Foreign counterparts utilized FTA negotiations as an opportunity to bring Korea's attention to their concerns in Korea, to expedite further liberalization in the Korean regulatory regime for their nationals' investment, and to introduce a mechanism to protect their investors. Specific substantive and procedural issues have been raised; in particular, the substantive issue of "indirect expropriation"[2] as well as the procedural issue of introducing ISDS proceedings have been hotly debated.

The issue of indirect expropriation is implicated when a government's otherwise legitimate regulation turns into an expropriation (or taking), *i.e.*, prompting just compensation for a victim. The perception that somehow foreign investors would be discriminated against in Korea even if the Korean market had been opened up by the FTAs has caused Korea's trading partners to raise these issues at the FTA negotiation table. The key concept here is that a seemingly legitimate government policy and measure could somehow be determined to be a measure targeting foreign investment in disguise. In the meantime, the ISDS procedure has also attracted attention in Korea because of its unique feature by which a foreign investor can bring an international legal action against another government, a situation that Korea has neither undergone nor fully thought about before. Korea's FTA partners' rationale behind this new procedural addition has been that their investors need a neutral international forum to lodge their legal claims against the Korean government when their investment is subject to discriminatory treatment in Korea.

In this process, the Korean government has become aware of the following: (i) major trading partners' continuing perception about the regulatory regime in Korea and role of the government, (ii) the close relationship between governmental regulation (most of the time non-investment related regulation) and foreign investment, and (iii) the increasing likelihood of future legal disputes in this area. This realization has apparently led the Korean government to understand that foreign investment is not a stand-alone issue anymore, but closely intertwined with the general regulatory power of the government.

Obviously, Korea's drive for more liberalization to lure foreign investment will be further boosted by its current effort to spread the FTA network among its major trading partners. Given that all FTAs have foreign investment promotion and protection as one of the key ingredients, an increasing number of FTAs basically means a more protected and more favorable environment for foreign investors in Korea. In fact, recent negotiations with other trading partners in the course of concluding the FTAs have helped clarify the concerns of foreign investors and identified measures to be adopted by the Korean government, including legislation for new laws and regulation and amendment of existing ones. It is widely expected that continuing reform measures in this regard will be able to transform Korea into a magnet for foreign investment in the region.

4) WTO vs. FTA: A Comparison

Currently, WTO and FTA are the two most utilized forums for trade liberalization among the member states. However, it is important to understand their nature and relationship in relation to trade liberalization. The WTO and FTAs have different characteristics and their relationship matters in promoting free trade. While the WTO stands out as a multilateral trade organization involving the majority of the international members, FTAs are meant to further liberalize trade between certain WTO members. The two systems have their own peculiar features and benefits that make them suitable for different issues. Issues more suitable to be addressed under the multilateral forum may not necessarily be suitable to be addressed under FTAs, and vice-versa. However, the rules of the WTO serve as boundaries within which FTAs can be concluded. As such, any FTA needs to be evaluated against the rules of the multilateral rules on trade liberalization.

5) Treatment of FTAs under the WTO Regime

This section looks into how FTAs are treated in the WTO regime. FTAs are still concluded within the rubric of the WTO regime. It is imperative, therefore, to understand that the obligations of FTAs are either in line with or are extensions of respective obligations of WTO Agreements. Korea, China and Japan have been loyal members of the WTO. They have been relatively faithful implementers of the obligations of the WTO Agreements. It would be indeed embarrasing if the implementation of FTAs would lead to a looser implementation of comparable or related WTO obligations of the three states. Interestingly, however, the focus of the three states recently has been placed on FTAs — either negotiations of FTA or implementation of FTAs with major trading partners. The WTO obligations have been put on the back burner.

(1) Article XXIV of GATT

The FTAs are indeed permitted under Article XXIV of the General Agreement on Tariffs and Trade 1994 (GATT 1994). Upon careful reading of Article XXIV, however, it becomes evident that what is permitted under this provision is a preferential measure that is "necessary for the formation of the FTA,"[3] which does not put other non-parties in a more disadvantageous position than before.[4] It may not cover *all* the consequences flowing from the creation of an FTA, however. For example, if a new situation occurs as a result of an FTA, it is not entirely clear whether such a situation would also be covered by Article XXIV because arguably the situation is not "necessary for the formation of the FTA." Thus, the proposition stating that anything relating to the FTAs can be covered by Article XXIV is thus not justified under the article. This rationale applies with equal force to instances in which the members adopt two different sets of rules affecting trade in their respective territories, as a result of concluding different FTAs.

As a corollary, systematic changes, taking place as a result of the adoption of new rules of an FTA, may lead to a situation where they cannot be justified by Article XXIV. In fact, Article X of GATT 1994 is also supportive of the proposition that uniformity is indeed one of the core elements of the trade norms of the member States.[5] The introduction of various new rules through FTAs now stands to implicate these other norms of the WTO Agreements that all the FTA partners are presumably supposed to abide by unless deviation is justified by Article XXIV.

(2) Article V of GATS

Article V of General Agreement on Trade in Services (GATS) is another avenue where preferential trade arrangement among WTO members can be justified. The provision allows WTO members to enter into a preferential trade arrangement in relation to trade in services. Unlike its counterpart under Article XXIV of GATT that presupposes a provisional arrangement the provision of GATS Article V seems to allow a permanent arrangement provided that the stated conditions are fulfilled. Therefore, regional efforts in market integration can also take this course in order to liberalize the trade in services.

6) Changing Perception of Multilateralism in East Asia

The three states are now displaying a changing view of multilateralism. They have been stout supporters of the multilateralism enshrined in the WTO Agreements. But over the past decade, their loyalty to multilateralism has been weakened and compromised. This change may affect how these three countries view their trading regimes with other trading partners through various FTAs and how they view internal trade among the three states as well.

However, things are changing on the other side of the world where the major trading partner of the three countries, the US, operates. The recent change of administration also brought about a change of attitude towards FTA and trade liberalization in general. The Trump administration is openly critical of various trade deals made by previous adminstrations and has vowed to abandon or renegotiate them. Prior to taking office, Donald Trump became famous for his unconventional trade policies. During his presidential campaign, he promised to declare China a "currency manipulator," to immediately pursue the renegotiation of the North American Free Trade Agreement (NAFTA), and to withdraw from the Trans-Pacific Partnership (TPP).[6] Along similar lines, Trump declared in his inaugural speech that "for many decades, we've enriched foreign industry at the expense of American industry; subsidized the armies of other countries, while allowing for the very sad depletion of our military. We've defended other nations' borders while refusing to defend our own." He also stated that "From this day forward, it's going to be only America first, America first," and that "protection will lead to great prosperity and strength."[7] As such, Trump has been labeled as a protectionist by the media, deviating from past presidents who were champions of free trade.[8,9,10] Addressing such remarks, Trump has argued that he "believe[s] strongly in free trade but it also has to be fair trade."[11] While Trump made some extreme remarks regarding trade policy, his policies seem to be taking a more conservative turn since he started his term as president. For instance, "The President's 2017 Trade Policy Agenda" released by the United States Trade Representative (USTR) in March 2017 does state that the Trump administration will "expand trade in a way that is freer and fairer for all Americans," but it does not make grand promises of sweeping change.[12] The media also pointed out that Trump became more conservative over the months regarding his trade policy, especially on Chinese relations and NAFTA.[13,14] Still, Trump continued to be adamant about decreasing trade deficits. (This point will be explained in more detail in sections below, in relation to NAFTA and Korea-US FTA) In addition to renegotiating NAFTA and Korea-US FTA, Trump focused on creating trade barriers to steel and aluminum imports to decrease trade deficits. Notably, Trump invoked *national security concerns* as the grounds for erecting trade barriers.[15] For instance, on April 20, 2017, the Secretary of Commerce announced that the Department of Commerce had initiated an investigation into the effect of steel imports on national security under Section 232 of the Trade Expansion Act of 1962.[16] Similarly, on April 27, 2017 Trump signed a memorandum on "aluminum imports and threats to national security."[17]

During his first six months in office, Trump repeatedly showed disregard for multilateralism. Trump withdrew from the TPP, a multilateral free trade agreement between more than 12 countries across the pacific, which was supported by the Obama administration.[18,19] The Trump administration was also reported to have stated that they will ignore anti-US WTO rulings, as "ever since the United States won its independence, it has been a basic principle of our country that American citizens are subject only to laws and regulations made by the US government — not rulings made by foreign governments or international bodies," according to a leaked report that was scheduled to be sent to Congress.[20] What are the reasons for the current administration's disregard for multilateralism? According to the Press briefing by Secretary of Commerce Wilbur Ross, the problem with the current WTO system is that it has a "most favored nation clause," which makes reciprocal tariff barriers difficult to erect. In addition, Ross also pointed out that the WTO does not effectively secure intellectual property rights and does not have an effective dispute resolution mechanism.[21] As such, deviating from multilateral agreements or organizations and turning to bilateral agreements can enable the US to get better deals with individual countries. Some reporters have criticized that the Trump administration's disregard for multilateralism stems from a belief that economic treaties are essentially a zero-sum situation rather than a win-win situation and that historically other countries have taken advantage of the United States, when in reality economic treaties can be a win-win situation.[22] Others have pointed out that such a disregard for multilateralism seems to be a product of both economic and political populism.[23]

Notably, in terms of trade policy, the Biden administration has maintained the basic stance of the former Trump administration. Thus, despite the inauguration of the new government, the United States is pursuing the same policy on trade — be it WTO, FTA, digital trade or confrontation with China.

(1) Providing New Platform for Access to Foreign Markets for SMEs

FTAs provide Small and Medium Enterprises (SME) with lowered tariffs and non-tariff barriers on goods, as well as less reduced restrictions on services. For this reason, SMEs can enjoy the benefit of FTA preferential tariff rates from FTA trading partners. For instance, in the case of textile products, SMEs can access foreign markets with lowered tariffs from 18% of the MFN rate to 0% of the FTA preferential rate according to the Korea-US FTA.

SMEs can also strengthen business relationships with foreign buyers by offering more favorable prices on goods subject to FTA preferential treatment, while foreign buyers' inquiries about Korean, Chinse or Japanese companies capable of FTA utilization is continuously increasing. For instance, US buyers have been reluctant to import Korean products related to power transmissions due to their relatively high prices. The Korea-US FTA has eliminated the tariff rate of the products from 7% to 0%. As a result, US buyers started to search for Korean suppliers capable of meeting the import requirements of the buyers. In addition, an FTA has a spill-over effect of increasing sales of domestic suppliers which provide materials and parts for the producers which export goods that receive FTA preferential treatment. An increase in exports by an FTA subsequently brings about an increase in sales of suppliers in the supply chain. The collaboration between producers of goods and suppliers in the supply chain to obtain FTA preferential status tends to provide business opportunities for suppliers as well as producers.

In addition, FTA networks offer suppliers of SMEs opportunities to join a global supply chain managed by global companies. For instance, Korean auto parts suppliers have been increasingly enlisted as vendors for global automotive makers such as GM and Ford in the US with the help of the Korea-US FTA. Already, several Korean suppliers have succeeded in expanding their vendor status to other areas such as Europe and India by utilizing the Korea-EU and Korea-India FTAs.

As such, the three countries have started to rely upon their FTAs as a new platform for their SMEs. In particular, the export-oriented tendency of the SMEs of the three countries has been facilitated and supported dramatically with the advent of the FTAs, numbering in the tens and dozens.

(2) Facilitating Attraction of Foreign Direct Investment

FTAs also bring about a favorable business environment for foreign investors by dismantling tariff and non-tariff barriers. The three states realized this crucial potential of FTAs. To them, the FTAs have turned out to be the best means of boosting foreign investment. The FTAs can have a domino effect in terms of establishing a web of cooperative networks. For example, suppose that a Swedish company which produces materials for cars has recently decided to invest in Korea. One of the factors considered in the decision-making process is to utilize Korea's global FTA network. In case the company sets up a plant in Korea, the business relationship with the car industry in Korea will become more solid. Also, the Swedish plant in Korea can import materials from Sweden with cheaper prices through the Korea-EU FTA. In addition, the plant can export automotive parts and materials to the ASEAN markets using the FTA preferential treatment.

More favorable business environments shaped by FTAs also appeal to Korean companies overseas making them consider returning to their home land. Some industries such as textile and footwear also recognize that the need for the return of missing links is necessary to meet FTA requirements regarding rules of origin. Specifically, in August 2012, 14 Korean jewelry companies jointly announced they would relocate their factories overseas to Iksan, North Jeolla Province, located in the Southern part of Korea. FTAs have triggered huge changes to Korea's investment environment, encouraging domestic firms to relocate from overseas to Korea. Many small-and-medium-sized companies are swiftly joining the trend. In addition, the Korean textile industry is seeking a way to attract garment companies overseas back home to meet the rules of origin requirements for textiles such as the yarn forward rule in the Korea-US FTA.

The same rationale identified in the above examples should equally apply to China and Japan, as their respective governments and corporations attempt to take advantage of these benefits of FTAs.

(3) Creating New Business Models through FTAs

Likewise, it is expected that the FTA networks can allow companies in Korea, China and Japan to gain competitive advantages by creating various types of new business models. Newly introduced alliance and cooperative regime, made possible through FTAs, will enable the entities of the three countries to participate more actively in global competition.

There are some exemplary types of collaboration among FTA partners. For instance, there is a possible case that intra-industry collaboration between companies in Korea and ASEAN can enter the EU market through the Korea-EU FTA. According to the Korea-EU FTA, rules of origin for textile products include the fabric forward criterion. In the case that ASEAN and Korean textile makers build up a collaboration in the international textile supply chain, a win-win effect is expected in entering the EU textile market. For example, ASEAN textile makers supply yarns for Korean textile makers through the Korea-ASEAN FTA. And then, Korean textile companies produce fabric and other textiles with yarns made in ASEAN, and also export the goods to the EU market through the Korea-EU FTA.

Collaboration in investment between Korean and ASEAN companies is also possible to help facilitate entry into the Chinese market through the ASEAN-China FTA. Korean companies may invest to set up production plants in the ASEAN region and then export products to China through the ASEAN-China FTA. With regard to production in ASEAN, companies located in Korea can collaborate by forming international supply chain relationships to supply parts and materials made in Korea to the plants located in ASEAN through the Korea-ASEAN FTA.

Also possible is a collaboration to fully utilize Korea-US, Korea-EU and Korea-ASEAN FTAs together. The US companies with a global brand of outdoor footwear can request Korean companies to produce OEM-based outdoor footwear. To this end, the Korean companies can import some parts and materials of the products from ASEAN suppliers through the Korea-ASEAN FTA. Finally, the finished products of outdoor footwear made in Korea with a US company's brand can be exported to the US and EU markets under the Korea-US and Korea-EU FTAs. In this case, outdoor footwear using a high-end brand of a US company can have stronger competitive advantages with a high level of quality and a good price by fully utilizing the Korea-US, Korea-EU and Korea-ASEAN FTAs together.

China and Japan are pursuing similar objectives. They also

regard the FTAs as a vehicle that will facilitate the introduction of and experiments with new business models for their key industries. Japan has been rather conservative in this respect because its technological edge has already been solid. Japan has also started to realize that the FTAs can provide a further boost for their companies' global competitiveness.

(4) Securing Dominance in the Global Trade Market

The FTAs will ultimately solidify the dominance of the three countries in the global trading market. China is the world's third largest trading country. Japan is the fourth and Korea is the seventh. As such, the combination of the three would occupy the critical mass of global trade. The three contries are of the view that FTAs will allow them to maintain their continuing dominance in the global trading market.

7) FTAs in East Asia

Korea's global FTA network is providing freer, speedier, and more competitive express ways for the global trade and investment community. Currently, the network is already in effect with 55 countries including the EU, the ASEAN, China and India as well as the United States. In addition, a regional FTA is under discussion between Korea, China and Japan. A mega FTA is also on the table that comprises the three countries as core members — the Regional Comprehensive Economic Partnership (RCEP). Korea's global FTA network connects 39% of the world's population (2,687 mil. people), 56% of the world's GDP and 60% of the world's trade. This network is larger than those of the EU, the US and Japan in terms of population, GDP and trade. For instance, the US FTA network connects 6% of the world's population (415 mil. people), 10% of the world's GDP and 13% of the world's trade.

The East Asian region is undergoing a remarkable change into a global marketplace from the world production base. The potentials of the region are fast growing. The economic size of

China, Japan and Korea in the region is already close to the size of the EU and US markets. This area is moving forward step by step toward regional integration in the future. In this context, Korea is striving to be the first mover towards a regional FTA in East Asia. To this end, Korea started FTA negotiations with China in May 2012. In addition, regional FTAs among Korea, China and Japan are under discussion.[24]

(1) FTA DSMs: Key Provisions and Characteristics

The recent phenomenon of the proliferation of FTAs started around the time when the WTO came in to being in 1995. From 1950, when the first FTA started, the then EC tried to introduce FTAs among EU members, i.e. a predecessor of the current EU. Other GATT members were not interested in FTAs until the 1980s. Many of the FTAs were signed recently, particularly between developing and developed countries. The signing of FTAs between developed countries was not so frequent because the number of developed countries is relatively small in the WTO. In addition, developed states have largely already signed their FTAs.

Newer generations of FTAs tend to have wider coverage. Before 1995, most of the FTAs were "regional trade agreements" (RTAs) that tended to be limited to a particular region. After 1995, of cross- or inter-regional FTAs emerged. Nowadays, any WTO member that starts signing FTAs tends to reach more than a dozen agreements. Because of the rise in the number of new FTAs, there is now a need for DSMs in FTAs: more trade tends to lead to more disputes. Some suggest using the existing WTO DSM in FTAs. According to DSU, the WTO DSM only applies to covered agreements,[25] which do not include FTAs. Other members may prefer different DSMs to those of the WTO, even if FTA chapters are covered by the WTO. They do not wish to go all the way to Geneva or object to the way the WTO handles a dispute.

There are two categories of models for settling disputes under an FTA, i.e. political and legal models. The political model calls for members to resort to political mechanisms, such as bilateral negotiations and consultation. In this model, disputes are typically handled directly between parties. The two parties do not have to follow strict legal procedures or draft complicated legal documents. Under this model, they can consider not only legal factors, but also political ones in resolving disputes. The advantage of the political model is, first, greater flexibility. Unlike the legal model in which the parties follow fixed procedures, the parties can decide what they want to do. Second, there is more control by the parties. The political model does not usually involve the use of lawyers from law firms. Thus, it is less costly. On the other hand, the political model tends to be power-oriented. For instance, strong states, such as the United States, may be tempted to abuse their power and strong-arm others into accepting their position. Under the political model, states tend to look at overall bilateral relations, rather than particular legal merits. Over time, this can weaken the international rule of law. This is not good news for smaller countries.

Under the legal model, on the other hand, an impartial third party decides a case on the basis of fixed law and jurisprudence. The advantage of the legal model is greater certainty. This creates a level playing field for everybody, regardless of its size. In the *US-Gambling* case,[26] for instance, Antigua and Barbuda won the case against the United States. In the long run, it promotes the international rule of law. The disadvantage of the model is that it is lengthy because of fixed procedures for the judicial process. It is also costly, as it involves external counselors. It does not take political factors into consideration. At the end of the day, a state may win a battle but lose the war. Resorting to the legal model can be problematic when the relationship of the parties is harmed by legal disputes.

The legal model can again be further broken down into two sub-categories. The first is the semi-judicial model, which will be the main focus of this discussion. The semi-judicial model utilizes ad hoc arbitration tribunals. When a state has a case, it will compose an arbitration panel on an ad hoc basis. The second model is the judicial model which is used in some FTAs. Under the judicial model, there is a permanent court that serves as a tribunal. Under this model a state does not need to compose a panel every time it has a case. Between the two models, the ad hoc model is actively utilized by Korea, China and Japan.

In many FTAs, the semi-judicial model is often the one most preferred. Out of 226 FTAs surveyed, 147 FTAs use the semi-judicial model, which accounts for 65% of all FTAs.[27] The judicial model is the least preferred approach, which accounts for only 5%.[28] The remainder adopt a political model or do not adopt a particular dispute settlement system. This is not surprising because the judicial model requires the establishment of a permanent court, which is costly. Judicial models are typically found in FTAs when there is a court that has been already established for other purposes, such as the European Court system of the EU. A state does not wish to create a tribunal just for FTAs, because there are not many FTA disputes and the expense cannot be justified. The semi-judicial model has been on the rise. After 2005, the frequency of using the quasi-judicial model exceeded that of using the political model.

More specifically, key provisions of the semi-judicial model are as follows: jurisdiction, consultation, panel & appellate review, implementation & remedies, administrative & institutional costs. As for jurisdiction, subject areas need to be discussed first. Most of the FTAs these days not only cover tariff measures, but also non-tariff measures such as Technical Barriers to Trade (TBT) and Sanitary and Phytosanitary measures (SPS). They also cover trade in goods, as well as trade in services and trade-related aspects of intellectual property rights. Many FTA DSMs only tend to cover tariff measures. According to the WTO study, 65% of the FTA DSMs exclude other measures, 46% exclude competition, and 38% exclude services. With respect to services, many FTAs tend to exclude the movement of natural persons (MNP) from the scope of DSM.[29] This is because MNP is closely related to immigration law and most countries do not want their immigration law to be challenged by foreigners. In addition, 33% of the FTA DSMs exclude sanitary and phytosanitary measures (SPS) and 20% excludes Anti-dumping (AD) and Countervailing Duties (CVD). For the types of measures, 61 FTAs (including the Canada-US FTA and NAFTA), cover proposed measures. As for the types of complaints, 56 FTAs cover non-violation claims, which accounts for 25% of all FTAs.

In most of the FTAs, only the government of a contracting party has standing. The only exception is Chapter 19 of the NAFTA, which allows private parties to challenge AD & CVD decisions of other parties. Another issue is choice of forum. If one measure is in violation of the WTO and FTA obligation, can a party bring a case before the WTO and FTA simultaneously? Different FTAs have different rules; there are some FTAs which require a party to use the FTA DSM. However, this could be a violation of the WTO obligation, as according to Article 23 of DSU, parties to the WTO must resort to the WTO DSM when there are disputes.[30] Therefore, if FTA parties exclude particular disputes from the WTO DSM, such an act may be a violation of the WTO obligation. Yet most FTAs do not take such an extreme approach. Instead, they take the so-called "fork-in-the-road" approach; once a party starts proceedings relying on one particular DSM, it must finish the proceedings before it invokes another DSM. This approach is found in 96 FTAs, which is about half of the total FTAs.

Another issue is consultation, which is typically stated as a compulsory first step in the DSM. Different FTAs provide different timeframes. Some provide 30 days, some 60 days and some 2-6 months. Consultation is usually bilateral in nature, but it may take place with the assistance of political bodies. Under FTAs panels are composed on an ad hoc basis. For the number of panelists, most FTAs provide 3 panelists, but it could be either 5 or 1. The United States and EU's FTAs usually provide rosters that include the name lists of panelists. Yet many other FTAs do not have them, and thus the parties nominate anyone they wish upon the initiation of their respective disputes. As for appointment procedure, each party nominates one panelist each, and both agree to nominate a chairman. If both panelists cannot agree, the chairman can be selected through a lot or a designated authority, such as the WTO Director General in the case of the ASEAN FTA. As for the qualification of panelists, they need to have expertise in law or international trade. As for nationalities, two panelists each would be nationals of complaining and respondent parties, and the chairman would not normally be a national of either party.

Regarding panel procedures and appellate reviews, once panels are composed, the panels would ask the parties to submit written submissions. Then the panel would hold hearings. In some FTAs, the panel would hold just one hearing, whereas in other FTAs, the panel would hold two hearings, just like in the WTO. During the panel hearings, the parties start making oral arguments individually and then make rebuttal arguments, after which the panel asks questions. 60% of the FTAs provide for an interim review.[31] After the interim review, the panel can revise its finding and issue a final report. The timeframe would typically be 120 days in most FTAs. In terms of language, many FTAs agree to use English or allow parties to agree on another common language, such as Spanish. Costs of panel procedures are usually equally shared by the parties. Yet the ASEAN FTA has established a fund for DSMs for ASEAN members. Some FTAs provide for the appellate review. It is carried out by a permanent body instead of an ad hoc body. The review is limited to the issues of law and legal interpretation, and not factual determination. The appellate body does not have remand power. Such appellate reviews are very rare and have only featured in three FTAs. The first is MERCOSUR, which is the only one functioning. The Southern African Development Community (SADC) used to have the appellate mechanism, but was suspended in 2010.[32] For ASEAN, the appellate mechanism exists on paper, but has not yet been realized.

In the implementation stage, the first issue is how long the DSM allows a losing party to implement a panel decision.

This could be determined by agreement or arbitration, similar to the WTO. There is also a possibility for the compliance review procedure. 64% FTAs of the global community surveyed allow the parties to bring an issue before the arbitration panel regarding whether the losing party complied with the panel decision. 46% FTAs surveyed provide for both pre-retaliation and post-retaliation stages.[33]

The next issue is compensation. 88% FTAs surveyed provide for cross-retaliation. Some US FTAs provide for financial compensation.[34] This is an innovation, compared to the WTO. In the WTO, compensation only refers to compensatory tariff reduction or market access. As for financial compensation in the FTAs, this means that the losing party pays money to the winning party. 74 FTAs solved the sequencing problem.[35] 68% FTAs provide for arbitration for retaliation.[36] In some FTAs, there is the merger of the compliance and compensation proceedings. The parties go to the panel once and get rulings on two issues — first, whether or not the losing party comply, and second, how much compensation the losing party should provide.

The last issue is both an administrative and an institutional one. Some FTAs have political bodies, such as a joint committee. The joint committee may assist in consultation if the parties have a dispute. Many FTAs also provide for contact points, usually used for the exchange of documents. Some FTAs, such as MERCOSUR, ASEAN and NAFTA, provide for a secretariat which may help the panel. Only five FTAs, including ASEAN-AUS-NZ and EU-ACP, mentioned S&D treatment.

For better or worse, DSMs in FTAs have largely remained dormant. American FTAs are the ones that have been most frequently utilized among FTAs globally. If issues are subject to both the WTO and FTA DSM, those are frequently brought before the WTO, instead of the FTA DSM. According to the WTO study, FTA disputes constitute 19% of WTO disputes. WTO dispute resolution mechanisms are often favored because of the institutional advantages of the WTO. It already has established institutions that are able to deal with institutional issues with which the parties do not have experience. FTAs also have limited precedential effect.

For factors that are considered when selecting FTA DSM models, states may first consider whether the scope of an FTA covers traditional issues only or the FTA also covers new issues. Most FTAs tend to exclude new issues from DSMs. If states do not want to create legally binding obligations, for new issues, this would be a natural choice. Another factor that should be considered is the extent of integration. For instance, there are different ways of negotiating over issues of standards. States can either have a mutual recognition agreement or reach harmonization by adopting the same standard among the FTA parties. If the parties have a common standard, it is easier for the panel to decide the case. As for alternative DSMs, in many FTAs parties may utilize domestic judicial mechanisms. For instance, parties may appeal against the decision of an Anti-Dumping authority before the domestic court. The other alternative is the WTO DSM. A third factor that should be considered is the availability of qualified experts. The last factor to be considered is costs. The cost of bringing a case to the WTO is basically free because the parties only pay for their lawyers. Yet for regional DSMs, the parties must pay for panelists and secretariat services.

In conclusion, the design of FTA DSMs is determined by many factors, such as level of development, asymmetry of power between parties, depth of integration and width of coverage and culture. Another issue is the rise of mega-FTAs, such as TPP and Transatlantic Trade and Investment Partnership (TTIP). It is important to assess whether such mega FTAs will make FTA DSMs more powerful. In the course of considering the choice of a given dispute settlement proceeding, there are two points worth mentioning here: motivation for choosing different DSMs and the question of integration and coherence. Regarding motivation under the legal dispute settlement, the majority of FTAs generally have quasi-judicial procedures. 65% FTAs choose quasi-judicial dispute settlement.[37] The differences between countries based on income and region can also have an impact on the choice of DSMs. Low and middle income countries tend to choose the political model. Only five of the 26 RTAs involving OECD high income countries use the political model.[38] The quasi-judicial model is not a feature of RTAs involving low income economies, yet is widely used among other income categories. There does appear to be some relationship between income and choices of political settlement. It seems clear in a question of whether there is a relationship between geographic regions and choices of political settlement. It has been found that in America, the quasi-judicial model is preferred. The same is true for Europe with the exception of Turkey's RTAs with Balkan countries.[39] In Asia, there is a cluster of Western Asian countries that use the political model for their inter-regional RTAs. All the other RTAs, except China's with Hong Kong and Macao, use the quasi-judicial model.[40] In CIS, there is a clear preference for the political model.[41] In Africa, there is generally a split between the judicial and quasi-judicial model. Many commentators allude to the benefits of the legal model.[42] These include stability and relationships and enhancement of the international rule of law. Asia Pacific Economic Cooperation (APEC) could consider providing some intensive capacity building funding in this area to help those followers catch up with the other APEC economies.

Regarding integration and coherence, academics and international lawyers tend to be concerned about the fragmentation of international law. States are expected to weigh in on some of the different options to clarify the relationship between the WTO and FTA DSMs. Article 23 of the DSU can be read to show that the DSB has an exclusive jurisdiction over the WTO issues. Thus, it is improper for FTA parties to handle those issues in the FTA DSMs. It is the case that several countries make reference to the WTO obligations in their FTAs, reaffirming them. They exclude some subject matter relating to jurisdiction from the competence of the FTA DSMs. Often there are exceptions for SPS, TBT and trade remedies. The Korea-EU FTA states that the panel may not adopt an interpretation inconsistent with WTO jurisprudence.[43] Similarly, in the Columbia-Canada

FTA, the panelists must take a note of the previous WTO cases.[44] It is argued that the "fork-in-the-road" approach is not enough to address new challenges arising from the new phenomenon. Arguably, it is not a solution that can stand on its own. There should be a stronger clarification of the relationship between the WTO and FTA DSMs.

With respect to jurisdiction-related issues, in the Korea-US FTA, non-actions claims are allowed. For example, Article 22.4 of the Korea-US FTA provides that dispute settlement proceedings shall apply whenever a party considers that a measure of the other party is inconsistent with FTA obligations or that the other party has failed to carry out FTA obligations.[45] When considering this phrase as referring to non-action claims, it seems that it opens up the coverage of jurisdiction in FTAs too broadly. There is a lack of precedent and experience in applying such non-action claims not only under FTAs but also under WTO DSMs. The fact that non-action claims are not covered by the WTO rules has serious implications that merit the attention of states.

With respect to a choice of forum, it is also related to a jurisdiction issue. Some FTAs, such as the Korea-EU FTA, explicitly state that FTA DSMs shall not be resorted to where a dispute is already intiated under WTO DSM.[46] In several chapters covering trade remedies, SPS, customs and trade facilitation, such FTAs provide that either party may have recourse to the dispute settlement chapter in the FTA for any matter arising under the section. This effectively seems to open up the possibility that the FTA parties should resort to the WTO DSM even for adjudicating FTA-specific obligations, which may not be covered by the WTO rules.

As for compensation, it is debatable whether monetary compensation is a desirable mechanism to deal with non-implementation. In fact, there has been a heated debate on retaliation as a means to induce compliance. Equally there has been a discussion about an alternative remedy of using monetary compensation. There may be some merits for doing this, but this alternative remedy has its own problems. In particular, in the Korea-US FTA, specifically Article 22.13 (non-implementation) provides that a complaining party may not retaliate if a respondent party pays an annual monetary assessment, and, furthermore, if the parties cannot agree on the amount of monetary compensation, it will be set at a level, equal to 50% of the level of the benefits the panel has determined, or if the panel has not determined the level, 50% of the level that the complaining party has proposed to suspend. This alternative form of remedy seems to have the effect of not only allowing a non-complying party to buy itself out of the obligations, but also to allow the paying of only half the level of the retaliation amount that has been determined. More serious considerations are necessary regarding the use of monetary compensation as an alternative remedy. Furthermore, when it involves less-developed countries and developing countries, as a respondent, especially in Asia, they may not have adequate financial resources to pay out of their obligations, as developed countries do. From this perspective, allowing monetary compensation would have the effect of accentuating the problem of imbalance.

With respect to S&D treatment in FTAs, it is doubtful that such S&D treatment and FTAs are compatible. In other words, the key objective of establishing an FTA is to deepen a bilateral trade relationship between parties to the agreement. In such a case, providing for the S&D treatment, mainly in the form of an exception or preferential treatment, may hinder or delay the deepening of the trade performances. It does not seem to meet the purpose of establishing an FTA in the first place. Therefore, because of the inherently conflicting nature of FTAs and the implications of S&D treatment, people may not see the inclusion of such S&D treatment in FTAs. In the case of trade facilitation provisions contained in FTAs, as a related example, despite the mandate for providing technical assistances and capacity building for developing countries, FTAs cannot realistically incorporate such assistance commitments, since actual costs are associated with the problem of free-riding. Regarding the implementation-related concerns of developing countries it may be more appropriately addressed in the WTO framework.

These various traits of global FTAs have recently found their way into the FTAs concluded by the three states of East Asia. As Korea is the only country that has concluded FTAs with both the United States and EU, Korea's FTAs with these two trading giants contain the most conspicuous traits. For instance, these two FTAs have unique provisions and chapters compared to other FTAs that Korea has concluded. They have rosters for panelists for dispute settlement mechanisms. New issues of trade norms are also included. Special DSMs are also present such as a dispute settlement mechanism for automobile trade and NTB mediation.

(2) Overview of Positions of China, Japan and Korea Regarding FTA

Judging from their statements and behavior, the three countries have become active supporter of FTAs. They will continue to maintain this course of policy for the time being. Still, the specific strategic positions of the three countries are slightly different.

i) China

China is an active utilizer of FTAs. Its FTA policy of course began as a trading strategy. It has now turned into its geopolitical tool helping a G-2 giant compete with the United States in many places in the world. China's FTA policy therefore has become more geared toward diplomatic and political implications compared to Korea or Japan.

① Policy in General

Over time, China tends to provide more generous preferential tariffs to the partners of its bilateral and regional trade agreements. While the offered rates to Hong Kong, Macao and Chinese Taipei have not changed since 2013, the average concessions for most of the other partners have been declining substantially since then. Currently, the ASEAN countries, Chile, New Zealand and a Costa Rica are facing the lowest average tariff rate of 0.7%. China has also started to grant duty-free treatment on 95 to 97% of all tariff lines to Least Developed Countries (LDCs) since 2015. As of December 2015, a total of 44 LDCs are benefitting from such arrangements.[47]

Most of the FTAs signed by China during the review period involved further liberalizing commitments in the telecommunication industry that goes beyond China's GATS commitments. The agreements between Guangdong and Hong Kong on Achieving Basic Liberalization of Trade in Services and the new agreements on services among mainland China, Hong Kong, and Macao signed in November 2015 are particular examples. The China-Australia FTA, signed in June 2015 and which entered into force in December 2015, also contains two supplementary commitments on telecommunication services regarding a) the permission to set up joint-ventures between the two countries or wholly owned enterprises in the CSPFTZ relating to information services, store and forward services, call centers and domestic multi-party communications, and b) the permission to set up joint ventures to undertake online data and transaction processing for profits from e-commerce. Yet, the Korea-China FTA does not contain any further commitments related to telecommunications beyond GATS commitments.[48]

All six of the FTAs signed by China during the review period contain further liberalization commitments with respect to securities. In particular, the agreements between Guangdong and Hong Kong on Achieving Basic Liberalization of Trade in Services and the new agreements on services among mainland China, Hong Kong, and Macao signed in November 2015 substantially liberalized limitations on equity and the scope of business. These agreements define national treatment obligations rather widely, while applying a negative list to commercial presence reservation and a positive list to supplementary commitments.[49]

China has achieved additional liberalization results through its FTAs with Korea and Australia. Commitments in these agreements include an increase from 33% (GATS commitment) to 49% of minority ownership allowed in joint ventures of companies engaged in the underwriting of A-shares and in the underwriting and trading of B-shares and H-shares. There are also improvements relating to the right to provide trading, advisory and portfolio management and custody services to Qualified Domestic institutional Investors (QDII). Furthermore, China may be granted permission to participate in the securitization business on a national treatment basis under the China-Australia FTA.[50]

China did not offer any concession regarding retirement homes under the GATS, but has undertaken commitments in the China-Australia FTA, the CEPAs and the agreements with Hong Kong and Macao.[51]

China believes that trade contributes strongly to sustainable development of the global economy. Within the Asia-Pacific region, China has emphasized that successful FTA negotiations are important for promoting liberalization and facilitation of trade and investment which would lead to regional integration and economic development. China is willing to cooperate with any system in accordance with the WTO rules and conducive to regional economic integration.[52] China is also willing to play a leading role within the multilateral trading system in order to promote balanced and inclusive development. Meanwhile, China strongly opposes trade protectionism. It will thus continue expediting the creation of high-standard global FTA networks.[53]

② FTA Conclusion/Negotiation Status

As of December 2015, China signed 15 preferential trade agreements. During the period under review, China signed two FTAs, one with Australia and the other with Korea, and two agreements, with Iceland and Switzerland respectively, entered into force. China also signed supplementary agreements to respective CEPAs with Hong Kong and Macao, in order to deepen their integration process.[54]

China is also an active participant in regional trade forums. It is a member of the APEC forum (1991) and a signatory of the Asia-Pacific Trade Agreement (APTA) (2001) as well as the Agreement on Trade in Goods of the Framework Agreement on Comprehensive Economic Cooperation between China and ASEAN (2004).[55]

China is currently engaged in a number of FTA negotiations, including China-Japan-Republic of Korea FTA, China-GCC FTA, China-Sri Lanka FTA, China-Israel FTA and so on. The China-Palestine FTA is in the second stage of negotiation and the Cross-straits Economic Co-operation Framework Agreement is proceeding to a follow-up negotiation.[56] China has been an active participant in regional and sub-regional economic cooperation forums including the APEC, Greater Mekong Sub-regional Economic Cooperation, and Greater Tumen Initiative. The negotiations of the China-US BIT moved smoothly to the stage of discussing negative lists. A China-EU BIT is also headed towards favorable agreements as part of the negotiations.[57]

③ Trade Remedy system: General Legal Structure and Characteristics

China has overseen a dramatic upgrade of its trade remedy legislations and system in the past decade. Chinsese companies that frequently participate in foreign trade remedy investigations have taught the Chinese government the importance and utility of those remedy investigations as well as the imposition of additional duties in the WTO regime as well as the FTA regime.

• Anti-Dumping Investigation: The Ministry of Commerce of the People's Republic of China (MOFCOM) is the investigating authority of China that conducts AD and CVD investigations in China. Some changes at the institutional level were made relating to China's AD and CVD investigations during the period under review. The Trade Remedy and Investigation Bureau (TRB) was established in April 2014, which aimed to consolidate the trade remedy investigation functions of the former Bureau of Fair

Trade for Imports and Exports (BOFT) and of the Investigation Bureau of Industry Injury (IBII). The authorities consider this reform as vital to bring about improved efficiency, reduce the burdens for interested parties involved in litigation, and better streamlining of investigation procedures. Most importantly, these benefits are expected to be realized while the independence of the bureau in determining the margin of dumping and injury remains uncompromised.[58]

The number of AD measures in place was lower than the previous period of review, but the average length of application was longer in the current period. With respect to the grown years of applications, the authorities reasonably assume that the AD measures imposed by China will normally be terminated after ten years. Imposed measures were concentrated in particular on chemical products, which accounted for over 60% of the total number of measures in place as of 31 December 2015.[59]

In China, the Foreign Trade Law, which entered into force on 1 July 2004, together with the relevant Regulations like the Anti-Dumping Regulations and a number of published Rules, some of which are provisional, provide the basis for investigating dumping cases and applying AD remedies.[60] MOFCOM is the governing agency regarding dumping practices and since April 2014, the Trade Remedy and Investigation Bureau (TRB), housed within the ministry, specifically conducts Anti-Dumping investigations, the determination of margins, and the imposition of AD measures. In the case of AD investigations on agricultural products, injury determination is conducted jointly with the Ministry of Agriculture, in exceptional cases.[61]

According to the Provisional Rules of the Ministry of Foreign Trade and Economic Co-operation on Initiation of Anti-dumping Investigations, an investigation can be initiated at the request of an interested party or self-initiated by MOFCOM. Petitions from natural or legal persons, or organizations representing domestic industry to initiate an AD investigation should be presented in written form to MOFCOM. MOFCOM should then decide whether to initiate an investigation within 60 days of the date of receipt of a petition and, if it decides to do so, a Public Notice should be issued. Non-confidential information will be publicly available. For confidential information, MOFCOM should be able to provide a non-confidential summary of any confidential information on request, subject to Article 22 of the Foreign Trade Law.[62]

MOFCOM publishes its preliminary determination of dumping and injury along with findings regarding the existence of any causal link between the two. An affirmative decision leads to a continuation of the investigation. If the investigation takes longer than 60 days from the date of publication of the initiation, provisional AD measures such as AD duties, deposits, bonds, and other forms of guarantee may be applied, based on guidance from MOFCOM. Provisional AD duties are determined by the State Council Tariff Commission (SCTC), following the recommendation of MOFCOM, but deposits, bonds, and other forms of guarantees are directly determined by MOFCOM. Provisional measures are valid up to four months in principle; however, some of the measures can be extended, when justified as "special circumstances." The authorities explain that these cases arise when the investigating authorities try to examine whether a duty lower than the margin would be sufficient to remove domestic injury.[63] When MOFCOM publishes its preliminary affirmative determination of injury and causality relationship between dumping and injury, exporters have the choice to offer price undertakings. Based on the examination of whether the suggested undertaking is sufficient to eliminate injury and has a low possibility of circumvention, MOFCOM can accept the offer and may also suspend or terminate the AD investigation.[64]

In the case of investigations involving a large number of exporters or producers, MOFCOM has the authority to utilize a sampling method instead of determining a separate dumping margin for each individual exporter, in order to make a timely determination. Exporters and producers selected for the sample by the faculty in MOFCOM are subject to individual determinations of dumping margins. The dumping margins for exporters and producers not selected as part of the sample will be determined based on the weighted average of determined margins for the sample, which excludes zero or *de minimis* (less than 2%) margins of dumping. The authorities reported that the sampling method has been used in three investigations between 2014 and 2015.[65]

An AD investigation should be completed within 12 months from the date of initiation, or within 18 months, under special circumstances. As MOFCOM determines the existence of dumping, injury, and causation, its findings and recommendations are sent to the SCTC, which makes the final decision on the imposition of AD duties. The final determination should be published accordingly.[66] Imposed AD duties may not exceed the determined margin of dumping since duties lower than the dumping margin is not precluded under China's AD regulations. Currently, the investigating authorities are not known to be examining if an imposed duty is sufficient to eliminate injury.[67]

If the interested parties are not satisfied with MOFCOM's decisions, MOFCOM may be requested an administrative reconsideration by the Department of Treaties and Law or the case may be brought directly to the court. Since 2010, it has been reported that there has been one AD case about an isotropic silicon electrical steel product that requested an administrative review and administrative litigation by two Russian companies. The case was withdrawn by the Russian companies in April 2014.[68] According to the Provisional Rules of the Ministry of Foreign Trade and Economic Cooperation on Refund of Anti-Dumping Duty, importers are allowed to apply for a refund within three months of payment of the duty if they can prove that the AD duty paid was higher than the dumping margin. MOFCOM examines the applications and makes a proposal for a decision to the SCTC. MOFCOM will provide a refund to the importer for the difference of the recalculated margin for the six-month period prior to the application and the paid duty, without interest. No request for refunds were reported during the period under review.[69]

Retaliatory measures are permitted under Article 56 of the Foreign Trade Law, in cases where Chinese producers were unjustly treated in foreign AD investigations. Chinese authorities have repeatedly stated that this article has never been invoked. China had replied during the course of question and answer sessions in the last review that Article 56 of China's AD Regulation and Article 17 of the ADA have no direct connection with each other. China reaffirmed in this review that it would resort to WTO dispute settlements before taking any unilateral counter measures.[70]

Final AD measures can be applied for a maximum of five years, while there may be extensions following the review. China's AD Regulations stipulate "expiry" (sunset) and "interim" reviews. MOFCOM publishes notice six months prior to the expiry date of the measure. This public notice can be important because sunset reviews are not automatic. MOFCOM initiates a review only when there are sufficient requests and evidence provided by the domestic industry. Without a petition, the AD measure is automatically terminated and a public notice is issued. MOFCOM may also initiate an interim review, *ex officio* or upon request, while the authorities have stated that this has never happened. Regarding sunset reviews, interim reviews must be completed within 12 months of the initiation date. Preliminary determinations are not mandatory and the utilization of sampling methods is permitted.[71]

• Countervailing Duty Investigation: The main legal framework for the application of countervailing measures in China is constituted by the Foreign Trade Law, the Regulations on Countervailing Measures (CVD Regulations), promulgated in 2001 and amended on 31 March 2004, and a number of provisional rules.[72]

Countervailing duty (CVD) investigations are subject to similar procedures, with only a few exceptions, to those applied to AD investigations. The major difference arises from the fact that the exporting country's government is involved in the investigations. There is a process of consultations with MOFCOM prior to initiation. If a mutually agreeable solution is found during consultations, an investigation may not be initiated. There are also some other differences, such as the absence of published rules for the use of the sampling method, for conducting interim or judicial reviews and for regulating the use of price undertakings.[73]

Interested parties should file a petition providing MOFCOM with a description of the alleged subsidy, including detailed information regarding the existence, nature and amount of the subsidy, as well as an estimation of the per unit subsidy. Public hearings for the determination of a subsidy are held unless otherwise decided by MOFCOM for cases involving classified information.[74]

"There has been only one initiation of CVD investigation in 2013 (wines from the EU), which was actually terminated due to the withdrawal of the petition. No other investigations had been initiated either in 2014 or 2015. As of December 2015, there were four CVD measures against imports from the EU and the US. As MOFCOM did not receive a request for a sunset review, the measure on grain-oriented flat-rolled electrical steel from the United States expired on 10 April 2014. By the end of 2015, the longest existing CVD measure had been imposed for more than five years. In August 2015, China initiated a sunset review of the measure on US broiler products.[75]

China and its particular RTA partners, Hong Kong and Macao, have waived the authority to use countervailing measures between the parties. But most other RTA partners with China, ASEAN, Australia, Chile, Costa Rica, Iceland, the Republic of Korea, New Zealand, Pakistan, Peru and Switzerland, have maintained their rights to use Anti-Dumping and countervailing measures as set out in the WTO Agreements.[76]

- Safeguards Investigation: The Foreign Trade Law and

the Regulations on Safeguards (SG Regulations) governs the investigations and imposition of safeguard measures in China. Along with the SG Regulations, the Provisional Rules for Initiation of Safeguards Investigations, the Provisional Rules for Conduct of Public Hearings in Safeguards Investigations, the Rules on Investigations and Determinations of Industry Injury for Safeguards, and the Rules on Public Hearings with regard to Investigations of Injury to Industry form the main structure of Chinese legal framework on safeguard measures.[77]

MOFCOM is responsible for safeguard investigation and injury determination along with causation analysis. In cases where agricultural products are subject to a safeguard investigation, the Ministry of Agriculture jointly determines the injury with MOFCOM. An interested party may submit a petition asking for the initiation of an investigation. The interested party should provide detailed information on the trend and reason for the increase in quantities of the imported product for a period of at least five years in the application. MOFCOM can also initiate an investigation *ex officio,* when there is sufficient evidence of injury. After reviewing evidence of injury provided by the interested party, MOFCOM decides whether to initiate an investigation within 60 days of receipt of the petition. Certain complicated cases may get an extension of this due period. The decision to initiate is notified publicly and to the WTO as well.[78]

In the case of affirmative preliminary decisions, MOFCOM may impose provisional safeguard measures, for no longer than 200 days. Tariff increases or quantitative restrictions can be imposed as final measures. MOFCOM directly decides whether to adopt quantitative restrictions, but for tariff measures, it only provides a recommendation and the SCTC makes the final decision of adoption. MOFCOM publishes a Ministerial Decree to notify the decision to implement a final safeguard measure.[79]

Final safeguard measures are applicable up to four years, otherwise under special circumstances. An extension can be made up to a total period of 10 years for an application, when the measure seems necessary to prevent or to remedy serious injury and not more restrictive than the former measure. Measures applied for more than a year should be scheduled to be progressively liberalized at regular intervals. MOFCOM should conduct a mid-term review for measures adopted for more than three years. The decisions by the authorities are not subject to any appeal mechanism.[80]

The RTAs with New Zealand and Singapore allow exemptions to the application of global safeguard measures against imports from the counterparties. In contrast, the RTAs with other partners, ASEAN, Australia, Chile, Costa Rica, Iceland, the Republic of Korea, Pakistan, Peru and Switzerland, uphold all the parties' rights under in GATT Article XIX and the WTO Agreement on Safeguards. Simultaneous imposition of global and bilateral safeguard is prohibited in all RTAs.[81]

• General Reaction or Perception: China's practice of trade remedy measures can be summarized as reflecting the conditions of rapid globalization and active application. It does not seem to worry about trade friction with trading partners as a result of trade remedy investigations and measures. This stance is also clear with respect to its relationship with Korea and Japan as well. It may be a matter of time before products from Korea and Japan become one of the major targets of trade remedy measures by China.

• Toward International Dispute Settlement Proceedings: All in all, China largely abides by the WTO rules and highly respects rulings by the WTO dispute settlement body. It has continuously strived to improve its investigation procedures in accordance with the comments by the Panels and the Appellate Body.[82] The export duties on some raw materials are in line with the WTO rules, since it is a within the spectrum of measures to strengthen environmental protection. China is willing to discuss any arising conflict through the WTO dispute settlement mechanism.[83] China sees itself as an important contributor to the multilateral trading system and has always been an active participant in the daily operation of the WTO and has respected the dispute settlement body ever since its accession. China has earnestly fulfilled its accession commitments and transparency obligations. It has also been a crucial supporter of WTO's monitoring and surveillance mechanism, which has been playing a significant role in restraining protectionism after the global financial crisis.[84]

• Toward Expanded Trade Remedy Measures: In recent years, the number of Anti-Dumping measures in effect in China has been increasing steadly. A total of 91 Anti-Dumping duty orders were in force as of December 2015, which was less than the 113 measures that were applied in December 2013. The orders affected imports from 13 countries or territories. Imports from the United States and Japan are the most frequently targeted products, succeeded by those from the EU, the Republic of Korea, and Chinese Taipei. Measures are concentrated in particular on chemical products, which accounted for more than 60% of the total number of AD orders in place as of December 2015. The average length of application seems to have been slightly longer than in the previous review period. There were no countervailing duty investigations initiated in 2014 or 2015. As of December 2015, four countervailing measures were imposed, targeting imports from the EU and the US. A countervailing measure placed for the longest period among those in effect by December 2015 was slightly over five years. No safeguard investigation was initiated during the period under review.[85]

ii) Korea

Korea has expended the most effort in the course of its FTA policies among the three states in East Asia. It has been the most dependent on exports among the three, so it has been in a sense forced to explore a more aggressive strategy when it comes to trade policies. FTAs have become the core survival plan for the country since the early 2000s. The basic stance still remains the same as of September 2017, even if different administrations have taken the helm over the almost two decades oscillitating between conservative and progressive governments.

① Policy in General

Korea actively pursues FTA negotiations based on the belief that trade liberalization strengthens national competitiveness. Korea has concluded eleven new FTAs since 2012, including those with the US and China. As of 2022, 18 FTAs connect Korea to a total of 58 countries throughout the world.[86] While signing FTAs with the US, the EU and China, the world's largest economies, Korea has always sought comprehensive and high-standard agreements. Korea is currently in the process of negotiating FTAs with China and Japan, Central America, and Ecuador.[87] Korea perceives that concluding RTAs along with cherishing the multilateral trade system correspond to upholding its commitment to pursuing a free and open economy based on market principles.[88]

In order to enhance the international competitiveness of its businesses and the economy, Korea has strived to expand its access to the main markets, through participating in multilateral negotiation rounds and RTA negotiations. The strategic goal of the Ministry of Trade, Industry and Energy (MOTIE) is to build a creative economy through expanding growth engines, facilitating quality employment and supporting balanced growth among industries. Policy priorities are as follows: 1) promote industrial convergence to maximize and create high-quality jobs; 2) foster small and medium-sized businesses, based on market principles; 3) revitalize local economies to balance regional growth; 4) improve communication channels and public debate on trade policy; 5) establish a safe and reliable energy system.[89]

② FTA Conclusion/Negotiation Status

Between 2013 and 2016, seven new RTAs, concluded with Colombia, China, New Zealand, Viet Nam, Canada, Australia, and Turkey, entered into force. Agriculture products are partially covered while rice is excluded from all the RTA concessions.[90] This makes a total of 18 FTAs in force with a total number of 58 states. An Additional eight FTAs including the three revisions with ASEAN, Chile and India are undergoing. These eight

Table 1. Korea FTAs (as of May 2020)

<table>
<tr><th>Phase</th><th>Trading Partner</th><th>Progress</th><th>Notes</th></tr>
<tr><td>In force (7)</td><td colspan="3">Chile (April 2004), Singapore (March 2006), EFTA (September 2006), ASEAN (September 2009), India (January 2010), Peru (August 2011), EU (December 2015)</td></tr>
<tr><td rowspan="8">Recently entered into force (8)</td><td>US</td><td>Entered into force in March 2012</td><td>Tariffs eliminated for 96% of all tariff lines within 5 years of entry into force</td></tr>
<tr><td>Turkey (Framework Agreement, Agreement on Trade in Goods)</td><td>Entered into force in May 2013</td><td>Tariffs eliminated for all tariff lines within 10 years of entry into force (Korea: 99.6%, Turkey: 100%)</td></tr>
<tr><td>Australia</td><td>Entered into force in December 2014</td><td>Tariffs eliminated for the majority of tariff lines within 10 years of entry into force (Australia: within 5 years)</td></tr>
<tr><td>Canada</td><td>Entered into force in January 2015</td><td>Tariffs eliminated for the majority of tariff lines within 10 years of entry into force (Korea, Canada: 97.5%)</td></tr>
<tr><td>China</td><td>Entered into force in December 2015</td><td>Tariffs eliminated for over 90% of all tariff lines within 20 years of entry into force
Services and investment: Follow-up negotiations on liberalization to begin within 2 years of entry into force</td></tr>
<tr><td>New Zealand</td><td>Entered into force in December 2015</td><td>New Zealand to eliminate tariffs within 7 years, and Korea within 15 years, of entry into force</td></tr>
<tr><td>Viet Nam</td><td>Entered into force in December 2015</td><td>Additional tariff reduction on sensitive and highly sensitive tariff lines that are not covered by the Korea-ASEAN FTA: 94.7% for Korea (+3 percentage points compared to Korea-ASEAN FTA), 92.2% for Vietnam (+6 percentage points compared to Korea-ASEAN FTA)
Product-specific rules of origin improved</td></tr>
<tr><td>Colombia</td><td>Entered into force in July 2016</td><td>Tariffs eliminated for the majority of tariff lines within 10 years of entry into force (Korea: 96.1%, Colombia: 96.7%)</td></tr>
</table>

Phase	Trading Partner	Progress	Notes
Negotiations concluded (1)	Turkey (Agreement on Services and Investment)	Concluded in 2014, officially signed in February 2015	
Under negotiation (5)	Korea-China-Japan FTA	10 rounds of official negotiations	
	Korea-Central America FTA	4 rounds of official negotiations	
	RCEP	13 rounds of official negotiations	Negotiations targeted for conclusion in 2016
	Korea-Ecuador SECA	2 rounds of official negotiations	
	Korea-Israel FTA	Negotiations launched in May 2016, 1 round of official negotiations	

WTO, *Trade Policy Review, Report by Republic of Korea*, WT/TPR/G/346/Rev.1 (Jan. 6, 2017), p. 11, Table 4.1 Overview of Korea's FTAs.

FTAs overall include 24 countries. Korea continues to actively negotiate RTAs with its major trading partners. During the review period, seven new FTAs entered into force.[91]

Despite the fact that the position of Korea remains intact towards FTAs, changes in policy on the part of its trading partners can have a significant impact on the existence and nature of FTAs. A case in point is the change of administration in the US and the change in the perception of FTAs by the new administration. Korea has an FTA in force with the United States that might be affected by the position of the new administration. Regarding Korea-US, Trump stated in an interview with Reuters that the agreement is "unacceptable" and "a horrible deal made by Hillary [Clinton]." Trump also stated that "It's a horrible deal, and we are going to renegotiate that or terminate it."[92] Similar to NAFTA, the Trump administration focuses on the fact that US trade deficits have increased post-Korea-US Initiated under the George W. Bush administration and renegotiated under the Obama administration, Korea-US decreased tariffs on 95% of the goods imported and exported between South Korea and the

US.[93] According to *The Economist*, the USTR originally predicted Korea-US would increase US exports by $10 billion, but in reality, the exports dropped by $3 billion from 2011 to 2016.[94] According to USTR representative Robert Lighthizer, the "trade deficit in goods with Korea has doubled from $13.2 billion to $27.6 billion, while US goods exports have actually gone down." As such, Lighthizer requested a special Joint-Committee as part of a process of renegotiating Korea-US in July 2017.[95]

③ Trade Remedy System: General Legal Structure and Characteristics

The *Customs Act* and the *Act on the Investigation of Unfair International Trade Practices and Remedy Against Injury to Industry* (2001) provide the legal framework for applying trade remedy measures. The Korea Trade Commission (KTC) under MOTIE, governs administration, investigation and the determination of dumping or subsidy. Under emergency safeguard provision, KTC investigates whether imports have caused or threatened to cause serious injury to domestic industry. Based on the determination made by KTC, the Ministry of Strategy and Finance (MOSF) decides whether or not to impose Anti-Dumping and countervailing duties.[96]

In first five RTAs Korea has brought into force since 2012, each agreement contains a specific trade remedies chapter that preserves the parties' rights under the WTO, while there are certain clarifications and requirement attached: (i) the possibility of exclusion of imports from FTAs from global safeguard measures; (ii) the written notice requirement prior to the initiation of an investigation; (iii) the possibility of having consultations prior to the initiation of an investigation; (iv) the written information regarding procedures for requesting price undertakings; (v) the re-consideration of Anti-Dumping measures that have been terminated after review within a year; (vi) the application of the *de minimis* dumping margin threshold new shipper reviews; and (vii) the creation of a Committee on Trade Remedies.[97]

• Safeguards investigation: The KTC takes into account the impact on the relevant industries, domestic price levels, consumer interests, and international trade relations when deciding on type and duration of safeguard measure. Safeguard measures can be applied for up to four years (200 days if provisional), while it may be extended for four more years based on a further review. The last safeguard investigation by Korea dates back to 1999.[98]

④ General Reaction or Perception: Toward a More Active Trade Remedy Investigation

It can be said that one of the most dramatic changes in Korea as a result of the FTA drive is the realization of the importance and usefulness of the trade remedy mechanism. This concern works both ways — Korean exports subject to foreign trade remedy investigations by other countries' investigating authorities and foreign exports subject to Korean trade remedy investigations by the KTC. The first category of concern — dealing with foreign trade remedy investigations againt Korean products — has been a core issue of the Korean trade policy, as Korea has been one of the major targets of such investigation traditionally. Korea has been placed second place after China in terms of the number of Anti-Dumping investigations globally. The situation still remains the same as more and more Korean products are destined to foreign markets as a result of the increase in the number of Korean FTAs. The United States offers a good example in this regard. With respect to the second category — dealing with unfair trade imports into the Korean market, Korea's stance is now changing rapidly. While this had not been the main subject of Korean trade policy due to a relatively small domestic market, the expansion of the size of Korean domestic market recently, the increasing penetration of the exports as a result of FTAs, and rising concerns over foreign competition in the domestic market has worked in the direction of realizing the importance of building up the infrastructure of KTC and undergoing more active investigations of trade remedy measures on behalf of Korean industry. In a sense, the policy is to use its authority under the WTO's Agreements more diligently than before.

By way of example, Korea's recourse to Anti-Dumping actions has doubled during the period under review. Between 2012 and 2015, Korea initiated 20 Anti-Dumping investigations. As of December 2015, 32 Anti-Dumping measures were in force on 12 products such as choline chloride (4 cases), ethanolamine (4 cases), ethyl acetate (3 cases), PET film (3 cases), oriented polypropylene film (3 cases), and stainless steel bar/plate (2 cases). The measures were on products mostly originating from Asia (28, mainly China (10), Japan (7), India (3), Malaysia (3), and Thailand (2)), while some were also from Canada, the EU (Spain) and the United States. Between 2012 and 2015, Korea extended 12 measures after a sunset review, while one of those reviewed was terminated. Three measures were terminated without a review. On 15 March 2016, Japan requested consultations with Korea under the dispute settlement system concerning measures imposing Anti-Dumping duties on valves for pneumatic transmission (pneumatic valves) from Japan.[99]

Since its last review, Korea has had more frequent recourse to special safeguard (SSG) measures. Korea reserves the right to take SSG action on 124 agricultural ten-digit tariff items (as of 2011) products under the WTO Agreement on Agriculture. The Special Safeguard Tariff Schedule is issued annually and, as from 2015, rice and rice items became eligible for volume- and/ or price-based action. Price-based SSG measures between 2011 and 2013 were on raw ginseng, white ginseng, and ginseng root. Volume-based SSG measures have been used on cereal flour and other worked grain for the first time since 2007. Korea notified its latest SSG measures to the WTO Committee on Agriculture in July 2016.[100]

iii) Japan

Japan was a relatively slow starter for the FTAs in this region. Japan has been a model state in the multilateral regime and its domestic market had been able to cater to the demand from its domestic market, so the temptation for a change may have been relatively weak for Japan compared to Korea and China, who have had to respond to changes in the trading landscape more promptly. At the same time, foreign imports had traditionally found it difficult getting into the domestic market of Japan, as a result of the traditionally strong preference of Japanese consumers for Japan's home-grown products and home-produced items.

① Policy in General

Japan pursues strengthening the multilateral trading system under the WTO as its main pillar of external economic policy. Japan also promotes regional and bilateral trade policies through Economic Partnership Agreements in order to complement the multilateral trading system.[101]

A negotiation of Economic Partnership Agreements (EPAs) is currently based on the Japan Revitalization Strategy, decided by the cabinet in 2013. Under this strategy, the government has a specific goal to increase the FTA ratio, defined as the percentage of the volume of trade among FTA partners in terms of a country's total trade volume, from 19% to 70% by 2018.[102]

Japan has 13 regional trade agreements or EPAs that entered into force. It displays a tendency to exclude a variety of agricultural products for further tariff reduction under these agreements.[103]

Japan promotes economic partnership as a basis of its global economic activities. It has concluded investment treaties with 33 nations or regions and is currently negotiating with nine countries including Oman, Angola and Algeria. When choosing a new EPA/FTA negotiation partner, Japan takes into account a comprehensive list of relevant factors including the progress of existing negotiations, economic and diplomatic relations, and the overall economic and political situation of a possible partner. Japan expects concluded EPAs and BITs to encourage an increase in future inward FDI.[104]

② FTA Conclusion/Negotiation Status (as of May 2020)

Table 2. Japan FTAs

Country	Date of the entry into force	Additional information
Entered into force		
Singapore (The Japan-Singapore Agreement for a New Age Economic Partnership)	30 November 2002	- The fourth and fifth Supervisory Committees were held in May 2013 and July 2014 respectively. - Joint Committees on Customs Procedures, Paperless Trading, Mutual Recognition, Mutual Recognition of Professional Qualifications, Intellectual Property, Financial Services Cooperation, ICT, Science and Technology, Trade and Investment Promotion, SMEs, Broadcasting, and Tourism have been held to date. - The amended Agreement came into effect in September 2007. - The partial amendment of the Annex (IIA "Product-Specific Rules" and IIB "Minimum Data Requirement for Certificate of Origin") came into effect in January 2008. - The amended Agreement came into effect in September 2007. - The partial amendment of the Annex (IIA "Product-Specific Rules" and IIB "Minimum Data Requirement for Certificate of Origin") came into effect in January 2008.
Mexico (The Agreement between Japan and the United Mexican States for the Strengthening of the Economic Partnership)	1 April 2005	- The Protocol between Japan and the United Mexican States related to Improvement of Market Access Conditions based on paragraphs 3 and 5 of Article 5 of the Agreement between Japan and the United Mexican States for the Strengthening of the Economic Partnership entered into force in April 2007. - The Protocol Amending the Agreement between Japan and the United Mexican States for the Strengthening of the Economic Partnership was signed in September 2011 and entered into force in April 2012. - Sub-Committees on Trade in Goods, SPS Measures, Technical Regulations, Standards and Conformity Assessment Procedures, Rules of Origin, Certificate of Origin and Customs Procedures, Cross-Border Trade in Services, Entry and Temporary Stay, Government Procurement, Cooperation in the Field of Trade and Investment Promotion, Cooperation in the Field of Agriculture, Cooperation in the Field of Tourism, and also the Special Sub-Committee on Steel Products and the

Country	Date of the entry into force	Additional information
		Committees for the Improvement of the Business Environment have been held to date.
Malaysia (The Agreement between the Government of Japan and the Government of Malaysia for an Economic Partnership)	13 July 2006	- The third Joint Committee was held in February 2013. - Sub-Committees on Trade in Services, Improvement of Business Environment, Cooperation, Rules of Origin, Intellectual Property, Sanitary and Phytosanitary, Investment, Trade in Goods, and Technical Regulations, Standards and Conformity Assessment Procedures have been held to date.
Chile (The Agreement between Japan and the Republic of Chile for a Strategic Economic Partnership)	3 September 2007	- Meetings of the Commission, Committees on Trade in Goods and Improvement of Business Environment and the Working Group on Fish and Fishery Products have been held to date.
Thailand (The Agreement between Japan and the Kingdom of Thailand for an Economic Partnership)	1 November 2007	- Sub-Committees on Trade in Services, Rules of Origin, Small and Medium Enterprises, Paperless Trading, Enhancement of Business Environment, Customs Procedures, Tourism, Agriculture, Forestry and Fisheries, Trade in Goods, and Movement of Natural Persons have been held to date.
Indonesia (The Agreement between Japan and the Republic of Indonesia for an Economic Partnership)	1 July 2008	- Sub-Committees on Rules of Origin, Trade in Goods, Trade in Services, Movement of Natural Persons, Cooperation, and Investment have been held to date.
Brunei Darussalam (The Agreement between Japan and Brunei Darussalam for an Economic Partnership)	31 July 2008	- Sub-Committees on Trade in Services and Cooperation have been held to date.
ASEAN (The Agreement on Comprehensive Economic Partnership among Japan and Member States of the Association of Southeast Asian Nations)	1 December 2008 (Lao People's Democratic Republic, Myanmar, Singapore, Viet Nam) 1 January 2009 (Brunei) 1 February 2009 (Malaysia) 1 June 2009 (Thailand) 1 December 2009 (Cambodia) 1 July 2010 (The Philippines)	- The 11th Joint Committee was held in March 2014. - Sub-Committees on Rules of Origin, Trade in Services, Investment and Economic Cooperation have been held to date. - The Agreement is a legally independent agreement in relation to the bilateral EPAs between Japan and individual ASEAN Member States and thus the entry into force of the Agreement does neither nullify nor integrate those bilateral EPAs.

Country	Date of the entry into force	Additional information
The Philippines (The Agreement between Japan and the Republic of the Philippines)	11 December 2008	- The fourth Joint Committee was held in March 2013. - Sub-Committees on Trade in Goods, Trade in Services, Rules of Origin, Investment, Movement of Natural Persons, Improvement of Business Environment, and Cooperation have been held to date.
Switzerland (The Agreement on Free Trade and Economic Partnership between Japan and the Swiss Confederation)	1 September 2009	
Viet Nam (The Agreement between Japan and the Socialist Republic of Viet Nam for an Economic Partnership)	1 October 2009	- Sub-Committees on Movement of Natural Persons have been held to date.
India (Comprehensive Economic Partnership Agreement between Japan and the Republic of India)	1 August 2011	- The sub-committee on Rules of Origin, Customs Procedures, TBT/SPS, Trade Services, Improvement of Business Environment has been held to date.
Peru (The Agreement between Japan and the Republic of Peru for an Economic Partnership)	1 March 2012	- Meeting of the Commission and the Sub-Committee on Improvement of the Business Environment have been held to date.
Signed		
Australia (The Agreement between Japan and Australia for an Economic Partnership) (The negotiations commenced in April 2007)	Signed on 8 July 2014	- Sixteen rounds of negotiations were held.
Under negotiation		
The Republic of Korea	Under negotiation (The negotiations commenced in December 2003)	- Six rounds of negotiations were held. - Although no negotiations have been held since the end of the sixth round held in November 2004, four rounds of the working-level consultation were held by December 2009 to consider the resumption of negotiations. Director-general level consultations for the EPA were held in September 2010 and in May 2011. Several rounds of working-level consultations have been held since 2012.
GCC (Gulf Cooperation Council)	Under negotiation (Formal negotiations commenced in September 2006)	- Two rounds of negotiations and four rounds of informal intermediate meetings were held. The latest meeting was held in March 2009.

Country	Date of the entry into force	Additional information
Mongolia	Reached an agreement in principle in the negotiations of the Agreement in July 2014. (The negotiations commenced in June 2012)	- Seven rounds of negotiations were held.
Canada	Under negotiation (The negotiations commenced in November 2012)	- Seven rounds of negotiations were held. The latest meeting was held in Tokyo in November 2014.
Colombia	Under negotiation (The negotiations commenced in December 2012)	- Eight rounds of negotiations were held. The latest meeting was held in Bogota in October 2014.
CJK (China, Japan and Republic of Korea)	Under negotiation (The negotiations commenced in March 2013)	- Six rounds of negotiations were held. The latest meeting was held in Tokyo in November 2014.
RCEP (Regional Comprehensive Economic Partnership)	Under negotiation (The negotiations commenced in May 2013)	- Six rounds of negotiations were held. The latest meeting was held in India in December 2014.
EU (European Union)	Under negotiation (The negotiations commenced in April 2013)	- Seven rounds of negotiations were held. The latest meeting was held in Brussels in October 2014.
TPP (Trans-Pacific Partnership	Under negotiation (Japan participated in TPP negotiations in July 2013)	- The latest ministerial meeting was held in November 2014 and the latest Chief Negotiators' meeting was held in September 2014.
Turkey	Under negotiation (The negotiations commenced in December 2014)	- The first round of negotiations was held in December 2014.

WTO, *Trade Policy Review, Report by Japan*, WT/TPR/G/310 (Jan. 19, 2015), p. 6, Table 2.1.

③ Investment Disputes

Japan believes that investment agreements create stable, equitable, favorable and transparent conditions for investment for both the investor and the country invested in. That is why Japan is also very eager to promote the conclusion of investment agreements. As of September 2014, Japan concluded bilateral and trilateral investment agreements with 21 countries and regions. The EPAs Japan concluded with 10 countries also contain investment chapters.[105]

Against the backdrop of an appreciating Japanese Yen, Japan believes that inward foreign direct investment will work as an important force in attracting global demand. Japan will continue negotiating investment agreements proactively and is willing to play a leading role in establishing new international investment rules.[106]

The Japanese government also strives to facilitate outward investment by concluding IIAs and Investment Chapters of EPAs. The Ministry of Land, Infrastructure, Transport and Tourism (MLIT) also established a new government funded agency called Japan Overseas Infrastructure Investment Corporation for Transport & Urban Development (JOIN) in 2014 in order to promote PPP infrastructure projects conducted abroad.[107]

④ Trade Remedy System: General Legal Structure and Characteristics

The Customs Tariff Law and the relevant Cabinet Orders and Guidelines define Japan's legal framework regarding the use of trade remedy measures.[108] All in all, considering the size of its economy and the domestic market, Japan has been a relatively calm and low-profile state in terms of the application of its trade remedy measures against foreign imports. Japan has had a relatively low number of Anti-Dumping investigations and very few countervailing duty investigations — a phenomenon that is distinct from other major trading partners globally. Trade remedy measures are imposed, both legally and practically, when there is a surge of imports that causes or threatens to cause material injury to domestic industries. The relatively low level of imports may have rendered trade remedy measures less appealing to the Japanese government and industries. This trend of course is now on the verge of changing because of the deeper and wider penetration of the FTAs. The TPP negotiations for instance focused on the identification and elimination of the NTBs on the part of Japan. These efforts by other countries may signal the change of the environment of the domestic market of

Japan in the long run. If that is the case, Japan's traditional view toward the trade remedy measures may also change accordingly.

• Anti-Dumping Investigation: According to Article 18 of Cabinet Order on Anti-Dumping Duty, Anti-Dumping investigations are carried out by ad hoc teams composed of relevant officials from the Ministry of Finance, Ministry of Economy, Trade, and Industry (METI) and other relevant Ministries. The Ministry of Finance authorizes tariff policy and customs administration and the METI is directly in charge of an investigation as it manages the trend in import and export. The three ministries should keep in close contact with each other in terms of their decisions. Any important determination should be made after consultation with each other.[109]

• Countervailing Duty Investigation: According to Article 14 of Cabinet Order on Countervailing Duty, countervailing investigations are carried out by ad hoc teams composed of relevant officials from the Ministry of Finance, METI and other relevant Ministries. The Ministry of Finance authorizes tariff policy and customs administration and the METI is directly in charge of an investigation as it manages the trend in import and export. The three ministries should keep in close contact with each other in terms of their decisions. Any important determination should be made after consultation with each other.[110]

• General Reaction or Perception — Less Attention to Domestic Trade Remedy Investigations and More attention to Foreign Trade Remedy Investigations: Japan has been a loyal member of the WTO when it comes to the utilization of the WTO Dispute Settlement system. It has actively engaged in the dispute settlement process both as a party and third party. At the same time, Japan has been prompt in bringing challenged measures into compliance once a decision has been rendered by a panel or the Appellate Body of the WTO. Japan has also been an active participant in amending the DSU, Anti-Dumping Agreement, SCM Agreement and Safeguards Agreement of the WTO, as all of them are directly related to the protection of the interests of Japanese businesses in foreign markets.[111] Japan's focus has been largely on how the authority of investigating authorities should be supervised or restrained as opposed to how it should be expanded. As such, Japan's position has been on the other side of the spectrum compared to that of members with large import markets such as the United States.

Notably, Japan has been keen in devising and upgrading DSM in the WTO regime. It has been an active participant in the DSU revision negotiations and actively participated in the negotiations since 1997. It submitted textual contributions on many occasions. For instance, Japan has submitted important proposals since 2007 in the area of a) procedural sequence of compliance determination and authorization of the suspension of obligations (documented in JOB (05)/71/Rev.1), and b) procedures for the termination of retaliation and monitoring of post-retaliation situation (documented in JOB (05)/47/REV.1 and JOB (05)/47/Rev.1/Corr.1). These textual contributions are reflected in the July 2008 text prepared by the Chair of the Special Session of the Dispute Settlement Body (JOB (08)/81) and was later reproduced as an attachment to the Chair's Report of 21 April 2011 to the Trade Negotiations Committee (TN/DS/25). Japan's active participaton in the DSU negotiation has been constant and it hopes that the DSU amendment is completed sooner rather later. In Japan's view the DSU is the critical component of the multilateral regime of global trade.[112] This traditional perception of Japan has also affected the creation and administration of the DSMs of FTAs that it has signed. Japan has been keen to maintain the smooth operation of the DSMs as a main pillar for the preservation of rule of law in a trading regime.

(3) Comparison of Positions of Three States Regarding FTAs

Among the three states, there is a clear commonality in terms of the FTA policy. That is, the unwavering understanding of the importance of FTAs in the their respective economic policies and trade strategies. While the three states have come to this common understanding through rather different paths and routes, they now share a common understanding on this issue. That said, the specific positions of the three states still sport some meaningful differences.

Korea views the FTAs as a major vehicle to maintain and expand its export volume to major trading partners. Korea, therefore, has focused on how to influence the adoption of greater liberalization in the domestic markets of other countries. Relatively less attention has been given to the idea of how to introduce new norms of trade or how to address other issues of global scale. On the other hand, China views the FTAs as a tool for its global geopolitical strategy. Its emphasis on the regional FTAs in Asia and expanded economic cooperation — whether through FTAs or otherwise — with countries in Afria and South America is the product of such stragetic thinking. Its interest, however, is in how to preserve and expand China's own interest as opposed to initiating an important discussion on global issues. Japan views the FTAs as a new way of reinvigorating multilateralism. The slow progress on the multilateral front have frustrated Japan in the past 17 years of the Doha Round Negotiations, and the FTAs may provide a new platform to re-initiate and re-invigorate many of the multilateral issues that Japan has been paying attention to. At the same time, Japan is more aware of the usefulness of FTAs as a tool to reform its own domestic economic policies, namely the agricultural sector and the fisheries sector.

So, the three countries in East Asia, while close neighbors among each other and major trading partners in the global market, have harbored different ideas and strategies when it comes to FTAs. These different views of FTAs have also affected the adoption of DSMs in their respecitve FTAs. When it comes to the actual utilization of and participation in DSMs, either bilaterally in FTAs and BITs or multilaterally in WTO, the different views have also played important roles in shaping the rationale and logic of the arguments of the three states and how they approach the DSMs.

(4) New Attempt of Economic Integration: Korea's "Eurasian Initiative" and China's "One Belt One Road"

The fact that Korea and China have been more innovative in terms of trading regime as opposed to Japan is further evidenced by the recent development of the two countries' trade projects. They have tried to explore something different from the traditional FTAs. Korea aims to establish a new economic cooperation network called the Eurasian Initiative (EI)[113] and China is putting a great deal of effort into its new One Belt One Road (OBOR) project.[114] Korea's EI and China's OBOR aim to cover basically similar or nearby regions in Central Asia, and all the way to Europe; and the two projects place their focus on the establishment and operation of infrastructure in the countries in the region covered with the stable supply of energy resources in mind.

These attempts have the traits of traditional FTAs and they also contain new elements that are not found in the current FTAs. These schemes stand out among the existing FTAs due to their unique market liberalization and integration potential. At the same time, as a new type of economic cooperation scheme, the EI and OBOR will also bring about various new practical and legal implications that will require the attention of the two countries in the future.

i) Two Projects' Objectives and Positive Consequences

FTAs continue to proliferate globally, and the multilateral trading regime enshrined in the WTO Agreements is facing a serious challenge. The Asia Pacific region has seen more robust activities in terms of negotiating and concluding FTAs of various sorts. All these FTAs adopt similar structures and contain similar provisions. Korea's EI and China's OBOR now seek to achieve different goals compared to those of conventional FTAs.[115]

For its part, Korea's EI is a new effort to connect the two Koreas, northern China, Russia, Central Asian countries and East European countries so as to facilitate transportation, communication and exchange of goods and services among the constituent States.[116] This initiative is distinct from existing FTAs in many key respects. The current FTAs, be they bilateral or multilateral, are arguably geared toward *opening* the domestic markets of contracting parties. How the other countries can reach the domestic markets thus opened is usually not addressed in the FTAs themselves. In fact, this is an area that is not regulated by the trade agreements per se. Nor is the issue of supply of energy resources and development. The EI, on the other hand, aims to fill this gap. It attempts to address how these respective States can be *connected* through transportation infrastructure and communication facilities that can help enhance the flow of goods, services, natural persons and corporations. Thus, the EI largely complements the current regime of FTAs in an important way. If the current FTAs can be called vehicles for "market liberalization," the EI is about "connection." As such, if properly implemented, the EI can further support the existing FTAs and facilitate enjoyment of the benefits of the FTAs.[117]

In some key respects, China's OBOR also aims to achieve a similar objective. The OBOR is also, by nature, designed to introduce and implement new kinds of economic cooperation in the Central Asian region to enhance *connection* or *connectivity* among the participating States in a way that can match the original "Silk Roads" of the past.[118] This endeavor by China represents its effort to initiate the exploration of a new regime of economic cooperation in the region that is different from that established by conventional FTAs.[119] Put simply, this can be called an effort to introduce an economic cooperation regime tailor-made for this region. While the specific contents are not entirely clear at the moment, the general direction and ultimate objectives are arguably clearly on the table. So, the new scheme of OBOR can also be said to be aimed at enhancing connections among states in the region both economically and culturally.[120]

Furthermore, Korea's EI and China's OBOR apparently do not seem to pursue the creation of an integrated market or a common market in the region, nor anything similar to the European Union or free trade zones, which may be a difficult objective given the relative absence of homogeneity of the societies in the countries along the old Silk Roads and their different levels of economic development.[121] Rather, the two projects seem to place emphasis on specific construction projects and the construction of infrastructure that can bring benefits to all participating States and facilitate the speedy transportation of goods and services.

As such, the EI and OBOR aim to pursue similar objectives in key respects. It is almost coincidental that the two countries have started to explore these initiatives almost simultaneously. Perhaps this temporal proximity is evidence of the fact that the current FTAs with their many partners do not necessarily satisfy the needs of the two countries in the long term.

At the same time, the two projects look at similar or nearby regions in Central Asia. Korea's EI aims to connect Asian and European countries through the establishment of networks of trade, transportation and energy supply.[122] By way of example, one of its planned projects is to connect rail and road networks from Busan to Europe. Trans-Korean Railways (TKR) and Trans-Siberian Railways (TSR) are such examples. Establishing new sea routes using the Arctic passage is yet another project that receives keen attention under the EI policy. Constructing networks of oil and gas pipelines and electric power grids in Korea and Russia through North Korea are also being explored.

On its part, China's OBOR aims to establish a new Silk Road connecting the Central Asian countries: that is, the land-based "Silk Road Economic Belt" and the ocean-based "Maritime Silk Road."[123] These two "Silk Roads" are said to enable China to increase its influence in global affairs and help expand its export market to absorb overproduction in China.[124] So China is aiming to construct a new bridge to Europe through OBOR.[125]

As such, to the extent that these two national projects look at Central Asia and all the way to Europe, they largely overlap in terms of geographical coverage. Despite the fact that Korea's EI places more emphasis on Northeast Asia while China's OBOR focuses on its neighboring States in Central Asia, the general direction moves along similar lines in their overall pictures. If the two projects were coordinated, a synergy effect could be expected in this respect: if the enhancement of connection is the priority, two routes are better than one route and several routes are better than two routes.

In addition, the EI and OBOR also pay attention to various infrastructure projects.[126] The vast connection projects under both the EI and OBOR require the establishment and construction of infrastructure in all of the participating states in the region. In fact, those states mostly find themselves currently in situations where national infrastructure development is in great demand. As such, the two national policy projects have commonalities with respect to their core elements. Here again, a synergy effect can be pursued by Korea and China through active application of FTAs in services and goods sectors and of increased mutual investments. China may be able to mobilize its vast capital and human resources, while Korea can provide technology and management skills based on its information technology (IT) capabilities and experience.

In the latter regard, the successful launch of the Asian Infrastructure Investment Bank (AIIB) in 2014 will be able to provide a financial platform for the implementation of these infrastructure construction projects.[127] Korea and China are indeed the two countries that stand to provide mutual benefit in the course of infrastructure construction and operation. The fact that the AIIB stands to play an important role in this Central Asian region offers another piece of evidence that this initiative is distinct from other conventional FTAs that China and Korea have concluded.

In summary, the EI and OBOR are designed to cover similar geographical locations and similar projects. As a new model for an international economic cooperation network, the two projects can benefit from each other's experience in the course of the implementation of the initiatives. More than anything else, the two projects support the proposition that a new breed of economic cooperation regime is needed at this juncture in this region. While these two national projects share some commonalities with existing FTAs, they are also distinguished from them in that their priorities are not placed on market liberalization or market penetration of the contracting parties. Rather, they are designed to "connect" the constituent states so that close economic cooperation can be ensured. Such a connection can take place either by creating transportation routes or other infrastructure or by exchanges of people and culture. Arguably, the focus of the two projects is therefore distinct from that of the FTAs. At the same time, to the extent that these two projects do not necessarily aim to create a common market — such as the EU — they are also distinguishable from such economic integration plans.

ii) Remaining Questions and Concerns

Despite the many positive aspects, there are some concerns and problems regarding the common pursuit of the EI and OBOR which need to be highlighted. It is natural that there should be logistical and legal hurdles to be overcome by the EI and OBOR as new attempts to establish international economic cooperation regimes. Unless efficiently managed, these problems may erode the benefits that could accrue from the co-existence of the projects.

There are also legal implications flowing from the new initiatives. While we cannot and do not have to find answers to these legal questions at this time, relevant analyses should be undertaken in order to structure the proper framework, noting that oftentimes economic cooperation issues lead to trade and investment disputes brought by other states and entities who are negatively affected by the advent of a new regime.

First of all, discussions should be undertaken to determine what kind of legal instruments are to be adopted to specifically implement the EI and OBOR. A new type of economic cooperation agreement can be contemplated. It may also carry the name of an FTA. It may simply lead to the adoption of an international agreement dealing with specific cooperation projects, such as specific infrastructure construction and financing projects as seen in the Economic Development Cooperation Fund (EDCF) agreements of many countries. In some instances, it may take the form of Official Development Assistance (ODA) agreements. The point is that there may be many different forms that the prospective legal instruments can take. Once the idea of the EI and OBOR becomes concrete, this issue should be the first to be considered.

Second, depending upon how the idea is implemented and through which legal vehicles, questions may be raised as to whether such a new cooperation agreement and regime is compatible with the WTO Agreements and existing FTAs and BITs. For instance, questions may be raised as to the new regimes' compatibility with the GATT 1994, if these new agreements contain preferential treatment among the participating countries. Depending upon the terms of existing arrangements, most-favored-nation (MFN) and national treatment (NT) issues may be implicated. Ordinary FTAs, of course, can rely upon the exception contained in Article XXIV of the GATT 1994, but it is not entirely clear whether these new types of cooperation networks and agreements can indeed satisfy this provision. Upon careful reading of Article XXIV, it is evident that what is permitted thereunder is a preferential measure that is "necessary for the formation of the FTA"[128] and which does not put other non-parties in a more disadvantageous position than before.[129] It arguably does not cover *all* the consequences flowing from the creation of an economic cooperation agreement.

Similar issues may also arise with respect to FTAs that

relevant countries have already concluded before their participation in the EI or OBOR. For instance, Korea's preferential treatment toward another country in the Eurasian region that is not codified in a separate FTA could constitute a possible violation of MFN or NT provisions contained in its FTA with Australia or New Zealand.

Also, noting that infrastructure projects are frequent venues for investment disputes, efforts to grant preferential treatment for the infrastructure projects of Eurasian States could well bring BITs into the equation as well. These agreements also contain MFN and NT provisions, as well as provisions covering fair and equitable treatment (FET); consequently, inter-state support and other arrangements offered under the EI and OBOR could potentially raise investment dispute issues.

Third, it seems that the two countries' EI and OBOR initiatives are based on the commitment and full support of their respective governments. As with any other national projects, it is quite likely that various kinds of governmental support measures will be introduced to encourage domestic companies and entities to take part in these projects. This is inevitable because it is, after all, individual businessmen and corporations that actually participate in the infrastructure projects of neighboring states and because they are only likely do so when they are sure to receive economic returns and benefits. Since such commercial returns and benefits are not always guaranteed, in particular in the initial stages of such projects as those contemplated by the EI and OBOR, governments may try to provide such incentives for participation as affordable loans, tax exemptions, loan guarantees and the provision of governmental goods and services. Such incentives, while necessary and appropriate within the context of the EI and OBOR, may run the risk of violating the WTO's SCM Agreement, which rather strictly regulates provision of such support to domestic industries and companies.[130]

These are just some examples of possible legal issues to be contemplated in the course of devising specific mechanisms for implementing the EI and OBOR. Thorough analyses and adequate preparation will enable avoidance or reduction of the possibility of raising various unintended legal issues. This, in fact, is another reason why close cooperation and coordination between Korea and China would be beneficial to both countries in designing and implementing their respective EI and OBOR.

iii) New Initiatives' Possible Implications for Regional Economic Cooperation

Korea and China have been actively pursuing their FTA policies to support their robust global trade. At present, they actively participate in various bilateral negotiations as well as negotiations for plurilateral FTAs called mega-FTAs. On top of this, they have also laid out plans to establish a new type of economic cooperation regime in the Eurasian region. Korea's EI and China's OBOR have arguably introduced a new breed of international economic cooperation scheme that will cover Asia and the eastern part of Europe. As these schemes are not necessarily about market liberalization in the constituent countries but rather about infrastructure construction, joint energy resources development and transportation/ communications systems, they are distinct from the traditional version of FTAs. They are in fact focused on ensuring enhanced "connection" — both figuratively and culturally — and, as such, aim to serve different purposes for the participating states. Furthermore, these new initiatives are designed and able to address geopolitical issues in the Asian region, including, for instance, most notably, long-term engagement with North Korea. While the EI and OBOR were initiated by Korea and China with different purposes and at different times, they do share considerable commonalities and similarities.

With the recent conclusion of the Korea–China FTA, cooperation between the two countries in various economic sectors has reached a new dimension, both quantitatively and qualitatively. This framework of cooperation can certainly help the two countries pursue coordination and cooperation with respect to their pursuits of the EI and OBOR. After all, they share the largely common goal of connecting various States in Asia all the way to Eastern Europe and the focus has been placed on infrastructure, energy supply and transportation. Synergy effects from the close cooperation and coordination of the two initiatives are evident both economically and geographically.

In the meantime, there are likely side effects as well. If the two countries and their business entities become engaged in fiercer competition as a result of the implementation of the EI and OBOR due to these projects' similar scopes of coverage, the benefits from both projects would be reduced and other countries may take advantage of the two countries' competition. On a different note, the legal implications flowing from these new initiatives cannot be ignored either. As with any other new attempt at establishing international economic cooperation schemes, a myriad of trade and investment agreements that apply to the two countries and other potential participating countries may apply to the EI and OBOR. This provides evidence of another reason for close coordination and cooperation between the two countries in the implementation of their projects.

iv) Areas of Convergence

Observing the FTA policy of Korea, China and Japan at present, a clear commonality emerges: the FTAs are all designed to ensure further penetration into the domestic markets of foreign trading partners and to protect their domestic market to the extent that such protection does not rise to the level of protectionism or otherwise in violation of trade agreements. As such, the basic formats and structures of the FTAs of the three countries largely share commonalities as well. A great deal of attention is paid to the tariff schedules, the core vehicle for market liberalization. A variety of mechanisms are introduced in these three states' FTAs to protect domestic industries from seemingly intensifying competition from foreign countries, most notably FTA partners.

From a wider perspective, there is a clear commonality

in terms of the FTA policy of the three countries — that is, the FTAs have become a core element of their respective economic policies and and strategies. The FTAs have become indispensable in formulating and implementing these economic policies and trade policies. As such, the FTA policies have become key domestic agenda of the three states, sometimes prompting fierce domestic controversies. With respect to DSMs specifically, the three countries also share the understanding that the DSMs are critically important for any FTA, and that active participation in them is critical in preserving their rights and interest in a given FTA. In other words, they are receptive, more receptive than other states in other parts of the globe, to the idea that DSMs should take center stage in any trade agreement.

v) Areas of Divergence

In the meantime, there are also areas of divergence as well. For instance, the domestic industries that are economically important and politically sensitive are all different among the three states. The automobile industry and agricultural industy are critical to Korea. The agricultural and fisheries industries are critical to Japan. While small and medium-sized exporters are the backbone of China's export industry.

Korea's approach to FTAs is said to be more technical. It looks at FTAs as a tool to maintain and expand its exports. Korea is not in a position to see beyond specific FTAs and look for something else. This technicality-oriented approach has made Korea flexible and elastic in terms of adapting to a changing environment quickly, a strong point for Korea. The downside of this approach is that short-term interest may blur long-term interest. Likewise, if the short term benefit does not materialize in a short period of time, frustration from the government and industry can flare up instantly.

On the other hand, China's approach is rather strategic. As a G-2 state, China has realized that FTAs can be a tool that can solidify its position globally and narrow the gap between itself and the United States and other developed states. It approached its FTAs with Korea and Australia with strategic considerations. It is also approaching the ongoing negotiations for RCEP and other FTAs with similar strategic considerations. This approach can ensure the long-term interest of China in the global market. The downside of the strategy is that it alerts its trading partners to see and question the real intent of China with respect to trade issues. It is also the case that China may rely upon its trade influence to achieve its political and diplomatic objectives. The strategic approach therefore can cut both ways.

Japan is said to be in-between. It looks at the technicalities of FTAs and it also considers the long term-interest of its position in the region and globally. If anything, Japan still harbors high hopes for a multilateral regime. The FTAs are stepping stones for future multilateralism. So its interest is not just directed at preserving its own interest but also at reviving the vitality of multilateralism. This trait does not seem obvious in the case of Korea and China.

Different approaches to FTAs have also led to some extent to a different understanding of DSMs. Korea's understanding of DSMs is mainly geared toward how to ensure liberalization of the export market. When it is necessary to adjust domestic policies as a result of an adverse ruling of a DSM, the general perception of the public and the legislature is rather negative, viewing it as an encroachment upon its national sovereignty. China has been more strategic when it comes to DSMs. Its offensive and defensive strategies in DSMs are timed and adjusted in response to other countries' actions, mainly that of the United States, the EU and Japan. Japan on the other other hand looks at DSMs as a vehicle for enhancing the rule of law in the global trading regime. At the same time, Japan has failed to correct some aspects not clearly stipulated in the trade agreements. NTB problems are examples of this. The NTBs of the Japanese market have been claimed to have vitiated the intended benefit of trade agreements. Japan has however been rather slow in handling these concerns mainly because they are not explicitly addressed or mentioned in the trade agreements at issue.

(5) Assessment of East Asian FTAs in the Global FTA Regime

All FTAs are important and throw light on each other. East Asian FTAs also play an important role. More than anything else the three countries constitute almost 50% of the global trading volume. So anything the three countries adopt in terms of trade will be meaningful and influential. At the same time the profiles of the three countries are also important. Japan represents the traditional bloc of developed countries who are the architect of today's global trading regime. China, on the other hand, is located at the other side of the spectrum: A massive developing state which challenges the hegemony of the existing developed states and their trading regime and norms. Korea is between the developing and developed group. Historically and culturally, it is closely related to China. Philosophically and geopolitically, on the other hand it is closely related to Japan. The different profiles of the three countries make the FTAs that these three countries adopt more colorful and diverse, which will provide an interesting guiding light to other countries in the world. The same logic equally applies to DSMs of FTAs of the three countries, with their unique approaches and experience in DSMs of various types.

8) Difficulty in Proper Evaluation of FTA's Impact

More than anything else, it is diffiuclt to assess the impact of an FTA. Any impact, whether positive or negative, requires a long-term assessment. There is some immediate impact of course, such as the effect of tariff rate elimination. At the same time, how the adjustment of industries takes place and how national resources are re-distributed are questions the answers to which require a significant amount of time. It is therefore not necessarily wise to state that a particular FTA is beneficial or not, unless a thorough and long-term analysis has been completed. The three countries are also struggling with this notion. Their domestic constituents are impatient in waiting for the benefits of FTAs. When the benefit is not immediate enough, the reaction from the general public becomes instantly negative. This makes the FTA policy of the three states more vulnerable to domestic political popularity.

A similar example can be found with the Korea-US FTA. The United States amended the FTA which has only been in place for five years. In particular, since the inauguration of the Trump Administration, South Korea held its breath. The dreaded term "termination" finally surfaced during President Trump's interview on April 28, 2017 where he described the trade pact as "a horrible deal that should've never been made," vowing re-negotiation and possible termination. This has put South Korea on scramble mode in preparation for the first encounter of the two governments to discuss this issue: the summit meeting between President Trump and President Moon was held in Washington, D.C. later that month.

A trade agreement can survive only if, and as long as, it can ensure a win-win situation for both parties. If one party believes it is being shortchanged, no words of friendship or goodwill can save it. At the end of the day, in a trade deal money talks. An aggrieved party has the option of triggering the kill switch (called a termination clause) embedded in a trade pact. The Korea-US FTA was no exception. So it is important and critical to read the balance sheet of the Korea-US FTA carefully and accurately when this issue is put on the table this coming June and onwards. If the balance sheet does indicate that one side stands to gain more systematically, then the playing field should be leveled at all costs. Otherwise, it would be simply a matter of time or a matter of patience before a 'losing' party invokes termination. In light of this, the negotiation provides a good occasion for candid discussions between the two major trading partners.

Reading the Korea-US balance sheet, however, requires an understanding of some unique aspects of the trade pact. First is how to account for a time gap between goods trade and services trade in terms of the "market opening" effect. All things being equal, the effect of goods trade liberalization (i.e., tariff cuts) is usually immediate: you just don't pay extra tax anymore at the border. Meanwhile, services trade commonly demands prior planning and a time-sequential process: in a foreign country you need to rent an office, hire staff, undergo a registration process, and run advertisements. So here market penetration takes more time.

Between the two countries, the United States had a competitive edge in services trade. And the five years' that has elapsed may not be sufficient yet for full penetration into the Korean market by competitive US service providers. USTR's own assessment in the National Trade Estimate of March 31, 2017 regards the Korea-US as "provid[ing] meaningful market access commitments across virtually all major services sectors" of Korea. While Washington has registered concerns over implementation of the services market opening in certain sectors of Korea, this 'time lag' in services trade is a factor was reflected in the Korea-US assessment.

Reading the balance sheet properly also required recognition that the pact is not just about market liberalization and tariff reduction. It is (at least intended to be) much more than that. The almost 1,000-page treaty texts cover virtually the entire spectrum of economic activities. For instance, facilitation and protection of foreign investment is a core concept. At least on the part of Korea, the Korea-US FTA had induced more Korean investment in the US, totaling 51 billion dollars during the five-year period, more than double that of US investment in Korea during the same period. Transparency and due process in the regulatory regime were other examples. Again at least on the part of Korea, the FTA played a pivotal role in attaining these objectives. The USTR's 2017 NTE attributes "improvements in the transparency of Korea's regulatory system" to Korea-US FTA. Granted, there is still a long way to go, but it seems to be working, albeit slowly.

Likewise, those assessing Korea-US FTA should not be oblivious to the geopolitical aspect of the treaty. Upon entry into force, the FTA was branded and touted as another milestone of the bilateral relations, a sequel to the Korea-US Mutual Defense Treaty of 1954. After five years, arguably this side of the agreement still remained valid. If anything, the increasing tension in Northeast Asia these days further underscores the need to tighten bolts and nuts between the two states. The FTA provides those bolts and nuts.

A final score sheet of Korea-US FTA will only be available when all these multiple facets of the agreement are fully taken into account. And yet, quite a few people in the two countries tend to look at only the tip of the iceberg such as trade surplus or deficit in a given year. One needs to look at what is below the water at the same time.

9) Specific Challenges for Korea, China and Japan: Balkanization of the Global Trading Regime

The three East Asian states have encountered the most difficult time in their trade policies. The multilateral trade regime in which the three have thrived has been weakening continuously. The WTO has now reached the lowest point as of March 2022. Its stellar dispute settlement system has also suffered a lot: the Appellate Body ceased to function as of December 11, 2019 because of the absence of Appellate Body Member as a result of the continuous blockings of appointment by the United States that began in May 2016.

In the meantime, FTAs and RTAs have sparead further and deeper globally. The number of FTAs and RTAs concluded by the three countries has also increased. In addition, new types of trade agreements, not falling under conventional FTAs or RTAs, have also emerged. The Japan-US Digital Trade Agreement of September 2019 is a good example. The two countries agreed on a bilateral trade agreement on a specific topic — digital trade. It is not clear whether this treaty can be categorized as an FTA or RTA under Article XXIV of the GATT 1994 or Article V of the GATSs. The CPTPP went into effect as of December 30, 2018, and introduced a series of new norms for countries in the Asia Pacific region. Only Japan is a party to the CPTPP, but Korea has been keen to acceding the trade agreement. The CPTPP stands out from the pack of FTAs because it is an 11-state multilateral FTA with a variety of trade norms. The three countries are also actively participating in RCEP, another mega-FTA in the region and in trilateral FTA among themselves. All thes horizontal and vertical overlappings of FTAs and RTAs have added layers of complexity to the three countries.

The demise of the WTO and the surge of FTAs and RTAs with comprehensive coverage and sectoral coverage have invited fragmented trade regime globally. The fragmented nature of the regime exerts significant impact on East Asia as well. The three countries are standing at the doorstep of a new era of a trade regime.

(1) Why Are Different Rules Included and Tested in Different FTAs?

These FTAs introduce new rules and norms for trade. They are not found in existing trade agreements. Existing trade agreements only focus on tariff elimination and trade liberalization. New FTAs, on the other hand, focus on establishing a new trade environment and adjusting domestic regulatory regimes of contracting parties. So, newer version of FTAs are not simply trade agreements, but they should be called to be "Bilateral (or Trilateral of Plurilateral) Economic Governance Agreement." From this perspective, such issues as exchange rate or labor standards are naturally falling under the jurisdiction of a trade agreement. Viewing an FTA as a mere trade liberalization treaty is not accurate or appropriate any more. This approach is now outdated and rendered incapable of dealing with some of the recent challenges and demands of the global community.[131] Just imagine the drastic and dramatic changes in the world that we have gone through during the past 20 years since the inception of the WTO in 1995. Also consider the array and scope of new issues being discussed at the moment, including national security as seen in Trump Administration and global health regulation as seen in the COVID-19. The scope of trade agreements have gone through a fundamental change.

As a matter of fact, the DDA has become bogged down not so much as because of the different views held by members on tariff rate reductions but because of the diversity of positions on how to adopt new rules in various sectors of global trade.[132] It is time to garner consensus on this new concept and role of trade agreements. Unfortunately, the three countries are merely following the trend of new norms in other parts of the world. They need to take a leadership role at least in some of the issues being discussed in this regard. The three states are mainly the targets countries of new norms — consider SOEs, fisheries subsidies or exchange rates. They need to take an initiative in this process, as opposed to the target or subject of critical discussions.

(2) Examples of New Experiments of DSMs in Recent FTAs of Korea, China and Japan

New rules do not simply stop at substantive part of FTAs. They also appear in procedural portion as well. As such, new rules appear in DSMs as well. Some of them are directly related to DSMs of FTAs and others are indirectly associated with the operation of DSMs. Various DSMs are inserted into and scattered around the texts of FTAs. Unlike substantive part, there is more leeway the three states can resort to: DSMs are still earlier stage of development and thus more susceptible to the suggestions and experiments. The three states need to take advantage of this situation. For instance, the three countries can devise and suggest various DSMs in a way that can address their existing and new concerns over the new trend of the global trade. Such suggestions will also help other countries in other parts of the global community as well. A few selected examples are as follows.

i) Ensuring Legitimate Policy Space

The most important task in formulating DSMs in FTAs is

how to ensure the contracting parties' authority to pursue and implement legitimate public policy objectives (so called LPPO). Any new DSM in an FTA should be able to sort out LPPO. This objective can be directly attained through changes and amendments of substantive provisions of FTA. DSMs can also play an important role in this regard. For instance, selection and appointments expertis with public policy background can help achieve this objective. Having an appellate mechanism is another way of ensuring fair assessment of Legitimate Public Policy Objectives (LPPO). Introducing mechanisms through which state parties can exercise control over panels of DSM can be yet another choice. The three states' endevour can focus on these practical elements in the future.

Most importantly, substantive provisions need to be changed and amended so as to ensure LPPO's ultimate survival at DSMs. For instance, some FTAs expand the scope of a general exceptions clause or introduce a new exceptions clause so as to explicitly carve out certain governmental measures from the coverage of the FTA.[133] Some of the FTAs also include provisions that stipulate favorable consideration of certain types of governmental measures.[134] Yet other FTAs clarify the discretion accorded to the governments of contracting parties with respect to particular types of measures.[135] Likewise, some types of measures are exempted from dispute settlement proceedings, which is another way of guaranteeing wide latitude of discretion of government agencies.[136] These changes and amendments of substantive norms can guarantee the protection of LPPO. But ultimate protection can only be guaranteed once procedural aspect of DSMs are changed simultaneously. This is the areas where the three countries can provide critical contribution.

ii) Non-Binding DSMs

Exploring non-binding dispute settlement mechanisms offers yet another example of experiments with new rules in the FTAs. In addition to the existing binding DSMs, non-binding ones can provide a complementary support for the general architecture of dispute settlement of the FTAs. For instance, the Korea-EU FTA and the Korea-China FTA adopted a non-binding mediation mechanism to deal with disputes over Non-Tariff Barriers (NTB).[137] These mediation mechanisms are innovative. They aim to resolve disputes as soon as possible without resorting to a lengthy and costly legal proceedings. And yet, these proceedings do not rule out the possibility of proceeding to legally binding DSMs, once mediations fail. As Korea, Japan and China are frequent subject states in NTB discussions, their experiments will carry important weight for other countries' own thinking as well. At this stage, the three countries' experiments are confined to NTBs. Over time, similar mediation mechanisms can be applied other types of ordinary trade disputes as well.

In a similar vein, parties to FTAs have started to strengthen the function of the Joint Committee, a bilateral consultative body of an FTA, in a way that can issue a 'binding' interpretation of the text of the FTA.[138] This is an avenue to control breakaway panels and panelists in FTA DSMs. State parties can maintain their control over the texts of the treaties. The problem, however, is the possibility of weakening rule of law. A Joint Committee is a political entity. A political entity's control of a judicial body may raise a structural problem. A proper balance needs to be found between protection of the principle of rule of law and state parties' authority to impose their intention as drafters of the texts. The three states are in a unique position to contribute in this regard.

iii) Fisheries Subsidies

Fisheries subsidies is one of the most controversial topics in new trade agreements. Fisheries subsidies norms aim to prohibit states' subsidy for the fisheries sector, because such subsidy is the main culprit of overfishing and ultimately global depletion of fish stocks. In that regard, prohibition of subsidies to fisheries sectors has been touted as the most efficient way of slowing down the depletion of marine species. As a result, this issue has become one of the core topics of DDA negotiations,[139] FTAs negotiations. States, however, have failed to reach consensus since, as with any other new issue, countries have different ideas about how to introduce new rules on fisheries subsidies.[140] In other words, they all agree on the need to protect fish stocks and they also agree to regulate and prohibit state subsidies in this regard. But they have not yet agreed on how to introduce specific rules to achieve the objective. The latest version of consensus is found in the CPTPP, a multilateral free trade agreement among 11 nations.[141] Japan is a party to the CPTPP. The norms contained in the CPTPP is quite skeletal and are far from being able to be applied with any level of predictability.

The controversial topic of fisheries subsidies also raises an important aspect for DSMs of FTA. First of all, interpretation of the fisheries subsidies norms in FTAs will be significantly affected by how states parties express their collective views. So, Joint Committees and environmental committees (or their equivalents) will play a critical role in this regard. If an FTA has contracting parties more than two, how to allow standing for fisheries subsidies disputes and non-Party third party submission will be important. Most importantly, how to collect and reflect scientific evidence in fisheries subsidies dispute is very critical. Formulation of DSMs in FTAs should consider unique traits of new substantive norms. Fisheries subsidies provide a useful example in this regard.

iv) Inserting Linchpins for Overlapping Issues

In devising DSMs in FTAs, it would be also critical to include a linchpin provision. This provision is to deal with overlapping norms from different treaties. As of now, there is no such provision, and panels are paralyzed for issues that are closely related to other agreements or treaties. This phenomenon stems from structural problems of international law, most notably fragmentation of international law and self-contained regimes. So, resolution of the problem goes beyond what can be expected of FTAs. Nonetheless, at least a provision that can alleviate the situation is still necessary and meaningful. In that regard, a provision can be explored that provides (i) the panel's authority to refer to other legal instruments outside the FTA as a legally binding source; (ii) the sequence of applying different norms in settling disputes under the FTA; (iii) the parties' right to explain legal obligations imposed on the from other international agreements and treaties and how those obligations have affected the measures at issue.

Korea, China and Japan have unique experience in dealing with these issues. They are well positioned to propose an article to be included in ther future FTAs. Other countries can rely upon the article as an example for their own FTAs.

(3) Side Effects of New Experiments in FTAs

Generally speaking, new experiments of DSMs in FTAs should be welcomed. Theese experiments reflect the demands of states and businesses. In particular, Korea, China and Japan are positioned to formulate and implement these DSMs in a proper direction. The three countries experience can certainly help other countries think about these issues more carefully and practically. Compared to substantive norms, procedural norms such as DSMs are more open to the three countries' contribution as well because they are still in the beginning stage of the evolution. So, the three countries are advised to pay more attention to the development and discussions of DSMs in their future FTAs. At the same time, there are also important side effects in developing and fine-tuning DSMs in the FTAs. They concern logistical, policy and legal aspects, respectively.

i) Logistical Aspect

Most importantly, introduction of new DSMs in an FTA means drastic increase of work for the government a contracting state. At the same time, there are numerous FTAs. So, together this means that the government should handle almost 10 to 20 times more disputes and dispute settlement proceedings than before. If the government still operates within the confinement of existing budgetary and human resources, it will be unable to handle all these new tasks efficiently. Few discussions have taken place in this regard, however.

The three states are advised to initiate projects to expand their infrastructure in dispute settlement proceedings as soon as possible. Increasing the number of FTAs without contemplating this logistical strain on the part of the dispute settlement proceedings may backfire in the near future. The three states are lagging behind their western counterparts when it comes to dispute settlement expertise. Unfortunately, these three states still heavily rely on the professional assistance of experts from the United States and EU. Unless this shallow depth of the pool of experts, the three countries will continue to face difficulties in the future, and more so in the new environment of fragmented and multiplied FTAs.

ii) Policy Aspect

From the domestic policy perspective, the surge of DSMs in FTAs suggests that each new legislation and policy decisions are put under a microscopic review by trading partners. Their enhanced interest in the domestic markets of an FTA counterpart incentivize deeper analysis of new legislations and policies. Not only bilateral SSDS, Joint Committes and chapter-specific committees convene regularly to talk about various issues. Government agencies are supposed to look over their shoulder whenever it contemplates a measure. To the extent this new environment enhances rule of law, it is development to be welcomed. On the other hand, this new environment can also turn out to be a source of chilling effect, negatively affecting the government's formulation and implementation of important national policies. It is important how government agencies deal with this new environment efficiently and effectively.

The three states of East Asia have shown relatively reasonable response until this point. They have coordinated domestic interest groups well. They have also implemented obligations flowing from FTAs relatively well. But this is just the initial stage and the circumstances may change as FTAs enter into a full swing stage. FTA counterparts of the three countries will now be impatient when certain promises are not met (in their view), followed by demand of changes and pressing demands on all fronts. The three states are now supposed to face heavier burdens on formulating, discussion and advertising and defending their legislations and policies.

iii) Legal Aspect

FTAs are indeed permitted under Article XXIV of the GATT 1994 and Article V of the GATS. Upon careful reading of Article XXIV and Article V, however, it becomes evident that what is permitted under this article is a preferential measure that is "necessary for the formation of the FTA,"[142] which does not put other non-parties in a more disadvantageous position than before.[143] How this cardinal rule applies to various DSMs included in FTAs. All FTAs have different DSMs. All FTA counterparts, therefore, are treated differently. Consequently, all business entities from these different FTA counterparts are also treated differently. It is not clear how this different treatment of FTA counterpart governments and business entities in terms of dispute settlement is assessed under Article XXIV of the GATT 1994 and and Article V of the GATS.

As a corollary, systematic changes taking place as a result of the adoption of new rules of DSMs in an FTA may lead to a situation where they cannot be justified by Article XXIV or Article V. In fact, Article X of GATT 1994 is also supportive of the proposition that uniformity is indeed one of the core elements of the obligations of member states in the administrative and adjudicatory process.[144] The introduction of various new rules through FTA DSMs stands to implicate these other norms of the WTO Agreements that some of the aggrieved WTO Members may raise going forward.

In short, these legal issues have not received adequate attention yet. DSMs of future FTAs should be devised with this legal implication in mind. It is questionable whether Article XXIV, adopted in 1947, does reflect the realities of 2020. But, still, it is the legal parameter within which current FTAs should operate. The three states in East Asia may analyze related legal issues and reflect the outcome in their respective FTAs. That can certainly provide guidance for other countries and even for WTO in this regard.

(4) New Experiments of DSMs in FTAs and New Challenges

The FTAs present useful fora to explore and examine DSMs of new types. The lesssons learned and data collected can be brought back to future negotiations of FTAs, so that a better version of DSMs can appear. Lessons from the better version can again be cycled for future development, and so on and so forth. This process can certainly improve FTAs in a way that resolves disputes between contracting parties fairly and efficiently and improve interpretation of substantive provisions of FTAs accurately and appropriately.

More importantly, such lessons and experience can also be brought back to the WTO. At the moment, reform of the WTO Agreement and WTO regime have become a global topic. Any reform of the WTO also requires attention to dispute settlement mechanism as well. So, any lesson, positive or negative, can be utilized in the amendment of existing WTO DSM and formulation of new DSMs at the WTO. An effective and workable DSM can help restore the status of the WTO and revive the sagging multilateralism. The endeavor to create and apply new DSMs in the FTAs may serve the noble cause of restoring multilateralism of the global trading regime.

It explains why the contribution of Korea, China and Japan is all the more important in this regard. Their robust participation in FTAs should not stop at market liberalization. They should not simply follow the lead of other western countries in the adoption of new norms, both substantive and procedural ones. They could and should play a leading role in the discussions of new DSMs in the FTAs. They can do so in their own FTAs with other countries, and FTAs among themselves or in which they participate together. This exercise can again contribute to the WTO's own DSM discussions and development currently underway.

2. Introduction to Dispute Settlement Procedures in Major FTAs

1) Historical Background Reflecting Views of Western Countries

Like any other international interaction, trade negotiations are affected by the policy directions of participating states. Legal and institutional arrangements in the international arena need to reflect the interests of participants. In other words, different ideologies and policy priorities are reflected in the outcomes of negotiations and the resulting legal and institutional setups. Most importantly, trade negotiations and the resulting agreements are a result of the economic principles of the dominant nations. When it comes to the development of FTAs, it can be said that most of them were dominated by the west and developed nations. In other words, historically it is the west and the developed nations that were active in setting the rules for the operations of most of the FTAs that entered into force. Therefore, it is important to understand the historical process in order to understand the rules incorporated within those FTAs and others that developed on the basis of them. It is important to look in their history to grasp the rationale behind those rules. It is very difficult to understand certain rules without tracing the philosophical underpinning behind those. And this is only possible through a study of the historical background of the rules in question.

2) Cultural Background Reflecting Litigation Cultures in Western Countries

Culture is one factor to be noted in the study of dispute

settlements. The litigation culture of participants in a given legal regime has an impact on the dispute settlement mechanism and its performances. The dispute settlement procedures and the conduct of the system as a whole reflects the litigation culture of the dominant participants. As indicated above, litigation in the WTO as well as the major FTAs are dominated by the west and developed nations. Thus, the litigation cultures prevailing in those countries have an impact on the administration of the disputes governed under those FTAs. To understand the impact of litigation culture it is important to understand its values in other cultures that are trying to utilize the systems. Therefore, participants in FTAs in South East Asia need to understand the existence of the cultural influences of the west so as to come up with a workable model to deal with the particular litigation culture prevailing in the region.

3) Legal Background Reflecting Anglo-American Jurisprudence

Legal traditions affect the legal and institutional setups of dispute settlement mechanisms. The dominance of a certain legal tradition in the development of an international legal regime can shape the dispute settlement mechanism of that particular regime. In preceeding parts, there has been a discussion of the different legal traditions in the world and their impact on international dispute settlements. Thus, the development of international agreements out of these legal traditions can have their own implication on the emerging dispute settlement mechanisms. Most FTAs are modeled after the legal structure of the WTO. As such they try to incorporate the precepts of the WTO dispute settlement mechanism as far as possible. Again, the WTO dispute settlement mechanism is dominated by legal precepts common in the west and developed nations. This is because the west and the developed nations were active participants in the development of the rules of the multilateral trading system. Therefore, the western countries being the leading participants in those processes had the chance to design those agreements in line with the dominant legal tradition of the west. That is why it is argued most of the time that provisions in most FTAs reflect the understanding in the west and the developed nations. Thus, understanding the historical background of a legal system is very important to understand the operation of a given legal regime. As such, one needs to have a better understanding of the historical background of a given legal regime in order to have a better understanding of the operation of the laws. Likewise, understanding the historical background of FTAs help in gaining an understanding of the antecedents of FTAs in South East Asia as well.

3. DSMs for Regional Trade: Lessons and Observations

A higher standard DSM makes a higher standard regional trade agreement. These days, a lot of focus and attention is given to the implementation stage of RTAs. A dispute settlement mechanism is highly related to securing a high standard implementation of FTA commitments. Creativity in RTAs can save a lot of time, energy and money to business people of the parties involved, especially high-tech industries to whom time is money. DSMs ought to be one of the areas in which a lot of WTO plus approach should be taken.

There is a disorganized and uncoordinated web of multiple FTAs in existence, not only in the Western hemisphere, but also in Asia. How to coordinate and effectively solve some complicated problems is a central issue. Dispute settlement could be one area where some countries can bring out creativity and solve problems in a consistent manner. Hopefully in the future, multiple FTAs can harmonize or converge into a common method of dispute settlement.

In general, a good DSM is one that is wider in terms of

scope of application, and that is an integrated system so that it can solve many similar subject matters at one time, and one that can prevent future disputes. Also, facilitation, neutrality and transparency are three important goals to achieve in the panel proceedings. Panel decisions must be well implemented and must be faster.

First, a wider scope of DSM is better. It has been established in international trade law that not only violation cases but also non-violation cases may be subject to certain dispute settlement mechanisms. Non-violation means a certain measure that nullifies or impairs benefits on a treaty by taking measures consistent with the treaty obligations. In the Korea-Chile FTA, for instance, any violation and non-violation between Korea and Chile can be settled through consultation and subsequent arbitral panel procedures. Any type of dispute is solved through a single, integrated DSM. The Korea-EU FTA prescribes 30 days of consultation, which is a lot shorter than the normal 60-day consultation in typical FTAs including the Korea-US FTA. According to the Korea-EU FTA, any dispute concerning the interpretation or application of the provisions of the agreement must be subject to two stages of the dispute settlement process. This language, "any dispute concerning the interpretation and application of the provisions of the agreement," includes not only violation, but also non-violation cases and possibly any other type of cases regarding the interpretation or application of the FTA.

The Korea-EU FTA sets up a single, relatively integrated scope of DSM, similar to the Korea-Chile FTA. Employing a similar integrated DSM approach, the Singapore-US FTA establishes a three, instead of two, stage DSM, having a joint committee procedure in between consultation and panel. It is somewhat redundant, because a joint committee is composed of officials from the two parties. It is quite a political, bureaucratic, and diplomatic process and can be hard in the consultation stage. Having another round of political and diplomatic stages of a joint committee would be somewhat redundant. In any event, the Singapore-US, Korea-US FTAs give more weight to the bilateral settlement stage than the arbitral panel stage.

In comparison, the Japan-Singapore FTA (JSEPA) takes a quite different approach. In the JSEPA, non-violation cases are subject to a separate track of DSM from that of the violation cases. Non-violation cases must be brought to the general consultation procedure to begin with, while violation cases may be brought to the special consultation process in addition to general consultation. Interestingly, the request of the general consultation does not have to be in writing. It is quite informal and more diplomatic than the special consultation. If non-violation cases are not settled during the general consultation, the consultative committee process follows. In comparison with an arbitral tribunal procedure for violation cases, which proceeds after the failure of the special consultation, it seems that the consultative committee process is a more political procedure than the arbitral tribunal procedure, which is judicial in nature. Therefore, it can be summarized that JESPA takes a separate, less judicial approach at least in settling non-violation cases.

Regarding a claim against a proposed measure, in the case of the Korea-Chile FTA, the answer is yes, yet only in the context of violation cases. In other words, non-violation cases can only be raised against an implemented measure, not against a proposed measure. A comparable system can be found in the NAFTA in which a party may request a consultation regarding any actual or proposed measure. If a NAFTA party prevails in the case of a proposed measure, the measure must not be implemented. It is quite a dramatic remedy against the violation of a proposed measure. This complaint against a proposed measure is only allowed for violation cases. The rationale to regulate proposed measures in addition to existing ones lies in the necessity that the role of the DSM in an FTA should extend to the area of prevention of future disputes beyond the traditional function of dealing with existing violation. Is there any reason that a complaint against a proposed measure must be limited only to violation cases? It's possible that a proposed measure consistent with the WTO could cause, in the near future, nullification or impairment of the benefits accruing to the party of a RTA. Possible ways should be discussed of including future violation and preventive functions of DSM.

Facilitation can take place from the stage of the selection of the panelist. According to the experience in various fora, the selection of a panelist is no easy task, because it is hardly going to be agreed upon by disputing parties. In order to solve this kind of problem, many FTAs have adopted some kind of automatic selection process. For example, NAFTA introduced a random method of panelist selection. This random selection method is followed by many subsequent FTAs with some variations. In this regard, it seems that it is not necessary for the Director General of the WTO to intervene in the process of the panel selection in the Singapore-EFTA FTA (S-EFTA FTA). In the Korea-Chile FTA and JSPEA, the random method was adopted. The Korea-Chile FTA even designates the person who does it all, i.e. the FTA chairman.

By contrast, the initial report and separate opinion system, employed in the Korea-Chile FTA, is not recommended. According to the experiences on the WTO dispute settlement process, the interim report system arguably tends to only delay the DSM. The separate opinion system in the FTA could provoke unnecessary resistance from the losing party. On the other hand, the termination of the panel proceedings stated in the JSPEA and S-EFTA FTA is to be recommended, as it can facilitate diplomatic settlement. Since international arbitration must respect the party's intention at any stage of proceedings, the complaining party should be allowed to unilaterally terminate the panel proceedings by withdrawing the complaint at any time before the last hearing is closed. This is stated in the S-EFTA FTA.

It is worth noting that the Korea-Chile FTA has detailed proceedings of the panel, which is also the case of the Korea-EU FTA as well as the Singapore-Australia FTA. These rules and procedures will enhance the predictability of panel proceedings and facilitate them. In addition, the Korea-Chile FTA designates the secretariat, i.e. the trade bureau of the foreign ministry, of each party. Notably, the secretariat of the defending party and not the complaining party is given a mandate to administer the entire proceedings of a specific dispute settlement as a responsible secreteriat. This is controversial because designating the agency of the defending party and not the complaining party as the administrating secretariat does not seem to be the best choice. This is because the agency of the complaining party will be more active in saving time, providing necessary support to the panels.

The Korea-Chile FTA confirms the panel's right to seek technical advice from experts. The Japan-Singapore FTA broadens the expert's role by establishing such a system as an advisory report from experts and participation by experts in the panel process with no right to vote. Given that more technical issues tend to be involved in the panel process, active roles by experts enhance the quality and neutrality of arbitral awards. Beyond expert participation, the Singapore-US FTA establishes a unique system of public participation. Under the system, each party must solicit and consider the views of the member's public upon the request of consultation. Interestingly, it goes further in opening the panel proceedings to the public. In addition, the party's submission must be made public in ten days.

The panel must consider a request from qualified NGOs to provide written views. This kind of arrangement greatly enhances the transparency of the DSM and institutionalizes NGO's practices of submitting *amicus curiae* briefs to the proceedings. It is doubtful that opening the panel hearing will always work as there might be a side effect. It seems inevitable that the panelist and representatives of disputing parties will face enormous pressure from domestic interest groups. As a result, neutrality and technicality of the panel decision might be harmed to a certain degree. For the sake of transparency, it seems sufficient to take submission from experts or NGOs and release the party's submission to the public as promptly as possible.

It is very important to discuss how to improve and facilitate the implementation of a panel report. Under most of the FTAs including JSPEA, a specific implementation period needs to be determined by a separate process including arbitration. On the other hand, the Korea-Chile FTA mandates the panel to specify the implementation period in its final report. This is a WTO-plus approach. By doing this, disputing parties can save time and energy and avoid another dispute regarding the implementation period. It is a recommended approach, if feasible. If there is no implementation or compensation, a prevailing party will have the right of suspension. With regard to the process of exercising the suspension right, variations exist. Under the JSEPA, a prevailing party has to turn to the original panel, the so-called compliance panel, which will determine the failure of implementation. With that determination, the prevailing party can finally take a retaliatory measure.

By contrast, the Korea-Chile FTA does not have such a compliance panel, and the Singapore-US FTA likewise. Either way, the so-called "sequencing problem" does not arise. This is because that JSPEA only adopts the DSU Article 21 track, while the other two agreements generalize the DSU Article 22 track. There is no possibility of mutual conflict between Article 21 and 22 of the DSU in any of these three agreements. By contrast, it seems that a sequencing problem does arise in the Singapore-Australia FTA. This is because the DSU Article 21 and 22 tracks are stated in parallel. Besides the sequencing issue, an interesting point is the relationship between the compliance and suspension panels. The compliance panel examines the legality of implementation by a losing party, whereas the suspension panel examines the legality of a retaliatory measure taken by a winning party. In this regard, it should be noted that JSEPA adopted the compliance panel as well as the suspension panel process.

It is true that this double arbitrary system makes the DSM cumbersome. To correct this problem, the foreign ministry of Korea has suggested the idea of frontloading, which is as follows:

if the compliance panel is mandated to examine in detail the existence or consistence of measures taken to comply with the DSU ruling, the compliance panel would not be overburdened if it were to be charged with additional tasks of determining the level of nullification or impairment. As the compliance and suspension panels are usually composed of the members of the original panel, they are already very familiar with the subject matter. Thus, if the compliance panel were required to determine the level of nullification or impairment upfront, it would importantly facilitate the eventual implementation of the ruling of the panel with or without the reference to the suspension panel process. Indeed, the pre-determined level of nullification or impairment is an essential parameter not only for the suspension concession but also for the conduct of compensation negotiation. In order to engage in a meaningful compensation negotiation, one should know how much nullification or impairment occurs. Deciding the level of nullification at an early stage will facilitate the entire process. The optimal timing for the determination of the level of nullification or impairment should be the point of the discussion.

There are an increasing number of non-implemented cases in the WTO. There are some cases that are not properly implemented and are subject to retaliation by large economies. Securing implementation, proper implementation and adequate implementation are major topics in the WTO. To this end, an alternative remedy, such as a monetary fine or damages, must be introduced into the WTO DSM. The rationale is that a retaliatory measure not only makes a losing party suffer, but also the winning party. It is not an economically sound way of solving the problem. If the losing party prefers to pay a certain amount of monetary assessment to the winning party, such a party will be exempted from being subject to retaliation by the winning party. Having the alternative system may solve a chronic problem of non-implementation. The Korea-US FTA already introduced this kind of system. However, under the WTO DSU, compensation, even though it is not monetary, is a temporary measure. Yet in the Korea-US FTA, monetary assessment is stated as a permanent measure, replacing the obligation to comply.

An important question is how long it will take to settle a dispute. In total, it takes approximately 185-200 days for Korea or Chile to obtain a final award under the Korea-Chile FTA. Japan or Singapore needs around 180-280 days under JSEPA. Under the Korea-EU FTA, it takes less time. The FTA DSP takes a lot less time than the WTO DSP, in which the procedure should lapse in one year. The shorter, the better.

In general, the FTAs concluded by major Asian countries reflect how making a better DSM is an important and urgent issue, especially in recent FTAs. Some insights are as follows:

First, when the RTA DSM covers more comprehensive disputes, it becomes a better RTA. Thus, most RTAs deal with non-violation claims, in addition to those concerning violation. In doing so, JSEPA presents a quite unique system, taking a separate, less judicial approach in settling non-violation cases. It remains to be seen whether this will be successful in dealing with non-violation disputes.

The importance of non-violation claims should be emphasized, because these days the focus of mutual interest is given to non-tariff barriers, which is closely related to non-violation cases. Under the Korea-Chile FTA, a complaint can be raised against not only existing measures, but also proposed measures. This is positive, yet the coverage of the DSM should be extended to allow non-violation claims against proposed measures.

Given the goals of facilitation, neutrality, and transparency, the automatic panel selection method is quite satisfying, while the initial interim report system is not. The complaining party's government agency should be designated as the administrating secretariat, instead of the defending party. The expense can be shared evenly by both parties. By the same token, the determination of the panel proceedings upon an agreement is okay. Enhancing the role of experts in the panel proceedings is a good idea. The acceptance of submission from qualified NGOs and the early publication of the party's submission will make the proceedings more transparent.

Regarding how to improve the implementation process, mandating the arbitral panel to specify an implementation period in each final report is a good idea. This approach, combined by the frontloading idea, will greatly facilitate the implementation of the panel decision. These invaluable lessons learned from the integration of Asia must be a basis to build a better RTA.

There are some lessons that we can take advantage of in this respect. First, there is a lack of uniformity in specific approaches the parties take to reform or amend DSMs in the RTAs. If there is one common theme, parties seem to focus on a pre-formal resolution process of consultation in order to minimize the role of dispute resolution. Second, there is a formalization of dispute resolution process through the means of quasi-judicial process, i.e. arbitration and some formal means of dispute resolution. Two of those concepts are already well built into many of the agreements, i.e. the notion of conciliation and of some type of formal arrangement whereby the tribunal will resolve the merits of the case. Third, there is some consistency in terms of the presentation of the cases and the development of rules in resolving disputes.

From these, it is possible to raise three practical questions. First, why do people need separate dispute settlement proceedings in an RTA? The vast majority of the RTA DSMs have not been used. Nevertheless, an RTA DSM plays a central role in the enforceability of the agreement, because the WTO DSM may not be available to enforce a deeper RTA commitment. The second question is a more practical one. How do RTA partners design the structure of RTA DSM? DSM in the RTA can be classified into two types. One is a state-state dispute and the other is an investor-state dispute. In case of a state-state dispute procedure, RTA DSMs generally follow the pattern of dispute settlement set out in the WTO and thus provide for initial consultations, a dispute panel, an implementation period, and remedies for non-compliance. Based on that, the RTA DSM contains WTO-plus features. Such features, in my observation, usually come from the member's experience in the WTO dispute proceedings and its positions at the WTO DSU negotiations. Sequencing is a good example. At the WTO, the United States and European Union have shown divergent views on whether the Article 21.5 panel process must precede the right of retaliation under Article 22. Similarly, FTAs by the US allow remedies for non-compliance through compliance review proceedings, while FTAs by EU preclude remedies for non-compliance before being determined through compliance review procedures. This is a general state-state dispute procedure. But some RTAs have a special state-state procedure. That example is Annex 22-A of the Korea-US FTA. It provides an automatic snap-back tariff increase as a remedy for disputes concerning motor vehicles. Another one which has not been fully explained in the session is an arbitral proceeding which can be initiated by an investor of a party. The third is, "what should the WTO do?" There are two points that we can consider. An immediate issue to be addressed is potential jurisdictional conflicts between the WTO and RTAs. It is believed that Article 23 of the DSU indicates that the WTO DSM not only has compulsory jurisdiction but also exclusive jurisdiction over matters arising under the covered agreements. Even if agreed under the RTA as forum selection, the WTO may not give up its jurisdiction over WTO matters. Although most scholars agree on this, the rule is not yet clear. It would be better if this issue was further clarified through multilateral discussions. Another important issue is to harmonize bilateral rules and procedures in RTAs. In my view, many divergences come from the lack of clarity or absence of rules in the WTO text. Thus, the WTO members need to double their efforts to make progress in the current DSU negotiations. Additionally, it is recommended that members seriously discuss an option to use the WTO dispute settlement mechanism as a venue for resolving RTA disputes.

4. Relationship with Multilateral Dispute Settlement Procedure under the WTO

1) Jurisdictional Division

In preceding parts, attempts were made to show how sources of disputes can determine the mode of dispute settlements as well as the jurisdictions of the tribunals entrusted with the resolution of the disputes. Likewise, trade relations are governed by various legal regimes deserving separate dispute settlement mechanisms that take into account their peculiar features. This is not the case, however, in areas where different sources give rise to legal relations on a similar or interconnected subject matter. This is true in the case of trade agreements. Likewise, investment relations can be addressed under the multilateral trade rules, bilateral investment treaties or FTAs. These different sources may give rise to a dispute provoking question regarding which tribunals have jurisdiction to resolve the case. Most importantly, distinguishing issues which fall under the various jurisdiction is a serious undertaking. The fact that many disputes arising from FTAs and WTO Agreements are overlapping gives rise to many issues that need to be addressed properly.

2) Forum Shopping Problem

There are important issues that should be considered in the administration of Trade Dispute Settlement. These are: forum shopping, appeal system, and transparency.

As for forum shopping, some define it as a litigant or claiming party's attempt to have an action tried in a particular court or jurisdiction where it is felt they will receive the most favorable judgment or verdict. Others state that it is an informal way of describing the practice adopted by a litigant or a claiming party to have its case heard in the forum thought most likely to provide a favorable judgment. The claiming party may forum shop if the case could be claimed before two or more forum or courts. As for the possibility of forum shopping, violations of obligations under the WTO Agreement are to be referred to the DSM under the DSU. The legal basis for this is Article 23 of the DSU. On the other hand, violations of obligations under FTAs are to be referred to the DSM under the relevant FTA. An example would be NAFTA Article 2004. If the facts given allow claims of a breach of obligations under two or more trade agreements, the claiming party may resort to two or more sets of dispute settlement mechanism allowing for forum shopping. For instance, there may be a Korean measure which could be alleged to be in violation of national treatment under GATS Article XVII and at the same time in violation under Korea-US FTA Article 12.2. In this case, the US may bring a case against Korea either before the WTO panel or FTA panel. If the given facts allow a claim of breach under a unique trade DSM, an issue of forum shopping does not arise. For instance, Korea-US FTA Chapter 10 Article 10.7 says that neither party may have recourse to a dispute settlement under this Agreement for any matter arising under this Article. It is about AD and CVD measures. If there is any dissatisfaction about Korea's measures with regard to AD or CVD measures, the US cannot bring a case under the Korea-US FTA, but it should utilize the WTO DSM. It is the same with the KO Korea-US RUS FTA Chapter 16 Article 16.8. It also says that neither party may have recourse to a dispute settlement under this Agreement for any matter arising under Article 16.1, 16.6, or 16.7.

As for things to consider when shopping for a forum, substantial obligations and exceptions in relevant trade agreements are the most important. Considering the given facts of a situation, those involved need to analyze the provisions precisely and see if there is any merit in bringing a case under the FTA. The second factor to consider is the future value of the case as a precedent. This means that a precedent can be brought by another party and affect a party's future policy. Another factor is the predictability of the outcome. The principle of *stare decisis* is not reflected in the WTO Agreement. In reality, succeeding panels have a strong preference to refer to awards given by previous panels. The outcome of preceding cases affects succeeding cases. The more cases, the more predictability. The fourth factor is the estimated time required for the full process. If there is an appeal system within the DSM, it will take a longer time. The fifth is measures that could be pursued as a remedy. Is retaliation the only remedy? Or is there an alternative such as monetary compensation?

As for some of the issues discussed and suggested, in developing countries there might be a scarcity of human and financial resources who can devote themselves to managing DSMs. To resolve this concern, the WTO provides many training programs for government officials in charge of WTO disputes. Some countries suggest that funds should be raised to support under-developed and developing countries and utilize the DSM. Another concern regarding forum shopping is a risk of conflicting rulings reducing the predictability and integrity of the DSM. In order to resolve this concern, people can consider the adoption of a "choice of forum" clause — *e.g.* Korea-US FTA Article 22.6. Paragraph 1 says that the complaining party may select the forum in which to settle the dispute. However, paragraph 2 says that the forum selected shall be used to the exclusion of other fora. Once a choice is made of one forum to resolve a dispute, the other forum cannot be used. The EU-Chile FTA Article 189.4(c) has a different version of "choice of forum". It says that when a party seeks redress of a violation of an obligation under this part of the Agreement which is equivalent in substance to an obligation under the WTO, it shall have recourse to the relevant rules and procedures of the WTO Agreement. This means that if a case can be brought both before the WTO panel and FTA panel, the party should bring the case under the WTO DSM.

Some suggest that the application of the "principle of *res judicata*" is one way to resolve these concerns. *Res judicata*, also known as claim preclusion, is the Latin term for "a matter already judged" and precludes continued litigation of such cases between the same parties. Some suggest that the application of the "principle of estoppel" is another way to resolve such concerns. The principle of estoppel precludes "a person from denying or asserting anything to the contrary of what has, in contemplation of law, been established as the truth, either by the acts of judicial or legislative officers, or by his own deed, acts, or representations, either express or implied.

These three methods can be used to resolve vertical consistency. Academics and practitioners differentiate between vertical consistency and horizontal consistency. Vertical consistency refers to consistency with regard to the same cases. Horizontal consistency refers to consistency in different cases. Through an appeal system, people can obtain horizontal consistency. As for the function of the DSM, it is to ensure that member states abide by and implement the obligations that have been agreed under the trade agreements. It is also to interpret provisions of the trade agreement to find its meanings to assist member states understand its obligation. In order to achieve these purposes, the DSM should warrant fair and just application of the agreement, and the application of the agreement should be consistent and the result should be predictable. Dispute settlement systems are being established under various FTAs and RTAs, yet most of them have not adopted an appeal system. As a result, different tribunals or courts can have conflicting results with regard to the same measure. For instance, with regard to the same measure against the US which could be alleged to be in violation of national treatment, Korea may file a case under the Korea-US FTA and Singapore file a case under the Singapore-US FTA. The panel established under the Korea-US FTA may rule that the US measure is consistent with the NT provision, whereas the panel under the Singapore-US FTA can find that the identical US measure is in violation. In this case, there is a conflicting ruling. An appeal system could assure the consistency of the awards issued by various tribunals and courts. To achieve this goal, it is advisable that all awards issued by first tier tribunals or courts be reviewed by the identical appellate body, or at least the results of the appellate body be binding to each other.

The final section regards transparency. Empirical studies show that when parties open up the process of consultation, parties tend to have difficulty in coming to an agreement. There must be a balance between transparency and confidentiality. This is the current status under the WTO. As for the formal request for consultation, the summary of the request, including a description of the contested measures, as well as the legal basis for the complaint is disclosed. Yet documents exchanged at the consultation are not disclosed. For the request of the establishment of a panel, the summary is disclosed. However, submissions are not disclosed. Awards are disclosed. Under Article 22.10 of the Korea-US FTA, parties must disclose submissions, subject to the protection of confidential information. This is a significant step that has been made under the FTA. Panel awards are also disclosed under the Korea-US FTA. Under the WTO, open hearings are exceptions, and not a rule. The first public hearing at the WTO took place in 2005 at the request of the main parties in the dispute in the US-Continued Suspension of Obligations and Canada-Continued Suspension of Obligations. Hearings before the panel and AB were open to the public. Article 17.10 of the DSU says that the AB proceedings should be confidential. The AB, however, overcame this Article, allowing public access to the hearing. Article 18.2 of the DSU provides contextual support for the view that the confidentiality rule in Article 17.10 is not absolute. Parties have the discretion to forge confidentiality with regard to their statements, including those made in the course of a hearing. Some third-party participants were not willing to make their statements public and thus the WTO allowed public viewing via closed circuit television or through delayed screening in another room.

Some progress was made under the Korea-US FTA. Under the Korea-US FTA, hearings are open to the public as a rule, not an exception. As long as confidential protection is protected, the panel hearings should be open to the public. The following suggestions are made by academics and practitioners to enhance the transparency of the DSM.

One suggestion is to establish clear rules under the WTO Agreement that enforces the parties to the dispute to disclose litigation documents submitted to the panel or the AB at the time those documents are presented and converts the public hearing as a rule and not an exception. These two are realized under the Korea-US FTA.

The second is to have all open hearings available to the public by webcast. This was discussed during the Korea-US FTA negotiations, but at the very last moment the parties dropped this provision. The third is to have hearings available via a delayed video feed on the Internet in order to facilitate participation by representatives from developing WTO member countries who are otherwise unable to attend in person. This is a good suggestion to give government officials in developing countries the chance to participate.

Endnotes

1. The first part of Work Program under the Doha Ministerial Declaration was dedicated to the implementation related issues and concerns, as follows: "We attach the utmost importance to the implementation-related issues and concerns raised by members and are determined to find appropriate solutions to them. In this connection, and having regard to the General Council Decisions of 3 May and 15 December 2000, we further adopt the Decision on Implementation-Related Issues and Concerns in document WT/MIN(01)/17 to address a number of implementation problems faced by members. We agree that negotiations on outstanding implementation issues shall be an integral part of the Work Programme we are establishing, and that agreements reached at an early stage in these negotiations shall be treated in accordance with the provisions of paragraph 47 below. In this regard, we shall proceed as follows: (a) where we provide a specific negotiating mandate in this declaration, the relevant implementation issues shall be addressed under that mandate; (b) the other outstanding implementation issues shall be addressed as a matter of priority by the relevant WTO bodies, which shall report to the Trade Negotiations Committee, established under paragraph 46 below, by the end of 2002 for appropriate action."

2. *See* Chapter 11, Annex B of the Korea-US FTA.

3. GATT 1994, art. XXIV, ¶ 5, chapeau.

4. *Ibid.*¶ 4, ¶ 5 (b).

5. GATT 1994. art. X (Publication and Administration of Trade Regulation). It provides that:

> 3. (a) Each contracting party shall administer in a uniform, impartial and reasonable manner all its laws, regulations, decisions and rulings of the kind described in paragraph 1 of this Article.

6. B. Applebaum (Feb. 24, 2017). "Trump is Off to a Slow Start on Trade Promises," *The New York Times*. Retrieved from https://www.nytimes.com/2017/02/24/business/economy/trump-trade-policy.html.

7. A. Blake (Jan. 20, 2017). "Trump's Full Inauguration Speech Transcript, Annotated," *The Washington Post*. Retrieved from https://www.washingtonpost.com/news/the-fix/wp/2017/01/20/donald-trumps-full-inauguration-speech-transcript-annotated/?utm_term=.ad1bf3491072.

8. K. Allen (Nov. 9, 2016). "Trump's Economic Policies: Protectionism, Low Taxes and Coal Mines," *The Guardian*. Retrieved from https://www.theguardian.com/us-news/2016/nov/09/trumps-economic-policies-protectionism-low-taxes-and-coal-mines.

9. S. Liesman (Jan. 31, 2017). "Trump's Protectionism Biggest Threat to US Economy's Growth, CNBC Fed Survey Respondents Say," *CNBC*. Retrieved from https://www.cnbc.com/2017/01/30/trumps-protectionism-biggest-threat-to-us-economys-growth-cnbc-fed-survey-respondents-say.html.

10. E. Curran (Jul. 6, 2017). "Global Trade Rebounds Despite Trump's Protectionist Threats," *Bloomberg Politics*. Retrieved from https://www.bloomberg.com/news/articles/2017-07-05/global-trade-rebounds-as-trump-s-protectionist-threat-lingers.

11. Remarks by President Trump in Joint Address to Congress. (Feb. 18, 2017). Retrieved from https://www.whitehouse.gov/the-press-office/2017/02/28/remarks-president-trump-joint-address-congress

12. The President's Trade Policy Agenda (Mar. 2, 2017). Retrieved from https://ustr.gov/sites/default/files/files/reports/2017/AnnualReport/Chapter%20I%20-%20The%20President%27s%20Trade%20Policy%20Agenda.pdf; Alden, E. (Mar. 01, 2017). Trump's 2017 Trade Agenda: Signs of a Sensible Direction. *Council on Foreign Relations*. Retrieved from https://www.cfr.org/blog/trumps-2017-trade-agenda-signs-sensible-direction.

13. Donald Trump's Trade Policy is in Disarray (Apr. 26, 2017). Retrieved from https://www.nytimes.com/2017/04/26/opinion/donald-trumps-trade-policy-is-in-disarray.html.

14. A. Griffin (Apr. 27, 2017). Donald Trump Admits He Backed Down on Nafta after Calls from Canada and Mexico's Leaders. *The Independent*. Retrieved from http://www.independent.co.uk/news/world/americas/us-politics/donald-trump-nafta-canada-mexico-justin-trudeau-leaders-enrique-pe-a-nieto-a7705311.html.

15. P. W. Watson (Jul. 19, 2017). Trump Has Found a Loophole to Rewrite

Trade Agreements Without Anyone's Permission. *Forbes*. Retrieved from https://www.forbes.com/sites/patrickwwatson/2017/07/19/trump-has-found-a-loophole-to-rewrite-trade-agreements-without-anyones-permission/#4084a12e2dd0.

16. Press Briefing by Secretary of Commerce Wilbur Ross on the Memorandum Regarding the Investigation Pursuant to Section 232 (B) of the Trade Expansion Act. Retrieved from https://www.whitehouse.gov/the-press-office/2017/04/20/press-briefing-secretary-commerce-wilbur-ross-memorandum-regarding.

17. President Trump Signs a Memorandum on Aluminum Imports and Threats to National Security. Retrieved from https://www.whitehouse.gov/featured-videos/video/2017/04/27/president-trump-signs-memorandum-aluminum-imports-and-threats.

18. Trans-Pacific Partnership (TPP). Retrieved from https://ustr.gov/trade-agreements/free-trade-agreements/trans-pacific-partnership.

19. Retrieved from https://www.nytimes.com/2017/01/23/us/politics/tpp-trump-trade-nafta.html.

20. E. Beech (Mar. 1, 2017). Trump Administration Would Ignore WTO Rulings It Sees as Anti-US: FT. *Reuters*. Retrieved from http://www.reuters.com/article/us-usa-trump-wto-idUSKBN16832U.

21. Press briefing by Secretary of Commerce Wilbur Ross on an executive order on trade agreement violations and abuses. Retrieved from https://www.whitehouse.gov/the-press-office/2017/04/28/press-briefing-secretary-commerce-wilbur-ross-executive-order-trade.

22. G. Gertz (Feb. 8, 2017). What will Trump's embrace of bilateralism mean for America's trade partners? *Brookings*. Retrieved from https://www.brookings.edu/blog/future-development/2017/02/08/what-will-trumps-embrace-of-bilateralism-mean-for-americas-trade-partners/.

23. D. W. Drezner (Mar. 9, 2017). Why the Trump administration hates multilateral trade agreements the most. *The Washington Post*. Retrieved from https://www.washingtonpost.com/posteverything/wp/2017/03/09/why-the-trump-administration-hates-multilateral-trade-agreements-the-most/?utm_term=.82335afddd20.

24. *See* Timeline of regional FTA among China, Japan and Korea (in Korean), *available at* https://fta.go.kr/cnjp/info/2/ (last visited May 11, 2020).

25. *See* DSU, art. 1.

26. *United States — Measures Affecting the Cross-Border Supply of Gambling and Betting Services*.

27. *See*, for instance, Claude Chase, Alan Yanovich, Jo-Ann Crawford, and Pamela Ugaz, *Mapping of Dispute Settlement Mechanisms in Regional Trade Agreements — Innovative or Variations on a Theme?*, World Trade Organization Staff Working Paper, No. ERSD-2013-07 (Jun. 10, 2013), p. 13.

28. *Ibid.*

29. Chase *et al.*, *supra* note 27, p. 13.

30. *See* DSU, art. 23.1.

31. Chase *et al.*, *supra* note 27, p. 30.

32. *See*, Erika de Wet, The Rise and Fall of the Tribunal of the Southern African Development Community: Implications for Dispute Settlement in Southern Africa, *available at* https://repository.up.ac.za/dspace/bitstream/handle/2263/21831/DeWet_Rise_2013.pdf?sequence=1 (last visited May 7, 2020).

33. Chase *et al.*, *supra* note 27, p. 39.

34. *Ibid.*, p. 37.

35. *Ibid.*, p. 39.

36. *Ibid.*

37. Chase *et al.*, *supra* note 27, p. 13.

38. Chase *et al.*, *supra* note 27, p. 15.

39. *Ibid.*, p. 16.

40. *Ibid.*, p. 17.

41. *Ibid.*

42. *Ibid.*

43. Korea-EU FTA, art. 14.16.

44. Canada-Colombia Free Trade Agreement, art. 2102, *available at* http://international.gc.ca/trade-commerce/trade-agreements-accords-commerciaux/agr-acc/colombia-colombie/fta-ale/21.aspx?lang=eng (last visited May 7, 2020).

45. *See*, Korea-US FTA, art. 22.4.

46. Korea-EU FTA, art. 14.19.2.

47. WTO, *Trade Policy Review, Report by the Secretariat, China*, WT/TPR/S/342/Rev.1 (Oct. 12, 2016), p. 51, para. 3.17.

48. *Ibid.*, p. 126, para. 4.35.

49. WTO, *Trade Policy Review, Report by the Secretariat, China*, WT/TPR/S/342/Rev.1 (Oct. 12, 2016), p. 137, para. 4.81.

50. *Ibid.*, p. 137, para. 4.82.

51. *Ibid.*, p. 140, para. 4.92.

52. WTO, *Trade Policy Review, China, Minutes of the Meeting, Addendum*, WT/TPR/M/342/Add.1 (Oct. 28, 2016), p. 236, Reply of Question 2.

53. WTO, *Trade Policy Review, Report by China*, WT/TPR/G/342 (Jun. 15,

2016), p. 26, para. 4.6.

54. WTO, *Trade Policy Review, Report by the Secretariat, China*, WT/TPR/S/342/Rev.1 (Oct. 12, 2016), p. 10, para. 12.

55. *Ibid.*, p. 37, para. 2.21.

56. WTO, *Trade Policy Review, China, Minutes of the Meeting, Addendum*, WT/TPR/M/342/Add.1 (Oct. 28, 2016), p.73, Reply of question 66; WTO, *Trade Policy Review, Report by China*, WT/TPR/G/342 (Jun. 15, 2016), p. 24, para. 3.56.

57. WTO, *Trade Policy Review, Report by China*, WT/TPR/G/342 (Jun. 15, 2016), p. 24, para. 3.57.

58. WTO, *Trade Policy Review, Report by the Secretariat, China*, WT/TPR/S/342/Rev.1 (Oct. 12, 2016), p. 11, para. 20.

59. *Ibid.*, p. 57, para. 3.31.

60. *Ibid.*, p. 57, para. 3.32.

61. *Ibid.*, p. 57, para. 3.33.

62. WTO, *Trade Policy Review, Report by the Secretariat, China*, WT/TPR/S/342/Rev.1 (Oct. 12, 2016), p. 57, para. 3.34.

63. *Ibid.*, pp. 57-58, para. 3.35.

64. *Ibid.*, p. 58, para. 3.36.

65. WTO, *Trade Policy Review, Report by the Secretariat, China*, WT/TPR/S/342/Rev.1 (Oct. 12, 2016), p. 58, para. 3.37.

66. *Ibid.*, para. 3.39.

67. *Ibid.*, para. 3.40.

68. *Ibid.*, para. 3.41.

69. *Ibid.*, pp. 58-59, para. 3.42.

70. WTO, *Trade Policy Review, Report by the Secretariat, China*, WT/TPR/S/342/Rev.1 (Oct. 12, 2016), p. 58, para. 3.43.

71. *Ibid.*, p. 58, para. 3.44.

72. *Ibid.*, p. 60, para. 3.49.

73. *Ibid.*, pp. 60-61, para. 3.50.

74. WTO, *Trade Policy Review, Report by the Secretariat, China*, WT/TPR/S/342/Rev.1 (Oct. 12, 2016), p. 61, para. 3.51.

75. *Ibid.*, p. 61, para. 3.52.

76. *Ibid.*, p. 61, para. 3.53.

77. *Ibid.*, p. 62, para. 3.55.

78. WTO, *Trade Policy Review, Report by the Secretariat, China*, WT/TPR/S/342/Rev.1 (Oct. 12, 2016), p. 62, para. 3.56.

79. *Ibid.*, p. 62, para. 3.57.

80. *Ibid.*, p. 62, para. 3.58.

81. *Ibid.*, p. 62, para. 3.59.

82. WTO, *Trade Policy Review, China, Minutes of the Meeting, Addendum*, WT/TPR/M/342/Add.1 (Oct. 28, 2016), p. 244, Reply of Question 6.

83. *Ibid.*, p. 441, Reply of Question on 3.2.2 Export taxes, charges, and levies.

84. WTO, *Trade Policy Review, Report by China*, WT/TPR/G/342 (Jun.15, 2016), p. 23, para. 3.48.

85. WTO, *Trade Policy Review, Report by the Secretariat, China*, WT/TPR/S/342/Rev.1 (Oct. 12, 2016), p. 11, para. 9.

86. WTO, *Trade Policy Review, Report by Republic of Korea*, WT/TPR/G/346/Rev.1 (Jan. 6, 2017), p. 11, para. 4.14.

87. *Ibid.*, p. 11, para. 4.15.

88. *Ibid.*, p. 28, para. 2.2.

89. WTO, *Trade Policy Review, Report by Republic of Korea*, WT/TPR/G/346/Rev.1 (Jan. 6, 2017), pp. 30-31, para. 2.17.

90. *Ibid.*, p. 28, para. 2.2.

91. *Ibid.*, p. 36, para. 2.36

92. S. J. Adler, J. Mason, and S. Holland (Apr. 28, 2017). Exclusive: Trump vows to fix or scrap South Korea trade deal, wants missile system payment. Retrieved from http://www.reuters.com/article/us-usa-trump-southkorea-exclusive-idUSKBN17U09M.

93. E. Holodny (Apr. 28, 2017). Trump says he'll revisit the 'horrible' US-South Korea trade deal—here's what you need to know. Retrieved from http://www.businessinsider.com/what-is-korea-us-trade-deal-korus-2017-4.

94. The South Korea-US trade agreement turns five. Retrieved from http://www.economist.com/news/finance-and-economics/21718894-though-not-many-are-celebrating-its-birthday-south-korea-us-trade-agreement.

95. USTR Calls a Special Session Under the US-Korea Free Trade Agreement. Retrieved from https://ustr.gov/about-us/policy-offices/press-office/press-releases/2017/july/ustr-calls-special-session-under-us.

96. WTO, *Trade Policy Review, Report by the Secretariat, Republic of Korea*, WT/TPR/S/346/Rev.1 (Jan. 6, 2017), p. 66, para. 3.64.

97. WTO, *Trade Policy Review, Report by the Secretariat, Republic of Korea*,

WT/TPR/S/346/Rev.1 (Jan. 6, 2017), p. 66, para. 3.65.

98. *Ibid.*, p. 67, para. 3.68.

99. WTO, *Trade Policy Review, Report by the Secretariat, Republic of Korea*, WT/TPR/S/346/Rev.1 (Jan. 6, 2017), pp. 66-67, para. 3.66.

100. *Ibid.*, pp. 67-68, para. 3.69.

101. WTO, *Trade Policy Review, Report by Japan*, WT/TPR/G/310 (Jan. 19, 2015), p. 8, para. 2.13.

102. WTO, *Trade Policy Review, Report by the Secretariat, Japan*, WT/TPR/S/310/Rev.1 (May 6, 2015), p. 20, para. 2.9.

103. *Ibid.*, pp. 20-21, para. 2.10.

104. WTO, *Trade Policy Review, Japan, Minutes of the Meeting, Addendum*, WT/TPR/M/310/Add.1 (Jun. 17, 2015), pp. 25-26, Response to Question 2.4 Investment regime.

105. WTO, *Trade Policy Review, Report by Japan*, WT/TPR/G/310 (Jan. 19, 2015), p. 12, para. 2.46.

106. *Ibid.*, p. 12, para. 2.47.

107. WTO, *Trade Policy Review, Japan, Minutes of the Meeting, Addendum*, WT/TPR/M/310/Add.1 (Jun. 17, 2015), p. 70, Response to Question 56.

108. WTO, *Trade Policy Review, Report by the Secretariat, Japan*, WT/TPR/S/310/Rev.1 (May 6, 2015), p. 32, para. 3.29.

109. WTO, *Trade Policy Review, Report by the Secretariat, Japan*, WT/TPR/S/310/Rev.1 (May 6, 2015), p. 32, para. 3.30; WTO, *Trade Policy Review, Japan, Minutes of the Meeting, Addendum*, WT/TPR/M/310/Add.1 (Jun. 17, 2015), p. 4, Response to Question on 3.1.6 Contingency trade measure.

110. WTO, *Trade Policy Review, Japan, Minutes of the Meeting, Addendum*, WT/TPR/M/310/Add.1 (Jun. 17, 2015), p. 4, Response to Question on 3.1.6 Contingency trade measure.

111. WTO, *Trade Policy Review, Report by Japan*, WT/TPR/G/310 (Jan. 19, 2015), p. 5, para. 2.10.

112. WTO, *Trade Policy Review, Japan, Minutes of the Meeting, Addendum*, WT/TPR/M/310/Add.1 (Jun. 17, 2015), p. 244, Response to Question 24.

113. Korea's Eurasia Initiative was first announced by President Park Geun-hye in her keynote address at an international conference in Seoul on Oct. 18, 2013. The key mantra for the project was "one continent, creative continent, and peaceful continent" through the creation of "a unified system of transport, energy, and trade networks across the vast Eurasian continents."

114. One Belt, One Road (also known as the Belt and Road Initiative; abbreviated OBOR) is a development strategy and framework proposed by the

People's Republic of China that focuses on connectivity and cooperation among countries primarily in Eurasia, which consists of two main components, the land-based "Silk Road Economic Belt" (SREB) and the oceangoing "Maritime Silk Road" (MSR). The strategy underlines China's push to take a bigger role in global affairs and its need to export China's production capacity in areas of overproduction, such as steel manufacturing.

115. *See* Kim Taehwan, "Beyond Geopolitics: South Korea's Eurasia Initiative as a New Nordpolitik," The ASAN Forum, 16 February 2015, *available at* http://www.theasanforum.org/beyond-geopolitics-south-koreas-eurasia-initiative-as-a-new-nordpolitik/ (last visited Oct. 29, 2015); Yuan Xintao, "Analysis of the National Strategy of One Belt and One Road Construction," (2014) *Around Southeast Asia*, Issue 8, pp. 3-8.

116. *See* Ministry of Foreign Affairs, *Eurasia Initiative*, Republic of Korea (Aug. 2, 2015), *available at* http://www.mofa.go.kr/ENG/image/common/title/res/0707_eurasia_bro.pdf (last visited Nov. 15, 2015).

117. *See* Kim, *supra* note 115, footnote 3.

118. Ping Ai, *One Belt One Road, New Diplomacy and Public Diplomacy, China and World*, 4 *International Understanding* (2014), p. 2.s

119. Ministry of Foreign Affairs of the People's Republic of China, *Foreign Ministry Spokesperson Hong Lei's Regular Press Conference*, (Apr. 17, 2015), *available at* http://www.fmprc.gov.cn/mfa_eng/xwfw_665399/s2510_665401/t1255670.shtml (last visited Nov. 2, 2015).

120. Ai, *supra* note 116, footnote 6, 3.CHdf

121. *See* Kim, *supra* note 115, footnote 3; Yuan, *supra* note 318, footnote 3, p. 44.

122. *Ibid.*

123. Xi Jinping, "Develop further the Silk Road Spirit and Deepen China-Arab Cooperation — the Speech at the Opening Ceremony of the Sixth Ministerial Conference of China-Arab Cooperation Forum," *People's Daily* (Jul. 6, 2014), p. 2.

124. *See* Scott Kennedy and David A. Parker, *Building China's "One Belt, One Road,"* CSIS (Apr. 3, 2015), available at http://csis.org/publication/building-chinas-one-belt-one-road (last visited Nov. 2, 2015).

125. "The Joint Statement to Deepen China-EU Comprehensive Strategic Partnership for Mutual Benefit and Win-win Cooperation," *People's Daily* (Apr. 1, 2014).

126. Ai, *supra* note 116, footnote 6, p. 3.

127. "Why China is creating a new 'World Bank' for Asia," *The Economist* (Nov. 11, 2014), *available at* http://www.economist.com/blogs/economist-explains/2014/11/economist-explains-6 (last visited Nov. 2, 2015).

128. GATT 1994, art. XXIV, para. 5, *chapeau*.

129. GATT 1994, art. XXIV, para. 4 and para. 5 (b).

130. *See* SCM Agreement, arts. 1, 2 and 14.

131. *See* World Trade Organization, Subjects Treated under the Doha Development Agenda, *available at* https://www.wto.org/english/tratop_e/dda_e/dohasubjects_e.htm (last visited Jul. 10, 2015).

132. *See* World Trade Organization, The Doha Round, *available at* https://www.wto.org/english/tratop_e/dda_e/dda_e.htm (last visited Jul. 10, 2015).

133. Consider general exception clause in the Korea-Australia FTA. This is the first instance where a general exceptions clause has been inserted in a trade agreement with respect to an investment chapter. *See* Korea-Australia FTA, *supra* note 90, art. 22.1, para. 3.

134. *See* Korea-EU FTA, art. 3.8, para. 3, art. 7.1, para. 2.

135. *See* Free Trade Agreement between the Republic of Korea and Canada (Korea-Canada FTA), entered into force on Jan. 1, 2015, art. 17.2.

136. *See* Korea-China FTA, art. 16.9.

137. *See* Korea-EU FTA, Annex 14-A, Korea-China FTA, art. 20.5, para. 4.

138. *See* Korea-Australia FTA, art. 11.21.4 (e).

139. The Doha Ministerial Declaration provided in paragraph 28 that discussions on clarifying and improving disciplines under the SCM Agreement were to move forward "while preserving the basic concepts, principles and effectiveness of these Agreements and their instruments and objectives." The Ministers further noted that, "in the context of these negotiations, participants should also aim to clarify and improve WTO disciplines on fisheries subsidies." The Doha Ministerial Declarations (WT/MIN(01)/DEC/1), adopted on November 20, 2001. In the Hong Kong Ministerial Declaration, paragraph 9 of Annex D, the cross-reference to trade and environment is reiterated along with the "broad agreement that the Group should strengthen disciplines on subsidies in the fisheries sector, *including* through the prohibition of certain forms of fisheries subsidies that contribute to overcapacity and over-fishing (*emphasis* added)." *See also* WTO Negotiating Group on Rules, *Draft Consolidated Chair Texts of the AD and the SCM Agreements,* TN/RL/W/213 (Nov. 30, 2007); WTO Negotiating Group on Rules, *New Draft Consolidated Chair Texts of the AD and the SCM Agreements,* TN/RL/W/236 (Dec. 19, 2007).

140. *See* World Trade Organization, WTO Negotiating Group on Rules, *New Draft Consolidated Chair Texts of the AD and the SCM Agreements,* TN/RL/W/236 (Dec. 19, 2008).

141. *See* art. SS.16, para. 6 of the draft text of the TPP, *available at* http://www.fao.org/fishery/topic/3195/en (last visited Jul. 10, 2015).

142. *See* GATT 1994, art. XXIV, para. 5, chapeau.

143. *See* GATT 1994, art. XXIV, para. 4, para. 5 (b).

144. Article X of the GATT 1994 provides that:

Article X: Publication and Administration of Trade Regulation

3. (*a*) Each contracting party shall administer in a uniform, impartial and reasonable manner all its laws, regulations, decisions and rulings of the kind described in paragraph 1 of this Article.

Chapter VI

An Anatomy of an East Asian FTA DSMs: Bilateral Proceedings

1. Unique Aspects of East Asia Concerning International Dispute Settlement

The DSMs contained in the FTAs and BITs of these three East Asian countries share the basic elements and general features of the DSMs of FTAs and BITs of other countries. Perhaps, therefore, the situation may not be that different for FTAs and BITs in other countries and other regions. These DSMs contain state-to-state dispute settlement proceedings and ISDS proceedings. Depending on specific partners of FTAs and BITs, the particular contents and nature of the provisions set forth in DSMs vary, but the three countries apparently have templates for DSMs in their respective agreements. These templates have not reached an official status or the firmness of model provisions, but they do seem to have secured the place as a starting point for new negotiations. It appears that these three countries make the effort to maintain their respective templates of DSMs as much as feasible.

There are, of course, some unique aspects as well that appear in the DSMs of these three East Asian countries. In order to understand the unique characteristics of the DSMs of the three countries, it is necessary to discuss how they perceive international dispute settlement proceedings generally. With respect to international dispute settlement proceeding generally, the three countries present the following traits:

- Litigation-averse attitude
- Cultural backgrounds
- Historical backgrounds
- Politicization of disputes and consequences
- Relative lack of an expert pool

These traits in turn have helped shape the DSMs of FTAs and BITs that these three countries negotiate and adopt. These traits continue to affect the DSMs of various kinds of the three countries. Unique characteristics of these three countries' DSMs can be summarized as follows:

- Effort to resolve disputes through diplomatic consultation
- Expectation of low utilization of DSMs
- Conservative approach when it comes to the formulation of DSMs
- Relative preference for WTO dispute settlement proceedings
- Increased sensitivity to investment arbitration and to introducing safeguards to protect regulatory autonomy

1) Asian Culture and Legal Disputes

It has been traditionally the case that East Asian countries have shunned official, legal disputes as much as possible. As the famous adage goes, "a person who can live without law" is among the highest praise that can be afforded a person. This adage reflects the Confucian tradition of teaching and guidance that is treasured by Asian countries, which emphasizes amicable resolution of a dispute. In many respects, the three countries have a different understanding of and approach to official legal proceedings as a mechanism to resolve outstanding disputes between individuals and entities. This view is in clear contrast with the views from other countries, particularly the views from western countries such as the United States and the European Union where legal disputes are understood to be one of the tools available to settle disputes in the environment of "business as usual." Discrepancies of this sort play an important role in formulating dispute settlement procedures domestically and internationally regarding the three countries.

The cultural discrepancy directly leads to a discrepancy in the legal systems as well, since the law is a reflection of the society it governs.[1] For instance, a disposition of a particular case may well be affected by this difference in culture and perspectives between the three countries and others.[2] Likewise, regulation of business entities and activities is not the same either. Traditionally, these three countries have relied on unofficial contact and policy coordination more than western countries. Even if key legislation and regulations are adopted in the FTA-era, one could still claim that agency practice and invisible norms still fail the purpose of the ostensibly FTA-consistent legislations and regulations. This is so, because the changes required by the FTA not only include statutes and regulations, but also policy guidelines and practice.[3] In the context of the three countries of East Asia, it may be the case that despite official changes and reforms, some critics might still dispute whether true changes have been made.[4]

Resorting to unofficial contacts and guidelines has been perceived by other western countries as evidence of a lack of transparency, which allegedly constitutes a significant challenge for businessmen from foreign countries operating in the three Asian countries' markets.[5,6] It is true that invisible guidelines should be avoided at all costs if it is used as a measure to circumvent otherwise applicable treaty provisions, but if it stems from cultural context it may take long time to eliminate them. This alleged non-transparency and unofficial regulation could turn into a source of increasing disputes between the three countries and other countries when fueled by an economic nationalistic tendency.[7]

Furthermore, the fact that countries have different legal systems (civil law systems and common law systems) sometimes further complicates the situation. For instance, in interpreting a provision of a treaty, the two systems have different approaches to statutory construction.[8] Judicial procedures, administrative investigations and administrative decision-making procedures for that matter, also expose differences: the role of the judge is different between the Korea and the US as the former follows the so-called "inquisitorial" approach while the latter follows the "adversarial" approach[9]; the judge possesses more leeway in pursuing the substantive truth in the East Asian countries and plea bargaining is basically not permitted in the three countries' criminal procedures. As such, businessmen from western states participating in administrative procedures in government agencies of the three countries sometimes complain that they cannot expect the same level of procedural protection through due process or that they have difficulty in solving a dispute promptly through a mutually agreeable solution.[10]

2) Asian Culture and International Legal Disputes

One of the fundamental principles of the treaty implementation is that a party to a treaty cannot rely on domestic regulation or legislation to justify a violation of its otherwise applicable treaty obligations.[11] This jurisprudence has also been consistently confirmed in the implementation of trade agreements as well.[12] So, when it comes to treaty implementation, what counts is the particular treaty provision at issue rather than having to look into the domestic laws of a party. Stated as such, this seems to be a relatively simple principle.

The situation, however, could be different if the nature of the obligation under a provision of a treaty in question somehow requires a pre-judgment on non-trade, national sovereignty-related issues. Resolving disputes of this sort invites inquiries into what is really going on in the decision-making process of the party concerned, which then leads to an examination of various aspects of domestic legal system and administrative system of that party. The situation would get worse if the parties to a treaty possess fundamental differences in their respective legal, administrative or political systems. Then, the legal dispute could easily turn into a value dispute as to whose approach to a particular issue is more appropriate and desirable.

Although there are a lot of similarities between the legal systems of the three countries and those of other countries such as the United States as a result of gradual convergence over the years,[13] there still remain fundamental, respective peculiarities. These peculiarities appear to stand ready to complicate the implementation of the FTAs of the three East Asian countries.

Likewise, dissimilarities in the respective legal systems would be more apparant if the legal services market is opened in Seoul, Tokyo and Beijing. The three East Asian countries are further opening up their legal markets to foreign attorneys and law firms.[14]

3) Historical Ramifications in East Asia and International Legal Disputes

The historical background of the three East Asian countries also plays a meaningful role in trade and investment disputes. Japan's annexation of Korea and invasion of China in the early 20th century still live on in the memories of the Korean and Chinese general public. The historical sentiment sometimes tends to blur the eyes of the governments and peoples of Korea and China when they encounter disputes with Japan. Once a dispute is lodged, the historical sentiment also invites unnecessary emotional and nationalistic responses from the general public, which is not regarded as a legtimate policy consideration by WTO Agreements or FTAs. Overcoming the historical ramifications and treating trade disputes as 'business as usual' are the first steps towards the stable and predictable regulation of trade relations among the three states in the region.

4) Unique Aspects in East Asia Relating to Trade Disputes

Recent disputes between Korea and the United States have

somehow been premised upon the cultural context: that is, different notions of the role of the government, the relationship between the governmental sector and the private sector and societal characteristics. One of the unique traits of Asian culture has been said to be that people view their government as having paternal authority and role.[15] Apparently, this trait still persists and affects the economic regulation of countries in such cultures. As a result, compared to its western counterparts, the governments in Asian countries are more directly involved in regulating the economic activities of private entities in their jurisdictions.[16]

Probably the same is also true of Korea. When it comes to the regulation of markets, the government of Korea has traditionally taken a hands-on policy to achieve governmental goals.[17] If a problem is observed in the market, the government has been usually quick in responding to the situation rather than waiting for the market to do it on its own. Sometimes, it works out but sometimes it does not.

This phenomenon, however, has caused constant concern on the part of foreign countries, particularly western countries including the United States or the European Union. The foreign countries tend to think that the government of Korea is illegitimately intervening in the market to drive governmental goals. They are of the view that the government orchestrates the players in the market for the purpose of artificially inflating the competitiveness of Korean companies while putting foreign companies in a disadvantageous position or sometimes keeping them out of the Korean market.[18] The government counters this argument by mentioning that it is simply adopting and implementing legitimate governmental policies as with any other government and dismisses such allegations.[19] As for Korea, this difference in culture and perspective has led to numerous legal disputes recently at international and domestic tribunals.

In short, regarding the proper role of a government, there seems to be a gap between Korea and western countries, which apparently stems from the difference in culture and perspectives regarding what a government can (or should) do and how a government can (or should) do it. This discrepancy would be underlined in a dispute where a government's intention and the appropriateness of its policy is extensively examined. When the disputes and debates heat up in the future, this discrepancy in cultural context could play an important role, for better or worse.

5) Unique Aspects in East Asia Relating to Investment Disputes

One of the key issues of the Korea-US FTA is the introduction of the investment-related provisions and its dispute settlement procedure in Chapter 11 of the agreement. Issues contained in this chapter had been on the negotiating table until the last minute of the bilateral negotiations.[20] More specifically, the Korea-US FTA has introduced an international dispute settlement mechanism under which an investor of a party can bring a legal action at an international tribunal against the government of the other party in which he or she made an investment when the government has violated the applicable provisions of the agreement in a manner that negates the purpose of the investment.[21]

One of the key issues to be reviewed in this procedure is the concept of "indirect expropriation," which occurs when a governmental measure is tantamount to an expropriation, even if an actual expropriation does not occur.[22] The problem with this inquiry is that it inevitably involves the examination of a wide range of national policies, such as environmental policies, security policies, financial policies, etc. as long as a foreign investor claims that his or her investment has been virtually evaporated because of the host government's policy at issue. This is a highly fact-specific inquiry and the reviewing panel should look into the whole spectrum of the governmental measure in question. It should thus examine the government's intent in adopting the measure, true objective of the measure, the impact of the measure on the market, the interaction of the government and interested groups in the course of formulating the measure in addition to the extent of the alleged loss by the foreign investor.

Obviously, this is not an easy question. The way Korea sees a particular issue may be quite different from the way the United States sees the same issue. Also, the way Korea (or the United States) sees the problem may be different from the way the panelists or arbitrators see the same issue.

2. Challenges Facing DSMs of East Asian FTAs

Many countries are currently facing challenges, both legal and logistical, when it comes to DSMs of FTAs and WTO. Korea, China and Japan are no exception in this regard. While the three countries are better situated than other developing states due to their economic success and strong national infrastructure, there are unique challenges that the three countries are facing and are trying to overcome at the moment in the new landscapce of international trade.

1) Sino-US Confrontation and Systemic Impact

Most importantly, the pendulum of global FTAs has indeed shifted from the "tariff reduction" to the "rule setting." Consider the following statements of President Obama of the United States in his State of the Union address in January 2015:

> Twenty-first century businesses, including small businesses, need to sell more American products overseas. Today, our businesses export more than ever, and exporters tend to pay their workers higher wages. But as we speak, *China wants to write the rules for the world's fastest-growing region.* That would put our workers and our businesses at a disadvantage. *Why would we let that happen? We should write those rules.* We should level the playing field. That's why I'm asking both parties to give me trade promotion authority to protect

> American workers, with strong new trade deals from Asia to Europe that aren't just free, but are also fair. It's the right thing to do.
>
> Look, I'm the first one to admit that past trade deals haven't always lived up to the hype, and that's why we've gone after countries *that break the rules* at our expense. But 95 percent of the world's customers live outside our borders. We can't close ourselves off from those opportunities. More than half of manufacturing executives have said they're actively looking to bring jobs back from China. In the Asia Pacific, we are modernizing alliances while making sure *that other nations play by the rules* — in how they trade, how they resolve maritime disputes, how they participate in meeting common international challenges like nonproliferation and disaster relief. (emphasis added)[23]

President Obama's reference to China in the context of trade was both direct and pointed. In his speech, he underscored that "China wants to write the rules for the world's fastest-growing region" in a way "that would put [US] workers and [US] businesses at a disadvantage." He then stated, the US "would [not] let that happen." He continues that the United States "should write those rules," instead to "level the playing field" in the area of global trade. After warning China's 'writing rules on trade,' he then moved on to ask for the Trade Promotion Authority — namely, fast track authority to negotiate trade deals under which US Congress can vote only up-or-down for completed deals, which he has just secured.[24] So, the collective reading of these statements indicates that "writing trade rules" is the critical objective of the US trade negotiation at the moment and such writing of rules is mainly is geared toward the fierce competition with China. If anything, President Obama's statement almost admits that one of the major goals of the TPP is to adopt new 'rules' on trade so as to counter the expansion of Chinese influence in this part of the world.

China has responded in kind. On its part, China has also

been pursuing its own network of FTAs where it can adopt new rules on trade as it deems appropriate. The RCEP and Free Trade Areas of Asia Pacific (FTAAP) are the mega-FTAs that China is currently advocating to help introduce new rules on trade.[25] In this respect, China is even pursuing a more comprehensive economic cooperation network spanning over Asia and Europe under the name of "OBOR" initiative which was unveiled in 2013 when President Xi Jinping visited Kazakhstan. China's OBOR aims to establish a new silk road connecting China, central Asia and Europe, composed of the land-based "Silk Road Economic Belt" and the ocean-based "Maritime Silk Road." This may be called a Chinese version of a 'mega-mega-FTA' that can potentially cover a sizable swath of Eurasian states. These two silk roads are said to enable China to increase its influence in global affairs and help expand its export market that can absorb the overproduction in China. As such, this new project is also, by nature, designed to introduce and implement new rules on economic cooperation including trade. According to a recent statement by a Chinese ambassador on OBOR:

> Some of you may wonder why we put forward the initiative. Well, it is not difficult to get a clue from the development momentum of today's world. First of all, the Belt and Road initiative answers the call of our time. We are now in a globalized world. The economic integration is accelerating and regional cooperation is on the upswing, but *global economy remains in a period of profound adjustment*, with risks of low growth, low inflation and low demand interwoven with risks of high unemployment, high debt and high level of bubbles. The performance and policies of major economies continue to diverge, and uncertainties in the economic climate remain prominent. The Belt and Road initiative will promote free flow of economic factors, highly efficient allocation of resources and deep integration of markets; encourage countries along the Belt and Road *to achieve economic policy coordination and carry out broader and more in-depth regional cooperation of higher standards; and jointly create an open, inclusive*

> *and balanced regional economic cooperation architecture* that benefits all. The initiative is a positive endeavor to seek *new models of international cooperation and global governance.*[26] (emphasis added)

The focus on rules is likely to intensify among states pursuing FTAs. States with hegemonic dominance tend to place more emphasis on the establishment of rules that would favor their goods and services. Other countries with less influence usually end up accepting new rules inserted and incorporated in respective FTAs.

More fundamentally, it seems that recent disputes between China and the United States have somehow been premised upon the cultural context: that is, different notions of the role of the government, the relationship between the governmental sector and the private sector, and societal characteristics. It has been said that one of the unique traits of Asian culture is that people ascribe to their government a paternal authority and role.[27] Apparently, this trait still persists and affects economic regulation by countries influenced by this culture such as China. As a result, compared with its Western counterparts, the governments in Asian countries are arguably more directly involved in regulating economic activities of private entities in their jurisdictions.[28]

Increasingly, it is observed that in a wide range of trade areas the United States and China possess different views and perspectives of this sort. The confrontation between the two trade giants has put other trading partners in a difficult position. Likewise, recent US-China disputes have also made other countries realize that a considerable discrepancy exists between the United States and China in their perceptions of some fundamental issues in the trade sector. This realization could also help these other countries prepare themselves to respond to their own disputes with the United States or China. Although the contexts and backgrounds may differ considerably, some of the issues raised by the United States *vis-à-vis* China could apply to others with some modifications. For example, the recent extensive US search for China's subsidy programs in both its central and provincial governments could also function as a preemptive warning for other countries, that to some extent may implement similar programs in various sectors.

China has been particularly critical of the WTO's possible infringement of its sovereignty.[29] In *China-Measures Affecting Trading Rights and Distribution Services (DS363)*, China referred to the *UNESCO Convention on the Protection and Promotion of the Diversity of Cultural Expressions*, adopted in October 2005, to stress that cultural goods are different from other non-cultural goods and that WTO members reserve the right to more leeway in regulating these goods.[30] China's point was that it could regulate foreign goods and services when it had a legitimate concern about preserving its cultural identity; this argument was consequently rejected by the WTO's panel.

Another example of national sovereign infringement argument proffered by China has been taking place at the WTO dispute settlement proceedings in terms of the scope of the general exceptions stipulated in Article XX of the *General Agreement on Tariffs and Trade 1994* (GATT 1994). As is well known, Article XX defense is considered to represent an important right of a WTO member. In the *China-Raw Materials* dispute, China took the position that this exception should cover measures adopted to conserve exhaustible natural resources,[31] and thus virtually any violation of substantive provisions of GATT 1994 should be justified. In the dispute, China argued that it adopted a multi-layered policy framework designed to meet a range of inter-related objectives regarding its sovereign natural resource endowments, which are virtually unreachable under the WTO.[32] The United States in that dispute starkly opposed such an interpretation.[33] The scope of Article XX defense is not entirely clear yet and is still arguably subject to the disputes between the United States and China.[34]

Yet another example concerns the subsidy disputes between the United States and China. The SCM Agreement does subject

WTO members' provision of illegitimate subsidies to specific private economic entities within their territories to a rigorous discipline. In fact, the SCM Agreement does not provide for any special treatment or consideration for any particular type of governmental programs since the provisions stipulating the so-called 'non-actionable' subsidies lapsed on December 31, 1999.[35] That said, however, the SCM Agreement is also mindful not to interfere with the inherent authority of the members' governments to pursue legitimate public objectives and economic policies within the parameters of various provisions of the agreement, which is well-summarized by the panel in *Canada-Aircraft*.[36] As a matter of fact, almost all governments are actively involved in numerous projects to foster the technological and scientific development of academic institutions and industries within their territories. Thus, the line between a government's legitimate function and an illegal subsidization scheme through various governmental projects is sometimes not entirely clear.[37] In fact, this very issue is being discussed in the course of the Doha Development Agenda (DDA) negotiations.[38]

Viewing these high-profile disputes between the United States and China, and fundamental differences in understanding key provisions of the WTO Agreements, some countries, on the one hand, clearly espouse the perspective held by the United States, which supports fuller promotion of private activity, further protection of private property rights, and more liberalization and deregulation of the market. Over time, these countries have made significant efforts to harmonize its perspectives and views with those of the United States in terms of economic regulation and policies.[39] On the other hand, however, there are some economic or trade issues in the spectrum with regards to which these countries seem to subscribe to perspectives that are closer to those of China. These issues may include the role of the government in regulating private activity in the market and the appropriateness of the government's intervention in the private sector.[40] This does not mean that individual countries support China in specific disputes involving such issues; in fact, developing countries may well have views different from China. Instead, it simply means that, irrespective of the possible violation of international trade agreements in technical terms, an argument can be made that other countries may at least understand the basic rationale of China in introducing certain economic or trade measures.

The role of the government in regulating the private market continues to flare up in the context of China's SOEs, which account for almost half of the China's GDP according to some recent statistics. The question then is how these unique enterprises should be treated in terms of treaty application and implementation.[41] Particularly vigilant here is the United States who have put this issue as one of its top priorities in its negotiations of various agreements including TPP that may have relevance to China, although China is not participating in the TPP negotiations. During the WTO's Trade Policy Review of China conducted in August 2012 at the WTO, questions concerning the SOEs took center stage.

In this respect, it should be noted that the International Law Commission itself has recognized that this kind of inquiry involves cultural background discussions and contextual analyses.[42] In fact, the ILC commentary on this issue states that "Article 5 [of the 2001 Draft Articles] does not attempt to identify precisely the scope of 'governmental authority' for the purpose of attributing the conduct of an entity to the State."[43] The ILC commentary further elaborates that "what is regarded as 'governmental' depends on the particular society, its history and traditions."[44] Thus, it denounces any categorical approach, but puts emphasis on the specific factual circumstances of the case, including cultural or societal background.

Thus, the position of other countries in these intense US-China disputes is necessarily nuanced — particularly among developing countries. As to some issues, developing countries seem to share the US position when the issues relate to further market openings in China. But for others, developing countries seem to side with the Chinese approach to the extent that preservation of national sovereignty is concerned. The developing world is therefore meticulously eyeing the current surge of trade friction between the two trade giants. The situation of Korea offers an example in this regard. For a long time, foreign governments have claimed that the government of Korea manages the Korean financial market to the benefit of Korean companies.[45] These interactions between Korea and other countries resemble those between China and the United States.

As such, US-China disputes present instances in which other countries realize the existence of a mismatch between the different perspectives regarding the same issue. WTO norms are not sufficient and detailed enough, so disputes between major trading partners (such as China and the United States) addressing WTO norms regarding new issues (such as trade and environment, trade and security, trade and financial sovereignty, and trade and culture) are bound to intensify, and the losing party will do whatever it takes to reject a ruling or to find an excuse to delay implementation of the ruling. Strong confrontations between the United States and China will continue to test these perspective-related trade issues. Other third countries' position in the midst of fierce confrontations will be likely to remain precarious.

Therefore, successful integration of economic entities through FTAs in East Asia requires a basic understanding of key differences between legal systems and the effort to harmonize the key differences in a mutually satisfactory manner. As discussed earlier, differences in legal systems has its own impact on dispute settlement mechanisms. Thus, understanding the different legal systems in each region and their salient feature helps to understand the key areas where integration efforts should be focused.

2) The Trap for FTA DSMs: Difficulty and Complexity of FTA Implementation

The advent of the FTA era has brought about significant

changes in Korea, China and Japan in terms of its trading policy and domestic regulation. The deep penetration of FTAs has alerted the three countries in a way that has not been seen in the WTO's multilateral regime. All three countries have become active players in FTAs, and likewise, all in all, they are all faithful contracting parties of these agreements. Most notably, they pay keen attention to the implementation of these agreements domestically. In the meantime, they are also facing new challenges in implementing these agreements domestically. The challenges are said to be twofold. The first one is the domestic controversy triggered by domestic constituents that stand to lose their business interests due to increased foreign competition. While the situation in China is different from Korea and Japan because China's economy is largely orchestrated by the central government and is generally not amenable to different voices from different economic entities, domestic concern in China has been increasing commensurate with the conclusion of new FTAs. Domestic responses in Korea and Japan have been more acute and assertive to the extent that accommodating the demands from domestic industries has become the most important priorities of the two countries in their FTA policies.

(1) Korea

i) Korea's FTA Drive and FTA Implementation Act

Free Trade Agreements (FTAs) have brought about significant changes in the Korean trade landscape. The sheer workload has increased dramatically in the course of negotiating, concluding and implementing the FTAs, and domestic controversies surrounding these FTAs have become all the more intensified. The new trade landscape in Korea has demanded a new domestic legislation to address the changed situation.[46] Having observed the far reaching impact of an FTA, core consensus has been formed inside the Korean National Assembly, the country's legislative body, in order to enact new legislation to regulate the entire proceeding of an FTA.[47] The concerns and opposition from the executive branch was brushed off and the need for more heightened legislative oversight over the FTAs has taken center stage. This legislative effort has led to the enactment of the *Act on Governing Procedures of Conclusion and Implementation of Trade Agreements* (FTA Implementation Act, or Act). This Act was passed by the National Assembly on December 30, 2011,[48] and went into effect on July 18, 2012 after a grace period of roughly six months. The Act applies to all sorts of trade agreements including FTAs in the entire segments of the life cycle of the trade agreements, from negotiation, to initialing, signing, conclusion, ratification, and implementation.[49] No similar act has been enacted in other areas of treaties or agreements in Korea. In that regard, this Act has drawn a great deal of attention from Korea and abroad since its inception. In fact, the introduction of the FTA Implementation Act has had a significant impact on the negotiation, conclusion and implementation of the FTAs.[50]

As the full title of the legislation signifies, this Act is designed to apply to "trade agreements" which is defined quite broadly, as discussed below. As it currently stands, the scope is so expansively defined that almost all trade agreements, whether in the WTO context or FTA context, can be potentially covered by the Act. Needless to say, as the Act has been adopted due to the domestic controversies swirling around the FTAs, the main target of the Act is the FTAs. Thus, the Act is simply abbreviated as "FTA Implementation Act." But it should be borne in mind that the Act could equally apply to other non-FTA trade agreements such as WTO Agreements or the Trade in Services Agreement (TISA). Once determined as falling under the scope of the Act, a series of rather stringent statutory requirements is then attached. The trade agreement at issue is placed under the constant supervision of the National Assembly and the government should engage in continuing dialogue with the legislative body to secure either cooperation or permission, as the case may be, regarding a particular trade agreement at issue. Furthermore, the coverage of the Act means that the legislative oversight will continue for as long as ten years after the effective date of the trade agreement. Likewise, there is significant statutory homework for the government to do with respect to the covered trade agreements, including the issuance of implementation assessment reports and adoption of remedial action for domestic industries, items which raise legal implications regarding WTO Agreements and various FTAs.

While the title of the Act uses the term "trade," this Act in fact goes beyond trade and encompasses many different subjects under the government's regulatory authority. This is so because modern FTAs are framed to cover the entire spectrum of national economic sectors including environment, competition, human rights, labor, investment, law enforcement, administration of judiciary, as well as conventional trade issues of tariff elimination. Thus, with the vehicle of FTAs, all these issues fall under the jurisdiction of the Act. Likewise, issues being raised in investment arbitration and sometimes commercial arbitration also potentially fall under the ambit of the Act since these arbitration proceedings increasingly constitute important elements of an FTA and its implementation. This means that the FTA Implementation Act of 2011 of Korea stands to affect not only trade sectors but also investment and commercial arbitration sectors. This Act therefore deserves careful attention from interested groups and entities both in Korea and abroad.

ii) Two Unique Aspects of the Act

The FTA Implementation Act is the first attempt of this kind in Korea, and a similar legislation is hard to find in other countries. There are pieces of domestic legislation in Korea and other countries addressing implementation of trade agreements, but few of them aim to provide tight legislative monitoring and supervision, as seen in the Act, for the entire life cycle of trade agreements, from the initiation of negotiation spanning over one decade after the agreements' going into effect. According to the scheme of the statute, a broadly defined "trade agreement" is only to be concluded and implemented in consultation with the National Assembly. This is indeed a novel idea given the increasing demand to reflect the views of the general public in the course of negotiations and conclusion of controversial trade agreements. However, it is quite another issue whether such direct and longstanding intervention by the legislature is logically feasible.[51] In particular, the new statute even requires the government to take remedial action when it becomes apparent that Korea's national interest is not adequately guaranteed through the implementation by the other contracting party of a trade agreement, such as an FTA.[52] If remedial action is indeed taken under this particular provision in the future, this may even raise the legal question of compliance with the FTA at issue or with the WTO Agreements.[53] Among many traits, the new legislation has two aspects that stand out, namely, (i) active and continuing participation by the National Assembly, and (ii) a vague and broad scope of application of the Act. Let us examine each of these aspects in detail.

iii) Active and Continuing Participation by the National Assembly

One of the fundamental traits of the Act is the participation of the National Assembly in virtually all proceedings of negotiating, concluding and implementing trade agreements.[54] The objective of the legislation is set forth in Article 1 of the Act, as follows:

> Article 1 (Objective) This Act aims to achieve, by stipulating necessary details concerning the conclusion and implementation process of trade agreements, improvement of transparency of the conclusion process of trade agreements by ensuring understanding and participation of the general public, pursuit of effective trade negotiation, and contribution to the development of a sound national economy by guaranteeing the rights and interests of Korea in terms of the implementation of trade agreements.[55]

As this provision clarifies, the three key words of the Act can be summarized as "transparency," "participation" and "national economic interest." The first two terms stand for the wider participation of the general public in the treaty negotiation, conclusion and implementation, and the third term signifies the focus on political and economic consideration of Korea;s long-term interest with respect to the particular trade agreements at issue. All of these three items, thus, stand to require more direct and broader participation of the National Assembly in the matters pertaining to trade agreements as a representative of the general public. Not surprisingly, this objective constitutes one of the key underpinnings of the Act.

The National Assembly thus either reviews, approves or discusses issues relating to broadly defined "trade agreements" throughout the entire segments of trade agreements including negotiation, initialing, signing, ratification, going into effect, and implementation.[56] In fact, this legislative monitoring continues as late as ten years after the effective date of a particular trade agreement.[57]

The legislative participation in itself is not new. In fact, under the Korean Constitution, the National Assembly's participation in treaty matters is guaranteed in the form of legislative consent to ratification with respect to certain key treaties.[58] What draws attention to the FTA Implementation Act is the scope of such participation by the National Assembly. While the constitutional participation of the National Assembly is limited to providing "consent to ratification" of certain treaties, the scheme of the Act covers proceedings both prior to and after such ratification procedures — prior to in that it covers treaty negotiations and signing — and after in that it covers a lengthy period after the treaty (trade agreement) goes into effect. As such, the newly-proposed participation by the National Assembly far exceeds the bounds of legislative participation as envisioned in the Constitution. Setting aside domestic constitutional issues attendant to the new statutory scheme, the wider participation of the National Assembly in treaty matters is the first attempt of this kind and poses new challenges to the government in terms of conducting FTA negotiations with other countries.[59] It is not clear whether the government can report all the issues discussed on the negotiating table to the National Assembly or whether the National Assembly is indeed in a position to approve or reject specific issues on the table. It is no secret that many issues on FTA negotiation tables are technical and complex, which would render the legislative intervention either impractical or unfeasible. It is one thing that legislative supervision is appropriate in a democratic state, but quite another thing that the legislative body actually participates in the negotiating process. This model departs from the previous structure in Korea and those in many other countries wherein it is mainly the executive branch that makes key decisions for a trade agreement, such as an FTA.

In short, for better or worse, the National Assembly has become a key decision maker under the new statutory scheme of Korea when it comes to the negotiation and conclusion of FTAs.[60] In particular, it should be noted that FTAs are viewed as an on-going process even after their conclusion.[61] Constant surveillance has thus become one of the key components of FTA implementation.[62] This post-conclusion monitoring is scheduled to be conducted by the National Assembly that stays vigilant of the status of domestic industries as a result of FTAs. Furthermore, the National Assembly has the authority to request that the government to take remedial action *vis-à-vis* a trading partner once it determines that domestic industries are being shortchanged after the conclusion of an FTA.[63] All in all, the unprecedented participation of the National Assembly in trade agreements represents the hallmark of the FTA Implementation Act of 2011.

iv) Vague and Broad Scope of Application

With respect to the temporal scope, this Act applies to trade agreements concluded within six months after the date of entry into force of the Act, which is July 18, 2013.[64] As such, the Act applies neither to the Korea-US FTA, which entered into force on March 15, 2012, nor to the Korea-EU FTA, which entered into force on July 1, 2011.[65] The Act, however, applies to many other FTAs including the Korea-Turkey FTA that entered force on May 1, 2013. While the Act contains a clear-cut provision on the temporal scope, it does not provide a clear definition of a "trade agreement." Article 2 of the Act provides the following:

> Article 2 (Definition) Definitions of the terms used in this Act are as follows:
> 1. A "trade agreement" means a treaty, as set forth below, which Korea concludes with other countries or by which Korea accedes to international organizations such as the World Trade Organization or other economic unions, and which is subject to the consent of the National Assembly for ratification in accordance with Article 60, paragraph 1 of the Korean Constitution.
>
> A. A treaty whose objective is to open up domestic market comprehensively through conclusion at the level of international organizations such as the World Trade Organization.
> B. A treaty concluded at the regional or bilateral levels, whose objective is to open up domestic market comprehensively.
> C. Other treaties that stand to cause a significant impact on the national economy through the market opening in various sectors of economy.[66]
>
> 2. "Trade negotiation" is negotiation that Korea conducts with other countries in order to conclude trade agreements.

As noted in the article quoted above, the Act is supposed to apply to a "trade agreement," but the definition of the term is arguably not as clear-cut as it should be. So, the door is wide open as to the trade agreements to be covered by the Act.[67] An ordinary FTA certainly falls under the definition of trade agreement provided for in the Act. What is less clear is what kind of trade agreements other than FTAs are also covered by the

Act. Likewise, it is unclear what kind of amendments of existing trade agreements would be covered by the Act, even if the original agreements are not covered by the Act as they went into effect before July 18, 2013. One immediate question that arises is whether a proposed amendment to the Korea-US FTA would fall under the scope of the Act, thereby becoming subject to the extensive monitoring requirement of the National Assembly for the years to come.[68]

In principle, *any* trade agreement with a comprehensive market opening effect, which is also subject to the National Assembly's consent to ratification under Article 60, paragraph 1 of the Korean Constitution is to be covered by the Act.[69] At the same time, *any* agreement that may significantly affect the national economy and to be subject to the National Assembly consent requirement under Article 60, paragraph 1 is also covered by the Act. Viewed from this angle, an amendment of an existing FTA may well constitute a "trade agreement" falling within the scope of application of the Act, (i) if the amendment leads to a comprehensive market opening effect, or (ii) if it otherwise affects the national economy significantly, and the proposed amendment requires the consent of the National Assembly for ratification.[70] Such statutory terms as "comprehensive market opening" or "national economy" are arguably vague and amorphous. Many situations could potentially satisfy these requirements. Consequently, not only FTAs or WTO Agreements but also non-FTA, non-WTO trade agreements may be regarded as "trade agreements" and may be covered by the Act.[71]

In summary, all conventional FTAs concluded after July 18, 2013 fall under the scope of the FTA Implementation Act. Other types of trade agreements may also be subject to the Act to the extent they exert significant influence on the national economy or entail comprehensive market opening situations and are subject to the National Assembly's consent requirement pursuant to Article 60 of the Constitution. Given the fact that virtually all trade agreements of the present day would easily satisfy these three requirements under the jurisprudence of the Korean Constitution and relevant statutes, many, if not all, non-FTA trade agreements could also be considered "trade agreements" within the meaning of the Act. This potentially broad scope of application offers another hallmark of the Act.

The combination of the two traits means that the Korean National Assembly is now authorized to intervene in negotiations, conclusion and implementation of a wide range of trade agreements of Korea. FTAs are main targets of the Act but other forms of trade agreements are not that different in essence. The National Assembly stands to reflect the political volatility of the country. This, in turn, signifies that more politicization of trade issues looms around the horizon in the long run.[72]

v) Legal Issues Arising from the Key Provisions of the Act

The key provisions contained in the FTA Implementation Act do raise many novel questions as this is the first attempt of its kind in terms of negotiating, concluding and implementing trade agreements. They also pose logistical challenges as the MOTIE as well as other government agencies and research institutions are expected to conduct close consultations with the National Assembly, prepare detailed assessment reports and take actions to provide remedy to domestic industries. At the same time, the new ideas contained in the Act also raise legal issues that require careful consideration by Korea in light of its obligations under the WTO Agreements and FTAs. It is true that to the extent some of the provisions simply provide discretion to the executive branch, an "as such" challenge may be successfully defended by Korea based on the WTO jurisprudence distinguishing between 'mandatory' and 'discretionary' legislation. Nonetheless, the fact that provisions that aim to override otherwise applicable trade agreements have been introduced in key domestic legislation itself draws the attention of other countries with respect to associated legal issues.[73]

① Implementation Assessment Reports

It is undeniable that implementation assessment reports to be prepared for respective FTAs will provide critical opportunities to evaluate the status of the domestic industries and to consider means to alleviate the harm inflicted upon them.[74] Notwithstanding this practical utility, a government-prepared report, including all key information on the situation of domestic industries as a result of the FTA in question, will turn out to be a key documentary piece of evidence for the measures taken by the Korean government. The contents and statistics contained in the report would operate as the database for trade remedy investigations and measures either under the WTO Agreements or the FTAs. Trade remedy investigations require an assessment of the domestic industries either in terms of the material injury or serious injury standard, and the assessment reports, for better or worse, would constitute some sort of self-initiated survey of any injury suffered by Korean industries because of trade liberalization. In respective trade remedy investigations, investigating authorities and domestic industries may be tempted to refer to the discussions in the assessment reports either in the applications, submissions and arguments. How much weight would and should be accorded to the discussions in these self-initiated and self-prepared reports is not entirely clear. It is, however, safe to say that discussions and analyses contained in such reports may potentially be utilized and referenced in various trade remedy investigations by the Korea Trade Commission, the investigating authority of Korea.

On the other hand, the fact that the Act clearly imposes an obligation on the government to take remedial action in cases where an assessment report shows that domestic industry has been harmed, a resulting investigation and imposition of trade remedy action may trigger accusations of protectionism from other contracting parties. The neutrality and fairness of the investigation may also be vulnerable to such criticism if a measure follows the release of an implementation assessment report. So, an implementation assessment report, useful as it may be, could still pose legal implications with respect to Korea's implementation of its obligations under the WTO Agreements and FTAs.

Similar situations may also arise with respect to investment issues and disputes. If a measure is taken by a governmental agency against foreign investors after the issuance of an implementation assessment report, foreign investors and their governments may cast a suspicious eye on Korea's intention behind the measure. After all, the measure is taken at that point as a result of the release of the report and accompanying demand by domestic constituents. The genuine intent of the measure would inevitably be challenged. This may then lead to disputes under BITs and FTAs. The fact that the government is actually preparing a document with a lot of legal implications under international trade law and international investment law has been largely ignored in the course of introducing this new Act.

② Provision of Assistance to Domestic Industries

The imposition of obligations on the government to provide assistance to certain domestic industries based on the outcome of an implementation assessment report (or independently from such a report) also raises an important legal question.[75] As is well known, provision of support to these industries may directly implicate the WTO SCM Agreement and FTAs which regulate or prohibit such provision of targeted assistance to domestic industries.[76] The SCM Agreement and FTAs do not include clauses that exempt such government assistance from scrutiny.[77] Therefore, any provision of statutory assistance may lead to a possible violation of international obligations assumed by Korea under such treaties. Viewed from this perspective, it does not seem prudent to include provisions with a strong mandate to support domestic industries. If it simply remains a piece of political rhetoric,[78] the provisions may not trigger controversies. If, however, the provisions are given serious consideration and are considered as requiring the government to explore various ways to support domestic industries and if such support is actually provided, other countries may take issue with Korea.

Also, within the context of providing support to domestic industries, the current provisions of the Act seem to indicate the possibility of adjusting the provisions of trade agreements if necessary.[79] Since unilateral adjustment is not feasible, this should mean an "amendment" of trade agreements. An amendment of treaty text can only be made possible through discussions and agreement between contracting parties. Practically speaking, it is almost unthinkable that the other contracting party would agree to the amendment of the provisions of a trade agreement at Korea's request so that the latter can provide assistance to its own domestic industries as required by the Act. This scheme, therefore, could be illusory. If unilateral action is taken without going through the stipulated amendment procedure, such action may well lead to a violation of trade agreements, such as FTAs.

③ Principle of Interpretation

In terms of legal aspects, the inclusion of a principle of interpretation applicable to trade agreements also merits careful scrutiny.[80] As noted above, the Act stipulates that interpretation of trade agreements should always be conducted in a way that preserves the economic interest of Korea. To the extent that this provision mandates interpretation that best serves Korea's trade interest and that this interpretation does not find a place in the general principles of treaty interpretation as codified in Article 31 of the Vienna Convention on the Law of Treaties, an argument for the violation of the agreements will be raised. While it is unambiguous that this declaration of interpretation principle cannot be sustained before international tribunals,[81] the existence of such a provision may encourage domestic industries to invoke it when a particular line of interpretation favors their interest. According to the prevailing jurisprudence of Korea, the reviewing domestic court would have to abide by the domestic statute in such circumstances.[82]

④ Counter-measures

Finally, the Act also allows the government to take unilateral retaliatory action against another country if implementation of the trade agreement is not faithful or if that country otherwise violates the trade agreement. While the provision is phrased in permissive terms, if action is taken under this provision, it may well lead to controversy concerning possible violation of various provisions of the WTO Agreements and FTAs. For instance, the WTO Agreements and FTAs are regarded as having so-called "self-contained regimes"[83] and the resolution of disputes can only be achieved through their dispute settlement mechanisms.[84] If no counter-measures are taken under the provision, the Act may overcome the scrutiny under the present jurisprudence of international trade law. Considering the strong language contained in the Act and the circumstances surrounding the enactment of the Act, it is more likely than not that the government would have to face a demand from domestic constituents and from the National Assembly to resort to the provision when needed. Again, as long as this provision is explicitly stipulated, the reviewing court would have to apply it over any contradictory provisions contained in the relevant trade agreements.[85]

vi) Application of the FTA Implementation Act to Korea-US FTA

With the respective inauguration of their new administrations, Korea and the United States agreed to begin re-negotiation of the Korea-US FTA that went in to effect on March 15, 2012 for a possible amendment of the agreement. The basic contour of the re-negotiation became clear after the summit meeting between the Presidents Moon and Trump in June 2017. Among others, the investment chapter of the Korea-US FTA emerged as a hot topic because this chapter was one of the deal breaker issues up to the last minute of the original negotiations in early 2007. The negotiation for the amendment was completed in September 2018, and the amended FTA went into effect Jan. 1, 2019.

A new legislation (FTA Implementation Act) that was adopted in the aftermath of the Korea-US FTA was not supposed to apply to the bilateral FTA (due to the problem of retrospective application) that triggered the legislation in the first place but is now ready to apply to an amended one because it was done in 2018.

In retrospect, fierce political controversies over the original Korea-US FTA during the 2007-2011 period evidenced the need to introduce a domestic statutory framework that governs the entire life span of an FTA. As a result, it introduces various procedural requirements for the Korean government agencies and the Korean National Assembly to follow during a full cycle of an FTA — that is, from a decision to initiate negotiations for an agreement, to the conclusion of an agreement, and even to the implementation of a concluded agreement,[86] which is unprecedented in previous Korean legislation and practice concerning treaty negotiation and conclusion.

According to the relevant provisions of the Act, any trade agreement with a comprehensive market opening purpose *and* to be subject to National Assembly's consent to ratification under Article 60, paragraph 1 of the Constitution is covered by the Act.[87] At the same time, any agreement that may significantly affect the national economy *and* to be subject to the "consent" requirement under Article 60, paragraph 1 is also covered by the Act. Such being the case, an amendment of an existing FTA (such as Korea-US FTA) can be found to fall under the category of the "trade agreement" eligible to be regulated by the Act, (i) if it leads to a comprehensive market opening effect, *or* (ii) if it otherwise affects the national economy significantly, *and* (iii) it is subject to the ratification "consent" requirement by the National Assembly under the Constitution. Considering the possibly significant impact of the Korea-US FTA on the Korea's national economy and the emotional importance attached to the agreement, these statutory requirements were easily satisfied with respect to the re-negotiation of the agreement in 2018. So, unlike the original negotiation of the Korea-US FTA in 2007-2001 the amended Korea-US FTA became subject to the scrutiny and monitoring by the National Assembly under the Act.

This then means that any changes in the investment chapter (Chapter 11) as a result of the amendment of the Korea-US FTA is also subject to the stringent requirements under the Act for a long time after the completion of the re-negotiation in 2018. It is possible that even after the conclusion of the re-negotiation and entry into effect of the amended Korea-US FTA, the government will continue to have to maintain dialogue with the National Assembly and the domestic interest groups in this regard until 2028. Such dialogue will certainly provide opportunities to re-assess and re-evaluate the agreement from the perspective of maximizing the national interest of Korea. The practical problem is that a treaty, once concluded or amended, is difficult to be re-opened for amendment. So, the domestic dialogue, even if it manages to generate consensus on specific topics or issues, will hardly be able to find its way into the text of the agreement. To the extent that discussions and dialogue in the post-amendment period do not lead to a tangible outcome, they may well lead to on-going domestic controversies and repeated frustration.

The amendment in 2018 was not conventional, and most treaties are not re-opened for amendment once concluded. What transpired at that time was a rather unexpected consequence of the surge of anti-globalization and unconventional trade policy of the then Trump administration. Even if amendment of a treaty is contemplated from time to time, it is usually suggested after the application of the treaty for a sufficient period of time, so that reliable data is accumulated that may justify adjustment of the terms of the treaty. An amendment proposal after only a five-year application for a highly complex and controversial trade agreement such as Korea-US FTA was unusual, if not entirely unthinkable.

Such being the case, under normal circumstances it is neither reasonable nor practical that contracting parties of a treaty contemplate an amendment in abstract or in advance, in the absence of a compelling reason. Although specific numbers are not readily available, few, if any, FTAs out of 400-plus FTAs concluded so far have been amended in the middle of their lifespan. Amendment or adjustment of an FTA at the discretion or desire of one party is arguably detached from reality. This realization of the treaty practice brings our attention to the basic formula of the Act. As noted above, the Act is premised upon the impractical notion that an FTA is subject to a continuous review and is open to a possibility of adjustment or amendment. This basic notion of the Act does not seem to reflect practice or reality.

This scheme then exposes the amended Korea-US FTA to constant assessment by the legislature, and most importantly to a continuing possibility of and pressure for further amendment. In this process, attention by the legislature and domestic interest groups will be directed at certain sensitive issues, including the investment chapter. In other words, investment chapter will continue to be a "hot" topic in the future. A perennial scrutiny of the investment chapter of the Korea-US FTA will then affect investment chapters of other FTAs (perhaps, pressure will mount to force other investment chapters to follow suit after the Korea-US FTA) and negotiation of investment chapters of new FTAs and texts of new BITs. So, the application of the Act has the potential to affect or even change the existing dynamics of the investment arbitration and investment agreements involving Korea.

Opening the texts of the Korea-US FTA to an amendment was a critical development for Korea given the possible economic consequences from such changes. At the same time, it has also brought long-lingering consequences for the application and implementation of the investment agreements, be it FTAs or BITs, of Korea.

vii) FTA Interpretation: Korean Supreme Court's View

In a recent dispute involving local governments' measures to impose a bi-weekly close-down requirement for large-size retailer shops, the Korean Supreme Court basically held for the local governments, the defendants in the dispute.[88] This case was brought by owners of large retailers,[89] who are subject to the bi-weekly mandatory close-down requirement of the local governments at issue (the "measure). Under the requirement, these stipulated Super Supermarkets (SSMs) are ordered to close down their shops twice a month. The measure at issue was an implementation, on the level of respective local governments, of the enabling act (*Act on the Development of Distribution Service Business of 2013*: the "Act"), and its enforcement decree (*Enforcement Decree of the Act on the Development of Distribution Service Business*: the "Enforcement Decree").

The plaintiff SSMs (more specifically, Lotte Shopping, E-Mart, Home Plus, etc.) argued that the ordinances of the local governments pronounced under the Act and the Enforcement Decree violate Korean Administrative Law principles (*i.e.*, abuse of discretion and disproportionate regulation), the WTO's GATS and the Korea-EU FTA (*i.e.*, regulation not authorized in the schedules of specific commitments applicable to services trade).[90] As the measure attempts to regulate retail distribution service provider operating in the Korean market, and as one of the plaintiffs is owned by an EU corporation (Home Plus), the dispute referred to the schedules of specific commitments of the GATS and the Korea-EU FTA.

The local governments at issue, the defendants, are various district offices of the Seoul Metropolitan City Government. The defendants issued respective ordinances following the enactment of the Act and the Enforcement Decree in 2013. The purpose of the Act and the Enforcement Decree was to maintain "good order in the distribution service industry," "health right of the employees working in the distributions service industry," and "the co-prosperity of the large corporation and SMEs," to name a few.[91] In particular, the Act authorizes the heads of respective local governments to impose a close-down requirement not exceeding twice a month.[92] The local governments thus adopted their respective ordinances mandating two close-downs per month for SSMs operating within their jurisdiction.

In a nutshell, the objective of the Act, Enforcement Decree and the ordinances is to protect the small retailers who stand to lose sales due to the penetration and expansion of the large retail shops, some of which are Korean and others foreign. Thus, the legal scheme aims to protect the interest of the SMEs in the retailing industry from the fierce competition caused by large retailers. It has been argued that the new scheme will ensure even distribution of wealth of the society. Arguably, no one would challenge the noble cause of equality in society, but the issue is whether such a measure is compatible with the Korean Administrative Law and international agreements that Korea has concluded.

In the proceeding of the Seoul Appeals Court, the plaintiffs prevailed: the court decided that the ordinances of the local governments constituted violation of Korean Administrative Law principles because they constituted abuse of discretion on the part of the agency and a disproportionate burden on certain corporations in the industry. In addition, the court also found that the measure constituted a violation of the GATS and the Korea-EU FTA because of a deviation from the schedules of specific commitments that Korea has submitted.

In its decision of November 10, 2015, however, the Supreme Court of Korea reversed the decision of the Seoul Appeals Court on both counts and remanded the case back to the lower court for reconsideration. In the decision, the Supreme Court held that the challenged ordinances are within the discretion of the local governments as empowered by the Act and the Enforcement Decree[93] and that they manage to maintain the conflicting interest between those regulated and that of the society at large.[94] Thus, the Supreme Court found them to be compatible with the Administrative Law principles requiring "reasonable regulation" by a governmental agency.

With respect to the issue of possible violation of international trade agreements, the Supreme Court basically held that as international agreements these cited trade agreements create rights and obligations *only* for the contracting parties (*i.e.*, governments of the contracting parties).[95] According to the court, the plaintiffs, as corporations, do not possess the right to bring legal action before the Korean domestic court based on the trade agreements at issue.[96] The court thus basically dismissed the claim of the plaintiffs to the extent that it referred to trade agreements without reaching the merit: that is, whether or not the said measure constituted a violation of schedules of specific commitments. So, in a sense, in this high-profile dispute attracting attention from the European Union and the United States, the Supreme Court managed to avoid addressing the difficult issue of evaluating the measures from the perspective of the international obligations assumed by Korea through trade agreements. Based on this decision, the Supreme Court remanded the case back to the lower court for further consideration.

All in all, the finding of the Supreme Court may arguably be a correct interpretation of the Korean Administrative Law principles. It is not entirely clear, however, whether the judgment can also be found to be consistent with the general understanding of treaty obligations imposed on Korea. The plaintiffs were arguably not attempting to exercise their rights under the trade agreements, a situation that the Supreme Court refers to in its judgment. Rather, it seems that the plaintiffs were invoking GATS and the Korea-EU FTA in an effort to point out that the legislative instruments and enforcement decrees should be interpreted in a way that is consistent with the obligations under international agreements. If that is the case, it may not be entirely appropriate to dismiss the issue simply because the plaintiffs were alluding to or relying upon treaties.

According to the rationale of the Supreme Court, only governmental agencies can cite Korea's trade agreements in domestic court proceedings as only the government can exercise the right under the agreements. Otherwise, the Korean courts will be able to hear a claim of violation of trade agreements only when the plaintiff before the Korean court is somehow a foreign sovereign government who is a contracting party of an agreement; this is highly unlikely because the foreign government will probably proceed to the WTO or FTA dispute settlement proceedings, if it believes that a Korean measure is somehow in violation of a trade agreement. So, the interpretation of the nature of an obligation of trade agreements of Korea, as pronounced by the Korean Supreme Court in this judgement, would render trade agreements virtually unreachable or unchallengeable by interested parties. This understanding would lead to an odd conclusion. The conclusion apparently would not dovetail with the provision of the Korean Constitution that stipulates that "treaties concluded and promulgated according to the Constitution shall possess the same legal effect as domestic law."[97]

As a matter of fact, regardless of the issue of "standing," the issue raised by the plaintiffs was whether the measure could be found to be compatible with major trade agreements. Arguably, the Court is obligated to review the issue and render a judgment on it.

In conclusion, the Korean Supreme Court's judgment of November 10, 2015 pronounced important jurisprudence in an important dispute. While the final outcome of the judgment may be appropriate and correct, its disposition and discussion of Korea's obligation of trade agreements and how Korean courts address this issue in domestic court proceedings may remain vulnerable to continuing criticism. Similar issues will continue to be raised in Korean domestic courts as the web of trade agreements is becoming more complex both in terms of quantity and in quality. The judgment of November 2015 in fact raises more questions and issues when new disputes involving trade agreements are brought to the review of the Korean courts.

viii) Continuing Disputes at the WTO

Korea's practice of international law in the field of international economic sector continued to be active even after the conclusion of FTAs with major trading partners. In particular, since 2012 when the FTAs with the United States and EU were concluded, Korea has been involved in multiple disputes at the WTO. So far Korea has participated in 21 disputes as a complainant 19 disputes as a respondent and 139 as a third-party participant. Among the 21 disputes it participated in as a complainant the majority of the disputes concentrate on trade remedy measures in particular on US Anti-Dumping measures. The other areas where Korea involved as a complainant relates to safeguard measures.

The first case, *United States — Anti-Dumping and Countervailing Measures on Large Residential Washers from Korea* (DS464), involved the Anti-Dumping and countervailing duty imposition by the United States against Korean residential washers. This case proceeded to the panel stage in 2014. WTO's Dispute Settlement Body (DSB) established a panel on January 22, 2014, wherein Brazil, Canada, China, the European Union, India, Japan, Norway, Thailand and Turkey participated as third parties. A panel was composed on June 20, 2014. Korea submitted its First Written Submissions on September 24, 2014, and the United States made its First Written Submission on November 26, 2014, respectively. The panel circulated its report on March 11, 2016. The case continued in the Appellate body and the Appellate Body Circulated its report on 7 September 2016. An Arbitration Proceeding under Article 21.3 (C) and the award of the Arbitrater was circulated on 13 April 2017 determining the reasonable period of time to be 15 months expiring on 26 December 2017.

United States — Anti-Dumping Measures on Certain Oil Country Tubular Goods from Korea (DS488) concerned anti-dumping duty imposition by the United States against special steel products from Korea. On December 22, 2014, Korea requested consultations with the United States regarding certain anti-dumping measures on oil country tubular goods (OCTG) from Korea and the investigation methodology underlying such measures. The DSB established a Panel on 25 March 2015. On 13 July, the parties agreed on the composition of the panel. The panel was expected to issue its report to the parties before the end of 2016, however, due to the resignation of the Chair of the panel the parties agreed on a new Chair and the panel proposed to issue its report to the parties by June 2017. Nevertheless, the panel did not issue its report to date. On 14 November 2017, the panel report was finally circulated. The report was adopted on 12 January 2018.

United States — Anti-Dumping Measures on Stainless Steel Plate in Coils and Stainless Steel Sheet and Strip from Korea (DS179) case relates to two separate Anti-Dumping measures involving stainless stell plate in coils and stainless steel sheet and strips in coils. On 30 July 1999, Korea requested consultation with the United States alleging that several errors were made by the US in the determination and calculation of Anti-Dumping margines which are inconsistent with the obligations of the United States under the provisions of the Anti-Dumping Agreement and Article VI of GATT 1994. The Dispute Settlement Body Established a panel at its meeting held on 19 November 1999. On 24 March 2000, the panel was composed and circulated its final report on 22 December 2000. The report of the panel was adopted by the DSB at its meeting of 1 February 2001. On 10 September 2001, the United States announced that it had implemented the recommendation of the DSB on 1 September 2001 and Korea acknowledged the implementation at the same meeting.

The Korea — Anti-Dumping Duties on Pneumatic Valves from Japan (DS504) case relates to Anti-Dumping measures imposed on valves from pneumatic transmission from Japan. In this case Japan claimed that the measures are inconsistent to Articles 1, 3.1, 3.2, 3.4, 3.5, 4.1, 6.5.1, 6.9, 12.2 and 12.2.2 of the Anti-Dumping Agreement and Article VI of the GATT 1994. The DSB established a panel at its meeting on 4 July 2016. The panel was composed on 29 August 2016 and the chair of the panel informed the DSB that the panel expected to issue its final report to the parties in the second half of 2017. However, the panel report was issued on 12 April 2018 and the Appellate Body report was adopted on 10 September 2019.

The Korea — Import Bans, and Testing and Certification Requirements for Radionuclides (DS495) case relates measures in

Table 1. Status of WTO Disputes of Korea

A. Korea as Complainant: 17 case(s):

	Case Name	The Other Party
1	United States— Anti-Dumping Duties on Imports of Colour Television Receivers from Korea(DS89)	US
2	United States — Anti-Dumping Duty on Dynamic Random Access Memory Semiconductors (DRAMS) of One Megabit or Above from Korea(DS99)	US
3	United States — Anti-Dumping measures on Stainless Steel Plate in Coils and Stainless Steel Sheet and Strip from Korea(DS179)	US
4	United States — Definitive Safeguard Measures on Imports of Circular Welded Carbon Quality Line Pipe from Korea(DS202)	US
5	Philippines — Anti-Dumping Measures Regarding Polypropylene Resins from Korea(DS215)	Philippines
6	United States — Continued Dumping and Subsidy Offset Act of 2000(DS217)	US
7	United States — Definitive Safeguard Measures on Imports of Certain Steel Products(DS251)	US
8	United States — Countervailing Duty Investigation on Dynamic Random Access Memory Semiconductors (DRAMS) from Korea(DS296)	US
9	European Communities — Countervailing Measures on Dynamic Random Access Memory Chips from Korea(DS299)	EU
10	European Communities — Measures Affecting Trade in Commercial Vessels(DS301)	EU
11	European Communities — Aid for Commercial Vessels(DS307)	EU
12	Japan — Import Quotas on Dried Laver and Seasoned Laver(DS323)	Japan
13	Japan — Countervailing Duties on Dynamic Random Access Memories from Korea(DS336)	Japan
14	United States — Use of Zeroing in Anti-Dumping Measures Involving Products from Korea(DS402)	US
15	United States — Anti-Dumping measures on corrosion-resistant carbon steel flat products from Korea(DS420)	US
16	United States — Anti-Dumping and Countervailing Measures on Large Residential Washers from Korea(DS464)	US
17	United States — Anti-Dumping Measures on Certain Oil Country Tubular Goods from Korea(DS488)	US

B. Korea as Respondent: 16 case(s):

	Case Name	The Other Party
1	Korea — Measures Concerning the Testing and Inspection of Agricultural Products (DS3)	US
2	Korea — Measures Concerning the Shelf-Life of Products(DS5)	US
3	Korea — Measures concerning Bottled Water(DS20)	Canada
4	Korea — Laws, Regulations and Practices in the Telecommunications Procurement Sector(DS40)	EC
5	Korea — Measures concerning Inspection of Agricultural Products(DS41)	US
6	Korea — Taxes on Alcoholic Beverages(DS75)	EC
7	Korea — Taxes on Alcoholic Beverages(DS84)	US
8	Korea — Definitive Safeguard Measure on Imports of Certain Dairy Products(DS98)	
9	Korea — Measures Affecting Imports of Fresh, Chilled and Frozen Beef(DS161)	US
10	Korea — Measures Affecting Government Procurement(DS163)	US
11	Korea — Measures Affecting Imports of Fresh, Chilled and Frozen Beef(DS169)	Australia
12	Korea — Measures Affecting Trade in Commercial Vessels(DS273)	EC
13	Korea — Anti-Dumping Duties on Imports of Certain Paper from Indonesia(DS312)	Indonesia
14	Korea — Measures Affecting the Importation of Bovine Meat and Meat Products from Canada(DS391)	Canada
15	Korea — Import Bans, and Testing and Certification Requirements for Radionuclides(DS495)	Japan
16	Korea — Anti-Dumping Duties on Pneumatic Valves from Japan(DS504)	Japan

See WTO Disputes by member, *available at* https://www.wto.org/english/tratop_e/dispu_e/dispu_by_country_e.htm (last visited May 7, 2020).

relation to a) import bans on certain food products; b) additional testing and certification requirements regarding the presence of certain radionuclides; and c) a number of alleged omissions concerning transparency obligations under the SPS Agreement. The alleged measures were adopted by Korea after the accident at the Fukushima Daiichi nuclear power plant in March 2011. Japan claimed that the measures are inconsistent with Articles

2.2, 2.3, 4, 5.1, 5.2, 5.5, 5.6, 5.7, 5.8, 7, and 8, paragraphs 1 and 3 of Annex B, and paragraphs 1(a), 1(c), 1€ and 1(g) of Annex C, of the SPS Agreement and Article XXIII:1 of the GATT 1994. The DSB established a panel at its meeting on 28 September 2015 and the panel was composed on 8 February 2016. The chair of the panel informed the DSB that the panel expected to issue its final report to the parties in June 2017. And on 29 May 2017, the chair of the panel informed the DSB that, due to the complex procedural and factual nature of the case as well as schedule conflicts, the panel expected to issue its final report to the parties in early October 2017. Yet, the issuance of the panel report was delayed to 22 February 2018. The Appellate Body report was adopted on 11 April 2019.

(2) China's FTA Implementation: Unique Situations[98]

Sometimes, FTA implementation and compliance may be constrained by the central-local protectionism. An increasing level of local power due to democratization is a new trend in many economies of Asia Pacific. In this practical environment, if a local government feels that the implementation of certain provisions is not conducive to its economic growth, it may be unwilling to genuinely enforce such provisions in its local territory. A typical example would be a local government's lax enforcement of environmental and labor commitments under FTAs. Attention should be paid among APEC economies to establishing an operative and effective implementation mechanism that is based on a cooperative spirit between central and local governments.

In 2001, China acceded to the WTO, and just before this event, China became a participating state of the Bangkok Agreement. Starting from the year 2002, China initiated its FTA policy and signed and implemented many RTAs or CEPAs with ASEAN, Singapore, Pakistan, New Zealand, Chile, Peru, Costa Rica, Hong Kong, Macau, Korea, Chinese Taipei and what not. In addition, more FTA negotiations are progressing.

In China, FTAs are considered as an executive agreement. No ratification therefore is needed. After a RTA is signed, it undergoes some administrative procedures to fulfill the requirements of the RTA. The pre-implementation preparation requires the active involvement of all government agencies concerned. Therefore, implementation of RTAs in China is subject to the approval by the State Council followed by the notice of the Ministry of Finance. Many administrative regulations need to be formulated for the implementation of an FTA in such areas including the general administration of customs, quality control, supervision, inspection, quarantine, lifting restrictions on the market access, and the national treatment to foreign entities. These regulations enacted by the State Council and ministries are ranked lower compared to the constitution and basic law.

FTA implementation in China is largely operated by the customs offices. Customs at every port in China are subordinate bodies to the General Customs Administrations (AQSIQ and CCPIT). These administrations have full control over every provincial and local customs. There might be challenges in implementing FTAs by other FTA partners. Since the implementation involves various government agencies and businesses, the continued task of coordination and cooperation is inevitable. In practice, most troubles or disputes are related to the difference between applied rate and expected rate of tariffs. If one party makes a different interpretation of a treaty commitment from the interpretation made by the other side, tariffs applied could be different from what traders might have expected. Sometimes, it may occur that a customs office may occasionally levy an erroneous rate of duty by a simple mistake. Imported goods might be declared using the wrong HS code or without a certificate of origin under an FTA. All these incidents may lead to impediments to FTA implementation.

Having traced common causes of such implementation problems, China made various efforts in collaboration with other parties of RTAs or through domestic coordination: (i) strengthening the pre-implementation mechanism, a mechanism to prepare for the implementation based on adequate discussions among eleven ministries; (ii) cooperating with counterpart economies of RTAs, (iii) human resource trainings, and (iv) promoting the benefits of RTAs. Workshops for traders have been organized at the provincial and local levels to help them make better use of RTAs. Ministry of Commerce set up an RTA website to disseminate information. Online inquiry services (fta.mofcom.gov.cn) were established. Through these efforts, RTAs have been implemented smoothly.

Speaking of general impacts of RTAs on trade, approximately one fourth of China's foreign trade has been liberalized through FTA implementation as of the end of 2011. Trade between China and its FTA partners is increasing faster than the rate of increase of China's total foreign trade. A key measurement to assess impact of FTA implementation is the utilization ratio of FTAs. Seen from the utilization ratio of RTAs implemented by China over the period of 2009 to 2011, the utilization ratio of China-ASEAN FTA is slowly gaining momentum. China-Pakistan FTA is utilized relatively well. On the other hand, the utilization of China-Chile FTA remains very low, except in 2007 when the ratio was around 27% due to the trade of copper. As the tariff for copper was adjusted to 0% in 2008, the utilization ratio has dropped since then. The China-Peru FTA was implemented in 2010, and it seems that there is a time lag between reduction of tariffs and responses from traders. It is expected that the ratio would increase along with the realization of tariff concessions. The China-Costa Rica FTA was implemented in 2011. The ratio is quite low since the agreement entered into force in August. The China-Hong Kong CEPA has been utilized at a stable level. It shows that the impact of implementation of RTAs remained almost the same, considering that some years have passed since the implementation date.

The utilization ratio depends on several factors: level of market access in FTA concession list, margin of preference between FTA rates and MFN rates, rules of origin to FTA, sectoral competitiveness, and time. Thanks to efforts to improve

Table 2. Utilization Ratio of RTAs implemented by China

RTA	Utilization Ratio (%)		
	2009	2010	2011
China-ASEAN FTA	9.6	11.9	13.9
China-Pakistan FTA	30.1	28.3	36.4
China-Chile FTA	1	2.1	3
China-New Zealand FTA	23	22.4	26.4
China-Peru FTA		0.7(March-December)	2.1
China-Costa Rica FTA			0.0035(August-December)
CEPA with Hong Kong	7.9	7.2	7.3
CEPA with Macao	1.7	6.8	7.4
ECFA			3.3
APTA	6.25	6.56	6.49

Table 3. Total value of RTA Certificates of Origin issued by AQSIQ and CCPIT

RTA	2011	
	Value (USD)	Increase rate compare to 2010(%)
China-ASEAN FTA	29.1 billion	59.7
China-Singapore FTA	214.1 million	10.6
China-Pakistan FTA	2.7 billion	37.7
China-Chile FTA	8.6 billion	32.9
China-New Zealand FTA	127.3 million	11.4
China-Peru FTA	1.8 billion	10.6
China-Costa Rica FTA	115.3 million	
ECFA	1.51 billion	
APTA	10.79 billion	31.3

public awareness for RTAs, total value of RTA certificates of origin issued by AQSIQ and CCPIT has increased year by year.

In order to fully utilize FTAs, rules need to be simplified, clear and operational. Parties to the trade agreements need to cooperate with each other to ensure a smooth implementation of the rules. Each party should take responsibility and contact each other directly and properly to deal with any problems. In addition, parties need to work jointly to promote the benefit of RTAs. It would be a good idea to establish an RTA export advisory mechanism to promote the benefits of RTAs and to disseminate information in an effective and accurate manner.

i) Local Governments as Key Decision Makers in China

Although the Chinese approach toward treaties seems to be close to the dualistic approach, it is impossible to define whether China follows monism or dualism. The State Council, China's cabinet, has the power to conclude treaties and agreements, which can be made in the name of the People's Republic of China (PRC), the PRC Government, or a department in the PRC Government. The Standing Committee of the National People's Congress (NPC) decides to approve or abolish treaties and 'important' agreements. Also, the NPC is in charge of examining where there is any violation. FTAs are not subject to this NPC examination, and FTAs do not need the consent of the PRC.

In general, treaties do not automatically become part of national law in China, and domestic implementing legislation needs to be enacted. Implicitly, the rank of the treaty is at the same level of the laws made by the relevant government authorities. Treaties made in the name of states have the same ranking as basic laws. Treaties made in the name of central governments could be equivalent to administrative regulations which are decrees issued by the central government. Treaties concluded in the name of government departments could be equivalent to ministerial rules.

Then what is the hierarchy between domestic law and international law at the same level? Many laws adopted at various levels contain the rule that "if any international treaty concluded or acceded to by the PRC contains provisions differing from those in the XXX laws of the PRC, the provisions of the international treaty shall apply, unless those provisions are the ones on which the PRC has declared reservations." Does this mean that international rules prevail over domestic law? It is hard to say that this is the general rule of hierarchy. Therefore, without such a built-in provision on hierarchy, every question on hierarchy becomes controversial.

In practice in China, there are three modalities to solve the problem: transformation into domestic law through legislation (dualistic style of solution), implementation through administrative measures, and direct application without legislation (monistic solution). First, the transformation style has two types: transformation by a special national legislation and incorporation into national law by an amendment. The former type is used when there is no pre-existing domestic law. Transformation of the WTO Agreements into domestic laws could be the example. Second, international agreements made between governments are usually implemented by the government or department directly through administrative measures. Third, treaties dealing with rights and duties of individuals may apply directly without legislation.

Speaking of FTA implementation in China, FTAs are considered to be international agreements that do not require congressional approval and are thus implemented through administrative measures. This means that FTAs are not regarded as "treaties" and cannot be directly applied in China. They do not confer rights and duties upon any individual and cannot be enforced by courts in China. It is obvious that FTAs do not take a high position in the Chinese legal system.

To compare the implementation process of the FTAs in several key economies of APEC, in China and Singapore, the parliament has little control over the implementation from the very beginning to the ratification and even the conclusion of FTAs. The power of enforcement is almost exclusively in the hands of the executive branch. In such unitary state economies, the central government holds many powers under the constitution, and any power not explicitly bestowed to the local government belongs to the central government. As a consequence, the central government can easily make international law in that it has a decisive power in many aspects.

Another aspect is that there is a close relationship between the state and industries in East Asia. States are providing a variety of assistance to companies other than subsidies. When a subsidy is determined as violating international obligations by an international tribunal, as occurred in the WTO double remedy case (Anti-Dumping duties and countervailing measures)[99] on Chinese products, the Chinese government tends to enforce the relevant provisions under the international agreement. In this sense, international tribunal decisions have an impact on domestic implementation of treaty obligations in China.

Implementation and compliance may also be constrained by the central-local protectionism. Most of East Asian countries are unitary states, but an increasing level of local power is a new trend. Although China is formally a unitary state, something akin to a *de facto* federalism is in place in China. In practice, it is a hierarchical political system in which the activities of the government are divided between the provinces and the center. Each level of government makes final decisions in certain fields. The provinces have primary responsibility over the economy and even politics within their jurisdictions. In this regulatory environment, if a local government feels that the implementation of certain provision is not conducive to its economic growth, it may not enforce such a provision in its territory. Given that it is local governments that provide many subsidies and aids to enterprises and that have much at stake in preserving IPR-infringing enterprises, it may easily occur that local governments are unwilling to implement international commitments made by the central government. Lax local enforcement of environmental and labor commitments under FTAs may also occur.

The last point is about nationalism. Occasionally, governments have launched so-called "trade wars" based on the nationalism sentiment. This tendency also provides fuel for undue retaliation. At any rate, it is true that domestic "rule of law" culture matters a lot in implementing FTA obligations. It is truer that congressional supervision and democratic accountability rarely exist. Attention should be paid among APEC economies to establishing an operative and effective implementation mechanism that is based on a cooperative spirit and better rule of law culture.

ii) China's Active Participation in the WTO Dispute Settlement Proceedings

As of May 31, 2020, China has participated in 54 disputes as a direct participant and in 140 disputes as a third party. Among the 54 disputes that China was involved in as a party, China was the complainant in 15 disputes, while it was the respondant in 39 disputes. Among the 15 disputes China has been involved in as a complainant, the majority of the disputes involve Anti-Dumping measures. From the disputes it can be observed that the majority of the cases in which China has been involved relates to trade in goods.[100] From the overall disputes that China has been involved in nearly half of the disputes relate to trade remedy measures. Regarding parties, most of the cases in which China has actively participated involves the US, EU and Canada. From the 15 disputes that China has participated as a complainant 10 of the disputes are with the United states while the remaining five are with the EU. In general, given its recent admission to the WTO as compared to other frequent users of the dispute settlement mechanism, China's involvement in the dispute settlement mechanism is quite significant.

Table 4. Status of WTO Disputes of China (as of May 2020)

A. China as Complainant: 15 Cases

	Case Name	The Other Party
1	United States — Definitive Safeguard Measures on Imports of Certain Steel Products (DS252)	US
2	United States — Preliminary Anti-Dumping and Countervailing Duty Determinations on Coated Free Sheet Paper from China (DS368)	US
3	United States — Definitive Anti-Dumping and Countervailing Duties on Certain Products from China (DS379)	US
4	United States — Certain Measures Affecting Imports of Poultry from China (DS392)	US
5	European Communities — Definitive Anti-Dumping Measures on Certain Iron or Steel Fasteners from China (DS397)	EU
6	United States — Measures Affecting Imports of Certain Passenger Vehicle and Light Truck Tyres from China (DS399)	US

	Case Name	The Other Party
7	European Union — Anti-Dumping Measures on Certain Footwear from China (DS405)	EU
8	United States — Anti-Dumping Measures on Shrimp and Diamond Sawblades from China (DS422)	US
9	United States — Countervailing Duty Measures on Certain Products from China (DS437)	US
10	United States — Countervailing and Anti-Dumping Measures on Certain Products from China (DS449)	US
11	European Union and Certain Member States — Certain Measures Affecting the Renewable Energy Generation Sector (DS452)	EU
12	United States — Certain Methodologies and their Application to Anti-Dumping Proceedings Involving China (DS471)	US
13	European Union — Measures Affecting Tariff Concessions on Certain Poultry Meat Products (DS492)	EU
14	United States — Measures Related to Price Comparison Methodologies (DS 515)	US
15	European Union — Measures Related to Price Comparison Methodologies (DS 516)	EU

B. China as Respondent: 39 Cases

	Case Name	The Other Party
1	China — Value-Added Tax on Integrated Circuits (DS309)	US
2	China — Measures Affecting Imports of Automobile Parts (DS339)	EC
3	China — Measures Affecting Imports of Automobile Parts (DS340)	US
4	China — Measures Affecting Imports of Automobile Parts (DS342)	Canada
5	China — Certain Measures Granting Refunds, Reductions or Exemptions from Taxes and Other Payments (DS358)	US
6	China — Certain Measures Granting Refunds, Reductions or Exemptions from Taxes and Other Payments (DS359)	Mexico
7	China — Measures Affecting Trading Rights and Distribution Services for Certain Publications and Audiovisual Entertainment Products (DS 362)	US
8	China — Measures Affecting Trading Rights and Distribution Services for Certain Publications and Audiovisual Entertainment Products (DS 363)	US
9	China — Measures Affecting Financial Information Services and Foreign Financial Information Suppliers (DS372)	EC
10	China — Measures Affecting Financial Information Services and Foreign Financial Information Suppliers (DS373)	US

	Case Name	The Other Party
11	China — Measures Affecting Financial Information Services and Foreign Financial Information Suppliers (DS378)	Canada
12	China — Grants, Loans and Other Incentives (DS387)	US
13	China — Grants, Loans and Other Incentives (DS388)	Mexico
14	China — Grants, Loans and Other Incentives (DS390)	Guatemala
15	China-Measure Related to the Exportation of Various Raw Materials (DS394)	US
16	China-Measure Related to the Exportation of Various Raw Materials (DS395)	EC
17	China — Measures Related to the Exportation of Various Raw Materials (DS398)	Mexico
18	China — Provisional Anti-Dumping Duties on Certain Iron and Steel Fasteners from the European Union (DS407)	EU
19	China-Certain Measures Affecting Electronic Payment (DS413)	US
20	China — Countervailing and Anti-Dumping Duties on Grain Oriented Flat-rolled Electrical Steel from the United States (DS414)	US
21	China — Measures concerning wind power equipment (DS419)	US
22	China — Definitive Anti-Dumping Duties on X-Ray Security Inspection Equipment from the European Union (DS425)	EU
23	China — Anti-Dumping and Countervailing Duty Measures on Broiler Products from the United States (DS427)	US
24	China — Measures Related to the Exportation of Rare Earths, Tungsten and Molybdenum (DS431)	US
25	China — Measures Related to the Exportation of Rare Earths, Tungsten and Molybdenum (DS432)	EU
26	China — Measures Related to the Exportation of Rare Earths, Tungsten and Molybdenum (DS433)	Japan
27	China — Anti-Dumping and Countervailing Duties on Certain Automobiles from the United States (DS440)	US
28	China — Certain Measures Affecting the Automobile and Automobile-Parts Industries (DS450)	US
29	China — Measures Relating to the Production and Exportation of Apparel and Textile Products (DS451)	Mexico
30	China — Measures Imposing Anti-Dumping Duties on High-Performance Stainless Steel Seamless Tubes (HP-SSST) from Japan (DS454)	Japan
31	China — Measures Imposing Anti-Dumping Duties on High-Performance Stainless Steel Seamless Tubes (HP-SSST) from the European Union (DS460)	EU
32	China — Anti-Dumping Measures on Imports of Cellulose Pulp from Canada (DS483)	Canada

	Case Name	The Other Party
33	China — Measures Related to Demonstration Bases and common Service Platforms Programmes (DS489)	US
34	China — Tax Measures Concerning Certain Domestically Produced Aircraft (DS501)	US
35	China — Export Duties on Certain Raw Materials (DS508)	US
36	China — Duties and other Measures concerning the Exportation of Certain Raw Materials (DS509)	EU
37	China — Domestic Support for Agricultural Producers (DS511)	US
38	China — Tariff Rate Quotas for Certain Agricultural Products (DS517)	US
39	China — Subsidies to Producers of Primary Aluminium (DS519)	US

See WTO Disputes by member, *available at* https://www.wto.org/english/tratop_e/dispu_e/dispu_by_country_e.htm (last visited May 7, 2020).

iii) China's Utilization of Trade Influence

Korea's deployment of the THAAD anti-missile system of the United States in Korean territory in late 2016 has raised a serious diplomatic controversy between Korea and China. In retaliation, China has imposed unilateral economic sanctions against Korea. The most drastic measure by China is the restriction or prohibition of tourism by its nationals destined for Korea. This measure is causing significant economic losses for Korea.

While this measure is not codified in law or regulation, nor is there a clear official governmental directive in this respect, the totality of circumstances canvassing all circumstantial evidence indicate that a governmental measure can be found under the prevailing jurisprudence of the WTO Agreements. As this measure affects trade in services (tourism and travel related services), the measure can implicate WTO's GATS.

The measure apparently violates China's obligation under its Schedules of Specific Commitments, in particular Mode 2 of tourism and travel related services, as China has not attached any conditions or reservations for this sector and for this mode. Consequently Article XVI (market access) and XVII (national treatment) appear to have been violated by China. Likewise, the

Chinese measure also appears to violate various provisions of the General Obligation of GATS, most notably the most favored nation treatment obligation of Article II.

Under the facts available at the moment, the Chinese measure at issue seems to have difficulty in satisfying the legal threshold of successfully invoking the General Exceptions defense of Article XIV or Security Exceptions defense of Article XIV *bis*. So, all in all, under the circumstances, China's restriction and prohibition of its tourists regarding their travel to and tourism in Korea seem to indicate China's possible violation of legal obligations under GATS.

(3) Japan's FTA Implementation: Faithful application with Increasing Dissatisfaction

All in all, Japan has faithfully implemented its obligations udner FTAs. Japan's implementation does not violate relevant provisions of FTAs on the surface. The written covenants of FTAs have been implemented. Nonetheless, the counterparts of Japan have not been so satisfied with the the level of market liberalization of the Japanese domestic market. This dissatisfaction has been largely triggered by the allegedly constant NTBs in the Japanese market. Many of the alleged NTBs do not constitute a violation of provisions of FTAs. At least, it is not entirely clear whether Japanese government's measures constitute a violation of FTAs. Rather, trading partners realize that that their original expectation is not met or their products and service providers face invisible and hidden barriers in the Japanese domestic market.

As such, one of the major issues facing Japan's trading partners in negotiating and formulating FTAs with Japan is how to identify and address NTBs. As the conventional DSMs are not able to address the NTBs properly, the demand for a new type of DSM has been on the increase.

Table 5. Status of WTO Disputes of Japan (as of May 2020)

A. Japan as Complainant: 23 case(s):

	Case Name	The Other Party
1	United States — Imposition of Import Duties on Automobiles from Japan under Sections 301 and 304 of the Trade act of 1974 (DS6)	US
2	Brazil — Certain Automotive Investment Measures(DS51)	Brazil
3	Indonesia-Certain Measures Affecting the Automobile Industry(DS55)	Indonesia
4	Indonesia-Certain Measures Affecting the Automobile Industry(DS64)	Indonesia
5	United States- Measure Affecting Government Procurement (DS95)	US
6	Canada-Certain Measures Affecting the Automotive Industry(DS139)	Canada
7	United States — Anti-Dumping Act of 1916 (DS162)	US
8	United States — Anti-Dumping Measures on Certain Hot-Rolled Steel Products from Japan (DS184)	US
9	United States — Continued Dumping and Subsidy Offset Act of 2000 (DS217)	US
10	United States — Sunset Review of Anti-Dumping Duties on Corrosion-Resistant Carbon Steel Flat Products from Japan (DS244)	US
11	United States — Definitive Safeguard Measures on Imports of Certain Steel Products (DS249)	US
12	United States — Measures Relating to Zeroing and Sunset Reviews (DS322)	US
13	European Communities-Tariff Treatment Certain Information Technology Products(DS376)	EC
14	Canada-Certain Measures Affecting Renewable Energy Generation Sector (DS412)	Canada
15	China — Measures Related to the Exportation of Rare Earths, Tungsten and Molybdenum (DS433)	China
16	Argentina — Measures Affecting the Importation of Goods (DS445)	Argentina
17	China — Measures Imposing Anti-Dumping Duties on High-Performance Stainless Steel Seamless Tubes (HP-SSST) from Japan (DS454)	China
18	Russian Federation — Recycling Fee on Motor Vehicles (DS463)	Russia
19	Ukraine — Definitive Safeguard Measures on Certain Passenger Cars (DS468)	Ukraine
20	Korea — Import Bans, and Testing and Certification Requirements for Radionuclides(DS495)	Korea
21	Brazil — Certain Measures Concerning Taxation and Charges(DS497)	Brazil

	Case Name	The Other Party
22	Korea — Anti-Dumping Duties on Pneumatic Valves from Japan(DS504)l	Korea
23	India — Certain Measures on Imports of Iron and Steel Products(DS518)	India

B. Japan as Respondent: 15 case(s):

	Case Name	The Other Party
1	Japan-Taxes On Alcoholic Beverage (DS8)	EC
2	Japan-Taxes On Alcoholic Beverage (DS10)	Canada
3	Japan-Taxes On Alcoholic Beverage (DS11)	US
4	Japan — Measures Affecting the Purchase of Telecommunications Equipment(DS15)	EC
5	Japan — Measures Concerning Sound Recordings(DS28)	US
6	Japan — Measures Concerning Sound Recordings(DS42)	EC
7	Japan — Measures Affecting Consumer Photographic Film and Paper(DS44)	US
8	Japan — Measures Affecting Distribution Services(DS45)	US
9	Japan-Measures Affecting Imports of Port(DS66)	EC
10	Japan — Procurement of a Navigation Satellite(DS73)	US
11	Japan — Measures Affecting Agricultural Products(DS76)	EC
12	Japan — Tariff Quotas and Subsidies Affecting Leather(DS147)	EC
13	Japan — Measures Affecting the Importation of Apples(DS245)	US
14	Japan — Import Quotas on Dried Laver and Seasoned Laver(DS323)	Korea
15	Japan — Countervailing Duties on Dynamic Random Access Memories from Korea(DS336)	Korea

See WTO Disputes by member, *available at* https://www.wto.org/english/tratop_e/dispu_e/dispu_by_country_e.htm (last visited May 6, 2020).

3. Key Characteristics of Bilateral DSMs in East Asia

This work aims to discuss various aspects of dispute settlement mechanisms contained in the Free Trade Agreements (FTAs) concluded by East Asian countries. The number of FTAs has surged dramatically in East Asia recently including, most notably, the Korea-China FTA and the China-Australia FTA. These FTAs all contain dispute settlement proceedings of various sorts so as to resolve trade and investment disputes between the contracted parties. The dispute settlement proceedings contained in East Asian countries' FTAs largely follow, in their form, the basic format of such proceedings found in FTAs concluded in other parts of the world such as those signed by the United States and the European Union.

But, at their core, specific contents and operating mechanisms of these East Asian countries' FTAs are distinct in nature from those in other regions, such as the US-led FTAs. Likewise, the practice surrounding the operation of dispute settlement proceedings in East Asian FTAs shows their own uniqueness. These unique characteristics contained and found in East Asian FTAs' dispute settlement proceedings sometimes exert a positive impact on the implementation of the FTA obligations, but they sometimes entail negative consequences on full implementation of the obligations as well.

While individual FTAs are negotiated and concluded in East Asia, few studies have been conducted to look into the uniqueness of East Asian FTAs' dispute settlement proceedings including both their strengths and weaknesses in an analytical manner. Rather, usually simple introductions have been offered of the provisions of dispute settlement proceedings for a particular FTA. This fragmented approach has failed to offer an analysis of dispute settlement proceedings of various FTAs in a comparative and horizontal manner, so as to help governments understand why and how the dispute settlement proceedings of East Asian countries' FTAs are the same as or different from other FTAs with non-East Asian states.

This structural mismatch harbors a possibility that prospective disputes between East Asian countries under applicable FTAs may not be resolved as efficiently as possible, failing to achieve the stated objectives of the dispute settlement proceedings. Such in-depth, multi-dimensional analyses will also enable states to kickstart more meaningful discussions of how to improve dispute settlement proceedings in the context of the FTAs of East Asian countries. Simply copying the proceedings developed and adopted by western countries may not always be appropriate for the management and settlement of disputes between Asian countries.

This work aims to discuss these issues and provide useful implication at this juncture. As the FTAs are spreading fast in this region, it is time to consider these structural issues of dispute settlement mechanism and suggest new elements to be contained in dispute settlement proceedings of East Asian countries' FTAs.

4. Commonalities of Bilateral DSMs in East Asia

The DSMs of the three countries share commonalities in essence. The attached table in the annex showing DSMs in the FTAs of Korea, China and Japan indicates that DSMs included in the FTAs of the three countries indeed share commonalities. This is the outcome of the reality that DSMs of FTAs have been largely copied from each other and reproduced as necessary. Such being the case, while there are differences and discrepancies among various FTAs, they also share strong commonalities. The national varitions, at least as regards DSMs, are relatively small in number.

5. National Variations

At the same time, among various DSMs of FTAs concluded by three countries, there are national variations as well. The three countries' unique variations are underlined in the table attached in the annex.

1) Korea

Korea's approach to DSMs is quite flexible depending on the other party to the FTA. In some FTAs, Korea adopts a roster system by which candiates of panelists are elected in advance. In other FTAs, no such roster is adopted. In response to the demand or request from the other party, Korea seems to be ready to accommodate DSMs of various sorts in response to the request from the other party. This reflects Korea's assmuption that DSMs of FTAs will rarely be used. But in fact, as noted earlier the likelihood of DSMs of FTAs being utilized has arguably increased recently.

Korea is also mindful of identifying and addressing NTBs, as it has experienced difficulties with NTBs for a long time. In that respect Korea is the more flexible among the three, in terms of experimenting with new DSMs. Korea and China introduced an NTB-specific mediation procedure in their FTA of 2015.

2) Japan

Japan's DSMs are largely homogeneous. There do not seem to be significant differences among the DSMs adopted by Japan in its FTAs. This shows Japan's ability to impose its own designs and architecture in terms of DSMs in its negotiations of FTAs. Japan is said to be conservative in its choice of DSMs, as Japan's DSMs are quite conventional and stable. ISDS proceedings are also quite conventional, by following traditional forms of ISDS proceedings.

3) China

China's DSM's also show a signifcant level of consistency. China also seems to believe that the DSMs in the FTAs will be rarely utilized in the future. As such, China shows relatively little interest in developing DSMs in its FTAs. In bilateral trade relations, China seems to be more confident in utilizing its own economic and diplomatic influence to resolve a dispute as opposed to utilzing the DSMs.

6. Utilization of the Bilateral DSMs

Bilateral DSMs have not been used by either of the three countries. It seems increasingly the case, however, that the likelihoold of resorting to these DSMs, whether these three countries like it or not, is increasing rapidly, as the FTAs become more complex and intertwined with other non-trade issues such as labor or environment than the previous ones. This means that FTA-specific issues are on the rise which again means that FTAs' DSMs will be the only vehicle that can deal with these new trade issues.

7. Systemic Problems and Weaknesses

At the same time, there are systemic problems and weaknesses in the DSMs of the three countries' FTAs. First of all, there is no secretariat that can handle the logistical aspects of a dispute. It is therefore difficult for the parties to advance their disputes through FTAs' DSMs. The three countries need to consider establishing infrastructure that can deal with logistical problems. Secondly, the pool of experts is also limited although the three countries have accumulated economic power over the years. Their economic development and trade volume, however, have not seen a proportionate development in trade law expertise and human resources.

8. Suggestions for Reform

In order to introduce DSMs that can better deal with disputes in the area of trade and investment in the future, it is imperative that the three countries become more enlightened regarding the importance of DSMs. They should be aware that the DSMs and active utilization of the system are critical for taking advantage of any FTA. The traditional stance to focus on tariff reductions and to disregard DSMs in FTAs as something subsidiary or ornamental should be re-considered for future FTAs of three countries. Specific areas of reform will be further discussed in the next chapter.

Endnotes

1. One scholar commented that "law is a form of cultural expression and is not readily transplantable from one culture to another without going through some process of indigenization. French law is as much a reflection of the French culture as Russian law is a reflection of Russian culture." Mary Ann Glendon, *et al., Comparative Legal Traditions in A Nutshell* (West Group, 1982), p. 10.

2. George C. Christie, *Some Key Jurisprudential Issues of the Twenty-First Century*, 8 Tul. J. Int'l & Comp. L. (2000), p. 217.

3. This is particularly the case, because under the Korea-US FTA, a "measure" is defined as any law, regulation, procedure, requirement, or practice. *See* art. 1.4 of the Korea-US FTA, *supra* note 37. For instance, in the FTA, the United States underscores the importance of the low-key guidance of the Financial Supervisory Service, a financial watch dog in Korea, in the context of financial regulation. *See* Annex 13-B, Section D of the Korea-US FTA.

4. For instance, although Japan has adopted various legislation in the 1993-2005 period for the restructuring of the corporate governance in Japan in response to increasing outside criticism of the Japanese culture, the opinions are quite divided as to the true extent and impact of such reform. *See generally* Luke Nottage, *Nothing New in the (North) East?: Interpreting the Rhetoric and Realithy of Japanese Corporate Governance*, CLPE Research Paper 1/2006, Vol. 2, No. 1 (2006).

5. For instance, the USTR states in the Korea section of its 2008 National Trade Estimate Report on Foreign Trade Barriers (2008 NTE) that lack of transparency in the financial regulatory system is problematic for all US financial services providers. Improvement in notice and comment periods is necessary for foreign suppliers to have input into the regulations that will be imposed upon them. It also states that "some US investors have raised concerns about a lack of transparency in investment related regulatory decisions, including by tax authorities, raising concerns about possible discrimination." Office of the United States Trade Representative, 2008 NTE, p. 343; *see also* Bruce Klingner and Anthony B. Kim, *Economic Lethargy: South Korea Needs a Second Wave of Reforms*, ackgrounder No. 2090, Heritage Foundation (Dec. 7, 2007), p. 1 ("Current performance

reflects a strengthening recovery, but inconsistent economic policies, lingering systemic deficiencies, and increasingly competitive rivals create significant long-term challenges."), p. 5 ("Layers of regulations and lingering government intervention persist, and the lack of economic opportunities, particularly among young people, encourages further frustration.").

6. A similar concern is also raised when it comes to Japan as well. Obviously, there should be difference between the situation in Korea and the situation in Japan, but there is a constant concern that regulation in Japan also is not so transparent as to cause barriers to trade. Scott Bradford, *An Analysis of a Possible Japan-US Free Trade Agreement* at *New Asia-Pacific Trade Initiatives Conference,* hosted by Japan Economic Foundation and PIIE (Nov. 27, 2007), pp. 21-22.

7. *Minister Regrets Negative Sentiment on Foreign Capital, Korea Times* (Feb. 16, 2006).

8. Christie, *supra* note 2, p. 219.

9. Moshe Cohen, The Burden of Proof in Comparative and International Human Rights Law: Civil and Common Law Approaches with Special Reference to the American and German Legal Systems, *93 Am. J. Int'l L.* (1999), pp. 556, 557.

10. *See* 2008 NTE, p. 344.

11. Article 27 of the 1969 Vienna Convention on the Law of the Treaties provides that:

Internal law and observance of treaties

A party may not invoke the provisions of its internal law as justification for its failure to perform a treaty...

12. *See, e.g.,*Panel Report, *United States — Sections 301-310 of the Trade Act of 1974*, WT/DS152/R (Dec. 22 1990), footnote 652; Appellate Body Report, *United States– Import Measures on Certain Products from the European Communities*, WT/DS165/R (Jul. 17, 2000), para 6.81; Panel Report, *Mexico-Measures Affecting Telecommunications Services,* WT/DS204/R (Apr. 2, 2004), para. 7.244.

13. Joseph J. Norton, "Banking law in the Twenty-First century" in Ross Cranston (ed.), *Making Commercial Law* (Clarendon Press, 1997), pp. 297, 302.

14. Indeed, a quite drastic change is currently taking place. As recently as in 2003, one observer commented that Korea seems to be a country which has in place one of the most restrictive stance toward the legal market opening. *See* Misasha Suzuki, *The Protectionist Bar Against Foreign Lawyers in Japan, China and Korea: Domestic Control in the Face of Internationalization*, 16 Columbia Journal of Asian Law (2003), pp. 385, 403. But, Korea has just adopted an "American-style" law school system which is now scheduled to open in March 2009, mainly in an effort to deal with fast changing legal environment and legal services market opening.

15. For instance, in Japan there is continuing tension between the new le-

gal regime and the traditional legal regime. The former has been affected by the influx of Anglo-American jurisprudence while the latter is based on the notion that not only profit maximization, but also other social values need to be taken into account when it comes to corporate governance. *See* Luke Nottage, *supra* note 4, p. 1.

16. *See, e.g.*, Panel Report, *Japan - Measures Affecting Consumer Photographic Film and Paper*, WT/DS44/R (Apr. 22, 1998), paras. 10.43-10.46.

17. *See* Anna Fifield, "OECD tells S Korea to Reform Economy," *Financial Times* (Jun. 20, 2007).

18. *See* Panel Report, *United States-Countervailing Duty Investigations on Dynamic Random Access Memory Semiconductors from Korea*, WT/DS296/R (Feb. 21, 2005) (US-DRAMs), paras. 7.6-7.8, 7.49-7.50, 7.59; Panel Report, *European Communities-Countervailing Measures on Dynamic Random Access Memory Chips from Korea*, WT/DS299/R (Jun. 17, 2005) (EC-DRAM), paras. 7.38-7.46.

19. *See US-DRAMs*, paras. 7.9, 7.48, 7.54, 7.57-7.58, *EC-DRAMs*, paras. 7.23-7.30.

20. Ministry of Foreign Affairs and Trade, *High Ranking Level Negotiations for Remaining Issues to Be Held in Seoul* (Press Release 07-175) (Mar. 26, 2007).

21. *See* Section B, Chapter 11 of the Korea-US FTA.

22. Annex 11-B, 3 of the Korea-US FTA defines indirect expropriation as "an action or a series of actions by a Party has an effect equivalent to direct expropriation without formal transfer of title or outright seizure."

23. The White House, *State of the Union Address 2015*, *available at* https://www.whitehouse.gov/sotu (last visited Jul. 10, 2015).

24. *See* The White House, *On Trade, Here is What the President Signed into Law*, *available at* https://www.whitehouse.gov/blog?page=1 (last visited Jul. 10, 2015).

25. Ministry of Foreign Affairs of the People's Republic of China, *Foreign Ministry Spokesperson Hong Lei's Regular Press Conference* (Apr. 17, 2015), *available at* http://www.fmprc.gov.cn/mfa_eng/xwfw_665399/s2510_665401/t1255670.shtml (last visited Jul. 10, 2015).

26. Ministry of Foreign Affairs of the People's Republic of China, *Speech on the Belt and Road Initiative by Chinese Ambassador Qu Zhe* (Chinese Ambassador to Estonia) (Apr. 13, 2015), *available at* http://www.fmprc.gov.cn/mfa_eng/wjb_663304/zwjg_665342/zwbd_665378/t1254259.shtml (last visited Jul. 10, 2015).

27. In Japan, for example, there is continuing tension between the new legal regime and the traditional legal regime. The former has been affected by the influx of Anglo-American jurisprudence while the latter is based on the notion that social values - not only profit maximization - need to be taken into account when it comes to corporate governance; *see* Luke Nottage, *supra* note 4, p. 1.

28. *See*, *Japan-Measures Affecting Consumer Photographic and Paper*, WT/DS44/R (Apr.22, 1998) (*Japan-Film*), paras. 10.43-10.46.

29. *See* Panel Report, *China-Measures Affecting the Protection and Enforcement of Intellectual Property Rights (China-IPR),* WT/DS362/R (Jan. 26, 2009), paras. 7.499–7.501. China argued that the WTO panel should not illegitimately intrude into an issue that is reserved to the domestic jurisdiction.

30. *China-IPR, supra* note 29.

31. *See* Panel Report, *China- Measures Related to the Exportation of Various Raw Materials* (WT/DS394/R), paras. 7.110, 7.356.

32. *Ibid.*, paras. 7.265, 7.365, 7.378-7.405.

33. *Ibid.* para. 7.111.

34. In fact, the Appellate Body also expressed this principle in *US-Gasoline*, addressing Article XX(g), in which it stated that:

WTO Members have a large measure of autonomy to determine their own policies on the environment (including its relationship with trade), their environmental objectives and the environmental legislation they enact and implement. So far as the WTO concerns, that autonomy is circumscribed only by the need to respect the requirements of the General Agreement and the other covered agreements.

Appellate Body Report, *United States — Standards for Reformulated and Conventional Gasoline* (WT/DS2/AB/R) / DSR 1996: I, 3, (May 20, 1996), p. 30.

35. *See* SCM Agreement, art. 31.

36. *See* Panel Report, *Canada — Measures Affecting the Export of Civilian Aircraft*, WT/DS70/R (Aug. 20, 1999), para. 9.119.

37. *See* Part IV & art. 31 of the SCM Agreement.

38. *See* World Trade Organization Negotiating Group on Rules, *Draft Consolidated Chair's Texts of AD and SCM Agreements*, TN/RL/W/213 (Nov. 30, 2007), Part IV of the SCM Agreement.

39. In the case of Korea, such an effort originally started with the financial and regulatory reform following the 1997 financial crisis, and it has been further expedited during the course of the FTA negotiations with the United States.

40. For instance, in a speech during his visit to Harvard University on Dec. 10, 2003, Premier Wen Jiabao stated that the traditional Chinese culture, both extensive and profound, starts far back and runs a long, long course.

More than 2,000 years ago, there emerged in China Confucianism, represented by Confucius and Mencius, Taoism represented by Lao Zi and Zhuang Zi, and many other theories and doctrines that figured prominently in the history of Chinese thought, all being covered by the famous term "the masters' hundred schools."From Confucius to Sun Yat-sen, the traditional Chinese culture presents many precious ideas and qualities, which are essentially populist and democratic.

For example, they lay stress on the importance of kindness and love in human relations, *on the interest of the community, on seeking harmony without uniformity and on the idea that the world is for all.*Especially, patriotism as embodied in the saying, "Everybody is responsible for the rise or fall of the country"; the populist ideas that "people are the foundation of the country" and that "people are more important than the monarch"; the code of conduct of "Don't do to others what you don't want others to do to you"; and the traditional virtues taught from generation to generation: suffer long and work hard, diligence and frugality in household management, and respect teachers and value education.All these have played a great role in binding and regulating the family, the country, and the society [emphasis added].

See also, generally, Alex Inkeles, "Continuity and Change: Popular Values on the Pacific Rim," *1 Stanford Journal of International Relations* (Summer/Fall 1998). With respect to the role of culture and societal traits in terms of trade disputes, *see Panel Report, Japan-Measures Affecting Consumer Photographic Film and Paper , WT/DS44/R* (Mar. 31, 1998), paras. 10.43-10.46.

41. Treaties only bind "governments" of the contracting states and do not reach private entities. *See Draft Articles on Responsibility of States for Internationally Wrongful Acts*, adopted by the ILC at its fifty-third session (2001), Official Records of the UN General Assembly, Fifty-sixth session, Supplement No. 10 (A/56/10), chp.IV.E.1 (2 Y.B. Int'l L. Comm'n 31, 84-85, U.N. Doc. A/56/10) (Nov. 2001), arts. 5 & 8. The Commentary to the 2001 ILC Draft Articles is *available at* http://untreaty.un.org/ilc/texts/instruments/english/commentaries/9_6_2001.pdf (last visited Mar. 1, 2013). This rule also applies to the WTO dispute settlement proceedings as the covered agreements only apply to "measures" by a Member. *See* Articles 3.3, 4.4 of the DSU. Increasingly, however, it is becoming more difficult to say which is which. In quite a few countries, the governmental sector and the private sector are sometimes closely intertwined to undertake joint tasks or achieve common policy objectives. This phenomenon is more observable in the economic sector where governmental entities and private players are more closely working together to ride out financial storms. This topic has recently flared up in the context of China. China has traditionally maintained a hoard of State-Owned Enterprises (SOEs) in key economic sectors, which account for almost half of the GDP according to some recent statistics. The question then is how these unique enterprises should be treated in terms of treaty application and implementation. Particularly vigilant here is the United States who puts this issue as one of the priorities in its negotiations of various agreements including TPP that may have relevance to China.

42. *See* ILC Commentary, *supra* note 41, p. 43.

43. Commentaries play a vital role in clarifying the meaning of the ILC Draft Articles. *See* Daniel Bodansky and John R. Crook, "Symposium: The ILC's State Responsibility Articles," 96 *American Journal of International Law* (Oct, 2002), pp. 773, 789.

44. *See* ILC Commentary, *supra* note 41, p. 43.

45. *See US-DRAMs*, paras. 7.6–7.8, 7.49–7.50, 7.59; *EC-DRAMs*, paras. 7.38–7.46.

46. *See* FTA Implementation Act, art. 1 (Objective); Maeil Economic Daily, *Imminent Conclusion of the Largest Free Trading Bloc (TPP)* (Nov. 26, 2013), *available at* http://news.mk.co.kr/newsRead.php?year=2013&no=1189898 (in Korean)(last visited Dec. 10, 2014).

47. *See* FTA Implementation Act, arts. 7 & 8.

48. Seoul Economic Daily, *The National Assembly Passes FTA Implementation Act* (Dec. 29, 2011), *available at* http://economy.hankooki.com/lpage/politics/201112/e2011122916421196380.htm (in Korean) (last visited Dec. 10, 2014); Maeil Economic Daily, *Interview with the New Trade Minister, Taeho Bark*, (Jan. 4, 2012), *available at* http://news.mk.co.kr/newsRead.php?year=2012&no=9278 (in Korean)(last visited Dec. 10, 2014).

49. *See* FTA Implementation Act, arts. 5 to 15.

50. *See* the Yonhap News, *The Trade Treaty Conclusion Procedure Act is Carried by the Foreign Affairs and Trade Committee of National Assembly* (Dec. 1, 2014), *available at* http://www.yonhapnews.co.kr/bulletin/2011/10/25/0200000000AKR20111025194951001.HTML (last visited Dec. 21, 2014).

51. *See* the Yonhap News, *Rice Tariff Discussion under the crippled operation of the National Assembly* (Sept. 28, 2014), *available at* http://www.yonhapnews.co.kr/politics/2014/09/28/0505000000AKR20140928057600001.HTML (last visited Dec. 21, 2014); Sera Jung, *Bureaucrats monopolizes FTA negotiation... Interest groups are neglected*, the Hankyoreh Daily (Nov. 11, 2014), *available at* http://www.hani.co.kr/arti/economy/economy_general/664073.html (last visited Dec. 20, 2014).

52. *See* FTA Implementation Act, arts. 17, 20.

53. *See, e.g.*, the Agreement Establishing the World Trade Organization, art. 16, paragraph 4.

54. *See* the flow of measures in sequence required under the FTA Implementation Act as stipulated in arts. 5 to 15 of the Act.

55. This English translation has been prepared by the author. An official translation of the Act does not exist as of this writing.

56. *See* FTA Implementation Act, arts. 6, 10, 12, 13, 15.

57. *Ibid.*, art. 15.

58. *See* Korean Constitution, art. 60, paragraph 1.

59. *See* Hong-ryeul Kim, *Andrew Robb, Australian Minister for Trade and Investment, said "Australian Parliament ratifies the Korea-Australia FTA... now it's Korean National Assembly's turn,"* The Korea Economic Daily (Oct. 5, 2014), *available at* http://www.hankyung.com/news/app/newsview.php?aid=2014100574691 (last visited Dec. 21, 2014).

60. *See* FTA Implementation Act, arts. 6, 10, 12, 13, 15.

61. *Ibid.*, art. 15.

62. *Ibid.*

63. *Ibid.*, arts. 17, 20.

64. *See* FTA Implementation Act, at Addendum at art. 1. Note that this provision was amended for immediate implementation as a result of the amendment of the Government Organization Act on Mar. 23, 2013.

65. *See* the Status of FTAs of Korea at the Korean Government's website, *available at* www.fta.go.kr (last visited Dec. 20, 2014).

66. This English translation has been prepared by the author. An official translation of the Act does not exist as of this writing.

67. *See* Byeong-il Choi *et al.*, *Trade Governance: research of the mid/long-term trade strategy for becoming the advanced country*, Korea Institute for International Economic Policy (Research material no. 06-04), pp. 95-99, *available at* http://www.kiep.go.kr/skin.jsp?bid=pub_main_view&grp=publication&tabValue=1&namuSub=&mode=viewjoin&num=177338 (last visited Dec. 21, 2014).

68. It seems that so far both contracting parties seem to be making efforts to avoid using the term "amendment", apparently feeling the pressure to be flowing from opening the controversial investment chapter for negotiations and debates again. Regardless of the specific term to be used, however, if the purpose of the discussion is to change the rights and obligations already contained in the existing agreement, it would arguably constitute "amendment" within the meaning of Article 40 of the Vienna Convention of the Law of Treaties.

69. *See* FTA Implementation Act, art. 2.

70. *See* FTA Implementation Act, art. 2.

71. For instance, the TISA, a plurilateral agreement on trade in services currently being negotiated by 22 states outside the WTO framework, may also found to be a "trade agreement" within the meaning of the Act.

72. *See* Jung-eun Kim, *The ruling and the opposition parties, Mutual consent of enacting the Trade Treaty Conclusion Procedure Act...but Conflict on another re-negotiation*, The Korea Economic Daily (Oct. 13, 2011), *available at* http://www.hankyung.com/news/app/newsview.php?aid=2011101393221 (last visited Dec. 21, 2014).

73. *See* Hankyoreh Daily, *Demanding for enacting the Trade Treaty Conclusion Procedure Act* (July 5, 2006), *available at* http://www.hani.co.kr/arti/society/society_general/138712.html (last visited Dec. 21, 2014).

74. *See* FTA Implementation Act, arts. 11, 15.

75. *See* FTA Implementation Act, arts. 17, 19.

76. *See* the SCM Agreement, art. 1, 2.

77. Some of the assistance measures may be covered by Part IV of the SCM Agreement as non-actionable subsidies, but that part has been terminated as of the end of 1999.

78. *See* Byeong-il Choi *et al.*, *Trade Governance: research of the mid/long-term trade strategy for becoming the advanced country*, Korea Institute for International Economic Policy (Research material no. 06-04), pp. 96-99, *available at* http://www.kiep.go.kr/skin.jsp?bid=pub_main_view&grp=publication&tabValue=1&namuSub=&mode=viewjoin&num=177338 (last visited Dec. 21, 2014).

79. *See* FTA Implementation Act, art. 17.

80. *Ibid.*, art. 16.

81. A contracting party is precluded from justifying its violation of a treaty provision based on its domestic statutes. *See, e.g.*, Vienna Convention, art. 27. This principle has also been referred to in *Case Concerning Factory at Chorzów* (Claim for Indemnity) (The Merits) (F.R.G. v Poland), 1928 P.C.I.J. (ser. A) No. 17, pp. 4-65 (Sept., 1928); *Concerning Rights of Nationals of the United States in Morocco*, (France v. US) 1952 I.C.J. 176 (Aug. 27); Appellate Body Report, *United States - Measures Relating to Zeroing and Sunset Reviews - Recourse to Article 21.5 of The DSU By Japan*, WT/DS322/AB/RW (Aug. 18, 2009), para. 182, footnote 463; Appellate Body Report, *Canada - Export Credits and Loan Guarantees for Regional Aircraft - Recourse to Arbitration by Canada under Article 22.6 of the DSU and Article 4.11 of the SCM Agreement*, Decision by the Arbitrator, WT/DS222/ARB (Feb. 17, 2003), paras. 3.103-3.104.

82. In particular, it should be noted that Article 3 declares the superiority of this Act over other statutes in case of contradiction. Article 3 thus provides:

Article 3 (Relation to Other Statutes)

This Act first applies to the conclusion and implementation process of trade agreements before other statues.

83. *See* WTO DSU, art. 3.2.

84. *Ibid.*, art. 23.

85. *See* Korean Supreme Court, Judgment No. 2008Du17936 (Jan. 30, 2009).

86. *See* FTA Implementation Act, arts. 5 to 15.

87. *See Ibid.*, art. 2.

88. *Case Concerning Revocation of Limitation of Operating Hours for Certain Retailers*, Supreme Court of the Republic of Korea, 2015DU295 (Nov. 10, 2015), available at http://www.scourt.go.kr/supreme/news/NewsViewAction2.work?currentPage=5&searchWord=&searchOption=&seqnum=5035&gubun=4 (last visited Jan. 10, 2016) (in Korean) (hereinafter "Judgment"), p. 18.

89. Retailers with the Size of 3,000 square meters or larger. *See* Judgement, *supra* note 88, p. 4.

90. *See* Judgment, *supra* note 88, pp. 3-5, 6, 8.

91. The Act, art, 12-2.

92. *See Ibid.*

93. *See* Judgment, *supra* note 88, pp. 14-15.

94. *Ibid.*, pp. 15-17.

95. *Ibid.*, p. 17.

96. *Ibid.*

97. *See* Korean Constitution, art. 6, para. 1.

98. This section is the clarified summary of a speech made by Director Wang Yan, FTA Division, Ministry of Commerce of China.

99. Appellate Body Report, *United States-Definitive Anti-Dumping and Countervailing Duties on Certain Products from China*, WT/DS379/AB/R (Mar. 11, 2011), p. 394.

100. *See also*, Chi Manjiao, "China's Participation in WTO Dispute Settlement over the Past Decade: Experiences and Impacts," 15 *Journal of International Economic Law* (2012), pp. 29-49.

Chapter VII

Formulating Future DSMs in FTAs of East Asia

The DSMs of the three East Asian states play an important role in many respects in terms of shaping new rules in the area of the international dispute settlement mechanism. The DSMs contained in the FTAs and BITs of these three East Asian countries share the basic elements and general features of the DSMs of FTAs and BITs of other countries. Perhaps the situation may not be that different for FTAs and BITs in other countries and other regions. These DSMs contain state-to-state dispute settlement proceedings and ISDS proceedings. Depending upon specific partners of FTAs and BITs, the specific contents and natures of the provisions set forth in DSMs vary, but the three countries apparently have templates for DSMs in their respective agreements. These templates have not reached official status or the firmness of model provisions, but they do seem to have secured the status of starting points for new negotiations. It appears that these three countries make efforts to maintain their respective templates of DSMs as much as is feasible.

There are, of course, some unique aspects as well that appear in the DSMs of these three East Asian countries. In order to understand the unique characteristics of the DSMs of the three countries, it is necessary to discuss how they perceive international dispute settlement proceedings generally. With respect to international dispute settlement proceedings generally, the three countries present the following shared traits:

- Avoiding litigation as much as possible
- Cultural backgrounds viewing legal proceedings disfavorably
- Relatively under-developed legal proceedings in history
- Political sentiments toward legal issues and legal proceedings
- Relatively smaller pool of legal experts and professionals

Not surprisingly, these traits in turn affect the DSMs of FTAs and BITs that these Not surprisingly, three countries adopt. As such, unique characteristics of these three countries' DSMs in agreements are:

- Favoring WTO proceedings over FTA/BIT proceedings
- Resolving disputes amicably if at all possible
- Legal proceedings as a last resort
- Favoring a conservative approach in formulating and devising DSMs for future application
- Avoiding initiation of a legal proceeding for unclear outcome
- Underscoring national sovereignty for regulatory autonomy

1. A Need for a Creative Approach

In devising DSMs for the future, it is advised that the three countries become more creative. Up until now, the three countries have largely incorporated DSMs developed by other countries, mainly the western states. These DSMs are able to deal with some of the disputes effectively. There are, however, also disputes that cannot be dealt with effectively by the existing DSMs. These disputes require rather innovative and creative approaches by the three states. As China is able to develop its own DSMs in its FTAs, it may consider exploring and adopting DSMs with new features and contents. China's experiment, if successful, will exert a positive impact on Korea and Japan as well, two countries that are more conservative than China.

1) Reflecting Unique Aspects of East Asian Culture and Situations

In devising new DSMs, the three countries may prefer to adopt DSMs that take into consideration unique aspects of the cultural background of East Asian countries. The three countries have tended to prefer non-binding, out-of-court dispute settlements. The traditional view is also applicable to disputes between states. Legal action by one state is received rather emotionally. Sometimes the fact that legal action has been taken itself may carry weight. As such, the three countries should consider adopting DSMs where such non-binding DSMs are actively explored. This does not mean that the regular DSMs should become any weaker. Regular or ordinary DSMs where legal action is treated as something of paramount importance should also be preserved. The suggestion is that the DSMs can only be considered after trials of various non-biding DSMs.

2) Reflecting Economic Vibrance of the Region in Global Trade

It is also important that the new DSMs of the three countries equally utilize the economic dominance of the three countries in global trade. If the three countries pool their economic capitals in a way that can push DSM's development in a certain direction, that will certainly be helpful. The three states' share in the global trade, however, has not been adequately reflected in the rule making process. Nor has it been reflected in the discussion of DSMs in FTAs. The three states should now have a clearer objective about DSMs in FTAs and the course of action to achieve such objective. With proper planning and rationale, improved DSMs can be incorporated into future FTAs. Up until now, the FTAs of these three countries have mainly followed what have been already inserted into FTAs of other countries.

3) Resolving Disputes Effectively

Any DSM should be effective in resolving disputes. A legally perfect DSM may not serve the interest of contracting states if it is proven practically problematic. So, legal aspect and practical aspect should receive balanced attention. A DSM skewed one way or another may only defeat the basic objective of the DSM. Likewise, it is not wise to have a DSM and make it ineffective because of the concern of the possibility of infringement of sovereignty of contracting states. Arguably, this is what is being observed in the recent development of WTO DSM. Startled by the authority of panels and the Appellate Body, some Members are proposing to reduce the authority of panels and the Appellate Body and make the decision making process less effective. Unfortunately, ineffective DSMs would only foster mistrust in the DSMs, which would then lead to a weakening of the credibility of DSMs, which in turn translates into the collapse of multilateralism. As such, DSMs, if introduced, should be effective in all respects. It may mean loss for a particular state in a specific case. It, however, means a sustainable benefit for all states over a long period of time.

Having an effective DSM does not mean that it should be the only DSM in an FTA. There are disputes which are better suited for legally binding and effective DSM, and there are others which are better suited for non-binding, conciliaory proceeding. The two should go hand-in-hand in future FTAs. As such, non-binding DSMs should be further explored and expanded in future FTAs. The three states have inherent advantage in formulating DSMs, both binding and non-binding because of their ample experience in trade disputes over the years in many fora including the WTO DSM.

4) Overcoming Structural Problems of the Present DSMs

In this respect, the three countries may be able to overcome structural problems of the present DSM at the WTO. There are discussions to reform the DSM of the WTO. The three countries have participated in the WTO's DSM quite frequently and intensively, which has enabled the three states to be aware of the problems of the present DSM of the WTO and areas for future reform. It has however taken a long time for negotiations in this area. It is still not clear when the proposed changes will become officially accepted and effectuate amendments. In this respect the three countries can conduct their own experiments in their own FTAs. These FTAs may cover those between or among the three countries, or those between one of the three countries and other trading partners in Europe or America.

(1) Resurrection of the Same Measures Found to be WTO-Inconsistent

Obviously, for a losing member to comply with the rulings and recommendations of the DSB, the member must "withdraw" or "eliminate" the measure, or take otherwise comparable action, *before* the expiration of the Reasonable Period of Time (RPT). If the challenged measure continues for whatever reason after the lapse of the RPT, the WTO member has simply failed to comply with the rulings and recommendations of panels and the Appellate Body.

For example, Korea has been of the view that a critical date for a 21.5 dispute should be the end of the RPT. In the case of a zeroing dispute involving Japanese steel products, for example, the 11-month RPT ended on December 24, 2007, and thus the existence or consistency of a US measure in this process should be examined as of that date. Therefore, if any aspect of the challenged measures which had been confirmed by the panel and the Appellate Body to be WTO-inconsistent continued after December 24, 2007, it would simply constitute a US failure to comply with the rulings and recommendations of the DSB. In this particular zeroing dispute, the recorded evidence proves that the USDOC has continued to apply the zeroing practice in the original investigations, periodic reviews and sunset reviews *after*

December 24, 2007. The United States, therefore, has failed to implement the DSB ruling and recommendations in due course. In Korea's view, this should be dispositive in this inquiry and the panel should find for Japan.

(2) Limitations of Prospective Remedy Only

Another trait of the present WTO DSM is its adoption of the prospective remedy only approach. The DSB's recommendations and rulings are applied only in a *prospective* manner. This has been repeatedly mentioned by the WTO's Appellate Body,[1] and, in fact, in deliberating the most recent dispute involving zeroing implementation, the Appellate Body confirmed this principle again.[2] It is widely accepted that this is exactly what the complainant was seeking in this dispute. The remedy sought by this state is none other than a prospective remedy. Contrary to what some member states argue, the date of entry into customs territory does not and should not dictate whether a remedy is retroactive or prospective in the WTO dispute settlement procedure. The critical point in time should be the expiry of an applicable RPT. If a member is required to take a measure before the RPT expiry, then one could argue for an illegitimate retroactive application of a remedy. In *US-Zeroing (EC) (21.5)* the Appellate Body considered this issue and held that the benchmark to determine whether a remedy is prospective or retroactive in the context of a zeroing dispute is the date when final dumping duty liabilities are assessed as opposed to the date of entry. The Appellate Body thus stated:

> Moreover, because compliance with the recommendations and rulings of the DSB implies cessation of zeroing in the assessment of final duty liability, and in the measures that, in the ordinary course of the imposition of Anti-Dumping duties, derive mechanically from the assessment of duties, *whether the implementation is prospective or retroactive should not be determined by reference to the date when liability arises, but rather by reference to the time when final dumping duty*

liabilities are assessed or when measures that result mechanically from the assessment of duties occur. (emphasis added)[3]

In the dispute, the Appellate Body then held that the date of entry is not determinative in this inquiry, because the "impact" from the zeroing-tainted assessment continues after the RPT and because what is critical here is "the time when final dumping duty liabilities are assessed."[4] The same logic and rationale applies to other disputes and measures as well.

(3) Lengthy DSM Proceedings

Under the current DSU system, it takes a long time to resolve a WTO dispute. Especially, regarding panel procedures, the current DSU sets a limit of 9 months as the maximum time frame for a panel ruling from the date of the panel establishment. In practice, however, panel procedures generally last 12 months. This extra time is, in practice, caused by the factual and legal complexity of the cases. Moreover, delays are also a consequence of the *ad hoc* panel composition process. As a result, from the consultation to the implementation dispute, it may take even two to three years at the moment.

(4) Prolonged Implementation Period

The ultimate implementation of the losing member at the WTO DSM is the ultimate destination and the hallmark of the entire proceeding. Nonetheless, it takes a lengthy period of time for a losing member to take an implementation measure. Every case has a different implementation period, but on average the implementation period is around eight months. This period is the one between the adoption of the panel and the Appellate Body reports at the DSB and the ultimate implementation. This procedure is currently regulated by Article 21 of the DSU. Members are now critical of the fact that sometimes implementation periods are unnecessarily long.

Table 1. Actual time Spent* for Domestic Subsidy and Prohibited Subsidy Disputes at the WTO

A. Domestic Subsidy

<table>
<tr><th rowspan="2">No.</th><th rowspan="2">Case</th><th colspan="2">Consultation Request to Panel Decision</th><th colspan="2">Consultation Request to AB Decision</th></tr>
<tr><th>Date of Consultation Request</th><th>Date of Panel Report Circulation</th><th>Date of Consultation Request</th><th>Date of AB Report Circulation</th></tr>
<tr><td rowspan="2">1</td><td rowspan="2">United States — Definitive Anti-Dumping and Countervailing Duties on Products from China (DS379)</td><td>Sep 19, 2008</td><td>Oct 22, 2010</td><td>Sep 19, 2008</td><td>March 11 2011</td></tr>
<tr><td colspan="2">764D</td><td colspan="2">903D</td></tr>
<tr><td rowspan="2">2</td><td rowspan="2">Mexico — Definitive Countervailing Measures on Olive Oil from the European Communities (DS341)</td><td>Mar 31, 2006</td><td>Sep 4, 2008</td><td colspan="2" rowspan="2">N/A</td></tr>
<tr><td colspan="2">889D</td></tr>
<tr><td rowspan="2">3</td><td rowspan="2">United States — Measures Related to Shrimp from Thailand (DS343)
United States — Customs Bond Directive for Merchandise Subject to Anti-Dumping/ Countervailing Duties (DS345)</td><td>Apr 24, 2006 (DS343)
Jun 6, 2006 (DS345)</td><td>Feb 29, 2008</td><td>Apr 24, 2006 (DS343)
Jun 6, 2006 (DS345)</td><td>Jul 16, 2008</td></tr>
<tr><td colspan="2">677D(DS343)
634D(DS345)</td><td colspan="2">815D(DS343)
772D(DS345)</td></tr>
<tr><td rowspan="2">4</td><td rowspan="2">Japan — Countervailing Duties on Dynamic Random Access Memories from Korea (DS336)</td><td>Mar 14, 2006</td><td>Jul 13, 2007</td><td>Mar 14, 2006</td><td>Nov 28, 2007</td></tr>
<tr><td colspan="2">487D</td><td colspan="2">625D</td></tr>
<tr><td rowspan="2">5</td><td rowspan="2">European Communities — Countervailing Measures on Dynamic Random Access Memory Chips from Korea (DS299)</td><td>Jul 25, 2003</td><td>Jun 17, 2005</td><td colspan="2" rowspan="2">N/A</td></tr>
<tr><td colspan="2">694D</td></tr>
<tr><td rowspan="2">6</td><td rowspan="2">United States — Countervailing Duty Investigation on Dynamic Random Access Memory Semiconductors (DRAMS) from Korea (DS296)</td><td>Jun 30, 2003</td><td>Feb 21, 2005</td><td>Jun 30, 2003</td><td>Jun 27, 2005</td></tr>
<tr><td colspan="2">603D</td><td colspan="2">729D</td></tr>
</table>

<table>
<tr><th rowspan="2">No.</th><th rowspan="2">Case</th><th colspan="2">Consultation Request to Panel Decision</th><th colspan="2">Consultation Request to AB Decision</th></tr>
<tr><th>Date of Consultation Request</th><th>Date of Panel Report Circulation</th><th>Date of Consultation Request</th><th>Date of AB Report Circulation</th></tr>
<tr><td rowspan="2">7</td><td rowspan="2">European Communities — Measures Affecting Trade in Commercial Vessels (DS301)</td><td>Sep 3, 2003</td><td>Apr 22, 2005</td><td colspan="2" rowspan="2">N/A</td></tr>
<tr><td colspan="2">598D</td></tr>
<tr><td rowspan="2">8</td><td rowspan="2">Korea — Measures Affecting Trade in Commercial Vessels (DS273)*</td><td>Oct 21, 2002</td><td>Mar 7, 2005</td><td colspan="2" rowspan="2">N/A</td></tr>
<tr><td colspan="2">869D</td></tr>
<tr><td rowspan="2">9</td><td rowspan="2">United States — Subsidies on Upland Cotton (DS267)*</td><td>Sep 27, 2002</td><td>Sep 8, 2004</td><td>Sep 27, 2002</td><td>Mar 3, 2005</td></tr>
<tr><td colspan="2">713D</td><td colspan="2">889D</td></tr>
<tr><td rowspan="2">10</td><td rowspan="2">United States — Investigation of the International Trade Commission in Softwood Lumber From Canada (DS277)</td><td>Dec 20, 2002</td><td>Mar 22, 2004</td><td colspan="2" rowspan="2">N/A</td></tr>
<tr><td colspan="2">459D</td></tr>
<tr><td rowspan="2">11</td><td rowspan="2">United States — Final Countervailing Duty Determination With Respect To Certain Softwood Lumber From Canada (DS257)</td><td>May 3, 2002</td><td>Aug 29, 2003</td><td rowspan="2">May 3, 2002</td><td rowspan="2">Jan 19, 2004</td></tr>
<tr><td colspan="2">484D</td></tr>
<tr><td colspan="2">Time Spent on Average</td><td colspan="2">656D</td><td colspan="2">742D</td></tr>
</table>

B. Prohibited Subsidy

No.	Case	Consultation Request to Panel Decision		Consultation Request to AB Decision	
		Date of Consultation Request	Date of Panel Report Circulation	Date of Consultation Request	Date of AB Report Circulation
1	European Communities — Export Subsidies on Sugar Complaint by Australia (DS265) European Communities — Export Subsidies on Sugar Complaint by Brazil (DS266) European Communities — Export Subsidies on Sugar Complaint by Thailand (DS283)	Sep 27, 2002 (DS265/DS266) Mar 14, 2003 (DS283)	Oct 15, 2004	Sep 27, 2002 (DS265/DS266) Mar 14, 2003 (DS283)	Apr 28, 2005
2	Canada — Export Credits and Loan Guarantees for Regional Aircraft (DS222)	Jan 22, 2001	Jan 28, 2002	N/A	
		372D			
3	Canada — Certain Measures Affecting the Automotive Industry Complaint by Japan (DS139) Canada — Certain Measures Affecting the Automotive Industry Complaint by European Communities (DS142)	Jul 3, 1998 (DS139) Aug 17, 1998 (DS142)	Feb 11, 2000	Jul 3, 1998 (DS139) Aug 17, 1998 (DS142)	May 31, 2000
		589D(DS139) 544D(DS142)		699D(139D) 654D(DS142)	
4	United States — Tax Treatment For "Foreign Sales Corporations" (DS108)	Nov 18, 1997	Oct 8, 1999	Nov 18, 1997	Feb 24, 2000
		690D		829D	

<table>
<tr><th rowspan="2">No.</th><th rowspan="2">Case</th><th colspan="2">Consultation Request to Panel Decision</th><th colspan="2">Consultation Request to AB Decision</th></tr>
<tr><th>Date of Consultation Request</th><th>Date of Panel Report Circulation</th><th>Date of Consultation Request</th><th>Date of AB Report Circulation</th></tr>
<tr><td rowspan="2">5</td><td rowspan="2">Canada — Measures Affecting the Importation of Milk and the Exportation of Dairy Products Complaint by United States (DS103)
Canada — Measures Affecting the Importation of Milk and the Exportation of Dairy Products Complaint by New Zealand (DS113)</td><td>Oct 8, 1997 (DS103)
Dec 29, 1997 (DS113)</td><td>May 17, 1999</td><td>Oct 8, 1997 (DS103)
Dec 29, 1997 (DS113)</td><td>Oct 13, 1999</td></tr>
<tr><td colspan="2">587D(DS103)
505D(DS113)</td><td colspan="2">736D(DS103)
654D(DS113)</td></tr>
<tr><td rowspan="2">6</td><td rowspan="2">Canada — Measures Affecting the Export of Civilian Aircraft (DS70)</td><td>Mar 10, 1997</td><td>Apr 14, 1999</td><td>Mar 10, 1997</td><td>Aug 2, 1999</td></tr>
<tr><td colspan="2">766D</td><td colspan="2">876D</td></tr>
<tr><td rowspan="2">7</td><td rowspan="2">Brazil — Export Financing Programme for Aircraft (DS46)</td><td>Jun 18, 1996</td><td>Apr 14, 1999</td><td>Jun 18, 1996</td><td>Aug 2, 1999</td></tr>
<tr><td colspan="2">1031D</td><td colspan="2">1141D</td></tr>
<tr><td rowspan="2">8</td><td rowspan="2">Australia — Subsidies Provided to Producers and Exporters of Automotive Leather (DS126)</td><td>May 4, 1998</td><td>May 25, 1999</td><td colspan="2" rowspan="2">N/A</td></tr>
<tr><td colspan="2">387D</td></tr>
<tr><td colspan="2">Time Spent on Average</td><td colspan="2">618D</td><td colspan="2">812D</td></tr>
</table>

* Time Spent for Recent Subsidy Disputes
Key: Indicates case in which both a domestic subsidy and prohibited subsidy are examined.

2. Traits of New DSMs

With these considerations in mind, future DSMs of the three East Asian countries should preferably explore various new options and improve their existing DSMs. Through these efforts, the three countries will be able to lead the global community in this respect. Elements that can be considered in future DSMs are discussed below. All these traits may not be reflected in future DSMs at once, of course. Nonetheless, discussions below may show which elements need careful consideration in future discussions. Perhaps some of the elements below can be adopted earlier than others depending upon contexts of negotiations of future FTAs.

1) Activation and Diversification of Non-binding DSMs

More than anything else, the three countries are encouraged to lead the current phenomenon of the global community where non-binding DSMs are increasingly underscored and tried. The three East Asian countries have had a strong preference for and long cultural backgrounds in resorting to and applying non-binding DSMs. Based on this experience, the three countries can lead the global discussion in the future. In particular, the three countries have the particualar experience in handling disputes where the surge of different views, evolving into complaints and finally turning into disputes in the trade relations between close trading partners, turns out to be grave perils and challenges for the entire FTA or the entire bilateral trade relationship. In the case of Korea and Japan, the two countries have arguably experienced a limitation in handling complex trade disputes involving many dimensions of diplomacy and domestic politics, through a regular WTO DSM. In the case of China, bilateral trade disputes with the United States recently have also exposed the limitations of WTO DSM as well as pure diplomatic negotiation. A dispute settlement path something in-between, that is non-binding DSM such as mediation, may have turned out to be useful in this regard.

Under the current circumstances of the FTA saturation, more disputes are bound to arise no matter what, as the expectation level of each state has risen much higher than before in all trade sectors. And yet, many of the disputes stem from a lack of preparation or understanding in the course of an FTA negotiations, applications and enforcement. For these disputes, an official DSM would run the risk of undermining the spirit of the FTA. It may solve the dispute but still ruin the bilateral relationship for a long time. Even to a winning state in binding DSM, a battle was won but the war is lost. So, it may not be a wise idea for some politically or diplomatically sensitive trade disputes. On the other hand, mere diplomatic consultation may not necessarily ensure an adequate amount of pressure so that each party is forced to make a serious effort to handle the concern from the other party. States may simply end up exchanging diplomatic conversation and leaving the dispute unresolved for the future. This may also cause another serious risk of deterioration of bilateral trade relationship. If anything, a non-binding mechanism seems to offer a viable 1.5 track solution of the situation wherein the two parties can discuss and resolve a dispute efficiently and amicably. It is more serious than diplomatic consultation but less formal than legally binding litigation. As such, in certain types of disputes mediation or conciliation would serve the interests of the contracting parties of FTAs much more efficiently.

2) Shortening the Timeframe

It is critical that the three states explore DSMs that can shorten the time needed for the proceedings of DSMs in the future. Prompt resolution of disputes is indispensable for an effective system of dispute settlement. This is also one of the important criteria to revive the trust of individuals and corporations participating in the global trading regime, whether bilateral or multilateral.

3) Standing Roster of Panel

The three countries should consider adopting a system that can further judicialize the system. A more judicialized system can possibly enhance the rule of law in the long run. In that respect, the three states can consider, most importantly, a bilateral DSM in an FTA which uses a roster of panelists that is prepared and finalized in advance. Panelists will then be selected from these pre-established rosters when actual disputes arise. Enhanced predictability and stability can be ensured.

4) Assurance of Effective Remedy

In addition, any remedy from a DSM should be effective. Some of the problems stemming from the conventional prospective remedy aspects of the DSM can be addressed in future DSMs. A wider acceptance of "compensation" could be explored in this regard.

5) Identification and Resolution of NTB Disputes

Focus should be placed on the identification and resolution of NTBs as they become the core topics of trade disputes at present. The three countries have been regarded as major utilizers of NTBs by other countries (mainly Western countries) and they have also been major victims of NTBs from other countries as well. So, future DSMs should be mobilized to deal with this particular problem effectively.

6) Establishment of an Appellate Mechanism

The possibility of introducing an appellate tribunal has long been one of the priority topics in the international trade dispute and international investment arbitration discussions.[5]

At the moment, the WTO dispute settlement proceeding and some of the recent FTA dispute settlement proceedings offer rare instances of having an appellate court system in place.[6] As much as important governmental measures are challenged at investment arbitrations, states have now started to think about having another round of judicial review after the original legal proceeding.[7] The sometimes conflicting decisions and jurisprudence have indeed put many governments in a state of confusion with respect to investment agreement negotiations and implementation.[8] This state of fragmented decisions in investment arbitrations has further underscored the need to have an appellate court which may have the authority to "straighten out" any differences in jurisprudence.[9] Reflecting this increasing consensus, the Korea-US FTA have particular provisions mentioning the possibility of adopting appellate tribunals in the context of the investment arbitration to be brought by the provisions of the bilateral FTA.[10]

When Korea and the United States initiate discussions on this issue of appellate mechanism in accordance with the provisions in the Korea-US FTA in the future,[11] the following four specific issues will immediately emerge that need prompt attention: namely, how to compose an appellate tribunal; how to understand the nature of an appellate tribunal; how to define the scope of an appeal; and finally, whether to accord remand authority to the appellate tribunal. The provisions currently contained in the Korea-US FTA merely state a general intention of the two countries in an abstract way and do not suggest how that intention will be in fact carried out. It is more important that the two countries codify specific provisions that will actually work.

First, with respect to the composition of an appellate tribunal, what should be determined at first by the two countries in this regard is the format and location of the new tribunal. Should it be established on a bilateral basis within the context of a particular BIT,[12] or should it be created as a multilateral entity such as a prospective addition of an appellate tribunal to the ICSID[13] regime? Yet another question is whether the tribunal should be an *ad hoc* one or a standing one. The WTO Appellate Body's experience, a standing appellate court, may provide a useful guideline in this respect,[14] but the experience of the WTO may not necessarily be appropriate to be transplanted to investment arbitration or FTA trade dispute DSMs without any change. Obviously, there are pluses and minuses in these different approaches, which the two countries need to examine carefully.[15]

Second, a more fundamental question to be addressed by Korea and the United States in considering the future appellate mechanism is how to understand the nature of an appeal in these particular proceedings. On the one hand, the two countries may wish to form an appellate mechanism as a way to offer a second bite at the apple — *i.e.*, one more chance to be heard, before a different set of experts — to alleviate the increasing concern of the governments of the two contracting parties.[16] On the other hand, the two countries may also wish to introduce an appellate court resembling a domestic appellate court in all material respects with stronger oversight and authority over the original arbitration tribunal or panel.[17] This decision on the nature of appeal, in fact, would affect many specific segments of a prospective appellate mechanism. For instance, this second avenue would be more amenable to a standing appellate mechanism with a remand authority.[18]

Third, how the two countries will determine the "scope of appeal" also merits careful consideration. This issue relates to whether the prospective appeal should accommodate only legal issues, or both legal and factual issues.[19] Depending upon which path is adopted, the logistical burden and timeframe for an appeal may be significantly changed.[20] As can be seen from many international litigations, it is sometimes quite difficult to segregate legal issues and factual ones in actual disputes.[21] This will be particularly the case in the context of trade disputes and investment disputes where the key provisions in BITs and FTAs themselves require and envisage an in-depth evaluation of complex factual issues — issues that frequently span over a long period of time in multiple countries.[22] Future trade disputes and investment arbitrations to be brought by the investment chapter of the Korea-US FTA would be no different.

Finally, another critical question to be addressed in the early stage of these discussions between the two countries is about the so-called "remand" authority. What should an appellate tribunal do when an underlying first instance tribunal has failed to apply a proper legal standard? Can the appellate tribunal complete the analysis *de novo*? Or should it send (*i.e.*, remand[23]) the case back to the original tribunal? What if factual information on the record is lacking or insufficient?[24] This question is thus closely related to the third issue mentioned above. A decision on the introduction or non-introduction of a remand will significantly alter the dynamics and structure of an appellate proceeding.[25] This issue has also been discussed at the WTO from the early days of its creation, so the discussions there could offer a benchmark in this regard.[26] As shown in remand discussions, various attendant issues are likely to increase the timeframe of trade and investment disputes, which would in turn further increase the cost of the proceedings, another chronic concern for the parties.[27]

These are some of the key issues to be raised when Korea and the United States initiate their initial discussions or negotiations concerning appellate mechanism in accordance with the relevant provisions of the Korea-US FTA. When sincere discussions on an appellate mechanism in international trade and investment disputes are initiated, these questions and issues should be carefully examined to determine what kind of format and structure would best serve the interest of the two countries and their traders and investors. An appellate mechanism, properly established, will be able to address some of the key concerns harbored by stakeholders in the area of international trade and investment. Most importantly, an appellate mechanism will be able to facilitate and foster accumulation of jurisprudence in international trade and investment disputes.

7) Cautious Approach to Expanded Transparency

Transparency has become a new trend in the DSMs globally. The importation of the concept into DSMs of the three East Asian states needs careful contemplation, however. Transparency has been there for some time. For instance, in the investment arbitration sector, according to the ICSID Convention Article 48(5), the Centre shall not publish the award without the consent of the parties. However, the ICSID Rules Article 48(4) obliges the Centre to promptly include in its publications excerpts of the legal reasoning of the tribunal.[28] As for commercial arbitration, UNCITRAL Rules on Transparency in Treaty-based Investor- State Arbitration, which became effective on 1 April 2014, provides the obligation to publish a much broader scope of information than required in the ICSID Convention.[29]

The Korea-US FTA adopts robust transparency provisions in its investment chapter. which are considered to be innovative by any measure. The transparency provisions have been used as a yardstick in international discussions of transparency enhancement in the international arbitrations. The other side of the coin of the transparency requirement is the protection of confidential governmental information. The more transparency is enhanced, the more important the provisions protecting confidential information become. Likewise, the Korea-US FTA also underscores the importance of protecting confidential information in exchange for the introduction of the innovative transparency enhancement provisions.[30] In fact, this kind of protection of confidential information is crucial for the examination of governmental policies.[31] Most of the internal discussion papers and documents in many governments are treated as confidential. At the same time, again, the Korea-US FTA adopts quite ambitious transparency provisions for investment arbitrations.[32] So, the combination of the two juxtaposed principles could have the potential of causing conflicting situations in the actual application, which needs careful consideration when the two countries start to discuss these issues in future disputes. For example, questions may arise as to how to adjust the open hearing when necessary, how to manage the submission of two different versions (public and confidential versions), and how to define the term 'confidential information.' These questions have been extensively discussed at other forums debating transparency provisions in the investment arbitration and trade dispute context. The lessons and experiences in these forums can and should be reflected in the prospective discussions of Korea and the United States.

With respect to the holding of the open hearing, it should be noted that the open hearing principle is important for transparency purposes.[33] This is also in line with a general trend for international litigation these days involving states and treaties such as ICJ, WTO, etc.[34] The Korea-US FTA also reflects this global trend. Basically, the hearings of all trade disputes and investment arbitrations under the FTA are scheduled to be open to the public.[35] Likewise, all documents are also open to the public.[36] This is in fact contrary to the practice of Korea so far as international litigation involving its own governmental measures is concerned.[37]

Still, despite the need to enhance transparency in terms of systematic consideration, open hearings will also have practical implications. Since an open hearing is likely to further encourage the participation of interested groups, it may increase domestic political sensitivity.[38] An open hearing will also affect the utilization of foreign attorneys during the open hearing, because the general public can watch the entire litigation in real time.[39] In order to avoid any future criticism, government officials should be forced to take more active roles in defending the cases than before.

An open hearing also affects the treatment of confidential information. In fact, an ISDS proceeding will involve a great deal of confidential information during the hearing[40] and this will have practical implications for the government, whether positive or negative. Now, in the context of implementing the Korea-US FTA's transparency provisions, there are a couple of specific ways to conduct a hearing under these circumstances. By way of example, the parties may decide to have two different sessions, comprising a public session and a confidential session.[41] Likewise, a method for the open hearing may be to conduct it as a one-room session or using a closed circuit transmission to another room.[42] This also entails the question of how to treat the transcript of the hearing as well. With respect to the submission of two different versions of documents, that is, submitting the original version and public version in the case of confidential submission, the following questions may arise. One of the problems concerns the preparation of exhibits which sometimes reach tens of thousands of pages or even more.[43] Organizing confidential information of this magnitude and non-confidential information of this magnitude is also quite challenging in practice. While the respondent government has discretion in determining and designating confidential information to be protected from disclosure, it has the obligation to provide a confidential version and a non-confidential version to the tribunal, the other party and the general public.[44] Given the size of documents to be provided in trade disputes and investment arbitration, creating two different versions would put a significant logistical burden on the respondent government. Of course, all these requirements apply to both disputing parties, but given the nature of the dispute, the respondent government will have to face a disproportionate burden in this regard. The burden for the respondent government will further increase through the translation of these documents and exhibits.[45]

How to reconcile the transparency provisions with existing statutes that restrict such public disclosure is yet another remaining question to be dealt with in future discussions. As for Korea, there are several provisions in domestic statutes that specifically prohibit the provision of information to anyone in the absence of a specific extraordinary situation such as a court order to that effect.[46] In addition, with respect to the designation of confidential information, basically a wide latitude of discretion is given to the parties.[47] Therefore, under the Korea-US

FTA a party submitting the information will have the authority to determine which information is confidential.[48] Sometimes this itself becomes an issue when a governmental agency is involved. A governmental agency would have a great level of comfort if it had the authority to say what is confidential and what is not. Arguably, as long as there is no specific guideline in this regard, an obvious temptation inside a government would be to favor and explore a broader designation,[49] which would ensure that only a minimum segment of the proceeding and hearing can be shown to the public so as to minimize the public exposure of the dispute.

The official language issue also requires careful contemplation in the context of transparency enhancement and confidentiality protection. Trade disputes and investment arbitration respect the parties' agreement about the language of proceedings. However, Article 22 of the ICSID Rules limits parties' autonomy by providing that if the parties agree on any language that is not an official language of the Centre (*i.e.*, English, French and Spanish), the tribunal, after consultation with the Secretary-General, has to give its approval to the parties' agreement. The Korea-US FTA permits both English and Korean as official languages of the ISDS proceedings. Oral hearings and submissions can be done in both languages.[50] Although it is not explicitly stated, apparently simultaneous translation during the oral hearings and submissions of translated documents throughout the proceedings are being contemplated.[51] This largely reflects Korea's concerns as its official language is not English.[52] Thus, theoretically, it is possible that Korea can defend itself in investment arbitration by speaking Korean and submitting original Korean documents only.

But one needs to examine how it would work in practice. First of all, there is an inherent limitation in simultaneous translation. Simultaneous translation sometimes is unable to convey nuances accurately. All statements made during investment arbitration and trade dispute proceedings may carry significant legal meaning, so that adopting a proper term will be crucial throughout the proceedings. This is particularly the case where, as here, complex governmental policies are at issue. In this regard, attention should also be directed to the increasing instances of parties' disputes over translation differences and variations. Similar issues will also arise in document submission. It may be the case that all documents in Korean should be translated into English regardless of the provision permitting Korean to be used as an official language of the proceeding under the Korea-US FTA. Submissions and briefs would have to be prepared in English anyway. As with any other countries, in prospective disputes, it is quite likely that foreign attorneys will be hired to represent the government of Korea.[53] They would prefer English over Korean in preparing and submitting documents, regardless of the provision of the Korea-US FTA.[54] Korean government officials and witnesses may want to use Korean in preparing documents, which is indeed permitted under the Korea-US FTA, but doing so would invite the risk of inaccurate translation of the words and languages in the documents. So, again the chances are that all parties, including Korea, will end up using English after all. It is possible that the double official language provisions may well become 'moot' in actual trade disputes and investment arbitrations. The question then is how to explore introducing provisions that may actually enable the use of the Korean language in hearings and submissions as much as possible.

The current provisions of the Korea-US FTA do not address these specific practical aspects of transparency and confidentiality protection principles. Once re-discussion or re-negotiation is initiated, the two countries need to calibrate these issues and include provisions to regulate them. Similar situations may also arise to China and Japan whose languages are also not generally used in international dispute settlement proceedings.

8) Accommodating New Development in Other FTAs

In September 2015 the European Union proposed a new scheme that would change the framework of the current international investment agreements and investor-state dispute settlement proceedings (ISDS proceedings) in a significant manner.[55] The EU proposal in particular presented new ideas to amend the current ISDS proceedings. What stands out among the new ideas is the suggestion to introduce a new standing court to resolve investment disputes.[56] There have since been robust discussions in the international community and scholars regarding this suggestion of a standing investment court. Some countries have agreed to the EU proposal and adopted an investment court and appellate mechanism in their respective FTAs or BITs. Canada[57] and Vietnam[58] offer such examples. On the other hand, other countries such as Japan and the United States seem to be rather cautious, if not entirely skeptical, about this EU proposal.[59]

There are obvious merits to introducing a standing investment court as it will accord enhanced trust on the decision-making process of international investment disputes.[60] Conflict of interest among the arbitrators can also be avoided more efficiently under the new scheme. The investment court may also be more susceptible to understanding the need to preserve the legitimate policy space of sovereign governments.[61]

At the same time, there are various legal problems and questions relating to this proposal. For instance, it is not clear whether the operation and administration of an investment court is compatible with provisions of the ICSID Convention.[62] It is also questionable whether a standing court indeed stays within the general parameter of an investment arbitration.[63] In addition, to the extent the core problems of the ISDS proceedings lie in the fragmented system of the international investment agreements, and unless and until this system itself is somehow amended as a result of introducing a multilateral regime in international investment law, the introduction of the court system alone may not be able to address these problems at their core. Any contribution, if at all, should arguably be minimal or marginal. If anything, the fragmentation phenomenon can become more acute with the introduction of bilateral investment courts from agreements to agreements.

In considering introducing an investment court, all these related legal and practical issues should be contemplated at the same time. Apparently, the current proposal of the EU and ensuing global debates have not addressed these legal and practical issues in an in-depth manner. In any event, it is time for Korea, China and Japan to keep abreast of various reform proposals for international investment agreements and ISDS proceedings. The three countries' final positions will significantly affect the fate of these new negotiations, given their combined share in the global economy.

Endnotes

1. *See* Art 21.5 DSU Panel Report, *United States — Subsidies on Upland Cotton — Recourse to Article 21.5 of the DSU by Brazil*, WT/DS267/AB/RW (Jun. 20, 2008), para. 243, footnote 494.

2. The Appellate Body held in Appellate Body Report, *United States — Laws, Regulations and Methodology for Calculating Dumping Margins ("Zeroing")*, WT/DS294/AB/RW (May 14, 2009)(*US-Zeroing (EC)(21.5)*) that:

> When a reasonable period of time for implementation has been determined, Article 21.3 of the DSU implies that the obligation to comply with the recommendations and rulings of the DSB has to be fulfilled by the end of the reasonable period of time at the latest, and that the WTO-inconsistency has to cease by the end of the reasonable period of time with *prospective effect* (emphasis added)

Ibid., para. 299.

3. *US-Zeroing (EC)(21.5),* para. 309.

4. *See Ibid.*

5. While there are some review features contained in investment arbitrations, they are limited to specific instances requiring such reviews and do not constitute the conventional appeal mechanism where the legal issues of underlying tribunals' decisions are challenged. As for ICSID Convention, *see* Measures

for Review Mechanism include Rectification (art. 49(2)), Interpretation (art. 50), Revision (art. 51), and annulment (art. 52). *See also* Jaemin Lee, *Introduction of an Appellate Review Mechanism for International Investment Disputes,* 11 Transnational Dispute Management (2014), p. 12; Article 60 of *the Statute of the International Court of Justice* available at the court's website, *available at* http://www.icj-cij.org/documents/index.php?p1 = 4&p2 = 2&p3 = 0 (last visited Jun. 10, 2014) (stipulating no appellate procedure at the ICJ). Likewise, state-to-state arbitrations do not have an appellate mechanism. *See, e.g.*, Article 32.2 of *the Optional Rules for Arbitrating Disputes between Two States*, available at the PCA's website, *available at* http://www.pca-cpa.org/showpage.asp?pag_id = 1188 (last visited Jun. 10, 2014). The International Criminal Court, the International Criminal Tribunals for Former Yugoslavia, and the International Criminal Tribunals for Rwanda have appellate procedures, but these are criminal courts designed to determine personal criminal liability for certain designated international crimes. *See e.g.*, Article 81 of the Rome Statute of the International Criminal Court available at the ICC's website, *available at* http://untreaty.un.org/cod/icc/statute/romefra.htm (last visited Jun. 10, 2014).

6. *See, e.g.*, Chapter 11 of the *North American Free Trade Agreement*; Chapter 11 of the Korea-US FTA, *supra* note 37; Chapter 14 of the Korea-EU FTA, *supra* note 186, *available at* http://www.fta.go.kr/eu/info/2/ (last visited May 7, 2020).

7. The US Model BIT of 2012 includes the appellate mechanism as one of the key items of the US BITs in the future. Lee, *supra* note 5, p. 12.

8. Lee, *supra* note 5, p. 12; *See Global Trading Resource Corp. and Globex International, Inc. v. Ukrsaine*, ICSID Case No. ARB/09/11, Award of Dec. 1, 2010 ("The existing case law has thrown up no uniform approach as to the identification and respective importance of the criteria that may be resorted to by ICSID tribunals having to define an investment for the purpose of Article 25(1).").

9. *See, e.g.,* European Court of Justice, *OHIM v. Wm Wrigley Company*, ECJ Case C-191/01P (Dec. 4, 2003); European Court of Justice, *Bertelsmann and Sony Corporation of America v. Impala*, ECJ Case C-413/06P (Jul. 10, 1998); US Supreme Court, *Indiana v. Edwards*, Slip Op. 07-208 (Jun. 19, 2008); US Supreme Court, *Powerex Corp. v. Reliant Energy Service Inc*, Slip Op 05-85 (Jun. 19, 2007).

10. In this regard, there are two specific provisions discussing the possibility of the introduction of the appellate mechanism in the future. Thus, Korea-US FTA, *supra* note 37, art. 11.20, para. 12, stipulates that:

ARTICLE 11.20: CONDUCT OF THE ARBITRATION

12. If a separate, multilateral agreement enters into force between the Parties that establish an appellate body for purposes of reviewing awards rendered by tribunals constituted pursuant to international trade or investment arrangements to hear investment disputes, the Parties shall strive to reach an agreement that would have such appellate body review awards rendered under Article 11.26 in arbitrations commenced after the multilateral agreement enters into force between the Parties.

Also, Annex 11-D of the Korea-US FTA, *supra* note 6, provides that:

POSSIBILITY OF A BILATERAL APPELLATE MECHANISM

Within three years after the date this Agreement enters into force, the Parties shall consider whether to establish a bilateral appellate body or similar mechanism to review awards rendered under Article 11.26 in arbitrations commenced after they establish the appellate body or similar mechanism.

11. *Ibid.*

12. Indeed, some commentators have argued that disputing parties' own selection of arbitrators has contributed to the enhancement of qualities of review by tribunals in charge of investment disputes. Jeswald W. Salacuse, *Is There a Better Way? Alternative Methods of Treaty-Based, Investor-State Dispute Resolution*, 31 Fordham Int'l L.J. (2007), p. 168.

13. *See* ICSID Convention, Regulations and Rules, *available at* https://icsid.worldbank.org/en/Pages/resources/ICSID-Convention,-Regulations-and-Rules.aspx (last visited May 7, 2020); ICSID proceeding takes up the majority of investment arbitrations at the moment. By way of example, in 2013, 31 out of 57 disputes were filed to ICSID. See UNCTAD, *Latest developments in investor-State dispute settlement*, IIA Monitor No.1 (Apr. 2014), p. 4.

14. *See* World Trade Organization, Appellate Body Annual Report for 2012, WT/AB/18 (Apr. 9, 2013), pp. 10-12.

15. As can be seen from the rarity of the prior examples, an appellate mechanism in international dispute settlement proceedings seems to have both pluses and minuses: by way of example, while an appellate mechanism obviously helps ensure the establishment and spread of key jurisprudence, it also translates into mobilization of more time and resources to settle disputes. Also, the introduction of an appellate mechanism would mean increased complexities — both substantively and procedurally — regarding the issues being examined.

16. *See* Jaemin Lee, 'The WTO Appellate Body as a Trailblazer — Facilitation of Appellate Mechanism Discussion in Other Intenrational Courts' in Chang-fa Lo, Junji Nakagawa, Tsai-fang Chen (eds.), *The Appellate Body of the WTO and Its Reform* (Springer, 2020), p. 304.

17. *See* Article 17 of the *Understanding on rules and procedures governing the settlement of disputes* (DSU); Katia Yannaca-Small, *Improving the System of Investor-State Dispute Settlement*, OECD Working Papers on International Investment (Jan. 2006), *available at* http://www.oecd-ilibrary.org/docserver/download/5l9x0xwx5nd8.pdf?expires=1386454606&id=id&accname=guest&checksum=1A83186C8792DD1B70D3F6B173A3457A (last visited Jun. 10, 2014) , pp. 8-9.

18. *See Ibid.*, DSU, art. 17.

19. *See* DSU, art. 17.6; Mélida Hodgson, *Elements Of An Architecture For A CAFTA Appellate Mechanism*, American Bar Association Section Of International Law Fall Meeting "Towards A CAFTA Appellate Mechanism" (2009), *available at*

http://apps.americanbar.org/intlaw/fall09/ materials/HodgsonCAFTAAppellate-Mechanism.pdf (last visited Jun. 10, 2014), p; 7. In this respect, it should be noted that the ICSID Convention does have a procedure that resembles an appellate mechanism to some extent in Article 52. But this "annulment procedure" is not an appellate mechanism *per se* and is rather a procedure which is invoked only when extraordinary situations are involved that raise question over the integrity of the procedure. *See Convention on the Settlement of Investment Disputes between States and Nationals of Other States* entered into force on Oct. 16, 1966 (ICSID Convention), art. 52.

20. For instance, inclusion of a remand may significantly increase the amount of time necessary for the completion of the appellate review. *See* art. 17 of the DSU for comparison.

21. For a similar discussion at the WTO, *see* Appellate Body Report, *Canada - Measures Affecting the Importation of Milk and the Exportation of Dairy Products,* Recourse to Article 21.5 of the DSU by New Zealand and the United States(WT/DS103,113/AB/RW) (Dec. 18, 2001), paras. 126, 127; Appellate Body Reports, *Canada/United States - Continued Suspension of Obligations in the EC - Hormones Dispute,* (WT/DS320/AB/R,WT/DS321/AB/R) (Nov. 14, 2008), paras. 736 (c) (vi), (d) (vi).

22. The factual intensive nature of investment disputes can be evidenced from the list of cases and awards from those handled by ICSID. *See* International Center for Settlement of Investment Disputes, *List of Concluded Cases, available at* https://icsid.worldbank.org/ICSID/FrontServlet?Request Type=GenCaseDtlsRH&actionVal=ListConcluded (last visited Jun. 10, 2014).

23. The Black's Law Dictionary defines 'remand' as "the act of an appellate court when it sends a case back to the trial court and orders the trial court to conduct limited new hearings or an entirely new trial, or to take some other further action." in *Black's Law Dictionary* (6th ed.) (West Publishing Co., St. Paul,1990), p. 1293. Other law dictionaries also provide similar definitions such as "sending a case back to a lower court after a higher court has given an opinion on it, in *Dictionary of Law* (2nd ed.), (Peter Collins Publishing Co., 1995), p. 206.

24. *See* Appellate Body Reports, *United States-Countervailing Duty Investigation on Dynamic Random Access Memory Semiconductors (DRAMs) from Korea (US-DRAMs),* WT/DS296/AB/R (Jun. 27, 2005), Rulings and Recommendation.

25. *See, e.g., OHIM v. Wm Wrigley Company,* ECJ Case C-191/01P (Dec. 4, 2003); *Bertelsmann and Sony Corporation of America v. Impala,* ECJ Case C-413/06P (July 10, 1998); *Indiana v. Edwards,* Slip Op. 07-208 (Jun. 19, 2008); *Powerex Corp. v. Reliant Energy Service Inc,* Slip Op 05-85 (Jun. 19, 2007).

26. *See* World Trade Organization, Special Session of the Dispute Settlement Body, *Report by the Chairman, Ambassador Ronald Saborío Soto, to the Trade Negotiations Committee,* TN/DS/25 (Apr. 21, 2011), art. 17.12 and 17 *bis*, A-11, A-12.

27. Leon E Trakman, *the ICSID under Siege,* 45 Cornell Int'l L.J. 603 (2013),

p. 616.

28. The ICSID Administrative and Financial Regulation Article 22(1): Publication "The Secretary-General shall appropriately publish information about the operation of the Centre, including the registration of all requests for conciliation or arbitration and in due course an indication of the date and method of the termination of each proceeding."

29. UNCITRAL Rules on Transparency in Treaty-based Investor-State Arbitration art. 3(1): Publication of documents "Subject to article 7, the following documents shall be made available to the public: the notice ofarbitration, the response to the notice of arbitration, the statement of claim, the statement of defense andany further written statements or written submissions by any disputing party; any written submissionsby the non-disputing Party (or Parties) to the treaty and by third persons, transcripts of hearings, where available; and orders, decisions and awards of the arbitral tribunal."

30. *See* Korea-US FTA, *supra* note 6, art. 7.6.

31. *See* UNCITRAL Transparency Rules, art. 7.

32. *See* Korea-US FTA, *supra* note 6, art. 11.21. Similar provisions are also found in China-Canada BIT, art. 27.

33. *See* UNCITRAL Transparency Rules, art. 6.

34. *See* Statutes of the International Court of Justice, art. 46, *available at* http://www.icj-cij.org/documents/index.php?p1=4&p2=2&p3=0 (last visited Jun. 15, 2014); DSU, art. 14, paragraph 1; World Trade Organization, *Special Session of the Dispute Settlement Body*, Report by the Chairman, Ambassador Ronald Saborío Soto, to the Trade Negotiations Committee, TN/DS/25 (Apr. 21, 2011).

35. *See* Ministry of Foreign Affairs and Trade, *Explanatory Materials for the Agreement of the Additional Negotiations of the Korea-US FTA* (Feb. 2011), pp. 22-26.

36. *Ibid.*

37. Korea has opposed to the opening its disputes and statements to the public. *See* Cases involving Korea as respondents and complainants from World Trade Organization, *Republic of Korea and the WTO*, available at https://www.wto.org/english/thewto_e/countries_e/korea_republic_e.htm (last visited May 7, 2020).

38. *See* World Trade Organization, Appellate Body Annual Report for 2012, WT/AB/18 (Apr. 9, 2013), pp. 10-12.

39. *See* discussions on members of the UNCITRAL Working Group regarding UNCITRAL Transparency Rules, on art. 6.

40. *See* discussions on members of the UNCITRAL Working Group regarding UNCITRAL Transparency Rules, on art. 7.

41. *See* Muthucumaraswamy Sornarajah, 'The Case against a Regime on International Investment Law', in *Leon Trakman and Nick Ranieri* (eds.), *Regionalism*

in International Investment Law (Oxford University Press, 2013), Chapter 16.

42. *Ibid.*

43. *See* discussions on members of the UNCITRAL Working Group regarding UNCITRAL Transparency Rules, on art. 3.

44. *See* Korea-US FTA, *supra* note 37, art. 11.13.

45. *See* discussions on members of the UNCITRAL Working Group regarding UNCITRAL Transparency Rules, on art. 3.

46. *See, e.g.,* National Basic Taxation Act, art. 81-13. Under this provision, government officials are prohibited from providing specific tax information relating to individual persons or individual corporations with respect to their tax payments or reductions. In the absence of any clearly defined justifying ground such as a disclosure order from the court, a National Taxation Service official violating the provision is subject to civil and criminal liability depending upon situations. Paragraph 1 of the Article provides in the pertinent part that:

A tax official shall not offer or disclose to others data which a taxpayer has submitted in order to fulfill his liability to taxation as prescribed by tax-related Acts or data which the tax officials has obtained for the purpose of taxation or collection of national tax, etc. in discharging his duties (hereinafter referred to as "taxation information"), shall not make use of it except for the prescribed purposes: provided that in cases falling under any of the following subparagraphs, he may offer the taxation information to be used for the prescribed purposes:

when a local government, etc. requests taxation information in order to use for taxation or collection of the taxes as prescribed by the laws;

when governmental authorities request taxation information to use for tax action or the prosecution of a tax evader;

when taxation information is requested by the submission order of a court or a warrant issued by a judge;

when the Commissioner of the National Statistical Office requests taxation information for producing national statistics; and

When the Commissioner of the Statics Korea requests tax information for the purpose of issuing a national statistics report...

47. *See* UNCITRAL Transparency Rules, art. 7.

48. *See* Korea-US FTA, *supra* note 6, art. 7.6.

49. *See* discussions on members of the UNCITRAL Working Group regarding UNCITRAL Transparency Rules, on art. 7.

50. *See* Korea-US FTA, *supra* note 6, art. 11.20, para. 3.

51. *See Ibid.*

52. *See Ibid.*, art. 11.20.

53. Indeed, it is reported that foreign attorneys have been hired in all the WTO disputes in which Korea has appeared as a party and that foreign attorneys are taking the leading role in the first investment arbitration case brought against

Korea by Lonestar. *See LSF-KEB Holdings SCA and Others v. Republic of Korea*, ICSID Case No. ARB/12/37, *available at* https://icsid.worldbank.org/ICSID/FrontServlet?requestType=GenCaseDtlsRH&action Val= ListPending (last visited Jun. 14, 2014).

54. *See* Korea-US FTA, *supra* note 6, art. 11.20, para. 3.

55. European Commission, *Commission Proposes New Investment Court System for TTIP and Other EU Trade and Investment Negotiations*, Press Release (Sept.16, 2015), *available at* http://trade.ec.europa.eu/doclib/press/index.cfm?id=1364 (last visited Nov. 23, 2016); Louise Woods, *Fit for purposes? The EU's Investment Court System* (Mar. 23, 2016), Kluwer Arbitration Blog, *available at* http://kluwerarbitrationblog.com/2016/03/23/to-be-decided/ (last visited Nov. 23, 2016).

56. *See* European Commission, *Transatlantic Trade and Investment Partnership: Trade in Services, Investment and E-Commerce, Chapter II- Investment*, Commission draft text TTIP — investment (Nov. 12, 2016), *available at* http://trade.ec.europa.eu/doclib/docs/2015/september/tradoc_153807.pdf (last visited Nov. 23, 2016), pp. 16-21.

57. *See* Isabelle Michou *et al.*, *TTIP: 12th Round of Negotiations Concludes, Investment Protection Remains High on the Agenda; Plus Newly Published CETA Text Includes EU's Investment Court System Proposal*, Herbert Smith Freehills Dispute Resolution Arbitration Notes (Feb. 29, 2016), *available at* http://hsfnotes.com/arbitration/2016/02/29/ttip-12th-round-of-negotiations-concludes-investment-protection-remains-high-on-the-agenda-plus-newly-published-ceta-text-includes-eus-investment-court-system-proposal/ (last visited Nov. 24, 2016); Government of Canada, *Joint Statement by European Commissioner for Trade and Canada's Minister of International Trade on Canada-EU Trade Agreement*, Global Affairs Canada (Feb. 29, 2016), *available at* http://news.gc.ca/web/article-en.do?mthd=index&crtr.page=1&nid=1036759_(last visited Nov. 24, 2016).

58. *See* European Commission, *The EU and Vietnam Finalise Landmark Trade Deal*, European Commission News Archive (Dec. 2, 2015), *available at* http://trade.ec.europa.eu/doclib/press/index.cfm?id=1409_(last visited Nov. 24, 2016); *Trade in Services, Investment and E-Commerce*, *available at* http://trade.ec.europa.eu/doclib/docs/2016/february/tradoc_154210.pdf (last visited Nov. 24, 2016); for the text of EU-Vietnam FTA; *See* Cecilia Malmstrom, Trade Commissioner, *Done Deal with Vietnam*, Commission and Its Priorities Blog Post, *available at* https://ec.europa.eu/commission/2014-2019/malmstrom/blog/done-deal-vietnam_en (last visited Nov. 24, 2016).

59. Krista Hughes & Philip Blenkinsop, *US Wary of EU Proposal for Investment Court in Trade Pact* (Oct. 29, 2015), Reuters Business News, *available at* http://www.reuters.com/article/us-trade-ttip-idUSKCN0SN2LH20151029 (last visited Nov. 24, 2016); *See* Stockholm Chamber of Commerce, *The U.S is Skeptical of the European Commission's ISDS Proposal*, ISDS Blog, *available at* http://isdsblog.com/2015/11/13/the-u-s-is-sceptical-of-the-european-commissions-isds-proposal/ (last visited Nov. 24, 2016).

60. European Commission, *Reading Guide to the Draft Text on Investment*

Protection and Investment Court System in the Transatlantic Trade and Investment Partnership (TTIP), available at http://trade.ec.europa.eu/doclib/press/index.cfm?id=1365 (last visited Nov. 23, 2016); European Parliament, *European Parliament Resolution of 8 July 2015 Containing the European Parliament's Recommendations to the European Commission on the Negotiations for the Transatlantic Trade and Investment Partnership (TTIP)* (2014/2228(INI)), S2(d)(xv), *available at* http://www.europarl.europa.eu/sides/getDoc.do?pubRef=-//EP//TEXT+TA+P8-TA-2015-0252+0+DOC+XML+V0//EN (last visited Nov. 24, 2016); Ingo Venzke, *Investor-State Dispute Settlement in TTIP from the Perspective of a Public Law Theory of International Adjudication,* 17 The Journal of World Investment & Trade (2016), p. 394; *See* Cecilia Malmström, Trade Commissioner, *Proposing and Investment Court System,* Commission and Its Priorities Blog Post (Sept. 16, 2015), *available at* https://ec.europa.eu/commission/2014-2019/malmstrom/blog/proposing-investment-court-system_en (last visited Nov. 24, 2016) ("What has clearly come out of the debate is that the old, traditional form of dispute resolution suffers from a fundamental lack of trust. However, EU investors are the most frequent users of the existing model, which individual EU countries have developed over time. This means that Europe must take the responsibility to reform and modernise it. We must take the global lead on the path to reform." "We want to establish a new system built around the elements that make citizens trust domestic or international courts. I'm making this proposal public at the same time that I send it to the European Parliament and the Member States. It's very important to have an open and transparent exchange of views on this widely debated issue.").

61. European Parliament, *European Parliament Resolution of 8 July 2015 Containing the European Parliament's Recommendations to the European Commission on the Negotiations for the Transatlantic Trade and Investment Partnership (TTIP)* (2014/2228(INI)), S2(d)(xv), *available at* http://www.europarl.europa.eu/sides/getDoc.do?pubRef=-//EP//TEXT+TA+P8-TA-2015-0252+0+DOC+XML+V0//EN (last visited Nov. 24, 2016); Venzke, *supra* note 60, p. 394.

62. *See* Mateus Aimoré Carreteiro, *Appellate Arbitral Rules in International Commercial Arbitration,* 33(2) Journal of International Arbitration 185 (2016); Barbara Helene Steindl, *ICSID Annulment vs. Set Aside by State Courts,* 4 YB on Int'l Arb. 181 (2015); Gloria Maria Alvarez, *et al., A Response to the Criticism against ISDS by EFILA,* 33(1) J. Int'l Arb. 1(2016), pp. 10-11.

63. J.J. Saulino and Josh Kallmer, "The Emperor Has No Clothes: A Critique of the Debate over Reform of the ISDS System," in Jean E. Kalicki and Anna Jubin-Bret (eds.), *Reshaping the Investor-State Dispute Settlement System: Journeys for the 21st Century* (Brill Nijhoff, 2015), p. 498; Eduardo Zuleta, "The Challenges of Creating a Sstanding International Investment Court," in Jean E. Kalicki and Anna Jubin-Bret (eds.), *Reshaping the Investor-State Dispute Settlement System: Journeys for the 21st Century* (Brill Nijhoff, 2015), p. 403.

Chapter VIII

Conclusion: FTAs and DSMs in East Asia and Contribution to the Global Trading Regime

Free Trade Agreements (FTAs) continue to proliferate globally and the multilateral trading regime enshrined in the World Trade Organization (WTO) Agreements is facing a serious challenge. The Asia Pacific region has seen more robust activities in terms of negotiating and concluding FTAs of various sorts. While all these FTAs adopt similar structures and share strong similarities, they also set forth different rules in certain areas and conduct new experiments. As a matter of fact, FTAs among like-minded friends are arguably the best place to carry out experiments of new rules that have been elusive in the multilateral fronts where competing interests of countries hardly converge.

As a matter of fact, at present international dispute settlement proceedings are actively utilized by states. These proceedings have contributed to the development of international law and have become a core element of important treaties. In particular, they play an important role in enforcing respective treaties, and developing and clarifying relevant provisions in the treaties.

In the meantime, as procedural loopholes and inconsistencies are identified with respect to these proceedings, efforts are being made to fill the loopholes and elaborate procedural rules of the proceedings. Along the lines of these efforts, various suggestions and proposals have been made, triggering lively discussions and debates. These efforts are generally to introduce further procedural rules and more detailed steps to the existing dispute settlement mechanism of international law. In a sense, this is to bring international dispute settlement proceedings one step closer to domestic court proceedings, so to speak.

For instance, with respect to the WTO's dispute settlement proceeding, negotiations have been underway for many years to amend the existing system codified in the *Understanding on Rules and Procedures Governing the Settlement of Disputes* (DSU).[1] Negotiations have focused on fixing structural problems identified through the application of the DSU since 1995 and introducing more detailed and coherent provisions in the DSU so as to enhance rule of law.[2] Given the rather strong consensus among the WTO members, the DSU amendment is regarded as one of the early harvest issues once a new round begins in the near future.[3]

Likewise, on the investment dispute settlement front (i.e., ISDS proceedings), new efforts are being made to upgrade and reform existing proceedings contained in IIAs (*i.e.*, either Bilateral Investment Treaties of Free Trade Agreements). Here also, various proposals have been made by many countries and inserted into respective IIAs one way or another. Most recently, the European Union proposed a new scheme that would change the framework of the current ISDS proceedings in a significant manner. Among the new ideas are suggestions to introduce a new standing court equipped with an appellate system, coupled with strong ethical rules for appointed judges. At the moment, robust discussions are taking place in the international community regarding these suggestions.[4]

At its core, the basic idea behind the current discussions seems to be an incorporation of similar rules and procedures found in the WTO DSU and relevant practice, even if the WTO does not adopt a "court" system.

Needless to say, there are obvious merits in these efforts to reform existing investment dispute settlement proceedings and introduce a standing international court, because proposed changes are expected to enhance trust in the decision-making process of international investment disputes. If anything, with this, perhaps the legitimate policy space of sovereign governments could be better preserved while guaranteeing the agreed level of protection for foreign investors.

This book does not claim to cover the entire spectrum of dispute settlement proceedings at the WTO and FTAs. Nor does it aim to address all issues of dispute settlement proceedings of the WTO and FTAs. Rather, it seeks to provide the readers with an opportunity to understand key principles of international law in the context of dispute settlement proceedings and apply them to the specific operating mechanisms of the WTO and FTA DSMs. It is hoped that this book will provide a meaningful stepping stone to cultivate knowledge in international law and skill in international litigation.

As of this writing, Korea has participated in the WTO DSM 40 times — 21 times as a responding party and 19 times as a complaining party. Korea also experienced the first investment arbitration due to the ISDS proceeding brought by Lonestar against the government of Korea based on the 2007 Korea-Belgium BIT. As long as Korea remains one of the active participants of the global markets and a robust magnet for foreign investment, these international disputes will continue to increase at the WTO DSM, FTA DSM and the ISDS proceedings.

This reality notwithstanding, legal experts and practicing attorneys in this field are still in short supply. Up until now, Korea has mainly been represented by foreign attorneys in these disputes.

Endnotes

1. *Understanding on Rules and Procedures Governing the Settlement of Disputes*, Marrakesh Agreement Establishing the World Trade Organization, Annex 2, 1869 U.N.T.S. 401, (Apr.15, 1994).

2. *See* World Trade Organization, *Ministerial Declarations*, WT/MIN(01)/EDC/1 (Nov. 14, 2001), para. 47; World Trade Organization, *Decision on the Application and Review of the Understanding on Rules and Procedures Governing the Settlements of Disputes, available at* https://www.wto.org/english/docs_e/legal_

e/53-ddsu_e.htm (last visited on Jan. 4, 2016). *See also Ministerial Declarations*, WT/MIN(01)/EDC/1, paras. 30, 47.

3. *See* WTO's Website *available at* https://www.wto.org/english/tratop_e/dispu_e/dispu_e.htm#negotiations (last visited Dec. 4, 2016).

4. *See* Stephan W. Schill, *The European Commission's Proposal of an "Investment Court System" for TTIP: Stepping Stone or Stumbling Block for Multilateralizing International Investment Law*? ASIL Insights, Vol. 20, Issue 9 (Apr. 22, 2016), *available at* https://www.asil.org/insights/volume/20/issue/9/european-commissions-proposal-investment-court-system-ttip-stepping (last visited Nov. 24, 2016); *See* M. Sornarajah, An International Investment Court: Panacea or Purgatory? *Columbia FDI Perspectives: Perspectives on Topical Foreign Direct Investment Issues*, No. 180 (Aug. 15, 2016), *available at* http://ccsi.columbia.edu/files/2013/10/No-180-Sornarajah-FINAL.pdf (last visited Nov. 24, 2016).

References

Agreement among the Government of Japan, the Government of the Republic of Korea and the Government of the People's Republic of China for the Promotion, Facilitation and Protection of Investment.

Agreement between Japan and the Republic of Peru for an Economic Partnership.

Agreement between Japan and the United Mexican States for the Strengthening of the Economic Partnership.

Agreement between the Government of Canada and the Government of the People's Republic of China for the Promotion and Reciprocal Protection of Investments.

Ai, Ping, *One Belt One Road, New Diplomacy and Public Diplomacy, China and World,* 4 International Understanding (2014).

Alvarez, Gloria Maria, *et al.*, *A Response to the Criticism against ISDS by EFILA,* 33(1) Journal of International Arbitration 1 (2016).

Anti-Dumping Agreement.

Akhtar, Shayerah Ilias & Martin A. Weiss, *U.S. International Investment Agreements: Issues for Congress*, CRS Report R43052 (Apr. 29, 2013).

Arrest Warrant of 11 April 2000 (Democratic Republic of the Congo v. Belgium), Judgment, I.C.J. Reports 2002.

Asia Development Bank, *How to Design, Negotiate and Implement a Free Trade Agreement in Asia* (Manila: Asia Development Bank, Office of Regional Economic Cooperation, 2008).

Black, Henry Campbell (ed.), *Black's Law Dictionary* (6th ed.), (West Publishing Co., St. Paul, 1990).

Bipartisan Congressional Trade Priorities and Accountability Act of 2015.

Bodansky, Daniel and John R. Crook, "Symposium: The ILC's State Responsibility Articles," 96 *American Journal of International Law*

(2002).

Bolle, Mary Jane and Ian F. Fergusson, *Worker Rights Provisions in Free Trade Agreements (FTAs)*, CRS Report IF10046 (June 18, 2015).

Border and Transborder Armed Actions (Nicaragua v. Honduras), Jurisdiction and Admissibility, Judgment, I.C.J. Reports 1988.

Bradford, Scott, *An Analysis of a Possible Japan-U.S. Free Trade Agreement*, Petersen Institute of International Economics (2013).

Canada — Export Credits and Loan Guarantees for Regional Aircraft — Recourse to Arbitration by Canada under Article 22.6 of the DSU and Article 4.11 of the SCM Agreement, Decision by the Arbitrator, WT/DS222/ARB (Feb. 17, 2003).

Canada — Measures Affecting the Export of Civilian Aircraft, WT/DS70/R (Aug. 20, 1999).

Canada — Measures Affecting the Importation of Milk and the Exportation of Dairy Products, Recourse to Article 21.5 of the DSU by New Zealand and the United States, WT/DS103,113/AB/RW (Dec. 18, 2001).

Canada/United States — Continued Suspension of Obligations in the EC — Hormones Dispute, WT/DS320/AB/R,WT/DS321/AB/R (Nov. 14, 2008).

Carreteiro, Mateus Aimoré, "Appellate Arbitral Rules in International Commercial Arbitration," 33(2) *Journal of International Arbitration 185* (2016).

Case Concerning Factory at Chorzów (Claim for Indemnity) (The Merits) (F.R.G. v Poland), 1928 P.C.I.J. (ser. A) No. 17 (Sept., 1928).

Case Concerning Revocation of Limitation of Operating Hours for Certain Retailers, Supreme Court of the Republic of Korea, 2015DU295, Nov. 10, 2015.

Cassese, Antonio, *International Law* (2nd ed.) (Oxford University Press, 2005).

Chase, Claude, Alan Yanovich, Jo-Ann Crawford, and Pamela Ugaz, *Mapping of Dispute Settlement Mechanisms in Regional Trade Agreements — Innovative or Variations on a Theme?* World Trade Organization Staff Working Paper, No. ERSD-2013-07 (Jun. 10, 2013).

Chevron U.S.A., Inc. v. NRDC (467 U.S. 837 (1984)), (Jun. 25, 1984).

China-Measures Affecting the Protection and Enforcement of Intellectual Property Rights, WT/DS362/R (Jan. 26, 2009).

China-Measures Affecting Trading Rights and Distribution Services for

Certain Publications and Audiovisual Entertainment Products, WT/DS363/AB/R (Dec. 21, 2009).

China- Measures Related to the Exportation of Various Raw Materials, WT/DS394/R (Jan. 30, 2012).

Choi, Byeong-il *et al.*, *Trade Governance: research of the mid/long-term trade strategy for becoming the advanced country*, Korea Institute for International Economic Policy (Research material no. 06-04).

Christie, George C., "Some Key Jurisprudential Issues of the Twenty-First Century," 8 *Tulane Journal of International and Comparative Law* (2000).

Colt Industries Operating Corporation v. Republic of Korea (ICSID Case No. ARB/84/2).

Compatibility of Ordinance of Jeollabukdo-province with GATT 1994, 2004 Do 2432, Decisions of the Korean Supreme Court (Sept. 14, 2005).

Comprehensive and Progressive Agreement for Trans-Pacific Partnership (hereinafter "CPTPP"), Entered into force on December 30, 2018.

Comprehensive Economic and Trade Agreement between the EU and Canada.

Concerning Rights of Nationals of the United States in Morocco (France v. U.S.), 1952 I.C.J. 176 (Aug. 27).

Constitution of the Republic of Korea.

Constitution of the United States.

Convention on the Settlement of Investment Disputes between States and Nationals of Other States.

Cooper, William H., *The Proposed U.S.-South Korea Free Trade Agreement (Korea-U.S. FTA): Provisions and Implications*, CRS Report RL34330.

Cranston, Ross (ed.), *Twenty-First Century, in Making Commercial Law* (Clarendon Press, 1997).

Draft Articles on Responsibility of States for Internationally Wrongful Acts.

Dictionary of Law (2nd ed.), (Peter Collins Publishing Co. 1995).

Difference Relating to Immunity from Legal Process of a Special Rapporteur of the Commission on Human Rights, Advisory Opinion, I.C.J. Reports 1999.

Dispute Settlement Understanding.

Eritrea Ethiopia Claims Commission, Partial Award (Diplomatic Claim:

Ethiopia's Claim 8) between the Federal Democratic Republic of Ethiopia and the State of Eritrea, (The Hague, December 19, 2005).

European Commission, *Commission Proposes New Investment Court System for TTIP and Other EU Trade and Investment Negotiations*, Press Release (Sept. 6, 2015).

____, *Investment Protection and Investor-to-State Dispute Settlement in EU Agreements — Fact Sheet* (Nov., 2013).

____, *Transatlantic Trade and Investment Partnership: Trade in Services, Investment and E-Commerce, Chapter II- Investment, Commission draft text TTIP — investment* (Nov. 12, 2016).

European Communities-Countervailing Measures on Dynamic Random Access Memory Chips from Korea, WT/DS299/R (Jun. 17, 2005).

European Parliament, *European Parliament Resolution of 8 July 2015 Containing the European Parliament's Recommendations to the European Commission on the Negotiations for the Transatlantic Trade and Investment Partnership (TTIP)* (2014/2228(INI)), S2(d)(xv).

Fergusson, Ian F. and Richard S. Beth, *Trade Promotion Authority (TPA): Frequently Asked Questions*, CRS Report (Jul. 2, 2015).

Framework Agreement Establishing a Free Trade Area between the Republic of Korea and the Republic of Turkey.

Franck, Susan D., "Foreign Direct Investment, Investment Treaty Arbitration, and the Rule of Law," 19 *Global Business & Development Law Journal* (2007).

Free Trade Agreement between the Government of the People's Republic of China and the Government of The Republic of Korea.

Free Trade Agreement between the Government of the Republic of Korea and the Government of Australia.

Free Trade Agreement between the Government of the Republic of Korea and the Government of Canada.

Free Trade Agreement between the Republic of Korea and EU.

Free Trade Agreement between the Republic of Korea and People's Republic of China.

Free Trade Agreement between the Republic of Korea and the Republic of Peru.

Free Trade Agreement between the Republic of Korea and the United States of America.

General exceptions to the jurisdictional immunity of a foreign state (28 U.S. Code § 1605).

Glendon, Mary Ann, Michael Wallace Gordon and Christopher Osakwe, *Comparative Legal Traditions in a Nutshell* (St. Paul, Minn.: West, 1982).

Global Trading Resource Corp. and Globex International, Inc. v. Ukraine, ICSID Case No. ARB/09/11, Award of Dec. 1, 2010.

Grimmett, Jeanne G., *Dispute Settlement Under the U.S.-Peru Trade Promotion Agreement: An Overview,* Congressional Research Service (Aug. 12, 2011).

Government of Canada, *Joint Statement by European Commissioner for Trade and Canada's Minister of International Trade on Canada-EU Trade Agreement, Global Affairs Canada* (Feb. 29, 2016).

Guatemala — Definitive Anti-Dumping Measures on Grey Portland Cement from Mexico, WT/DS156/R (Nov. 17, 2000).

Hodgson, Mélida, *Elements Of An Architecture For A CAFTA Appellate Mechanism,* American Bar Association Section Of International Law Fall Meeting "Towards A CAFTA Appellate Mechanism" (2009).

Hoffman, Adam, "Corralling Constitutional Fact: De Novo Fact Review in Federal Appeals Court," 50 *Duke Law Journal* (2001).

Hornbeck, J. F., *The Proposed U.S.-Panama Free Trade Agreement,* CRS Report RL32540.

Hanocal Holding B.V. and IPIC International B.V. v. Republic of Korea (ICSID Case No. ARB/15/17).

Hwang GeumJoo v. Japan (542 U.S.901 (2004)), Supreme Court of United States (Jun. 14, 2004).

International Centre for Settlement and Investment Disputes Convention, Regulations and Rules.

International Labour Organization Declaration on Fundamental Principles and Rights at Work and its Follow-up.

Inkeles, Alex, *Continuity and Change: Popular Values on the Pacific Rim,* 1 Stanford Journal of International Relations (Summer/Fall 1998).

Interpretation of the Peace Treaties with Bulgaria, Hungary and Romania, Advisory Opinion: I.C.J. Reports 1950.

Japan — Australia Economic Partnership Agreement.

Japan — Measures Affecting Consumer Photographic Film and Paper, WT/DS44/R (Apr. 22, 1998).

Jeonju District Court 2007gahap3553 decision on the SOFA (Agreement on The Status of U.S. Forces in The Republic of

Korea).

Jurisdictional Immunities of the State (Germany v. Italy: Greece intervening), Judgment, I.C. J. Reports 2012.

Kalicki, Jean E. & Anna Jubin-Bret (eds.), *Reshaping the Investor-State Dispute Settlement System: Journeys for the 21st Century* (Boston: Brill Nijhoff, 2015).

Kennedy, Scott and David A. Parker, *Building China's "One Belt, One Road*, CSIS (Apr. 3, 2015).

Klingner, Bruce and Anthony B. Kim, *Economic Lethargy: South Korea Needs a Second Wave of Reforms*, No. 2090, Heritage Foundation (Dec. 7, 2007).

Kim, Taehwan, *Beyond Geopolitics: South Korea's Eurasia Initiative as a New Nordpolitik*, The ASAN Forum, 16 February 2015.

Korea — Anti-Dumping Duties on Imports of Certain Paper from Indonesia, WT/DS312/R (Nov. 28, 2005).

Korean Constitutional Court, Case No. 97 Hunba 65 (Nov. 26, 1998).

Lapidoth, Ruth Escehlbacher, *International Law at the Time of Its Codification: Essays In Honour of Robert Ago* (Giuffrè Editore, 1987).

Lattanzio, Richard K. and Ian F. Fergusson, *Environmental Provisions in Free Trade Agreements* (FTAs), CRS Report IF10166 (Jun. 18, 2015).

Lee, Jaemin, *A Brief Comparison of Antidumping Investigation in Korea and China*, 18 Trade Remedy 11.

____, *Introduction of an Appellate Review Mechanism forInternational Investment Disputes*, 11 Transnational Dispute Management (2014).

Lo, Chang-fa, Junji Nakagawa, and Tsai-fang Chen (eds.), *The Appellate Body of the WTO and Its Reform* (Springer, 2020).

LSF-KEB Holdings SCA and others v. Republic of Korea (ICSID Case No. ARB/12/37).

Manjiao, Chi, "China's Participation in WTO Dispute Settlement over the Past Decade: Experiences and Impacts," 15 *Journal of International Economic Law* (2012).

Marrakesh Agreement Establishing the WTO.

Mexico-Measures Affecting Telecommunications Services, WT/DS204/R (Apr. 2, 2004).

Mohammad Reza Dayyani and others v. Republic of Korea, PCA Case No. 2015-38.

Michou, Isabelle, *et al.*, *TTIP: 12th Round of Negotiations Concludes, Investment Protection Remains High on the Agenda; Plus Newly Published CETA Text Includes EU's Investment Court System Proposal*, Herbert Smith Freehills Dispute Resolution Arbitration Notes (Feb. 29, 2016).

Ministry of Foreign Affairs, *Eurasia Initiative* (Aug. 2, 2015).

Ministry of Foreign Affairs and Trade, *Explanatory Materials for the Agreement of the Additional Negotiations of the Korea-U.S. FTA* (Feb. 2011).

Ministry of Foreign Affairs of the People's Republic of China, *Foreign Ministry Spokesperson Hong Lei's Regular Press Conference* (Apr. 17, 2015).

Nottage, Luke, *Nothing New in the (North) East?: Interpreting the Rhetoric and Reality of Japanese Corporate Governance*, CLPE Research Paper 1/2006, Vol. 02, No. 01 (2006).

Nottebohm case (Liechtenstein v. Guatemala) (Second phase), Judgment of April 6th, 1955: I.C.J. Reports 1955.

Office of the United States Trade Representative, *2007 National Trade Estimate Report on Foreign Trade Barriers* (Apr. 2, 2007).

____, *2012 National Trade Estimate Report on Foreign Trade Barriers* (Mar., 2012).

Organisation for Economic Cooperation and Development, *International Investment Perspectives* (OECD Publishing, 2006).

Paik, Choong Hyun (ed.), *International Law in Korean Perspective* (Seoul National University Press, 2004).

Panhuys, F. van, W.P. Heere, J.W. Josephus Jitta Ko Swan Sik and A.M. Stuyt, *International Law in the Netherlands, Vol. III* (Alphen aan den Rijn: Sijthoff & Noordhoff, 1980).

Philip Morris Asia Ltd v The Commonwealth of Australia, UNCITRAL, PCA No 2012-12.

Republic of Austria v. Altmann (541 U.S. 677 (2004)), Supreme Court of the United States (Jun. 7, 2004).

Salacuse, Jeswald W., "Is There a Better Way? Alternative Methods of Treaty-Based, Investor-State Dispute Resolution," 31 *Fordham International Law Journal* (2007).

Schill, Stephan W., *The European Commission's Proposal of an "Investment Court System" for TTIP: Stepping Stone or Stumbling Block for Multilateralizing International Investment Law?* ASIL Insights, Vol. 20, Issue 9 (Apr. 22, 2016).

Seoul Administrative Court, Case No. 2006 Guhab 29782.

____, Case No. 2008 Guha 40363.

____, 2007guhap37285 decision on Corporate Tax; Seoul Administrative Court 2007guhap16875 decision on Resident Tax.

____, 2007guhap37650 and Seoul High Court 2009nu8016 decision on Transfer Income Tax.

____, 2008guhap17110 decision on Corporate Tax.

Shaw, Malcolm N., *International Law* (Cambridge University Press, 2008).

Sornarajah, M., *An International Investment Court: Panacea or Purgatory?,* Columbia FDI Perspectives: Perspectives on Topical Foreign Direct Investment Issues, No. 180 (Aug. 15, 2016).

Statute of the International Court of Justice.

Steindl, Barbara Helene, *ICSID Annulment vs. Set Aside by State Courts,* 4 Yearbook on International Arbitration 181 (2015).

Supreme Court of Korea, Case No. 2008 Du 17936 (Jan. 30, 2009).

Suzuki, Misasha, "The Protectionist Bar Against Foreign Lawyers in Japan, China and Korea: Domestic Control in the Face of Internationalization," 16 *Columbia Journal of Asian Law* (2003).

The Mavriommatis Palestine Concessions, Collection of Judgments, Series A, No. 2 (Aug. 30, 1924).

Trakman, Leon E., "the ICSID under Siege," 45 *Cornell International Law Journal 603* (2013).

Trakman, Leon and Nick Ranieri (eds.), *Regionalism in International Investment Law* (Oxford University Press, 2013).

United Nations, *Yearbook of the International Law Commission,* Report of the Commission to the General Assembly on the work of its thirty-second session, Volume II, Part Two, A/CN.4/SER.A/1980/Add.l (Part 2), New York (1981).

United Nations Commission on International Trade Law, UNCITRAL Transparency Rules in Treaty-based Investor-State Arbitration (2014).

United Nations Convention on Transparency in Treaty-based Investor-State Arbitration (2014).

United Nations Conference on Trade and Development, *Non-Tariff Measures to Trade: Economic and Policy Issues for Developing Countries* (2013).

United States — Countervailing Duty Investigations on Dynamic Random Access Memory Semiconductors from Korea, WT/DS296/R (Feb. 21,

2005).

United States — Countervailing Duty Measures on Certain Products from China, WT/DS437/1, G/L/988, G/SCM/D90/1 (May 30, 2012).

United States Diplomatic and Consular Staff in Tehran, Judgment, I.C.J. Reports 1980.

United States Department of Commerce, *Press briefing by Secretary of Commerce Wilbur Ross on an executive order on trade agreement violations and abuses* (Apr. 29, 2017).

United States — Laws, Regulations and Methodology for Calculating Dumping Margins ("Zeroing"), WT/DS294/AB/RW (May 14, 2009).

United States — Import Measures on Certain Products from the European Communities, WT/DS165/R (Jul. 17, 2000).

United States — Measures Affecting the Cross-Border Supply of Gambling and Betting Services, WT/DS285/AB/R (Apr. 7, 2005).

United States — Measures Relating to Zeroing and Sunset Reviews — Recourse to Article 21.5 of The DSU By Japan, WT/DS322/AB/RW (Aug. 18, 2009).

United States — Sections 301-310 of the Trade Act of 1974, WT/DS152/R (Dec. 22 1990).

United States — Subsidies on Upland Cotton — Recourse to Article 21.5 of the DSU by Brazil, WT/DS267/AB/RW (Jun. 20, 2008).

United States — Sunset Review of Anti-Dumping Duties on Corrosion-Resistant Carbon Steel Flat Products from Japan, WT/DS244/R (Jan. 9, 2004).

United States — Sunset Reviews of Anti-Dumping Measures on Oil Country Tubular Goods from Argentina, WT/DS268/AB/R (Nov. 29, 2004).

United States Trade Representative, *USTR to Request First-Ever Environment Consultations Under the U.S.-Korea Free Trade Agreement (KORUS) in Effort to Combat Illegal Fishing* (2019).

U.S.- China Economic and Security Review Commission, *China's Response to U.S.-South Korean Missile Defense system Deployment and its Implications* (Jul. 26, 2017).

Vattenfall AB and others v Federal Republic of Germany, ICSID Case No ARB/12/12, Notice of Arbitration (May 31, 2012).

Venzke Ingo, "Investor-State Dispute Settlement in TTIP from the Perspective of a Public Law Theory of International Adjudication," 17 *The Journal of World Investment & Trade* (2016).

Vienna Convention on the Law of Treaties, 1155 U.N.T.S. 331(May

23, 1969).

Villarreal, M. Angeles, *Proposed U.S.-Colombia Free Trade Agreement: Background and Issues*, CRS Report RL34470.

Walde, Thomas W., "The "Umbrella" Clause in Investment Arbitration — A Comment on Original Intentions and Recent Cases," 6 *The Journal of World Investment & Trade* (2005).

White House, *Press Briefing by Secretary of Commerce Wilbur Ross on the Memorandum Regarding the Investigation Pursuant to Section 232 (B) of the Trade Expansion Act* (Apr. 20, 2017).

White House Office of the Press Secretary, *G-20 Leaders Declaration, summarizing the discussion at the latest G-20 meeting held in Los Cabos on June 18-19, 2012* (2012).

World Trade Organization, *Appellate Body Annual Report for 2012*, WT/AB/18 (Apr. 9, 2013).

____, *Ministerial Declarations*, WT/MIN(01)/EDC/1 (Nov. 14, 2001).

____, *Reports on Recent Trade Developments* (2012).

____, *Special Session of the Dispute Settlement Body, Report by the Chairman, Ambassador Ronald Saborío Soto, to the Trade Negotiations Committee*, TN/DS/25 (Apr. 21, 2011).

____, *Trade Policy Review, China, Minutes of the Meeting, Addendum*, WT/TPR/M/342/Add.1 (Oct. 28, 2016).

____, *Trade Policy Review, Japan, Minutes of the Meeting, Addendum*, WT/TPR/M/310/Add.1 (Jun. 17, 2015).

____, *Trade Policy Review, Report by China*, WT/TPR/G/342 (Jun. 15, 2016).

____, *Trade Policy Review, Report by Japan*, WT/TPR/G/310 (Jan. 19, 2015).

____, *Trade Policy Review, Report by Republic of Korea*, WT/TPR/G/346/Rev.1 (Jan. 6, 2017).

____, *Trade Policy Review, Report by the Secretariat, China*, WT/TPR/S/342/Rev.1 (Oct. 12, 2016).

____, *Trade Policy Review, Report by the Secretariat, Japan*, WT/TPR/S/310/Rev.1 (May 6, 2015).

____, *WTO Negotiating Group on Rules, Draft Consolidated Chair's Texts of AD and SCM Agreements*, TN/RL/W/213 (Nov. 30, 2007).

____, *WTO Negotiating Group on Rules, New Draft Consolidated Chair Texts of the AD and the SCM Agreements*, TN/RL/W/236 (Dec. 19, 2008).

World Trade Organization Negotiating Group on Rules, *Draft Con-*

solidated Chair Texts of the AD and the SCM Agreements, TN/RL/W/213 (Nov. 30, 2007).

____, *New Draft Consolidated Chair Texts of the AD and the SCM Agreements*, TN/RL/W/236 (Dec. 19, 2007).

Yannaca-Small, Katia, *Improving the System of Investor-State Dispute Settlement*, OECD Working Papers on International Investment (Jan., 2006).

Yang, Florence Wen-Ting, *Asymmetrical Interdependence and Sanction: China's Economic Retaliation over South Korea's THADD Deployment*, 55 Issues and Studies (2019).

Yuan, Xintao, *Analysis of the National Strategy of One Belt and One Road Construction*, Around Southeast Asia, Issue 8 (2014).

Additional References

*Following articles and book chapters have been written by the author previously, which have been referenced as necessary in this book.

Lee, Jaemin, "A Clash Between IT Giants and the Changing Face of International Law: The Samsung vs. Apple Litigation and Its Jurisdictional Implications," *Journal of East Asia and International Law*, Vol. 5, No. 1 (Spring 2012), pp. 117-142.

____, "A Counterweight to the FTA Drive? Korea's FTA Implementation Act of 2011 and Its Implications," *Journal of Trade and Arbitration Law*, Vol. 4, Iss. 2 (2015), pp. 207-230.

____, "An Analysis of Legal Issues Relating to Instruments That Local Governments Conclude," *Oregon Review of International Law,* Vol. 9, No. 2 (Mar. 2007), pp. 431-476.

____, "An Important First Stride, But Beware the Pitfalls — A Critical Analysis of the ISDS Mechanism of the 2012 Korea-China-Japan Trilateral Investment Treaty," *Chinese Journal of Itnernational Law*, Vol. 12, Iss. 3 (Sept. 2013), pp. 509-541.

____, "A Pragmatic Approach for Determining Overfishing and Overfished Condition for Assessing Data-Deficient Fisheries," 『수산해양연구(*The Korean Society Fisheries and Sciences Education*)』, Vol. 25, No. 2 (2013), pp. 1009-1019.

____, "Back on the Negotiating Table Again? — Recalibrating Provisions of the Korea-U.S. FTA ISDS Proceedings through a Prospective 'Amendment'," 『국제거래법연구(*Korean Fodum on International Trade and Business Law*)』, Vol. 23, No. 1 (2014), pp. 171-200.

____, "Bracing for the Hidden Fallout: Systemic Implications of the Sino-US Trade Disputes at a Time of Changing International Trade Paradigms," *Journal of East Asia and International Law* (May

2013), pp. 53-79.

____, "Chapter 3: Korea," in Mark Williams, *The Political Economy of Competition Law in Asia* (Edward Elgar, 2013).

____, "Chapter 7. Increasing Interaction between Investment and Trade in Korea," in Seung Wha Chang, Won-Mog Choi, *Trade Law and Regulation in Korea* (Edward Elgar, 2011).

____, "Chapter 9. Korea," in Derk Beinen *et al.*, *Guide to International Anti-Dumping Practice* (Kluwer Law International, 2013).

____, "Chapter 16. Korea: Increasing Attention and New Challenges," in Müslüm Yilmaz, *Domestic Judicial Review of Trade Remedies Experience of the Most Active WTO Members* (Cambridge University Press, 2013).

____, "Chapter 20. Introduction of an Appellate Review Mechanism for International Investment Disputes: Expected Benefits and Remaining Tasks," in Jean E. Kallicki and Anna Joubin-Bret (eds.), *Reshaping the Investor-State Dispute Settlement System: Journeys for the 21st Century* (Brill Nijhoff, 2015).

____, "Complementing Each Other or Stoking Further Complexity? — Interaction between International Investment Law and International Trade Law," *Journal of World Trade*, Vol. 47 (2013), pp. 421-445.

____, "Commercializing National Security? — National Security Exceptions' Outer Parameter under GATT Article XXI," *Asian Journal of WTO & International Health Law and Policy*, Vol. 13, No. 2 (2018), pp. 277-310.

____, "Dispute Settlement Mechanisms in U.S. Free Trade Agreements with Korea, Panama, Peru and Colombia: Basic Designs, Key Characteristics and Implications," *British Journal of American Legal Studies,* Vol. 5, Iss. 2 (2016), pp. 487-504.

____, "Incorporation and Implementatio of Treaties in South Korea," in Curtis A. Bradley (ed.), *Oxford Handbook of Comparative Foreign Relations Law* (Oxford University Press, 2019), pp. 221-238.

____, "International Trade Disputes in the Republic of Korea," in Lee Jang-Hie (ed.), *Korean Yearbook of International Law*, Vol. 3 (Ilchokak, 2017).

____, "International Trade Disputes Relating to the Republic of Korea," in Lee Jang-Hie (ed.), *Korean Yearbook of International Law*, Vol. 2 (Ilchokak, 2016).

____, "International Treaties in the Korean Constitutional Court:

A Review of Recent Decisions," in *Beyond Globalization — In Commemoration of the 70th Anniversaty of the Institute of Comparative Law in Japan* (Chuo University Press, 2020).

____, "Judicial Review of Trade Remedies in the United States: Litigation in the U.S. Court of International Trade," 『무역구제 (*Trade Remedy Review*)』, Vol. 29 (2008), pp. 149-180.

____, "Korea-U.S. Bilateral Trade Relations at Crossroads U.S. Trade Remedy Investigations and Ensuing WTO Litigation," in Lee Jang-Hie (ed.), *Korean Yearbook of International Law*, Vol. 5 (Ilchokak, 2018).

____, "Korea-U.S. Economic Relationship With or Without an FTA: KORUS FTA as a Better Alternative to Manage the Bilateral Economic Relationship," *Shifting Strategic and Political Relations with the Koreas*, Korea Economic Institutue & New York University Center for Japan -U.S. Business Relationship (Oct. 2008), pp. 159-176.

____, "Minimizing the Aftershocks of the Korea-U.S. FTA: How to Manage Disputes Arising from the Two Countries' Discrepant Perspectives and Legal Systems," *KEI Academic Paper Series*, Vol. 2, Korea Economic Institute (Jan. 2009), pp. 29-48.

____, "Past and Present of the Korean Telecommunication Regulation: Market Liberalization and Broadband Permeation," *Global Trade and Customs Journal*, Vol. 2, Iss. 11/12 (Oct. 2007), pp. 393-403.

____, "Putting a Square Peg into a Round Hole? Assessment of the "Umbrella Clause" from the Perspective of Public International Law," *Chinese Journal of International Law*, Vol. 14, Iss. 2 (2015), pp. 341-373.

____, "Revisiting the ISD Procedure: Beyond Sovereign Immunity, Substantial Evidence and Chevron," 『사법(*Sabub*)』, Vol. 1 (Sep. 2007), pp. 163-191.

____, "Settling International Disputes Through Mediation — Establishing a New International Organization in Asia Pacific and Jurisdictional Issues," *Asian Journal of WTO & International Health Law and Policy*, Vol. 13, No. 1 (2018), pp. 81-122.

____, "The Belt and Road Initiative under Existing Trade Agreement," in Yun Zhao (ed.), *International Governance and the Rule of Law in China under the Belt and Road Initiative* (Cambridge University Press, 2018), pp. 59-80.

____, "The Other Side of the FTAs: China's Multilateralism and the

Balkanization of the Global Trading Rules," *China and WTO Review*, Vol. 1, No. 2 (Sept. 2015), pp. 251-268.

____ *et al*, "The United States — Korea Free Trade Agreement Path to Common Economic Prosperity or False Promise," *University of Pennsylvania East Asia Law Review*, Vol. 7 (Apr. 2011), pp. 111-162.

____, "Turning Private Action into State Action — Discrepancy Between WTO's Jurisprudence and 2001 ILC Draft Articles on State Responsibility," 『국제법학회논총(*Korean Journal of International Law*)』, Vol. 56, No. 4 (2011), pp. 341-373.

____, "Two Bites at the Same Apple? — Derivative ISDS Proceedings in the Revised Korea-U.S. FTA," *Journal of East Asia and International Law*, Vol. 12, Iss. 1 (2019), pp. 107-130.

____, "What Can We Learn from Our Struggling Cousin?: Recent Discussions on Reform of International Investment Law and Investment Dispute Settlement Proceedings" in Meredith Kolsky Lewis *et el.*, *A Post-WTO International Legal Order: Utopian, Dystopian and Other Scenarios* (Springer, 2020).

Appendix I

Provisions Governing Dispute Settlement Mechanisms (as of May 2020)

1. Japan

1. Agreement between Japan and the Republic of Singapore for a New-Age Economic Partnership*

Bilateral Dispute Settlement Provisions	Investment Dispute Settlement (ISDS) Provisions
CHAPTER 21 DISPUTE AVOIDANCE AND SETTLEMENT Article 139 Scope of Chapter 21 1. This Chapter shall apply with respect to the avoidance and settlement of disputes between the Parties concerning the interpretation or application of this Agreement or the Implementing Agreement. 2. Nothing in this Chapter shall prejudice any rights of the Parties to have recourse to dispute settlement procedures available under any other international agreement to which they are parties. 3. Notwithstanding paragraph 2 above, once a dispute settlement procedure has been initiated under this Chapter or under any other international agreement to which the Parties are parties with respect to a particular dispute, that procedure shall be used to the exclusion of any other procedure for that particular dispute. However, this does not apply if substantially separate and distinct rights or obligations under different international agreements are in dispute. 4. Paragraph 3 above shall not apply where the Parties expressly agree to the use of more than one dispute settlement procedure in respect of a particular dispute. Article 140 General Consultations for the Avoidance and Settlement of Disputes	CHAPTER 8 INVESTMENT Article 82 Settlement of Investment Disputes between a Party and an investor of the other Party 1. For the purposes of this Chapter, an investment dispute is a dispute between a Party and an investor of the other Party that has incurred loss or damage by reason of, or arising out of, an alleged breach of any right conferred by this Chapter with respect to the investments of the investor of that other Party. 2. In the event of an investment dispute, such investment dispute shall, as far as possible, be settled amicably through consultations between the parties to the investment dispute. 3. If an investment dispute cannot be settled through such consultations within five months from the date on which the investor requested for the consultations in writing, and if the investor concerned has not submitted the investment dispute for resolution (i) under administrative or judicial settlement, or (ii) in accordance with any applicable, previously agreed dispute settlement procedures, that investor may either: (a) request the establishment of an arbitral tribunal in accordance with the procedures set out in Annex Vc and submit the investment dispute to that tribunal;

Bilateral Dispute Settlement Provisions	Investment Dispute Settlement (ISDS) Provisions
1. For the purpose of avoiding disputes, a Party may request consultations with the other Party with regard to any matter on the interpretation or application of this Agreement or the Implementing Agreement. 2. When a Party requests consultations pursuant to paragraph 1 above, the other Party shall afford adequate opportunity for consultations and shall reply promptly to the request and enter into consultations in good faith. 3. If the Parties fail to resolve any matter through consultations, either Party may request a meeting of the Consultative Committee established pursuant to paragraph 4 below. The Consultative Committee shall convene within 30 days after the date of receipt of the request, with a view to a prompt and satisfactory resolution of the matter. 4. To facilitate the implementation of this Chapter, the Parties establish the Consultative Committee, which shall consist of representatives of each Party, including one legal expert designated by each Party. 5. The procedure provided for in this Article shall not be applicable if, in respect of the same dispute, the procedure provided for in Article 142 has already been initiated. Article 141 Good Offices, Conciliation or Mediation 1. Good offices, conciliation or mediation may be requested at any time by either Party. They may begin at any time if the Parties agree. The use of good offices, conciliation or mediation may be terminated at any time at the request of either Party. 2. If the Parties agree, good offices, conciliation or mediation may continue while procedures of the arbitral tribunal provided for in this Chapter are in progress.	(b) submit the investment dispute to conciliation or arbitration in accordance with the provisions of the Convention on the Settlement of Investment Disputes between States and Nationals of Other States done at Washington, March 18, 1965 (hereinafter referred to in this Chapter as "the ICSID Convention"), so long as the ICSID Convention is in force between the Parties, or conciliation or arbitration under the Additional Facility Rules of the International Centre for Settlement of Investment Disputes (hereinafter referred to in this Chapter as "ICSID") so long as the ICSID Convention is not in force between the Parties; or (c) submit the investment dispute to arbitration under the Arbitration Rules of the United Nations Commission on International Trade Law, adopted by the United Nations Commission on International Trade Law on April 28, 1976. 4. Each Party hereby consents to the submission of investment disputes to international conciliation or arbitration as provided for in paragraph 3 above, in accordance with the provisions of this Article, provided that: (a) less than three years have elapsed since the date the investor knew or ought to have known, whichever is the earlier, of the loss or damage which, it is alleged, has been incurred by the investor; and (b) in the case of arbitration in accordance with the provisions of the ICSID Convention referred to in sub-paragraph (b) of paragraph 3 above, if the Chairman of ICSID is asked to appoint an arbitrator or arbitrators pursuant to Article 38 or 56(3) of the ICSID Convention, the Chairman: (i) allows both the Party and the investor to each indicate up to three nationalities, the appointment of arbitrators of which pursuant to Article 38 or 56(3) of the ICSID Convention is unacceptable to it; and (ii) does not appoint as arbitrator any person who is, by virtue of sub-paragraph (i) above, excluded by either the Party or the investor or both the Party and the investor. 5. When the condition set out in sub-paragraph (a) of paragraph 4 above is not met,

Bilateral Dispute Settlement Provisions	Investment Dispute Settlement (ISDS) Provisions
Article 142 Special Consultations for Dispute Settlement 1. For the purpose of settling disputes, either Party may make a request in writing for consultations to the other Party if the requesting Party considers that any benefit accruing to it directly or indirectly under this Agreement or the Implementing Agreement is being nullified or impaired, as a result of failure of the requested Party to carry out its obligations, or as a result of the application by the requested Party of measures which conflict with its obligations, under this Agreement or the Implementing Agreement. 2. Unless the Parties agree otherwise, the requested Party shall: (a) enter into consultations within 30 days after the date of receipt of the request for consultations made pursuant to paragraph 1 above; or (b) enter into consultations within 10 days after the date of receipt of the request for consultations made pursuant to paragraph 1 above if the procedure provided for in Article 140 was utilised in respect of the same dispute and 60 days or more have elapsed from the date of the initiation of consultations under that Article. 3. The Parties shall make every effort to reach a mutually satisfactory resolution through consultations. 4. Where there is an infringement of the obligations assumed under this Agreement or the Implementing Agreement, such infringement is considered prima facie to constitute a case of nullification or impairment. Article 143 Establishment of Arbitral Tribunals	the consent given in paragraph 4 above shall be invalidated. 6. When the conditions set out in sub-paragraph (b) of paragraph 4 of this Article are not met, the consent to arbitration by ICSID given in paragraph 4 of this Article shall be invalidated. In such circumstances, a different method of dispute settlement can be chosen from among those methods provided for in paragraph 3 of this Article other than ICSID arbitration. 7. Paragraphs 3 and 4 of this Article shall not apply if an investor which is an enterprise of a Party owned or controlled by persons of non-Parties submits an investment dispute with respect to its investments in the territory of the other Party, unless the investments concerned have been established, acquired or expanded in the territory of that other Party. 8. An investor to an investment dispute who intends to submit an investment dispute pursuant to paragraph 3 of this Article shall give to the Party that is a party to the investment dispute written notice of intent to do so at least 90 days before the claim is submitted. The notice of intent shall specify: (a) the name and address of the investor concerned; (b) the specific measures of that Party at issue and a brief summary of the factual and legal basis of the dispute sufficient to present the problem clearly, including the provisions of this Chapter alleged to have been breached; and (c) the dispute settlement procedures set forth in sub-paragraph (a), (b) or (c) of paragraph 3 of this Article which the investor will seek. 9. When an investor of a Party submits an investment dispute pursuant to paragraph 3 of this Article and the disputing Party invokes Article 84 or 85, the arbitrators to be selected shall, on the request of the disputing Party or investor, have the necessary expertise relevant to the specific financial matters under dispute.

Bilateral Dispute Settlement Provisions	Investment Dispute Settlement (ISDS) Provisions
1. Unless otherwise agreed by the Parties, if the Parties fail to resolve a dispute through consultations provided for in Article 142 above, either Party may request the establishment of an arbitral tribunal in respect of that dispute: (a) after 60 days from the date on which the requested Party receives the request for consultations made pursuant to subparagraph (a) of paragraph 2 of Article 142 above; or (b) after 30 days from the date on which the requested Party receives the request for consultations made pursuant to subparagraph (b) of paragraph 2 of Article 142 above. 2. Any request to establish an arbitral tribunal pursuant to this Article shall identify: (a) the legal basis of the complaint including the provisions of this Agreement or the Implementing Agreement alleged to have been breached and any other relevant provisions; and (b) the factual basis for the complaint. 3. The Parties shall, within 30 days after the date of receipt of the request for the establishment of an arbitral tribunal, appoint one arbitrator each. If one Party fails to so appoint an arbitrator, the legal expert designated by that Party pursuant to paragraph 4 of Article 140 shall be appointed as an arbitrator. 4. The Parties shall agree on and designate a third arbitrator, who shall chair the arbitral tribunal. If the Parties fail to agree on the third arbitrator, each Party shall prepare and exchange with the other Party, a list of five persons whom that Party can accept as the third arbitrator. The third arbitrator shall be chosen in the following manner: (a) if only one name is common to both lists, that person, if available, will be	10. (a) The award shall include: (i) a judgement whether or not there has been a breach by a Party of any rights conferred by this Chapter in respect of the investor of the other Party and its investments; and (ii) a remedy if there has been such breach. (b) The award rendered in accordance with sub-paragraph (a) above shall be final and binding upon the Party and the investor, except to the extent provided for in sub-paragraphs (c) and (d) below. (c) Where an award provides that there has been a breach by a Party of any rights conferred by this Chapter in respect of the investor of the other Party and its investments, the Party to the dispute is entitled to implement the award through one of the following remedies, in lieu of the remedy indicated pursuant to (ii) of sub-paragraph (a) of this paragraph: (i) pecuniary compensation, including interest from the time the loss or damage was incurred until time of payment; (ii) restitution in kind; or (iii) pecuniary compensation and restitution in combination, provided that: (A) the Party notifies the investor, within 30 days after the date of the award, that it will implement the award through one of the remedies indicated in (i), (ii) or (iii) of this sub-paragraph; and (B) where the Party chooses to implement the award in accordance with (i) or (iii) of this sub-paragraph, the Party and the investor agree as to the amount of pecuniary compensation, or in lieu of such agreement, a decision pursuant to sub-paragraph (d) below is made. (d) If the Party and the investor are unable to agree, within 60 days after the date of the award, as to the amount of pecuniary compensation as provided for in (B) of sub-paragraph (c) above, the matter may be referred, by either the Party or the investor, to the arbitral tribunal that rendered the award. The award on the amount of pecuniary compensation in accordance with this paragraph is final and binding on both the Party and the investor.

Bilateral Dispute Settlement Provisions	Investment Dispute Settlement (ISDS) Provisions
chosen as the third arbitrator; (b) if more than one name appears on both lists, the Parties shall consult for the purpose of agreeing on the third arbitrator from such names; (c) if the Parties are not able to reach agreement in accordance with sub-paragraph (b) above or if there is no name common to both lists, or the arbitrator agreed upon or chosen is not available and the Parties cannot decide on a replacement for the arbitrator that is not available, then the two arbitrators appointed pursuant to paragraph 3 above shall agree on the third arbitrator; and (d) if the arbitrators are not able to reach agreement on the third arbitrator, the third arbitrator shall be chosen by random drawing in accordance with the procedure agreed to by the Parties for this purpose in the Implementing Agreement. 5. The third arbitrator shall be appointed within 40 days after the date of appointment of the second arbitrator. 6. The third arbitrator shall not, unless the Parties agree otherwise, be a national of either of the Parties, nor have his or her usual place of residence in the territory of either of the Parties, nor be employed by either Party, nor have dealt with the dispute in any capacity. 7. The arbitral tribunal should be composed of arbitrators with relevant technical or legal expertise. Article 144 Functions of Arbitral Tribunals 1. The arbitral tribunal established pursuant to Article 143 above:	(e) The award shall be executed by the applicable laws and regulations concerning the execution of such awards in force in the Party in whose territory such execution is sought. 11. Nothing in this Article shall be construed so as to prevent an investor to an investment dispute from seeking administrative or judicial settlement within the territory of the Party that is a party to the investment dispute. 12. Neither Party shall give diplomatic protection, or bring an international claim, in respect of an investment dispute which one of its investors and the other Party shall have consented to submit or shall have submitted to arbitration under this Article, unless such other Party shall have failed to abide by and comply with the award rendered in such dispute. Diplomatic protection, for the purposes of this paragraph, shall not include informal diplomatic exchanges for the sole purpose of facilitating a settlement of the dispute.

Bilateral Dispute Settlement Provisions	Investment Dispute Settlement (ISDS) Provisions
(a) should consult with the Parties as appropriate and provide adequate opportunities for the development of a mutually satisfactory resolution; (b) shall make its award in accordance with this Agreement, the Implementing Agreement, and applicable rules of international law; (c) shall set out, in its award, its findings of law and fact, together with the reasons therefor; and (d) may, apart from giving its findings, include in its award suggested implementation options for the Parties to consider in conjunction with Article 147. 2. The Parties agree that the award of the arbitral tribunal shall be final and binding on the Parties. 3. The arbitral tribunal may seek, from the Parties, such relevant information as it considers necessary and appropriate. The Parties shall respond promptly and fully to any request by an arbitral tribunal for such information as the arbitral tribunal considers necessary and appropriate. 4. The arbitral tribunal may seek information from any relevant source and may consult experts to obtain their opinion on certain aspects of the matter. With respect to factual issues concerning a scientific or other technical matter raised by a Party, the arbitral tribunal may request advisory reports in writing from an expert or experts. The arbitral tribunal may, at the request of a Party or proprio motu, select, in consultation with the Parties, no fewer than two scientific or technical experts who shall assist the arbitral tribunal throughout its proceedings, but who shall not have the right to vote in respect of any decision to be made by the arbitral tribunal, including its award. 5. The deliberations of the arbitral tribunal shall be confidential. The award of the	

Bilateral Dispute Settlement Provisions	Investment Dispute Settlement (ISDS) Provisions
arbitral tribunal shall be drafted without the presence of the Parties, and in the light of the information provided and the statements made. 6. The arbitral tribunal shall issue its award within 120 days of its establishment, unless the dispute is settled otherwise or the proceeding of the arbitral tribunal is terminated in accordance with Article 146. When the arbitral tribunal is unable to issue its award within 120 days, the arbitral tribunal may, in consultation with the Parties, agree to delay the issuance of its award by no more than 30 days. 7. The arbitral tribunal shall accord equal opportunity to the Parties to review the award in draft form. 8. The arbitral tribunal shall attempt to make its decisions, including its award, by consensus but may also make such decisions, including its award, by majority vote. Article 145 Proceedings of Arbitral Tribunals 1. The arbitral tribunal shall meet in closed session. 2. The deliberations of the arbitral tribunal and the documents submitted to it shall be kept confidential. 3. Notwithstanding paragraph 2 above, either Party may make public statements as to its views regarding the dispute, but shall treat as confidential, information and written submissions submitted by the other Party to the arbitral tribunal which that other Party has designated as confidential. Where a Party has provided information or written submissions designated to be confidential, the other Party may request a non-confidential summary of the information or written submissions which may be disclosed publicly. The Party to whom such a request is made may agree to such a request and submit such a summary, or refuse the request without needing to ascribe any reasons or justification.	

Bilateral Dispute Settlement Provisions	Investment Dispute Settlement (ISDS) Provisions
4. The Parties shall be given the opportunity to attend any of the presentations, statements or rebuttals in the proceeding. Any information or written submissions submitted by a Party to the arbitral tribunal, including any comments on the descriptive part of the draft award and responses to questions put by the arbitral tribunal, shall be made available to the other Party. Article 146 Termination of Proceedings Even if the arbitral tribunal has been established and is proceeding with the procedure provided for in Article 145 above, the Parties may agree to terminate the proceedings at any time by jointly so notifying the chair of the arbitral tribunal. Article 147 Implementation of Chapter 21 1. The award of the arbitral tribunal made pursuant to Article 144 (hereinafter referred to in this Chapter as "the original award") shall be complied with promptly. A Party which is required by the arbitral tribunal to comply with its award (hereinafter referred to in this Chapter as "the implementing Party") shall, within 20 days after the date of issuance of the original award, notify the other Party (hereinafter referred to in this Chapter as "the other Party") as to the period which it assesses to be reasonable and necessary in order to implement the original award. Such period may: (a) extend to 12 months only if administrative or legislative measures have to be undertaken; (b) be extended or shortened if the Parties agree that special circumstances so justify; or (c) give rise to a request for consultations if the other Party considers the	

Bilateral Dispute Settlement Provisions	Investment Dispute Settlement (ISDS) Provisions
period notified to be unacceptable, in which case the Parties shall enter into consultations within 10 days after the date of receipt of the request. 2. If the implementing Party considers that compliance with the original award is impracticable, it shall, instead of notifying the period for implementing the award in accordance with paragraph 1 above, promptly enter into consultations with the other Party, with a view to developing a mutually acceptable resolution, through compensation or any alternative arrangement, and agreeing on a reasonable period to implement such resolution. 3. If the other Party considers that the measures taken by the implementing Party to comply with the original award do not comply with the original award, it may request consultations. 4. Either Party may refer matters arising from the implementation of the original award to an arbitral tribunal if: (a) consultations were initiated under sub-paragraph (c) of paragraph 1 of this Article, and the Parties fail to reach agreement on the period for implementation within 20 days after the date of receipt of the request; (b) consultations were initiated under paragraph 2 of this Article, and the Parties fail to reach agreement on a mutually acceptable resolution or the period for its implementation within 30 days after the date of the initiation of consultations; (c) consultations were initiated under paragraph 3 above, and the Parties fail to resolve the matter, and at least 30 days have elapsed since the date of the expiration of the period for implementation provided for in paragraph 1 of this Article; or (d) the Party that is requested to enter into consultations refuses to do so	

Bilateral Dispute Settlement Provisions	Investment Dispute Settlement (ISDS) Provisions
where required pursuant to paragraph 1, 2 or 3 above. 5. If the arbitral tribunal convened pursuant to sub-paragraph (c) of paragraph 4 above confirms that the implementing Party has failed to comply with the original award within the implementation period as determined pursuant to paragraph 1 or sub-paragraph (a) of paragraph 4 above, the other Party may, within 30 days from the date of such confirmation by the arbitral tribunal, notify the implementing Party that it intends to suspend the application to the implementing Party of the obligations of the other Party under this Agreement or the Implementing Agreement. 6. If the implementing Party has failed to implement the compensation or other alternative arrangement within the implementation period as determined pursuant to paragraph 2 or sub-paragraph (b) of paragraph 4 of this Article, the other Party may, within 30 days from the date of the expiration of such implementation period, notify the implementing Party that it intends to suspend the application to the implementing Party of the obligations of the other Party under this Agreement or the Implementing Agreement. 7. Suspension pursuant to paragraphs 5 and 6 above may only be implemented at least 30 days after the date of the notification in accordance with that paragraph. Such suspension: (a) shall not be effected if, in respect of the dispute to which the suspension relates, consultations, or proceedings before an arbitral tribunal are in progress; (b) shall be temporary, and shall be discontinued when the Parties reach a mutually satisfactory resolution or where compliance with the original award is effected; (c) shall be restricted to the level of nullification or impairment that is attributable to the failure to comply with the original award; and	

Bilateral Dispute Settlement Provisions	Investment Dispute Settlement (ISDS) Provisions
(d) shall be restricted to the same sector or sectors to which the nullification or impairment relates, unless it is not practicable or effective to suspend obligations in such sector or sectors. 8. If the implementing Party considers that the requirements in paragraph 5, 6 or 7 above have not been met, it may request consultations with the other Party. The other Party shall enter into consultations within 10 days after the date of receipt of the request. If the Parties fail to resolve matters within 30 days after the date of receipt of the request for consultations pursuant to this paragraph, either Party may refer the matter to an arbitral tribunal. 9. The arbitral tribunal that is convened for the purpose of this Article shall, wherever possible, have as its members, the members of the original arbitral tribunal. If this is not possible, then the members to the arbitral tribunal shall be appointed pursuant to paragraphs 3 to 7 of Article 143. Unless the Parties agree to a different period, such arbitral tribunal shall issue its award within 60 days after the date when the matter is referred to it. Article 148 Expenses Unless the Parties agree otherwise, the expenses of the arbitral tribunal, including the remuneration of its members, shall be borne by the Parties in equal shares.	

* Entered into force on November 30, 2002.

1.2 Agreement between Japan and the United Mexican States for the Strengthening of the Economic Partnership*

Bilateral Dispute Settlement Provisions	Investment Dispute Settlement (ISDS) Provisions
CHAPTER 15 DISPUTE SETTLEMENT Article 150 Scope and Coverage Except as otherwise provided for in this Agreement, this Chapter shall apply with respect to the settlement of all disputes between the Parties regarding the interpretation or application of this Agreement. Article 151 Choice of Dispute Settlement Procedure 1. Nothing in this Chapter shall prejudice any rights of the Parties to have recourse to dispute settlement procedures available under any other international agreement to which both Parties are parties. 2. Notwithstanding paragraph 1 above, once a dispute settlement procedure has been initiated under this Chapter or under any other international agreement to which both Parties are parties with respect to a particular dispute, that procedure shall be used to the exclusion of any other procedure for that particular dispute. However, this does not apply if substantially separate and distinct rights or obligations under different international agreements are in dispute. 3. For the purposes of paragraph 2 above, a dispute settlement procedure under this Chapter shall be deemed to be initiated by a Party's request for the establishment of an arbitral tribunal pursuant to paragraph 1 of Article 153. 4. For the purposes of paragraph 2 above, a dispute settlement procedure under the WTO Agreement shall be deemed to be initiated by a Party's request for the	CHAPTER 7 INVESTMENT SECTION 2 SETTLEMENT OF INVESTMENT DISPUTES BETWEEN A PARTY AND AN INVESTOR OF THE OTHER PARTY Article 75 Purpose Without prejudice to the rights and obligations of the Parties under Chapter 15, this Section establishes a mechanism for the settlement of investment disputes that assures both equal treatment among investors of the Parties and due process before an impartial tribunal. Article 76 Claim by an Investor 1. An investor of a Party: (a) on its own behalf, may submit to arbitration under this Section a claim that the other Party has breached an obligation under Section 1 and that the investor has incurred loss or damage by reason of, or arising out of, that breach; and (b) on behalf of an enterprise of the other Party that is a legal person that the investor owns or controls directly or indirectly, may submit to arbitration under this Section a claim that the other Party has breached an obligation under Section 1 and that the enterprise has incurred loss or damages by reason of, or arising out of, that breach.

Bilateral Dispute Settlement Provisions	Investment Dispute Settlement (ISDS) Provisions
establishment of a panel pursuant to Article 6 of the Understanding on Rules and Procedures Governing the Settlement of Disputes in Annex 2 to the WTO Agreement, as may be amended. Article 152 Consultations 1. Each Party may request in writing consultations with the other Party regarding any matter on the interpretation or application of this Agreement. 2. When a Party requests consultations pursuant to paragraph 1 above, the other Party shall reply to the request and enter into consultations in good faith within 30 days after the date of receipt of the request, with a view to a prompt and satisfactory resolution of the matter. In a case of consultations regarding perishable goods, the requested Party shall enter into consultations within 15 days after the date of receipt of the request. Article 153 Establishment of Arbitral Tribunals 1. The complaining Party that requested consultations under Article 152 above may request in writing the establishment of an arbitral tribunal to the Party complained against: (a) if the Party complained against does not enter into such consultations within 30 days after the date of its receipt of the request for consultations under that Article; or 120 (b) if the Parties fail to resolve the dispute through such consultations under that Article within 60 days after the date of receipt of the request for such consultations, provided that the complaining Party considers that any benefit accruing to it directly or indirectly under this Agreement is being nullified or	2. An investment may not make a claim under this Section. Article 77 Consultation and Negotiation The disputing parties should first attempt to settle a claim through consultation or negotiation. Article 78 Written Request 1. The disputing investor shall submit to the disputing Party a written request for consultations with a view to settling the claim amicably at least 180 days before the claim may be submitted to arbitration. Such a request shall specify: (a) the name and address of the disputing investor and, where a claim is submitted by an investor of a Party on behalf of an enterprise, the name and address of the enterprise; (b) the provisions of this Agreement alleged to have been breached and any other relevant provisions; (c) the issues and the factual and legal basis for the claim, including specific measures adopted by the disputing Party; and (d) the relief sought and the approximate amount of damages claimed. 2. The disputing investor may not submit its written request referred to in paragraph 1 above before the events giving rise to a claim have occurred. Article 79 Submission of a Claim to Arbitration

Bilateral Dispute Settlement Provisions	Investment Dispute Settlement (ISDS) Provisions
impaired as a result of the failure of the Party complained against to carry out its obligations, or as a result of the application by the Party complained against of measures which are in conflict with the obligations of that Party, under this Agreement. 2. Any request for the establishment of an arbitral tribunal pursuant to this Article shall identify: (a) the legal basis of the complaint, including the provisions of this Agreement alleged to have been breached and any other relevant provisions; and (b) the factual basis for the complaint. 3. The arbitral tribunal shall comprise 3 arbitrators. 4. Each Party shall, within 30 days after the date of receipt of the request for the establishment of an arbitral tribunal, appoint one arbitrator who may be its national and propose up to 3 candidates to serve as the third arbitrator who shall be the chair of the arbitral tribunal. The third arbitrator shall not be a national of either Party, nor have his or her usual place of residence in either Party, nor be employed by either Party. 5. The Parties shall agree on and appoint the third arbitrator within 45 days after the date of receipt of the request for the establishment of an arbitral tribunal, taking into account the candidates proposed pursuant to paragraph 4 above. 6. If a Party has not appointed one arbitrator pursuant to paragraph 4 above or if the Parties fail to agree on and appoint the third arbitrator pursuant to paragraph 5 above, such arbitrator or such third arbitrator shall be chosen by lot within further 7 days from the candidates proposed pursuant to paragraph 4 above. 7. The date of the establishment of an arbitral tribunal shall be the date on which the	1. Subject to the compliance of the requirements established under Article 78 the disputing investor may submit the claim to: (a) arbitration under the ICSID Convention provided that both the disputing Party and the Party of the investor are parties to the ICSID Convention; (b) arbitration under the ICSID Additional Facility Rules, as may be amended, provided that either the disputing Party or the Party of the investor, but not both, is a party to the ICSID Convention; (c) arbitration under the UNCITRAL Arbitration Rules; or (d) if agreed by the disputing parties, any arbitration in accordance with other arbitration rules. 2. The applicable arbitration rules shall govern the arbitration under this Section except to the extent modified by this Section. Article 80 Consent to Arbitration 1. Each Party consents to the submission of a claim to arbitration in accordance with the procedures set out in this Section. 2. The consent given by paragraph 1 above and the submission by a disputing investor of a claim to arbitration shall satisfy the requirement of: (a) Chapter II of the ICSID Convention (Jurisdiction of the Centre) and the Additional Facility Rules for written consent of the parties; and (b) Article II of the New York Convention for an agreement in writing. Article 81 Conditions and Limitations on Consent of Each Party

Bilateral Dispute Settlement Provisions	Investment Dispute Settlement (ISDS) Provisions
chair is appointed. 8. Unless the Parties otherwise agree within 20 days from the date of receipt of the request for the establishment of the arbitral tribunal, the terms of reference of such arbitral tribunal shall be: "To examine, in the light of the relevant provisions of this Agreement, the matter referred to in the request for the establishment of an arbitral tribunal pursuant to this Article, to rule on the consistency of the measures at issue with this Agreement, and, where the arbitral tribunal reaches the conclusion that the measure is inconsistent with this Agreement, to make recommendations that the Party complained against bring the measure into conformity with this Agreement. When making recommendations, the arbitral tribunal may not suggest specific ways in which the Party complained against could implement the recommendations." 9. The Parties shall promptly deliver the terms of reference pursuant to paragraph 8 above to the arbitral tribunal. 10. If an arbitrator dies, withdraws or is removed, a replacement shall be appointed within 30 days in accordance with the appointment procedure provided for in paragraphs 4 to 6 above, which shall be applied, respectively, mutatis mutandis. In such a case, any time period applicable to the arbitral tribunal proceeding shall be suspended for a period beginning on the date the arbitrator dies, withdraws or is removed and ending on the date the replacement is appointed. Article 154 Award of Arbitral Tribunals 1. The arbitral tribunal shall meet in closed session. 2. The deliberations of the arbitral tribunal, the documents submitted to it and the draft award referred to in paragraph 4 below shall be kept confidential. 3. Nothing in this Chapter shall preclude a Party from disclosing statements of	1. No claim may be submitted to arbitration under this Section if more than 3 years have elapsed from the date on which the investor (for claims brought under subparagraph 1 (a) of Article 76) or the enterprise (for claims brought under subparagraph 1(b) of Article 76) first acquired, or should have first acquired knowledge of the breach alleged under Article 76 and knowledge that the investor (for claims brought under subparagraph 1(a) of Article 76), or the enterprise (for claims brought under subparagraph 1(b) of Article 76) had incurred loss or damage. 2. No claim may be submitted to arbitration under this Section unless: (a) (i) for claims submitted to arbitration under subparagraph 1(a) of Article 76, the investor consents in writing to arbitration in accordance with the procedures set out in this Section; 76 (ii) for claims submitted to arbitration under subparagraph 1(b) of Article 76, the investor and the enterprise agree upon the submission of a claim on behalf of the enterprise by the investor with respect to the claim and both of them consent in writing to arbitration in accordance with the procedures set out in this Section; (b) for claims submitted to arbitration under subparagraph 1(a) of Article 76, the investor and, where the claim is for loss or damage to an interest in an enterprise of the other Party that is a legal person that the investor owns or controls directly or indirectly, the enterprise, waive in writing their right to initiate or continue before any administrative tribunal or court under the law of either Party, or other dispute settlement procedures, any proceedings with respect to any measure alleged to constitute a breach referred to in paragraph 1 of Article 76; (c) for claims submitted to arbitration under subparagraph 1(b) of Article 76, both the investor and the enterprise waive in writing their right to initiate or continue before any administrative tribunal or court under the law of either Party, or other dispute settlement procedures, any proceedings with respect to any measure alleged to constitute a breach referred to in paragraph 1 of Article

Bilateral Dispute Settlement Provisions	Investment Dispute Settlement (ISDS) Provisions
its own position to the public. Each Party shall treat as confidential, information submitted by the other Party to the arbitral tribunal which that other Party has designated as confidential. A Party shall also, upon request of the other Party, provide a nonconfidential summary of the information contained in its written submissions that could be disclosed to the public. 4. The arbitral tribunal shall, within 90 days after the date of its establishment, submit to the Parties its draft award, including both descriptive part and its findings and conclusions, for the purposes of enabling the Parties to review precise aspects of the draft award. When the arbitral tribunal considers that it cannot submit to the Parties its draft award within the aforementioned 90 day period, it may extend that period with the consent of the Parties. However, in no case should the period from the establishment of the arbitral tribunal to the submission of the draft award to the Parties exceed 150 days. A Party may submit comments in writing to the arbitral tribunal on the draft award within 15 days after the date of the submission of the draft award. 5. The arbitral tribunal shall issue its award within 30 days after the date of the submission of the draft award. 6. In the case that the matters referred to the arbitral tribunal are those concerning perishable goods, the arbitral tribunal shall make every effort to issue its award to the Parties within 90 days after the date of its establishment. In no case should it do so later than 120 days. 7. The arbitral tribunal shall take its decisions including its award by majority vote. 8. The award of the arbitral tribunal shall be final and binding on the Parties. Article 155 Termination of Proceedings of the Arbitral Tribunal While the proceedings of the arbitral tribunal are in progress, the Parties may agree	76; and (d) where the investor (for claims brought under subparagraph 1(a) of Article 76) or the enterprise (for claims brought under subparagraph 1(b) of Article 76) has initiated any proceedings before any administrative tribunal or court referred to in subparagraphs (b) and (c) above, those proceedings are withdrawn in accordance with the laws of that Party. 3. Notwithstanding subparagraphs (b) and (c) above, the investor (for claims submitted to arbitration under subparagraph 1(a) of Article 76) and both the investor and the enterprise (for claims submitted to arbitration under subparagraph 1(b) of Article 76), may initiate or continue an action that seeks interim injunctive relief or other extraordinary relief that does not involve the payment of damages before an administrative tribunal or court under the law of the disputing Party. 4. With respect to the submission of a claim to arbitration: (a) an investor of a Party may not allege that the other Party has breached an obligation under Section 1, both in an arbitration under this Section and in proceedings before an administrative tribunal or court under the law of either Party; and (b) where an enterprise of a Party that is a legal person that an investor of the other Party owns or controls directly or indirectly alleges in proceedings before an administrative tribunal or court under the law of either Party that such a Party has breached an obligation under Section 1, the investor may not allege the breach in an arbitration under this Section. Article 82 Constitution of a Tribunal 1. Except in respect of a Tribunal established under Article 83, and unless the

Bilateral Dispute Settlement Provisions	Investment Dispute Settlement (ISDS) Provisions
to terminate the proceedings at any time by jointly so notifying the chair of the arbitral tribunal. Article 156 Implementation of Award 1. The Party complained against shall promptly comply with the award of the arbitral tribunal issued pursuant to Article 154. 2. The Party complained against shall, within 20 days after the date of issuance of the award, notify the complaining Party of the period of time for implementing the award. If the complaining Party considers the period of time notified to be unacceptable, it may refer the matter to an arbitral tribunal. 3. If the Party complained against fails to comply with the award within the implementation period as determined pursuant to paragraph 2 above, the Party complained against shall no later than the expiry of that implementation period enter into consultations with the complaining Party, with a view to developing mutually acceptable compensation. If no satisfactory compensation has been agreed within 20 days after the date of expiry of that implementation period, the complaining Party may notify the Party complained against that it intends to suspend the application to the Party complained against of concessions or other obligations under this Agreement. 4. If the complaining Party considers that measures taken by the Party complained against for implementing the award do not comply with the award within the implementation period as determined pursuant to paragraph 2 above, it may refer the matter to an arbitral tribunal. 5. If the arbitral tribunal to which the matter is referred pursuant to paragraph 4 above confirms that the Party complained against has failed to comply with the award within the implementation period as determined pursuant to paragraph 2	disputing parties otherwise agree, the Tribunal shall comprise 3 arbitrators, one arbitrator appointed by each of the disputing parties and the third, who shall be the presiding arbitrator, appointed by agreement of the disputing parties. 2. The Secretary-General shall serve as appointing authority for an arbitration under this Section. 3. If the Tribunal, other than the Tribunal established under Article 83, has not been constituted within 90 days from the date on which a claim was submitted to arbitration, the Secretary-General, on the request of either disputing party, shall appoint, in his discretion, the arbitrator or arbitrators not yet appointed except that the presiding arbitrator shall be appointed in accordance with paragraph 4 below. 4. The Secretary-General shall appoint the presiding arbitrator from the roster of presiding arbitrators referred to in paragraph 5 below or, if not available, from the ICSID Panel of Arbitrators, provided that in both cases the presiding arbitrator shall not be a national of the disputing Party or a national of the Party of the disputing investor. 5. The Parties may establish, and thereafter maintain, a roster of 20 presiding arbitrators experienced in international law and investment matters. The roster members shall be appointed by agreement of the Parties and without regard to nationality. Article 83 Consolidation of Multiple Claims 1. When a disputing party considers that two or more claims submitted to arbitration under Article 76 have a question of law or fact in common, the disputing party may seek a consolidation order in accordance with the terms of paragraphs 2 through 9 below.

Bilateral Dispute Settlement Provisions	Investment Dispute Settlement (ISDS) Provisions
above, the complaining Party may, within 30 days after the date of such confirmation by the arbitral tribunal, notify the Party complained against that it intends to suspend the application to the Party complained against of concessions or other obligations under this Agreement. 6. Suspension of the application of concessions or other obligations under paragraphs 3 and 5 above may only be implemented at least 30 days after the date of the notification in accordance with those paragraphs. Such suspension shall: (a) not be effected if, in respect of the dispute to which the suspension relates, consultations, or proceedings before an arbitral tribunal are in progress; (b) be temporary, and be discontinued when the Parties reach a mutually satisfactory resolution or where compliance with the award is effected; (c) be restricted to the same level of nullification or impairment that is attributable to the failure to comply with the award; and (d) be restricted to the same sector or sectors to which the nullification or impairment relates, unless it is not practicable or effective to suspend the application of concessions or other obligations in such sector or sectors. 7. If the Party complained against considers that the requirements for the suspension of the application to it of concessions or other obligations under this Agreement by the complaining Party set out in paragraph 3, 5 or 6 above have not been met, it may refer the matter to an arbitral tribunal. 8. The arbitral tribunal that is established for the purposes of this Article shall, wherever possible, have as its arbitrators, the arbitrators to the original arbitral tribunal. If this is not possible, then the arbitrators to the arbitral tribunal that is established for the purposes of this Article shall be appointed pursuant to paragraphs 4 to 6 of Article 153. Unless the Parties agree to a different period, such	2. A disputing party that seeks a consolidation order under this Article shall deliver, in writing, a request to the Secretary-General to establish a Tribunal under this Article. The request shall: (a) specify the nature of the order sought and the grounds on which the order is sought; and (b) be accompanied by a request for arbitration made under paragraph 1 of Article 36 of the ICSID Convention or a notice of arbitration submitted under Article 2 of Schedule C of the ICSID Additional Facility Rules, as may be amended. 3. Within 60 days of receipt of the request, the Secretary-General shall establish a Tribunal comprising 3 arbitrators. One arbitrator shall be a national of the disputing Party, the second arbitrator shall be a national of the Party of the disputing investor, and the presiding arbitrator shall not be a national of any of the Parties. 4. A Tribunal established under this Article shall be established under the ICSID Convention or the ICSID Additional Facility Rules as may be amended, as appropriate, and shall conduct its proceedings in accordance with the provisions thereof, except as modified by this Section. 5. Any disputing investor that has submitted a claim to arbitration and considers that such a claim raises questions of law or fact which are common to those upon which the consolidation under paragraph 2 above has been requested, but has not been named in a request made under paragraph 2 above, may request to the Tribunal established under this Article to consider the consolidation of his claim. The request shall comply with the requirements established in paragraph 2 above. 6. The disputing investor referred to in paragraph 5 above shall deliver to the disputing Party or disputing investors with respect to whom the order is sought, a copy of the request made under paragraph 5 above.

Bilateral Dispute Settlement Provisions	Investment Dispute Settlement (ISDS) Provisions
arbitral tribunal shall issue its award within 30 days after the date when the matter is referred to it. The award of the arbitral tribunal established under this Article shall be binding on the Parties.	7. On application of a disputing party, a Tribunal established under this Article may order the adjourning of the proceedings related to claims referred to in paragraphs 1 and 5 above.
Article 157 Modification of Time Periods Any time period provided for in this Chapter may be modified by mutual consent of the Parties.	8. A Tribunal established under this Article may, in the interests of fair and efficient resolution of the dispute, and after hearing the disputing parties, by order: (a) assume jurisdiction over, and hear and determine together, all or part of the claims referred to in paragraphs 1 and 5 above; or (b) assume jurisdiction over, and hear and determine one or more of the claims referred to in paragraphs 1 and 5 above, the determination of which it believes would assist in the resolution of the others.
Article 158 Expenses Unless the Parties agree otherwise, the expenses of the arbitral tribunal, including the remuneration of its arbitrators, shall be borne by the Parties in equal shares.	9. A Tribunal established under Article 79 shall not have jurisdiction to decide a claim, or a part of a claim, over which a Tribunal established under this Article has assumed jurisdiction in the terms of paragraph 8 above.[1]
Article 159 Rules of Procedure	Article 84 Governing Law 1. A Tribunal established under this Section shall decide the issues in dispute in accordance with this Agreement and applicable rules of international law.
Unless the Parties agree otherwise, the details and procedures for the arbitral tribunal provided for in this Chapter shall be in accordance with the Rules of Procedure to be adopted by the Joint Committee within the first year of the date of entry into force of this Agreement.	2. An interpretation of a provision of this Agreement adopted by the Joint Committee shall be binding on a Tribunal established under this Section. Such interpretation shall be made publicly available through the means that each Party considers appropriate.
	Article 85 Notice A disputing Party shall deliver to the other Party: (a) written notice of a claim that has been submitted to arbitration no later

Bilateral Dispute Settlement Provisions	Investment Dispute Settlement (ISDS) Provisions
	than 30 days after the date on which the claim was submitted; and (b) copies of all pleadings filed in the arbitration. Article 86 Participation by a Party On written notice to the disputing parties, the Party other than the disputing Party may make submissions to a Tribunal on a question of interpretation of this Agreement. Article 87 Documents 1. The Party other than the disputing Party shall be entitled to receive from the disputing Party, at the cost of the requesting Party a copy of: (a) the evidence that has been tendered to the Tribunal; and (b) the written argument of the disputing parties. 2. The Party receiving information pursuant to paragraph 1 above shall treat the information as if it were a disputing Party. Article 88 Place of Arbitration Unless the disputing parties agree otherwise, a Tribunal shall hold an arbitration in a country that is a party to the New York Convention. Article 89 Interpretation of Annexes

Bilateral Dispute Settlement Provisions	Investment Dispute Settlement (ISDS) Provisions
	1. Where a disputing Party asserts as a defense that the measure alleged to be a breach is within the scope of a reservation or exception set out in Annex 6, Annex 7, Annex 8 or Annex 9, on request of the disputing Party, the Tribunal shall request the Joint Committee to adopt an interpretation on the issue. The Joint Committee, within 60 days of delivery of the request, shall adopt an interpretation and submit in writing its interpretation to the Tribunal. 2. Further to Article 84, an interpretation adopted and submitted under paragraph 1 above shall be binding on the Tribunal. If the Joint Committee fails to submit an interpretation within 60 days, the Tribunal shall decide the issue. Article 90 Expert Reports Without prejudice to the appointment of other kinds of experts where authorized by the applicable arbitration rules, a Tribunal, at the request of a disputing party or, unless the disputing parties disapprove, on its own initiative, may appoint one or more experts in the fields of environmental, health, safety or other scientific matters to report to it in writing on any factual issue concerning matters of their expertise raised by a disputing party in a proceeding, subject to such terms and conditions as the disputing parties may agree. Article 91 Interim Measures of Protection A Tribunal may order an interim measure of protection to preserve the rights of a disputing party, or to facilitate the conduct of arbitral proceedings, including an order to preserve evidence in the possession or control of a disputing party. A Tribunal may not order attachment or enjoin the application of the measure alleged to constitute a breach referred to in paragraph 1 of Article 76.

Bilateral Dispute Settlement Provisions	Investment Dispute Settlement (ISDS) Provisions
	Article 92 Final Award 1. Where a Tribunal makes a final award against a disputing Party, the Tribunal may award, separately or in combination, only: (a) monetary damages and any applicable interest; or (b) restitution of property, in which case the award shall provide that the disputing Party may pay monetary damages and any applicable interest in lieu of restitution. A Tribunal may also award costs in accordance with the applicable arbitration rules. 2. Subject to paragraph 1 above, where a claim is made under subparagraph 1 (b) of Article 76: (a) an award of monetary damages and any applicable interest shall provide that the sum be paid to the enterprise; and (b) an award of restitution of property shall provide that restitution be made to the enterprise. 3. A Tribunal may not order a Party to pay punitive damages. Article 93 Finality and Enforcement of an Award 1. Any arbitral award rendered pursuant to Article 92 shall be final, and binding on the disputing parties in respect of the particular case. 2. Subject to the applicable revision, annulment or set aside procedures, a disputing party shall abide by and comply with an award without delay.

Bilateral Dispute Settlement Provisions	Investment Dispute Settlement (ISDS) Provisions
	3. If a disputing Party fails to abide by or comply with a final award, the Party whose investor was a party to the arbitration may have recourse to the dispute settlement procedure under Chapter 15. In this event, the requesting Party may seek: (a) a determination that the failure to abide by or comply with the final award is inconsistent with the obligations of this Agreement; and (b) a recommendation that the Party abide by or comply with the final award. Article 94 General 1. A claim is submitted to arbitration under this Section when: (a) the request for arbitration under paragraph (1) of Article 36 of the ICSID Convention has been received by the Secretary-General; (b) the notice of arbitration under Article 2 of Schedule C of the ICSID Additional Facility Rules, as may be amended, has been received by the Secretary-General; or (c) the notice of arbitration given under the UNCITRAL Arbitration Rules is received by the disputing Party. The disputing parties shall otherwise agree in relation to subparagraph 1 (d) of Article 79. 2. Delivery of notice and other documents on a Party shall be made: (a) in the case of Mexico: through the Directorate General of Foreign Investment of the Ministry of Economy; and (b) in the case of Japan: through the Ministry of Foreign Affairs.

Bilateral Dispute Settlement Provisions	Investment Dispute Settlement (ISDS) Provisions
	3. In an arbitration under this Section, a Party shall not assert, as a defense, counterclaim, right of setoff or otherwise, that the disputing investor has received or will receive, pursuant to an insurance or guarantee contract, indemnification or other compensation for all or part of its alleged damages. 4. Either disputing party may make available to the public in a timely manner all documents, including an award, submitted to, or issued by, a Tribunal established under this Section, subject to redaction of: (a) confidential business information; (b) information which is privileged or otherwise protected from disclosure under the applicable law of either Party; and (c) information which the Party must withhold pursuant to the relevant arbitral rules, as applied. Note: For greater certainty, it is confirmed by both Parties that a Party may share with officials of its central or local government in the case of Japan, and its federal or state government in the case of Mexico, all relevant documents in the course of dispute settlement under this Section, including confidential information and that the disputing parties may disclose to other persons in connection with the arbitral proceedings the documents submitted to, or issued by, a Tribunal established under this Section, as they consider necessary for the preparation of their cases; provided that they shall ensure that those persons protect the confidential information in such documents. Article 95 Exceptions from Dispute Settlement Procedure 1. Without prejudice to the applicability or nonapplicability of the dispute settlement provisions of this Section or of Chapter 15 to other actions taken by a Party pursuant to Article 169, a decision by a Party to prohibit or restrict the acquisition of an investment in its Area by an investor of the other Party, or its investment, pursuant to

Bilateral Dispute Settlement Provisions	Investment Dispute Settlement (ISDS) Provisions
	that Article shall not be subject to such provisions. 2. In the case of Mexico, the dispute settlement provisions of this Section and of Chapter 15 shall not apply to a decision by the National Commission on Foreign Investment ("Comisión Nacional de Inversiones Extranjeras") following a review pursuant to Annex 6, reservation 3 set out in the Schedule of Mexico, with respect to whether or not to permit an acquisition that is subject to review.

* Entered into force on April 1, 2005.

1) *This provision may be notable as it does not appear in any other ISDS provisions Japan has concluded.*

1.3 Agreement between Japan and the Kingdom of Thailand for an Economic Partnership*

Bilateral Dispute Settlement Provisions	Investment Dispute Settlement (ISDS) Provisions
CHAPTER 14 DISPUTE SETTLEMENT Article 159 Scope and Coverage	Article 106 Settlement of Investment Disputes between a Party and an Investor of the Other Party
1. Unless otherwise provided for in this Agreement, this Chapter shall apply with respect to the settlement of disputes between the Parties concerning the interpretation or application of this Agreement.	1. For the purposes of this Chapter, an investment dispute is a dispute between a Party and an investor of the other Party concerning a claim that the investor has incurred loss or damage by reason of, or arising out of, an alleged breach of an obligation under this Chapter by the former Party.
2. Nothing in this Chapter shall prejudice any rights of the Parties to have recourse to dispute settlement procedures available under any other international agreement to which both Parties are parties.	2. In the event of an investment dispute, such investment dispute shall, as far as possible, be settled amicably through consultations between the parties to the investment dispute.
3. Notwithstanding paragraph 2 above, once a dispute settlement procedure has been initiated under this Chapter or under any other international agreement to which both Parties are parties with respect to a particular dispute, that procedure shall be used to the exclusion of any other procedure for that particular dispute. However, this shall not apply if substantially separate and distinct rights or obligations under different international agreements are in dispute.	3. If the investment dispute cannot be settled through such consultations within 6 months from the date on which the investor requested for the consultations in writing and if the investor concerned has not submitted the investment dispute for resolution to courts of justice or administrative tribunals under the law of the Party that is a party to the investment dispute (hereinafter referred to in this Article as the "disputing Party"), that investor may submit the investment dispute to one of the following international conciliations or arbitrations:
4. Paragraph 3 above shall not apply where the Parties expressly agree to the use of more than one dispute settlement procedure in respect of a particular dispute. Article 160 Consultations	(a) conciliation or arbitration in accordance with the provisions of the Convention on the Settlement of Investment Disputes between States and Nationals of Other States done at Washington, 18 March 1965, as may be amended (hereinafter referred to in this Article as "the ICSID Convention"), provided that both Parties are parties to the ICSID Convention;
1. Each Party may request in writing consultations with the other Party with regard to any matter on the interpretation or application of this Agreement.	(b) conciliation or arbitration under the Additional Facility Rules of the International Centre for Settlement of Investment Disputes, as may be amended provided that one of the Parties is a party to the ICSID Convention; or

Bilateral Dispute Settlement Provisions	Investment Dispute Settlement (ISDS) Provisions
2. When a Party requests consultations pursuant to paragraph 1 above, the other Party shall reply promptly to the request and enter into consultations in good faith within 30 days after the date of receipt of the request, with a view to a prompt and satisfactory resolution of the matter. Article 161 Good Offices, Conciliation or Mediation 1. Good offices, conciliation or mediation may be requested at any time by either Party. They may begin at any time if the Parties agree and, at the request of either Party, be terminated at any time. 2. If the Parties agree, good offices, conciliation or mediation may continue while procedures of the arbitral tribunal provided for in this Chapter are in progress. Article 162 Establishment of Arbitral Tribunals 1. The complaining Party that requested consultations under Article 160 may request in writing the establishment of an arbitral tribunal to the Party complained against: (a) if the Party complained against does not enter into such consultations within 30 days after the date of receipt of the request for consultations under that Article; or (b) if the Parties fail to resolve the dispute through such consultations under that Article within 60 days after the date of receipt of the request for such consultations, provided that the complaining Party considers that any benefit accruing to it directly or indirectly under this Agreement is being nullified or impaired as a result of the failure of the Party complained against to carry out its obligations, or as a result of	(c) arbitration under the Arbitration Rules of the United Nations Commission on International Trade Law, adopted by the United Nations Commission on International Trade Law on 28 April 1976, as may be amended. In respect of a particular claim, exercise of the right under this paragraph to submit an investment dispute to an arbitration shall be deemed to have been made to the exclusion of any other dispute settlement procedures specified in this paragraph and proceedings before courts of justice or administrative tribunals under the law of the disputing Party, unless the arbitration proceedings have been terminated before a final award on the merit of the case has been rendered. 4. The applicable arbitration rules shall govern the arbitration referred to in this Article except to the extent modified by this Article. 5. An investor that is a party to an investment dispute who intends to submit an investment dispute pursuant to subparagraph 3(a), (b) or (c) above (hereinafter referred to in this Article as the "disputing investor") shall give to the disputing Party written notice of intent to do so at least 90 days before the claim is submitted. The notice of intent shall specify: (a) the name and address of the disputing investor; (b) the specific measures of the disputing Party at issue and a brief summary of the factual and legal basis of the dispute sufficient to present the problem clearly, including the provisions of this Chapter alleged to have been breached; and (c) the dispute settlement procedures set forth in subparagraph 3(a), (b) or (c) above which the disputing investor intends to choose. 6. Each Party hereby consents to the submission of investment disputes to international conciliation or arbitration as provided for in this Article. If more than

Bilateral Dispute Settlement Provisions	Investment Dispute Settlement (ISDS) Provisions
the application by the Party complained against of measures which are in conflict with the obligations of that Party, under this Agreement. 2. Any request for the establishment of an arbitral tribunal pursuant to this Article shall identify: (a) the specific measures at issue; and (b) the legal basis of the complaint including the provisions of this Agreement alleged to have been breached and any other relevant provisions.	2 years have elapsed since the date the disputing investor knew or ought to have known, whichever is the earlier, of the loss or damage which, it is alleged, has been incurred by the disputing investor, the consent above shall be invalidated. 7. Paragraph 3 above shall not prevent the disputing investor from initiating or continuing an action that seeks interim injunctive relief that does not involve the payment of damages before courts of justice or administrative tribunals under the law of the disputing Party provided that the action is brought for the sole purpose of preserving the disputing investor's rights and interests while the arbitration is pending.
3. Each Party shall within 30 days after the date of receipt of the request for the establishment of an arbitral tribunal, appoint one arbitrator who may be its national and propose up to 3 candidates to serve as the third arbitrator who shall be the chair of the arbitral tribunal. The third arbitrator shall not be a national of either Party, nor have his or her usual place of residence in either Party, nor be employed by either Party. 4. The Parties shall agree on and appoint the third arbitrator within 45 days after the date of receipt of the request for the establishment of an arbitral tribunal, taking into account the candidates proposed pursuant to paragraph 3 above.	8. Unless the disputing investor and the disputing Party (hereinafter referred to in this Article as the "disputing parties") agree otherwise, the arbitral tribunal shall comprise 3 arbitrators, one arbitrator appointed by each of the disputing parties and the third, who shall be the presiding arbitrator, appointed by agreement of the disputing parties. If the disputing investor or the disputing Party fails to appoint an arbitrator within 75 days from the date on which the investment dispute was submitted to arbitration, the Secretary-General of the International Centre for Settlement of Investment Disputes, upon request by either of the disputing parties, shall appoint, in his or her discretion, the arbitrator or arbitrators not yet appointed subject to the requirement of paragraphs 9 and 10 below.
5. If a Party has not appointed one arbitrator pursuant to paragraph 3 above, or if the Parties fail to agree on and appoint the third arbitrator pursuant to paragraph 4 above, such arbitrator or such third arbitrator shall be chosen by lot within a further period of 7 days from the candidates proposed pursuant to paragraph 3 above.	9. Unless the disputing parties agree otherwise, the third arbitrator shall not be of the same nationality as the disputing investor, nor be a national of the disputing Party, nor have his or her usual place of residence in the Area of either of the Parties, nor be employed by either of the disputing parties at the time of his or her appointment.
6. The arbitral tribunal should be composed of arbitrators with relevant technical or legal expertise. Article 163 Functions of Arbitral Tribunals	10. Each of the disputing parties may indicate up to 3 nationalities, the appointment of arbitrators of which is unacceptable to it. In this event, the Secretary-General of the International Centre for Settlement of Investment Disputes may not appoint as an arbitrator any person whose nationality is indicated by any of the disputing parties.

Bilateral Dispute Settlement Provisions	Investment Dispute Settlement (ISDS) Provisions
1. The arbitral tribunal established pursuant to Article 162: (a) should consult with the Parties as appropriate and provide adequate opportunities for the development of a mutually satisfactory resolution; (b) shall make its award in accordance with this Agreement and applicable rules of international law; (c) shall set out, in its award, its findings of law and fact, together with the reasons therefor; and (d) may, apart from giving its findings, include in its award suggested implementation options for the Parties to consider in conjunction with Article 166. 2. The arbitral tribunal may seek, from the Parties, such relevant information as it considers necessary and appropriate. The Parties shall respond promptly and fully to any request by an arbitral tribunal for such information. 3. The arbitral tribunal may seek information from any relevant source and may consult experts to obtain their opinion on certain aspects of the matter. With respect to factual issues concerning a scientific or other technical matter raised by a Party, the arbitral tribunal may request advisory reports in writing from an expert or experts. The arbitral tribunal may, at the request of a Party or on its own initiative, select, in consultation with the Parties, no fewer than 2 scientific or technical experts who shall assist the arbitral tribunal throughout its proceedings, but who shall not have the right to vote in respect of any decision to be made by the arbitral tribunal, including its award. 4. The award of the arbitral tribunal shall be drafted without the presence of the Parties, and in the light of the information provided and the statements made.	11. Any arbitration under this Article shall be held in a country that is a party to the Convention on the Recognition and Enforcement of Foreign Arbitral Awards, done at New York on 10 June 1958, as may be amended. 12. Where an arbitral tribunal makes a final award against a disputing Party, it may award, separately or in combination, only: (a) payment of monetary damages and applicable interest; and (b) restitution of property, in which case the award shall provide that the disputing Party may pay monetary damages and any applicable interest in lieu of restitution. Costs may also be awarded in accordance with the applicable arbitration rules. 13. Any arbitral award rendered pursuant to this Article shall be final and binding upon the disputing parties. Each Party shall carry out without delay the provisions of any such award and provide in its Area for the enforcement of such award in accordance with its relevant laws and regulations. 14. In an arbitration under this Article, a Party shall not assert, as a defense, counterclaim, right of set-off or otherwise, that the disputing investor has received or will receive, pursuant to an insurance or guarantee contract, indemnification or other compensation for all or part of its alleged damages. 15. This Article shall not apply to investment disputes: (a) arising out of events which occurred, or to investment disputes which had been settled, prior to the entry into force of this Agreement; (b) with respect to obligations under Article 97; and

Bilateral Dispute Settlement Provisions	Investment Dispute Settlement (ISDS) Provisions
5. The arbitral tribunal shall, within 90 days after the date of its establishment, submit to the Parties its draft award, including both descriptive part and its findings and conclusions, for the purpose of enabling the Parties to review precise aspects of the draft award. When the arbitral tribunal considers that it cannot submit to the Parties its draft award within the afore-mentioned 90 days period, it may extend that period with the consent of the Parties. However, in no case should the period from the establishment of the arbitral tribunal to the submission of the draft award to the Parties exceed 150 days. A Party may submit comments in writing to the arbitral tribunal on the draft award within 15 days after the date of submission of the draft award. 6. The arbitral tribunal shall issue its award, within 30 days after the date of submission of the draft award. 7. The arbitral tribunal shall attempt to make its decisions, including its award, by consensus but may also make such decisions, including its award, by majority vote. 8. The award of the arbitral tribunal shall be final and binding on the Parties. Article 164 Proceedings of Arbitral Tribunal 1. The arbitral tribunal shall meet in closed session. 2. The deliberations of the arbitral tribunal, the documents submitted to it and the draft award referred to in paragraph 5 of Article 163 shall be kept confidential. 3. Notwithstanding paragraph 2 above, either Party may make public statements as to its views regarding the dispute, but shall treat as confidential, information and written submissions submitted by the other Party to the arbitral tribunal which that other Party has designated as confidential. Where a Party has provided information or written submissions designated to be confidential, the other Party may request	(c) with respect to measures other than those relating to the management, conduct, operation, maintenance, use, enjoyment, and sale or other disposition of investments.

Bilateral Dispute Settlement Provisions	Investment Dispute Settlement (ISDS) Provisions
a non-confidential summary of the information or written submissions which may be disclosed publicly. The Party to whom such a request is made may agree to such a request and submit such a summary, or deny the request without providing any reasons or justification. 4. The Parties shall be given the opportunity to attend any of the presentations, statements or rebuttals in the proceeding. Any information or written submissions submitted by a Party to the arbitral tribunal, including any comments on the descriptive part of the draft award and responses to questions put by the arbitral tribunal, shall be made available to the other Party. Article 165 Termination of Proceedings The Parties may agree to terminate the proceedings of the arbitral tribunal at any time by jointly so notifying the chair of the arbitral tribunal. Article 166 Implementation of Award 1. The Party complained against shall promptly comply with the award issued pursuant to Article 163. 2. The Party complained against shall, within 20 days after the date of issuance of the award, notify the complaining Party of the period of time for implementing the award. If the complaining Party considers the period of time notified to be unacceptable, it may refer the matter to an arbitral tribunal. 3. If the Party complained against considers it impracticable to comply with the award within the implementation period as specified pursuant to paragraph 2 above, the Party complained against shall, no later than the expiry of that implementation period, enter into consultations with the complaining Party, with a view to	

Bilateral Dispute Settlement Provisions	Investment Dispute Settlement (ISDS) Provisions
developing mutually acceptable compensation. If no satisfactory compensation has been agreed within 20 days after the date of expiry of that implementation period, the complaining Party may notify the Party complained against that it intends to suspend the application of concessions or other obligations under this Agreement. 4. If the complaining Party considers that the Party complained against has failed to comply with the award within the implementation period as specified pursuant to paragraph 2 above, it may refer the matter to an arbitral tribunal. If the arbitral tribunal confirms that the Party complained against has failed to comply with the award within the implementation period as specified pursuant to paragraph 2 above, the complaining Party may, within 30 days after the date of such confirmation by the arbitral tribunal, notify the Party complained against that it intends to suspend the application of concessions or other obligations under this Agreement. 5. Suspension of the application of concessions or other obligations under paragraphs 3 and 4 above may only be implemented at least 30 days after the date of notification in accordance with those paragraphs. Such suspension shall: (a) not be effected if, in respect of the dispute to which the suspension relates, consultations, or proceedings before an arbitral tribunal are in progress; (b) be temporary, and be discontinued when the Parties reach a mutually satisfactory resolution or where compliance with the original award is effected; (c) be restricted to the same level of nullification or impairment that is attributable to the failure to comply with the original award; and (d) be restricted to the same sector or sectors to which the nullification or impairment relates, unless it is not practicable or effective to suspend the application of concessions or other obligations in such sector or sectors. 6. If the Party complained against considers that the requirements for the suspension	

Bilateral Dispute Settlement Provisions	Investment Dispute Settlement (ISDS) Provisions
of the application of concessions or other obligations under this Agreement by the complaining Party set out in paragraph 3, 4, or 5 above have not been met, it may request consultations with the complaining Party. The complaining Party shall enter into consultations within 10 days after the date of receipt of the request. If the Parties fail to resolve the matters within 30 days after the date of receipt of the request for consultations pursuant to this paragraph, the Party complained against may refer the matter to an arbitral tribunal. 7. The arbitral tribunal under this Article shall, wherever possible, be composed of the arbitrators of the original arbitral tribunal. If any of the arbitrators is not available, then that arbitrator shall be replaced by an arbitrator appointed pursuant to paragraphs 3 through 5 of Article 162. Unless the Parties agree to a different period, the arbitral tribunal under this Article shall issue its award within 60 days after the date when the matter is referred to it. The award of the arbitral tribunal under this Article shall be final and binding on the Parties. Article 167 Expenses Unless the Parties agree otherwise, the expenses of the arbitral tribunal, including the remuneration of the arbitrators, shall be borne by the Parties in equal shares.	

* Entered into force on November 1, 2007.

1.4 Agreement between Japan and the Socialist Republic of Viet Nam for an Economic Partnership*

Bilateral Dispute Settlement Provisions	Investment Dispute Settlement (ISDS) Provisions
CHAPTER 13 DISPUTE SETTLEMENT Article 116 Scope 1. Unless otherwise provided for in this Agreement, this Chapter shall apply with respect to the settlement of disputes between the Parties concerning the interpretation or application of this Agreement. 2. Nothing in this Chapter shall prejudice any rights of the Parties to have recourse to dispute settlement procedures available under any other international agreement to which both Parties are parties. 3. Notwithstanding paragraph 2, once a dispute settlement procedure has been initiated under this Chapter or under any other international agreement to which both Parties are parties with respect to a particular dispute, that procedure shall be used to the exclusion of any other procedure for that particular dispute. However, this shall not apply if substantially separate and distinct rights or obligations under different international agreements are in dispute. 4. For the purposes of paragraphs 2 and 3, a dispute settlement procedure shall be deemed to have been initiated when a Party has requested the establishment of, or referred a dispute to, an arbitral tribunal or a dispute settlement panel, in accordance with this Chapter or any other international agreement to which the Parties are parties. Article 117 Consultations	N/A

Bilateral Dispute Settlement Provisions	Investment Dispute Settlement (ISDS) Provisions
1. Either Party may make a request in writing for consultations to the other Party concerning any matter on the interpretation or application of this Agreement. 2. Any request for consultations shall be submitted in writing, containing the identification of the specific measures at issue and indication of the factual and legal basis (including, if applicable, the provisions of this Agreement alleged to have been breached and any other relevant provisions) of the complaint. 3. When a Party makes a request for consultations pursuant to paragraph 1, the other Party shall reply to the request and enter into consultations in good faith within 30 days after the date of receipt of the request, with a view to reaching a prompt and mutually satisfactory resolution of the matter. In case of consultations regarding perishable goods, the other Party shall enter into consultations within 15 days after the date of receipt of the request. Article 118 Good Offices, Conciliation, or Mediation 1. Good offices, conciliation, or mediation may be requested at any time by either Party. They may begin at any time by agreement of the Parties and be terminated at any time upon the request of either Party. 2. If the Parties agree, good offices, conciliation, or mediation may continue while the proceedings of the arbitral tribunal provided for in this Chapter are in progress. Article 119 Establishment of Arbitral Tribunals 1. The complaining Party that made a request for consultations under Article 117 may request in writing the establishment of an arbitral tribunal to the Party complained against:	

Bilateral Dispute Settlement Provisions	Investment Dispute Settlement (ISDS) Provisions
(a) if the Party complained against does not enter into such consultations within 30 days, or within 15 days in case of consultations regarding perishable goods, after the date of receipt of the request for such consultations; or (b) if the Parties fail to resolve the dispute through such consultations within 60 days, or within 30 days in case of consultations regarding perishable goods, after the date of receipt of the request for such consultations, provided that the complaining Party considers that any benefit accruing to it under this Agreement is being nullified or impaired as a result of the failure of the Party complained against to carry out its obligations under this Agreement, or as a result of the application by the Party complained against of measures which are in conflict with its obligations under this Agreement. 2. Any request for the establishment of an arbitral tribunal pursuant to this Article shall identify: (a) the legal basis of the complaint including the provisions of this Agreement alleged to have been breached and any other relevant provisions; and (b) the factual basis for the complaint. 3. Each Party shall, within 30 days after the date of receipt of the request for the establishment of an arbitral tribunal, appoint one arbitrator who may be its national and propose up to three candidates to serve as the third arbitrator who shall be the chair of the arbitral tribunal. The third arbitrator shall not be a national of either Party, nor have his or her usual place of residence in either Party, nor be employed by either Party, nor have dealt with the dispute in any capacity. 4. The Parties shall agree on and appoint the third arbitrator within 45 days after the date of receipt of the request for the establishment of an arbitral tribunal, taking into account the candidates proposed pursuant to paragraph 3.	

Bilateral Dispute Settlement Provisions	Investment Dispute Settlement (ISDS) Provisions
5. If either Party has not appointed an arbitrator pursuant to paragraph 3, or if the Parties fail to agree on and appoint the third arbitrator pursuant to paragraph 4, the Director-General of the World Trade Organization shall immediately be requested to make the necessary appointments. In the event that the Director-General is a national of either Party, the Deputy Director-General or the officer next in seniority who is not a national of either Party shall be requested to make the necessary appointments. 6. The date of the establishment of an arbitral tribunal shall be the date on which the chair is appointed. 7. An arbitral tribunal should be composed of arbitrators with relevant technical or legal expertise. Article 120 Functions of Arbitral Tribunals 1. The arbitral tribunal established pursuant to Article 119: (a) should consult with the Parties as appropriate and provide adequate opportunities for the development of a mutually satisfactory resolution; (b) shall make its award in accordance with this Agreement and applicable rules of international law; (c) shall set out, in its award, its findings of law and fact, together with the reasons therefor; and (d) may, apart from giving its findings, include in its award suggested implementation options for the Parties to consider in conjunction with Article 123.	

Bilateral Dispute Settlement Provisions	Investment Dispute Settlement (ISDS) Provisions
2. The arbitral tribunal may seek, from the Parties, such relevant information as it considers necessary and appropriate. The Parties shall respond promptly and fully to any request by the arbitral tribunal for such information. 3. The arbitral tribunal may seek information from any relevant source and may consult experts to obtain their opinion on certain aspects of the matter. With respect to factual issues concerning a scientific or other technical matter raised by a Party, the arbitral tribunal may request advisory reports in writing from experts. The arbitral tribunal may, at the request of a Party or on its own initiative, select, in consultation with the Parties, no fewer than two scientific or technical experts who shall assist the arbitral tribunal throughout its proceedings, but who shall not have the right to vote in respect of any decision to be made by the arbitral tribunal, including its award. Article 121 Proceedings of Arbitral Tribunals 1. The rules and procedures as set out in this Article shall apply to the proceedings of an arbitral tribunal. 2. The Parties, in consultation with the arbitral tribunal, may agree to adopt additional rules and procedures not inconsistent with the provisions of this Article. 3. After consulting the Parties, the arbitral tribunal shall as soon as practicable and whenever possible within seven days after the establishment of the arbitral tribunal, fix the timetable for the arbitral tribunal process. The timetable fixed for the arbitral tribunal shall include precise deadlines for written submissions by the Parties. Modifications to such timetable may be made by the agreement of the Parties in consultation with the arbitral tribunal. 4. The venue for the arbitral tribunal proceedings shall be decided by mutual agreement between the Parties. If there is no agreement, the venue shall alternate between the capitals of the Parties with the first meeting of the arbitral tribunal	

Bilateral Dispute Settlement Provisions	Investment Dispute Settlement (ISDS) Provisions
proceedings to be held in the capital of the Party complained against. 5. The arbitral tribunal shall meet in closed session. The Parties shall be present at the meetings only when invited by the arbitral tribunal to appear before it. 6. The Parties shall be given the opportunity to attend any of the presentations, statements or rebuttals in the proceedings. Any information provided or written submissions made by a Party to the arbitral tribunal, including any comments on the descriptive part of the draft award and responses to questions put by the arbitral tribunal, shall be made available to the other Party. 7. The deliberations of the arbitral tribunal and the documents submitted to it shall be kept confidential. 8. Notwithstanding paragraph 7, either Party may make public statements as to its views regarding the dispute, but shall treat as confidential, information provided and written submissions made by the other Party to the arbitral tribunal which that other Party has designated as confidential. Where a Party has provided information or made written submissions designated to be confidential, that Party shall, upon request of the other Party, provide a non-confidential summary of the information or written submissions which may be disclosed publicly. 9. The award of the arbitral tribunal shall be drafted without the presence of the Parties, and in the light of the information provided and the statements made. 10. The arbitral tribunal shall, within 90 days after the date of its establishment, submit to the Parties its draft award, including both the descriptive part and its findings and conclusions, for the purposes of enabling the Parties to review it. When the arbitral tribunal considers that it cannot submit its draft award within the aforementioned 90 day period, it may extend that period with the consent of the Parties. A Party may submit comments in writing to the arbitral tribunal on the draft award within 15 days after the date of submission of the draft award.	

Bilateral Dispute Settlement Provisions	Investment Dispute Settlement (ISDS) Provisions
11. The arbitral tribunal shall issue its award within 30 days after the date of submission of the draft award. 12. The arbitral tribunal shall attempt to make its decisions, including its award, by consensus but may also make its decisions, including its award, by majority vote. 13. The award of the arbitral tribunal shall be final and binding on the Parties. Article 122 Termination of Proceedings The Parties may agree to terminate the proceedings of the arbitral tribunal by jointly so notifying the chair of the arbitral tribunal at any time before the issuance of the award to the Parties. Article 123 Implementation of Award 1. The Party complained against shall promptly comply with the award of the arbitral tribunal issued pursuant to Article 121. 2. The Party complained against shall, within 20 days after the date of issuance of the award, notify the complaining Party of the period of time in which to implement the award. If the complaining Party considers the period of time notified to be unacceptable, it may refer the matter to an arbitral tribunal which then determines the reasonable implementation period. 3. If the Party complained against considers it impracticable to comply with the award within the implementation period as determined pursuant to paragraph 2, the Party complained against shall, no later than the expiry of that implementation period, enter into consultations with the complaining Party, with a view to developing mutually satisfactory compensation. If no satisfactory compensation has	

Bilateral Dispute Settlement Provisions	Investment Dispute Settlement (ISDS) Provisions
been agreed within 20 days after the date of expiry of that implementation period, the complaining Party may notify the Party complained against that it intends to suspend the application to the Party complained against of concessions or other obligations under this Agreement. 4. If the complaining Party considers that the Party complained against has failed to comply with the award within the implementation period as determined pursuant to paragraph 2, it may refer the matter to an arbitral tribunal to confirm the failure. 5. If the arbitral tribunal to which the matter is referred pursuant to paragraph 4 confirms that the Party complained against has failed to comply with the award within the implementation period as determined pursuant to paragraph 2, the complaining Party may, within 30 days after the date of such confirmation by the arbitral tribunal, notify the Party complained against that it intends to suspend the application to the Party complained against of concessions or other obligations under this Agreement. 6. The suspension of the application of concessions or other obligations under this Agreement pursuant to paragraphs 3 and 5 may only be implemented at least 30 days after the date of the notification in accordance with those paragraphs. Such suspension shall: (a) not be effected if, in respect of the dispute to which the suspension relates, consultations or proceedings before the arbitral tribunal are in progress; (b) be temporary, and be discontinued when the Parties reach a mutually satisfactory resolution or where compliance with the award is effected; (c) be restricted to the same level of nullification or impairment that is attributable to the failure to comply with the award; and (d) be restricted to the same sector or sectors to which the nullification or	

Bilateral Dispute Settlement Provisions	Investment Dispute Settlement (ISDS) Provisions
impairment relates, unless it is not practicable or effective to suspend the application of concessions or other obligations under this Agreement in such sector or sectors. 7. If the Party complained against considers that the requirements for the suspension of the application to it of concessions or other obligations under this Agreement by the complaining Party set out in paragraph 6 have not been met, it may request consultations with the complaining Party. The complaining Party shall enter into consultations within 10 days after the date of receipt of the request. If the Parties fail to resolve the matter within 30 days after the date of receipt of the request for consultations pursuant to this paragraph, the Party complained against may refer the matter to an arbitral tribunal. 8. The arbitral tribunal that is established for the purposes of this Article shall, wherever possible, have, as its arbitrators, the arbitrators of the original arbitral tribunal. If this is not possible, then the arbitrators to the arbitral tribunal that is established for the purposes of this Article shall be appointed pursuant to paragraphs 3 through 5 of Article 119. Unless the Parties agree to a different period, the arbitral tribunal established for the purposes of this Article shall issue its award within 60 days after the date when the matter is referred to it. Such award shall be binding on the Parties. Article 124 Expenses Each Party shall bear the costs of the arbitrator appointed by it and its representation in the proceedings of the arbitral tribunal. The other costs of the arbitral tribunal shall be borne by the Parties in equal shares, unless otherwise agreed by the Parties.	

* Entered into force on December 1, 2008.

1.5 Agreement on Free Trade and Economic Partnership between Japan and the Swiss Confederation*

Bilateral Dispute Settlement Provisions	Investor-State Dispute Settlement (ISDS) Provisions
CHAPTER 14 DISPUTE SETTLEMENT Article 137 General Provisions The Parties shall at all times endeavour to reach a mutually satisfactory resolution of any matter concerning the interpretation and application of this Agreement through cooperation, expert consultations or other means provided for in this Agreement. Article 138 Scope and Coverage 1. Unless otherwise provided for in this Agreement, this Chapter shall apply with respect to the settlement of disputes between the Parties concerning the interpretation or application of this Agreement. 2. Nothing in this Chapter shall prejudice any rights of the Parties to have recourse to dispute settlement procedures available under any other international agreement to which both Parties are parties. 3. Notwithstanding paragraph 2, once the complaining Party has requested the establishment of an arbitral tribunal under this Chapter or a panel under Article 6 of the Understanding on Rules and Procedures Governing the Settlement of Disputes in Annex 2 to the WTO Agreement with respect to a particular dispute, the arbitral tribunal or panel selected shall be used to the exclusion of the other procedure for that particular dispute. Article 139 Consultations	CHAPTER 9 INVESTMENT Article 94 Settlement of Investment Disputes between an Investor and a Party 1. For the purposes of this Chapter, "investment dispute" means a dispute between a Party and an investor of the other Party that has incurred loss or damage by reason of, or arising out of, an alleged breach by the former Party of any obligation under this Chapter with respect to the investor or its investment. This Article shall not apply to disputes arising out of events which occurred prior to the entry into force of this Agreement. 2. Any investment dispute shall, as far as possible, be settled amicably through consultations between the investor and the disputing Party (hereinafter collectively referred to in this Article as "the disputing parties") at the request of the investor. 3. If the investment dispute cannot be settled through consultations within six months from the date on which the disputing investor requested such consultations in writing, the disputing investor may submit the investment dispute to international conciliation or arbitration at the following institutions or under the following rules: (a) the International Centre for Settlement of Investment Disputes (hereinafter referred to in this Article as "ICSID") established by the Convention on the Settlement of Investment Disputes between States and Nationals of other States done at Washington, on 18 March 1965; (b) the Additional Facility Rules of ICSID, provided that either Party, but not both, is a party to the ICSID Convention; or

Bilateral Dispute Settlement Provisions	Investor-State Dispute Settlement (ISDS) Provisions
1. A Party may request in writing consultations with the other Party if it considers that a measure applied by that other Party is inconsistent with this Agreement or that any benefit accruing to it directly or indirectly under this Agreement is impaired or nullified by such measure. The Party requesting consultations shall set out the reasons for the request, including identification of the measure at issue and an indication of the legal basis for the complaint. 2. When a Party requests consultations pursuant to paragraph 1, the other Party shall reply promptly and enter into consultations in good faith within 30 days after the date of receipt of the request, with a view to a prompt and satisfactory resolution of the matter. In case of a matter concerning perishable products, the other Party shall enter into consultations within 15 days after the date of receipt of the request. Article 140 Good Offices, Conciliation or Mediation 1. Good offices, conciliation or mediation may be requested at any time by either Party. They may begin at any time if the Parties agree and, at the request of either Party, be terminated at any time. 2. If the Parties agree, good offices, conciliation or mediation may continue while procedures of the arbitral tribunal provided for in this Chapter are in progress. 3. Proceedings involving good offices, conciliation or mediation and positions taken by the Parties during these proceedings shall be confidential and without prejudice to the rights of either Party in any further proceedings. Article 141 Establishment of Arbitral Tribunals 1. The complaining Party that requested consultations under Article 139 may address a written request to the Party complained against for the establishment of an arbitral	(c) an ad hoc arbitral tribunal which, unless otherwise agreed upon by the disputing parties, shall be established under the arbitration rules of the United Nations Commission on International Trade Law (UNCITRAL) adopted on 28 April 1976. 4. Each Party hereby gives its consent to the submission of an investment dispute by a disputing investor to international conciliation or arbitration referred to in paragraph 3 regarding an investment made. 5. Notwithstanding paragraph 4, no investment dispute may be submitted to conciliation or arbitration under paragraph 3, if more than five years have elapsed since the date on which the disputing investor acquired or should have first acquired, whichever is the earlier, knowledge of the incurred loss or damage referred to in paragraph 1. 6. A disputing investor may submit the investment dispute to international conciliation or arbitration if: (a) the disputing investor has not initiated any proceedings for the resolution of the investment dispute before courts of justice or administrative tribunals or agencies of the disputing Party; or (b) where the disputing investor has initiated any proceedings for the resolution of the investment dispute before courts of justice or administrative tribunals or agencies of the disputing Party, the disputing investor withdraws the investment dispute from such proceedings. For the purpose of withdrawal, a written waiver shall be included in the written request for conciliation or arbitration by which the disputing investor waives any right to initiate or continue before any courts of justice or administrative tribunals or agencies under the law of either Party, any proceeding with respect to any alleged breach of this Chapter. It is understood that a disputing investor may initiate or continue an action that seeks interim injunctive relief and does not involve the payment of

Bilateral Dispute Settlement Provisions	Investor-State Dispute Settlement (ISDS) Provisions
tribunal: (a) if the Party complained against does not enter into such consultations within 30 days, or within 15 days in case of a matter concerning perishable products, after the date of receipt of the request for consultations under that Article; or (b) if the Parties fail to resolve the matter through such consultations under that Article within 60 days after the date of receipt of the request for such consultations. 2. Any request for the establishment of an arbitral tribunal pursuant to this Article shall identify: (a) the specific measures at issue; and (b) the legal basis of the complaint including, if applicable, the provisions of this Agreement alleged to have been breached and any other relevant provisions. The arbitral tribunal may also be requested to propose implementation options, which will be attached to its award. 3. The arbitral tribunal shall consist of three arbitrators with relevant technical or legal expertise. 4. Each Party shall, within 30 days after the date of receipt of the request for the establishment of an arbitral tribunal, appoint one arbitrator who may be its national and propose up to three candidates to serve as the third arbitrator who shall be the chair of the arbitral tribunal. The third arbitrator shall not be a national of either Party, nor have his or her usual place of residence in either Party, nor be employed by either Party, nor have dealt with the dispute in any capacity. 5. The Parties shall agree on and appoint the third arbitrator within 45 days after the	monetary damages before a judicial or administrative tribunal of the disputing Party, provided that the action is brought for the sole purpose of preserving the disputing investor's rights and interests while the conciliation or arbitration is pending. 7. Unless the disputing parties agree otherwise, the arbitration shall be held in a country that is a party to the Convention on the Recognition and Enforcement of Foreign Arbitral Awards, done at New York on 10 June 1958. 8. The arbitral tribunal shall decide the investment dispute in accordance with this Chapter and applicable rules of international law. Where the investment dispute includes a claim based on paragraph 2 of Article 86, the arbitral tribunal shall decide on that claim in accordance with this Chapter and the following: (a) the rules of law specified in the pertinent investment contract, or other rules of law the disputing parties may agree upon; or (b) in the absence of rules of law referred to in subparagraph (a): (i) such rules of international law as may be applicable; and (ii) the law of the respondent, including its rules on the conflict of laws. 9. The disputing Party shall notify the other Party in writing of the investment dispute submitted to international conciliation or arbitration no later than 30 days after the date on which it was submitted, and provide that other Party with copies of all pleadings filed in the arbitration. 10. Upon written notice to the disputing parties, the Party which is not the disputing Party may make submissions to the arbitral tribunal on a question of interpretation of this Chapter. 11. The disputing Party may not assert as a defence its immunity or the fact that the disputing investor has received or will receive, by virtue of an insurance contract,

Bilateral Dispute Settlement Provisions	Investor-State Dispute Settlement (ISDS) Provisions
date of receipt of the request for the establishment of an arbitral tribunal, taking into account the candidates proposed pursuant to paragraph 4. 6. If a Party has not appointed the one arbitrator pursuant to paragraph 4, or if the Parties fail to agree on the third arbitrator pursuant to paragraph 5, the necessary appointments shall be made at the request of either Party by the SecretaryGeneral of the Permanent Court of Arbitration within a further 30 days. 7. The date of the establishment of an arbitral tribunal shall be the date on which the chair of the arbitral tribunal is appointed. Article 142 Functions of Arbitral Tribunals 1. The arbitral tribunal established pursuant to Article 141: (a) shall examine the matter referred to in the request for the establishment of the arbitral tribunal pursuant to paragraph 2 of Article 141; (b) shall make its award in accordance with this Agreement and applicable rules of international law; (c) shall set out, in its award, its findings of law and fact, together with the reasons therefor; (d) shall, if requested by the complaining Party pursuant to paragraph 2 of Article 141, attach to its award suggested implementation options for the Parties to consider in conjunction with Article 145; and (e) should consult with the Parties, as appropriate, with a view to providing adequate opportunities for the development of a mutually satisfactory resolution.	guarantee or indemnity, a compensation covering, in whole or in part, the incurred loss or damage. 12. Neither Party shall give diplomatic protection, or bring an international claim, in respect of an investment dispute submitted to international arbitration, unless the disputing Party has failed to abide by and comply with the award rendered. Diplomatic protection, for the purposes of this paragraph, shall not include informal diplomatic exchanges for the sole purpose of facilitating a settlement of the investment dispute. 13. The decision of arbitration shall be final and binding upon the disputing parties and shall be executed without delay in accordance with the law of the disputing Party.

Bilateral Dispute Settlement Provisions	Investor-State Dispute Settlement (ISDS) Provisions
2. The award of the arbitral tribunal shall be final and binding on the Parties. Article 143 Proceedings of Arbitral Tribunals 1. Unless the Parties have agreed otherwise, the arbitral tribunal shall decide on whether its proceedings are to be held in Japan or Switzerland, and the complaining Party shall provide the secretariat services. The language of the proceedings and the documents submitted to and produced by the tribunal, including the award, shall be English. 2. The arbitral tribunal shall meet in closed session. Hearings shall be open to the public, unless either Party objects. 3. The deliberations of the arbitral tribunal, the documents submitted to it and the draft award referred to in paragraph 8 shall be kept confidential. 4. Notwithstanding paragraph 3, either Party may make public statements as to its views regarding the dispute, but shall treat as confidential, information provided and written submissions made by the other Party to the arbitral tribunal which that other Party has designated as confidential. Where a Party has provided information or made written submissions designated to be confidential, that Party shall, upon request of the other Party, provide a non-confidential summary of the information or written submissions which may be disclosed publicly. 5. Each Party has the right to at least one hearing before the arbitral tribunal as well as the opportunity to provide initial and rebuttal written submissions. The arbitral tribunal may seek from the Parties such relevant information as it considers necessary and appropriate. The Parties shall respond promptly and fully to any request by an arbitral tribunal for such information. 6. The arbitral tribunal may seek information from any relevant source and may	

Bilateral Dispute Settlement Provisions	Investor-State Dispute Settlement (ISDS) Provisions
consult experts to obtain their opinion on certain aspects of the matter. 7. The Parties shall be given the opportunity to attend any of the presentations, statements or rebuttals in the proceeding. Any information provided or written submissions made by a Party to the arbitral tribunal, including any comments on the descriptive part of the draft award and responses to questions put by the arbitral tribunal, shall be made available to the other Party. 8. The arbitral tribunal shall, within 90 days after the date of its establishment, submit to the Parties its draft award, including both the descriptive part and its findings and conclusions, for the purpose of enabling the Parties to review it. When the arbitral tribunal considers that it cannot submit to the Parties its draft award within the afore-mentioned 90 days period, it may extend that period with the consent of the Parties. A Party may submit comments in writing to the arbitral tribunal on the draft award within 15 days after the date of submission of the draft award. 9. The arbitral tribunal shall issue its award within 30 days after the date of submission of the draft award. 10. The arbitral tribunal shall attempt to make its decisions, including its award, by consensus but may also make such decisions, including its award, by majority vote. 11. The award of the arbitral tribunal shall be made public. Article 144 Suspension or Termination of Proceedings of Arbitral Tribunals 1. The Parties may agree to suspend the work of the arbitral tribunal at any time before the issuance of the award for a period not exceeding twelve months following the date of such agreement. If the work of the tribunal has been suspended for more than twelve months, the authority of the arbitral tribunal to examine the dispute shall lapse, unless the Parties agree otherwise.	

<table>
<tr><th>Bilateral Dispute Settlement Provisions</th><th>Investor-State Dispute Settlement (ISDS) Provisions</th></tr>
<tr><td>2. The Parties may agree to terminate the proceedings of the arbitral tribunal at any time before the issuance of the award to the Parties by jointly so notifying the chair of the arbitral tribunal.

Article 145
Implementation of Award

1. The Party complained against shall promptly comply with the award issued by the arbitral tribunal pursuant to Article 143.

2. The Party complained against shall, within 20 days after the date of issuance of the award, notify the complaining Party of the means and the period of time for implementing the award, taking into account, if applicable, the implementation options attached to the award. If the complaining Party considers the notified means or period of time to be unacceptable, it may request the Party complained against to hold consultations with a view to reaching a mutually satisfactory solution on the matter. If no such solution has been agreed upon within 20 days after the date of receipt of the request, the complaining Party may refer the matter to an arbitral tribunal, which then shall determine a reasonable means or period of time for implementing the award. The determination of the arbitral tribunal shall be presented within 15 days from the referral of the matter to the arbitral tribunal.

3. If the Party complained against considers it impracticable to comply with the award, it shall notify the complaining Party accordingly within 20 days after the issuance of the award and enter into consultations, with a view to agreeing on mutually satisfactory compensation. If no such compensation has been agreed upon within 20 days after the date of the notification, the complaining Party may notify the Party complained against that it intends to suspend the application of concessions or other obligations under this Agreement.

4. If the Party complained against has failed to notify the means and the period of time for implementing the award pursuant to paragraph 2 or if the complaining</td><td></td></tr>
</table>

Bilateral Dispute Settlement Provisions	Investor-State Dispute Settlement (ISDS) Provisions
Party considers that the Party complained against has failed to comply with the award within the implementation period as specified pursuant to paragraph 2, the complaining Party may notify the Party complained against that it intends to suspend the application of concessions or other obligations under this Agreement. 5. The notification pursuant to paragraph 3 or 4 shall indicate when the suspension of the application of concessions or other obligations under this Agreement shall commence and the application of what concessions or other obligations under this Agreement is to be suspended. Such suspension shall: (a) only be implemented at least 30 days after the date of notification; (b) not be effected if, in respect of the dispute to which the suspension relates, consultations or proceedings before an arbitral tribunal are in progress; (c) be restricted to benefits equivalent to the level of failure to comply with the award; and (d) be restricted to the same sector or sectors to which the inconsistency with the provisions of, or the nullification or impairment of a benefit under, this Agreement relates, unless it is not practicable or effective to suspend the application of concessions or other obligations in such sector or sectors. 6. If the Party complained against considers that the requirements for the suspension of the application of concessions or other obligations under this Agreement by the complaining Party set out in paragraph 5 have not been met, it may request consultations with the complaining Party within ten days after the receipt of the notification in accordance with paragraph 3 or 4. The complaining Party shall enter into consultations within ten days after the date of receipt of the request. If the Parties fail to resolve the matter within 30 days after the date of receipt of the request for consultations pursuant to this paragraph, the Party complained against may refer the matter to an arbitral tribunal. The ruling of the arbitral tribunal shall be given	

Bilateral Dispute Settlement Provisions	Investor-State Dispute Settlement (ISDS) Provisions
within 15 days from that referral. Application of concessions or other obligations under this Agreement shall not be suspended until the arbitral tribunal has issued its ruling. 7. The suspension of the application of concessions or other obligations under this Agreement following notification pursuant to paragraph 3 or 4 shall be discontinued when the Parties reach a mutually satisfactory resolution or where compliance with the award is effected. 8. A Party may request an arbitral tribunal to rule on the conformity with the award of any implementing measures adopted after the suspension of the application of concessions or other obligations under this Agreement and, in light of such ruling, whether the suspension should be terminated or modified. The ruling of the arbitral tribunal shall be given within 15 days from the date of such request. 9. The arbitral tribunal under this Article shall, wherever possible, be composed of the arbitrators of the original arbitral tribunal. If any of the arbitrators is not available, that arbitrator shall be replaced by an arbitrator appointed pursuant to paragraphs 4 to 6 of Article 141. Article 146 Expenses Unless the Parties agree otherwise, the expenses of the arbitral tribunal, including the remuneration of the arbitrators, shall be borne by the Parties in equal shares. Article 147 Other Provisions Any time period mentioned in this Chapter may be modified by agreement between the Parties.	

* Entered into force September 1, 2009.

1.6 Economic Partnership Agreement between the EU and Japan*

Bilateral Dispute Settlement Provisions	Investor-State Dispute Settlement (ISDS) Provisions
CHAPTER XX DISPUTE SETTLEMENT SECTION 1 Objective, Scope and Definitions Article [1] Objective The objective of this Chapter is to establish an effective and efficient mechanism for settling disputes between the Parties concerning the interpretation and application of this Agreement with a view to reaching a mutually agreed solution. Article [2] Scope Unless otherwise provided for in this Agreement, this Chapter shall apply with respect to the settlement of any dispute between the Parties concerning the interpretation and application of the provisions of this Agreement. Article [3] Definitions For the purposes of this Chapter: (a) "arbitrator" means a member of a panel; (b) "Code of Conduct" means the Code of Conduct for Members of a Panel referred to in Article [30] (Rules of Procedure and Code of Conduct); (c) "complaining Party" means the Party that requests the establishment of a	N/A

Bilateral Dispute Settlement Provisions	Investor-State Dispute Settlement (ISDS) Provisions
panel pursuant to Article [7] (Establishment of the Panel); (d) "covered provisions" means the provisions of this Agreement covered by this Chapter in accordance with Article [2] (Scope); (e) "days" means calendar days; (f) "DSB" means the Dispute Settlement Body of the WTO; (g) "panel" means a panel established pursuant to Article [7] (Establishment of the Panel); (h) "Party complained against" means the Party against which a dispute has been brought before a panel pursuant to Article [7] (Establishment of the Panel); and (i) "Rules of Procedure" means the Rules of Procedure of a Panel referred to in Article [30] (Rules of Procedure and Code of Conduct). SECTION 2 Consultations and Mediation Article [4] Request for information Before a request for consultations or mediation is made pursuant to Article [5] (Consultations) or [6] (Mediation) respectively, a Party may request in writing any relevant information with respect to a measure at issue. The Party to which such request is made shall make all efforts to provide the requested information in a written response to be submitted within 20 days. Article [5] Consultations	

Bilateral Dispute Settlement Provisions	Investor-State Dispute Settlement (ISDS) Provisions
1. The Parties shall endeavour to resolve any dispute referred to in Article [2] (Scope) through consultations in good faith with a view to reaching a mutually agreed solution. 2. Either Party may seek consultations concerning any dispute referred to in Article [2] (Scope). Any request for consultations shall be submitted in writing to the other Party. In the request for consultations, the Party which requested consultations shall give the reasons for the request, including identification of the measure at issue and an indication of its factual basis and its legal basis specifying the relevant provisions. 3. During consultations each Party shall provide sufficient information to enable a full examination of the measure at issue including how it might affect the operation and application of this Agreement. 4. The Party to which the request for consultations is made shall reply to the request within 10 days after the date of its receipt. The Parties shall enter into consultations in good faith within 30 days after the date of receipt of the request. Consultations shall be deemed to be concluded within 45 days after the date of receipt of the request unless the Parties agree otherwise. Where both Parties consider that the case concerns matters of urgency, including those which concern goods or services that rapidly lose their quality, current condition or commercial value in a short period of time, consultations shall be deemed to be concluded within 25 days after the date of receipt of the request unless the Parties agree otherwise. 5. Consultations may be held in person or by any other means agreed by the Parties. Unless otherwise agreed by the Parties, consultations, if held in person, shall take place in the Party to which the request is made. 6. Consultations, including all information disclosed and positions taken by the Parties during these proceedings, shall be confidential and without prejudice to the rights of either Party in any further proceedings.	

Bilateral Dispute Settlement Provisions	Investor-State Dispute Settlement (ISDS) Provisions
Article [6] Mediation 1. A Party may request the other Party at any time to enter into a mediation procedure with respect to any matter falling within the scope of this Chapter as referred to in Article [2] (Scope), where the matter concerns a measure that adversely affects trade or investment between the Parties. 2. The mediation procedure may begin at any time by agreement of the Parties. It shall be initiated, conducted and terminated in accordance with the Mediation Procedure, adopted by the Joint Committee pursuant to subparagraph [X] of paragraph [Y] of Article [Z] (Joint Committee) of Chapter [XX] (General/Institutional Provisions). 3. If the Parties agree, the mediation procedure may continue while procedures of the panel provided for in this Chapter are in progress. SECTION 3 Panel Procedure Article [7] Establishment of the Panel 1. The Party that sought consultations pursuant to Article [5] (Consultations) may request the establishment of a panel if: (a) the Party to which the request for consultations is made does not respond to such request within 10 days after the date of its receipt, or does not enter into consultations within 30 days after the date of receipt of the request; (b) the Parties agree not to have consultations; or	

Bilateral Dispute Settlement Provisions	Investor-State Dispute Settlement (ISDS) Provisions
(c) the Parties fail to resolve the dispute through the consultations within 45 days, or within 25 days in cases of urgency, including those which concern goods or services that rapidly lose their quality, current condition or commercial value in a short period of time, after the date of receipt of the request for consultations unless the Parties agree otherwise. 2. The request for the establishment of a panel pursuant to paragraph 1 shall be made in writing to the Party complained against. The complaining Party shall explicitly identify in its complaint: (a) the measure at issue; (b) the legal basis specifying the covered provisions which are relevant and in a manner sufficient to present clearly how such measure is in breach of those provisions; and (c) the factual basis. Article [8] Composition of the Panel 1. A panel shall be composed of three arbitrators. 2. Within 10 days of the date of receipt by the Party complained against of the request for the establishment of a panel, the Parties shall consult with a view to reaching an agreement on the composition of the panel. 3. If the Parties do not reach an agreement on the composition of the panel within the time period provided for in paragraph 2, each Party shall appoint an arbitrator from the sub-list for that Party established pursuant to Article [9] (List of Arbitrators) within 5 days from the expiry of the time period provided for in paragraph 2. If a Party fails to appoint an arbitrator within that time period, the co-chair of the Joint	

Bilateral Dispute Settlement Provisions	Investor-State Dispute Settlement (ISDS) Provisions
Committee from the complaining Party shall select by lot, within 5 days from the expiry of the time period, an arbitrator from the sub-list for the Party that has failed to appoint an arbitrator, established pursuant to Article [9] (List of Arbitrators). The co-chair of the Joint Committee from the complaining Party may delegate such selection by lot of the arbitrator. 4. If the Parties do not reach an agreement on the chairperson of the panel within the time period provided for in paragraph 2, upon request of either Party, the co-chair of the Joint Committee from the complaining Party shall select by lot, within 5 days after the request, the chairperson of the panel from the sub-list of chairpersons established pursuant to Article [9] (List of Arbitrators). The request shall be copied to the other Party. The co-chair of the Joint Committee from the complaining Party may delegate such selection by lot of the chairperson of the panel. 5. Should any of the lists provided for in Article [9] (List of Arbitrators) not be established or not contain at least nine individuals as referred to in that Article, the following procedures applies: (a) for the selection of the chairperson: (i) when the sub-list of chairpersons contains at least two individuals agreed by the Parties, the co-chair of the Joint Committee from the complaining Party shall select by lot the chairperson from those individuals within 5 days from the request referred to in paragraph 4; or (ii) when the sub-list of chairpersons contains one individual agreed by the Parties, that individual shall act as chairperson; or (iii) when a chairperson cannot be selected pursuant to subparagraphs (i) or (ii) or when the sub-list of chairpersons contains no individual agreed by the Parties, the co-chair of the Joint Committee from the complaining Party shall, within 5 days from the request of a Party, select by lot the chairperson from the up to six individuals who had been formally proposed as chairperson by one or both Parties at the time of establishing or updating the list of arbitrators referred to in Article 9 (List of Arbitrators). A Party may propose a new individual if an individual who had been formally proposed for a chairperson by that Party is no longer available.	

Bilateral Dispute Settlement Provisions	Investor-State Dispute Settlement (ISDS) Provisions
(b) for the selection of an arbitrator other than the chairperson: (i) when the sub-list of a Party contains at least two individuals agreed by the Parties, that Party shall select an arbitrator from those individuals within 5 days from the expiry of the time period provided in paragraph 2; or (ii) when the sub-list of a Party contains one individual agreed by the Parties, that individual shall act as an arbitrator; or (iii) when an arbitrator cannot be selected pursuant to subparagraphs (i) or (ii) or when the sub-list of arbitrators for a Party contains no individual agreed by the Parties, the co-chair of the Joint Committee from the complaining Party shall select an arbitrator applying mutatis mutandis the procedure referred to in subparagraph 5(a). 6. The date of establishment of the panel shall be the date on which the last of the three arbitrators has notified to the Parties the acceptance of his or her appointment. Article [9] List of Arbitrators 1. The Joint Committee shall, at its first meeting held pursuant to paragraph 2 of Article [X] (Joint Committee) of Chapter [XX] (General/Institutional Provisions), establish a list of at least nine individuals who are willing and able to serve as arbitrators. The list shall be composed of three sub-lists: one sub-list for each Party and one sub-list of individuals who are not nationals of either Party and who shall act as the chairperson of the panel. Each sub-list shall include at least three individuals. For the establishment or an update of the sub-list of chairpersons, each Party may propose up to three individuals. The Joint Committee will ensure that the list is always maintained at this level. 2. The Joint Committee may establish an additional list, consisting of individuals with demonstrated expertise in specific sectors covered by this Agreement, which may be used to compose the panel subject to the agreement of the Parties.	

Bilateral Dispute Settlement Provisions	Investor-State Dispute Settlement (ISDS) Provisions
Article [10] Qualifications of Arbitrators All arbitrators shall: (a) have demonstrated expertise in law, international trade, and other matters covered by this Agreement. The chairperson shall also have experience in arbitration proceedings; (b) be independent of, and not be affiliated with or take instructions from, either Party; (c) serve in their individual capacities and not take instructions from any organisation or government with regard to matters related to the dispute; and (d) comply with the Code of Conduct. Article [11] Replacement of Arbitrators If in an arbitration proceeding under this Chapter, any of the arbitrators of the original panel is unable to participate, withdraws, or needs to be replaced because he or she does not comply with the requirements of the Code of Conduct, the procedure set out in Article [8] (Composition of the Panel) shall apply. Article [12] Functions of the Panel The panel established pursuant to Article [7] (Establishment of the Panel): (a) shall make an objective assessment of the matter before it, including an objective assessment of the facts of the case and the applicability of and	

Bilateral Dispute Settlement Provisions	Investor-State Dispute Settlement (ISDS) Provisions
conformity with the covered provisions; (b) shall set out, in its decisions, the findings of fact and law and the rationale behind any findings and conclusions that it makes; and (c) should consult regularly with the Parties and provide adequate opportunities for the development of a mutually agreed solution. Article [13] Terms of Reference[1)] 1. Unless the Parties agree otherwise within 10 days after the date of the establishment of the panel, the terms of reference of the panel shall be: "to examine, in the light of the relevant provisions of this Agreement cited by the Parties, the matter referred to in the request for the establishment of the panel, to decide on the conformity of the measure at issue with the relevant provisions of this Agreement and to issue a report in accordance with Articles [18] (Interim Report) and [19] (Final Report)." 2. If the Parties agree on other terms of reference than those referred to in paragraph 1, they shall notify the agreed terms of reference to the panel within 3 days of their agreement. Article [14] Decision on Urgency[2)] If a Party so requests, the panel shall decide, within 15 days of its establishment, whether the case concerns matters of urgency. Article [15] Panel Proceedings	

Bilateral Dispute Settlement Provisions	Investor-State Dispute Settlement (ISDS) Provisions
1. Any hearing of the panel shall be open to the public, unless the Parties agree otherwise or unless the submission and arguments of a Party contains confidential information. When hearings are held in closed session their confidentiality shall be respected. 2. The venue for the hearings shall be decided by mutual agreement between the Parties. If there is no agreement, the venue shall alternate between the Parties with the first hearing to be held in the Party complained against. 3. The panel and the Parties shall treat as confidential any information submitted to the panel by a Party or received from any other source which has been designated as confidential. Where that Party submits a confidential version of its written submissions to the panel, it shall also, upon request of the other Party, provide a non-confidential summary of the information contained in its submissions that could be disclosed to the public with an explanation why the non-disclosed information is confidential. 4. The deliberations of the panel shall be kept confidential. 5. The Parties shall be given the opportunity to attend any of the presentations, statements, arguments or rebuttals in the proceedings. The Parties shall make available to each other any information or written submissions submitted to the panel, including any comments on the descriptive part of the interim report and responses to questions of the panel as well as written comments on those responses. 6. The interim report and the final report shall be drafted without the presence of the Parties, and in the light of the information provided and the statements made. The arbitrators shall assume full responsibility for the drafting of the reports and shall not delegate this responsibility to any other person. 7. The panel shall attempt to make its decisions, including its final report, by consensus. It may also make its decisions, including its final report, by majority vote	

Bilateral Dispute Settlement Provisions	Investor-State Dispute Settlement (ISDS) Provisions
where a decision cannot be arrived at by consensus. In no case shall dissenting opinions of arbitrators be published. 8. The decisions of the panel shall be final and binding on the Parties. They shall be unconditionally accepted by the Parties. They shall not add to or diminish the rights and obligations of the Parties under this Agreement. They shall not be construed as creating rights and obligations to natural or legal persons. Article [16] Rules of Interpretation The panel shall interpret the covered provisions in accordance with customary rules of interpretation of public international law, including those codified in the Vienna Convention on the Law of Treaties. The panel shall also take into account relevant interpretations in reports of panels and the Appellate Body adopted by the DSB. Article [17] Receipt of Information 1. At the request of a Party, or upon its own initiative, the panel may seek, from the Parties, relevant information it considers necessary and appropriate. The Parties shall respond promptly and fully to any request by the panel for such information. 2. Upon the request of a Party or its own initiative, the panel may seek any information, including confidential information, it deems appropriate from any source. The panel also has the right to seek the opinion of experts as it deems appropriate. 3. The panel may receive amicus curiae submissions from natural persons of a Party or legal persons established in a Party in accordance with the Rules of Procedure. 4. Any information obtained by the panel under this Article shall be made available	

Bilateral Dispute Settlement Provisions	Investor-State Dispute Settlement (ISDS) Provisions
to the Parties and the Parties may provide comments on that information. Article [18] Interim Report 1. The panel shall issue an interim report to the Parties setting out the descriptive part and its findings and conclusions within 120 days after the date of its establishment in a manner enabling the Parties to review it. When the panel considers that this deadline cannot be met, the chairperson of the panel shall notify the Parties in writing, stating the reasons for the delay and the date on which the panel plans to issue its interim report. Under no circumstances shall the period of the delay exceed 30 days after the deadline. 2. Each Party may submit to the panel written comments and a written request to review precise aspects of the interim report within 15 days after the date of issuance of the interim report. After considering any written comments and request by each Party on the interim report, the panel may modify the interim report and make any further examination it considers appropriate. 2. In cases of urgency, including those which concern goods or services that rapidly lose their quality, current condition or commercial value in a short period of time, (a) the panel shall make every effort to issue its interim report within 60 days and, in any case, no later than 75 days after the date of its establishment; and (b) each Party may submit to the panel written comments and a written request to review precise aspects of the interim report, within 7 days of the issuance of the interim report. Article [19] Final Report 1. The panel shall issue its final report to the Parties within 30 days after the date of the issuance of the interim report. When the panel considers that this deadline cannot be met, the chairperson of the panel shall notify the Parties in writing, stating	

Bilateral Dispute Settlement Provisions	Investor-State Dispute Settlement (ISDS) Provisions
the reasons for the delay and the date on which the panel plans to issue its final report. Under no circumstances shall the period of the delay exceed 30 days after the deadline. 2. In cases of urgency, including those which concern goods or services that rapidly lose their quality, current condition or commercial value in a short period of time, the panel shall make every effort to issue its final report within15 days and, in any case, no later than 30 days after the date of the issuance of the interim report. 3. The final report shall include a sufficient discussion of the written comments and request made by the Parties on the interim report. The panel may, in its final report, suggest ways in which the final report could be implemented. 4. The Parties shall make the final report publicly available in their entirety within 10 days of its issuance. The Parties may decide to publish the final report only in parts, or not to publish the final report, in order to protect confidential information. Article [20] Compliance with the Final Report 1. The Party complained against shall take any measure necessary to comply promptly and in good faith with the final report issued pursuant to Article [19] (Final Report). 2. The Party complained against shall, within 30 days after the date of issuance of the final report, notify the complaining Party of the length of the reasonable period of time for complying with the final report and the Parties shall endeavour to agree on the time required for compliance. If there is disagreement between the Parties on the length of the reasonable period of time for complying with the final report, the complaining Party may, within 20 days after the receipt of the notification made under this paragraph by the Party complained against, request in writing the original panel to determine the length of the reasonable period of time. Such request shall	

Bilateral Dispute Settlement Provisions	Investor-State Dispute Settlement (ISDS) Provisions
be notified simultaneously to the other Party. The original panel shall notify its determination to the Parties within 30 days from the date of the submission of the request. 3. The length of the reasonable period of time may be extended by mutual agreement of the Parties. 4. The Party complained against shall inform the complaining Party in writing of its progress to comply with the final report at least one month before the expiry of the reasonable period of time, unless otherwise agreed by the Parties. Article [21] Compliance Review 1. The Party complained against shall notify the complaining Party no later thanthe expiry of the reasonable period of time of any measure that it has taken to comply with the final report. 2. Where there is disagreement as to the existence or consistency with the covered provisions of measures taken to comply with the final report, the complaining Party may request in writing the original panel to examine the matter. The request shall be notified simultaneously to the Party complained against. 3. The request under paragraph 2 shall provide the factual and legal basis for the complaint, including the specific measures at issue and in a manner to present clearly how such measures are inconsistent with the covered provisions. 4. The panel shall notify its decision to the Parties within 90 days after the date of the referral of the matter. Article [22] Temporary Remedies in Case of Non-Compliance	

Bilateral Dispute Settlement Provisions	Investor-State Dispute Settlement (ISDS) Provisions
1. The Party complained against shall, upon request of the complaining Party, enter into consultations with a view to developing mutually satisfactory compensation or any alternative arrangement if: (a) in accordance with Article [21] (Compliance Review), the original panel finds that the measures taken to comply with the final report as notified by the Party complained against is inconsistent with the covered provisions; (b) the Party complained against fails to notify any measure taken to comply with the final report before the expiry of the reasonable period of time determined in accordance with paragraph 2 of Article 20 (Compliance with the Final Report); or (c) the Party complained against notifies the complaining Party that it is impracticable to comply with the final report within the reasonable period of time determined in accordance with paragraph 2 of Article 20 (Compliance with the Final Report). 2. If the complaining Party decides not to make a request under paragraph 1, or, in case such request is made, if no mutually satisfactory compensation or any alternative arrangement has been agreed within 20 days after the date of receipt of the request made in accordance with paragraph 1, the complaining Party may notify the Party complained against in writing that it intends to suspend the application to the Party complained against of concessions or other obligations under the covered provisions. The notification shall specify thelevel of intended suspension of concessions or other obligations. 3. The complaining Party shall have the right to implement the suspension of concessions or other obligations referred to in paragraph 2 15 days after the date of receipt of the notification by the Party complained against, unless the Party complained against has requested arbitration under paragraph 6.	

Bilateral Dispute Settlement Provisions	Investor-State Dispute Settlement (ISDS) Provisions
4. The suspension of concessions or other obligations: (a) shall be at a level equivalent to the nullification or impairment that is caused by the failure of the Party complained against to comply with the final report; and (b) may be applied to other sectors covered by this Chapter in accordance with Article [2] (Scope) than the sector or sectors in which the panel has found nullification or impairment, in particular if the complaining Party is of the view that such suspension is effective in inducing compliance. 5. The suspension of concessions or other obligations or the compensation or any alternative arrangement referred to in this Article shall be temporary and shall only apply until the inconsistency of the measure with the covered provisions which has been found in the final report has been removed, or the Parties have reached a mutually agreed solution. 6. If the Party complained against objects to the level of intended suspension of concessions or other obligations, it may request in writing the original panel to examine the matter. The request shall be notified simultaneously to the complaining Party. The original panel shall notify to the Parties its decision on the appropriate level of suspension of concessions or other obligations within 30 days after the date of the submission of the request. Concessions or other obligations shall not be suspended until the original panel has notified its decision. The suspension of concessions or other obligations shall be consistent with the decision. 7. If the Party complained against considers that the suspension of concessions or other obligations does not comply with paragraph [4], it may request the original panel to examine the matter. The panel shall notify to the Parties its decision on the matter within 30 days after the date of the submission of the request.	

Bilateral Dispute Settlement Provisions	Investor-State Dispute Settlement (ISDS) Provisions
Article [23][3)] Compliance Review after the Adoption of Temporary Remedies 1. Upon the notification by the Party complained against to the complaining Party of the measure it has taken to comply with the final report of the panel, (a) in a situation where the right to suspend concessions or other obligations has been exercised by the complaining Party in accordance with Article [22] (Temporary Remedies in Case of Non-Compliance), the complaining Party shall terminate the suspension of concessions or other obligations within 30 days from the receipt of the notification, with the exception of cases under paragraph 2; or (b) in a situation where mutually satisfactory compensation or alternative arrangement has been agreed, the Party complained against may terminate the application of such compensation or arrangement after 30 days from its notification, with the exception of cases under paragraph 2. 2. If the Parties do not reach an agreement on whether the notified measure is consistent with the covered provisions within 30 days of the date of receipt of the notification, the complaining Party shall request in writing the original arbitration panel to examine the matter. The request shall be notified simultaneously to the Party complained against. The decision of the panel shall be notified to the Parties within 45 days of the date of the submission of the request. If the panel decides that the measure taken to comply is consistent with the covered provisions, the suspension of concessions or other obligations, or compensation or any alternative arrangement, shall be terminated within 15 days. Where relevant, the level of suspension of concessions or other obligations, or of compensation or any alternative arrangement, shall be adapted in light of the decision of the panel. Article [24] Suspension and Termination of Proceedings	

Bilateral Dispute Settlement Provisions	Investor-State Dispute Settlement (ISDS) Provisions
When the Parties make a joint request, the proceedings of the panel shall be suspended at any time for a period agreed by the Parties not exceeding 12 consecutive months. In the event of such a suspension, the relevant time periods shall be extended by theamount of time for which the proceedings of the panel were suspended. The proceedings of the panel shall be resumed at any time upon the joint request of the Parties, or at the end of the agreed suspension period at the written request of either Party. The request shall be addressed to the chairperson of the panel, as well as to the other Party, where applicable. If the proceedings of the panel have been suspended for more than 12 consecutive months, the authority for establishment of the panel shall lapse and the proceedings of the panel shall be terminated. The Parties may agree to terminate the proceedings of the panel at any time by a joint notification to the chairperson of the panel. SECTION 4 General Provisions Article [25] Administration of the Dispute Settlement Procedure 1. Each Party shall: (a) designate an office that shall be responsible for the administration of the dispute settlement procedure under this Chapter; (b) be responsible for the operation and costs of its designated office; and (c) notify the other Party in writing of the office's location and contact information within [x months] after the entry into force of this Agreement. 2. Notwithstanding paragraph 1, the Parties may agree to entrust jointly an external body to provide support for certain administrative tasks for the dispute settlement procedure under this Chapter.	

Bilateral Dispute Settlement Provisions	Investor-State Dispute Settlement (ISDS) Provisions
Article [26] Mutually Agreed Solution 1. The Parties may reach a mutually agreed solution at any time with respect to any dispute referred to in Article [2] (Scope). 2. If a mutually agreed solution is reached during panel proceedings or a mediation procedure, the Parties shall jointly notify any such solution to thechairperson of the panel or the mediator, respectively. Upon such notification, the panel proceedings or the mediation procedure shall be terminated. 3. Each Party shall take measures necessary to implement the mutually agreed solution within the agreed time period. 4. No later than the expiry of the agreed time period the implementing Party shall inform the other Party in writing of any measure that it has taken to implement the mutually agreed solution. Article [27] Choice of Forum 1. Where a dispute arises regarding a particular measure in alleged breach of an obligation under this Agreement and a substantially equivalent obligation under any other international agreement to which both Parties are parties, including the WTO Agreement, the complaining Party may select the forum in which to settle the dispute. 2. Once a Party has selected the forum and initiated a dispute settlement procedure under this Chapter or under the other international agreement with respect to the particular measure referred to in paragraph 1, that Party shall not initiate a dispute settlement procedure in another forum with respect to that particular measure, unless the forum selected first fails to make findings on the issues in dispute for jurisdictional or procedural reasons.	

Bilateral Dispute Settlement Provisions	Investor-State Dispute Settlement (ISDS) Provisions
3. For the purposes of paragraph 2: (a) a dispute settlement procedure under this Chapter is deemed to be initiated when a Party requests the establishment of a panel in accordance with paragraph 1 of Article [7] (Establishment of the Panel); (b) a dispute settlement procedure under the WTO Agreement is deemed to be initiated when a Party requests the establishment of a panel in accordance with Article 6 of the Understanding on Rules and Procedures Governing the Settlement of Disputes of the WTO; and (c) a dispute settlement procedure under any other agreement is deemed to be initiated in accordance with the relevant provisions of that agreement. 4. Nothing in this Agreement shall preclude a Party from implementing the suspension of concessions or other obligations authorised by the DSB. The WTO Agreement shall not be invoked to preclude a Party from suspending concessions or other obligations under the covered provisions. Article [28] Time Period 1. All time periods provided for in this Chapter shall be counted in calendar days from the day following the act to which they refer. 2. Any time period provided for in this Chapter may be modified for a particular dispute by mutual consent of the Parties. The panel may at any time propose to the Parties to modify any time limit referred to in this Chapter, stating the reasons for the proposal. Upon requests from either Party, the panel shall decide whether to modify the time period referred to in paragraphs 2 and 3(b) of Article 18 (Interim Report), stating the reasons therefor, inter alia, in view of the complexity of the particular dispute.	

Bilateral Dispute Settlement Provisions	Investor-State Dispute Settlement (ISDS) Provisions
Article [29] Expenses Unless the Parties agree otherwise, the expenses of the panel, including the remuneration of its arbitrators, shall be borne by the Parties in equal shares in accordance with the Rules of Procedure. Article [30] Rules of Procedure and Code of Conduct The panel proceedings provided for in this Chapter shall be conducted in accordance with the Rules of Procedure of a Panel and the Code of Conduct for Members of a Panel, adopted by the Joint Committee pursuant to subparagraph [X] of paragraph [Y] of Article [Z] (Joint Committee) of Chapter [XX].	

* Not yet in force; as agreed and published on July 6, 2017. *Dispute Settlement chapter of this agreement includes several novel provisions worth noting, as they are not observant in any previously existing agreement.*

1) *This provision is notable since bilateral FTAs usually do not have a separate terms of reference provision. Other agreements usually have this element in an article on the functions of arbitral panel.*
2) *This is the only provision found among FTAs of three countries that allow a Party to request urgent decision as fast as within 15 days of the panel.*
3) *Articles 21-23 are unique to this agreement as much as the compliance review and five-year review provisions to KORUS FTA.*

2. Korea

2.1 Free Trade Agreement between the Government of the Republic of Korea and the Government of the Republic of Chile*

Bilateral Dispute Settlement Provisions	Investment Dispute Settlement (ISDS) Provisions
CHPTER 19 DISPUTE SETTLEMENT Article 19.1 Cooperation The Parties shall at all times endeavour to agree on the interpretation and application of this Agreement, and shall make every attempt through cooperation and consultations to arrive at a mutually satisfactory resolution of any matter that might affect its operation. Article 19.2 Scope of Application Except as otherwise provided in this Agreement, the provisions of this Chapter shall apply: (a) with respect to the avoidance and settlement of disputes between the Parties regarding the interpretation or application of this Agreement; or (b) wherever a Party considers that an existing or proposed measure of the other Party is or would be inconsistent with the obligations of this Agreement or causes nullification or impairment in the sense of Annex 19.2. Article 19.3 Choice of Forum	SECTION C SETTLEMENT OF DISPUTES BETWEEN A PARTY AND AN INVESTOR OF THE OTHER PARTY Article 10.19 Purpose Without prejudice to the rights and obligations of the Parties under Chapter 19, this Section establishes a mechanism for the settlement of investment disputes that assures both equal treatment among investors of the Parties in accordance with the principle of international reciprocity and due process before an impartial tribunal. Article 10.20 Claim by an Investor of a Party on Its Own Behalf 1. Subject to Annex 10.20, an investor of a Party may submit to arbitration under this Section a claim that the other Party has breached an obligation under Section B or Article 14.8, and that the investor has incurred loss or damage by reason of, or arising out of, that breach. 2. An investor may not make a claim if more than three years have elapsed from the date on which the investor first acquired, or should have first acquired, knowledge of the alleged breach and knowledge that the investor has incurred loss or damage. Article 10.21 Claim by an Investor of a Party on Behalf of an Enterprise

Bilateral Dispute Settlement Provisions	Investment Dispute Settlement (ISDS) Provisions
1. Disputes regarding any matter arising under both this Agreement and the WTO Agreement, any agreement negotiated thereunder, or any successor agreement, may be settled in the forum selected by the complaining Party. 2. Once dispute settlement procedures have been initiated under Article 19.6 or dispute settlement proceedings have been initiated under the WTO Agreement, the forum selected shall be used to the exclusion of the other. 3. For purposes of this Article, dispute settlement proceedings under the WTO Agreement are deemed to be initiated upon a request for a panel by a Party. Article 19.4 Consultations 1. A Party may request in writing consultations with the other Party regarding any existing or proposed measure or any other matter that it considers might affect the operation and application of this Agreement. 2. The Party that requests consultations according to paragraph 1 shall indicate the provisions of the Agreement that it considers relevant and deliver the request to the other Party. 3. Consultations on matters regarding perishable agricultural goods shall commence within 15 days of the date of delivery of the request. 4. The Parties shall: (a) provide information to enable a full examination of how the existing or proposed measure or other matter might affect the operation and application of this Agreement; and (b) give confidential treatment to any information exchanged in the course of	1. Subject to Annex 10.20, an investor of a Party, on behalf of an enterprise of the other Party that is a juridical person that the investor owns or controls, directly or indirectly, may submit to arbitration under this Section a claim that the other Party has breached an obligation under Section B or Article 14.8, and that the enterprise has incurred loss or damage by reason of, or arising out of, that breach. 2. An investor may not make a claim on behalf of an enterprise described in paragraph 1 if more than three years have elapsed from the date on which the enterprise first acquired, or should have first acquired, knowledge of the alleged breach and knowledge that the enterprise has incurred loss or damage. 3. Where an investor makes a claim under this Article and the investor or a non-controlling investor in the enterprise makes a claim under Article 10.20 arising out of the same events that gave rise to the claim under this Article, and two or more of the claims are submitted to arbitration under Article 10.24, the claims should be heard together by a Tribunal established under Article 10.30, unless the Tribunal finds that the interests of a disputing party would be prejudiced thereby. 4. An investment may not make a claim under this Section. Article 10.22 Settlement of a Claim through Consultation and Negotiation The disputing parties should first attempt to settle a claim through consultation or negotiation. Article 10.23 Notice of Intent to Submit a Claim to Arbitration The disputing investor shall deliver to the disputing Party written notice of its intention to submit a claim to arbitration at least 90 days before the claim is submitted, which notice shall specify:

Bilateral Dispute Settlement Provisions	Investment Dispute Settlement (ISDS) Provisions
consultations. Article 19.5 Good Offices, Conciliation and Mediation 1. Good offices, conciliation and mediation are procedures undertaken voluntarily if the Parties so agree. 2. Proceedings involving good offices, conciliation and mediation, and in particular positions taken by the Parties during these proceedings, shall be confidential, and without prejudice to the rights of either Party in any further proceedings under these procedures. 3. Good offices, conciliation or mediation may be requested at any time by any Party. They may begin at any time and be terminated at any time. Once procedures for good offices, conciliation or mediation are concluded without an agreement between the Parties, the complaining Party may request the establishment of a panel. Article 19.6 Request for an Arbitral Panel 1. A Party may request in writing the establishment of an arbitral panel if the matter has not been resolved pursuant to Article 19.4, within: (a) 45 days of delivery of a request for consultations; (b) 30 days of delivery of a request for consultations in matters regarding perishable agricultural goods; or (c) such other period as the Parties may agree.	(a) the name and address of the disputing investor and, where a claim is made under Article 10.21, the name and address of the enterprise; (b) the provisions of this Agreement alleged to have been breached and any other relevant provisions; (c) the issues and the factual basis for the claim; and (d) the relief sought and the approximate amount of damages claimed. Article 10.24 Submission of a Claim to Arbitration 1. Provided that six months have elapsed since the events giving rise to a claim, a disputing investor may submit the claim to arbitration under: (a) the ICSID Convention, provided that both the disputing Party and the Party of the investor are parties to the Convention; (b) the Additional Facility Rules of ICSID, provided that either the disputing Party or the Party of the investor, but not both, is a party to the ICSID Convention; or (c) the UNCITRAL Arbitration Rules. 2. The applicable arbitration rules shall govern the arbitration except to the extent modified by this Section. Article 10.25 Conditions Precedent to Submission of a Claim to Arbitration 1. A disputing investor may submit a claim under Article 10.20 to arbitration only if:

Bilateral Dispute Settlement Provisions	Investment Dispute Settlement (ISDS) Provisions
2. A Party may also request in writing the establishment of an arbitral panel where consultations have been held pursuant to Article 8.12. 3. Upon delivery of the request, an arbitral panel shall be established. 4. Unless otherwise agreed by the Parties, the panel shall be established and perform its functions in accordance with the provisions of this Chapter. Article 19.7 Roster 1. The Parties shall establish, by mutual agreement, no later than six months after the entry into force of this Agreement a roster of up to 15 individuals, one-third of whom shall not be nationals of either Party, who are willing and qualified to serve as panelists. The roster members shall be appointed for a term of three years, and will automatically be reappointed for an additional three-year term, unless either Party objects. 2. Roster members shall: (a) have expertise or experience in law, international trade, other matters covered by this Agreement or the resolution of disputes arising under international trade agreements; (b) be chosen strictly on the basis of objectivity, reliability and sound judgment; (c) be independent of, not be affiliated with or take instructions from, either Party; and (d) comply with the Code of Conduct set out in Annex 19.7.	(a) the investor and the enterprise, that is a juridical person that the investor owns or controls, directly or indirectly, have not submitted the same claim before any administrative tribunal or court of the disputing Party; (b) the investor consents to arbitration in accordance with the procedures set out in this Agreement; and (c) the investor and, where the claim is for loss or damage to an interest in an enterprise of the other Party that is a juridical person that the investor owns or controls, directly or indirectly, the enterprise, waive their right to initiate before any administrative tribunal or court under the law of a Party, or other dispute settlement procedures, any proceedings with respect to the measure of the disputing Party that is alleged to be a breach referred to in Article 10.20, except for proceedings for injunctive, declaratory or other extraordinary relief, not involving the payment of damages, before an administrative tribunal or court under the law of the disputing Party. 2. A disputing investor may submit a claim under Article 10.21 to arbitration only if: (a) both the investor and the enterprise that is a juridical person that the investor owns or controls, directly or indirectly, have not submitted the same claim before any administrative tribunal or court of the disputing Party; (b) both the investor and the enterprise consent to arbitration in accordance with the procedures set out in this Agreement; and (c) both the investor and the enterprise waive their rights to initiate before any administrative tribunal or court under the law of a Party, or other dispute settlement procedures, any proceedings with respect to the measure of the disputing Party that is alleged to be a breach referred to in Article 10.21, except for proceedings for injunctive, declaratory or other extraordinary relief, not involving the payment of damages, before an administrative tribunal or court

Bilateral Dispute Settlement Provisions	Investment Dispute Settlement (ISDS) Provisions
Article 19.8 Qualifications of Panelists 1. All panelists shall meet the qualifications set out in Article 19.7.2. 2. Individuals may not serve as panelists for a dispute in which they have participated pursuant to Article 19.5. Article 19.9 Panel Selection 1. The panel shall comprise three members. 2. Each Party shall select one panelist within 15 days from the delivery of the request for the establishment of the panel. 3. Within 15 days of the selection of the panelists under paragraph 2, the Parties shall agree on the chair of the panel. If the Parties are unable to agree on the chair within this period, the chairperson of the Commission shall select by lot the chair of the panel within five days, from among the roster members who are not nationals of either Party. 4. If a Party fails to select its panelist within the period indicated in paragraph 2, the chairperson of the Commission shall select by lot the panelist within five days, from among the roster members who are nationals of that Party. 5. Panelists shall normally be selected from the roster. 6. If a Party believes that a panelist is in violation of the Code of Conduct set out in Annex 19.7, the Parties shall consult and if they agree, the panelist shall be removed and a new panelist shall be selected in accordance with this Article.	under the law of the disputing Party. 3. Once a disputing investor concerned submits the dispute for resolution before any administrative tribunal or court under the law of a Party, the investor may not thereafter allege the measure to be such a breach referred to in Article 10.20 or 10.21 in an arbitration under this Section. 4. A consent and waiver required by this Article shall be in writing, shall be delivered to the disputing Party and shall be included in the submission of a claim to arbitration. 5. Only where a disputing Party has deprived a disputing investor of control of an enterprise: (a) a waiver from the enterprise under subparagraph 1(c) or 2(c) shall not be required; and (b) Article 10.24.1(b) shall not be applicable. Article 10.26 Consent to Arbitration 1. Each Party consents to the submission of a claim to arbitration in accordance with the procedures set out in this Agreement. 2. The consent given under paragraph 1 and the submission by a disputing investor of a claim to arbitration shall satisfy the requirements of: (a) Chapter II of the ICSID Convention (Jurisdiction of the Centre) and the Additional Facility Rules for written consent of the parties; and (b) Article II of the New York Convention for an agreement in writing.

Bilateral Dispute Settlement Provisions	Investment Dispute Settlement (ISDS) Provisions
Article 19.10 Model Rules of Procedure 1. Unless the Parties otherwise agree, the panel shall conduct its proceedings in accordance with the Model Rules of Procedure set out in Annex 19.10. 2. The Commission may amend when it considers necessary the Model Rules of Procedure referred to in paragraph 1. Article 19.11 Information and Technical Advice Upon request of a Party, or on its own initiative, the panel may seek information and technical advice from any person or body that it deems appropriate. Any information and technical advice so obtained shall be submitted to the Parties for comments. Article 19.12 Initial Report 1. Unless the Parties otherwise agree, the panel shall base its report on the relevant provisions of this Agreement, on the submissions and arguments of the Parties, and on any information before it, pursuant to Article 19.11. 2. Unless the Parties otherwise agree, the panel shall, within 90 days after the last panelist is selected, present to the Parties an initial report containing: (a) findings of fact, including any findings pursuant to a request under Rule 8 of Annex 19.10; (b) its determination as to whether the measure at issue is or would be inconsistent with the obligations of this Agreement or cause nullification or impairment in the sense of Annex 19.2, or any other determination requested in	Article 10.27 Number of Arbitrators and Method of Appointment Except in respect of a Tribunal established under Article 10.30, and unless the disputing parties otherwise agree, the Tribunal shall comprise three arbitrators, one arbitrator appointed by each of the disputing parties and the third, who shall be the presiding arbitrator, appointed by agreement between the disputing parties. Article 10.28 Constitution of a Tribunal When a Party Fails to Appoint an Arbitrator or the Disputing Parties are Unable to Agree on a Presiding Arbitrator 1. The Secretary-General shall serve as appointing authority for an arbitration under this Section. 2. If a Tribunal, other than a Tribunal established under Article 10.30, has not been constituted within 90 days from the date that a claim is submitted to arbitration, the Secretary General, on the request of either disputing party, shall appoint, in his or her discretion, the arbitrator or arbitrators not yet appointed, except that the presiding arbitrator shall be appointed in accordance with paragraph 3. 3. The Secretary-General shall appoint the presiding arbitrator from the roster of presiding arbitrators referred to in paragraph 4, provided that the presiding arbitrator shall not be a national of the disputing Party or a national of the Party of the disputing investor. In the event that no such presiding arbitrator is available to serve, the Secretary-General shall appoint, from the ICSID Panel of Arbitrators, a presiding arbitrator who is not a national of either of the Parties. 4. On the date of entry into force of this Agreement, the Parties shall establish, and thereafter maintain, a roster of 30 presiding arbitrators, none of whom may be a national of a Party, meeting the qualifications of the Convention and rules referred to in Article 10.24 and experienced in international law and investment matters. The

Bilateral Dispute Settlement Provisions	Investment Dispute Settlement (ISDS) Provisions
the terms of reference; and (c) its recommendations, if any, for resolution of the dispute. 3. Panelists may furnish separate opinions on matters not unanimously agreed. 4. The Parties may submit written comments on the initial report within 14 days of its presentation. 5. In case that such written comments by the Parties are received as provided for in paragraph 4, the panel, on its own initiative or at the request of a Party, may reconsider its report and make any further examination that it considers appropriate after considering such written comments. Article 19.13 Final Report 1. The panel shall present a final report to the Parties, including any separate opinions on matters not unanimously agreed, within 30 days of presentation of the initial report, unless the Parties otherwise agree. 2. No panel may, either in its initial report or its final report, disclose which panelists are associated with the majority or minority of the opinions. 3. The final report of the panel shall be made publicly available within 15 days of its delivery to the Parties. Article 19.14 Implementation of Final Report 1. The final report of a panel shall be binding on the Parties and shall not be subject to appeal. Unless the Parties decide otherwise, they shall implement the decision	roster members shall be appointed by mutual agreement. Article 10.29 Agreement to Appointment of Arbitrators For purposes of Article 39 of the ICSID Convention and Article 7 of Schedule C to the ICSID Additional Facility Rules, and without prejudice to an objection to an arbitrator based on Article 10.28.3 or on a ground other than nationality: (a) the disputing Party agrees to the appointment of each individual member of a Tribunal established under the ICSID Convention or the ICSID Additional Facility Rules; (b) a disputing investor referred to in Article 10.20 may submit a claim to arbitration, or continue a claim, under the ICSID Convention or the ICSID Additional Facility Rules, only on condition that the disputing investor agrees in writing to the appointment of each individual member of the Tribunal; and (c) a disputing investor referred to in Article 10.21.1 may submit a claim to arbitration, or continue a claim, under the ICSID Convention or the ICSID Additional Facility Rules, only on condition that the disputing investor and the enterprise agree in writing to the appointment of each individual member of the Tribunal. Article 10.30 Consolidation 1. A Tribunal established under this Article shall be established under the UNCITRAL Arbitration Rules and shall conduct its proceedings in accordance with those Rules, except as modified by this Section. 2. Where a Tribunal established under this Article is satisfied that claims have been

Bilateral Dispute Settlement Provisions	Investment Dispute Settlement (ISDS) Provisions
contained in the final report of the panel in the manner and within the time-frame that it orders. 2. Notwithstanding paragraph 1, where the final report of the panel states that a measure is not in compliance with this Agreement, or is causing nullification or impairment in the sense of Annex 19.2, the responding Party, wherever possible, shall abstain from executing the measure or shall abrogate it. Article 19.15 Non-Implementation - Suspension of Benefits 1. The complaining Party may suspend the application of benefits of equivalent effect to the Party complained against if the panel resolves: (a) that a measure is inconsistent with the obligations of this Agreement and the responding Party does not implement the final report within 30 days following the expiration of the time-frame established in such a report; or (b) that a measure causes nullification or impairment in the sense of Annex 19.2 and the Parties do not reach a mutually satisfactory agreement on the dispute within 30 days following the expiration of the time-frame established in the final report. 2. The suspension of benefits shall last until the responding Party implements the decision of the panel's final report or until the Parties reach a mutually satisfactory agreement on the dispute, depending on the case. 3. In considering what benefits to suspend pursuant to paragraph 1: (a) the complaining Party should first seek to suspend benefits in the same sector(s) as that affected by the measure or other matter that the panel has found to be inconsistent with the obligations derived of this Agreement or to	submitted to arbitration under Article 10.24 that have a question of law or fact in common, the Tribunal may, in the interests of fair and efficient resolution of the claims, and after hearing the disputing parties, by order: (a) assume jurisdiction over, and hear and determine together, all or part of the claims; or (b) assume jurisdiction over, and hear and determine one or more of the claims, the determination of which it believes would assist in the resolution of the others. 3. A disputing party that seeks an order under paragraph 2 shall request the Secretary General to establish a Tribunal and shall specify in the request: (a) the name of the disputing Party or disputing investors against which the order is sought; (b) the nature of the order sought; and (c) the grounds on which the order is sought. 4. The disputing party shall deliver to the disputing Party or disputing investors against which the order is sought a copy of the request. 5. Within 60 days of receipt of the request, the Secretary-General shall establish a Tribunal comprising three arbitrators. The Secretary-General shall appoint the presiding arbitrator from the roster referred to in paragraph 4 of Article 10.28. In the event that no such presiding arbitrator is available to serve, the Secretary-General shall appoint, from the ICSID Panel of Arbitrators, a presiding arbitrator who is not a national of either Party. The Secretary-General shall appoint the two other members from the roster referred to in paragraph 4 of Article 10.28 and to the extent not available from that roster, from the ICSID Panel of Arbitrators, and to the extent not

Bilateral Dispute Settlement Provisions	Investment Dispute Settlement (ISDS) Provisions
have caused nullification or impairment in the sense of Annex 19.2; and (b) if the complaining Party considers that it is not practicable or effective to suspend benefits in the same sector(s), it may suspend benefits in other sectors. The communication in which it announces such a decision shall indicate the reasons on which it is based. 4. Upon written request of the Party concerned, the original panel shall determine whether the level of benefits suspended by the complaining Party is excessive pursuant to paragraph 1. If the panel cannot be established with its original members, the proceeding set out in Article 19.9 shall be applied. 5. The panel shall present its determination within 60 days from the request made pursuant to paragraph 4, or if a panel cannot be established with its original members, from the date on which the last panelist is selected. The ruling of the panel shall be final and binding. It shall be delivered to the Parties and be made publicly available.	available from that Panel, in the discretion of the Secretary-General. One member shall be a national of the disputing Party and one member shall be a national of the Party of the disputing investors. 6. Where a Tribunal has been established under this Article, a disputing investor that has submitted a claim to arbitration under Article 10.20 or 10.21 and that has not been named in a request made under paragraph 3 may make a written request to the Tribunal that it be included in an order made under paragraph 2, and shall specify in the request: (a) the name and address of the disputing investor; (b) the nature of the order sought; and (c) the grounds on which the order is sought. 7. A disputing investor referred to in paragraph 6 shall deliver a copy of its request to the disputing parties named in a request made under paragraph 3. 8. A Tribunal established under Article 10.24 shall not have jurisdiction to decide a claim, or a part of a claim, over which a Tribunal established under this Article has assumed jurisdiction. 9. On application of a disputing party, a Tribunal established under this Article, pending its decision under paragraph 2, may order that the proceedings of a Tribunal established under Article 10.24 be stayed, unless the latter Tribunal has already adjourned its proceedings. Article 10.31 Notice 1. A disputing Party shall deliver to the Secretariat, within 15 days of receipt by the

Bilateral Dispute Settlement Provisions	Investment Dispute Settlement (ISDS) Provisions
	disputing Party, a copy of: (a) a request for arbitration made under paragraph (1) of Article 36 of the ICSID Convention; (b) a notice of arbitration made under Article 2 of Schedule C of the ICSID Additional Facility Rules; or (c) a notice of arbitration given under the UNCITRAL Arbitration Rules. 2. A disputing Party shall deliver to the Secretariat a copy of a request made under paragraph 3 of Article 10.30: (a) within 15 days of receipt of the request, in the case of a request made by a disputing investor; or (b) within 15 days of making the request, in the case of a request made by the disputing Party. 3. A disputing Party shall deliver to the Secretariat a copy of a request made under paragraph 6 of Article 10.30 within 15 days of receipt of the request. 4. The Secretariat shall maintain a public register of the documents referred to in paragraphs 1, 2 and 3. 5. A disputing Party shall deliver to the other Party: (a) written notice of a claim that has been submitted to arbitration no later than 30 days after the date that the claim is submitted; and (b) copies of all pleadings filed in the arbitration. Article 10.32: Participation by a Party Upon written notice to the disputing parties, a Party may make submissions to a Tribunal on a question of interpretation of this Agreement. Article 10.33: Documents 1. A Party shall be entitled to receive from the disputing Party, at the cost of the requesting Party, a copy of:

Bilateral Dispute Settlement Provisions	Investment Dispute Settlement (ISDS) Provisions
	(a) the evidence that has been tendered to the Tribunal; and (b) the written argument of the disputing parties. 2. A Party receiving information pursuant to paragraph 1 shall treat the information as if it were a disputing Party. Article 10.34 Place of Arbitration Unless the disputing parties agree otherwise, a Tribunal shall hold an arbitration in the territory of a Party that is party to the New York Convention, selected in accordance with: (a) the ICSID Additional Facility Rules if the arbitration is under those Rules or the ICSID Convention; or (b) the UNCITRAL Arbitration Rules if the arbitration is under those Rules. Article 10.35 Governing Law 1. A Tribunal established under this Section shall decide the issues in dispute in accordance with this Agreement and applicable rules of international law. 2. An interpretation by the Commission of a provision of this Agreement shall be binding on a Tribunal established under this Section. Article 10.36 Interpretation of Annexes

Bilateral Dispute Settlement Provisions	Investment Dispute Settlement (ISDS) Provisions
	1. Where a disputing Party asserts as a defense that the measure alleged to be a breach is within the scope of a reservation or exception set out in Annex I or Annex II, upon request of the disputing Party, the Tribunal shall request the interpretation of the Commission on the issue. The Commission, within 60 days of delivery of the request, shall submit in writing its interpretation to the Tribunal. 2. Further to paragraph 2 of Article 10.35, a Commission interpretation submitted under paragraph 1 shall be binding on the Tribunal. If the Commission fails to submit an interpretation within 60 days, the Tribunal shall decide the issue. Article 10.37 Expert Reports Without prejudice to the appointment of other kinds of experts where authorized by the applicable arbitration rules, a Tribunal, at the request of a disputing party or, unless the disputing parties disapprove, on its own initiative, may appoint one or more experts to report to it in writing on any factual issue concerning environmental, health, safety or other scientific matters raised by a disputing party in a proceeding, subject to such terms and conditions as the disputing parties may agree. Article 10.38 Interim Measures of Protection A Tribunal may order an interim measure of protection to preserve the rights of a disputing party, or to ensure that the Tribunal's jurisdiction is made fully effective, including an order to preserve evidence in the possession or control of a disputing party or to protect the Tribunal's jurisdiction. A Tribunal may not order attachment or enjoin the application of the measure alleged to constitute a breach referred to in Article 10.20 or 10.21. For purposes of this paragraph, an order includes a recommendation.

Bilateral Dispute Settlement Provisions	Investment Dispute Settlement (ISDS) Provisions
	Article 10.39 Final Award 1. Where a Tribunal makes a final award against a Party, the Tribunal may award, separately or in combination, only: (a) monetary damages and any applicable interest; and (b) restitution of property, in which case the award shall provide that the disputing Party may pay monetary damages and any applicable interest in lieu of restitution. 2. A Tribunal may also award costs in accordance with the applicable arbitration rules. 3. Subject to paragraphs 1 and 2, where a claim is made under Article 10.21.1: (a) an award of restitution of property shall provide that restitution be made to the enterprise; (b) an award of monetary damages and any applicable interest shall provide that the sum be paid to the enterprise; and (c) the award shall provide that it is made without prejudice to any right that any person may have in the relief under applicable domestic law. 4. A Tribunal may not order a Party to pay punitive damages. Article 10.40 Finality and Enforcement of an Award 1. An award made by a Tribunal shall have no binding force except between the disputing parties and in respect of the particular case.

Bilateral Dispute Settlement Provisions	Investment Dispute Settlement (ISDS) Provisions
	2. Subject to paragraph 3 and the applicable review procedure for an interim award, a disputing party shall abide by and comply with an award without delay. 3. A disputing party may not seek enforcement of a final award until: (a) in the case of a final award made under the ICSID Convention: (i) 120 days have elapsed from the date the award was rendered and no disputing party has requested revision or annulment of the award; or (ii) revision or annulment proceedings have been completed; and (b) in the case of a final award under the ICSID Additional Facility Rules or the UNCITRAL Arbitration Rules: (i) three months have elapsed from the date the award was rendered and no disputing party has commenced a proceeding to revise, set aside or annul the award; or (ii) a court has dismissed or allowed an application to revise, set aside or annul the award and there is no further appeal. 4. Each Party shall provide for the enforcement of an award in its territory. 5. If a disputing Party fails to abide by or comply with a final award, the Commission, on delivery of a request by a Party whose investor was a party to the arbitration, shall establish a panel under Article 19.6. The requesting Party may seek in such proceedings: (a) a determination that the failure to abide by or comply with the final award is inconsistent with the obligations of this Agreement; and (b) a recommendation that the Party abide by or comply with the final award. 6. A disputing investor may seek enforcement of an arbitration award under the ICSID Convention or the New York Convention regardless of whether proceedings have been taken under paragraph 5.

Bilateral Dispute Settlement Provisions	Investment Dispute Settlement (ISDS) Provisions
	7. A claim that is submitted to arbitration under this Section shall be considered to arise out of a commercial relationship or transaction for purposes of Article I of the New York Convention. Article 10.41 General Provision Time when a Claim is Submitted to Arbitration 1. A claim is submitted to arbitration under this Section when: (a) the request for arbitration under paragraph 1 of Article 36 of the ICSID Convention has been received by the Secretary-General; (b) the notice of arbitration under Article 2 of Schedule C of the ICSID Additional Facility Rules has been received by the Secretary-General; or (c) the notice of arbitration given under the UNCITRAL Arbitration Rules is received by the disputing Party. 2. Delivery of notice and other documents on a Party shall be made to the place named for that Party in Annex 10.41.2. 3. In an arbitration under this Section, a Party shall not assert, as a defense, counterclaim, right of setoff or otherwise, that the disputing investor has received or will receive, pursuant to an insurance or guarantee contract, indemnification or other compensation for all or part of its alleged damages. 4. Annex 10.41.4 applies to the Parties specified in that Annex with respect to publication of an award. Article 10.42 Exclusions

Bilateral Dispute Settlement Provisions	Investment Dispute Settlement (ISDS) Provisions
	Without prejudice to the applicability or non-applicability of the dispute settlement provisions of this Section or of Chapter 19 to other actions taken by a Party pursuant to Article 20.2, a decision by a Party to prohibit or restrict the acquisition of an investment in its territory by an investor of the other Party, or investment of such an investor, pursuant to that Article shall not be subject to such provisions.

* Entered into force on April 1, 2004.

2.2 Free Trade Agreement between the Republic of Korea and the United States of America*

Bilateral Dispute Settlement Provisions	Investment Dispute Settlement (ISDS) Provisions
SECTION A INSTITUTIONAL PROVISIONS AND ADMINISTRATION	SECTION B INVESTOR-STATE DISPUTE SETTLEMENT
Article 22.1 Contact Points	Article 11.15 Consultation and Negotiation
1. Each Party shall designate a contact point or points to facilitate communications between the Parties on any matter covered by this Agreement. 2. On request of the other Party, a Party's contact point shall identify the office or official responsible for the matter and assist, as necessary, in facilitating communications with the other Party.	In the event of an investment dispute, the claimant and the respondent should initially seek to resolve the dispute through consultation and negotiation, which may include the use of non-binding, third-party procedures. Article 11.16 Submission of A Claim to Arbitration
Article 22.2 Joint Committee	1. In the event that a disputing party considers that an investment dispute cannot be settled by consultation and negotiation:
1. The Parties hereby establish a Joint Committee comprising officials of each Party, which shall be co-chaired by the United States Trade Representative and the Minister for Trade of Korea, or their respective designees. 2. The Joint Committee shall:	(a) the claimant, on its own behalf, may submit to arbitration under this Section a claim (i) that the respondent has breached (A) an obligation under Section A, (B) an investment authorization, or (C) an investment agreement; and (ii) that the claimant has incurred loss or damage by reason of, or arising out of, that breach; and
(a) supervise the implementation of this Agreement; (b) supervise the work of all committees, working groups, and other bodies established under this Agreement; (c) consider ways to further enhance trade relations between the Parties; (d) seek to resolve disputes that may arise regarding the interpretation or	(b) the claimant, on behalf of an enterprise of the respondent that is a juridical person that the claimant owns or controls directly or indirectly, may submit to arbitration under this Section a claim (i) that the respondent has breached (A) an obligation under Section A, (B) an investment authorization, or (C) an investment agreement; and (ii) that the enterprise has incurred loss or damage by reason of, or arising out of, that breach, provided that a claimant may submit pursuant to subparagraph (a)(i)(C) or (b)(i)(C) a claim for breach of an investment agreement only if the subject matter of the claim and the claimed damages directly relate

Bilateral Dispute Settlement Provisions	Investment Dispute Settlement (ISDS) Provisions
application of this Agreement; (e) establish the amount of remuneration and expenses that will be paid to panelists; and (f) consider any other matter that may affect the operation of this Agreement. 3. The Joint Committee may: (a) establish and delegate responsibilities to ad hoc and standing committees, working groups, or other bodies; (b) seek the advice of non-governmental persons or groups; (c) consider amendments to this Agreement or make modifications to the commitments therein; (d) issue interpretations of the provisions of this Agreement, including as provided in Articles 11.22 (Governing Law) and 11.23 (Interpretation of Annexes); (e) adopt its own rules of procedure; and (f) take such other action in the exercise of its functions as the Parties may agree. 4. Unless the Parties otherwise agree, the Joint Committee shall convene: (a) in regular session every year, with such sessions to be held alternately in the territory of each Party; and (b) in special session within 30 days of the request of a Party, with such sessions to be held in the territory of the other Party or at such location as the Parties may agree.	to the covered investment that was established or acquired, or sought to be established or acquired, in reliance on the relevant investment agreement. 2. At least 90 days before submitting any claim to arbitration under this Section, a claimant shall deliver to the respondent a written notice of its intention to submit the claim to arbitration (notice of intent). The notice shall specify: (a) the name and address of the claimant and, where a claim is submitted on behalf of an enterprise, the name, address, and place of incorporation of the enterprise; (b) for each claim, the provision of this Agreement, investment authorization, or investment agreement alleged to have been breached and any other relevant provisions; (c) the legal and factual basis for each claim; and (d) the relief sought and the approximate amount of damages claimed. 3. Provided that six months have elapsed since the events giving rise to the claim, a claimant may submit a claim referred to in paragraph 1: (a) under the ICSID Convention and the ICSID Rules of Procedure for Arbitration Proceedings, provided that both the respondent and the non-disputing Party are parties to the ICSID Convention; (b) under the ICSID Additional Facility Rules, provided that either the respondent or the non-disputing Party is a party to the ICSID Convention; (c) under the UNCITRAL Arbitration Rules; or (d) if the claimant and respondent agree, to any other arbitration institution or

Bilateral Dispute Settlement Provisions	Investment Dispute Settlement (ISDS) Provisions
5. Each Party shall treat any confidential information exchanged in relation to a meeting of the Joint Committee or any body created under paragraph 3(a) on the same basis as the Party providing the information. 6. Recognizing the importance of transparency and openness, the Parties affirm their respective practices of considering the views of members of the public in order to draw on a broad range of perspectives in the implementation of this Agreement. 7. All decisions of the Joint Committee and all committees, working groups, and other bodies established under this Agreement shall be taken by consensus of the Parties.[1)] SECTION B DISPUTE SETTLEMENT PROCEEDINGS Article 22.3 Cooperation The Parties shall endeavor to agree on the interpretation and application of this Agreement, and shall make every attempt through cooperation and consultations to arrive at a mutually satisfactory resolution of any matter that might affect its operation. Article 22.4 Scope of Application Except as otherwise provided in this Agreement or as the Parties otherwise agree, this Section shall apply with respect to the avoidance or settlement of all disputes between the Parties regarding the interpretation or application of this Agreement or wherever a Party considers that: (a) a measure of the other Party is inconsistent with its obligations under this	under any other arbitration rules. 4. A claim shall be deemed submitted to arbitration under this Section when the claimant's notice of, or request for, arbitration (notice of arbitration): (a) referred to in paragraph 1 of Article 36 of the ICSID Convention is received by the Secretary-General; (b) referred to in Article 2 of Schedule C of the ICSID Additional Facility Rules is received by the Secretary-General; (c) referred to in Article 3 of the UNCITRAL Arbitration Rules, together with the statement of claim referred to in Article 18 of the UNCITRAL Arbitration Rules, are received by the respondent; or (d) referred to under any arbitral institution or arbitral rules selected under paragraph 3(d) is received by the respondent. A claim asserted by the claimant for the first time after such notice of arbitration is submitted shall be deemed submitted to arbitration under this Section on the date of its receipt under the applicable arbitral rules. 5. The arbitration rules applicable under paragraph 3, and in effect on the date the claim or claims were submitted to arbitration under this Section, shall govern the arbitration except to the extent modified by this Agreement. 6. The claimant shall provide with the notice of arbitration: (a) the name of the arbitrator that the claimant appoints; or (b) the claimant's written consent for the Secretary-General to appoint that arbitrator.

Bilateral Dispute Settlement Provisions	Investment Dispute Settlement (ISDS) Provisions
Agreement; (b) the other Party has otherwise failed to carry out its obligations under this Agreement; or (c) a benefit the Party could reasonably have expected to accrue to it under Chapter Two (National Treatment and Market Access for Goods), Three (Agriculture), Four (Textiles and Apparel), Six (Rules of Origin and Origin Procedures), Twelve (Cross-Border Trade in Services), Seventeen (Government Procurement), or Eighteen (Intellectual Property Rights)1 is being nullified or impaired as a result of a measure that is not inconsistent with this Agreement, except that neither Party may invoke this subparagraph with respect to a benefit under Chapter Twelve (Cross- Border Trade in Services) or Eighteen (Intellectual Property Rights) if the measure is subject to an exception under Article 23.1 (General Exceptions). Article 22.5 Administration of Dispute Settlement Proceedings Each Party shall designate an office that shall be responsible for providing administrative assistance to panels established under Article 22.9. Each Party shall be responsible for the operation and costs of its designated office and shall notify the other Party of its location. Article 22.6 Choice of Forum 1. Where a dispute regarding any matter arises under this Agreement and under the WTO Agreement or any other agreement to which both Parties are party, the complaining Party may select the forum in which to settle the dispute. 2. Once the complaining Party has requested the establishment of, or referred a	Article 11.17 Consent of Each Party to Arbitration 1. Each Party consents to the submission of a claim to arbitration under this Section in accordance with this Agreement. 2. The consent under paragraph 1 and the submission of a claim to arbitration under this Section shall satisfy the requirements of: (a) Chapter II (Jurisdiction of the Centre) of the ICSID Convention and the ICSID Additional Facility Rules for written consent of the parties to the dispute; and (b) Article II of the New York Convention for an "agreement in writing." Article 11.18 Conditions and Limitations on Consent of Each Party 1. No claim may be submitted to arbitration under this Section if more than three years have elapsed from the date the claimant first acquired, or should have first acquired, knowledge of the breach alleged under Article 11.16.1 and knowledge that the claimant (for claims brought under Article 11.16.1(a)) or the enterprise (for claims brought under Article 11.16.1(b)) has incurred loss or damage. 2. No claim may be submitted to arbitration under this Section unless: (a) the claimant consents in writing to arbitration in accordance with the procedures set out in this Agreement; and (b) the notice of arbitration is accompanied, (i) for claims submitted to arbitration under Article 11.16.1(a), by the claimant's written waiver, and (ii) for claims submitted to arbitration under Article 11.16.1(b), by the claimant's and the enterprise's written waivers of any right to initiate or continue before any

Bilateral Dispute Settlement Provisions	Investment Dispute Settlement (ISDS) Provisions
matter to, a dispute settlement panel under an agreement referred to in paragraph 1, the forum selected shall be used to the exclusion of other fora. Article 22.7 Consultations 1. Either Party may request consultations with the other Party with respect to any matter described in Article 22.4 by delivering written notification to the other Party. The complaining Party shall set out the reasons for the request, including identification of the measure or other matter at issue and an indication of the legal basis for the complaint. The other Party shall reply promptly to the request and enter into consultations. 2. Promptly after requesting or receiving a request for consultations pursuant to this Article, each Party shall seek the views of interested parties and other members of the public on the matter in order to draw on a broad range of perspectives. 3. Each Party shall: (a) provide sufficient information in the consultations to enable a full examination of how the matter subject to consultations might affect the operation of this Agreement; and (b) treat any confidential information exchanged in the course of consultations on the same basis as the Party providing the information. 4. A Party may request the other Party to make available during consultations under this Article personnel of its government agencies or other regulatory bodies who have expertise in the matter subject to consultations. Article 22.8 Referral to The Joint Committee	administrative tribunal or court under the law of either Party, or other dispute settlement procedures, any proceeding with respect to any measure alleged to constitute a breach referred to in Article 11.16. 3. Notwithstanding paragraph 2(b), the claimant (for claims brought under Article 11.16.1(a)) and the claimant or the enterprise (for claims brought under Article 11.16.1(b)) may initiate or continue an action that seeks interim injunctive relief and does not involve the payment of monetary damages before a judicial or administrative tribunal of the respondent, provided that the action is brought for the sole purpose of preserving the claimant's or the enterprise's rights and interests during the pendency of the arbitration. 4. (a) An investor of a Party may not initiate or continue a claim under this Section if a claim involving the same measure or measures alleged to constitute a breach under Article 11.16 and arising from the same events or circumstances is initiated or continued pursuant to an agreement between the respondent and a non-Party by: (i) a person of a non-Party that owns or controls, directly or indirectly, the investor of a Party; or (ii) a person of a non-Party that is owned or controlled, directly or indirectly, by the investor of a Party. (b) Notwithstanding subparagraph (a), the claim may proceed if the respondent agrees that the claim may proceed, or if the investor of a Party and the person of a non-Party agree to consolidate the claims under the respective agreements before a tribunal constituted under this Section. Article 11.19 Selection of Arbitrators

Bilateral Dispute Settlement Provisions	Investment Dispute Settlement (ISDS) Provisions
1. If the Parties fail to resolve a matter within 60 days of the delivery of a request for consultations under Article 22.7, or 20 days where the matter concerns perishable goods, either Party may refer the matter to the Joint Committee by delivering written notification to the other Party. 2. If the Parties fail to resolve a matter within 60 days of the delivery of a request for consultations under Article 19.7 (Labor Consultations) or 20.9 (Environmental Consultations and Panel Procedure), either Party may also refer the matter to the Joint Committee by delivering written notification to the other Party. 3. The Joint Committee shall promptly meet and endeavor to resolve the matter.[2)] Article 22.9 Establishment of Panel 1. If the Joint Committee has not resolved a matter within 60 days after delivery of a notification described in Article 22.8, within 30 days where the matter concerns perishable goods, or within such other period as the Parties may agree, the complaining Party may refer the matter to a dispute settlement panel by delivering written notification to the other Party. The complaining Party shall set out the reasons for the request, including identification of the measure or other matter at issue and a brief summary of the legal basis for the complaint sufficient to present the problem clearly. 2. Unless the Parties otherwise agree, the Parties shall apply the following procedures in selecting a panel: (a) The panel shall have three members. (b) Each Party shall propose one panelist within 28 days after the matter has been referred to a panel. If a Party fails to propose a panelist within that period, the Parties shall meet within seven days and select a panelist by lot from among	1. Unless the disputing parties otherwise agree, the tribunal shall comprise three arbitrators, one arbitrator appointed by each of the disputing parties and the third, who shall be the presiding arbitrator, appointed by agreement of the disputing parties. 2. The Secretary-General shall serve as appointing authority for an arbitration under this Section. 3. If a tribunal has not been constituted within 75 days of the date a claim is submitted to arbitration under this Section, the Secretary-General, on the request of a disputing party, shall appoint, in his or her discretion, the arbitrator or arbitrators not yet appointed. The Secretary-General shall not appoint a national of either Party as the presiding arbitrator unless the disputing parties otherwise agree. 4. For purposes of Article 39 of the ICSID Convention and Article 7 of Schedule C to the ICSID Additional Facility Rules, and without prejudice to an objection to an arbitrator on a ground other than nationality: (a) the respondent agrees to the appointment of each individual member of a tribunal established under the ICSID Convention or the ICSID Additional Facility Rules; (b) a claimant referred to in Article 11.16.1(a) may submit a claim to arbitration under this Section, or continue a claim, under the ICSID Convention or the ICSID Additional Facility Rules, only on condition that the claimant agrees in writing to the appointment of each individual member of the tribunal; and (c) a claimant referred to in Article 11.16.1(b) may submit a claim to arbitration under this Section, or continue a claim, under the ICSID Convention or the ICSID Additional Facility Rules, only on condition that the claimant and the enterprise agree in writing to the appointment of each individual member of the tribunal.

Bilateral Dispute Settlement Provisions	Investment Dispute Settlement (ISDS) Provisions
the members of the contingent list established under paragraph 3 who are nationals of that Party.	Article 11.20 Conduct of The Arbitration
(c) A Party may exercise a peremptory challenge against any individual not on the contingent list within 14 days after the individual has been proposed as a panelist. If a Party has exercised three peremptory challenges, the other Party shall select a panelist from the contingent list.	1. The disputing parties may agree on the legal place of any arbitration under the arbitral rules applicable under Article 11.16.3. If the disputing parties fail to reach agreement, the tribunal shall determine the place in accordance with the applicable arbitral rules, provided that the place shall be in the territory of a State that is a party to the New York Convention.
(d) The Parties shall endeavor to agree on a third panelist who shall serve as chair. 3. Within 180 days of the date this Agreement enters into force, the Parties shall establish a contingent list of individuals who are willing and able to serve as panelists. Unless the Parties otherwise agree, the contingent list shall include at least six nationals of each Party and at least eight individuals who are not nationals of either Party. An individual on the contingent list shall be appointed by agreement of the Parties for a minimum term of three years, and shall remain on the list until the individual is replaced or is unable to serve. The Parties shall review the contingent list every three years and may replace individuals on the list as appropriate. The Parties may also appoint a replacement where a member of the contingent list is no longer available to serve.	2. At the request of a disputing party, and unless the disputing parties otherwise agree, the tribunal may determine the place of meetings, including consultations and hearings, taking into consideration appropriate factors, including the convenience of the parties and the arbitrators, the location of the subject matter, and the proximity of evidence. The preceding sentence is without prejudice to any appropriate factors a tribunal may consider under paragraph 1. 3. Unless the disputing parties otherwise agree, English and Korean shall be the official languages to be used in the entire arbitration proceedings, including all hearings, submissions, decisions, and awards. 4. The non-disputing Party may make oral and written submissions to the tribunal regarding the interpretation of this Agreement. On the request of a disputing party, the non-disputing Party should resubmit its oral submission in writing.
4. Individuals appointed to a panel pursuant to paragraph 2 or to the contingent list pursuant to paragraph 3 shall: (a) be chosen strictly on the basis of objectivity, reliability, and sound judgment; (b) have expertise or experience in law, international trade, or the resolution of disputes arising under international trade agreements; (c) be independent of, and not be affiliated with or take instructions from,	5. After consulting the disputing parties, the tribunal may allow a party or entity that is not a disputing party to file a written amicus curiae submission with the tribunal regarding a matter within the scope of the dispute. In determining whether to allow such a filing, the tribunal shall consider, among other things, the extent to which: (a) the *amicus curiae* submission would assist the tribunal in the determination of a factual or legal issue related to the proceeding by bringing a perspective, particular knowledge, or insight that is different from that of the disputing

Bilateral Dispute Settlement Provisions	Investment Dispute Settlement (ISDS) Provisions
either Party; and	parties;
(d) comply with a code of conduct to be established by the Joint Committee. In addition, in any dispute arising under Chapter Nineteen (Labor) or Twenty (Environment), panelists other than those chosen by lot from the contingent list shall have expertise or experience relevant to the subject matter under dispute. Paragraph 2(c) shall not apply to disputes arising under Chapter Nineteen or Twenty.	(b) the *amicus curiae* submission would address a matter within the scope of the dispute; and (c) the *amicus curiae* has a significant interest in the proceeding.
Article 22.10 Rules of Procedure	The tribunal shall ensure that the *amicus curiae* submission does not disrupt the proceeding or unduly burden or unfairly prejudice either disputing party, and that the disputing parties are given an opportunity to present their observations on the *amicus curiae* submission.
1. By the date this Agreement enters into force, the Parties shall establish model rules of procedure, which shall ensure: (a) a right to at least one hearing before the panel;	6. Without prejudice to a tribunal's authority to address other objections as a preliminaryquestion, a tribunal shall address and decide as a preliminary question any objection by the respondent that, as a matter of law, a claim submitted is not a claim for which an award in favor of the claimant may be made under Article 11.26 or that a claim is manifestly without legal merit.
(b) that, subject to subparagraph (f), any hearing before the panel shall be open to the public; (c) an opportunity for each Party to provide initial and rebuttal submissions;	(a) Such objection shall be submitted to the tribunal as soon as possible after the tribunal is constituted, and in no event later than the date the tribunal fixes for the respondent to submit its counter-memorial or, in the case of an amendment to the notice of arbitration, the date the tribunal fixes for the respondent to submit its response to the amendment.
(d) that each Party's written submissions, written versions of its oral statements, and written responses to a request or questions from the panel shall be made available to the public within seven days after they are submitted, subject to subparagraph (f);	(b) On receipt of an objection under this paragraph, the tribunal shall suspend any proceedings on the merits, establish a schedule for considering the objection consistent with any schedule it has established for considering any other preliminary question, and issue a decision or award on the objection, stating the grounds therefor.
(e) that the panel shall consider requests from non-governmental entities located in the Parties' territories to provide written views regarding the dispute that may assist the panel in evaluating the submissions and arguments of the Parties; and	(c) In deciding an objection under this paragraph that a claim submitted is not a claim for which an award in favor of the claimant may be made under

Bilateral Dispute Settlement Provisions	Investment Dispute Settlement (ISDS) Provisions
(f) the protection of confidential information. 2. Unless the Parties otherwise agree, the panel shall follow the model rules of procedure and may, after consulting with the Parties, adopt additional rules of procedure not inconsistent with the model rules. 3. Unless the Parties otherwise agree within 20 days from the date of the delivery of the request for the establishment of the panel, the panel's terms of reference shall be: "To examine, in the light of the relevant provisions of this Agreement, the matter referenced in the request for the establishment of the panel, to make findings, determinations, and recommendations as provided in paragraphs 1 and 2 of Article 22.11, and to present the written reports referred to in paragraphs 1 and 4 of Article 22.11." 4. On request of a Party, or on its own initiative, the panel may seek information and technical advice from any person or body that it deems appropriate, provided that the Parties so agree and subject to such terms and conditions as the Parties may agree. Article 22.11 Panel Report 1. Unless the Parties otherwise agree, the panel shall, within 180 days after the chair is appointed, present to the Parties an initial report containing findings of fact and its determination as to: (a) (i) whether the measure at issue is inconsistent with the obligations of this Agreement; (ii) whether a Party has otherwise failed to carry out its obligations under this Agreement; or (iii) whether the measure at issue is causing nullification or impairment in the sense of Article 22.4(c); and (b) any other matter that the Parties have jointly requested that the Panel	Article 11.26, the tribunal shall assume to be true claimant's factual allegations in support of any claim in the notice of arbitration (or any amendment thereof) and, in disputes brought under the UNCITRAL Arbitration Rules, the statement of claim referred to in Article 18 of the UNCITRAL Arbitration Rules. The tribunal may also consider any relevant facts not in dispute. (d) The respondent does not waive any objection as to competence or any argument on the merits merely because the respondent did or did not raise an objection under this paragraph or make use of the expedited procedure set out in paragraph 7. 7. In the event that the respondent so requests within 45 days of the date the tribunal isconstituted, the tribunal shall decide on an expedited basis an objection under paragraph 6 and any objection that the dispute is not within the tribunal's competence. The tribunal shall suspend any proceedings on the merits and issue a decision or award on the objection(s), stating the grounds therefor, no later than 150 days after the date of the request. However, if a disputing party requests a hearing, the tribunal may take an additional 30 days to issue the decision or award. Regardless of whether a hearing is requested, a tribunal may, on a showing of extraordinary cause, delay issuing its decision or award by an additional brief period, which may not exceed 30 days. 8. When it decides a respondent's objection under paragraph 6 or 7, the tribunal may, ifwarranted, award to the prevailing disputing party reasonable costs and attorney's fees incurred in submitting or opposing the objection. In determining whether such an award is warranted, the tribunal shall consider whether either the claimant's claim or the respondent's objection was frivolous, and shall provide the disputing parties a reasonable opportunity to comment. 9. For greater certainty, if an investor of a Party submits a claim under Section B, including aclaim alleging that a Party breached Article 11.5, the investor has the burden of proving all elements of its claims, consistent with general principles of

Bilateral Dispute Settlement Provisions	Investment Dispute Settlement (ISDS) Provisions
address, as well as the reasons for its findings and determinations. 2. The panel shall base its report on the relevant provisions of this Agreement and the submissions and arguments of the Parties. The panel shall consider this Agreement in accordance with customary rules of interpretation of public international law, which are reflected in Articles 31 through 33 of the Vienna Convention on the Law of Treaties (1969). The panel may, at the request of the Parties, make recommendations for the resolution of the dispute. 3. Each Party may submit written comments to the panel on its initial report within 14 days of the presentation of the report. After considering any written comments by the Parties on the initial report, the panel may modify its report and make any further examination it considers appropriate. 4. The panel shall present a final report to the Parties within 45 days of presentation of the initial report, unless the Parties otherwise agree. The Parties shall make the final report available to the public within 15 days thereafter, subject to the protection of confidential information. Article 22.12 Implementation of The Final Report 1. On receipt of the final report of a panel, the Parties shall agree on the resolution of the dispute, which normally shall conform with the determinations and recommendations, if any, of the panel. 2. If, in its final report, the panel determines that a Party has not conformed with its obligations under this Agreement or that a Party's measure is causing nullification or impairment in the sense of Article 22.4(c), the resolution, whenever possible, shall be to eliminate the non-conformity or the nullification or impairment.	international law applicable to international arbitration. 10. A respondent may not assert as a defense, counterclaim, or right of set-off, or for any otherreason, that the claimant has received or will receive indemnification or other compensation for all or part of the alleged damages pursuant to an insurance or guarantee contract, except with respect to any subrogation as provided for in Article 11.14. 11. A tribunal may order an interim measure of protection to preserve the rights of a disputingparty, or to ensure that the tribunal's jurisdiction is made fully effective, including an order to preserve evidence in the possession or control of a disputing party or to protect the tribunal's jurisdiction. A tribunal may not order attachment or enjoin the application of a measure alleged to constitute a breach referred to in Article 11.16. For purposes of this paragraph, an order includes a recommendation. 12. (a) In any arbitration conducted under this Section, at the request of a disputing party, a tribunal shall, before issuing a decision or award on liability, transmit its proposed decision or award to the disputing parties and to the non-disputing Party. Within 60 days after the date the tribunal transmits its proposed decision or award, the disputing parties may submit written comments to the tribunal concerning any aspect of its proposed decision or award. The tribunal shall consider any such comments and issue its decision or award not later than 45 days after the date the 60-day comment period expires. (b) Subparagraph (a) shall not apply in any arbitration conducted pursuant to this Section for which an appeal has been made available pursuant to paragraph 13 or Annex 11-D. 13. If a separate, multilateral agreement enters into force between the Parties that establishesan appellate body for purposes of reviewing awards rendered by tribunals constituted pursuant to international trade or investment arrangements to hear investment disputes, the Parties shall strive to reach an agreement that would have

Bilateral Dispute Settlement Provisions	Investment Dispute Settlement (ISDS) Provisions
Article 22.13 Non-Implementation 1. If a panel has made a determination of the type described in Article 22.12.2, and the Parties are unable to reach agreement on a resolution pursuant to Article 22.12.1 within 45 days of receiving the final report, or such other period as the Parties agree, the Party complained against shall enter into negotiations with the complaining Party with a view to developing mutually acceptable compensation. 2. If the Parties: (a) are unable to agree on compensation within 30 days after the period for developing such compensation has begun; or (b) have agreed on compensation or on a resolution pursuant to Article 22.12.1 and the complaining Party considers that the Party complained against has failed to observe the terms of the agreement, the complaining Party may at any time thereafter provide written notice to the Party complained against that it intends to suspend the application to the Party complained against of benefits of equivalent effect. The notice shall specify the level of benefits that the complaining Party proposes to suspend. Subject to paragraph 5, the complaining Party may begin suspending benefits 30 days after the later of the date on which it provides notice to the other Party under this paragraph or the panel issues its determination under paragraph 3, as the case may be. 3. If the Party complained against considers that: (a) the level of benefits that the complaining Party has proposed to be suspended is manifestly excessive; or (b) it has eliminated the non-conformity or the nullification or impairment that the panel has found, it may, within 30 days after the complaining Party provides	such appellate body review awards rendered under Article 11.26 in arbitrations commenced after the multilateral agreement enters into force between the Parties. Article 11.21 Transparency of Arbitral Proceedings 1. Subject to paragraphs 2, 3, and 4, the respondent shall, after receiving the following documents, promptly transmit them to the non-disputing Party and make them available to the public: (a) the notice of intent; (b) the notice of arbitration; (c) pleadings, memorials, and briefs submitted to the tribunal by a disputing party and any written submissions submitted pursuant to Article 11.20.4 and 11.20.5 and Article 11.25; (d) minutes or transcripts of hearings of the tribunal, where available; and (e) orders, awards, and decisions of the tribunal. 2. The tribunal shall conduct hearings open to the public and shall determine, in consultation with the disputing parties, the appropriate logistical arrangements. However, any disputing party that intends to use information designated as protected information in a hearing shall so advise the tribunal. The tribunal shall make appropriate arrangements to protect the information from disclosure. 3. Nothing in this Section requires a respondent to disclose protected information or to furnish or allow access to information that it may withhold in accordance with Article 23.2 (Essential Security) or Article 23.4 (Disclosure of Information).

Bilateral Dispute Settlement Provisions	Investment Dispute Settlement (ISDS) Provisions
notice under paragraph 2, request that the panel be reconvened to consider the matter. The Party complained against shall deliver its request in writing to the complaining Party. The panel shall reconvene as soon as possible after delivery of the request and shall present its determination to the Parties within 90 days after it reconvenes to review a request under either subparagraph (a) or (b), or within 120 days for a request under both subparagraphs (a) and (b). If the panel determines that the level of benefits proposed to be suspended is manifestly excessive, it shall determine the level of benefits it considers to be of equivalent effect. 4. The complaining Party may suspend benefits up to the level the panel has determined under paragraph 3 or, if the panel has not determined the level, the level the Party has proposed to suspend under paragraph 2, unless the panel has determined that the Party complained against has eliminated the non-conformity or the nullification or impairment. 5. The complaining Party may not suspend benefits if, within 30 days after it provides written notice of intent to suspend benefits or, if the panel is reconvened under paragraph 3, within 20 days after the panel provides its determination, the Party complained against provides written notice to the other Party that it will pay an annual monetary assessment. The Parties shall consult, beginning no later than ten days after the Party complained against provides notice, with a view to reaching agreement on the amount of the assessment. If the Parties are unable to reach an agreement within 30 days after consultations begin, the amount of the assessment shall be set at a level, in U.S. dollars, equal to 50 percent of the level of the benefits the panel has determined under paragraph 3 to be of equivalent effect or, if the panel has not determined the level, 50 percent of the level that the complaining Party has proposed to suspend under paragraph 2. 6. Unless the Joint Committee decides otherwise, a monetary assessment shall be paid to the complaining Party in U.S. currency, or in an equivalent amount of Korean currency, in equal, quarterly installments beginning 60 days after the Party	4. Any protected information that is submitted to the tribunal shall be protected from disclosure in accordance with the following procedures: (a) Subject to subparagraph (d), neither the disputing parties nor the tribunal shall disclose to the non-disputing Party or to the public any protected information where the disputing party that provided the information clearly designates it in accordance with subparagraph (b); (b) Any disputing party claiming that certain information constitutes protected information shall clearly designate the information at the time it is submitted to the tribunal; (c) A disputing party shall, at the time it submits a document containing information claimed to be protected information, submit a redacted version of the document that does not contain the information. Only the redacted version shall be provided to the non-disputing Party and made public in accordance with paragraph 1; (d) The tribunal shall decide any objection by a disputing party regarding the designation of information claimed to be protected information. If the tribunal determines that such information was not properly designated, the disputing party that submitted the information may (i) withdraw all or part of its submission containing such information, or (ii) agree to resubmit complete and redacted documents with corrected designations in accordance with the tribunal's determination and subparagraph (c). In either case, the other disputing party shall, whenever necessary, resubmit complete and redacted documents which either remove the information withdrawn under (i) by the disputing party that first submitted the information or redesignate the information consistent with the designation under (ii) of the disputing party that first submitted the information; and (e) At the request of a disputing Party, the Joint Committee shall consider

Bilateral Dispute Settlement Provisions	Investment Dispute Settlement (ISDS) Provisions
complained against gives notice that it intends to pay an assessment. Where the circumstances warrant, the Joint Committee may decide that an assessment shall be paid into a fund established by the Joint Committee and expended at the direction of the Joint Committee for appropriate initiatives to facilitate trade between the Parties, including by further reducing unreasonable trade barriers or by assisting a Party in carrying out its obligations under this Agreement. 7. If the Party complained against fails to pay a monetary assessment, the complaining Party may suspend the application to the Party complained against of benefits in accordance with paragraph 4. Article 22.14 Compliance Review 1. Without prejudice to the procedures set out in Article 22.13.3, if the Party complained against considers that it has eliminated the non-conformity or the nullification or impairment that the panel has found, it may refer the matter to the panel by providing written notice to the complaining Party. The panel shall reconvene as soon as possible after delivery of the request and shall issue its report on the matter within 90 days after the Party complained against provides notice. 2. If the panel decides that the Party complained against has eliminated the non-conformity or the nullification or impairment, the complaining Party shall promptly reinstate any benefits it has suspended under Article 22.13, and the Party complained against shall no longer be required to pay any monetary assessment it has agreed to pay under Article 22.13.5. Article 22.15 Five-Year Review[3)] The Joint Committee shall review the operation and effectiveness of Article 22.13 not later than five years after the date this Agreement enters into force, or within six	issuing a decision in writing regarding a determination by the tribunal that information claimed to be protected was not properly designated. If the Joint Committee issues a decision within 60 days of such a request, it shall be binding on the tribunal, and any decision or award issued by the tribunal must be consistent with that decision. If the Joint Committee does not issue a decision within 60 days, the tribunal's determination shall remain in effect only if the non-disputing Party submits a written statement to the Joint Committee within that period that it agrees with the tribunal's determination. 5. Nothing in this Section requires a respondent to withhold from the public information required to be disclosed by its laws. Article 11.22 Governing Law 1. Subject to paragraph 3, when a claim is submitted under Article 11.16.1(a)(i)(A) or Article 11.16.1(b)(i)(A), the tribunal shall decide the issues in dispute in accordance with this Agreement and applicable rules of international law. 2. Subject to paragraph 3 and the other terms of this Section, when a claim is submitted under Article 11.16.1(a)(i)(B) or (C), or Article 11.16.1(b)(i)(B) or (C), the tribunal shall apply: (a) the rules of law specified in the pertinent investment authorization or investment agreement, or as the disputing parties may otherwise agree; or (b) if the rules of law have not been specified or otherwise agreed, (i) the law of the respondent, including its rules on the conflict of laws; and (ii) such rules of international law as may be applicable. 3. A decision of the Joint Committee declaring its interpretation of a provision of this Agreement under Article 22.2.3(d) (Joint Committee) shall be binding on a tribunal,

Bilateral Dispute Settlement Provisions	Investment Dispute Settlement (ISDS) Provisions
months after benefits have been suspended or monetary assessments have been paid in five proceedings initiated under this Chapter, whichever occurs first.	and any decision or award issued by a tribunal must be consistent with that decision. Article 11.23 Interpretation of Annexes 1. Where a respondent asserts as a defense that the measure alleged to be a breach is within the scope of an entry set out in Annex I or Annex II, the tribunal shall, on request of the respondent, request the interpretation of the Joint Committee on the issue. The Joint Committee shall submit in writing any decision declaring its interpretation under Article 22.2.3(d) (Joint Committee) to the tribunal within 60 days of delivery of the request. 2. A decision issued by the Joint Committee under paragraph 1 shall be binding on the tribunal, and any decision or award issued by the tribunal must be consistent with that decision. If the Joint Committee fails to issue such a decision within 60 days, the tribunal shall decide the issue. Article 11.24 Expert Reports Without prejudice to the appointment of other kinds of experts where authorized by the applicable arbitration rules, a tribunal, at the request of a disputing party or, unless the disputing parties disapprove, on its own initiative, may appoint one or more experts to report to it in writing on any factual issue concerning environmental, health, safety, or other scientific matters raised by a disputing party in a proceeding, subject to such terms and conditions as the disputing parties may agree. Article 11.25 Consolidation 1. Where two or more claims have been submitted separately to arbitration under Article 11.16.1 and the claims have a question of law or fact in common and arise out

Bilateral Dispute Settlement Provisions	Investment Dispute Settlement (ISDS) Provisions
	of the same events or circumstances, any disputing party may seek a consolidation order in accordance with the agreement of all the disputing parties sought to be covered by the order or the terms of paragraphs 2 through 10. 2. A disputing party that seeks a consolidation order under this Article shall deliver, in writing, a request to the Secretary-General and to all the disputing parties sought to be covered by the order and shall specify in the request: (a) the names and addresses of all the disputing parties sought to be covered by the order; (b) the nature of the order sought; and (c) the grounds on which the order is sought. 3. Unless the Secretary-General finds within 30 days after receiving a request under paragraph 2 that the request is manifestly unfounded, a tribunal shall be established under this Article. 4. Unless all the disputing parties sought to be covered by the order otherwise agree, a tribunal established under this Article shall comprise three arbitrators: (a) one arbitrator appointed by agreement of the claimants; (b) one arbitrator appointed by the respondent; and (c) the presiding arbitrator appointed by the Secretary-General, provided, however, that the presiding arbitrator shall not be a national of either Party. 5. If, within 60 days after the Secretary-General receives a request made under paragraph 2, the respondent fails or the claimants fail to appoint an arbitrator in accordance with paragraph 4, the Secretary-General, on the request of any disputing

Bilateral Dispute Settlement Provisions	Investment Dispute Settlement (ISDS) Provisions
	party sought to be covered by the order, shall appoint the arbitrator or arbitrators not yet appointed. If the respondent fails to appoint an arbitrator, the Secretary-General shall appoint a national of the disputing Party, and if the claimants fail to appoint an arbitrator, the Secretary-General shall appoint a national of the non-disputing Party. 6. Where a tribunal established under this Article is satisfied that two or more claims that have been submitted to arbitration under Article 11.16.1 have a question of law or fact in common, and arise out of the same events or circumstances, the tribunal may, in the interest of fair and efficient resolution of the claims, and after hearing the disputing parties, by order: (a) assume jurisdiction over, and hear and determine together, all or part of the claims; (b) assume jurisdiction over, and hear and determine one or more of the claims, the determination of which it believes would assist in the resolution of the others; or (c) instruct a tribunal previously established under Article 11.19 to assume jurisdiction over, and hear and determine together, all or part of the claims, provided that: (i) that tribunal, at the request of any claimant not previously a disputing party before that tribunal, shall be reconstituted with its original members, except that the arbitrator for the claimants shall be appointed pursuant to paragraphs 4(a) and 5; and (ii) that tribunal shall decide whether any prior hearing shall be repeated. 7. Where a tribunal has been established under this Article, a claimant that has submitted a claim to arbitration under Article 11.16.1 and that has not been named in a request made under paragraph 2 may make a written request to the tribunal that it be included in any order made under paragraph 6, and shall specify in the request: (a) the name and address of the claimant;

Bilateral Dispute Settlement Provisions	Investment Dispute Settlement (ISDS) Provisions
	(b) the nature of the order sought; and (c) the grounds on which the order is sought. The claimant shall deliver a copy of its request to the Secretary-General. 8. A tribunal established under this Article shall conduct its proceedings in accordance with the UNCITRAL Arbitration Rules, except as modified by this Section. 9. A tribunal established under Article 11.19 shall not have jurisdiction to decide a claim, or a part of a claim, over which a tribunal established or instructed under this Article has assumed jurisdiction. 10. On application of a disputing party, a tribunal established under this Article, pending its decision under paragraph 6, may order that the proceedings of a tribunal established under Article 11.19 be stayed, unless the latter tribunal has already adjourned its proceedings.[4)] Article 11.26 Awards 1. Where a tribunal makes a final award against a respondent, the tribunal may award, separately or in combination, only: (a) monetary damages and any applicable interest; and (b) restitution of property, in which case the award shall provide that the respondent may pay monetary damages and any applicable interest in lieu of restitution. 2. A tribunal may also award costs and attorney's fees in accordance with this Section and the applicable arbitration rules.

Bilateral Dispute Settlement Provisions	Investment Dispute Settlement (ISDS) Provisions
	3. Subject to paragraph 1, where a claim is submitted to arbitration under Article 11.16.1(b): (a) an award of restitution of property shall provide that restitution be made to the enterprise; (b) an award of monetary damages and any applicable interest shall provide that the sum be paid to the enterprise; and (c) the award shall provide that it is made without prejudice to any right that any person may have in the relief under applicable domestic law. 4. A tribunal may not award punitive damages. 5. An award made by a tribunal shall have no binding force except between the disputing parties and in respect of the particular case. 6. Subject to paragraph 7 and the applicable review procedure for an interim award, a disputing party shall abide by and comply with an award without delay. 7. A disputing party may not seek enforcement of a final award until: (a) in the case of a final award made under the ICSID Convention, (i) 120 days have elapsed from the date the award was rendered and no disputing party has requested revision or annulment of the award; or (ii) revision or annulment proceedings have been completed; and (b) in the case of a final award under the ICSID Additional Facility Rules, the UNCITRAL Arbitration Rules, or the rules selected pursuant to Article 11.16.3(d), (i) 90 days have elapsed from the date the award was rendered and no disputing party has commenced a proceeding to revise, set aside, or annul the award; or (ii) a court has dismissed or allowed an application to revise, set aside, or annul the

Bilateral Dispute Settlement Provisions	Investment Dispute Settlement (ISDS) Provisions
	award and there is no further appeal. 8. Each Party shall provide for the enforcement of an award in its territory. 9. If the respondent fails to abide by or comply with a final award, on delivery of a request by the non-disputing Party, a panel shall be established under Article 22.9 (Establishment of Panel). The requesting Party may seek in such proceedings: (a) a determination that the failure to abide by or comply with the final award is inconsistent with the obligations of this Agreement; and (b) in accordance with Article 22.11 (Panel Report), a recommendation that the respondent abide by or comply with the final award. 10. A disputing party may seek enforcement of an arbitration award under the ICSID Convention or the New York Convention regardless of whether proceedings have been taken under paragraph 9. 11. A claim that is submitted to arbitration under this Section shall be considered to arise out of a commercial relationship or transaction for purposes of Article I of the New York Convention. Article 11.27 Service of Documents Delivery of notice and other documents on a Party shall be made to the place named for that Party in Annex 11-C.

* Entered into force on March15, 2012. Protocol between the Government of the Republic of Korea and the Government of the United States of America Amending the Free Trade Agreement between the Republic of Korea and the United States of America entered into force on January 1, 2019.

1) *This provision on joint committee is unique to the KORUS FTA.*
2) *In accordance to the unique joint committee facility in the agreement, this provision is also unique to KORUS FTA.*
3) *Articles 22.14 and 22.15 are notable as it refers to an additional compliance review as well as a five-year review, which is unique to the KORUS FTA.*
4) *This provision is present in Japan-Mexico FTA. It is also observed in Korea-Australia FTA as well.*

2.3 Free Trade Agreement between the Republic of Korea and EU*

Bilateral Dispute Settlement Provisions	Non-Tariff Barrier (NTB) Mediation Mechanism
CHAPTER 14 DISPUTE SETTLEMENT SECTION A OBJECTIVE AND SCOPE Article 14.1 Objective The objective of this Chapter is to avoid and settle any dispute between the Parties concerning the good faith application of this Agreement and to arrive at, where possible, a mutually agreed solution. Article 14.2 Scope This Chapter applies to any dispute concerning the interpretation and application of the provisions of this Agreement unless otherwise provided. SECTION B CONSULTATIONS Article 14.3 Consultations 1. The Parties shall endeavour to resolve any dispute regarding the interpretation and application of the provisions referred to in Article 14.2 by entering into consultations in good faith with the aim of reaching a mutually agreed solution. 2. A Party shall seek consultations by means of a written request to the other	MEDIATION MECHANISM FOR NON-TARIFF MEASURES Article 1 Objective The objective of this Annex is to facilitate the finding of a mutually agreed solution to nontariff measures adversely affecting trade between the Parties through a comprehensive and expeditious procedure with the assistance of a mediator. Article 2 Scope The mediation mechanism shall apply to any measure, other than customs duties, which a Party believes adversely affects trade between the Parties and which is related to any matter falling under market access in goods1 including under Chapter Two (National Treatment and Market Access for Goods) and the Annexes pertaining thereto. SECTION A PROCEDURE UNDER THE MEDIATION MECHANISM Article 3 Initiation of The Mediation Procedure 1. A Party may request, at any time, that the other Party enter into a mediation procedure. Such request shall be addressed to the other Party in writing. The request shall be sufficiently detailed to present clearly the concerns of the requesting Party and shall: (a) identify the specific measure at issue;

Bilateral Dispute Settlement Provisionst	Non-Tariff Barrier (NTB) Mediation Mechanism
Party identifying any measure at issue and the provisions of the Agreement that it considers applicable. A copy of the request for consultations shall be delivered to the Trade Committee.	(b) provide a statement of the alleged adverse effects that the requesting Party believes the measure has on trade between the Parties; and
3. Consultations shall be held within 30 days of the date of the submission of the request and take place, unless the Parties agree otherwise, in the territory of the Party complained against. The consultations shall be deemed concluded within 30 days of the date of the submission of the request, unless the Parties agree to continue consultations. All information disclosed during the consultations shall remain confidential. 4. Consultations on matters of urgency, including those regarding perishable or seasonal goods shall be held within 15 days of the date of the submission of the request, and shall be deemed concluded within 15 days of the date of the submission of the request.	(c) explain how the requesting Party considers that those trade effects are linked to the measure. 2. The Party to which such request is addressed shall favourably consider the request and provide a written reply to the request within 15 days of its receipt. 1 For the purposes of this Annex, market access in goods covers non-agricultural market access (NAMA) and its related trade rules including trade remedies, technical barriers to trade, sanitary and phytosanitary measures, trade facilitation, rules of origin, safeguards and the Sectoral Annexes to Chapter Two (National Treatment and Market Access for Goods). It excludes trade in agricultural products, services and establishment, cultural cooperation, government procurement, competition, intellectual property rights, payments and capital movements and trade and sustainable development.
5. If consultations are not held within the time frames laid down in paragraph 3 or 4 respectively, or if consultations have been concluded and no mutually agreed solution has been reached, the complaining Party may request the establishment of an arbitration panel in accordance with Article 14.4. SECTION C DISPUTE SETTLEMENT PROCEDURES SUB-SECTION A ARBITRATION PROCEDURE Article 14.4 Initiation of The Arbitration Procedure	Article 4 Selection of Mediator 1. Upon launch of the mediation procedure, the Parties are encouraged to agree on a mediator no later than 15 days after the receipt of the reply to the request. If the Parties cannot agree on the mediator within the established time frame, either Party may request appointment of the mediator by lot. Within five days of the submission of the request, each Party shall establish a list of at least three persons who are not nationals of that Party, fulfill the conditions of paragraph 2 and may act as mediator. Within five days of submission of the list, each Party shall select at least one name from the other Party's list. The chair of the Trade Committee or the chair's delegate shall then select the mediator by lot among the selected names. The selection by lot shall be made in the presence of representatives of the Parties and within 15 days of the submission of the request for appointment by lot.
1. Where the Parties have failed to resolve the dispute by recourse to consultations as provided for in Article 14.3, the complaining Party may request the establishment of an arbitration panel. 2. The request for the establishment of an arbitration panel shall be made in writing to the Party complained against and the Trade Committee. The complaining Party shall identify in its request the specific measure at issue, and it	2. The mediator shall be an expert on the subject matter to which the measure in question relates.2 The mediator shall assist, in an impartial and transparent manner,

Bilateral Dispute Settlement Provisions	Non-Tariff Barrier (NTB) Mediation Mechanism
shall explain how such measure constitutes a breach of the provisions referred to in Article 14.2. Article 14.5 Establishment of The Arbitration Panel 1. An arbitration panel shall be composed of three arbitrators. 2. Within 10 days of the date of the submission of the request for the establishment of an arbitration panel to the Trade Committee, the Parties shall consult in order to reach an agreement on the composition of the arbitration panel. 3. In the event that the Parties are unable to agree on the composition of the arbitration panel within the time frame laid down in paragraph 2, either Party may request the chair of the Trade Committee, or the chair's delegate, to select all three members by lot from the list established under Article 14.18, one among the individuals proposed by the complaining Party, one among the individuals proposed by the Party complained against and one among the individuals selected by the Parties to act as chairperson. Where the Parties agree on one or more of the members of the arbitration panel, any remaining members shall be selected by the same procedure. 4. The date of establishment of the arbitration panel shall be the date on which the three arbitrators are selected. Article 14.6 Interim Panel Report 1. The arbitration panel shall issue to the Parties an interim report setting out the findings of facts, the applicability of the relevant provisions and the basic rationale behind any findings and recommendations that it makes, within 90 days of the date of establishment of the arbitration panel. Where it considers that this deadline	the Parties in bringing clarity to the measure and its possible trade effects, and in reaching a mutually agreed solution. Article 5 Rules of The Mediation Procedure 1. In the initial stage of the procedure, within 10 days of the appointment of the mediator, the Party having launched the mediation procedure shall present, in writing, a detailed description of the problem to the mediator and to the other Party, in particular of the operation of the measure at issue and its trade effects. Within 20 days of the date of delivery of this submission, the other Party may provide, in writing, its comments to the description of the problem. Either Party may include in its description or comments any information that it deems relevant. 2. The mediator may decide on the most appropriate way of conducting the initial stage, in particular whether to consult the Parties jointly or individually, seek the assistance of or consult with relevant experts and stakeholders. 3. Following the initial stage, the mediator may provide an advisory opinion and propose a solution for the Parties' consideration. In any such opinion, the mediator shall not consider whether the measure at issue is consistent or not with this Agreement; nor shall the mediator question the legitimacy of the policy objectives of the measure. The mediator may meet individually or jointly with the Parties in order to facilitate a mutually agreed solution. This stage of the procedure shall normally be completed within 60 days of the date of the appointment of the mediator. 4. The procedure shall be confidential and shall take place in the territory of the Party to which the request was addressed, or by a mutual agreement in any other location or by any other means. 5. The procedure shall be terminated:

Bilateral Dispute Settlement Provisions	Non-Tariff Barrier (NTB) Mediation Mechanism
cannot be met, the chairperson of the arbitration panel must notify the Parties and the Trade Committee in writing, stating the reasons for the delay and the date on which the panel plans to issue its interim report. Under no circumstances should the interim report be issued later than 120 days after the date of the establishment of the arbitration panel. 2. Any Party may submit a written request for the arbitration panel to review precise aspects of the interim report within 14 days of its issuance. 3. In cases of urgency, including those involving perishable or seasonal goods, the arbitration panel shall make every effort to issue its interim report and any Party may submit a written request for the arbitration panel to review precise aspects of the interim report, within half of the respective time frames under paragraphs 1 and 2. 4. After considering any written comments by the Parties on the interim report, the arbitration panel may modify its report and make any further examination it considers appropriate. The final arbitration panel ruling shall include a discussion of the arguments made at the interim review stage. Article 14.7 Arbitration Panel Ruling 1. The arbitration panel shall issue its ruling to the Parties and to the Trade Committee within 120 days of the date of the establishment of the arbitration panel. Where it considers that this deadline cannot be met, the chairperson of the arbitration panel must notify the Parties and the Trade Committee in writing, stating the reasons for the delay and the date on which the panel plans to issue its ruling. Under no circumstances should the ruling be issued later than 150 days after the date of the establishment of the arbitration panel. 2. In cases of urgency, including those involving perishable or seasonal goods, the arbitration panel shall make every effort to issue its ruling within 60 days of the date	(a) by the signature of a settlement agreement by the Parties, on the date of that 2 For example, in cases concerning standards and technical requirements, the mediator should have expertise in the area of relevant international standard setting bodies. signature; (b) by a mutual agreement of the Parties at any stage of the procedure, on the date of that agreement; (c) by a written declaration of the mediator, after consultation with the Parties, that further efforts at mediation are no longer justified; or (d) by a written declaration of a Party after exploring mutually agreed solutions under the mediation procedure and after having considered any advisory opinions and proposals by the mediator. SECTION B IMPLEMENTATION Article 6 Implementation of A Mutually Agreed Solution 1. Where the Parties have agreed to a solution, each Party shall take any measure necessary to implement the mutually agreed solution without undue delay. 2. The implementing Party shall inform the other Party in writing of any steps or measures taken to implement the mutually agreed solution. SECTION C GENERAL PROVISIONS Article 7 Relationship to Dispute Settlement

Bilateral Dispute Settlement Provisions	Non-Tariff Barrier (NTB) Mediation Mechanism
of its establishment. Under no circumstances should it take longer than 75 days after its establishment. The arbitration panel may give a preliminary ruling within 10 days of its establishment on whether it deems the case to be urgent. SUB-SECTION B COMPLIANCE Article 14.8 Compliance with The Arbitration Panel Ruling Each Party shall take any measure necessary to comply in good faith with the arbitration panel ruling, and the Parties will endeavour to agree on the period of time to comply with the ruling. Article 14.9 The Reasonable Period of Time For Compliance 1. No later than 30 days after the issuance of the arbitration panel ruling to the Parties, the Party complained against shall notify the complaining Party and the Trade Committee of the time it will require for compliance. 2. If there is disagreement between the Parties on the reasonable period of time to comply with the arbitration panel ruling, the complaining Party shall, within 20 days of the notification made under paragraph 1 by the Party complained against, request in writing the original arbitration panel to determine the length of the reasonable period of time. Such request shall be notified to the other Party and to the Trade Committee. The arbitration panel shall issue its ruling to the Parties and to the Trade Committee within 20 days of the date of the submission of the request. 3. In the event that any member of the original arbitration panel is no longer available, the procedures set out in Article 14.5 shall apply. The time limit for issuing the ruling shall be 35 days from the date of the submission of the request referred to	1. The procedure under this mediation mechanism is not intended to serve as a basis for dispute settlement procedures under this Agreement or another agreement. A Party shall not rely on or introduce as evidence in such dispute settlement procedures: (a) positions taken by the other Party in the course of the mediation procedure; (b) the fact that the other Party has indicated its willingness to accept a solution to the non-tariff measure subject to mediation; or (c) proposals made by the mediator. 2. The mediation mechanism is without prejudice to the Parties' rights and obligations under Chapter Fourteen (Dispute Settlement). Article 8 Time Limits Any time limit referred to in this Annex may be extended by mutual agreement of the Parties. Article 9 Costs 1. Each Party shall bear its own expenses derived from the participation in the mediation procedure. 2. The Parties shall share the expenses derived from organisational matters, including the expenses of the mediator. Article 10 Review

Bilateral Dispute Settlement Provisions	Non-Tariff Barrier (NTB) Mediation Mechanism
in paragraph 2. 4. The Party complained against will inform the complaining Party in writing of its progress to comply with the arbitration panel ruling at least one month before the expiry of the reasonable period of time. 5. The reasonable period of time may be extended by mutual agreement of the Parties. Article 14.10 Review of Any Measure Taken to Comply with The Arbitration Panel Ruling 1. The Party complained against shall notify the complaining Party and the Trade Committee before the end of the reasonable period of time of any measure that it has taken to comply with the arbitration panel ruling. 2. Where there is disagreement between the Parties as to the existence of a measure or consistency with the provisions referred to in Article 14.2 of any measure notified under paragraph 1, the complaining Party may request in writing the original arbitration panel to rule on the matter. Such request shall identify the specific measure at issue and it shall explain how such measure is incompatible with the provisions referred to in Article 14.2. The arbitration panel shall issue its ruling within 45 days of the date of the submission of the request. 3. In the event that any member of the original arbitration panel is no longer available, the procedures set out in Article 14.5 shall apply. The time limit for issuing the ruling shall be 60 days from the date of the submission of the request referred to in paragraph 2. Article 14.11 Temporary Remedies in Case of Non-Compliance	1. The Parties agree that any matter not falling within the scope defined in Article 14.2 shall become subject to the mediation mechanism if WTO Members agree on the establishment of a corresponding mechanism that covers such matter. The extension of the scope of application shall be as from the date of application of the latter agreement. This shall also apply to any further extensions of the scope of application of the WTO corresponding mechanism. 2. Five years after the entry into force of this Agreement, the Parties shall consult each other on the need to modify the mediation mechanism in light of the experience gained and the development of a corresponding mechanism in the WTO.

Bilateral Dispute Settlement Provisions	Non-Tariff Barrier (NTB) Mediation Mechanism
1. If the Party complained against fails to notify any measure taken to comply with the arbitration panel ruling before the expiry of the reasonable period of time, or if the arbitration panel rules that no measure taken to comply exists or that the measure notified under Article 14.10.1 is inconsistent with that Party's obligations under the provisions referred to in Article 14.2, the Party complained against shall, if so requested by the complaining Party, present an offer for temporary compensation. 2. If no agreement on compensation is reached within 30 days of the end of the reasonable period of time or of the issuance of the arbitration panel ruling under Article 14.10 that no measure taken to comply exists or the measure notified under Article 14.10.1 is inconsistent with the provisions referred to in Article 14.2, the complaining Party shall be entitled, upon notification to the Party complained against and to the Trade Committee, to suspend obligations arising from any provision referred to in Article 14.2 at a level equivalent to the nullification or impairment caused by the violation. The notification shall specify the level of obligations that the complaining Party intends to suspend. The complaining Party may implement the suspension 10 days after the date of the notification, unless the Party complained against has requested arbitration under paragraph 4. 3. In suspending obligations, the complaining Party may choose to increase its tariff rates to the level applied to other WTO Members on a volume of trade to be determined in such a way that the volume of trade multiplied by the increase of the tariff rates equals the value of the nullification or impairment caused by the violation. 4. If the Party complained against considers that the level of suspension is not equivalent to the nullification or impairment caused by the violation, it may request in writing the original arbitration panel to rule on the matter. Such request shall be notified to the complaining Party and to the Trade Committee before the expiry of the 10 day period referred to in paragraph 2. The original arbitration panel shall issue its ruling on the level of the suspension of obligations to the Parties and to the Trade Committee within 30 days of the date of the submission of the request. Obligations shall not be suspended until the original arbitration panel has issued its ruling, and	

Bilateral Dispute Settlement Provisions	Non-Tariff Barrier (NTB) Mediation Mechanism
any suspension shall be consistent with the arbitration panel ruling. 5. In the event that any member of the original arbitration panel is no longer available, the procedures laid down in Article 14.5 shall apply. The period for issuing the ruling shall be 45 days from the date of the submission of the request referred to in paragraph 4. 6. The suspension of obligations shall be temporary and apply only until any measure found to be inconsistent with the provisions referred to in Article 14.2 has been withdrawn or amended so as to bring it into conformity with those provisions, as established under Article 14.12, or until the Parties have agreed to settle the dispute. Article 14.12[1)] Review of Any Measure Taken to Comply After The Suspension of Obligations 1. The Party complained against shall notify the complaining Party and the Trade Committee of any measure it has taken to comply with the ruling of the arbitration panel and of its request for the termination of the suspension of obligations applied by the complaining Party. 2. If the Parties do not reach an agreement on the compatibility of the notified measure with the provisions referred to in Article 14.2 within 30 days of the date of the notification, the complaining Party shall request in writing the original arbitration panel to rule on the matter. Such request shall be notified to the Party complained against and to the Trade Committee. The arbitration panel ruling shall be issued to the Parties and to the Trade Committee within 45 days of the date of the submission of the request. If the arbitration panel rules that any measure taken to comply is in conformity with the provisions referred to in Article 14.2, the suspension of obligations shall be terminated. 3. In the event that any member of the original arbitration panel is no longer available, the procedures laid down in Article 14.5 shall apply. The period for issuing	

Bilateral Dispute Settlement Provisions	Non-Tariff Barrier (NTB) Mediation Mechanism
the ruling shall be 60 days from the date of the submission of the request referred to in paragraph 2. SUB-SECTION C COMMON PROVISIONS Article 14.13 Mutually Agreed Solution The Parties may reach a mutually agreed solution to a dispute under this Chapter at any time. They shall notify the Trade Committee of any such solution. Upon notification of the mutually agreed solution, the procedure shall be terminated. Article 14.14 Rules of Procedure 1. Dispute settlement procedures under this Chapter shall be governed by Annex 14-B. 2. Any hearing of the arbitration panel shall be open to the public in accordance with Annex 14-B. Article 14.15 Information and Technical Advice At the request of a Party, or upon its own initiative, the arbitration panel may obtain information from any source, including the Parties involved in the dispute, as it deems appropriate for the arbitration panel proceeding. The arbitration panel also has the right to seek the relevant opinion of experts as it deems appropriate. Any information obtained in this manner must be disclosed to both Parties which may submit comments. Interested natural or legal persons of the Parties are authorised to submit amicus curiae briefs to the arbitration panel in accordance with Annex 14-B.	

Bilateral Dispute Settlement Provisions	Non-Tariff Barrier (NTB) Mediation Mechanism
Article 14.16 Rules of Interpretation Any arbitration panel shall interpret the provisions referred to in Article 14.2 in accordance with customary rules of interpretation of public international law, including those codified in the Vienna Convention on the Law of Treaties. Where an obligation under this Agreement is identical to an obligation under the WTO Agreement, the arbitration panel shall adopt an interpretation which is consistent with any relevant interpretation established in rulings of the WTO Dispute Settlement Body (hereinafter referred to as the "DSB"). The rulings of the arbitration panel cannot add to or diminish the rights and obligations provided for in the provisions referred to in Article 14.2. Article 14.17 Arbitration Panel Decisions and Rulings 1. The arbitration panel shall make every effort to take any decision by consensus. Where, nevertheless, a decision cannot be arrived at by consensus, the matter at issue shall be decided by majority vote. In no case shall dissenting opinions of arbitrators be published. 2. Any ruling of the arbitration panel shall be binding on the Parties and shall not create any rights or obligations for natural or legal persons. The ruling shall set out the findings of fact, the applicability of the relevant provisions of this Agreement and the basic rationale behind any findings and conclusions that it makes. The Trade Committee shall make the arbitration panel rulings publicly available in its entirety unless it decides not to do so. SECTION D GENERAL PROVISIONS	

Bilateral Dispute Settlement Provisions	Non-Tariff Barrier (NTB) Mediation Mechanism
Article 14.18 List of Arbitrators 1. The Trade Committee shall, no later than six months after the entry into force of this Agreement, establish a list of 15 individuals who are willing and able to serve as arbitrators. Each Party shall propose five individuals to serve as arbitrators. The Parties shall also select five individuals who are not nationals of either Party and shall act as chairperson to the arbitration panel. The Trade Committee will ensure that the list is always maintained at this level. 2. Arbitrators shall have specialised knowledge or experience of law and international trade. They shall be independent, serve in their individual capacities and not take instructions from any organisation or government with regard to matters related to the dispute, or be affiliated with the government of any Party, and shall comply with Annex 14-C. Article 14.19 Relation with WTO Obligations[2)] 1. Recourse to the dispute settlement provisions of this Chapter shall be without prejudice to any action in the WTO framework, including dispute settlement action. 2. However, where a Party has, with regard to a particular measure, initiated a dispute settlement proceeding, either under this Chapter or under the WTO Agreement, it may not institute a dispute settlement proceeding regarding the same measure in the other forum until the first proceeding has been concluded. In addition, a Party shall not seek redress of an obligation which is identical under this Agreement and under the WTO Agreement in the two forums. In such case, once a dispute settlement proceeding has been initiated, the Party shall not bring a claim seeking redress of the identical obligation under the other Agreement to the other forum, unless the forum selected fails for procedural or jurisdictional reasons to make findings on the claim seeking redress of that obligation.	

Bilateral Dispute Settlement Provisions	Non-Tariff Barrier (NTB) Mediation Mechanism
3. For the purposes of paragraph 2: (a) dispute settlement proceedings under the WTO Agreement are deemed to be initiated by a Party's request for the establishment of a panel under Article 6 of the Understanding on Rules and Procedures Governing the Settlement of Disputes contained in Annex 2 of the WTO Agreement (hereinafter referred to as the "DSU") and are deemed to be concluded when the DSB adopts the Panel's report, and the Appellate Body's report as the case may be, under Articles 16 and 17.14 of the DSU; and (b) dispute settlement proceedings under this Chapter are deemed to be initiated by a Party's request for the establishment of an arbitration panel under Article 14.4.1 and are deemed to be concluded when the arbitration panel issues its ruling to the Parties and to the Trade Committee under Article 14.7. 4. Nothing in this Agreement shall preclude a Party from implementing the suspension of obligations authorised by the DSB. The WTO Agreement shall not be invoked to preclude a Party from suspending obligations under this Chapter. Article 14.20 Time Limits 1. All time limits laid down in this Chapter, including the limits for the arbitration panels to issue their rulings, shall be counted in calendar days, the first day being the day following the act or fact to which they refer. 2. Any time limit referred to in this Chapter may be extended by mutual agreement of the Parties.	

* Entered into force on July1,2011. *NTB mediation mechanism itself is a unique innovation within the FTA framework.*

1) *Articles 14.10-12 are similar to the developments in the Japan-EU FTA where they have multiple compliance review mechanisms. Yet the names of the provision seem to have deviated from these articles.*

2) *This provision is notable in this agreement. Not all agreements have separate provision allegedly defining the relationship with the WTO.*

2.4 Free Trade Agreement between the Government of the Republic of Korea and the Government of the People's Republic of China*

Bilateral Dispute Settlement Provisions	Investment Dispute Settlement (ISDS) Provisions
CHAPTER 20 DISPUTE SETTLEMENT Article 20.1 Cooperation The Parties shall at all times endeavor to agree on the interpretation and application of this Agreement, and shall make every attempt through cooperation and consultations to arrive at a mutually satisfactory resolution of any matter that might affect its operation when a dispute occurs. Article 20.2 Scope Unless otherwise provided in this Agreement or as the Parties otherwise agree, this Chapter shall apply with respect to the settlement of all disputes between the Parties regarding the interpretation and application of this Agreement or wherever a Party considers that: (a) a measure of the other Party is inconsistent with its obligations under this Agreement; or (b) the other Party has otherwise failed to carry out its obligations under this Agreement. Article 20.3 Choice of Forum 1. Where a dispute arises under this Agreement and under the WTO Agreement or any other agreement to which both Parties are party, the complaining Party may	CHAPTER 12 INVESTMENT Article 12.12 Settlement of Investment Disputes between a Party and an Investor of the Other Party 1. For the purposes of this Article, an investment dispute is a dispute between a Party and an investor of the other Party that has incurred loss or damage by reason of, or arising out of, an alleged breach of any obligation of the former Party under this Chapter with respect to the investor or its covered investments in the territory of the former Party. 2. Any investment dispute shall, as far as possible, be settled amicably through consultation between the investor who is a party to the investment dispute (hereinafter referred to in this Article as "disputing investor") and the Party that is a party to the investment dispute (hereinafter referred to in this Article as "disputing Party"). A written request for consultation shall be submitted to the disputing Party by the disputing investor before the submission of the investment dispute to the arbitration set out in paragraph 3. Such a written request shall specify: (a) the name and address of the disputing investor; (b) the obligations under this Chapter alleged to have been breached; (c) a brief summary of the facts of the investment dispute; and (d) the relief sought and the approximate amount of damages. 3. The investment dispute shall on the request of the disputing investor be submitted

Bilateral Dispute Settlement Provisions	Investment Dispute Settlement (ISDS) Provisions
select the forum in which to settle the dispute. 2. Once the complaining Party has requested the establishment of a dispute settlement panel under an agreement referred to in paragraph 1, the forum selected shall be used to the exclusion of other fora. Article 20.4 Consultations 1. The Parties shall make every attempt to arrive at a mutually satisfactory resolution of any dispute through consultations under this Article or other consultative provisions of this Agreement. 2. Either Party may request consultations with the other Party with respect to any matter described in Article 20.2 by delivering written notification to the other Party. The requesting Party shall set out the reasons for the request, including identification of the measure at issue and an indication of the legal basis for the complaint, in the written notification. If a request for consultations is made, the other Party shall reply in writing to the request within 10 days after the date of its receipt. 3. Consultations shall be held in good faith within 30 days after the date of receipt of the request with a view of reaching a mutually satisfactory solution and take place, unless the Parties otherwise agree, in the territory of the requested Party. 4. If the requested Party does not reply within 10 days or does not enter into consultations within 30 days from the date of receipt of the request for consultations, then the requesting Party may proceed directly to request the establishment of a panel in accordance with Article 20.6. 5. Each Party shall: (a) provide sufficient information in the consultations to enable a full	to either: (a) a competent court of the disputing Party; (b) arbitration in accordance with the ICSID Convention, if the ICSID Convention is available; (c) arbitration under the ICSID Additional Facility Rules, if the ICSID Additional Facility Rules are available; (d) arbitration under the UNCITRAL Arbitration Rules; or (e) if agreed with the disputing Party, any arbitration in accordance with other arbitration rules, provided that, for the purposes of subparagraphs (b) through (e): (i) the investment dispute cannot be settled through the consultation referred to in paragraph 2 within four months from the date of the submission of the written request for consultation to the disputing Party; and (ii) the requirement concerning the domestic administrative review procedure set out in paragraph 7, where applicable, is met. 4. Each Party hereby gives its consent to the submission of an investment dispute by a disputing investor to the arbitration set out in paragraph 3 in accordance with the provisions of this Article. 5. Once the disputing investor has submitted an investment dispute to the competent court of the disputing Party or to one of the arbitrations set out in paragraph 3, the choice of the disputing investor shall be final and the disputing investor may not submit thereafter the same dispute to the other arbitrations set out in paragraph 3. 6. Notwithstanding paragraphs 3 and 4, no claim may be submitted to the arbitration set out in paragraph 3 unless the disputing investor gives the disputing Party written

Bilateral Dispute Settlement Provisions	Investment Dispute Settlement (ISDS) Provisions
examination of how the matter subject to consultations might affect the operation of this Agreement; and (b) treat any confidential information exchanged in the course of consultations on the same basis as the Party providing the information. 6. Consultations shall be confidential and without prejudice to the rights of the Parties in any further proceedings under this Chapter. Article 20.5 Good Offices, Conciliation or Mediation 1. Good offices, conciliation, and mediation are procedures undertaken voluntarily if the Parties so agree. 2. Proceedings involving good offices, conciliation, and mediation, and in particular positions taken by the Parties during these proceedings, shall be confidential and without prejudice to the rights of either Party in any further proceedings. 3. Good offices, conciliation, or mediation may be requested at any time by any Party. They may begin at any time and be terminated at any time. If the Parties agree, procedures for good offices, conciliation or mediation may continue while the dispute proceeds for resolution before a panel established under Article 20.6. 4. The Parties are encouraged to enter into a mediation procedure in particular when a Party believes that a certain non-tariff measure adversely affects trade between the Parties and that such measure is related to the matter falling under market access of goods of this Agreement and is subject to this Chapter, unless the Parties otherwise agree. 5. The Parties should endeavor to participate in the mediation procedure provided for in paragraph 4 in an expeditious way and with the aim to reach a mutually	waiver of any right to initiate before any competent court of the disputing Party with respect to any measure of the disputing Party alleged to constitute a breach referred to in paragraph 1. 7. When the disputing investor submits a written request for consultation to the disputing Party under paragraph 2, the disputing Party may require, without delay, the investor concerned to go through the domestic administrative review procedure specified by the laws and regulations of that Party before the submission to the arbitration set out in paragraph 3. The domestic administrative review procedure shall not exceed four months from the date on which an application for the review is filed. If the procedure is not completed by the end of the four months, it shall be deemed to be completed and the disputing investor may submit the investment dispute to the arbitration set out in paragraph 3. The investor may file an application for the review unless the four months consultation period as provided in paragraph 3 has elapsed. 8. The applicable arbitration rules shall govern the arbitration set out in paragraph 3 except to the extent modified in this Article. 9. The award rendered by an arbitral tribunal established under paragraph 3 (hereinafter referred to in this Article as the "Tribunal") shall include: (a) a finding whether or not there has been a breach by the disputing Party of any obligation under this Chapter with respect to the disputing investor and its covered investments; and (b) one or both of the following remedies, only if the disputing investor's loss or damage is attributed to such breach: (i) monetary damages and applicable interest; and (ii) restitution of property, in which case the award shall provide that the disputing Party may pay monetary damages and any applicable interest, in lieu of restitution.

Bilateral Dispute Settlement Provisions	Investment Dispute Settlement (ISDS) Provisions
agreed solution within a reasonable period of time with the assistance of a mediator designated or appointed by the Parties upon agreement. Where the Parties have agreed to a solution, each Party should take any measure necessary to implement the mutually agreed solution. 6. The mediation procedure provided for in paragraph 4 is not intended to serve as a basis for dispute settlement procedures under this Agreement or any other agreement in which the Parties participate as parties. Article 20.6 Establishment of Panel 1. If the consultations referred to in Article 20.4 fail to resolve a matter within 60 days after the date of receipt of the request for consultations or within such other period as the Parties may agree, the complaining Party may deliver a written request to establish a panel to the other Party. 2. The complaining Party shall indicate in the request whether consultations were held, identify the specific measure at issue and provide a brief summary of the legal basis for the complaint sufficient to present the problem clearly. 3. A panel shall be established upon the date of receipt of the request referred to in paragraph 1. Article 20.7 Composition of Panel 1. Unless the Parties otherwise agree, the Parties shall apply the following procedures in selecting a panel: (a) the panel shall comprise three members;	10. The award which is rendered by the Tribunal shall be final and binding upon both parties to the investment dispute. This award shall be executed in accordance with the applicable laws and regulations concerning the execution of award in force, in the country in whose territory such execution is sought. 11. Notwithstanding paragraph 3, no claim may be submitted to the arbitration set out in that paragraph, if more than three years have elapsed from the date on which the disputing investor first acquired, or should have first acquired, whichever is the earlier, the knowledge that the disputing investor had incurred the loss or damage referred to in paragraph 1.

Bilateral Dispute Settlement Provisions	Investment Dispute Settlement (ISDS) Provisions
(b) each Party shall appoint one panelist respectively within 15 days after the establishment of the panel. If a Party fails to appoint a panelist within that period, the panelist shall be appointed by the other Party, unless the Parties otherwise decide; (c) the Parties shall endeavor to agree on the third panelist, who shall serve as the chair, within 30 days after the establishment of the panel; and (d) if the Parties are unable to agree on the chair within 30 days after the establishment of the panel, on the request of any Party to the dispute, the Director General of the WTO is expected to designate the chair within a further period of 30 days. In the event that the Director General of the WTO is a national of either Party or unable to perform this task, the Deputy Director-General of the WTO who is not a national of either Party shall be requested to perform such task. 2. The chair of the panel shall not be a national of either Party, nor have his or her usual place of residence in the territory of either Party, nor be employed by either Party, nor have dealt with the matter in any capacity. 3. If a panelist appointed under this Article resigns or becomes unable to serve on the panel, a successor shall be appointed within 15 days in accordance with the selection procedure of the original panelist and the successor shall have all the powers and duties of the original panelist. In such a case, any time period applicable to the panel proceedings shall be suspended during the appointment of the successor. 4. All panelists shall: (a) have expertise or experience in law, international trade, other matters covered by this Agreement, or the resolution of disputes arising under international trade agreements;	

Bilateral Dispute Settlement Provisions	Investment Dispute Settlement (ISDS) Provisions
(b) be chosen strictly on the basis of objectivity, reliability, and sound judgment; (c) be independent of, and not be affiliated with or take instructions from, either Party; and (d) comply with a code of conduct established in Annex 20-B (Code of Conduct for Panelists and Mediators). 5. Where a Party considers that a panelist does not comply with the requirements of Annex 20-B (Code of Conduct for Panelists and Mediators), the Parties shall consult and, if so agreed, replace that panelist in accordance with paragraph 3. Article 20.8 Functions of Panel 1. The function of a panel is to make an objective assessment of the dispute before it, including an examination of the facts of the case and the applicability of and conformity with this Agreement. 2. Where a panel concludes that a measure is inconsistent with this Agreement, it shall recommend that the Party complained against bring the measure into conformity with this Agreement. Article 20.9 Rules of Procedure 1. Unless the Parties otherwise agree, a panel shall follow the Rules of Procedure set out in Annex 20-A (Rules of Procedure) and may, after consulting with the Parties, adopt additional rules of procedure not inconsistent with the Annex 20-A (Rules of Procedure).	

Bilateral Dispute Settlement Provisions	Investment Dispute Settlement (ISDS) Provisions
2 Unless the Parties otherwise agree within 20 days from the date of receipt of the request for the establishment of the panel, the panel's terms of reference shall be: "To examine, in the light of the relevant provisions of this Agreement, the matter referred to in the request for the establishment of the panel pursuant to Article 20.6 and to make findings of law and fact together with the reasons therefore for the resolution of the dispute, conclusions, and recommendations." 3. On the request of a Party, or on its own initiative, the panel may seek information and technical advice from any person or body that it deems appropriate, provided that the Parties so agree. 4. Unless the Parties otherwise agree, the remuneration of the panelists and other expenses of the panel shall be borne by the Parties in equal shares. Article 20.10 Suspension or Termination of Panel Proceedings 1. The Parties may agree that a panel suspends its work at any time for a period not exceeding 12 months from the date of such agreement. In the event of such a suspension, all relevant timeframes set out in this Chapter shall be extended by the amount of time that the work was suspended. If the work of the panel has been suspended for more than 12 months, the authority for establishment of the panel shall lapse, unless the Parties otherwise agree. 2. The Parties may agree to terminate the proceedings of a panel. Article 20.11 Panel Report 1. Unless the Parties otherwise agree, a panel shall, within 120 days after the last panelist is appointed, issue to the Parties an interim report.	

Bilateral Dispute Settlement Provisions	Investment Dispute Settlement (ISDS) Provisions
2. In exceptional cases, if the panel considers it cannot issue its interim report within the period of 120 days, it shall inform the Parties in writing of the reasons for the delay together with an estimate of the period within which it will release its report. Any delay shall not exceed a further period of 30 days unless the Parties otherwise agree. 3. The panel shall base its report on the relevant provisions of this Agreement and the submissions and arguments of the Parties. The panel shall consider this Agreement in accordance with customary rules of interpretation of public international law, including those codified in the Vienna Convention on the Law of Treaties (1969). 4. Each Party may submit written comments to the panel on its interim report within 15 days of the presentation of the report. After considering any written comments by the Parties on the interim report, the panel may modify its report and make any further examination it considers appropriate. 5. The panel shall present a final report to the Parties within 45 days of the presentation of the interim report, unless the Parties otherwise agree. The Parties shall make the final report available to the public within 15 days after the issuance of the final report, subject to the protection of confidential information, unless the Parties decide not to do so. 6. The panel shall make every effort to take its decision by consensus. If the panel is unable to reach consensus, it may take its decision by majority vote. Panelists may furnish dissenting or separate opinions on matters not unanimously agreed. All opinions expressed in the panel report by individual panelists shall be anonymous. 7. The final report of the panel shall be final and binding on the Parties for the dispute and shall not create any rights or obligations for persons. The final report shall set out the findings of fact, the applicability of the relevant provisions of this Agreement and the basic rationale behind any findings and conclusions that the panel makes.	

Bilateral Dispute Settlement Provisions	Investment Dispute Settlement (ISDS) Provisions
Article 20.12 Implementation of the Final Report of the Panel 1. If in its final report the panel determines that a Party has not conformed with its obligations under this Agreement, the resolution, whenever possible, shall be to eliminate the non-conformity. 2. Unless the Parties otherwise agree, the Party complained against shall eliminate the non-conformity as determined in the final report of the panel immediately, or if this is not practicable, within a reasonable period of time referred to in Article 20.13. Article 20.13 Reasonable Period of Time 1. The reasonable period of time shall be mutually determined by the Parties, or where the Parties fail to agree on the reasonable period of time within 30 days of the issuance of the final report of the panel, either Party may, to the extent possible, refer the matter to the original panel, which shall determine the reasonable period of time. 2. The panel shall provide its report to the Parties within 30 days after the date of the referral of the matter to it. When the panel considers that it cannot provide its report within this timeframe, it shall inform the Parties in writing of the reasons for the delay together with an estimate of the period within which it will submit its report. Any delay shall not exceed a further period of 30 days unless the Parties otherwise agree. 3. The reasonable period of time normally should not exceed 15 months from the date of issuance of the final report of the panel. 4. The Party complained against will inform the complaining Party in writing of its progress to comply with the final report of the panel at least 30 days before the expiry of the reasonable period of time.	

Bilateral Dispute Settlement Provisions	Investment Dispute Settlement (ISDS) Provisions
Article 20.14 Compliance Review 1. The Party complained against shall notify the complaining Party before the end of the reasonable period of time of any measures that it has taken to comply with the final report of the panel. 2. Where there is disagreement as to the existence or consistency with this Agreement of measures taken to comply with the recommendations of the panel, such dispute shall be referred to a panel proceeding, including wherever possible by resort to the original panel. 3. The panel shall provide its report to the Parties within 60 days after the date of the referral of the matter to it. When the panel considers that it cannot provide its report within this timeframe, it shall inform the Parties in writing of the reasons for the delay together with an estimate of the period within which it will submit its report. Any delay shall not exceed a further period of 30 days unless the Parties otherwise agree. 4. Articles concerning panel procedures in this Agreement shall apply mutatis mutandis to the procedure under this Article. Article 20.15 Suspension of Concessions or Other Obligations 1. If the panel under Article 20.14 finds that the Party complained against fails to bring the measure found to be inconsistent with this Agreement into compliance with the recommendations of the panel within the reasonable period of time established, or if the Party complained against expresses in writing that it will not implement the recommendations, or if no measure taken to comply exists, and the Parties fail to reach an agreement on compensation within 20 days after entering into negotiations for compensation, the complaining Party may suspend the application of concessions or other obligations to the Party complained against.	

Bilateral Dispute Settlement Provisions	Investment Dispute Settlement (ISDS) Provisions
The complaining Party shall notify the Party complained against 30 days before suspending concessions or other obligations. The notification shall indicate the level and scope of the suspension of concessions or other obligations. 2. Compensation and suspension of concessions or other obligations are temporary measures available in the event that the recommendations and determinations are not implemented within the reasonable period of time. However, neither compensation nor suspension of concessions or other obligations is preferred to full implementation of a recommendation to bring a measure into conformity with this Agreement. Compensation shall be consistent with this Agreement. 3. In considering concessions or other obligations to suspend: (a) the complaining Party should first seek to suspend concessions or other obligations in the same sector or sectors that affected by the measure that the panel has found to be inconsistent with the obligations derived of this Agreement; and (b) if the complaining Party considers that it is not practicable or effective to suspend concessions or other obligations in the same sector or sectors, it may suspend concession or other obligations in other sectors. 4. The level of suspension of concessions or other obligations shall be equivalent to the level of the nullification or impairment. 5. If the Party complained against considers that the level of suspension of concessions or other obligations is not equivalent to the nullification or impairment, it may request in writing to the original panel. On the written request of the Party complained against, the original panel shall determine whether the level of concessions or other obligations to be suspended by the complaining Party is excessive pursuant to paragraph 4. If the panel cannot be established with its original panelists, the proceeding set out in Article 20.6 shall be applied.	

Bilateral Dispute Settlement Provisions	Investment Dispute Settlement (ISDS) Provisions
6. The panel shall present its determination within 60 days after the date of receipt of the request, or if the panel cannot be established with its original panelists, from the date on which the last panelist is appointed. 7. The complaining Party may not suspend the application of concessions or other obligations before the issuance of the panel's determination pursuant to this Article. Article 20.16 Post Suspension 1. Without prejudice to the procedure in Article 20.15, if the Party complained against considers that it has eliminated the non-conformity that the panel has found, it may provide a written notice to the complaining Party with description of how nonconformity has been removed. If the complaining Party disagrees, it may refer the matter to the original panel within 60 days after receipt of such written notice. Otherwise, the complaining Party shall promptly stop the suspension of concessions or other obligations. 2. The panel shall issue its report within 60 days after the referral of the matter. 3. If the panel determines that the Party complained against has eliminated the nonconformity, the complaining Party shall promptly stop the suspension of concessions or other obligations. Article 20.17 Private Rights Neither party may provide for a right of action under its domestic law against the other Party on the ground that a measure of the other Party is inconsistent with this Agreement.	

* Entered into force on December 20, 2015.

2.5 Free Trade Agreement between the Government of the Republic of Korea and the Government of Australia*

Bilateral Dispute Settlement Provisions	Investment Dispute Settlement (ISDS) Provisions / Non-Tariff Barrier (NTB) Mediation Mechanism
CHAPTER 20 DISPUTE SETTLEMENT Article 20.1 Cooperation The Parties shall endeavour to agree on the interpretation and application of this Agreement, and shall make every attempt through cooperation to arrive at a mutually satisfactory resolution of any matter that might affect its operation. Article 20.2 Scope Unless otherwise provided in this Agreement or otherwise agreed by the Parties, this Chapter shall apply with respect to the avoidance or settlement of all disputes between the Parties regarding the implementation, interpretation or application of this Agreement or wherever a Party considers that: (a) a measure of the other Party is inconsistent with its obligations under this Agreement; (b) the other Party has otherwise failed to carry out its obligations under this Agreement; or (c) a benefit the Party could reasonably have expected to accrue to it under Chapter 2 (Trade in Goods), 3 (Rules of Origin and Origin Procedures), 4 (Customs Administration and Trade Facilitation), 7 (Cross-Border Trade in Services), or 12 (Government Procurement), is being nullified or impaired as a result of a measure that is not inconsistent with this Agreement.	CHAPTER 11 INVESTMENT SECTION B INVESTOR-STATE DISPUTE SETTLEMENT Article 11.15 Consultation and Negotiation In the event of an investment dispute, the claimant and the respondent should initially seek to resolve the dispute through consultation and negotiation, which may include the use of nonbinding, third party procedures. Article 11.16 Submission of A Claim to Arbitration 1. In the event that a disputing party considers that an investment dispute cannot be settled by consultation and negotiation: (a) the claimant, on its own behalf, may submit to arbitration under this Section a claim: (i) that the respondent has breached: (A) an obligation under Section A; (B) an investment authorisation; or (C) an investment agreement; and (ii) that the claimant has incurred loss or damage by reason of, or arising out of, that breach; and (b) the claimant, on behalf of an enterprise of the respondent that is a juridical person that the claimant owns or controls directly or indirectly, may submit to arbitration under this Section a claim: (i) that the respondent has breached: (A) an obligation under Section A; (B) an investment authorisation; or (C) an

Bilateral Dispute Settlement Provisions	Investment Dispute Settlement (ISDS) Provisions / Non-Tariff Barrier (NTB) Mediation Mechanism
Article 20.3 Contact Points 1. Each Party shall designate a contact point to facilitate communications between the Parties with respect to any dispute initiated under this Chapter. 2. Any request, notification, written submission or other document made in accordance with this Chapter shall be delivered to the other Party through its designated contact point. Article 20.4 Choice of Forum 1. Recourse to the dispute settlement provisions of this Chapter shall be without prejudice to any action in the WTO framework, including dispute settlement action. 2. However, where a Party has, with regard to a particular measure, initiated a dispute settlement proceeding, either under this Agreement or under the WTO Agreement, it shall not initiate a dispute settlement proceeding regarding the same measure in the other forum until the first proceeding has been concluded or terminated by the complaining Party. In addition, where a Party has initiated a dispute settlement proceeding either under this Agreement or under the WTO Agreement to seek redress of an obligation which is identical or substantially identical under the two Agreements, it shall not initiate a dispute settlement proceeding to seek redress of the identical or substantially identical obligation in the other forum until the first proceeding has been concluded or terminated by the complaining Party. 3. Notwithstanding paragraph 2, a Party may initiate a dispute settlement proceeding in the other forum if the first forum selected fails for procedural or jurisdictional reasons to make findings on the claim. 4. For the purposes of paragraphs 2 and 3:	investment agreement; and (ii) that the enterprise has incurred loss or damage by reason of, or arising out of, that breach, provided that a claimant may submit pursuant to subparagraph (a)(i)(C) or (b)(i)(C) a claim for breach of an investment agreement only if the subject matter of the claim and the claimed damages directly relate to the covered investment that was established or acquired, or sought to be established or acquired, in reliance on the relevant investment agreement. 2. At least 90 days before submitting any claim to arbitration under this Section, a claimant shall deliver to the respondent a written notice of its intention to submit the claim to arbitration (notice of intent). The notice shall specify: (a) the name and address of the claimant and, where a claim is submitted on behalf of an enterprise, the name, address and place of incorporation of the enterprise; (b) for each claim, the provision of this Agreement, investment authorisation or investment agreement alleged to have been breached and any other relevant provisions; (c) the legal and factual basis for each claim; and (d) the relief sought and the approximate amount of damages claimed. 3. Provided that six months have elapsed since the events giving rise to the claim, a claimant may submit a claim referred to in paragraph 1: (a) under the ICSID Convention and the ICSID Rules of Procedure for Arbitration Proceedings, provided that both the respondent and the non-disputing Party are parties to the ICSID Convention; (b) under the ICSID Additional Facility Rules, provided that either the

Bilateral Dispute Settlement Provisions	Investment Dispute Settlement (ISDS) Provisions / Non-Tariff Barrier (NTB) Mediation Mechanism
(a) dispute settlement proceedings under the WTO Agreement are deemed to be initiated by a Party's request for the establishment of a panel under Article 6 of the Understanding on Rules and Procedures Governing the Settlement of Disputes, in Annex 2 of the WTO Agreement (hereinafter referred to as the "DSU") and are deemed to be concluded when the WTO Dispute Settlement Body (hereinafter referred to as the "DSB") adopts the Panel's report, and the Appellate Body's report, as the case may be, under Articles 16 and 17.14 of the DSU; and (b) dispute settlement proceedings under this Chapter are deemed to be initiated by a Party's request for the establishment of a dispute settlement panel under Article 20.8 and are deemed to be concluded when the panel present a final report to the Parties under Article 20.11. Article 20.5 Rules of Interpretation Any panel shall interpret this Agreement in accordance with customary rules of interpretation of public international law, including as reflected in the Vienna Convention on the Law of Treaties. Where an obligation under this Agreement is identical or substantially identical to an obligation under the WTO Agreement, the panel shall adopt an interpretation which is consistent with any relevant interpretation established in rulings of the DSB. The rulings of the panel cannot add to or diminish the rights and obligations provided for in this Agreement. Article 20.6 Consultations 1. Either Party may request consultations with the other Party with respect to any matter described in Article 20.2 by delivering written notification to the other Party. The complaining Party shall set out the reasons for the request, including identification of the measure at issue and an indication of the legal basis for the	respondent or the non-disputing Party is a party to the ICSID Convention; (c) under the UNCITRAL Arbitration Rules; or (d) if the claimant and respondent agree, to any other arbitration institution or under any other arbitration rules. 4. A claim shall be deemed submitted to arbitration under this Section when the claimant's notice of, or request for, arbitration (notice of arbitration): (a) referred to in paragraph 1 of Article 36 of the ICSID Convention is received by the Secretary-General; (b) referred to in Article 2 of Schedule C of the ICSID Additional Facility Rules is received by the Secretary-General; (c) referred to in Article 3 of the UNCITRAL Arbitration Rules, together with the statement of claim referred to in Article 18 of the UNCITRAL Arbitration Rules, are received by the respondent; or (d) referred to under any arbitral institution or arbitral rules selected under paragraph 3(d) is received by the respondent. A claim asserted by the claimant for the first time after such notice of arbitration is submitted shall be deemed submitted to arbitration under this Section on the date of its receipt under the applicable arbitral rules. 5. The arbitration rules applicable under paragraph 3, and in effect on the date the claim or claims were submitted to arbitration under this Section, shall govern the arbitration except to the extent modified by this Agreement. 6. The claimant shall provide with the notice of arbitration:

Bilateral Dispute Settlement Provisions	Investment Dispute Settlement (ISDS) Provisions / Non-Tariff Barrier (NTB) Mediation Mechanism
complaint, and any other issue of concern. The other Party shall reply promptly to the request and enter into consultations. 2. Each Party shall: (a) provide sufficient information in the consultations to enable a full examination of the matter subject to consultations, including how the measure at issue might affect the operation of this Agreement; and (b) treat any confidential information exchanged in the course of consultations on the same basis as the Party providing the information. Article 20.7 Referral to The Joint Committee 1. If the Parties fail to resolve a matter within 60 days of the delivery of a request for consultations under Article 20.6, either Party may refer the matter to the Joint Committee by delivering written notification to the other Party. 2. The Joint Committee shall promptly convene and endeavour to resolve the matter.[1)] Article 20.8 Establishment of Panel 1. If the matter has not been resolved within 60 days of the delivery of a notification described in Article 20.7, or within such other period as the Parties may agree, the complaining Party may request the establishment of a panel to consider the matter by delivering written notification to the other Party. The complaining Party shall set out the reasons for the request, including identification of the specific measure at issue and a brief summary of the factual and legal basis for the complaint sufficient	(a) the name of the arbitrator that the claimant appoints; or (b) the claimant's written consent for the Secretary-General to appoint that arbitrator. Article 11.17 Consent of Each Party to Arbitration 1. Each Party consents to the submission of a claim to arbitration under this Section in accordance with this Agreement. 2. The consent under paragraph 1 and the submission of a claim to arbitration under this Section shall satisfy the requirements of: (a) Chapter II (Jurisdiction of the Centre) of the ICSID Convention and the ICSID Additional Facility Rules for written consent of the parties to the dispute; and (b) Article II of the New York Convention for an "agreement in writing." Article 11.18 Conditions and Limitations on Consent of Each Party 1. No claim may be submitted to arbitration under this Section if more than three years have elapsed from the date the claimant first acquired, or should have first acquired, knowledge of the breach alleged under Article 11.16.1 and knowledge that the claimant (for claims brought under Article 11.16.1(a)) or the enterprise (for claims brought under Article 11.16.1(b)) has incurred loss or damage. 2. No claim may be submitted to arbitration under this Section unless: (a) the claimant consents in writing to arbitration in accordance with the

Bilateral Dispute Settlement Provisions	Investment Dispute Settlement (ISDS) Provisions / Non-Tariff Barrier (NTB) Mediation Mechanism
to present the problem clearly. 2. Within five days of the date of delivery of the written notification requesting the establishment of a panel as provided in paragraph 1, the Parties shall enter into consultations with a view to reaching agreement on the procedures for selecting a panel. If the Parties are unable to reach agreement on the procedures for selecting the panel within 15 days of the date of delivery of the written notification referring a matter to a panel as provided in paragraph 1, either Party may at any time thereafter notify the other Party that it wishes to use the procedures set forth in subparagraphs (a) and (b). Where such a notification is made, the panel shall be composed in accordance with subparagraphs (a) and (b): (a) the panel shall have three panellists. Within 30 days of the date of delivery of the written notification requesting the establishment of a panel as provided in paragraph 1, each Party shall appoint one panellist, who may be its national, and provide to the other Party a list of up to three nominees for appointment as the third panellist who shall be the chair of the panel. The Parties shall then consult with each other with the objective of appointing the third panellist, taking into account the lists of nominees; and (b) if all of the panellists have not been appointed within 45 days of the date of delivery of the written notification requesting the establishment of a panel as provided in paragraph 1, any of the remaining panellists shall be appointed on request of either Party by random drawing from the lists of nominees for appointment as chair or as a regular panellist. 3. If a panellist appointed under this Article resigns or becomes unable to act, a successor panellist shall be appointed in the same manner as prescribed for the appointment of the original panellist and shall have all the powers and duties of the original panellist. The work of the panel shall be suspended during the appointment of the successor panellist.	procedures set out in this Agreement; and (b) the notice of arbitration is accompanied: (i) for claims submitted to arbitration under Article 11.16.1(a), by the claimant's written waiver; and (ii) for claims submitted to arbitration under Article 11.16.1(b), by the claimant's and the enterprise's written waivers, of any right to initiate or continue before any administrative tribunal or court under the law of either Party, or other dispute settlement procedures, any proceeding with respect to any measure alleged to constitute a breach referred to in Article 11.16. 3. Notwithstanding paragraph 2(b), the claimant (for claims brought under Article 11.16.1(a)) and the claimant or the enterprise (for claims brought under Article 11.16.1(b)) may initiate or continue an action that seeks interim injunctive relief and does not involve the payment of monetary damages before a judicial or administrative tribunal of the respondent, provided that the action is brought for the sole purpose of preserving the claimant's or the enterprise's rights and interests during the pendency of the arbitration. Article 11.19 Selection of Arbitrators 1. Unless the disputing parties otherwise agree, the tribunal shall comprise three arbitrators, one arbitrator appointed by each of the disputing parties and the third, who shall be the presiding arbitrator, appointed by agreement of the disputing parties. 2. The Secretary-General shall serve as appointing authority for an arbitration under this Section. 3. If a tribunal has not been constituted within 75 days of the date a claim is submitted to arbitration under this Section, the Secretary-General, on request of a

Bilateral Dispute Settlement Provisions	Investment Dispute Settlement (ISDS) Provisions / Non-Tariff Barrier (NTB) Mediation Mechanism
4. The date of establishment of the panel shall be the date the last panellist is appointed in accordance with paragraph 2. 5. Individuals appointed to a panel in accordance with this Article shall: (a) be chosen strictly on the basis of objectivity, reliability, and sound judgment; (b) have expertise or experience in law, international trade, other matters covered by this Agreement or the resolution of disputes arising under international trade agreements; (c) be independent of, and not be affiliated with or take instructions from, either Party; (d) not have dealt with the matter in any capacity; (e) disclose to the Parties information which may give rise to justifiable doubts as to their independence or impartiality; and (f) comply with the code of conduct set out in Annex 20-A. 6. Unless the Parties otherwise agree, the chair shall not be a national of either Party. 7. Where a panel is reconvened under Article 20.13.4, 20.14.5, 20.14.6 or 20.15.1 the reconvened panel shall, where possible, have the same panellists as in the original panel. If the panel cannot be reconvened with all of its original panellists, the procedures for selection of the panellists set out in paragraphs 2 through 6 shall apply.	disputing party, shall appoint, in his or her discretion, the arbitrator or arbitrators not yet appointed. The Secretary General shall not appoint a national of either Party as the presiding arbitrator unless the disputing parties otherwise agree. 4. For the purposes of Article 39 of the ICSID Convention and Article 7 of Schedule C to the ICSID Additional Facility Rules, and without prejudice to an objection to an arbitrator on a ground other than nationality: (a) the respondent agrees to the appointment of each individual member of a tribunal established under the ICSID Convention or the ICSID Additional Facility Rules; (b) a claimant referred to in Article 11.16.1(a) may submit a claim to arbitration under this Section, or continue a claim, under the ICSID Convention or the ICSID Additional Facility Rules, only on condition that the claimant agrees in writing to the appointment of each individual member of the tribunal; and (c) a claimant referred to in Article 11.16.1(b) may submit a claim to arbitration under this Section, or continue a claim, under the ICSID Convention or the ICSID Additional Facility Rules, only on condition that the claimant and the enterprise agree in writing to the appointment of each individual member of the tribunal. Article 11.20 Conduct of the Arbitration 1. The disputing parties may agree on the legal place of any arbitration under the arbitral rules applicable under Article 11.16.3. If the disputing parties fail to reach agreement, the tribunal shall determine the place in accordance with the applicable arbitral rules, provided that the place shall be in the territory of a State that is a party to the New York Convention.

Bilateral Dispute Settlement Provisions	Investment Dispute Settlement (ISDS) Provisions / Non-Tariff Barrier (NTB) Mediation Mechanism
Article 20.9 Functions Of Panels 1. A panel shall make an objective assessment of the matter before it, including an objective assessment of: (a) the facts of the case; (b) the applicability of the relevant provisions of this Agreement cited by the Parties; and (c) whether: (i) the measure at issue is inconsistent with the obligations of this Agreement; (ii) a Party has otherwise failed to carry out its obligations under this Agreement; or (iii) the measure at issue is causing nullification or impairment in the sense of Article 20.2(c). 2. Unless the Parties otherwise agree within 20 days of the date of the delivery of the request for the establishment of the panel, the panel's terms of reference shall be: "To examine, in the light of the relevant provisions of this Agreement cited by the Parties, the matter referenced in the request for the establishment of the panel, to make findings, determinations, and, if applicable, recommendations as provided in Articles 20.11.1 and 20.11.2 and to present the written reports referred to in Articles 20.11.1 and 20.11.4." 3. This Article shall not apply to a panel reconvened under Article 20.13.4, 20.14.5, 20.14.6 or 20.15.1. Article 20.10 Rules of Procedure 1. Unless the Parties otherwise agree and subject to paragraph 3, the panel shall follow the model rules of procedure set out in Annex 20-B.	2. At the request of a disputing party, and unless the disputing parties otherwise agree, the tribunal may determine the place of meetings, including consultations and hearings, taking into consideration appropriate factors, including the convenience of the parties and the arbitrators, the location of the subject matter, and the proximity of evidence. The preceding sentence is without prejudice to any appropriate factors a tribunal may consider under paragraph 1. 3. Unless the disputing parties otherwise agree, English and Korean shall be the official languages to be used in the entire arbitration proceedings, including all hearings, submissions, decisions, and awards. 4. The non-disputing Party may make oral and written submissions to the tribunal regarding the interpretation of this Agreement. On request of a disputing party, the non-disputing Party should resubmit its oral submission in writing. 5. After consulting the disputing parties, the tribunal may allow a party or entity that is not a disputing party to file a written amicus curiae submission with the tribunal regarding a matter within the scope of the dispute. In determining whether to allow such a filing, the tribunal shall consider, among other things, the extent to which: (a) the amicus curiae submission would assist the tribunal in the determination of a factual or legal issue related to the proceeding by bringing a perspective, particular knowledge, or insight that is different from that of the disputing parties; (b) the amicus curiae submission would address a matter within the scope of the dispute; and (c) the amicus curiae has a significant interest in the proceeding. The tribunal shall ensure that the amicus curiae submission does not disrupt the proceeding or unduly burden or unfairly prejudice either disputing party, and that the

Bilateral Dispute Settlement Provisions	Investment Dispute Settlement (ISDS) Provisions / Non-Tariff Barrier (NTB) Mediation Mechanism
2. The panel may, after consulting with the Parties, adopt additional rules of procedure not inconsistent with the model rules. 3. A panel reconvened under Article 20.13.4, 20.14.5, 20.14.6 or 20.15.1 may establish its own procedures, in consultation with the Parties, which do not conflict with this Chapter or the model rules of procedure. Article 20.11 Panel Report 1. Unless the Parties otherwise agree, the panel shall, within 180 days of the date the chair is appointed, present to the Parties an initial report containing its findings on the facts of the case and on the applicability of the provisions of this Agreement, and its determination as to: (a) whether (i) the measure at issue is inconsistent with the obligations of this Agreement; (ii) a Party has otherwise failed to carry out its obligations under this Agreement; or (iii) the measure at issue is causing nullification or impairment in the sense of Article 20.2(c); and (b) any other issue of concern that the Parties have jointly requested that the panel address, as well as the reasons for its findings and determinations. 2. The panel shall base its report on the relevant provisions of this Agreement, the submissions and arguments of the Parties and any information or technical advice it has obtained in accordance with its rules of procedure. The panel may, on the joint request of the Parties, make recommendations for the resolution of the dispute. 3. Each Party may submit written comments to the panel on its initial report within 14 days of the presentation of the report. After considering any written comments by the Parties on the initial report, the panel may modify its report and make any further	disputing parties are given an opportunity to present their observations on the amicus curiae submission. 6. Without prejudice to a tribunal's authority to address other objections as a preliminary question, a tribunal shall address and decide as a preliminary question any objection by the respondent that, as a matter of law, a claim submitted is not a claim for which an award in favour of the claimant may be made under Article 11.26: (a) such objection shall be submitted to the tribunal as soon as possible after the tribunal is constituted, and in no event later than the date the tribunal fixes for the respondent to submit its counter-memorial or, in the case of an amendment to the notice of arbitration, the date the tribunal fixes for the respondent to submit its response to the amendment; (b) on receipt of an objection under this paragraph, the tribunal shall suspend any proceedings on the merits, establish a schedule for considering the objection consistent with any schedule it has established for considering any other preliminary question, and issue a decision or award on the objection, stating the grounds therefor; (c) in deciding an objection under this paragraph, the tribunal shall assume to be true the claimant's factual allegations in support of any claim in the notice of arbitration (or any amendment thereof) and, in disputes brought under the UNCITRAL Arbitration Rules, the statement of claim referred to in Article 18 of the UNCITRAL Arbitration Rules. The tribunal may also consider any relevant facts not in dispute; (d) the respondent does not waive any objection as to competence or any argument on the merits merely because the respondent did or did not raise an objection under this paragraph or make use of the expedited procedure set out in paragraph 7. 7. In the event that the respondent so requests within 45 days

Bilateral Dispute Settlement Provisions	Investment Dispute Settlement (ISDS) Provisions / Non-Tariff Barrier (NTB) Mediation Mechanism
examination it considers appropriate. 4. The panel shall present a final report to the Parties within 45 days of presentation of the initial report, unless the Parties otherwise agree. The Parties shall make the final report available to the public within 15 days thereafter, subject to the protection of confidential information. 5. Paragraphs 1, 3 and 4 shall not apply to a panel reconvened under Article 20.13.4, 20.14.5, 20.14.6 or 20.15.1. Article 20.12 Suspension and Termination of Proceedings 1. The Parties may agree that the panel suspend its work at any time for a period not exceeding 12 months from the date of such agreement. Within this period, the suspended panel shall be resumed upon the request of either Party. If the work of the panel has been continuously suspended for more than 12 months, the authority for establishment of the panel shall lapse unless the Parties otherwise agree. 2. The Parties may agree to terminate the proceedings of a panel in the event that a mutually satisfactory solution to the dispute has been found. 3. Before the panel presents its final report, it may at any stage of the proceedings propose to the Parties that the dispute be settled amicably. Article 20.13 Implementation of The Final Report 1. Where the final report of a panel contains: (a) a determination that the measure at issue is inconsistent with the	of the date the tribunal is constituted, the tribunal shall decide on an expedited basis an objection under paragraph 6 and any objection that the dispute is not within the tribunal's competence. The tribunal shall suspend any proceedings on the merits and issue a decision or award on the objection(s), stating the grounds therefor, no later than 150 days after the date of the request. However, if a disputing party requests a hearing, the tribunal may take an additional 30 days to issue the decision or award. Regardless of whether a hearing is requested, a tribunal may, on a showing of extraordinary cause, delay issuing its decision or award by an additional brief period, which may not exceed 30 days. 8. When it decides a respondent's objection under paragraph 6 or 7, the tribunal may, if warranted, award to the prevailing disputing party reasonable costs and attorney's fees incurred in submitting or opposing the objection. In determining whether such an award is warranted, the tribunal shall consider whether either the claimant's claim or the respondent's objection was frivolous, and shall provide the disputing parties a reasonable opportunity to comment. 9. A respondent may not assert as a defence, counterclaim, or right of set-off, or for any other reason, that the claimant has received or will receive indemnification or other compensation for all or part of the alleged damages pursuant to an insurance or guarantee contract, except with respect to any subrogation as provided for in Article 11.14. 10. A tribunal may order an interim measure of protection to preserve the rights of a disputing party, or to ensure that the tribunal's jurisdiction is made fully effective, including an order to preserve evidence in the possession or control of a disputing party or to protect the tribunal's jurisdiction. A tribunal may not order attachment or enjoin the application of a measure alleged to constitute a breach referred to in Article 11.16. For the purposes of this paragraph, an order includes a recommendation.

Bilateral Dispute Settlement Provisions	Investment Dispute Settlement (ISDS) Provisions / Non-Tariff Barrier (NTB) Mediation Mechanism
obligations of this Agreement, or that the Party complained against has otherwise failed to carry out its obligations under this Agreement, the Party complained against has an obligation to bring the measure into conformity with this Agreement; or (b) a determination of non-violation nullification or impairment in the sense of Article 20.2(c), the Party complained against has an obligation to eliminate the nullification or impairment or reach a mutually satisfactory solution with the complaining Party. 2. Within 20 days of the issuance of the final report of the panel, the Party complained against shall notify the complaining Party: (a) of its intentions with respect to implementation, including an indication of possible actions it may take to comply with paragraph 1; (b) whether such implementation can take place immediately; and (c) if such implementation cannot take place immediately, the reasonable period of time the Party complained against would need to implement. 3. If a reasonable period of time is required, it shall, whenever possible, be mutually determined by the Parties. Where the Parties are unable to agree on the reasonable period of time within 30 days of the issuance of the final report, either Party may request the panel to determine the reasonable period of time. Unless the Parties otherwise agree, such requests shall be made within 120 days of the issuance of the final report. 4. Where a request is made in accordance with paragraph 3, the panel shall present to the Parties a report containing a determination of the reasonable period of time and the reasons for such determination within 45 days of the date of the request. Prior to	11. In any arbitration conducted under this Section, on request of a disputing party, a tribunal shall, before issuing a decision or award on liability, transmit its proposed decision or award to the disputing parties and to the non-disputing Party. Within 60 days after the date the tribunal transmits its proposed decision or award, the disputing parties may submit written comments to the tribunal concerning any aspect of its proposed decision or award. The tribunal shall consider any such comments and issue its decision or award not later than 45 days after the date the 60day comment period expires. 12. Paragraph 11 shall not apply in any arbitration conducted pursuant to this Section for which an appeal has been made available pursuant to paragraph 13 or Annex 11-E. 13. If a separate, multilateral agreement enters into force between the Parties that establishes an appellate body for the purposes of reviewing awards rendered by tribunals constituted pursuant to international trade or investment arrangements to hear investment disputes, the Parties shall strive to reach an agreement that would have such appellate body review awards rendered under Article 11.26 in arbitrations commenced after the multilateral agreement enters into force between the Parties. Article 11.21 Transparency of Arbitral Proceedings 1. Subject to paragraphs 2, 3 and 4, the respondent shall, after receiving the following documents, promptly transmit them to the non-disputing Party and make them available to the public: (a) the notice of intent; (b) the notice of arbitration;

Bilateral Dispute Settlement Provisions	Investment Dispute Settlement (ISDS) Provisions / Non-Tariff Barrier (NTB) Mediation Mechanism
making this determination, the panel shall seek written submissions from the Parties, and if requested by either Party, hold a meeting with the Parties where each Party will be given an opportunity to present its submission. As a guideline, the reasonable period of time determined by the panel should not exceed 15 months from the date of the issuance of the panel's final report. However, such reasonable period of time may be shorter or longer, depending upon the particular circumstances. Unless the Parties otherwise agree, the principles applied in arbitrations under Article 21.3(c) of the DSU shall apply mutatis mutandis. Article 20.14 Non-Implementation 1. The Party complained against shall enter into negotiations with the complaining Party with a view to developing mutually acceptable compensation where: (a) the reasonable period of time referred to in Article 20.13 has elapsed; or (b) the Party complained against has notified the complaining Party that it does not intend to comply with the obligation in Article 20.13.1. 2. If the Parties: (a) are unable to agree on compensation within 30 days of the date the period for developing such compensation has begun; or (b) have agreed on compensation and the complaining Party considers that the Party complained against has failed to observe the terms of the agreement, the complaining Party may at any time thereafter provide written notification to the Party complained against that it intends to suspend the application to the Party complained against of benefits of equivalent effect to the level of non-conformity, or nullification or impairment that the panel has found.	(c) pleadings, memorials and briefs submitted to the tribunal by a disputing party and any written submissions submitted pursuant to Article 11.20.4 and 11.20.5 and Article 11.25; (d) minutes or transcripts of hearings of the tribunal, where available; and (e) orders, awards, and decisions of the tribunal. 2. The tribunal shall conduct hearings open to the public and shall determine, in consultation with the disputing parties, the appropriate logistical arrangements. However, any disputing party that intends to use information designated as protected information in a hearing shall so advise the tribunal. The tribunal shall make appropriate arrangements to protect the information from disclosure. 3. Without prejudice to Article 22.2 (Essential Security) and Article 22.4 (Disclosure of Information), nothing in this Section requires a Party to furnish or allow access to information, the disclosure of which: (a) would impede law enforcement; (b) would be contrary to its law regarding treatment of official information or matters relating to personal privacy; or (c) it considers to be contrary to its essential security interests. 4. Any protected information that is submitted to the tribunal shall be protected from disclosure in accordance with the following procedures: (a) subject to subparagraph (d), neither the disputing parties nor the tribunal shall disclose to the non-disputing Party or to the public any protected information where the disputing party that provided the information clearly

Bilateral Dispute Settlement Provisions	Investment Dispute Settlement (ISDS) Provisions / Non-Tariff Barrier (NTB) Mediation Mechanism
The notification shall specify the level of benefits that the complaining Party proposes to suspend. The complaining Party may begin suspending benefits 30 days after the later of the date it provides notification to the other Party under this paragraph or the panel issues its determination under paragraph 5, as the case may be. 3. A right to suspend benefits which arises under paragraph 2 shall not be exercised while a compliance review proceeding is being undertaken under Article 20.15. 4. In considering what benefits to suspend in accordance with paragraph 2: (a) a complaining Party should first seek to suspend benefits in the same sector or sectors as that affected by the measure that the panel has found to be inconsistent with the obligations of this Agreement or in the same sector or sectors where nullification or impairment in the sense of Article 20.2(c) has been found to exist; and (b) a complaining Party that considers it is not practicable or effective to suspend benefits in the same sector or sectors may suspend benefits in other sectors. 5. If the Party complained against considers that: (a) the level of benefits that the complaining Party has proposed to be suspended is not equivalent to the level of non-conformity, or nullification or impairment that the panel has found; or (b) it has eliminated the non-conformity, or the nullification or impairment that the panel has found, it may, within 30 days of the date the complaining Party provides notification under paragraph 2, request that the panel be reconvened to consider the matter. The Party complained against shall deliver its request in writing to the complaining Party. The panel shall reconvene as soon as	designates it in accordance with subparagraph (b); (b) any disputing party claiming that certain information constitutes protected information shall clearly designate the information at the time it is submitted to the tribunal; (c) a disputing party shall, at the time it submits a document containing information claimed to be protected information, submit a redacted version of the document that does not contain the information. Only the redacted version shall be provided to the non-disputing Party and made public in accordance with paragraph 1; (d) the tribunal shall decide any objection by a disputing party regarding the designation of information claimed to be protected information. If the tribunal determines that such information was not properly designated, the disputing party that submitted the information may: (i) withdraw all or part of its submission containing such information; or (ii) agree to resubmit complete and redacted documents with corrected designations in accordance with the tribunal's determination and subparagraph (c), in either case, the other disputing party shall, whenever necessary, resubmit complete and redacted documents which either remove the information withdrawn under subparagraph(d)(i) by the disputing party that first submitted the information or redesignate the information consistent with the designation under subparagraph(d)(ii) of the disputing party that first submitted the information; and (e) on request of a disputing Party, the Joint Committee shall consider issuing a decision in writing regarding a determination by the tribunal that information claimed to be protected was not properly designated. If the Joint Committee issues a decision within 60 days of such a request, it shall be binding on the tribunal, and any decision or award issued by the tribunal must be consistent with that decision. If the Joint Committee does not issue a decision within 60

Bilateral Dispute Settlement Provisions	Investment Dispute Settlement (ISDS) Provisions / Non-Tariff Barrier (NTB) Mediation Mechanism
possible after delivery of the request and shall present its determination to the Parties within 90 days of the date it reconvenes to review a request under either subparagraph (a) or (b), or within 120 days of a request under both subparagraphs (a) and (b). If the panel determines that the level of benefits proposed to be suspended is not equivalent to the level of non-conformity, or nullification or impairment that the panel has found, it shall determine the level of benefits it considers to be equivalent to the level of nonconformity, or nullification or impairment. 6. Where the right to suspend benefits has been exercised under this Article, if the Party complained against considers that the level of benefits suspended by the complaining Party is not equivalent to the level of non-conformity, or the nullification or impairment that the panel has found, it may request that the panel be reconvened to consider the matter. Where the panel reconvenes in accordance with this paragraph, the timeframes in paragraph 5 shall apply. If the panel determines that the level of benefits suspended by the complaining Party is not equivalent to the level of non-conformity, or nullification or impairment that the panel has found, it shall determine the level of benefits it considers to be equivalent to the level of non-conformity, or nullification or impairment. 7. The complaining Party may suspend benefits up to the level the panel has determined under paragraph 5 or 6 or, if the panel has not determined the level, the level the Party has proposed to suspend under paragraph 2, unless the panel has determined that the Party complained against has eliminated the non-conformity, or the nullification or impairment. Article 20.15 Compliance Review 1. Without prejudice to the procedures set out in Article 20.14.5, if the Party complained against considers that it has eliminated the non-conformity, or the	days, the tribunal's determination shall remain in effect only if the nondisputing Party submits a written statement to the Joint Committee within that period that it agrees with the tribunal's determination. 5. Nothing in this Section requires a respondent to withhold from the public information required to be disclosed by its laws. Article 11.22 Governing Law 1. Subject to paragraph 3, when a claim is submitted under Article 11.16.1(a)(i)(A) or Article 11.16.1(b)(i)(A), the tribunal shall decide the issues in dispute in accordance with this Agreement and applicable rules of international law. 2. Subject to paragraph 3 and the other terms of this Section, when a claim is submitted under Article 11.16.1(a)(i)(B) or 11.16.1(a)(i)(C), or Article 11.16.1(b)(i)(B) or 11.16.1(a)(i)(C), the tribunal shall apply: (a) the rules of law specified in the pertinent investment authorisation or investment agreement, or as the disputing parties may otherwise agree; or (b) if the rules of law have not been specified or otherwise agreed: (i) the law of the respondent, including its rules on the conflict of laws43; and (ii) such rules of international law as may be applicable. 43 For the purposes of this subparagraph, the "law of the respondent" means the law that a domestic court or tribunal of proper jurisdiction would apply in the same case. 3. A decision of the Joint Committee declaring its interpretation of a provision of this Agreement under Article 21.3.3(c) shall be binding on a tribunal, and any decision or award issued by a tribunal must be consistent with that decision.

Bilateral Dispute Settlement Provisions	Investment Dispute Settlement (ISDS) Provisions / Non-Tariff Barrier (NTB) Mediation Mechanism
nullification or impairment that the panel has found, it may refer the matter to the panel by providing written notification to the complaining Party. The panel shall reconvene as soon as possible after delivery of the request and shall issue its report on the matter within 90 days of the date of delivery of the written notification. 2. If the panel decides that the Party complained against has eliminated the non-conformity, or the nullification or impairment, the complaining Party shall promptly reinstate any benefits it has suspended under Article 20.14. 3. A panel reconvened in accordance with this Article or in relation to Article 20.14.5(b) shall make an objective assessment of the matter before it, including an objective assessment of: (a) the facts of any measure taken by the Party complained against to comply with the obligation in Article 20.13.1; and (b) whether the Party complained against has complied with the obligation in Article 20.13.1. 4. A panel reconvened in accordance with this Article or in relation to Article 20.14.5(b) shall set out in its report its findings on: (a) the facts of the case; and (b) whether the Party complained against has complied with the obligation in Article 20.13.1. Article 20.16 Private Rights Neither Party shall provide for a right of action under its law against the other Party	Article 11.23 Interpretation of Annexes 1. Where a respondent asserts as a defence that the measure alleged to be a breach is within the scope of an entry set out in Annex I or Annex II, the tribunal shall, on request of the respondent, request the interpretation of the Joint Committee on the issue. The Joint Committee shall submit in writing any decision declaring its interpretation under Article 21.3.3(c) to the tribunal within 60 days of delivery of the request. 2. A decision issued by the Joint Committee under paragraph 1 shall be binding on the tribunal, and any decision or award issued by the tribunal must be consistent with that decision. If the Joint Committee fails to issue such a decision within 60 days, the tribunal shall decide the issue. Article11.24 Expert Reports Without prejudice to the appointment of other kinds of experts where authorized by the applicable arbitration rules, a tribunal, on request of a disputing party or, unless the disputing parties disapprove, on its own initiative, may appoint one or more experts to report to it in writing on any factual issue concerning environmental, health, safety or other scientific matters raised by a disputing party in a proceeding, subject to such terms and conditions as the disputing parties may agree. Article 11.25 Consolidation 1. Where two or more claims have been submitted separately to arbitration under Article 11.16.1 and the claims have a question of law or fact in common and arise out of the same events or circumstances, any disputing party may seek a consolidation

Bilateral Dispute Settlement Provisions	Investment Dispute Settlement (ISDS) Provisions / Non-Tariff Barrier (NTB) Mediation Mechanism
on the ground that a measure of the other Party is inconsistent with this Agreement. Article 20.17 Expenses Unless the Parties otherwise agree, the expenses of a panel, including the remuneration of the panellists, shall be borne by the Parties in equal share. Article 20.18 Time Periods Unless otherwise specified, any time periods provided for in this Chapter may be modified by mutual agreement of the Parties.	order in accordance with the agreement of all the disputing parties sought to be covered by the order or the terms of paragraphs 2 through 10. 2. A disputing party that seeks a consolidation order under this Article shall deliver, in writing, a request to the Secretary-General and to all the disputing parties sought to be covered by the order and shall specify in the request: (a) the names and addresses of all the disputing parties sought to be covered by the order; (b) the nature of the order sought; and (c) the grounds on which the order is sought. 3. Unless the Secretary-General finds within 30 days after receiving a request under paragraph 2 that the request is manifestly unfounded, a tribunal shall be established under this Article. 4. Unless all the disputing parties sought to be covered by the order otherwise agree, a tribunal established under this Article shall comprise three arbitrators: (a) one arbitrator appointed by agreement of the claimants; (b) one arbitrator appointed by the respondent; and (c) the presiding arbitrator appointed by the Secretary-General, provided, however, that the presiding arbitrator shall not be a national of either Party. 5. If, within 60 days after the Secretary-General receives a request made under paragraph 2, the respondent fails or the claimants fail to appoint an arbitrator in accordance with paragraph 4, the Secretary-General, on request of any disputing party sought to be covered by the order, shall appoint the arbitrator or arbitrators not

Bilateral Dispute Settlement Provisions	Investment Dispute Settlement (ISDS) Provisions / Non-Tariff Barrier (NTB) Mediation Mechanism
	yet appointed. If the respondent fails to appoint an arbitrator, the Secretary-General shall appoint a national of the disputing Party, and if the claimants fail to appoint an arbitrator, the Secretary-General shall appoint a national of the non-disputing Party. 6. Where a tribunal established under this Article is satisfied that two or more claims that have been submitted to arbitration under Article 11.16.1 have a question of law or fact in common, and arise out of the same events or circumstances, the tribunal may, in the interest of fair and efficient resolution of the claims, and after hearing the disputing parties, by order: (a) assume jurisdiction over, and hear and determine together, all or part of the claims; (b) assume jurisdiction over, and hear and determine one or more of the claims, the determination of which it believes would assist in the resolution of the others; or (c) instruct a tribunal previously established under Article 11.19 to assume jurisdiction over, and hear and determine together, all or part of the claims, provided that: (i) that tribunal, on request of any claimant not previously a disputing party before that tribunal, shall be reconstituted with its original members, except that the arbitrator for the claimants shall be appointed pursuant to paragraphs 4(a) and 5; and (ii) that tribunal shall decide whether any prior hearing shall be repeated. 7. Where a tribunal has been established under this Article, a claimant that has submitted a claim to arbitration under Article 11.16.1 and that has not been named in a request made under paragraph 2 may make a written request to the tribunal that it be included in any order made under paragraph 6, and shall specify in the request: (a) the name and address of the claimant;

Bilateral Dispute Settlement Provisions	Investment Dispute Settlement (ISDS) Provisions / Non-Tariff Barrier (NTB) Mediation Mechanism
	(b) the nature of the order sought; and (c) the grounds on which the order is sought. The claimant shall deliver a copy of its request to the Secretary-General. 8. A tribunal established under this Article shall conduct its proceedings in accordance with the UNCITRAL Arbitration Rules, except as modified by this Section. 9. A tribunal established under Article 11.19 shall not have jurisdiction to decide a claim, or a part of a claim, over which a tribunal established or instructed under this Article has assumed jurisdiction. 10. On application of a disputing party, a tribunal established under this Article, pending its decision under paragraph 6, may order that the proceedings of a tribunal established under Article 11.19 be stayed, unless the latter tribunal has already adjourned its proceedings. Article 11.26 Awards 1. Where a tribunal makes a final award against a respondent, the tribunal may award, separately or in combination, only: (a) monetary damages and any applicable interest; and (b) restitution of property, in which case the award shall provide that the respondent may pay monetary damages and any applicable interest in lieu of restitution. 2. A tribunal may also award costs and attorney's fees in accordance with this Section and the applicable arbitration rules. 3. Subject to paragraph 1, where a claim is

Bilateral Dispute Settlement Provisions	Investment Dispute Settlement (ISDS) Provisions / Non-Tariff Barrier (NTB) Mediation Mechanism
	submitted to arbitration under Article 11.16.1(b): (a) an award of restitution of property shall provide that restitution be made to the enterprise; (b) an award of monetary damages and any applicable interest shall provide that the sum be paid to the enterprise; and (c) the award shall provide that it is made without prejudice to any right that any person may have in the relief under applicable domestic law. 4. A tribunal may not award punitive damages. 5. An award made by a tribunal shall have no binding force except between the disputing parties and in respect of the particular case. 6. Subject to paragraph 7 and the applicable review procedure for an interim award, a disputing party shall abide by and comply with an award without delay. 7. A disputing party may not seek enforcement of a final award until: (a) in the case of a final award made under the ICSID Convention: (i) 120 days have elapsed from the date the award was rendered and no disputing party has requested revision or annulment of the award; or (ii) revision or annulment proceedings have been completed; and (b) in the case of a final award under the ICSID Additional Facility Rules, the UNCITRAL Arbitration Rules, or the rules selected pursuant to Article 11.16.3(d): (i) 90 days have elapsed from the date the award was rendered and no disputing party has commenced a proceeding to revise, set aside, or annul the award; or (ii) a court has dismissed or allowed an application to revise, set aside, or annul the

Bilateral Dispute Settlement Provisions	Investment Dispute Settlement (ISDS) Provisions / Non-Tariff Barrier (NTB) Mediation Mechanism
	award and there is no further appeal. 8. Each Party shall provide for the enforcement of an award in its territory. 9. If the respondent fails to abide by or comply with a final award, on delivery of a request by the non-disputing Party, a panel shall be established under Article 20.8 (Establishment of Panel). The requesting Party may seek in such proceedings: (a) a determination that the failure to abide by or comply with the final award is inconsistent with the obligations of this Agreement; and (b) in accordance with Article 20.11 (Panel Report), a recommendation that the respondent abide by or comply with the final award. 10. A disputing party may seek enforcement of an arbitration award under the ICSID Convention or the New York Convention regardless of whether proceedings have been taken under paragraph 9. 11. A claim that is submitted to arbitration under this Section shall be considered to arise out of a commercial relationship or transaction for the purposes of Article I of the New York Convention. Article 11.27 Service Of Documents Delivery of notice and other documents on a Party shall be made to the place named for that Party in Annex 11-H.

* Entered into force December12, 2014.

1) *The provisions on joint committee were uniquely observant in KORUS FTA and this agreement seems to duplicate such mechanism.*

3. China

3.1 Free Trade Agreement between the Government of the People's Republic of China and the Government of the Islamic Republic of Pakistan*

Bilateral Dispute Settlement Provisions	Investment Dispute Settlement Provisions (ISDS)
CHAPTER X DISPUTE SETTLEMENT Article 57 Cooperation The Parties shall at all times endeavor to agree on the interpretation and application of this Agreement, and shall make every attempt through cooperation and consultations to arrive at a mutually satisfactory resolution of any matter that might affect its operation. Article 58 Scope of Application Except as otherwise provided in this Agreement, the dispute settlement provisions of this Chapter shall apply: (a) with respect to the avoidance or settlement of all disputes between the Parties regarding the interpretation or application of this Agreement; and (b) wherever a Party considers that a measure of the other Party is inconsistent with the obligations of this Agreement or that the other Party has failed to carry out its obligations under this Agreement. Article 59 Consultations 1. Either Party may request in writing consultations with the other Party with respect	CHAPTER IX INVESTMENT Article 54 Settlement of Disputes between Investors and one Party 1. Any legal dispute between an investor of one Party and the other Party in connection with an investment in the territory of the other Party shall, as far as possible, be settled amicably through negotiations between the parties to the dispute. 2. If the dispute cannot be settled through negotiations within six months from the date, it has been raised by either party to the dispute, it shall be submitted by the choice of the investor: (a) to the competent court of the Party that is a party to the dispute; (b) to International Center for Settlement of Investment Disputes (ICSID) under the Convention on the Settlement of Disputes between States and Nationals of Other States, done at Washington on March 18,1965, provided that the Party involved in the dispute may require the investor concerned to go through the domestic administrative review procedures specified by the laws and regulations of that Party before the submission to the ICSID. Once the investor has submitted the dispute to the competent court of the Party concerned or to the ICSID, the choice of the forum shall be final. 3. The arbitration award shall be based on the law of the Party to the dispute including its rules on the conflict of laws, the provisions of this Agreement as well as

Bilateral Dispute Settlement Provisions	Investment Dispute Settlement Provisions (ISDS)
to any measure that it considers might affect the operation of this Agreement.	the universally accepted principles of international law.
2. The requesting Party shall deliver the request to the other Parties and to the Commission (Chapter XI).	4. The arbitration award shall be final and binding upon the parties to the dispute. Both Parties shall commit themselves to the enforcement of the award.
3. Each Party shall accord adequate opportunity for consultations with another Party with respect to any matter affecting the implementation, interpretation or application of this Agreement. Any differences shall as far as possible be settled through consultation between the Parties.	
4. The requesting Party shall set out the reasons for the request, including identification of the measure at issue and an indication of the legal basis for the complaint, and shall deliver the request to the other Party.	
5. If a request for consultations is made, the Party to which the request is made shall reply to the request in writing within 7 days after the date of its receipt and shall 35 enter into consultations within a period of not more than: (a) 15 days after the date of receipt of the request for matters concerning perishable goods; or (b) 30 days after the date of receipt of the request for all other matters.	
6. The Parties shall make every attempt to arrive at a mutually satisfactory resolution of any matter through consultations under this Article or other consultative provisions of this Agreement. To this end, the Parties shall: (a) provide sufficient information to enable a full examination of how the measure might affect the operation and application of this Agreement; and (b) treat any confidential information exchanged in the course of consultations on the same basis as the Party providing the information.	

Bilateral Dispute Settlement Provisions	Investment Dispute Settlement Provisions (ISDS)
7. In consultations under this Article, a Party may request the other Party to make available personnel of its government agencies or other regulatory bodies who have expertise in the subject matter of consultations. 8. The consultations shall be confidential and without prejudice to the rights of any Party in any further proceedings. Article 60 Choice of Forum 1. This section is without prejudice to the rights of the Parties to have recourse to dispute settlement procedures available under other agreements to which they are parties. 2. Where a dispute regarding any matter arises under this Agreement and under another agreement to which the disputing Parties are party, the complaining Party may select the forum in which to settle the dispute. 3. Once the complaining Party has requested a particular forum, the forum selected shall be used to the exclusion of other possible fora. Article 61 Good Offices, Conciliation, and Mediation 1. The Parties to the dispute may at any time agree to good offices, conciliation or mediation by the Commission. They may begin at any time and be terminated at any time. 2. If the Parties agree, good offices, conciliation or mediation may continue while the dispute proceeds for resolution before an arbitral panel convened under Article 62.	

Bilateral Dispute Settlement Provisions	Investment Dispute Settlement Provisions (ISDS)
3. The proceedings under this Article and the positions taken by the Parties during these proceedings shall be confidential and are without prejudice to the rights of any Party in any further proceedings. Article 62 Request for an Arbitral Panel 1. If the Parties fail to resolve a matter within: (a) 60 days after receipt of the request for consultations under Article 59; (b) 30 days after receipt of the request for consultations under Article 59 in a matter regarding perishable goods; or (c) such other period as the Parties agree, either Party may request in writing the establishment of an arbitral panel to consider the matter. 2. The requesting Party shall state in the request the measure complained of and indicate the provisions of this Agreement that it considers relevant, and shall deliver the request to the other Party. An arbitral panel shall be established upon receipt of a request. Article 63 Composition of an Arbitral Panel 1. An arbitral panel shall comprise three members. 2. The complaining Party and the responding Party shall each appoint one panelist within 30 days from the deliverance of the request made under Article 62. 3. The Parties shall designate by common agreement the appointment of the third panelist within 30 days of the appointment of the second panelist. The panelist thus appointed shall chair the arbitral panel. 4. If one of the Parties does not appoint a panelist within 30 days from the date of deliverance of the request referred to in paragraph 2, at the request of the other	

Bilateral Dispute Settlement Provisions	Investment Dispute Settlement Provisions (ISDS)
Party to the dispute the designation shall be made by the Director-General of the WTO within a further 30 days. 5. If the chairperson of the arbitral panel has not been designated within the period according to paragraph 3, the Director General of the WTO shall at the request 37 of either Party appoint the chairperson of the arbitral panel within 30 days of the request. 6. All panelist shall: (a) have expertise or experience in law, international trade, other matters covered by this Agreement, or the resolution of disputes arising under international trade agreements; (b) be chosen strictly on the basis of objectivity, reliability, and sound judgment; (c) be independent of, and not be affiliated with or take instructions from, any Party; and (d) comply with the code of conduct in conformity with WTO Understanding on the Rules and Procedures Governing the Settlement of Disputes, and the rules established in the document WT/DSB/RC/1 of the WTO. 7. The chairperson of the arbitral tribunal shall: (a) not be a national of a Party (b) not have his or her usual place of residence in the territory of a Party (c) not have dealt with the matter in any capacity.	

Bilateral Dispute Settlement Provisions	Investment Dispute Settlement Provisions (ISDS)
8. If a panelist appointed under this Article resigns or becomes unable to act, a successor panelist shall be appointed in the same manner as prescribed for the appointment of the original panelist and the successor shall have all the powers and duties of the original panelist. Article 64 Functions of Arbitral Panel 1. The function of an arbitral panel is to make an objective assessment of the dispute before it, including an examination of the facts of the case and their applicability and conformity with this Agreement. 2. Unless the Parties otherwise agree within 20 days from the date of receipt of the request for the establishment of the arbitral panel, the terms of reference shall be: "To examine, in the light of the relevant provisions of this Agreement, the matter referred to in the request for the establishment of an arbitral panel pursuant to Article63 and to make findings of law and fact together with the reasons therefore for the resolution of the dispute." 3. Where an arbitral panel concludes that a measure is inconsistent with this Agreement, it may recommend that the responding Party bring the measure into conformity with this Agreement. In addition to its recommendations the arbitral panel may suggest ways in which the responding Party could implement the recommendations. 4. The arbitral panel, in their findings and recommendations, cannot add to subtract from or alter the rights and obligations provided in this Agreement. Article 65 Rules of Procedure of an Arbitral Panel 1. Unless the Parties agree otherwise, the arbitral panel proceedings shall be	

Bilateral Dispute Settlement Provisions	Investment Dispute Settlement Provisions (ISDS)
conducted in accordance with the rules or procedure set out in Annex III. 2. The arbitral panel shall, apart from the matters set out in this Article, regulate its own procedures in relation to the rights of the Parties to be heard and its deliberations in consultation with the Parties. 3. The arbitral panel shall endeavor to take its decisions by consensus; provided that where an arbitral panel is unable to reach consensus it may take its decisions by a majority vote. Article 66 Expenses 1. Unless the Parties otherwise agree, the costs of the arbitral panel and other expenses associated with the conduct of its proceedings shall be borne equally by the Parties. 2. Each Party shall bear its own expenses and legal costs of the arbitral proceedings. Article 67 Suspension or Termination of Proceedings 1. The Parties may agree that the arbitral panel suspends its work at any time for a period not exceeding 12 months from the date of such agreement. If the work of the arbitral panel has been suspended for more than 12 months, the authority for establishment of the arbitral panel shall lapse unless the Parties agree otherwise. 2. The Parties may agree to terminate the proceedings of an arbitral panel in the event that a mutually satisfactory solution to the dispute has been found. Article 68 Experts and Technical Advice	

Bilateral Dispute Settlement Provisions	Investment Dispute Settlement Provisions (ISDS)
1. On request of a disputing Party, or on its own initiative, the panel may seek information and technical advice from any person or body that it deems appropriate, provided that the disputing parties so agree and subject to such terms and conditions as such Parties may agree. 2. Before an arbitral panel seeks information or technical advice, it shall establish appropriate procedures in consultation with the Parties. The arbitral panel shall provide the Parties: (a) advance notice of, and an opportunity to provide comments to the arbitral panel on, proposed requests for information and technical advice pursuant to paragraph 1; and (b) a copy of any information or technical advice submitted in response to a request pursuant to paragraph 1 and an opportunity to provide comments. 3. Where the arbitral panel takes the information or technical advice into account in the preparation of its report, it shall also take into account any comments by the Parties on the information or technical advice. Article 69 Initial Report 1. The arbitral panel shall base its report on the relevant provisions of this Agreement and the submissions and arguments of the Parties and on any information before it pursuant to Article 68. 2. Unless the Parties otherwise agree, the arbitral panel shall: (a) within 90 days after the last panelist is selected; or (b) in case of urgency including those relating to perishable goods within 60	

Bilateral Dispute Settlement Provisions	Investment Dispute Settlement Provisions (ISDS)
days after the last panelist is selected, present to the Parties an initial report. 3. The initial report is to contain: (a) findings of fact; (b) its conclusions as to whether the measure at issue has not conformed with the obligations under this Agreement or any other determination if requested in the terms of reference; and (c) the recommendation, if any, for the resolution of the dispute. 4. In exceptional cases, if the arbitral panel considers it cannot release its initial report within 90 days or within 60 days in cases of urgency, it shall inform the Parties in writing of the reasons for the delay together with an estimate of the period within which it will release its report. Any delay shall not exceed a further period of 30 days unless the Parties otherwise agree. 5. Panelists may furnish separate opinions on matters not unanimously agreed upon. 6. A Party may submit written comments to the arbitral panel on its initial report within 14 days of presentation of the report or within such other period as the Parties may agree. 7. After considering any written comments on the initial report, the arbitral panel may reconsider its report and make any further examination it considers appropriate. Article 70 Final Report 1. The arbitral panel shall present a final report to the Parties, including any separate opinions on matters not agreed to by consensus, within 30 days of presentation of	

Bilateral Dispute Settlement Provisions	Investment Dispute Settlement Provisions (ISDS)
the initial report, unless the Parties otherwise agree. 2. No arbitral panel may, either in its initial report or its final report, disclose which panelists are associated with majority or minority opinions. 3. The disputing Parties shall transmit to the Commission on the final report of the panel, as well as any written views that a disputing Party desires to be appended, on a confidential basis within a reasonable period of time after it is presented to them. 4. Unless the Commission decides otherwise, the final report of the panel shall be published 15 days after it is transmitted to the Commission. Article 71 Implementation of Final Report 1. On receipt of the final report of an arbitral panel, the Parties shall agree on the resolution of the dispute, which normally shall conform with the findings and recommendation of the Panel. 2. Wherever possible, the resolution shall be removal of a major not conforming with this Agreement or a non-implementation of such a measure or, failing such a resolution, compensation. Article 72 Non implementation – Suspension of Benefits 1. If in its final report a panel has determined that a measure is inconsistent with the obligations of this Agreement and the Party complained against has not reached agreement with the complaining Party on a mutually satisfactory resolution pursuant to Article 71 (implementation of final report) within 30 days of receiving the final report, such complaining Party may suspend the application to the responding Party of benefits of equivalent effect until such time as they have reached agreement on a	

Bilateral Dispute Settlement Provisions	Investment Dispute Settlement Provisions (ISDS)
resolution of the dispute or the responding Party has brought its measures at issue into conformity with its obligations under this Agreement. 2. In considering what benefits to suspend pursuant to paragraph1: (a) a complaining Party should first seek to suspend benefits in the same sector or sectors as that affected by the measure or other matter that the Panel has found to be inconsistent with the obligations of this Agreement; and (b) a complaining Party that considers it is not practicable or effective to suspend benefits in the same sector or sectors may suspend benefits in other sectors. 3. On the written request of any disputing Party delivered to the other Party, a panel shall be established, which should be the original panel when possible, to determine whether the level of benefits suspended by a Party pursuant to paragraph 1 is manifestly excessive. 4. The panel shall present its determination within 60 days after the panel is established or such other period as the disputing Parties may agree. Article 73 Compliance Review 1. If the responding Party considers that it has eliminated the non-conformity that the arbitral panel has found, it may provide written notice to the complaining Party with a description of how non-conformity has been removed. If the complaining Party has disagreement, it may refer the matter to the original arbitral panel within 60 days after receipt of such written notice. 2. The arbitral panel shall release its report within 90 days after the referral of the matter.	

Bilateral Dispute Settlement Provisions	Investment Dispute Settlement Provisions (ISDS)
Article 74 Private Rights Any question regarding conformity of a measure taken by either Party under this Agreement shall be submitted and proceeded with as provided under Chapter X of this Agreement.	

* Entered into force on July1, 2007.

3.2 Free Trade Agreement between the Government of the People's Republic of China and the Government of New Zealand*

Bilateral Dispute Settlement Provisions	Investment Dispute Settlement (ISDS) Provisions / Non-Tariff Barrier (NTB) Mediation Mechanism
CHAPTER 16 DISPUTE SETTLEMENT Article 183 Objectives 1. The objectives of this Chapter are: (a) to encourage the Parties at all times to endeavour to reach a mutually satisfactory resolution of disputes arising under this Agreement through cooperation and consultations; and (b) to provide an effective, efficient and transparent process for consultations and settlement of disputes between the Parties concerning their rights and obligations under this Agreement. 2. Notwithstanding anything else in this Chapter, the Parties may, at any time, reach a mutually satisfactory resolution of the dispute. Article 184 Scope of Application 1. Except as otherwise provided in this Agreement, this Chapter shall apply to the avoidance or settlement of disputes between the Parties concerning their rights and obligations under this Agreement, except for Chapter 14 (Cooperation). 2. Any action taken pursuant to Articles 59 or 65.3 shall be without prejudice to the rights and obligations of the Parties under this Chapter.	CHAPTER 11 INVESTMENT SECTION 2 INVESTOR – STATE DISPUTE SETTLEMENT Article 152 Consultation and Negotiation Any legal dispute arising under this Chapter between an investor of one Party and the other Party, directly concerning an investment by that investor in the territory of that other Party, shall, as far as possible, be settled amicably through consultations and negotiations between the investor and that other Party, which may include the use of non-binding third-party procedures, where this is acceptable to both parties to the dispute. A request for consultations and negotiations shall be made in writing and shall state the nature of the dispute. Article 153 Consent to Submission of a Claim 1. If the dispute cannot be settled as provided for in Article 152 within 6 months from the date of request for consultations and negotiations then, unless the parties to the dispute agree otherwise, it shall, by the choice of the investor, be submitted to: (a) conciliation or arbitration by the International Centre for the Settlement of Investment Disputes (ICSID) under the Convention on the Settlement of Disputes between States and Nationals of Other States, done at Washington on March 18, 1965; or

Bilateral Dispute Settlement Provisions	Investment Dispute Settlement (ISDS) Provisions / Non-Tariff Barrier (NTB) Mediation Mechanism
Article 185 Choice of Forum 1. Except as provided in this Article, this Chapter is without prejudice to the rights of the Parties to have recourse to dispute settlement procedures available under other agreements to which they are party. 2. Where a dispute regarding any matter arises under this Agreement and under another agreement to which both Parties are party, the complaining Party may select the forum in which to settle the dispute. 3. Once the complaining Party has requested a particular forum, the forum selected shall be used to the exclusion of other possible fora. 4. For the purposes of this Article, a Party shall be deemed to have selected a forum when it has requested the establishment of, or referred a matter to, a dispute settlement panel or arbitral tribunal. Article 186 Consultations 1. The Parties shall make every effort to reach a mutually satisfactory resolution of any matter through consultations. Each Party shall accord adequate opportunity for consultations with the other Party with respect to any matter affecting the implementation, interpretation or application of this Agreement. Any differences shall as far as possible be settled through consultation between the Parties. 2. A request for consultations shall be submitted in writing and shall set out the reasons for the request, including identification of the measure at issue and an indication of the legal basis for the complaint. The complaining Party shall deliver the request to the other Party.	(b) arbitration under the rules of the United Nations Commission on International Trade Law (UNCITRAL); provided that the investor shall give the state party 3 months' notice prior to submitting the claim to arbitration under paragraph 1(a) or 1(b). 2. Upon the receipt of a notice referred to in paragraph 1, the state party may require the investor concerned to go through any applicable domestic administrative review procedures specified by the laws and regulations of the state party, which may not exceed 3 months, before the submission of the claim to arbitration under paragraph 1(a) or 1(b). 3. In case a dispute has been submitted to a competent domestic court, it may be submitted to international dispute settlement, on the condition that the investor concerned has withdrawn its case from the domestic courts before a final judgment has been reached in the case. 4. The arbitration rules applicable under paragraph 1, and in effect on the date the claim or claims were submitted to arbitration under this Section, shall govern the arbitration except to the extent modified by this Section. 5. The arbitration award shall be final and binding upon both parties to the dispute. Each party shall commit itself to the enforcement of the award. Article 154 Admissibility of Claims and Preliminary Objections 1. No claim may be submitted to arbitration under this Chapter if more than 3 years have elapsed between the time at which the disputing investor became aware, or should reasonably have become aware, of a breach of obligation under this Chapter causing loss or damage to the investor or its investments and the date of submission of the request for consultations and negotiations referred to in Article 152.

Bilateral Dispute Settlement Provisions	Investment Dispute Settlement (ISDS) Provisions / Non-Tariff Barrier (NTB) Mediation Mechanism
3. If a request for consultations is made, the Party to which the request is made shall reply to the request in writing within 10 days after the date of its receipt and shall enter into consultations in good faith, with a view to reaching a mutually satisfactory solution, within a period of no more than: (a) 15 days after the date of receipt of the request for matters concerning perishable goods; or (b) 30 days after the date of receipt of the request for all other matters. 4. If the Party complained against does not respond within the aforesaid 10 days, or does not enter into consultations within the timeframe specified in paragraph 3(a) or 3(b), then the complaining Party may proceed directly to request the establishment of an arbitral tribunal. 5. The consultations shall be confidential and are without prejudice to the rights of either Party in any further proceedings. 6. In conducting the consultations, the Parties shall: (a) provide sufficient information to enable a full examination of how the matter might affect the operation and application of this Agreement; and (b) treat any confidential or proprietary information exchanged in the course of consultations on the same basis as the Party providing the information. 7. The complaining Party may request the responding Party to make available for the consultations personnel of its government agencies or other regulatory bodies who have expertise in the matter under consultation.	2. A state party may, no later than 30 days after the constitution of the tribunal, file an objection that a claim is manifestly without merit or is otherwise outside the jurisdiction or competence of the tribunal. The state party shall specify as precisely as possible the basis for the objection. 3. The tribunal shall address any such objection as a preliminary question apart from the merits of the claim. The parties shall be given a reasonable opportunity to present their views and observations to the tribunal. If the tribunal decides that the claim is manifestly without merit, or is otherwise not within the jurisdiction or competence of the tribunal, it shall render a decision to that effect. 4. The tribunal may, if warranted, award the prevailing party reasonable costs and fees incurred in submitting or opposing the objection. In determining whether such an award is warranted, the tribunal shall consider whether either the claim or the objection was frivolous or manifestly without merit, and shall provide the parties a reasonable opportunity to comment. Article 155 Interpretation of Agreement 1. The tribunal shall, on request of the state party, request a joint interpretation of the Parties of any provision of this Agreement that is in issue in a dispute. The Parties shall submit in writing any joint decision declaring their interpretation to the tribunal within 60 days of delivery of the request. 2. A joint decision issued under paragraph 1 by the Parties shall be binding on the tribunal, and any award must be consistent with that joint decision. If the Parties fail to issue such a decision within 60 days, the tribunal shall decide the issue on its own account.

Bilateral Dispute Settlement Provisions	Investment Dispute Settlement (ISDS) Provisions / Non-Tariff Barrier (NTB) Mediation Mechanism
Article 187 Good Offices, Mediation and Conciliation 1. The Parties may at any time agree to good offices, conciliation or mediation. They may begin at any time and be terminated at any time. 2. If both Parties agree, good offices, conciliation or mediation may continue while the dispute proceeds for resolution before an arbitral tribunal convened under Article 188. 3. If both Parties agree, they may seek assistance of the FTA Joint Commission regarding good offices, mediation and conciliation. Article 188 Establishment of an Arbitral Tribunal 1. If the consultations fail to resolve a dispute within: (a) 30 days after the date of receipt of the request for consultations regarding a matter concerning perishable goods; or (b) 60 days after the date of receipt of the request for consultations regarding any other matter; the Party that made the request for consultations may request in writing the establishment of an arbitral tribunal to consider the matter. 2. The request to establish an arbitral tribunal shall identify: (a) the specific measures at issue; and (b) the legal basis of the complaint including the provisions of this Agreement alleged to have been breached and any other relevant provisions, sufficient to	Article 156 Consolidation of Claims Where two or more investors notify an intention to submit claims to arbitration which have a question of law or fact in common and arise out of the same events or circumstances, the disputing parties shall consult with a view to harmonising the procedures to apply, where all disputing parties agree to the consolidation of the claims, including with respect to the forum chosen to hear the dispute. Article 157 Publication of Information and Documents Relating to Arbitral Proceedings 1. Subject to paragraph 2, the state party may, as it considers appropriate, ensure public availability of all tribunal documents. 2. Any information that is submitted to the tribunal and that is specifically designated as confidential information shall be protected from disclosure. Article 158 Awards 1. Where a tribunal makes a final award against a state party, the tribunal may award, separately or in combination, only: (a) monetary damages and any applicable interest; (b) restitution of property, in which case the award shall provide that the state party may pay monetary damages and any applicable interest in lieu of restitution. 2. A tribunal may also award costs and fees in accordance with this Chapter and the

Bilateral Dispute Settlement Provisions	Investment Dispute Settlement (ISDS) Provisions / Non-Tariff Barrier (NTB) Mediation Mechanism
present the problem clearly. 3. An arbitral tribunal shall be established upon receipt of a request. Article 189 Composition of an Arbitral Tribunal 1. An arbitral tribunal shall comprise 3 members. 2. Within 15 days after the establishment of a tribunal, both Parties shall designate one member of that arbitral tribunal respectively. 3. The Parties shall designate by common agreement the appointment of the third arbitrator within 30 days after the establishment of a tribunal. The arbitrator thus appointed shall chair the arbitral tribunal. 4. If any member of the arbitral tribunal has not been designated or appointed within 30 days after the establishment of a tribunal, either Party may request that the Director-General of the WTO designate a member within 30 days of that request. 5. All arbitrators shall: (a) have expertise or experience in law, international trade, other matters covered by this Agreement, or the resolution of disputes arising under international trade agreements; (b) be chosen strictly on the basis of objectivity, reliability, and sound judgement; (c) be independent of, and not be affiliated with or take instructions from, either Party; and	applicable arbitration rules. 3. A tribunal may not award punitive damages. 4. An award made by a tribunal shall have no binding force except between the disputing parties and in respect of the particular case. 5. A disputing party may not seek enforcement of a final award until all applicable review procedures have been completed. 6. Subject to paragraph 5, a disputing party shall abide by and comply with an award without delay.

Bilateral Dispute Settlement Provisions	Investment Dispute Settlement (ISDS) Provisions / Non-Tariff Barrier (NTB) Mediation Mechanism
(d) comply with the WTO Rules of Conduct for the Understanding on Rules and Procedures Governing the Settlement of Disputes.	
6. The chair of the arbitral tribunal shall:	
(a) not be a national of either Party;	
(b) not have his or her usual place of residence in the territory of either Party; and	
(c) not have dealt with the matter in any capacity.	
7. If an arbitrator appointed under this Article resigns or becomes unable to act, a successor arbitrator shall be appointed in the same manner as prescribed for the appointment of the original arbitrator and the successor shall have all the powers and duties of the original arbitrator. The work of the arbitral tribunal shall be suspended during the appointment of the successor arbitrator.	
Article 190 Functions of Arbitral Tribunals	
1. The function of an arbitral tribunal is to make an objective assessment of the dispute before it, including an objective assessment of the facts of the case and the applicability of and conformity with this Agreement, and make such factual findings necessary for the resolution of the dispute.	
2. Where the tribunal makes a finding that a measure is inconsistent with this Agreement, that finding shall be binding on the Parties and the responding Party shall have the obligation to remove the non-conformity.	
3. For the avoidance of doubt, the Parties agree that the provisions of this Agreement	

Bilateral Dispute Settlement Provisions	Investment Dispute Settlement (ISDS) Provisions / Non-Tariff Barrier (NTB) Mediation Mechanism
shall be clarified in accordance with the customary rules of treaty interpretation of public international law. 4. The arbitral tribunal, in its findings, cannot add to or diminish the rights and obligations provided in this Agreement. Article 191 Rules of Procedure of an Arbitral Tribunal 1. Within 14 days of its composition, the arbitral tribunal shall establish rules of procedure, which shall, inter alia, ensure: (a) a right to at least 1, but no more than 2, hearings before the tribunal; (b) an opportunity for the complaining and responding Parties to provide initial and rebuttal submissions; (c) that any other procedural elements referred to in this Chapter or mutually agreed by the Parties to the dispute are provided for; (d) the protection of business confidential information, including in the final report. 2. Each Party has the right to make public its written submissions, written versions of its oral statements and written responses to a request or questions from the tribunal, subject to paragraph 3. 3. Each Party shall treat as confidential information submitted by the other Party to the arbitral tribunal which that Party has designated as confidential. 4. The arbitral tribunal may at any time put questions to the Parties and ask them for	

Bilateral Dispute Settlement Provisions	Investment Dispute Settlement (ISDS) Provisions / Non-Tariff Barrier (NTB) Mediation Mechanism
explanations or further information, either in the course of a meeting or in writing. A Party shall respond promptly and fully to any request by an arbitral tribunal for such information as the arbitral tribunal considers necessary and appropriate. There shall be no ex parte communications with the arbitral tribunal concerning matters under its consideration. 5. The arbitral tribunal shall have the right to seek information and technical advice from any individual or body which it deems appropriate. The arbitral tribunal shall provide the Parties with a copy of the information or technical advice received and an opportunity to provide comments. Where the arbitral tribunal takes the information or technical advice into account in the preparation of its report, it shall also take into account any comments by the Parties on the information or technical advice. 6. Unless the Parties otherwise agree within 20 days from the date of the establishment of the arbitral tribunal, the terms of reference shall be: "To examine, in the light of the relevant provisions of this Agreement, the matter referred to in the request for the establishment of an arbitral tribunal pursuant to Article 188 and to make findings of law and fact together with the reasons therefor for the resolution of the dispute." 7. The arbitral tribunal shall take its decisions by consensus; provided that where an arbitral tribunal is unable to reach consensus, it may take its decisions by majority vote. Any opinions expressed in the tribunal report by individual arbitrators shall be anonymous. 8. The arbitral tribunal shall, apart from the matters set out in this Article, regulate its own procedures in relation to the rights of the Parties to be heard and its deliberations, in consultation with the Parties. Article 192 Expenses	

Bilateral Dispute Settlement Provisions	Investment Dispute Settlement (ISDS) Provisions / Non-Tariff Barrier (NTB) Mediation Mechanism
Unless the Parties determine otherwise because of the particular circumstances of the case, the expenses of the tribunal, including the remuneration of its members, shall be borne by the Parties in equal shares. Article 193 Suspension or Termination of Proceedings 1. The Parties may agree that the arbitral tribunal suspend its work at any time for a period not exceeding 12 months from the date of such agreement. If the work of the arbitral tribunal has been suspended for more than 12 months, the authority for establishment of the tribunal shall lapse, unless the Parties agree otherwise. 2. The Parties may agree to terminate the proceedings of an arbitral tribunal in the event that a mutually satisfactory solution to the dispute has been found. In such event the Parties shall jointly notify the chair of the arbitral tribunal. Article 194 Report of Arbitral Tribunal 1. The report of the arbitral tribunal shall be drafted without the presence of the Parties in the light of the information provided and the statements made to the arbitral tribunal. 2. In order to enable the Parties to have an opportunity for review and comment, the arbitral tribunal shall present the Parties its initial report within 90 111 days of the tribunal's formation setting out its findings of facts and its determination as to whether a disputing Party has conformed with its obligations under this Agreement. In exceptional cases, if the arbitral tribunal considers it cannot release its initial report within 90 days, it shall inform the Parties in writing of the reasons for the delay together with an estimate of the period within which it will issue its report. Any delay shall not exceed a further period of 30 days, unless the Parties otherwise agree.	

Bilateral Dispute Settlement Provisions	Investment Dispute Settlement (ISDS) Provisions / Non-Tariff Barrier (NTB) Mediation Mechanism
3. A Party may submit written comments to the arbitral tribunal within 10 days of receiving the initial report. After considering these written comments by the Parties and making any further examination it considers appropriate, the arbitral tribunal shall present the Parties its final report within 30 days of presentation of the initial report, unless the Parties otherwise agree. The final report of the arbitral tribunal shall be made available as a public document after the lapse of 10 days from the date of its release. 4. The arbitral report is final. Article 195 Implementation of Arbitral Report 1. The Party concerned shall comply with the findings of the tribunal. If it is not practicable to comply immediately, the Party concerned shall implement the findings contained in the report of the arbitral tribunal within a reasonable period of time. 2. Where the tribunal makes a finding that a measure is inconsistent with this Agreement, the Party concerned shall have the obligation to eliminate the non-conformity. Article 196 Reasonable Period of Time 1. The reasonable period of time shall be mutually determined by the Parties, or where the Parties fail to agree on the reasonable period of time within 45 days of the release of the arbitral tribunal's report, either Party may refer the matter to the original arbitral tribunal (to the extent this is possible), which shall determine the reasonable period of time following consultation with the Parties. 2. The arbitral tribunal shall provide its report to the Parties within 60 days after the	

Bilateral Dispute Settlement Provisions	Investment Dispute Settlement (ISDS) Provisions / Non-Tariff Barrier (NTB) Mediation Mechanism
date of the referral of the matter to it. When the arbitral tribunal considers that it cannot provide its report within this timeframe, it shall inform the Parties in writing of the reasons for the delay together with an estimate of the period within which it will submit its report. Any delay shall not exceed a further period of 30 days, unless the Parties otherwise agree. Article 197 Compliance Review 1. Where there is disagreement as to the existence or consistency with this Agreement of measures taken within the reasonable period of time to comply with the findings of the arbitral tribunal, such dispute shall be referred to an arbitral tribunal proceeding under this Chapter, including wherever possible by resort to the original arbitral tribunal. 2. The arbitral tribunal shall provide its report to the Parties within 60 days after the date of the referral of the matter to it. When the arbitral tribunal considers that it cannot provide its report within this timeframe, it shall inform the Parties in writing of the reasons for the delay together with an estimate of the period within which it will submit its report. Any delay shall not exceed a further period of 30 days unless the Parties otherwise agree. Article 198 Compensation and Suspension of Concessions and Obligations 1. If the Party concerned fails to bring the measure found to be inconsistent with this Agreement into compliance with the findings of the arbitral tribunal within the reasonable period of time or if the Party complained against expresses in writing that it will not implement the findings, that Party shall, if so requested, enter into negotiations with the complaining Party with a view to reaching a mutually satisfactory agreement on any necessary compensation.	

Bilateral Dispute Settlement Provisions	Investment Dispute Settlement (ISDS) Provisions / Non-Tariff Barrier (NTB) Mediation Mechanism
2. If the Parties do not reach agreement on compensation as set forth by paragraph 1 within 30 days, the complaining Party may suspend the application of concessions and obligations of equivalent effect to the responding Party, with 30 days' notice in writing after the end of the reasonable period of time established in accordance with Article 196. Concessions and obligations may not be suspended while the complaining Party is pursuing negotiations under paragraph 1. 3. Any suspension of concessions and obligations shall be restricted to benefits accruing to the other Party under this Agreement. 4. In considering what concessions and obligations to suspend pursuant to paragraph 2: (a) the complaining Party should first seek to suspend concessions and obligations in the same sector(s) as that affected by the measure that the arbitral tribunal has found to be inconsistent with the obligations of this Agreement; and (b) if the complaining Party considers that it is not practicable or effective to suspend concessions and obligations in the same sector(s), it may suspend concessions and obligations in other sectors. The communication in which it announces such a decision shall indicate the reasons on which it is based. 5. The suspension of benefits shall be temporary and shall only be applied until such time as the measure found to be inconsistent with this Agreement has been removed, or the Party that must implement the arbitral tribunal's findings has done so, or a mutually satisfactory solution is reached. 6. Upon written request of the Party concerned, the original arbitral tribunal shall determine whether the level of concessions and obligations to be suspended by the complaining Party pursuant to paragraph 2 is excessive. If the arbitral tribunal cannot	

Bilateral Dispute Settlement Provisions	Investment Dispute Settlement (ISDS) Provisions / Non-Tariff Barrier (NTB) Mediation Mechanism
be established with its original members, the proceeding set out in Article 189 shall be applied. 7. The arbitral tribunal shall present its determination within 60 days from the request made pursuant to paragraph 6, or if an arbitral tribunal cannot be established with its original members, from the date on which the last arbitrator is selected. The decision of the arbitral tribunal shall be final and binding. It shall be delivered to the Parties and be made publicly available. Article 199 Post Suspension 1. Without prejudice to the procedures in Article 198, if the responding Party considers that it has eliminated the non-conformity that the arbitral tribunal has found, it may provide written notice to the complaining Party with a description of how non-conformity has been removed. If the complaining Party disagrees, it may refer the matter to the original arbitral tribunal within 60 days after receipt of such written notice. Otherwise, the complaining Party shall promptly stop the suspension of concessions and obligations. 2. The arbitral tribunal shall release its report within 60 days after the referral of the matter. If the arbitral tribunal concludes that the responding Party has eliminated the non-conformity, the complaining Party shall promptly stop the suspension of concessions and obligations.	

* Entered into force October 1, 2008.

3.3 Free Trade Agreement between the Government of the People's Republic of China and the Government of the Republic of Peru*

Bilateral Dispute Settlement Provisions	Investment Dispute Settlement (ISDS) Provisions / Non-Tariff Barrier (NTB) Mediation Mechanism
CHAPTER 15 DISPUTE SETTLEMENT Article 173 Cooperation The Parties shall at all times endeavor to agree on the interpretation and application of this Agreement, and shall make every attempt through cooperation or consultations to arrive at a mutually satisfactory resolution of any matter that might affect its operation when a dispute occurs. Article 174 Scope of Application Except as otherwise provided in this Agreement, the dispute settlement provisions of this Chapter shall apply with respect to the settlement of all disputes between the Parties regarding the interpretation or application of this Agreement, whenever a Party considers that the other Party has failed to carry out its obligations under this Agreement. Article 175 Choice of Forum 1. Where a dispute arises under this Agreement and under another free trade agreement to which both Parties are parties or the WTO Agreement, the complaining Party may select the forum to settle the dispute. 2. Once the complaining Party has requested a Panel under other agreements referred to in paragraph 1, the forum selected shall be used to the exclusion of the	CHAPTER 10 INVESTMENT Article 138 Settlement of Disputes between the Parties 1. Any dispute between the Parties concerning the interpretation or application of this Chapter shall, as far as possible, be settled with consultation through diplomatic channel. 2. If a dispute cannot thus be settled within 6 months, it shall, upon the request of either Party, be submitted to an ad hoc arbitral tribunal. 3. Such tribunal comprises of 3 arbitrators. Within 2 months of the receipt of the written notice requesting arbitration, each Party shall appoint one arbitrator. Those 2 arbitrators shall, within further 2 months, together select a national of a third State having diplomatic relations with both Parties who, upon approval by the Parties, shall be appointed as Chairman of the arbitral tribunal. 4. If the arbitral tribunal has not been constituted within 4 months from the receipt of the written notice requesting arbitration, either Party may, in the absence of any other agreement, invite the President of the International Court of Justice to make any necessary appointments. If the President is a national of either Party or is otherwise prevented from discharging the said functions, the Member of the International Court of Justice next in seniority who is not a national of either Party or is not otherwise prevented from discharging the said functions shall be invited to make such necessary appointments. 5. The arbitral tribunal shall determine its own procedure. The arbitral tribunal

Bilateral Dispute Settlement Provisions	Investment Dispute Settlement (ISDS) Provisions / Non-Tariff Barrier (NTB) Mediation Mechanism
others in respect of that matter. Article 176 Consultations 1. A Party may request in writing consultations with the other Party with respect to any matter referred to in Article 174 (Scope of Application). 2. The requesting Party shall deliver the request to the other Party, and shall set out the reasons for the request, including identification of the measure or other matter at issue and an indication of the legal basis for the complaint. 3. The requested Party shall reply to the request in writing within 25 days following the date of receipt of the request. 4. The Parties shall enter into consultations in good faith within: (a) 35 days following the date of receipt of the request for consultations regarding urgent matters; or (b) 40 days following the date of receipt of the request for consultations for all other matters. 5. The consulting Parties shall make every attempt to arrive at a mutually satisfactory resolution of any matter raised through consultations under this Article or other consultative provisions of this Agreement. 6. If the requested Party does not respond the consultation request within 25 days or does not enter into consultations within the timeframe set in paragraph 4 of this Article, the requesting Party may request directly the establishment of a Panel without waiting for the completion of the period established in paragraph 4 or it may act according to Article 177 (Request for a Panel).	shall reach its award in accordance with the provisions of this Agreement and the principles of international law recognized by both Parties. 6. The arbitral tribunal shall reach its award by a majority of votes. Such award shall be final and binding upon both Parties. The arbitral tribunal shall, upon the request of either Party, explain the reasons of its award. 7. Each Party shall bear the costs of its appointed arbitrator and of its representation in arbitral proceedings. The relevant costs of the Chairman and tribunal shall be borne in equal parts by the Parties. Article 139 Investor-State Dispute Settlement 1. Any dispute between an investor of one Party and the other Party in connection with an investment in the territory of the other Party shall, as far as possible, be settled amicably through negotiations between the parties to the dispute. 2. If the dispute cannot be settled through negotiations within 6 months from the date on which the disputing investor requested for the consultation or negotiation in writing, and if the disputing investor has not submitted the dispute for resolution to the competent court or any other binding dispute settlement mechanism of the Party receiving the investment, it may be submitted to one of the following international conciliation or arbitration fora by the choice of the investor: (a) conciliation or arbitration in accordance with the International Center for Settlement of Investment Disputes (ICSID), under the Convention on the Settlement of Disputes between States and Nationals of Other States, done at Washington on March 18th, 1965; (b) conciliation or arbitration under the Additional Facility Rules of the

Bilateral Dispute Settlement Provisions	Investment Dispute Settlement (ISDS) Provisions / Non-Tariff Barrier (NTB) Mediation Mechanism
7. Consultations may be held in person or by any technological means available to the Parties. Unless otherwise agreed by the consulting Parties, if in person, consultations shall be held in a rotating basis between cities of each country. The city for such meetings will be defined by the hosting country. In person meetings will begin to be held in a city of the requested Party. 8. In a consultation, each Party shall: (a) provide sufficient information to enable a full examination of how the measure in force or other matter at issue might affect the operation and application of this Agreement; and (b) treat any confidential information exchanged in the course of consultations on the same basis as the Party providing the information. 9. The consultations shall be confidential and without prejudice to the rights of any Party in any further proceedings. Article 177 Request for a Panel 1. Unless the Parties agree on a different period for consultations, a complaining Party may request in writing the establishment of a Panel if the consultation referred to in the Article 176 (Consultations) fails to resolve a matter within 60 days, after the date of receipt of the request for consultations or 50 days in case of urgent matters. 2. The complaining Party shall deliver the request to the other Party, indicating at least, the reason of the request, the identification of the measure, an indication of the provision of this Agreement that it considers relevant and an indication of the legal basis of the complaint. The Panel will be considered as established on the date of receipt of the corresponding request to the other Party.	International Centre for Settlement of Investment Disputes so long as the ICSID Convention is not in force between the Parties; (c) arbitration under the arbitration Rules of the United Nations Comission on International Trade Law; and (d) if agreed with the disputing Party, any arbitration in accordance with other arbitration rules. For more clarity, the election of one dispute settlement fora shall be definitive and exclusive. 3. An arbitral tribunal established under paragraph 2 shall decide the issues in dispute in accordance with this Agreement and applicable rules of international law. 4. The disputing investor who intends to submit the dispute to conciliation or arbitration pursuant to paragraph 2 shall give to the disputing Party written notice of its intent to do so at least 90 days before the claim is submitted. The notice of intent shall specify: (a) the name and address of the disputing investor; (b) the specific measures of the disputing Party at issue and a brief summary of the factual and legal basis of the investment dispute sufficient to present the problem clearly, including the obligations under this Chapter alleged to have been breached; (c) the waiver of the disputing investor from the right to initiate any proceedings before any of the other dispute settlement for referred to in paragraph 2 in relation to the matter under dispute; (d) conciliation or arbitration set forth in paragraph 2 which the disputing investor will choose; and

Bilateral Dispute Settlement Provisions	Investment Dispute Settlement (ISDS) Provisions / Non-Tariff Barrier (NTB) Mediation Mechanism
3. Unless otherwise agreed by the disputing Parties, the Panel shall be selected and perform its functions in a manner consistent with the provisions of this Chapter. Article 178 Qualifications of Panelists All Panelists shall: (a) have expertise or experience in law, international trade, other matters covered by this Agreement, or the resolution of disputes arising under international trade agreements relevant to the subject matter of the dispute; (b) be chosen strictly on the basis of objectivity, impartiality, reliability, and sound judgment; (c) be independent of, and not be affiliated with or take instructions from, any Party; (d) not delegate their responsibilities to any other person; and (e) comply with the Model Rules of Procedure established in Annex 12 (Model Rules of Procedure). Article 179 Panel Selection 1. The Parties shall apply the following procedures in selecting a Panel: (a) the Panel shall comprise 3 members; (b) within 15 days following the date of the establishment of the Panel, each	(e) the relief sought and the approximate amount of expropriation claimed. 5. Notwithstanding paragraph 4, no claim may be submitted to conciliation or arbitration set forth in paragraph 2, if more than 3 years have elapsed since the date on which the disputing investor became aware, or should reasonably have become aware, of a breach of an obligation under this Chapter causing loss or damage to the disputing investor or its investment referred to in paragraph 1. 6. The arbitration award shall be final and binding upon both parties to the dispute. Both Parties shall commit themselves to the enforcement of the award. 7. Where a tribunal makes a final award against a respondent, the tribunal may award, separately or in combination, only: (a) monetary damages and any applicable interest; and (b) restitution of property, in which case the award shall provide that the respondent may pay monetary damages and any applicable interest in lieu of restitution. A tribunal may also award costs and attorney's fees in accordance with the applicable arbitration rules. 8. Any disputing investor shall serve notices and other documents on disputes under this Article: (a) for China, to the: Ministry of Commerce 2, East Chang An Avenue 100731, Beijing, People's Republic of China; (b) for Peru, to the: Division of International Economy, Competition and Private Investment Affairs Ministry of Economy and Finance Jirón Lampa 277, floor 5th Lima, Peru.

Bilateral Dispute Settlement Provisions	Investment Dispute Settlement (ISDS) Provisions / Non-Tariff Barrier (NTB) Mediation Mechanism
Party shall nominate a Panelist; (c) the Parties shall endeavor to agree on a third Panelist who shall serve as chair within 30 days following the date of the establishment of the Panel; (d) if any member of the Panel has not been designated or appointed within 30 days following the date of the establishment of the Panel, at the request of any Party to the dispute, the Director-General of the WTO is expected to designate a member within a further 30 days; and (e) the chair of the Panel shall not be a national of any of the Parties, nor have his or her usual place of residence in the territory of any of the Parties, nor be or have been employed by any of the Parties, nor have dealt in any capacity with the subject raised on the dispute, unless the Parties otherwise agree. 2. If a Panelist appointed under this Article resigns or becomes unable to act, a successor Panelist shall be appointed within 30 days in accordance with the selection procedure as prescribed for the appointment of the original Panelist and the successor shall have all the powers and duties of the original Panelist. The work of the Panel shall be suspended during the appointment of the successor Panelist. Article 180 Role of the Panel 1. The role of the Panel shall be to make an objective assessment of the dispute under its consideration, including an examination of the facts of the case and the applicability of and conformity with this Agreement, incorporating necessary findings for settling the dispute. 2. The report of the Panel shall be binding on the disputing Parties.	

Bilateral Dispute Settlement Provisions	Investment Dispute Settlement (ISDS) Provisions / Non-Tariff Barrier (NTB) Mediation Mechanism
3. The Panel shall take its decisions by consensus. However, if the Panel is unable to reach consensus, it may take its decisions by majority vote. 4. Where a Panel concludes that a measure is inconsistent with this Agreement, it shall recommend that the Party complained against bring the measure into conformity with this Agreement. In addition to these recommendations, the Panel will be entitled to suggest ways in which the Party complained against could implement the recommendations. 5. The Panel, in its findings and recommendations, may not add to or diminish the rights and obligations provided in this Agreement. Article 181 Model Rules of Procedure 1. The procedure before the Panel shall be conducted in accordance with the Model Rules of Procedure set out in Annex 12 (Model Rules of Procedure). Exceptionally, the disputing Parties may agree on different rules to be applied by the Panel. 2. The Model Rules of Procedure are necessary for the good development of all the steps in this Chapter. In addition, these rules shall regulate the development of the procedure, pursuant to the following principles: (a) the procedures shall ensure the right to at least one hearing before the Panel, as well as the opportunity for each disputing Party to provide initial and rebuttal written submissions, and allow the use of any technological means to ensure its authenticity; and (b) the hearings before the Panel, the deliberations, as well as all the submissions and communications submitted during the hearings, shall be confidential.	

Bilateral Dispute Settlement Provisions	Investment Dispute Settlement (ISDS) Provisions / Non-Tariff Barrier (NTB) Mediation Mechanism
3. If needed, the Panel shall, apart from the matters set out in this Article and in Annex 12 (Model Rules of Procedure), regulate its own procedures in relation to the settlement of the dispute in consultation with the Parties. 4. Unless otherwise agreed by the disputing Parties within 20 days following the establishment of the Panel, the terms of reference shall be: "To examine, in light of the relevant provisions of this Agreement, the matter referred to in the request for the establishment of a Panel pursuant to Article 177 (Request for a Panel) and to make findings of law and fact together with the reasons therefore for the resolution of the dispute, as well as a recommendation for its implementation, if needed." 5. Unless otherwise agreed by the disputing Parties, the hearings shall be held in a rotating basis between cities of each country. The city for such meetings will be defined by the hosting country. In person meetings will begin to be held in a city of the Party complained against. 6. The working language of the dispute settlement proceedings shall be English. Whenever a document is presented in either Chinese or Spanish, the Party presenting the document shall file a translation to English. Article 182 Role of Experts 1. On request of a disputing Party, or on its own initiative, the Panel may seek information and technical advice from any person or body that it deems appropriate. The requirements set out in subparagraphs (b) and (c) of Article 178 (Qualifications of Panelists) shall apply to the selection of experts or groups, as appropriate. 2. Before the Panel seeks information or technical advice, appropriate procedures shall be established in consultation with the disputing Parties. The Panel shall:	

Bilateral Dispute Settlement Provisions	Investment Dispute Settlement (ISDS) Provisions / Non-Tariff Barrier (NTB) Mediation Mechanism
(a) notify the Parties, in advance, of its intention to seek information or technical advice pursuant to paragraph 1, establishing an adequate time period for the Parties to make the comments and observations that they deem convenient; and (b) provide the disputing Parties with a copy of any information or technical advice received pursuant to paragraph 1, and with a period of time for the Parties to submit its comments. 3. When the Panel takes into consideration the information or technical advice sought pursuant to paragraph 1 for the preparation of its report, it shall also take into account any comments or observations submitted by the disputing Parties with respect to such information or technical advice. Article 183 Report of the Panel 1. Unless the Parties otherwise agree, the Panel shall base its report on the relevant provisions of this Agreement, the submissions and arguments of the disputing Parties, and on any information received by it pursuant to Article 181 (Model Rules of Procedure). 2. Unless the Parties otherwise agree, the Panel shall present the report to the disputing Parties, within 120 days, or 90 days in the event of urgent matters, after the last Panelist is selected. 3. Only in exceptional cases, if the Panel considers it cannot release its report within 120 days or 90 days in the event of urgent matters, it shall inform the Parties in writing of the justifying reasons for the delay together with an estimate of the period within which it will release its report. Any delay shall not exceed a further period of 30 days unless the Parties otherwise agree.	

Bilateral Dispute Settlement Provisions	Investment Dispute Settlement (ISDS) Provisions / Non-Tariff Barrier (NTB) Mediation Mechanism
4. The report shall contain: (a) the finding along with its factual and legal basis; (b) the determination as to whether a Party has not conformed with its obligations under this Agreement or any other determination requested in the terms of reference; and (c) its recommendations for the implementation of the decision pursuant to paragraph 4 of Article 180 (Role of the Panel). 5. The Panelists may furnish separate opinions on matters not unanimously agreed. 6. No Panel may disclose which Panelists are associated with majority or minority opinions. 7. Unless the Parties agree otherwise, the report shall be available to the public within 30 days thereafter, subject to the protection of confidential information. Article 184 Request for Clarification of the Report 1. Within 10 days of the release of the report, either of the disputing Parties may submit a written request to the Panel, a copy of which shall be sent to the other Party, for clarification of any items the Party considers requires further explanation or definition. 2. The Panel shall respond to the request within 10 days following the submission of such request. The clarification of the Panel shall only be a more precise explanation or definition of the original contents of the report, and not an amendment of such report.	

Bilateral Dispute Settlement Provisions	Investment Dispute Settlement (ISDS) Provisions / Non-Tariff Barrier (NTB) Mediation Mechanism
3. The filing of this request for clarification will not postpone the effect of the Panel report nor the deadline for compliance of the adopted decision, unless the Panel decides otherwise. Article 185 Suspension and Termination of Procedure 1. The disputing Parties may agree to suspend the work of the Panel at any time for a period not exceeding 12 months following the date of such agreement. In any event, if the work of the Panel has been suspended for more than 12 months, the authority of the Panel shall lapse, unless the disputing Parties agree otherwise. If the authority of the Panel lapses and the disputing Parties have not reached an agreement on the settlement of the dispute, nothing in this Article shall prevent a Party from requesting a new proceeding regarding the same matter. 2. At any time prior to the release of the Panel report, the Parties may agree to terminate the procedures before a Panel by jointly notifying the chair of the Panel on this respect. Article 186 Implementation of the Report 1. The Panel report shall be final and binding on the disputing Parties. 2. If the report issued by the Panel determines that a Party has not conformed with its obligations under this Agreement, the Party complained against shall eliminate the non-conformity. 3. The Party complained against shall comply with the recommendation of the Panel promptly or, if not practicable, within a reasonable period of time. The Parties shall agree on reasonable period of time within 30 days of the notification of the report of	

Bilateral Dispute Settlement Provisions	Investment Dispute Settlement (ISDS) Provisions / Non-Tariff Barrier (NTB) Mediation Mechanism
the Panel. In any case, such reasonable period of time shall not exceed 300 calendar days after the release of the report. Article 187 Examination of Implementation 1. Without prejudice to the procedures set out in Article 188 (Compensation), once the period of time set out in paragraph 3 of Article 186 (Implementation of the Report) has expired, and there is disagreement between the disputing Parties as to the existence or consistency of the measures taken to comply with the Panel report, such dispute shall be referred to the original Panel wherever possible. If not possible, the procedure pursuant to Article 179 (Panel Selection) shall be followed to appoint a new Panel, in which event the periods set out thereof shall be reduced by half. 2. This Panel shall issue its report on the matter within 60 days after the date of the referral of the matter to it. When the Panel considers that it cannot provide its report within this timeframe, it shall inform the Parties in writing of the reasons for the delay together with an estimate of the period within which it will submit its report. Any delay shall not exceed a further period of 30 days unless the Parties otherwise agree. Article 188 Compensation 1. If the Party complained against does not comply with the Panel report within the period of time set forth in paragraph 3 of the Article 186 (Implementation of the Report), any of the disputing Parties may request in writing negotiations with the other Party with a view to establishing a mutually acceptable compensation. The disputing Parties shall initiate negotiations within a period no longer than 10 days following the receipt of the written request. 2. This compensation shall be effective as of the moment the Parties agree to it and	

Bilateral Dispute Settlement Provisions	Investment Dispute Settlement (ISDS) Provisions / Non-Tariff Barrier (NTB) Mediation Mechanism
until the Party complained against complies with the Panel report. Article 189 Suspension of Benefits 1. The complaining Party may, at any time thereafter, communicate in writing to the Party complained against its intention to suspend the application of benefits in 30 days upon reception of such communication, if: (a) the disputing Parties are unable to agree on a compensation within 30 days after the period for establishing such compensation has begun, or the Party complained against has failed to observe the terms of the agreed compensation within 30 days following such agreement; (b) the Panel under the Article 187 (Examination of the Implementation) finds that the Party complained against fails to bring the measure found to be inconsistent with this Agreement into compliance with the recommendations of the Panel within the period of time established; or (c) the Party complained against expresses in writing that it will not implement the recommendations. 2. The complaining Party may initiate the suspension of benefits within 30 days following the latest date between the date of the communication pursuant to paragraph 1 of this Article and the date when the Panel issued its report pursuant to Article 190 (Examination of Benefit Suspension Level). 3. The level of benefits to be suspended shall have an equivalent effect to the benefits not being received.	

Bilateral Dispute Settlement Provisions	Investment Dispute Settlement (ISDS) Provisions / Non-Tariff Barrier (NTB) Mediation Mechanism
4. In considering what benefits to suspend pursuant to paragraph 1: (a) the complaining Party should first seek to suspend benefits in the same sector or sectors affected by the measure; and (b) if the complaining Party considers that it is not practicable or effective to suspend benefits in the same sector or sectors, it may suspend benefits in other sectors. The communication in which it announces such a decision shall indicate the reasons on which it is based. Article 190 Examination of the Benefit Suspension Level 1. If the Party complained against considers that the level of benefits suspended is excessive, it may request in writing the original Panel to examine the level of suspension of benefits. If this is not possible, the procedure established in Article 179 (Panel Selection) shall be followed, in which event the periods set out thereof shall be reduced by half. 2. This Panel shall issue its ruling within 60 days following the date of the referral of the matter to it. When the Panel considers that it cannot provide its report within this timeframe, it shall inform the Parties in writing of the reasons for the delay together with an estimate of the period within which it will submit its report. Any delay shall not exceed a further period of 30 days unless the Parties otherwise agree. The ruling of the Panel shall be final and binding. It shall be delivered to the Parties and be made publicly available. 3. If the Panel finds that the level of benefits which the complaining Party has suspended is excessive, it shall determine the appropriate level of benefits it considers to be of equivalent effect.	

Bilateral Dispute Settlement Provisions	Investment Dispute Settlement (ISDS) Provisions / Non-Tariff Barrier (NTB) Mediation Mechanism
Article 191 Post Suspension 1. Without prejudice to the procedures in Article 190 (Examination of the Benefit Suspension Level), if the Party complained against considers that it has eliminated the non-conformity that the Panel has found, it may provide written notice to the complaining Party with a description of how non-conformity has been removed. If the complaining Party has disagreement, it may refer the matter to the original Panel within 60 days after receipt of such written notice. Otherwise, the complaining Party shall promptly stop the suspension of benefits. 2. The Panel shall release its report within 60 days after the referral of the matter. If the Panel concludes that the Party complained against has eliminated the non-conformity, the complaining Party shall promptly stop the suspension of benefits. Article 192 Private Rights Neither party may provide for a right of action under its domestic law against the other Party on the ground that a measure of the other Party is inconsistent with this Agreement.	

* Entered into force on March 1, 2010.

3.4 Free Trade Agreement between the Government of the Republic of Korea and the Government of the People's Republic of China*

Bilateral Dispute Settlement Provisions	Investment Dispute Settlement (ISDS) Provisions / Non-Tariff Barrier (NTB) Mediation Mechanism
CHAPTER 20 DISPUTE SETTLEMENT Article 20.1 Cooperation The Parties shall at all times endeavor to agree on the interpretation and application of this Agreement, and shall make every attempt through cooperation and consultations to arrive at a mutually satisfactory resolution of any matter that might affect its operation when a dispute occurs. Article 20.2 Scope Unless otherwise provided in this Agreement or as the Parties otherwise agree, this Chapter shall apply with respect to the settlement of all disputes between the Parties regarding the interpretation and application of this Agreement or wherever a Party considers that: (a) a measure of the other Party is inconsistent with its obligations under this Agreement; or (b) the other Party has otherwise failed to carry out its obligations under this Agreement. Article 20.3 Choice of Forum 1. Where a dispute arises under this Agreement and under the WTO Agreement or	CHAPTER 12 INVESTMENT Article 12.12 Settlement of Investment Disputes between a Party and an Investor of the Other Party 1. For the purposes of this Article, an investment dispute is a dispute between a Party and an investor of the other Party that has incurred loss or damage by reason of, or arising out of, an alleged breach of any obligation of the former Party under this Chapter with respect to the investor or its covered investments in the territory of the former Party. 2. Any investment dispute shall, as far as possible, be settled amicably through consultation between the investor who is a party to the investment dispute (hereinafter referred to in this Article as "disputing investor") and the Party that is a party to the investment dispute (hereinafter referred to in this Article as "disputing Party"). A written request for consultation shall be submitted to the disputing Party by the disputing investor before the submission of the investment dispute to the arbitration set out in paragraph 3. Such a written request shall specify: (a) the name and address of the disputing investor; (b) the obligations under this Chapter alleged to have been breached; (c) a brief summary of the facts of the investment dispute; and (d) the relief sought and the approximate amount of damages.

Bilateral Dispute Settlement Provisions	Investment Dispute Settlement (ISDS) Provisions / Non-Tariff Barrier (NTB) Mediation Mechanism
any other agreement to which both Parties are party, the complaining Party may select the forum in which to settle the dispute. 2. Once the complaining Party has requested the establishment of a dispute settlement panel under an agreement referred to in paragraph 1, the forum selected shall be used to the exclusion of other fora. Article 20.4 Consultations 1. The Parties shall make every attempt to arrive at a mutually satisfactory resolution of any dispute through consultations under this Article or other consultative provisions of this Agreement. 2. Either Party may request consultations with the other Party with respect to any matter described in Article 20.2 by delivering written notification to the other Party. The requesting Party shall set out the reasons for the request, including identification of the measure at issue and an indication of the legal basis for the complaint, in the written notification. If a request for consultations is made, the other Party shall reply in writing to the request within 10 days after the date of its receipt.	3. The investment dispute shall on the request of the disputing investor be submitted to either: (a) a competent court of the disputing Party; (b) arbitration in accordance with the ICSID Convention, if the ICSID Convention is available; (c) arbitration under the ICSID Additional Facility Rules, if the ICSID Additional Facility Rules are available; (d) arbitration under the UNCITRAL Arbitration Rules; or (e) if agreed with the disputing Party, any arbitration in accordance with other arbitration rules, provided that, for the purposes of subparagraphs (b) through (e): (i) the investment dispute cannot be settled through the consultation referred to in paragraph 2 within four months from the date of the submission of the written request for consultation to the disputing Party; and (ii) the requirement concerning the domestic administrative review procedure set out in paragraph 7, where applicable, is met.
3. Consultations shall be held in good faith within 30 days after the date of receipt of the request with a view of reaching a mutually satisfactory solution and take place, unless the Parties otherwise agree, in the territory of the requested Party.	4. Each Party hereby gives its consent to the submission of an investment dispute by a disputing investor to the arbitration set out in paragraph 3 in accordance with the provisions of this Article.
4. If the requested Party does not reply within 10 days or does not enter into consultations within 30 days from the date of receipt of the request for consultations, then the requesting Party may proceed directly to request the establishment of a panel in accordance with Article 20.6. 5. Each Party shall:	5. Once the disputing investor has submitted an investment dispute to the competent court of the disputing Party or to one of the arbitrations set out in paragraph 3, the choice of the disputing investor shall be final and the disputing investor may not submit thereafter the same dispute to the other arbitrations set out in paragraph 3.

Bilateral Dispute Settlement Provisions	Investment Dispute Settlement (ISDS) Provisions / Non-Tariff Barrier (NTB) Mediation Mechanism
(a) provide sufficient information in the consultations to enable a full examination of how the matter subject to consultations might affect the operation of this Agreement; and (b) treat any confidential information exchanged in the course of consultations on the same basis as the Party providing the information. 6. Consultations shall be confidential and without prejudice to the rights of the Parties in any further proceedings under this Chapter. Article 20.5 Good Offices, Conciliation or Mediation 1. Good offices, conciliation, and mediation are procedures undertaken voluntarily if the Parties so agree. 2. Proceedings involving good offices, conciliation, and mediation, and in particular positions taken by the Parties during these proceedings, shall be confidential and without prejudice to the rights of either Party in any further proceedings. 3. Good offices, conciliation, or mediation may be requested at any time by any Party. They may begin at any time and be terminated at any time. If the Parties agree, procedures for good offices, conciliation or mediation may continue while the dispute proceeds for resolution before a panel established under Article 20.6. 4. The Parties are encouraged to enter into a mediation procedure in particular when a Party believes that a certain non-tariff measure adversely affects trade between the Parties and that such measure is related to the matter falling under market access of goods of this Agreement and is subject to this Chapter, unless the Parties otherwise agree.	6. Notwithstanding paragraphs 3 and 4, no claim may be submitted to the arbitration set out in paragraph 3 unless the disputing investor gives the disputing Party written waiver of any right to initiate before any competent court of the disputing Party with respect to any measure of the disputing Party alleged to constitute a breach referred to in paragraph 1. 7. When the disputing investor submits a written request for consultation to the disputing Party under paragraph 2, the disputing Party may require, without delay, the investor concerned to go through the domestic administrative review procedure specified by the laws and regulations of that Party before the submission to the arbitration set out in paragraph 3. The domestic administrative review procedure shall not exceed four months from the date on which an application for the review is filed. If the procedure is not completed by the end of the four months, it shall be deemed to be completed and the disputing investor may submit the investment dispute to the arbitration set out in paragraph 3. The investor may file an application for the review unless the four months consultation period as provided in paragraph 3 has elapsed. 8. The applicable arbitration rules shall govern the arbitration set out in paragraph 3 except to the extent modified in this Article. 9. The award rendered by an arbitral tribunal established under paragraph 3 (hereinafter referred to in this Article as the "Tribunal") shall include: (a) a finding whether or not there has been a breach by the disputing Party of any obligation under this Chapter with respect to the disputing investor and its covered investments; and (b) one or both of the following remedies, only if the disputing investor's loss or damage is attributed to such breach: (i) monetary damages and applicable interest; and (ii) restitution of property, in which case the award shall provide

Bilateral Dispute Settlement Provisions	Investment Dispute Settlement (ISDS) Provisions / Non-Tariff Barrier (NTB) Mediation Mechanism
5. The Parties should endeavor to participate in the mediation procedure provided for in paragraph 4 in an expeditious way and with the aim to reach a mutually agreed solution within a reasonable period of time with the assistance of a mediator designated or appointed by the Parties upon agreement. Where the Parties have agreed to a solution, each Party should take any measure necessary to implement the mutually agreed solution. 6. The mediation procedure provided for in paragraph 4 is not intended to serve as a basis for dispute settlement procedures under this Agreement or any other agreement in which the Parties participate as parties. Article 20.6 Establishment of Panel 1. If the consultations referred to in Article 20.4 fail to resolve a matter within 60 days after the date of receipt of the request for consultations or within such other period as the Parties may agree, the complaining Party may deliver a written request to establish a panel to the other Party. 2. The complaining Party shall indicate in the request whether consultations were held, identify the specific measure at issue and provide a brief summary of the legal basis for the complaint sufficient to present the problem clearly. 3. A panel shall be established upon the date of receipt of the request referred to in paragraph 1. Article 20.7 Composition of Panel 1. Unless the Parties otherwise agree, the Parties shall apply the following procedures in selecting a panel:	that the disputing Party may pay monetary damages and any applicable interest, in lieu of restitution. 10. The award which is rendered by the Tribunal shall be final and binding upon both parties to the investment dispute. This award shall be executed in accordance with the applicable laws and regulations concerning the execution of award in force, in the country in whose territory such execution is sought. 11. Notwithstanding paragraph 3, no claim may be submitted to the arbitration set out in that paragraph, if more than three years have elapsed from the date on which the disputing investor first acquired, or should have first acquired, whichever is the earlier, the knowledge that the disputing investor had incurred the loss or damage referred to in paragraph 1.

Bilateral Dispute Settlement Provisions	Investment Dispute Settlement (ISDS) Provisions / Non-Tariff Barrier (NTB) Mediation Mechanism
(a) the panel shall comprise three members; (b) each Party shall appoint one panelist respectively within 15 days after the establishment of the panel. If a Party fails to appoint a panelist within that period, the panelist shall be appointed by the other Party, unless the Parties otherwise decide; (c) the Parties shall endeavor to agree on the third panelist, who shall serve as the chair, within 30 days after the establishment of the panel; and (d) if the Parties are unable to agree on the chair within 30 days after the establishment of the panel, on the request of any Party to the dispute, the Director General of the WTO is expected to designate the chair within a further period of 30 days. In the event that the Director General of the WTO is a national of either Party or unable to perform this task, the Deputy Director-General of the WTO who is not a national of either Party shall be requested to perform such task. 2. The chair of the panel shall not be a national of either Party, nor have his or her usual place of residence in the territory of either Party, nor be employed by either Party, nor have dealt with the matter in any capacity. 3. If a panelist appointed under this Article resigns or becomes unable to serve on the panel, a successor shall be appointed within 15 days in accordance with the selection procedure of the original panelist and the successor shall have all the powers and duties of the original panelist. In such a case, any time period applicable to the panel proceedings shall be suspended during the appointment of the successor. 4. All panelists shall: (a) have expertise or experience in law, international trade, other matters	

Bilateral Dispute Settlement Provisions	Investment Dispute Settlement (ISDS) Provisions / Non-Tariff Barrier (NTB) Mediation Mechanism
covered by this Agreement, or the resolution of disputes arising under international trade agreements; (b) be chosen strictly on the basis of objectivity, reliability, and sound judgment; (c) be independent of, and not be affiliated with or take instructions from, either Party; and (d) comply with a code of conduct established in Annex 20-B (Code of Conduct for Panelists and Mediators). 5. Where a Party considers that a panelist does not comply with the requirements of Annex 20-B (Code of Conduct for Panelists and Mediators), the Parties shall consult and, if so agreed, replace that panelist in accordance with paragraph 3. Article 20.8 Functions of Panel 1. The function of a panel is to make an objective assessment of the dispute before it, including an examination of the facts of the case and the applicability of and conformity with this Agreement. 2. Where a panel concludes that a measure is inconsistent with this Agreement, it shall recommend that the Party complained against bring the measure into conformity with this Agreement. Article 20.9 Rules of Procedure 1. Unless the Parties otherwise agree, a panel shall follow the Rules of Procedure set	

Bilateral Dispute Settlement Provisions	Investment Dispute Settlement (ISDS) Provisions / Non-Tariff Barrier (NTB) Mediation Mechanism
out in Annex 20-A (Rules of Procedure) and may, after consulting with the Parties, adopt additional rules of procedure not inconsistent with the Annex 20-A (Rules of Procedure). 2 Unless the Parties otherwise agree within 20 days from the date of receipt of the request for the establishment of the panel, the panel's terms of reference shall be: "To examine, in the light of the relevant provisions of this Agreement, the matter referred to in the request for the establishment of the panel pursuant to Article 20.6 and to make findings of law and fact together with the reasons therefore for the resolution of the dispute, conclusions, and recommendations." 3. On the request of a Party, or on its own initiative, the panel may seek information and technical advice from any person or body that it deems appropriate, provided that the Parties so agree. 4. Unless the Parties otherwise agree, the remuneration of the panelists and other expenses of the panel shall be borne by the Parties in equal shares. Article 20.10 Suspension or Termination of Panel Proceedings 1. The Parties may agree that a panel suspends its work at any time for a period not exceeding 12 months from the date of such agreement. In the event of such a suspension, all relevant timeframes set out in this Chapter shall be extended by the amount of time that the work was suspended. If the work of the panel has been suspended for more than 12 months, the authority for establishment of the panel shall lapse, unless the Parties otherwise agree. 2. The Parties may agree to terminate the proceedings of a panel.	

Bilateral Dispute Settlement Provisions	Investment Dispute Settlement (ISDS) Provisions / Non-Tariff Barrier (NTB) Mediation Mechanism
Article20.11 Panel Report 1. Unless the Parties otherwise agree, a panel shall, within 120 days after the last panelist is appointed, issue to the Parties an interim report. 2. In exceptional cases, if the panel considers it cannot issue its interim report within the period of 120 days, it shall inform the Parties in writing of the reasons for the delay together with an estimate of the period within which it will release its report. Any delay shall not exceed a further period of 30 days unless the Parties otherwise agree. 3. The panel shall base its report on the relevant provisions of this Agreement and the submissions and arguments of the Parties. The panel shall consider this Agreement in accordance with customary rules of interpretation of public international law, including those codified in the Vienna Convention on the Law of Treaties (1969). 4. Each Party may submit written comments to the panel on its interim report within 15 days of the presentation of the report. After considering any written comments by the Parties on the interim report, the panel may modify its report and make any further examination it considers appropriate. 5. The panel shall present a final report to the Parties within 45 days of the presentation of the interim report, unless the Parties otherwise agree. The Parties shall make the final report available to the public within 15 days after the issuance of the final report, subject to the protection of confidential information, unless the Parties decide not to do so. 6. The panel shall make every effort to take its decision by consensus. If the panel is unable to reach consensus, it may take its decision by majority vote. Panelists may furnish dissenting or separate opinions on matters not unanimously agreed. All	

Bilateral Dispute Settlement Provisions	Investment Dispute Settlement (ISDS) Provisions / Non-Tariff Barrier (NTB) Mediation Mechanism
opinions expressed in the panel report by individual panelists shall be anonymous. 7. The final report of the panel shall be final and binding on the Parties for the dispute and shall not create any rights or obligations for persons. The final report shall set out the findings of fact, the applicability of the relevant provisions of this Agreement and the basic rationale behind any findings and conclusions that the panel makes. Article 20.12 Implementation of the Final Report of the Panel 1. If in its final report the panel determines that a Party has not conformed with its obligations under this Agreement, the resolution, whenever possible, shall be to eliminate the non-conformity. 2. Unless the Parties otherwise agree, the Party complained against shall eliminate the non-conformity as determined in the final report of the panel immediately, or if this is not practicable, within a reasonable period of time referred to in Article 20.13. Article 20.13 Reasonable Period of Time 1. The reasonable period of time shall be mutually determined by the Parties, or where the Parties fail to agree on the reasonable period of time within 30 days of the issuance of the final report of the panel, either Party may, to the extent possible, refer the matter to the original panel, which shall determine the reasonable period of time. 2. The panel shall provide its report to the Parties within 30 days after the date of the referral of the matter to it. When the panel considers that it cannot provide its report within this timeframe, it shall inform the Parties in writing of the reasons for the delay together with an estimate of the period within which it will submit its report. Any delay shall not exceed a further period of 30 days unless the Parties otherwise agree.	

Bilateral Dispute Settlement Provisions	Investment Dispute Settlement (ISDS) Provisions / Non-Tariff Barrier (NTB) Mediation Mechanism
3. The reasonable period of time normally should not exceed 15 months from the date of issuance of the final report of the panel. 4. The Party complained against will inform the complaining Party in writing of its progress to comply with the final report of the panel at least 30 days before the expiry of the reasonable period of time. Article 20.14 Compliance Review 1. The Party complained against shall notify the complaining Party before the end of the reasonable period of time of any measures that it has taken to comply with the final report of the panel. 2. Where there is disagreement as to the existence or consistency with this Agreement of measures taken to comply with the recommendations of the panel, such dispute shall be referred to a panel proceeding, including wherever possible by resort to the original panel. 3. The panel shall provide its report to the Parties within 60 days after the date of the referral of the matter to it. When the panel considers that it cannot provide its report within this timeframe, it shall inform the Parties in writing of the reasons for the delay together with an estimate of the period within which it will submit its report. Any delay shall not exceed a further period of 30 days unless the Parties otherwise agree. 4. Articles concerning panel procedures in this Agreement shall apply mutatis mutandis to the procedure under this Article. Article 20.15 Suspension of Concessions or Other Obligations	

Bilateral Dispute Settlement Provisions	Investment Dispute Settlement (ISDS) Provisions / Non-Tariff Barrier (NTB) Mediation Mechanism
1. If the panel under Article 20.14 finds that the Party complained against fails to bring the measure found to be inconsistent with this Agreement into compliance with the recommendations of the panel within the reasonable period of time established, or if the Party complained against expresses in writing that it will not implement the recommendations, or if no measure taken to comply exists, and the Parties fail to reach an agreement on compensation within 20 days after entering into negotiations for compensation, the complaining Party may suspend the application of concessions or other obligations to the Party complained against. The complaining Party shall notify the Party complained against 30 days before suspending concessions or other obligations. The notification shall indicate the level and scope of the suspension of concessions or other obligations. 2. Compensation and suspension of concessions or other obligations are temporary measures available in the event that the recommendations and determinations are not implemented within the reasonable period of time. However, neither compensation nor suspension of concessions or other obligations is preferred to full implementation of a recommendation to bring a measure into conformity with this Agreement. Compensation shall be consistent with this Agreement. 3. In considering concessions or other obligations to suspend: (a) the complaining Party should first seek to suspend concessions or other obligations in the same sector or sectors that affected by the measure that the panel has found to be inconsistent with the obligations derived of this Agreement; and (b) if the complaining Party considers that it is not practicable or effective to suspend concessions or other obligations in the same sector or sectors, it may suspend concession or other obligations in other sectors. 4. The level of suspension of concessions or other obligations shall be equivalent to	

Bilateral Dispute Settlement Provisions	Investment Dispute Settlement (ISDS) Provisions / Non-Tariff Barrier (NTB) Mediation Mechanism
the level of the nullification or impairment. 5. If the Party complained against considers that the level of suspension of concessions or other obligations is not equivalent to the nullification or impairment, it may request in writing to the original panel. On the written request of the Party complained against, the original panel shall determine whether the level of concessions or other obligations to be suspended by the complaining Party is excessive pursuant to paragraph 4. If the panel cannot be established with its original panelists, the proceeding set out in Article 20.6 shall be applied. 6. The panel shall present its determination within 60 days after the date of receipt of the request, or if the panel cannot be established with its original panelists, from the date on which the last panelist is appointed. 7. The complaining Party may not suspend the application of concessions or other obligations before the issuance of the panel's determination pursuant to this Article. Article 20.16 Post Suspension 1. Without prejudice to the procedure in Article 20.15, if the Party complained against considers that it has eliminated the non-conformity that the panel has found, it may provide a written notice to the complaining Party with description of how nonconformity has been removed. If the complaining Party disagrees, it may refer the matter to the original panel within 60 days after receipt of such written notice. Otherwise, the complaining Party shall promptly stop the suspension of concessions or other obligations. 2. The panel shall issue its report within 60 days after the referral of the matter. 3. If the panel determines that the Party complained against has eliminated the	

Bilateral Dispute Settlement Provisions	Investment Dispute Settlement (ISDS) Provisions / Non-Tariff Barrier (NTB) Mediation Mechanism
nonconformity, the complaining Party shall promptly stop the suspension of concessions or other obligations. Article 20.17 Private Rights Neither party may provide for a right of action under its domestic law against the other Party on the ground that a measure of the other Party is inconsistent with this Agreement.	

* Entered into force on December 20, 2015.

3.5 Free Trade Agreement between the Government of Australia and the Government of the People's Republic of China*

Bilateral Dispute Settlement Provisions	Investment Dispute Settlement (ISDS) Provisions
CHAPTER 15 DISPUTE SETTLEMENT Article 15.1 Cooperation The Parties shall endeavour to agree on the interpretation and application of this Agreement, and shall make every attempt through cooperation to arrive at a mutually satisfactory resolution of any matter that might affect its operation. Article 15.2 Scope of Application Unless otherwise provided in this Agreement, this Chapter shall apply to the settlement of disputes between the Parties regarding the implementation, interpretation and application of this Agreement or wherever a Party considers that: (a) a measure of the other Party is inconsistent with its obligations under this Agreement; or (b) the other Party has otherwise failed to carry out its obligations under this Agreement. Article 15.3 Contact Points 1. Each Party shall designate a contact point to facilitate communications between the Parties with respect to any dispute initiated under this Chapter. 2. Any request, notification, written submission or other document made in	CHAPTER 9 INVESTMENT SECTION B INVESTOR-STATE DISPUTE SETTLEMENT Article 9.10 Definitions For the purposes of this Chapter: (a) claimant means an investor of a Party that is a party to an investment dispute with the other Party; (b) disputing parties means the claimant and the respondent; (c) disputing Party means a Party against which a claim is made under Section B (Investor-State Dispute Settlement); (d) ICSID Additional Facility Rules means the Rules Governing the Additional Facility for the Administration of Proceedings by the Secretariat of the International Centre for Settlement of Investment Disputes; (e) ICSID Convention means the Convention on the Settlement of Investment Disputes between States and Nationals of Other States, done at Washington, 18 March 1965; (f) non-disputing Party means the Party that is not a party to an investment dispute;

Bilateral Dispute Settlement Provisions	Investment Dispute Settlement (ISDS) Provisions
accordance with this Chapter shall be delivered to the other Party through its designated contact point. Article 15.4 Choice of Forum 1. Unless otherwise provided in this Article, this Chapter is without prejudice to the rights of the Parties to have recourse to dispute settlement procedures available under other international trade agreements to which they are both parties. 2. Where a dispute regarding any matter arises under this Agreement and under another international trade agreement to which both Parties are party, the complaining Party may select the forum in which to settle the dispute. 3. Once the complaining Party has requested the establishment of, or referred a matter to, a dispute settlement panel or arbitral tribunal, the forum selected shall be used to the exclusion of the others. Article 15.5 Consultations 1. Either Party may request consultations with the other Party with respect to any matter described in Article 15.2 by delivering written notification to the other Party. 2. In this notification, the complaining Party shall set out the reasons for the request, including identification of the measure at issue and an indication of the factual and legal basis for the complaint. 3. If a request for consultations is made, the Party to which the request is made shall reply promptly to the request and shall enter into consultations in good faith, with a view to reaching a mutually satisfactory solution, within a period of no more than:	(g) protected information means confidential business information or information that is privileged or otherwise protected from disclosure under a Party's law; (h) respondent means the Party that is a party to an investment dispute; (i) Secretary-General means the Secretary-General of ICSID; and (j) UNCITRAL Arbitration Rules means the arbitration rules of the United Nations Commission on International Trade Law. Article 9.11 Consultations 1. In the event of an investment dispute, after two months since the occurrence of the measure or event giving rise to the dispute, the claimant may deliver to the respondent a written request for consultations. The request shall: (a) specify the name and address of the claimant and, where a claim is submitted on behalf of an enterprise of the respondent that is a juridical person that the claimant owns or controls directly or indirectly, the name, address, and place of incorporation of the enterprise; (b) for each claim, identify the provision of this Chapter alleged to have been breached and any other relevant provisions; (c) for each claim, identify the measures or events giving rise to the claim; (d) for each claim, indicate whether the claim is made on its own behalf or on behalf of the enterprise; (e) for each claim, provide a brief summary of the legal and factual basis

Bilateral Dispute Settlement Provisions	Investment Dispute Settlement (ISDS) Provisions
(a) 10 days after the date of receipt of the request for matters of urgency concerning perishable goods; or (b) 30 days after the date of receipt of the request for all other matters. 4. The consultations shall be confidential and are without prejudice to the rights of either Party in any further proceedings. 5. In conducting the consultations, the Parties shall: (a) provide sufficient information to enable a full examination of how the matter might affect the operation and application of this Agreement; and (b) treat any confidential or proprietary information exchanged in the course of consultations on the same basis as the Party providing the information. 6. If the Party complained against does not enter into consultations within the timeframe specified in paragraph 3(a) or 3(b), then the complaining Party may proceed directly to request the establishment of an arbitral tribunal. Article 15.6 Good Offices, Mediation and Conciliation 1. The Parties may at any time agree to good offices, conciliation or mediation. They may begin at any time and be terminated at any time. 2. If the Parties agree, good offices, conciliation or mediation may continue while the dispute proceeds for resolution before an arbitral tribunal convened under Article 15.7. Article 15.7 Establishment and Composition of an Arbitral Tribunal	sufficient to present the problem clearly; and (f) specify the relief sought, the approximate amount of damages claimed and its standard or basis for calculation. 2. After a request for consultations is made in accordance with this Section, the claimant and the respondent shall initially seek to resolve the dispute through consultations. 3. If the disputing parties reach a mutually agreed solution to a dispute, or certain claims thereof, formally raised under this Section, they shall abide by and comply with the mutually agreed solution reached under this Article without delay. 4. Measures of a Party that are non-discriminatory and for the legitimate public welfare objectives of public health, safety, the environment, public morals or public order shall not be the subject of a claim under this Section. 5. The respondent may, within 30 days of the date on which it receives a request for consultations (as provided for in paragraph 1), state that it considers that a measure alleged to be in breach of an obligation under Section A is of the kind described in paragraph 4, by delivering to the claimant and to the non-disputing Party a notice specifying the basis for its position (a 'public welfare notice'). 6. The issuance of a public welfare notice shall trigger a 90 day period during which the respondent and the non-disputing Party shall consult. The dispute resolution procedure contemplated by this Section shall be automatically suspended for this 90 day period. 7. The issuance of a public welfare notice is without prejudice to the respondent's right to invoke the procedures described in Article 9.16.5 or Article 9.16.6. The respondent shall promptly inform the claimant, and make available to the public, the outcome of any consultations.

Bilateral Dispute Settlement Provisions	Investment Dispute Settlement (ISDS) Provisions
1. If the consultations fail to resolve a dispute within: (a) 20 days after the date of receipt of the request for consultations regarding a matter of urgency concerning perishable goods; or (b) 60 days after the date of receipt of the request for consultations regarding any other matter; the Party that made the request for consultations may request, in writing, the establishment of an arbitral tribunal to consider the matter. 2. The request to establish an arbitral tribunal shall identify: (a) the specific measures at issue; and (b) the factual and legal basis of the complaint, including the provisions alleged to have been breached and any other relevant provisions of this Agreement, sufficient to present the problem clearly. 3. When a request is made by the complaining Party in accordance with paragraph 1, an arbitral tribunal shall be established. 4. An arbitral tribunal shall be composed of three arbitrators. 5. Within 15 days after the establishment of an arbitral tribunal, each Party shall appoint one arbitrator, who may be its national. 6. The Parties shall, by common agreement, designate the third arbitrator within 30 days after the establishment of the arbitral tribunal. The arbitrator thus appointed shall be the Chair of the arbitral tribunal. 7. If any arbitrator of the arbitral tribunal has not been designated or appointed within 30 days after the establishment of the arbitral tribunal, either Party may request that the Director-General of the WTO designate an arbitrator within 30 days	8. In any proceeding brought pursuant to this Section, the tribunal shall not draw any adverse inference from the non-issuance of a public welfare notice by the respondent, or from the absence of any decision between the respondent and the nondisputing Party as to whether a measure is of a kind described in paragraph 4.[1)] Article 9.12 Submission of A Claim to Arbitration 1. This Section applies where there is a dispute between a Party and an investor of the other Party relating to a covered investment made in accordance with the Party's laws, regulations and investment policies. 2. In the event that an investment dispute cannot be settled by consultations under Article 9.11 within 120 days after the date of receipt of the request for consultations, (a) the claimant, on its own behalf, may submit to arbitration under this Section a claim: (i) that the respondent has breached an obligation in Article 9.3; and (ii) that the claimant has incurred loss or damage by reason of, or arising out of, that breach; or (b) the claimant, on behalf of an enterprise of the respondent that is a juridical person that the claimant owns or controls directly or indirectly, may submit to arbitration under this Section a claim: (i) that the respondent has breached an obligation under Article 9.3; and (ii) that the enterprise has incurred loss or damage by reason of, or arising out of, that breach. 3. A claimant cannot submit or continue to pursue a claim under this Section where the investment of the claimant in the territory of the respondent is owned or controlled indirectly by an investor of a non-party, and the investor of the non-party submits or has submitted a claim with respect to the same measure or event under any agreement between the respondent and that non-party.

Bilateral Dispute Settlement Provisions	Investment Dispute Settlement (ISDS) Provisions
of that request. 8. All arbitrators shall: (a) have expertise or experience in law, international trade, other matters covered by this Agreement, or the resolution of disputes arising under international trade agreements; (b) be chosen strictly on the basis of objectivity, reliability, and sound judgement; (c) be independent of, and not be affiliated with or take instructions from, either Party; (d) not have dealt with the matter in any capacity; and (e) comply with the code of conduct set out in Annex 15-A. 9. The Chair of the arbitral tribunal shall: (a) not be a national of either Party; and (b) not have his or her usual place of residence in the territory of either Party. 10. If an arbitrator appointed in accordance with this Article resigns or becomes unable to act, a successor arbitrator shall be appointed in the same manner as prescribed for the appointment of the original arbitrator and the successor shall have all the powers and duties of the original arbitrator. The work of the arbitral tribunal shall be suspended during the appointment of the successor arbitrator. 11. Where an arbitral tribunal is reconvened in accordance with Articles 15.15 through 15.17, the reconvened arbitral tribunal shall, where possible, have the	4. A claimant may submit a claim referred to in paragraph 2: (a) under the ICSID Convention and the ICSID Rules of Procedure for Arbitration Proceedings, provided that both the respondent and the non-disputing Party are parties to the ICSID Convention; (b) under the ICSID Additional Facility Rules, provided that either the respondent or the non-disputing Party is a party to the ICSID Convention; (c) under the UNCITRAL Arbitration Rules, except as modified by this Agreement and the Side Letter on Transparency Rules Applicable to ISDS; or (d) if the claimant and respondent agree, to any other arbitration institution or under any other arbitration rules. 5. Where a claim is submitted to arbitration under paragraph 4(b), (c) and (d) (except where a claim is submitted to any other arbitration institution under paragraph 4(d)), the disputing parties and the tribunal constituted thereunder shall request ICSID to provide administrative services for the arbitration proceedings. Both Parties shall endeavour to make proper institutional arrangements with ICSID to accommodate such requests following the entry into force of this Agreement. 6. A claim shall be deemed submitted to arbitration under this Section when the claimant's notice of or request for arbitration ("notice of arbitration"): (a) referred to in paragraph 1 of Article 36 of the ICSID Convention is received by the Secretary-General; (b) referred to in Article 2 of Schedule C of the ICSID Additional Facility Rules is received by the Secretary-General; (c) referred to in Article 3 of the UNCITRAL Arbitration Rules, together with the

Bilateral Dispute Settlement Provisions	Investment Dispute Settlement (ISDS) Provisions
same arbitrators as in the original arbitral tribunal. If the arbitral tribunal cannot be reconvened with its original arbitrators, the procedures for selection of arbitrators set out in this Article shall apply. Article 15.8 Functions of Arbitral Tribunals 1. The function of an arbitral tribunal is to make an objective assessment of the matter before it, including an objective assessment of: (a) the facts of the case; (b) the applicability of the relevant provisions of this Agreement cited by the Parties; and (c) whether: (i) the measure at issue is inconsistent with the obligations of this Agreement; or (ii) a Party has otherwise failed to carry out its obligations under this Agreement. 2. Unless the Parties otherwise agree within 20 days after the date of the establishment of the arbitral tribunal, the terms of reference shall be: "To examine, in the light of the relevant provisions of this Agreement, the matter referred to in the request for the establishment of an arbitral tribunal pursuant to Article 15.7 and to make findings of law and fact together with the reasons therefor for the resolution of the dispute." 3. The findings of the arbitral tribunal shall be binding on the Parties. Article 15.9 Rules of Interpretation 1. The arbitral tribunal shall interpret this Agreement in accordance with customary	statement of claim referred to in Article 20 of the UNCITRAL Arbitration Rules, are received by the respondent; or (d) referred to under any arbitral institution or arbitral rules selected under paragraph 4(d) is received by the respondent, provided that no claim shall be deemed submitted under this Section if that claim is asserted by the claimant for the first time after such notice of arbitration is submitted. 7. A notice of arbitration shall: (a) specify the name and address of the claimant and, where a claim is submitted on behalf of an enterprise of the respondent that is a juridical person that the claimant owns or controls directly or indirectly, the name, address, and place of incorporation of the enterprise; (b) for each claim, identify the provision of this Chapter alleged to have been breached and any other relevant provisions; (c) for each claim, identify the measure or event giving rise to the claim; (d) for each claim, indicate whether the claim is made on the claimant's own behalf or on behalf of an enterprise; (e) for each claim, provide a brief summary of the legal and factual basis sufficient to present the problem clearly; and (f) specify the relief sought, the approximate amount of damages claimed and its standard or basis for calculation. 8. The claimant shall provide with the notice of arbitration: (a) the name of the arbitrator that the claimant appoints; or

Bilateral Dispute Settlement Provisions	Investment Dispute Settlement (ISDS) Provisions
rules of interpretation of public international law, including as reflected in the Vienna Convention on the Law of Treaties, done at Vienna on 23 May 1969. 2. The arbitral tribunal shall have regard to any relevant interpretation established in rulings and recommendations of the WTO Dispute Settlement Body. 3. The rulings and recommendations of the arbitral tribunal cannot add to or diminish the rights and obligations provided for in this Agreement. Article 15.10 Rules of Procedure of an Arbitral Tribunal 1. Unless the Parties otherwise agree, the arbitral tribunal shall follow the model rules of procedure set out in Annex 15-B. 2. The arbitral tribunal may, after consulting with the Parties, adopt additional rules of procedure not inconsistent with the model rules. Article 15.11 Suspension or Termination of Proceedings 1. The Parties may agree that the arbitral tribunal suspend its work at any time for a period not exceeding 12 months from the date of such agreement. Within this period, the tribunal shall resume its work if requested by either Party. If the work of the arbitral tribunal has been suspended for more than 12 months, the authority for establishment of the tribunal shall lapse, unless the Parties otherwise agree. 2. The Parties may agree to terminate the proceedings of the arbitral tribunal in the event that a mutually satisfactory solution to the dispute has been found. In such event the Parties shall jointly notify the Chair of the arbitral tribunal. 3 Before the arbitral tribunal presents its final report, it may at any stage of the	(b) the claimant's written consent for the Secretary-General to appoint that arbitrator. 9. The arbitration rules applicable under paragraph 4, and in effect on the date the claim or claims were submitted to arbitration under this Section, shall govern the arbitration except to the extent modified by this Agreement and the Side Letter on Transparency Rules Applicable to ISDS. Article 9.13 Consent of Each Party To Arbitration 1. Each Party consents to the submission of a claim to arbitration under this Section in accordance with this Agreement. Failure to meet any of the conditions and limitations provided for in Article 9.12.4 shall nullify that consent. 2. The consent under paragraph 1 and the submission of a claim to arbitration under this Section shall satisfy the requirements of Chapter II of the ICSID Convention (Jurisdiction of the Centre) and the ICSID Additional Facility Rules for written consent of the parties to the dispute. Article 9.14 Conditions and Limitations on Consent of Each Party 1. No claim may be submitted to arbitration under this Section if more than three years have elapsed from the date on which the claimant first acquired, or should have first acquired, knowledge of the breach alleged under Article 9.12.2 and knowledge that the claimant (for claims brought under Article 9.12.2(a)) or the enterprise (for claims brought under Article 9.12.2(b)) has incurred loss or damage. In no event may a claim be submitted to arbitration under this Section after four years since the occurrence of the measures and/or events giving rise to the breach alleged under Article 9.12.2.

Bilateral Dispute Settlement Provisions	Investment Dispute Settlement (ISDS) Provisions
proceedings propose to the Parties that the dispute be settled amicably. Article 15.12 Report of The Arbitral Tribunal 1. In order to enable the Parties to have an opportunity for review and comment, the arbitral tribunal shall present the Parties with its initial report within 90 days of appointment of the final arbitrator setting out its findings of facts, its reasoning, and its determination as to whether: (a) the measure at issue is inconsistent with the obligations of this Agreement; (b) a Party has otherwise failed to carry out its obligations under this Agreement. 2. The arbitral tribunal shall base its report on the relevant provisions of this Agreement, the submissions and arguments of the Parties and any information or technical advice it has obtained in accordance with its rules of procedure. The arbitral tribunal may also, on the joint request of the Parties, suggest ways in which the Party complained against could implement the recommendations. 3. In exceptional cases, if the arbitral tribunal considers it cannot present its initial report within 90 days, it shall inform the Parties in writing of the reasons for the delay, together with an estimate of the period within which it will issue its report. Any delay shall not exceed a further period of 30 days, unless the Parties otherwise agree. 4. Each Party may submit written comments to the arbitral tribunal within 10 days of the presentation of the initial report. After considering these written comments by the Parties and making any further examination it considers appropriate, the arbitral tribunal shall present the Parties its final report within 30 days of presentation of the initial report, unless the Parties otherwise agree.	2. No claim may be submitted to arbitration under this Section unless: (a) the claimant has complied with the rules and procedures set forth in Articles 9.12.1 and 9.12.2; (b) the claim has been explicitly included in the request for consultations submitted by the claimant in accordance with Article 9.11.1; (c) the claimant consents in writing to arbitration in accordance with the procedures set out in this Agreement; and, (d) the notice of arbitration is accompanied, (i) for claims submitted to arbitration under Article 9.12.2(a), by the claimant's written waiver, and (ii) for claims submitted to arbitration under Article 9.12.2(b), by the claimant's and the enterprise's written waivers, and written waiver by all persons through which the claimant owns or controls the enterprise, of any right to initiate or continue before any administrative tribunal or court under the law of either Party, or other dispute settlement procedures, any proceeding with respect to any measure or event alleged to constitute a breach referred to in Article 9.12.2. 3. Notwithstanding paragraph 2(d)(ii), a waiver from the enterprise shall not be required only if the respondent has deprived the claimant of its control of the enterprise and the claimant is unable to provide such a waiver as a result. 4. Notwithstanding paragraph 2(d), the claimant (for claims brought under Article 9.12.2(a)) and the claimant or the enterprise (for claims brought under Article 9.12.2(b)) may, in accordance with the laws of the respondent, initiate or continue an action that seeks interim injunctive relief and does not involve the payment of monetary damages before a judicial or administrative tribunal of the respondent, provided that the action is brought for the sole purpose of preserving the claimant's or the enterprise's rights and interests during the pendency of the arbitration.

Bilateral Dispute Settlement Provisions	Investment Dispute Settlement (ISDS) Provisions
5. The final report of the arbitral tribunal shall be made available to the public within 10 days from the date of its presentation to the Parties. Article 15.13 Implementation of The Final Report 1. Where the arbitral tribunal makes a finding that a measure is inconsistent with this Agreement, or that a Party has otherwise failed to carry out its obligations under this Agreement, the Party complained against shall bring the measure into conformity with this Agreement. 2. Within 30 days of the presentation of the final report of the arbitral tribunal to the Parties, the Party complained against shall inform the complaining Party of its intentions with respect to implementation of the findings of the arbitral tribunal. If it is impracticable to comply immediately with the findings, the Party complained against shall have a reasonable period of time in which to do so. Article 15.14 Reasonable Period of Time 1. The reasonable period of time shall be mutually determined by the Parties. Where the Parties fail to agree on the reasonable period of time within 45 days of the presentation of the arbitral tribunal's final report, either Party may refer the matter to the original arbitral tribunal, to the extent this is possible, which shall determine the reasonable period of time. 2. The arbitral tribunal shall provide its determination to the Parties within 30 days after the date of the referral of the matter to it. Prior to making its determination, the arbitral tribunal shall seek written submissions from the Parties and, if requested by either Party, hold a meeting with the Parties where each will be given an opportunity to present its submission. As a guideline, the reasonable period of time should not exceed 15 months from the date of the issuance of the arbitral tribunal's final	Article 9.15 Constitution of The Tribunal 1. Unless the disputing parties have agreed to appoint a sole arbitrator, the tribunal shall comprise three arbitrators, one arbitrator appointed by each of the disputing parties and the third, who shall be the chairperson, appointed by agreement of the disputing parties. 2. The Secretary-General shall serve as appointing authority for an arbitration under this Section. 3. If the disputing parties agree to appoint a sole arbitrator, the disputing parties shall seek to agree on the sole arbitrator. If they fail to do so within 90 days of the day on which the respondent gave its agreement to submit the dispute to a sole arbitrator, the sole arbitrator shall be drawn by the appointing authority on the request of a disputing party from the list of chairpersons established pursuant to paragraph 5 below. 4. If a tribunal has not been constituted within 90 days from the date that a claim is submitted to arbitration under this Section, the appointing authority, on the request of a disputing party, shall appoint, in his or her discretion, the remaining arbitrators from the list established pursuant to paragraph 5 below. 5. The Committee on Investment shall, no later than 2 years after the entry into force of this Agreement, establish a list of individuals who are willing and able to serve as arbitrators. The Committee on Investment shall ensure that at all times the list includes at least 20 individuals. 6. For purpose of the list referred to in paragraph 5, each Party shall select at least five individuals to serve as arbitrators. The Parties shall also jointly select at least 10 individuals who are not nationals of either Party to act as chairperson of the tribunals.

Bilateral Dispute Settlement Provisions	Investment Dispute Settlement (ISDS) Provisions
report. However, that time may be shorter or longer depending upon the particular circumstances. 3. When the arbitral tribunal considers that it cannot provide its determination within this timeframe, it shall inform the Parties in writing of the reasons for the delay together with an estimate of the period within which it will provide its determination. Any delay shall not exceed a further period of 15 days, unless the Parties otherwise agree. Article 15.15 Compliance Review 1. Where the Parties disagree on the existence or consistency with this Agreement of measures taken to comply with the obligations in Article 15.13.1, such dispute shall be referred to an arbitral tribunal under this Chapter, including wherever possible by resort to the original arbitral tribunal. 2. Such request may only be made after: (a) the expiry of the reasonable period of time; or (b) the Party complained against has given written notification to the complaining Party that it has complied with the obligations in Article 15.13.1. 3. The arbitral tribunal convened under this Article shall reconvene as soon as possible after the delivery of the request and shall issue its final report on the matter within 60 days of the date of delivery of the written notification. 4. The arbitral tribunal shall make an objective assessment of the matter before it, including an objective assessment of: (a) the facts of any implementation action taken by the Party complained	7. In the event that the Secretary-General is required to appoint an arbitrator or arbitrators under paragraph 3 or 4, and the list referred to in paragraph 5 has not been established, the Secretary-General shall appoint, in his or her discretion, the arbitrator or arbitrators not yet appointed. The Secretary-General shall not appoint a national of either Party as the presiding arbitrator unless the disputing parties otherwise agree. 8. All arbitrators appointed pursuant to this Section shall have expertise or experience in public international law, international trade or international investment rules, or the resolution of disputes arising under international trade or international investment agreements. They shall be independent, serve in their individual capacities and not take instructions from any organisation or government with regard to matters related to the dispute, or be affiliated with the government of either Party or any disputing party, and shall comply with Annex 9-A. Arbitrators who serve on the list established pursuant to paragraph 5 shall not, for that reason alone, be deemed to be affiliated with the government of either Party. 9. For purposes of Article 39 of the ICSID Convention and Article 7 of Schedule C to the ICSID Additional Facility Rules, and without prejudice to an objection to an arbitrator on a ground other than nationality: (a) the respondent agrees to the appointment of each individual member of a tribunal established under the ICSID Convention or the ICSID Additional Facility Rules; (b) a claimant referred to in Article 9.12.2(a) may submit a claim to arbitration under this Section, or continue a claim, under the ICSID Convention or the ICSID Additional Facility Rules, only on condition that the claimant agrees in writing to the appointment of each individual member of the tribunal; and (c) a claimant referred to in Article 9.12.2(b) may submit a claim to arbitration under this Section, or continue a claim, under the ICSID Convention or the ICSID

Bilateral Dispute Settlement Provisions	Investment Dispute Settlement (ISDS) Provisions
against to comply with the obligations in Article 15.13.1; and (b) whether the Party complained against has complied with the obligations in Article 15.13.1, and set out its findings on both elements in its report. Article 15.16 Compensation and Suspension of Concessions and Obligations 1. If the Party complained against: (a) fails to comply with the findings of the arbitral tribunal within the reasonable period of time; (b) expresses in writing that it will not comply with the findings of the arbitral tribunal, or (c) has been found through the compliance review process set out in Article 15.15 to have not complied with the obligations in Article 15.13.1, that Party shall, if so requested, enter into negotiations with the complaining Party with a view to reaching a mutually satisfactory agreement on any necessary compensation. 2. If the Parties do not reach agreement on compensation in accordance with paragraph 1 within 20 days, the complaining Party may provide written notification to the Party complained against that it intends to suspend the application to the Party complained against of concessions and obligations under this Agreement of equivalent effect to the level of non-conformity that the arbitral tribunal has found. The notification shall specify the level of concessions or other obligations that the complaining Party proposes to suspend. 3. The complaining Party may begin suspending concessions and obligations 30 days after it provides notification of its intention to suspend, or after an arbitral tribunal	Additional Facility Rules, only on condition that the claimant and the enterprise agree in writing to the appointment of each individual member of the tribunal. Article 9.16 Conduct of The Arbitration 1. The disputing parties may agree on the legal place of any arbitration under the arbitral rules applicable under Article 9.12.4. If the disputing parties fail to reach agreement, the tribunal shall determine the place in accordance with the applicable arbitral rules. 2. The non-disputing Party may make oral and written submissions to the tribunal regarding the interpretation of this Chapter. 3. With the written agreement of the disputing parties, the tribunal may allow a party or entity that is not a disputing party to file a written amicus curiae submission with the tribunal regarding a matter within the scope of the dispute. In determining whether to allow such a filing, the tribunal shall consider, among other things, the extent to which: (a) the amicus curiae submission would assist the tribunal in the determination of a factual or legal issue related to the proceeding by bringing a perspective, particular knowledge, or insight that is different from that of the disputing parties; (b) the amicus curiae submission would address a matter within the scope of the dispute; and (c) the amicus curiae has a significant interest in the proceeding. 4. Each submission in accordance with paragraph 3 of this Article shall identify the author, disclose any affiliation, direct or indirect, with any disputing party, and

Bilateral Dispute Settlement Provisions	Investment Dispute Settlement (ISDS) Provisions
issues its determination under paragraph 6. 4. Any suspension of concessions and obligations shall be restricted to benefits accruing to the other Party under this Agreement. 5. In considering what concessions and obligations to suspend in accordance with paragraph 2, the complaining Party shall apply the following principles: (a) the complaining Party should first seek to suspend concessions and obligations in the same sector(s) as that affected by the measure that the arbitral tribunal has found to be inconsistent with the obligations of this Agreement; and (b) if the complaining Party considers that it is not practicable or effective to suspend concessions and obligations in the same sector(s), it may suspend concessions and obligations in other sectors. The communication in which it announces such a decision shall indicate the reasons on which it is based. 6. If the Party complained against objects to the level of suspension proposed, or considers that the principles set out in paragraph 5 have not been applied, it may make a written request to reconvene the original arbitral tribunal to examine the matter. The arbitral tribunal shall determine whether the level of concessions and obligations to be suspended by the complaining Party in accordance with paragraph 2 is equivalent to the level of non-conformity. If the arbitral tribunal cannot be established with its original arbitrators, the proceeding set out in Article 15.7 shall be applied. 7. The arbitral tribunal shall present its determination within 60 days of the request made in accordance with paragraph 6 or, if an arbitral tribunal cannot be established with its original arbitrators, from the date on which the last arbitrator is designated. The determination of the arbitral tribunal shall be final and binding and shall be made publicly available.	identify any person, government, or other entity that has provided, or will provide, any financial or other assistance in preparing the submission. Each submission shall be in a language of the arbitration, and comply with any page limits and deadlines set by the tribunal. The tribunal shall ensure that the amicus curiae submission does not disrupt the proceeding or unduly burden or unfairly prejudice either disputing party, and that the disputing parties are given an opportunity to present their observations on the amicus curiae submission. 5. Without prejudice to a tribunal's authority to address other objections as a preliminary question, a tribunal shall address and decide as a preliminary question any objection by the respondent that, as a matter of law, a claim submitted is not a claim for which an award in favour of the claimant may be made under Article 9.12. (a) Such objection shall be submitted to the tribunal as soon as possible after the tribunal is constituted, and in no event later than the date the tribunal fixes for the respondent to submit its counter-memorial. (b) On receipt of an objection under this paragraph, the tribunal shall suspend any proceedings on the merits, establish a schedule for considering the objection consistent with any schedule it has established for considering any other preliminary question, and issue a decision or award on the objection, stating the grounds therefor. (c) In deciding an objection under this paragraph, the tribunal shall assume to be true claimant's factual allegations in support of any claim in the notice of arbitration and, in disputes brought under the UNCITRAL Arbitration Rules, the statement of claim referred to in Article 20 of the UNCITRAL Arbitration Rules. The tribunal may also consider any relevant facts not in dispute. (d) The respondent does not waive any objection as to competence or any argument on the merits merely because the respondent did or did not raise an objection under this paragraph or make use of the expedited procedure set out

Bilateral Dispute Settlement Provisions	Investment Dispute Settlement (ISDS) Provisions
8. The suspension of concessions and obligations shall be temporary and shall only be applied until such time as the measure found to be inconsistent with this Agreement has been removed, or a mutually satisfactory solution is reached. Article 15.17 Post Suspension Review 1. Where the right to suspend concessions and obligations has been exercised in accordance with Article 15.16, if the Party complained against considers that it has complied with its obligations in Article 15.13.1, it may provide written notice to the complaining Party with a description of how it has complied. If the complaining Party disagrees, it may refer the matter to the original arbitral tribunal within 30 days after receipt of such written notice. If the arbitral tribunal cannot be established with its original arbitrators, the proceeding set out in Article 15.7 shall be applied. Otherwise, the complaining Party shall promptly stop the suspension of concessions and obligations. 2. The arbitral tribunal shall release its report within 60 days after the referral of the matter. If the arbitral tribunal concludes that the Party complained against has eliminated the non-conformity, the complaining Party shall promptly stop the suspension of concessions and obligations.	in paragraph 6. 6. In the event that the respondent so requests within 45 days after the tribunal is constituted, the tribunal shall decide on an expedited basis an objection under paragraph 5 and any objection that the dispute is not within the tribunal's competence. The tribunal shall suspend any proceedings on the merits and issue a decision or award on the objection(s), stating the grounds therefor, no later than 150 days after the date of the request. However, if a disputing party requests a hearing, the tribunal may take an additional 30 days to issue the decision or award. Regardless of whether a hearing is requested, a tribunal may, on a showing of extraordinary cause, delay issuing its decision or award by an additional brief period, which may not exceed 30 days. 7. When it decides a respondent's objection under paragraph 5 or 6, the tribunal may, if warranted, award to the prevailing disputing party reasonable costs and attorney's fees incurred in submitting or opposing the objection. In determining whether such an award is warranted, the tribunal shall consider whether either the claimant's claim or the respondent's objection was frivolous, and shall provide the disputing parties a reasonable opportunity to comment. 8. A respondent may not assert as a defence, counterclaim, right of set-off, or for any other reason that the claimant or the enterprise referred to in Article 9.12.2(b) has received or will receive indemnification or other compensation for all or part of the alleged damages pursuant to an indemnity, guarantee or insurance contract. Article 9.17 Transparency of Arbitral Proceedings 1. Subject to paragraphs 3, 4 and 5, the respondent shall, after receiving the following documents, promptly transmit them to the non-disputing Party: (a) the request for consultations;

Bilateral Dispute Settlement Provisions	Investment Dispute Settlement (ISDS) Provisions
	(b) the notice of arbitration; (c) pleadings, memorials, and briefs submitted to the tribunal by a disputing party and any written submissions submitted pursuant to Article 9.21; (d) minutes or transcripts of hearings of the tribunal, where available; and (e) orders, awards, and decisions of the tribunal. 2. Subject to paragraphs 3, 4 and 5, the respondent: (a) shall make the documents referred to in paragraph 1 (a), (b) and (e) available to the public; (b) may make the documents referred to in paragraph 1(c) and (d) available to the public; (c) may make any written submissions submitted pursuant to Article 9.16.2 available to the public provided that prior consent is obtained from the non-disputing Party. 3. With the agreement of the respondent, the tribunal shall conduct hearings open to the public and shall determine, in consultation with the disputing parties, the appropriate logistical arrangements. However, any disputing party that intends to use information designated as protected information in a hearing shall so advise the tribunal. The tribunal shall make appropriate arrangements to protect the information from disclosure. 4. Nothing in this Section requires a respondent to disclose protected information or to furnish or allow access to information that it may withhold in accordance with Article 16.1 (Disclosure and Confidentiality of Information) or Article 16.3 (Security Exceptions) of Chapter 16 (General Provisions and Exceptions).

Bilateral Dispute Settlement Provisions	Investment Dispute Settlement (ISDS) Provisions
	5. Any protected information that is submitted to the tribunal shall be protected from disclosure in accordance with the following procedures: (a) Neither the disputing parties nor the tribunal shall disclose to the nondisputing Party or to the public any protected information where the disputing party that provided the information clearly designates it in accordance with subparagraph (b); (b) Any disputing party claiming that certain information constitutes protected information shall clearly designate the information at the time it is submitted to the tribunal; (c) A disputing party shall, within 7 days after it submits a document containing information claimed to be protected information, submit a redacted version of the document that does not contain the information. Only the redacted version may be provided to the non-disputing Party and made public in accordance with paragraphs 1 and 2. Article 9.18 Governing Law 1. Subject to paragraphs 2 and 3, when a claim is submitted under Article 9.12, the tribunal shall decide the issues in dispute in accordance with this Agreement as interpreted in accordance with customary rules of treaty interpretation of public international law, as codified in the Vienna Convention on the Law of Treaties done at Vienna on 23 May 1969. Where relevant and appropriate, the tribunal shall also take into consideration the law of the respondent. 2. A joint decision of the Parties, acting through the Committee on Investment, declaring their interpretation of a provision of this Agreement shall be binding on a tribunal of any ongoing or subsequent dispute, and any decision or award issued by such a tribunal must be consistent with that joint decision.

Bilateral Dispute Settlement Provisions	Investment Dispute Settlement (ISDS) Provisions
	3. A decision between the respondent and the non-disputing Party that a measure is of the kind described in Article 9.11.4 shall be binding on a tribunal and any decision or award issued by a tribunal must be consistent with that decision. Article 9.19 Interpretation Of Annexes 1. Where a respondent asserts as a defence that the measure alleged to be a breach is within the scope of an entry set out in Section A or B of its Schedule of NonConforming Measures in Annex III, the tribunal shall, on request of the respondent, request the interpretation of the Parties on the issue. The Parties shall submit in writing any joint decision declaring their interpretation to the tribunal within 90 days of delivery of the tribunal's request. 2. A joint decision issued under paragraph 1 by the Parties, acting through the Committee on Investment, shall be binding on the tribunal, and any decision or award issued by the tribunal must be consistent with that joint decision. If the Parties fail to issue such a decision within 90 days, the tribunal shall decide the issue. In such a case, the tribunal shall draw no inference from the fact that the Parties fail to issue such a decision. 3. A joint decision issued under paragraph 1 by the Parties shall also be binding on the tribunal of any dispute subsequent to the date of the joint decision to the extent applicable and not modified by another joint decision issued pursuant to paragraph 1 subsequent to the first said joint decision. Article 9.20 Expert Reports Without prejudice to the appointment of other kinds of experts where authorised by the applicable arbitration rules, a tribunal, at the request of a disputing party or, unless the disputing parties disapprove, on its own initiative, may appoint one or

Bilateral Dispute Settlement Provisions	Investment Dispute Settlement (ISDS) Provisions
	more experts to report to it in writing on any factual issue concerning environmental, health, safety, or other scientific matters raised by a disputing party in a proceeding, subject to such terms and conditions as the disputing parties may agree. Article 9.21 Consolidation 1. Where two or more claims have been submitted separately to arbitration under Article 9.12.2 and the claims have a question of law or fact in common and arise out of the same events or circumstances, any disputing party may seek a consolidation order in accordance with the agreement of all the disputing parties sought to be covered by the order or the terms of paragraphs 2 through 11. 2. A disputing party that seeks a consolidation order under this Article shall deliver, in writing, a request to the Secretary-General and to all the disputing parties sought to be covered by the order and shall specify in the request: (a) the names and addresses of all the disputing parties sought to be covered by the order; (b) the nature of the order sought; and (c) the grounds on which the order is sought. 3. Unless the Secretary-General finds within 30 days after receiving a request under paragraph 2 that the request is manifestly unfounded, a tribunal shall be established under this Article. 4. Unless all the disputing parties sought to be covered by the order otherwise agree, a tribunal established under this Article shall comprise three arbitrators: (a) one arbitrator appointed by agreement of the claimants;

Bilateral Dispute Settlement Provisions	Investment Dispute Settlement (ISDS) Provisions
	(b) one arbitrator appointed by the respondent; and (c) the presiding arbitrator appointed by the Secretary-General from the list of chairpersons established pursuant to Article 9.15.5. 5. If, within 60 days after the Secretary-General receives a request made under paragraph 2, the respondent fails or the claimants fail to appoint an arbitrator in accordance with paragraph 4, the Secretary-General, on the request of any disputing party sought to be covered by the order, shall appoint the arbitrator or arbitrators not yet appointed from the list of arbitrations established pursuant to Article 9.15.5. 6. In the event that the Secretary-General is required to appoint an arbitrator or arbitrators under paragraph 4 or 5, and the list referred to in Article 9.15.5 has not been established, the Secretary-General shall appoint, in his or her discretion, the arbitrator or arbitrators not yet appointed. The Secretary-General shall not appoint a national of either Party as the presiding arbitrator unless the disputing parties otherwise agree. 7. Where a tribunal established under this Article is satisfied that two or more claims that have been submitted to arbitration under Article 9.12.2 have a question of law or fact in common, and arise out of the same events or circumstances, the tribunal may, in the interest of fair and efficient resolution of the claims, and after hearing the disputing parties, by order: (a) assume jurisdiction over, and hear and determine together, all or part of the claims; (b) assume jurisdiction over, and hear and determine one or more of the claims, the determination of which it believes would assist in the resolution of the others; or

Bilateral Dispute Settlement Provisions	Investment Dispute Settlement (ISDS) Provisions
	(c) instruct a tribunal previously established under Article 9.15 to assume jurisdiction over, and hear and determine together, all or part of the claims, provided that (i) that tribunal, at the request of any claimant not previously a disputing party before that tribunal, shall be reconstituted with its original members, except that the arbitrator for the claimants shall be appointed pursuant to paragraphs 4(a), 5 and 6; and (ii) that tribunal shall decide whether any prior hearing shall be repeated. 8. Where a tribunal has been established under this Article, a claimant that has submitted a claim to arbitration under Article 9.12.2 and that has not been named in a request made under paragraph 2 may make a written request to the tribunal that it be included in any order made under paragraph 7, and shall specify in the request: (a) the name and address of the claimant; (b) the nature of the order sought; and (c) the grounds on which the order is sought. The claimant shall deliver a copy of its request to the Secretary-General. 9. A tribunal established under this Article shall conduct its proceedings in accordance with the UNCITRAL Arbitration Rules, except as modified by this Agreement and the Side Letter on Transparency Rules Applicable to ISDS. 10. A tribunal established under Article 9.15 shall not have jurisdiction to decide a claim, or a part of a claim, over which a tribunal established or instructed under this Article has assumed jurisdiction. 11. On application of a disputing party, a tribunal established under this Article, - 105 - pending its decision under paragraph 7, may order that the proceedings of a tribunal established under Article 9.15 be stayed, unless the latter tribunal has

Bilateral Dispute Settlement Provisions	Investment Dispute Settlement (ISDS) Provisions
	already adjourned its proceedings. Article 9.22 Awards 1. Where a tribunal makes an award against a respondent, the tribunal may award, separately or in combination, only: (a) monetary damages and any applicable interest; and (b) restitution of property, in which case the award shall provide that the respondent may pay monetary damages and any applicable interest in lieu of restitution. 2. A tribunal may also award costs and attorney's fees in accordance with this Section and the applicable arbitration rules. 3. Subject to paragraph 1, where a claim is submitted to arbitration under Article 9.12.2(b): (a) an award of restitution of property shall provide that restitution be made to the enterprise; (b) an award of monetary damages and any applicable interest shall provide that the sum be paid to the enterprise; and (c) the award shall provide that it is made without prejudice to any right that any person may have in the relief under applicable laws and regulations provided that such relief does not grant or result in duplicated remedies to any person in light of the award rendered. 4. A tribunal may not award punitive damages.

Bilateral Dispute Settlement Provisions	Investment Dispute Settlement (ISDS) Provisions
	5. An award made by a tribunal shall have no binding force except between the disputing parties and in respect of the particular case. 6. Subject to paragraph 7, a disputing party shall abide by and comply with an award without delay. 7. A disputing party may not seek enforcement of an award until: (a) in the case of a final award made under the ICSID Convention: (i) 120 days have elapsed from the date the award was rendered and no disputing party has requested revision or annulment of the award; or (ii) revision or annulment proceedings have been completed; and (b) in the case of an award made under the ICSID Additional Facility Rules, the UNCITRAL Arbitration Rules, or the rules selected pursuant to Article 9.12.4(d), (i) 90 days have elapsed from the date the award was rendered and no disputing party has commenced a proceeding to revise, set aside, or annul the award; or (ii) a court has dismissed or allowed an application to revise, set aside, or annul the award and there is no further appeal. 8. Each Party shall provide for the enforcement of an award in its territory. Article 9.23 Appellate Review[2)] Within three years after the date of entry into force of this Agreement, the Parties shall commence negotiations with a view to establishing an appellate mechanism to review awards rendered under Article 9.22 in arbitrations commenced after any such appellate mechanism is established. Any such appellate mechanism would hear appeals on questions of law.

Bilateral Dispute Settlement Provisions	Investment Dispute Settlement (ISDS) Provisions
	Article 9.24 Annexes and Footnotes The Annexes and footnotes shall form an integral part of this Agreement. Article 9.25 Service of Documents Delivery of notice and other documents on a Party shall be made to the place named for that Party in Annex 9-B.

* Entered into force on December 20, 2015.

1) *Many other agreements include a subparagraph noting that parties should go through consultations before filing a ISDS case. However, the provision in this agreement is unique to have established a specific procedure ane requirements for consultation.*

2) *This provision is unique to China-Australia FTA.*

Appendix II

List of Investment Disputes Involving East Asian Countries (as of May 2020)

1. Japan

1.1 Japan as home State

No.	Year of Initiation	Short case name	Summary	Outcome of original proceedings	Respondent State	Home State of investor
1	2016	Eurus Energy v. Spain	Investment: Investments in a renewable energy generation enterprise. Summary: Claims arising out of a series of energy reforms undertaken by the Government affecting the renewables sector, including a 7 per cent tax on power generators' revenues and a reduction in subsidies for renewable energy producers.	Pending	Spain	Japan Netherlands
2	2015	JGC v. Spain	Investment: Shareholding in two solar thermal power plants in Cordoba, Spain. Summary: Claims arising out of a series of energy reforms undertaken by the Government affecting the renewables sector, including a 7 per cent tax on power generators' revenues and a reduction in subsidies for renewable energy producers.	Pending	Spain	Japan

2. Korea

2.1 Korea as home state*

No.	Year of Initiation	Short case name	Summary	Outcome of original proceedings	Respondent State	Home State of investor
1	2015	Samsung v. Oman	Investment: Deposit in connection with the bid for a refinery improvement project. Summary: Claims arising out of the alleged discriminatory treatment by the State towards the claimant in connection with the bidding process to undertake improvements to the Sohar refinery in northern Oman run by the state-owned Oman Refineries and Petroleum Industries Company (ORPIC) in 2013.	Pending	Oman	Korea, Republic of
2	2014	Ansung Housing v. China	Investment: Capital expenditure of over USD 15 million for the development of a golf and country club in China. Summary: Claims arising out of the provincial government's alleged actions in relation to Ansung's investment in the construction of a golf and country club and condominiums in Sheyang-Xian, Jiangsu province.	Pending	China	Korea, Republic of
3	2013	Beck v. Kyrgyzstan	Investment: Rights under certain lease agreements. Summary: Claims arising out of the alleged expropriation of claimant's investment by terminating certain lease agreements with respect to various land plots to develop a theme park in Bishkek.	Decided in favour of investor	Kyrgyzstan	Korea, Republic of

* http://investmentpolicyhub.unctad.org/ISDS/CountryCases/111?partyRole=1

2.2 Koreas as respondent State*

No.	Year of Initiation	Short case name	Summary	Outcome of original proceedings	Respondent State	Home State of investor
1	2015	Dayyani v. Korea	Investment: Agreement for the acquisition of a majority stake in Daewoo Electronics and 10 per cent down payment of the price. Summary: Claims arising out of Korea Asset Management Corporation's termination of an agreement for the sale of a majority stake in Daewoo Electronics to the claimants' company Entekhab and alleged non-return of the claimants' US$50 million deposit.	Pending	Korea, Republic of	Iran, Islamic Republic of
2	2015	Hanocal and IPIC International v. Korea	Investment: Majority shareholding in Hyundai Oilbank, a petroleum and refinery company based in the city of Seosan. Summary: Claims arising out of the alleged tax levied on the 2010 sale of the claimants' controlling stake in Hyundai Oilbank, a petroleum and refinery company based in the city of Seosan.	Discontinued	Korea, Republic of	Netherlands
3	2012	LSF-KEB v. Korea	Investment: Majority shareholding in a South Korean financial institution; shareholding in Seoul's Star Tower; interests in an engineering and construction manufacturer. Summary: Claims arising out of the alleged failure by Korean regulatory authorities over a period of several years to approve the purchase by third parties of claimant's stake in Korea Exchange Bank, and the alleged imposition of arbitrary capital gains taxes on the sale by Korean tax authorities.	Pending	Korea, Republic of	Belgium Luxembourg

* http://investmentpolicyhub.unctad.org/ISDS/CountryCases/111?partyRole=2

3. China

3.1 China as home State*

No.	Year of Initiation	Short case name	Summary	Outcome of original proceedings	Respondent State	Home State of investor
1	2014	Beijing Urban Construction v. Yemen	Investment: Rights under an agreement concluded between claimant and the Yemeni civil aviation and meteorology authority for the construction of an airport terminal. Summary: Claims arising out of the alleged forced deprivation of claimant's assets and contract concerning a project for the construction of an airport terminal in Sana'a.	Pending	Yemen	China
2	2012	Ping An v. Belgium	Investment: Largest shareholding in the Belgian-Dutch financial institution Fortis. Summary: Claims arising out of the Government's bailout, and subsequent nationalisation and sale to a third party, of the financial institution in which the claimants had invested, in the context of the 2008 financial crisis.	Decided in favour of State	Belgium	China
3	2010	China Heilongjiang v. Mongolia	Investment: Rights under a mining licence. Summary: Claims arising out of the cancellation of licenses held by the claimants in the Tumurtei iron ore mine in 2012.	Pending	Mongolia	China

No.	Year of Initiation	Short case name	Summary	Outcome of original proceedings	Respondent State	Home State of investor
4	2007	Tza Yap Shum v. Peru	Investment: Majority shareholding in a Peruvian company engaged in the purchase and export of fish flour to Asian markets. Summary: Claims arising out of the seizure of the bank account of claimant's enterprise due to tax debt and other alleged actions undertaken by Peruvian tax authorities that resulted in the substantive deprivation of claimant's investment.	Decided in favour of investor	Peru	China

* http://investmentpolicyhub.unctad.org/ISDS/CountryCases/111?partyRole=2

3.2 China as respondent State*

No.	Year of Initiation	Short case name	Summary	Outcome of original proceedings	Respondent State	Home State of investor
1	2014	Ansung Housing v. China	Investment: Capital expenditure of over USD 15 million for the development of a golf and country club in China. Summary: Claims arising out of the provincial government's alleged actions in relation to Ansung's investment in the construction of a golf and country club and condominiums in Sheyang-Xian, Jiangsu province.	Pending	China	Korea, Republic of
2	2011	Ekran v. China	Investment: Rights under a 70 year lease over 900 hectares of land in the Chinese province of Hainan held by Ekran Berhad's local subsidiary. Summary: Claims arising out of the Government's revocation of claimant's subsidiary rights to a leasehold land due to an alleged failure to develop the land as stipulated under local legislation.	Settled	China	Malaysia

* http://investmentpolicyhub.unctad.org/ISDS/CountryCases/111?partyRole=2

Appendix III

List of Trade Disputes Involving East Asian Countries (as of May 2020)

1. Japan

1.1 Japan, cases as complainant

Case N.	RoC	Short title	Summary	Current status	Complaiant	Respondent	Third Parties
DS6	17 May 1995	N/A	United States — Imposition of Import Duties on Automobiles from Japan under Sections 301 and 304 of the Trade act of 1974 Complaint by Japan. On 17 May 1995, Japan requested consultations with the United States alleging that certain import surcharges on automobiles from Japan violated Articles I and II of the GATT 1994.	Settled or terminated (withdrawn, mutually agreed solution) on 19 July 1995.	Japan	US	N/A
DS51	30 July 1996	N/A	Brazil — Certain Automotive Investment Measures Complaint by Japan. On 30 July 1996, Japan requested consultations with Brazil concerning certain automotive investment measures taken by the Brazilian government. Violations of the TRIMs Agreement Article 2, GATT Articles I:1, III:4 and XI:1 as well as the Subsidies Agreement Articles 3, 27.2 and 27.4 are alleged. In addition, Japan made a non-violation claim under GATT Article XXIII:1(b).	In consultations on 30 July 1996	Japan	Brazil	N/A

Case N.	RoC	Short title	Summary	Current status	Complaiant	Respondent	Third Parties
DS55	4 October 1996	Indonesia — Autos	Indonesia — Certain Measures Affecting the Automobile Industry Complaints by the European Communities (WT/DS54), Japan (WT/DS55 and WT/DS64), and the United States (WT/DS59). On 3 October 1996, the EC requested consultations with Indonesia, on 4 October 1996 and 29 November 1996, Japan requested consultations with Indonesia, and on 8 October 1996, the US requested consultations with Indonesia concerning Indonesia's National Car Programme. The EC alleged that the exemption from customs duties and luxury taxes on imports of "national vehicles" and components thereof, and related measures were in violation of Indonesia's obligations under Articles I and III of GATT 1994, Article 2 of the TRIMs Agreement and Article 3 of the SCM Agreement. Japan contended that these measures were in violation of Indonesia's obligations under Articles I:1, III:2, III:4 and X:3(a) of GATT 1994, as well as Articles 2 and 5.4 of the TRIMs Agreement. The US contended that the measures were in violation of Indonesia's obligations under Article I and III of GATT 1994, Article 2 of the TRIMs Agreement, Article 3, 6 and 28 of the SCM Agreement and Articles 3, 20 and 65 of the TRIPS Agreement.	Implementation notified by respondent on 26 July 1999	Japan	Indonesia	India; Korea, Republic of; United States

Case N.	RoC	Short title	Summary	Current status	Complaiant	Respondent	Third Parties
DS64	29 November 1996	Indonesia — Autos	Indonesia — Certain Measures Affecting the Automobile Industry Complaints by the European Communities (WT/DS54), Japan (WT/DS55 and WT/DS64), and the United States (WT/DS59). On 3 October 1996, the EC requested consultations with Indonesia, on 4 October 1996 and 29 November 1996, Japan requested consultations with Indonesia, and on 8 October 1996, the US requested consultations with Indonesia concerning Indonesia's National Car Programme. The EC alleged that the exemption from customs duties and luxury taxes on imports of "national vehicles" and components thereof, and related measures were in violation of Indonesia's obligations under Articles I and III of GATT 1994, Article 2 of the TRIMs Agreement and Article 3 of the SCM Agreement. Japan contended that these measures were in violation of Indonesia's obligations under Articles I:1, III:2, III:4 and X:3(a) of GATT 1994, as well as Articles 2 and 5.4 of the TRIMs Agreement. The US contended that the measures were in violation of Indonesia's obligations under Article I and III of GATT 1994, Article 2 of the TRIMs Agreement, Article 3, 6 and 28 of the SCM Agreement and Articles 3, 20 and 65 of the TRIPS Agreement.	Implementation notified by respondent on 26 July 1999	Japan	Indonesia	India; Korea, Republic of; United States

Case N.	RoC	Short title	Summary	Current status	Complaiant	Respondent	Third Parties
DS95	18 July 1997	US — Procurement	United States — Measure Affecting Government Procurement Complaint by Japan. This request, dated 18 July 1997, is in respect of the same issued raised by the EC in WT/DS88.	Authority for panel lapsed on 11 February 2000	Japan	US	Japan
DS139	3 July 1998	Canada — Autos	Canada — Certain Measures Affecting the Automotive Industry Complaint by Japan. On 3 July 1998, Japan requested consultations with Canada in respect of measures being taken by Canada in the automotive industry. Japan contended that under Canadian legislation implementing an automotive products agreement (Auto Pact) between the US and Canada, only a limited number of motor vehicle manufacturers are eligible to import vehicles into Canada duty free and to distribute the motor vehicles in Canada at the wholesale and retail distribution levels. Japan further contended that this duty-free treatment is contingent on two requirements: i a Canadian value-added (CVA) content requirement that applies to both goods and services; and ii a manufacturing and sales requirement. Japan	Implementation notified by respondent on 12 March 2001	Japan	Canada	India; Korea, Republic of; United States

Case N.	RoC	Short title	Summary	Current status	Complaiant	Respondent	Third Parties
			alleges that these measures are inconsistent with Articles I:1, III:4 and XXIV of GATT 1994, Article 2 of the TRIMs Agreement, Article 3 of the SCM Agreement, and Articles II, VI and XVII of GATS. On 17 August 1998, the EC requested consultations with Canada in respect of the same measures raised by Japan in WT/DS139 and cites the same provisions alleged to be in violation, except for Article XXIV of GATT 1994, which was cited by Japan but is not cited by the EC.				
DS162	10 February 1999	US — 1916 Act (Japan)	United States — Anti-Dumping Act of 1916 Complaint by Japan. (See also DS136) On 10 February 1999, Japan requested consultations with the United States in respect of the US Anti-Dumping Act of 1916, 15 U.S.C. 72 (1994), (US 1916 Act). Japan alleged that the US 1916 Act stipulates that the importation or sale of imported goods within the US market in certain circumstances is unlawful, constituting a criminal offence and inviting civil liability. Japan further alleged that judicial decisions under the US 1916 Act are made without the procedural safeguards provided for in the Anti-Dumping Agreement. Japan stated that a court action had been brought under the US 1916 Act against affiliates of Japanese companies. Japan contended that the US 1916 Act is inconsistent with Articles III, VI and XI of the GATT 1994, and the Anti-Dumping Agreement.	Implementation notified by respondent on 26 November 2004	Japan	US	European Communities; India

Case N.	RoC	Short title	Summary	Current status	Complainant	Respondent	Third Parties
DS184	18 November 1999	US — Hot-Rolled Steel	United States — Anti-Dumping Measures on Certain Hot-Rolled Steel Products from Japan Complaint by Japan. On 18 November 1999, Japan requested consultations with the United States in respect of the preliminary and final determinations of the US Department of Commerce and the US International Trade Commission on the Anti-Dumping investigation of Certain Hot Rolled Steel Products from Japan issued on 25 and 30 November 1998, 12 February 1999, 28 April 1999 and 23 June 1999. Japan considered that these determinations are erroneous and based on deficient procedures under the US Tariff Act of 1930 and related regulations. The Japanese complaint also concerned certain provisions of the Tariff Act of 1930 and related regulations. Japan claimed violations of Articles VI and X of the GATT 1994 and Articles 2, 3, 6 (including Annex II), 9 and 10 of the Anti-Dumping Agreement.	Report(s) adopted, with recommendation to bring measure(s) into conformity on 23 August 2001	Japan	US	Brazil; Canada; Chile; European Communities; Korea, Republic of
DS217	21 December 2000	US — Offset Act (Byrd Amendment)	United States — Continued Dumping and Subsidy Offset Act of 2000 Joint complaint by Australia, Brazil, Chile, European Communities, India, Indonesia, Japan, Korea and Thailand. On 21 December 2000 and 21 May 2001 respectively, the complainants requested consultations with the US concerning the amendment to the Tariff Act of	Authorization to retaliate granted on 26 November 2004	Australia; Brazil; Chile; European Communities; India; Indonesia; Japan; Korea, Republic of; Thailand	US	Argentina; Canada; Costa Rica; Hong Kong, China; Israel; Mexico; Norway

Case N.	RoC	Short title	Summary	Current status	Complaiant	Respondent	Third Parties
			1930 signed on 28 October 2000 with the title of "Continued Dumping and Subsidy Offset Act of 2000" (the "Act") usually referred to as "the Byrd Amendment". According to the complainants the Act is inconsistent with the obligations of the United States under several provisions of the GATT, the AD Agreement, the SCM Agreement, and the WTO Agreement. In particular, the Act is alleged to be inconsistent with the obligations of the United States under: (i) Article 18.1 of the ADA in conjunction with Article VI:2 of the GATT and Article 1 of the ADA; (ii) Article 32.1 of the SCM Agreement, in conjunction with Article VI:3 of the GATT and Articles 4.10, 7.9 and 10 of the SCM Agreement; (iii) Article X(3)(a) of the GATT; (iv) Article 5.4 of the ADA and Article 11.4 of the SCM Agreement; (v) Article 8 of the ADA and Article 18 of the SCM Agreement; (vi) Article 5 of the SCM Agreement; and (vii) Article XVI:4 of the Marrakesh Agreement establishing the WTO, Article 18.4 of the ADA and Article 32.5 of the SCM Agreement.				
DS244	30 January 2002	US — Corrosion-Resistant Steel Sunset Review	United States — Sunset Review of Anti-Dumping Duties on Corrosion-Resistant Carbon Steel Flat Products from Japan Complaint by Japan. On 30 January 2002, Japan requested consultations with the United States in respect of the final determinations of both the United States Department of Commerce (DOC) and the United	Report(s) adopted, no further action required on 9 January 2004	Japan	US	Brazil; Canada; Chile; European Communities; India; Korea, Republic of; Norway

Case N.	RoC	Short title	Summary	Current status	Complaiant	Respondent	Third Parties
			States International Trade Commission in the full sunset review of the Anti-Dumping duties imposed on imports of corrosion-resistant carbon steel flat products from Japan. These determinations were issued on 2 August 2000 and 21 November 2000, respectively. • Japan claimed that these determinations were erroneous and based on deficient rulings, procedures and provisions pertaining to the United States Tariff Act of 1930, as amended (the Act) and related regulations. • Japan further claimed that the procedures and provisions of the Act and related regulations as well as the above determinations were inconsistent with, inter alia, Articles VI and X of GATT 1994; Articles 2, 3, 5, 6 (including Annex II), 11, 12, and 18.4 of the Anti-Dumping Agreement; and Article XVI:4 of the WTO Agreement.				
DS249	20 March 2002	US — Steel Safeguards	United States — Definitive Safeguard Measures on Imports of Certain Steel Products On 20 March 2002, Japan (WT/DS249) requested consultations with the United States also with regard to the definitive safeguard measures imposed by the US on the imports of certain steel products and claimed violations of Articles 2.1, 2.2, 3.1, 3.2, 4.1, 4.2, 5.1, 7.1, 7.4. 8.1, 12.1, 12.2, 12.3 of the Agreement on Safeguards and Articles I:1, II, X:3, XIII and XIX:2 of GATT 1994. On 27 March, Norway requested to join	Report(s) adopted, no further action required on 10 December 2003	Japan	US	Brazil; Canada; China; Chinese Taipei; European Communities; Korea, Republic of; Mexico; New Zealand; Norway; Switzerland; Thailand; Turkey;

Case N.	RoC	Short title	Summary	Current status	Complaiant	Respondent	Third Parties
			the consultations. On 5 April, Mexico requested to join the consultations. On 9 April 2002, New Zealand requested to join the consultations. The US informed the DSB that it had accepted the requests of Mexico, New Zealand and Norway to join the consultations.				Venezuela, Bolivarian Republic of
DS322	24 November 2004	US — Zeroing (Japan)	United States — Measures Relating to Zeroing and Sunset Reviews Complaint by Japan. On 24 November 2004, Japan requested consultations with the United States concerning (1) the USDOC's "zeroing" practice in Anti-Dumping investigations, administrative reviews, sunset reviews, and also in assessing the final Anti-Dumping duty liability on entries upon liquidation; (2) the USDOC's "irrefutable presumption" in sunset reviews; and (3) the waiver provisions of US law, which, in sunset reviews, oblige the USDOC, in certain situations, to find a likelihood of continuation or recurrence of dumping without performing a substantive review. According to the request for consultations from Japan, the US violates its WTO obligations with respect to the following measures: • the Tariff Act of 1930, in particular, sections 731, 751, 752, 771(7), 771(35)(A), 771(35)(B) and 777A(d); • the Statement of Administrative Action that accompanied the Uruguay Round Agreements Act;	Report(s) adopted, with recommendation to bring measure(s) into conformity on 12 September 2012	Japan	US	Argentina; China; European Communities; Hong Kong, China; India; Korea, Republic of; Mexico; New Zealand; Norway; Chinese Taipei; Thailand

Case N.	RoC	Short title	Summary	Current status	Complaiant	Respondent	Third Parties
			• the USDOC implementing regulations, 19 C.F.R. section 351, in particular sections 351.218 and 351.414; • the Import Administration Anti dumping Manual, including the computer program(s) to which it refers; — the USDOC's Policy Bulletin 98.3 (Sunset Policy Bulletin); • the methodology of the United States for determining dumping margins and material injury in anti dumping investigations; • the methodology of the United States for determining dumping margins in administrative reviews; and • the methodology of the United States, in sunset reviews, for determining whether revocation of Anti-Dumping orders would be likely to lead to continuation or recurrence of dumping, and continuation or recurrence of material injury within a reasonably foreseeable time. Japan wishes to consult with the United States not only on the above-mentioned measures "as such", but also on the applications of these measures in 16 specific instances. Japan considers that these US measures are inconsistent with, inter alia, Articles 1, 2.1, 2.4, 2.4.2, 3, 5.8, 6.1, 6.2, 9, 11, 18.3 and 18.4 of the Anti-Dumping Agreement; Articles VI:1 and VI:2 of the GATT; and Article XVI:4 of the WTO Agreement.				

Case N.	RoC	Short title	Summary	Current status	Complainant	Respondent	Third Parties
DS376	28 May 2008	EC — IT Products	European Communities and its Member States — Tariff Treatment of Certain Information Technology Products Complaint by Japan. (See DS375 and DS377) On 28 May 2008, Japan requested consultations with the European Communities and its member States with respect to their tariff treatment of certain information technology products. Japan claimed that the tariff treatment the European Communities and its member States accord to certain information technology products does not respect their commitments to provide duty-free treatment for these products under the Information Technology Agreement (ITA). According to Japan , the European Communities and its member States now impose duties on these products contrary to their scheduled duty-free tariff concessions arising from the ITA. Japan asserted that a number of EC customs classification legal instruments, alone or in combination with Council Regulation (EEC) No. 2658/87 of 23 July 1987 on the tariff and statistical nomenclature and on the Common Customs Tariff, including all annexes thereto, as amended, appear to be inconsistent with the EC's and its member States' obligations under Article II:1(a) and II:1(b) of the GATT 1994 and their Schedules, and therefore nullify or impair benefits accruing to Japan under the GATT 1994.	Implementation notified by respondent on 20 July 2011	Japan	European Communities	Australia; Brazil; China; Costa Rica; Hong Kong, China; India; Korea, Republic of; Philippines; Singapore; Chinese Taipei; Thailand; Turkey; United States; Viet Nam

Case N.	RoC	Short title	Summary	Current status	Complaint	Respondent	Third Parties
DS412	13 September 2010	Canada — Renewable Energy	Canada — Certain Measures Affecting the Renewable Energy Generation Sector Complaint by Japan. (See also DS426) On 13 September 2010, Japan requested consultations with Canada regarding Canada's measures relating to domestic content requirements in the feed-in tariff program (the "FIT Program"). Japan claimed that the measures are inconsistent with Canada's obligations under Article III:4 and III:5 of the GATT 1994 because they appear to be laws, regulations or requirements affecting the internal sale, offering for sale, purchase, transportation, distribution, or use of equipment for renewable energy generation facilities that accord less favorable treatment to imported equipment than that accorded to like products originating in Ontario; that the measures could be internal quantitative regulations relating to the mixture, processing or use of a specified amount or proportion of equipment for renewable energy generation facilities which require that equipment for renewable energy generation facilities be supplied from Ontario sources; and that the measures appear to require the mixture, processing or use of equipment for renewable energy generation facilities supplied from Ontario in specified amounts or proportions, being applied so as to afford protection to Ontario production of such equipment, contrary to the principles of Article III:1 of the GATT 1994. Japan also claimed that the measures appear to be inconsistent with Article 2.1 of the TRIMs Agreement	Implementation notified by respondent on 5 June 2014	Japan	Canada	Australia; Brazil; China; El Salvador; European Union; Honduras; India; Saudi Arabia, Kingdom of; Korea, Republic of; Mexico; Norway; Chinese Taipei; United States

Case N.	RoC	Short title	Summary	Current status	Complaiant	Respondent	Third Parties
			because they appear to be trade-related investment measures that are inconsistent with the provisions of Article III of the GATT 1994. Finally, Japan alleged that it appears that a subsidy is granted under the measures because there would be a financial contribution or a form of income or price support, and a benefit is thereby conferred. It is also claimed that the subsidy would be a prohibited subsidy under Articles 3.1(b) and 3.2 of the SCM Agreement because it appears to be provided "contingent … upon the use of domestic over imported goods", namely contingent upon the use of equipment for renewable energy generation facilities produced in Ontario over such equipment imported from countries such as Japan.				
DS433	13 March 2012	China — Rare Earths	China — Measures Related to the Exportation of Rare Earths, Tungsten and Molybdenum Complaint by Japan. (See also DS431 and DS432) On 13 March 2012, Japan requested consultations with China with respect to China's restrictions on the export of various forms of rare earths, tungsten and molybdenum. The request refers to materials falling under but not limited to 212 eight-digit Chinese Customs Commodity Codes and over 30 measures. The request also refers to a number of Chinese published as well as unpublished measures that, operating separately or collectively, allegedly impose and administer export restrictions. These restrictions include export duties, export quotas, minimum export price requirements, export licensing	Implementation notified by respondent on 20 May 2015	Japan	China	Brazil; Canada; Colombia; European Union; India; Korea, Republic of; Norway; Oman; Saudi Arabia, Kingdom of; Chinese Taipei; United States; Viet Nam; Argentina; Australia; Indonesia;

Case N.	RoC	Short title	Summary	Current status	Complaiant	Respondent	Third Parties
			requirements and additional requirements and procedures in connection with the administration of the quantitative restrictions. Japan claims that these measures are inconsistent with: • Articles VII, VIII, X and XI of the GATT 1994; and • paragraphs 2(A)2, 2(C)1, 5.1, 5.2, 7.2, 8.2 and 11.3 of Part I of China's Protocol of Accession, as well as China's obligations under paragraph 1.2 of Part I of the Protocol of Accession.				Turkey; Peru; Russian Federation
DS445	21 August 2012	Argentina — Import Measures	Argentina — Measures Affecting the Importation of Goods Complaint by Japan. (See also DS438, DS444 and DS446) On 21 August 2012, Japan requested consultations with Argentina concerning certain measures imposed by Argentina on the importation of goods. Japan challenges: (i) the requirement to present for approval of a non-automatic import licence: Declaración Jurada Anticipada de Importación (DJAI); (ii) non-automatic licences required in the form of Certificados de Importación (CIs) for the importation of certain goods; (iii) requirements imposed on mporters to undertake certain trade-restrictive commitments; and (iv) the alleged systematic delay in granting import approval or refusal to grant such approval, or the grant of import approval subject to importers undertaking to comply with certain	Report(s) adopted, with recommendation to bring measure(s) into conformity on 26 January 2015	Japan	Argentina	Australia; Canada; China; Ecuador; European Union; Guatemala; India; Israel; Japan; Korea, Republic of; Norway; Saudi Arabia, Kingdom of; Switzerland; Chinese Taipei; Thailand; Turkey; United States

Case N.	RoC	Short title	Summary	Current status	Complaiant	Respondent	Third Parties
			iallegedly trade-restrictive commitments. Japan claims that the challenged measures appear to be inconsistent with: • Articles III:4, VIII, X:1, X:2, X:3 and XI:1 of the GATT 1994; • Articles 2 and 6.1 of the TRIMs Agreement; • Articles 1.2, 1.3, 1.4, 1.5, 1.6, 1.7, 2.2, 3.2, 3.3, 3.4, 3.5, 5.1, 5.2, 5.3 and 5.4 of the Agreement on Import Licensing Procedures; and • Article 11 of the Safeguards Agreement.				
DS454	20 December 2012	China — HP-SSST (Japan)	China — Measures Imposing Anti-Dumping Duties on High-Performance Stainless Steel Seamless Tubes (HP-SSST) from Japan Complaint by Japan. (See also DS460) On 20 December 2012, Japan requested consultations with China concerning measures imposing Anti-Dumping duties on high-performance stainless steel seamless tubes (HP-SSST) from Japan, as set forth in Ministry of Commerce of the People's Republic of China (MOFCOM) Notice No. 21 [2012] and Notice No. 72 [2012], including any and all annexes and any amendments thereof. Japan claims that the measures are inconsistent with: • Articles 1, 3.1, 3.2, 3.4, 3.5, 5.3, 5.8, 6.5, 6.5.1, 6.8, 6.9, 7.4, 12.2 and 12.2.2 of the Anti-Dumping Agreement;	Report(s) adopted, with recommendation to bring measure(s) into conformity on 28 October 2015	Japan	China	European Union; India; Korea, Republic of; Russian Federation; United States; Turkey; Saudi Arabia, Kingdom of

Case N.	RoC	Short title	Summary	Current status	Complainant	Respondent	Third Parties
			and • Article VI of the GATT 1994.				
DS463	24 July 2013	N/A	Russian Federation — Recycling Fee on Motor Vehicles Complaint by Japan. (See also DS462) On 24 July 2013, Japan requested consultations with the Russian Federation regarding the Russian Federation's measures relating to a charge, the so called "recycling fee", imposed on motor vehicles. The legal instruments cited by Japan include: • Federal Law No. 128-FZ of 28 July 2012, on production and consumption wastes, and Article 51 of the Budget Code of the Russian Federation; • Government Decree No. 870 of 30 August 2012 on recycling fee for wheeled transport vehicles; • Joint Order of the Ministry of Internal Affairs No. 496, the Ministry of Economic Development and Trade No. 134 and the Ministry of Industry and Energy No. 192, on vehicle registration passports and chassis registration passports (23 June 2005), as amended by Joint Order of the Ministry of Internal Affairs No. 828, the Ministry of Industry and Trade No. 1227 and the Federal Customs Service No. 1744 (30 August 2012); and,	In consultations on 24 July 2013	Japan	Russian Federation	N/A

Case N.	RoC	Short title	Summary	Current status	Complaiant	Respondent	Third Parties
			• Resolution of the Government of the Russian Federation No. 520 of 20 June 2013 on, inter alia, rules for granting subsidies from the federal budget to organizations and individual entrepreneurs to reimburse expenses related to their handling of wastes resulting from the loss of consumer good characteristics of wheeled means of transport for which the recycling fee was paid (1 July 2013). According to Japan, the Russian Federation imposes the recycling fee on imported and domestic motor vehicles. The Russian Federation, however, exempts from the fee vehicles that are manufactured by companies: (a) that are registered in the Russian Federation; (b) that have committed to produce their vehicles in the Russian Federation involving certain specific manufacturing operations in the territory of the Russian Federation, Belarus or Kazakhstan. Japan also argues that the recycling fee treats imported vehicles less favourably than domestic vehicles, because the fee differentiates between "new vehicles" and "vehicles produced more than 3 years ago". Japan claims that the measures appear to be inconsistent with: • Articles I:1, II:1(a), II:1(b), III:2 and III:4 of the GATT 1994; • Article 2.1 and 2.2 of the TRIMs Agreement; and • Article 2.1 and 2.2 of the TBT Agreement.				

Case N.	RoC	Short title	Summary	Current status	Complaiant	Respondent	Third Parties
DS468	30 October 2013	Ukraine — Passenger Cars	Ukraine — Definitive Safeguard Measures on Certain Passenger Cars Complaint by Japan. On 30 October 2013, Japan requested consultations with Ukraine regarding the definitive safeguard measures imposed by Ukraine on imports of certain passenger cars and the investigation that led to the imposition of those measures. Japan claims that the measures are inconsistent with: • Articles 2.1, 3.1, 4.1(a), 4.1(b), 4.2(a), 4.2(b), 4.2(c), 5.1, 7.1, 7.4, 8.1, 11.1(a), 12.1, 12.2 and 12.3 of the Agreement on Safeguards; and • Articles II:1(b) and XIX:1(a) of the GATT 1994.	Report(s) adopted, with recommendation to bring measure(s) into conformity on 20 July 2015	Japan	Ukraine	European Union; India; Korea, Republic of; Russian Federation; Turkey; Australia; United States
DS495	21 May 2015	Korea — Radionuclides (Japan)	Korea — Import Bans, and Testing and Certification Requirements for Radionuclides Complaint by Japan. On 21 May 2015, Japan requested consultations with Korea regarding: (a) import bans on certain food products; (b) additional testing and certification requirements regarding the presence of certain radionuclides; and (c) a number of alleged omissions concerning transparency obligations under the SPS Agreement. Korea's measures were adopted subsequent to the accident at the Fukushima Daiichi nuclear power plant in March 2011. Japan claims that the measures are inconsistent with:	Panel composed on 8 February 2016	Japan	Korea, Republic of	United States; European Union; Norway; New Zealand; India; Russian Federation; Chinese Taipei; China; Guatemala; Canada; Brazil

Case N.	RoC	Short title	Summary	Current status	Complainant	Respondent	Third Parties
			• Articles 2.2, 2.3, 4, 5.1, 5.2, 5.5, 5.6, 5.7, 5.8, 7, and 8, paragraphs 1 and 3 of Annex B, and paragraphs 1(a), 1(c), 1(e) and 1(g) of Annex C, of the SPS Agreement; and • Article XXIII:1 of the GATT 1994.				
DS497	2 July 2015	Brazil — Taxation (Japan)	Brazil — Certain Measures Concerning Taxation and Charges Complaint by Japan. (See also DS472) On 2 July 2015, Japan requested consultations with Brazil with respect to certain measures concerning taxation and charges in the automotive sector, the electronics and technology industry, and tax advantages for exporters. Japan claims that the measures are inconsistent with: • Articles I:1, II:1(b), III:2, III:4 and III:5 of the GATT 1994; • Articles 3.1(a), 3.1(b) and 3.2 of the SCM Agreement; and • Articles 2.1 and 2.2 of the TRIMs Agreement.	Panel composed on 29 September 2015	Japan	Brazil	Argentina; Australia; Canada; China; Colombia; European Union; India; Korea, Republic of; Russian Federation; Singapore; Turkey; Ukraine; United States
DS504	15 March 2016	Korea — Pneumatic Valves	Korea — Anti-Dumping Duties on Pneumatic Valves from Japan Complaint by Japan On 15 March 2016, Japan requested consultations with Korea regarding measures imposing anti-dumping duties on valves for pneumatic	Panel composed on 29 August 2016	Japan	Korea, Republic of	Brazil; China; Ecuador; European Union; Norway; Singapore; Turkey; United

Case N.	RoC	Short title	Summary	Current status	Complainant	Respondent	Third Parties
			transmission from Japan and the documents and factual information underlying the imposition of those duties. Japan claims that the measures are inconsistent with: • Articles 1, 3.1,3.2,3.4, 3.5, 4.1, 6.5, 6.5.1, 6.9, 12.2 and 12.2.2 of the Anti-Dumping Agreement; and • Article VI of the GATT 1994.				States; Viet Nam
DS518	20 December 2016	N/A	India — Certain Measures on Imports of Iron and Steel Products Complaint by Japan On 20 December 2016, Japan requested consultations with India concerning certain measures imposed by India on imports of iron and steel products into India. Japan claimed that the measures appear to be inconsistent with: • Articles 2.1, 3.1, 4.1(a), 4.1(b), 4.1(c), 4.2(a), 4.2(b), 4.2(c), 5.1, 7.1, 11.1(a), 12.1, 12.2, 12.3 and 12.4 of the Agreement on Safeguards; and • Articles I:1, II:1(b), XI:1 and XIX:1(a) of the GATT 1994.	In consultations on 20 December 2016	Japan	India	N/A

Sourse:
DS6: https://www.wto.org/english/tratop_e/dispu_e/cases_e/ds6_e.htm
DS51: https://www.wto.org/english/tratop_e/dispu_e/cases_e/ds51_e.htm
DS55: https://www.wto.org/english/tratop_e/dispu_e/cases_e/ds55_e.htm
DS64: https://www.wto.org/english/tratop_e/dispu_e/cases_e/ds64_e.htm

DS95: https://www.wto.org/english/tratop_e/dispu_e/cases_e/ds95_e.htm
DS139: https://www.wto.org/english/tratop_e/dispu_e/cases_e/ds139_e.htm
DS162: https://www.wto.org/english/tratop_e/dispu_e/cases_e/ds162_e.htm
DS184: https://www.wto.org/english/tratop_e/dispu_e/cases_e/ds184_e.htm
DS217: https://www.wto.org/english/tratop_e/dispu_e/cases_e/ds217_e.htm
DS244: https://www.wto.org/english/tratop_e/dispu_e/cases_e/ds244_e.htm
DS249: https://www.wto.org/english/tratop_e/dispu_e/cases_e/ds249_e.htm
DS322: https://www.wto.org/english/tratop_e/dispu_e/cases_e/ds6_e.htm
DS376: https://www.wto.org/english/tratop_e/dispu_e/cases_e/ds376_e.htm
DS412: https://www.wto.org/english/tratop_e/dispu_e/cases_e/ds6_e.htm
DS433: https://www.wto.org/english/tratop_e/dispu_e/cases_e/ds433_e.htm
DS445: https://www.wto.org/english/tratop_e/dispu_e/cases_e/ds445_e.htm
DS454: https://www.wto.org/english/tratop_e/dispu_e/cases_e/ds454_e.htm
DS464: https://www.wto.org/english/tratop_e/dispu_e/cases_e/ds463_e.htm
DS468: https://www.wto.org/english/tratop_e/dispu_e/cases_e/ds468_e.htm
DS495: https://www.wto.org/english/tratop_e/dispu_e/cases_e/ds495_e.htm
DS497: https://www.wto.org/english/tratop_e/dispu_e/cases_e/ds497_e.htm
DS504: https://www.wto.org/english/tratop_e/dispu_e/cases_e/ds504_e.htm
DS518: https://www.wto.org/english/tratop_e/dispu_e/cases_e/ds518_e.htm

1.2 Japan as respondent

Case N.	RoC	Short title	Summary	Current status	Complaiant	Respondent	Third Parties
DS8	21 June 1995	Japan — Alcoholic Beverages II	Japan — Taxes on Alcoholic Beverages Complaints by the European Communities, Canada and the United States. The EC requested consultations on 21 June 1995, and Canada and the US on 7 July 1995. The complainants claimed that spirits exported to Japan were discriminated against under the Japanese liquor tax system which, in their view, levies a substantially lower tax on "shochu" than on whisky, cognac and white spirits.	Mutually acceptable solution on implementation notified on 9 January 1998	European Communities	Japan	N/A
DS10	21 June 1995	Japan — Alcoholic Beverages II	Japan — Taxes on Alcoholic Beverages Complaints by the European Communities, Canada and the United States. The EC requested consultations on 21 June 1995, and Canada and the US on 7 July 1995. The complainants claimed that spirits exported to Japan were discriminated against under the Japanese liquor tax system which, in their view, levies a substantially lower tax on "shochu" than on whisky, cognac and white spirits.	Mutually acceptable solution on implementation notified on 9 January 1998	Canada	Japan	N/A

Case N.	RoC	Short title	Summary	Current status	Complaiant	Respondent	Third Parties
DS11	21 June 1995	Japan — Alcoholic Beverages II	Japan — Taxes on Alcoholic Beverages Complaints by the European Communities, Canada and the United States. The EC requested consultations on 21 June 1995, and Canada and the US on 7 July 1995. The complainants claimed that spirits exported to Japan were discriminated against under the Japanese liquor tax system which, in their view, levies a substantially lower tax on "shochu" than on whisky, cognac and white spirits.	Mutually acceptable solution on implementation notified on 9 January 1998	US	Japan	N/A
DS15	18 August 1995	N/A	Japan — Measures Affecting the Purchase of Telecommunications Equipment Complaint by the European Communities. This request for consultations, dated 18 August 1995, claims that a 1994 agreement reached between the United States and Japan concerning telecommunications equipment is inconsistent with GATT Articles I:1, III:4 and XVII:1(c), and nullifies or impairs benefits accruing to the EC. The United States has joined in the consultations.	In consultations on 31 August 1995	European Communities	Japan	N/A
DS28	9 February 1996	N/A	Japan — Measures Concerning Sound Recordings Complaint by the United States. This request, dated 9 February 1996, is the first WTO dispute settlement case involving the TRIPS Agreement. The United States claims that Japan's copyright regime for the protection of intellectual	Settled or terminated (withdrawn, mutually agreed solution) on 24 January 1997	US	Japan	N/A

Case N.	RoC	Short title	Summary	Current status	Complaiant	Respondent	Third Parties
			property in sound recordings is inconsistent with, inter alia, the TRIPS Agreement Article 14 (protection of performers, producers of phonograms and broadcasting organizations).				
DS42	28 May 1996	N/A	Japan — Measures Concerning Sound Recordings Complaint by the European Communities. This request for consultations, dated 24 May 1996, concerns the intellectual property protection of sound recordings under GATT Article XXII:1. Violations of Articles 14.6 and 70.2 of the TRIPS Agreement are alleged. Earlier, the United States requested consultations with Japan on the same issue (WT/DS28), in which the EC joined.	Settled or terminated (withdrawn, mutually agreed solution) on 7 November 1997	European Communities	Japan	N/A
DS44	13 June 1996	Japan — Film	Japan — Measures Affecting Consumer Photographic Film and Paper Complaint by the United States. On 13 June 1996, the United States requested consultations with Japan concerning Japan's laws, regulations and requirements affecting the distribution, offering for sale and internal sale of imported consumer photographic film and paper. The US alleged that: • the Japanese Government treated imported film and paper less favourably through these measures, in violation of GATT Articles III and X. • these measures nullify or impair benefits accruing to the US (a non-violation claim).	Report(s) adopted, no further action required on 22 April 1998	US	Japan	European Communities; Mexico

Case N.	RoC	Short title	Summary	Current status	Complaiant	Respondent	Third Parties
DS45	13 June 1996	N/A	Japan — Measures Affecting Distribution Services Complaint by the United States. On 13 June 1996, the US requested consultations with Japan concerning Japan's measures affecting distribution services (not limited to the photographic film and paper sector) through the operation of the Large-Scale Retail Store Law, which regulates the floor space, business hours and holidays of supermarkets and department stores. Violations of the GATS Article III (Transparency) and Article XVI (Market Access) are alleged. The US also alleged that these measures nullify or impair benefits accruing to the US (a non-violation claim). The US requested further consultations with Japan on 20 September 1996, expanding the factual and legal basis of its claim.	In consultations on 13 June 1996	US	Japan	N/A
DS66	25 January 1997	N/A	Japan — Measures Affecting Imports of Pork Complaint by the European Communities. On 15 January 1997, the EC requested consultations with Japan in respect of certain measures affecting imports of pork and its processed products imposed by Japan. The EC contended that these measures are in violation of Japan's obligations under Articles I, X:3 and XIII of the GATT 1994. The EC also contended that these measures nullify or impair benefits accruing to it under the GATT 1994.	In consultations on 15 January 1997	European Communities	Japan	N/A

Case N.	RoC	Short title	Summary	Current status	Complaiant	Respondent	Third Parties
DS73	26 March 1997	N/A	Japan — Procurement of a Navigation Satellite Complaint by the European Communities. This request, dated 26 March 1997, is in respect of a procurement tender published by the Ministry of Transport (MoT) of Japan to purchase a multi-functional satellite for Air Traffic Management. The EC contends that the specifications in the tender were not neutral but referred explicitly to US specifications. This meant, the EC contends, that European bidders could effectively not participate in the tender. The EC alleges inconsistency of this tender with Annex I of Appendix I of Japan's commitments under the Government Procurement Agreement (GPA). The EC also alleges violations of Articles VI(3) and XII(2) of the GPA.	Settled or terminated (withdrawn, mutually agreed solution) on 31 July 1997	European Communities	Japan	N/A
DS76	7 April 1997	Japan — Agricultural Products II	Japan — Measures Affecting Agricultural Products Complaint by the United States. On 7 April 1997, the US requested consultations with Japan in respect of the latter's prohibition, under quarantine measures, of imports of certain agricultural products. The US alleged that Japan prohibits the importation of each variety of a product requiring quarantine treatment until the quarantine treatment has been tested for that variety, even if the treatment has proved to be effective for other varieties of the same product.	Mutually acceptable solution on implementation notified on 25 September 2001	US	Japan	Brazil; European Communities; Hungary

Case N.	RoC	Short title	Summary	Current status	Complaiant	Respondent	Third Parties
			The US alleged violations of Articles 2, 5 and 8 of the SPS Agreement, Article XI of GATT 1994, and Article 4 of the Agreement on Agriculture. In addition, the US made a claim for nullification and impairment of benefits.				
DS147	8 October 1998	N/A	Japan — Tariff Quotas and Subsidies Affecting Leather Complaint by the European Communities. On 8 October 1998, the EC requested consultations with Japan concerning the management of the tariff quotas for leather and the subsidies allegedly benefiting the leather industry and "Dowa" regions in Japan. The EC stated that the management of the three tariff quotas is specified in a notice published every year by the Ministry of International Trade & Industry (MITI), which is based on Article 6 of the Ministerial Order on the tariff quota system for heavy oil, crude oil, etc. The EC contended that: • the complexity of the management of the tariff quota system, as well as the fact that applications for licenses may only be submitted on a single day, appears open to criticism; • many licenses are granted for quantities without real economic interest, and some have a very short validity period; • the system leads to a situation that deters foreign	In consultations on 8 October 1998	European Communities	Japan	N/A

Case N.	RoC	Short title	Summary	Current status	Complaiant	Respondent	Third Parties
			companies from establishing in Japan for purposes of importing leather directly; • subsidies were granted on the basis of the "Law concerning Special Fiscal Measures", which extended the duration of 15 subsidy programmes; and • these subsidies are specific and that the total value of these different subsidy programmes is liable to cause serious prejudice to its interests. The EC alleged violations of Articles 1(6), 3(5)(g), (h), (i) and (j) of the Import Licensing Agreement, and Article 6 of the Subsidies Agreement.				
DS245	1 March 2002	Japan — Apples	Japan — Measures Affecting the Importation of Apples Complaint by the United States. On 1 March 2002, the United States requested consultations with Japan regarding restrictions allegedly imposed by Japan on imports of apples from the United States. The United States' complaint arose from the maintenance by Japan of quarantine restrictions on apples imported into Japan, which restrictions were said to be necessary to protect against introduction of fire blight. Among the measures the United States complained of were the prohibition of imported apples from orchards in which any fire blight was detected, the requirement that export orchards be inspected three times yearly for the presence of fire	Mutually acceptable solution on implementation notified on 30 August 2005	US	Japan	Australia; Brazil; China; Chinese Taipei; European Communities; New Zealand

Case N.	RoC	Short title	Summary	Current status	Complaiant	Respondent	Third Parties
			blight and the disqualification of any orchard from exporting to Japan should fire blight be detected within a 500 meter buffer zone surrounding such orchard. The United States claimed that these measures might be inconsistent with the obligations of Japan under: • Article XI of the GATT 1994, • Articles 2.2, 2.3, 5.1, 5.2, 5.3, 5.6, 6.1, 6.2 and 7 and Annex B of the SPS Agreement, and • Article 14 of the Agreement on Agriculture.				
DS323	1 December 2004	Japan — Quotas on Laver	Japan — Import Quotas on Dried Laver and Seasoned Laver Complaint by Korea. On 1 December 2004, Korea requested consultations with Japan concerning Japan's import quotas on dried laver and seasoned laver. According to the request for consultations, Korea believes that Japan's extremely restrictive import quotas on dried laver and seasoned laver are inconsistent with, inter alia: • Articles X.3 and XI of the GATT 1994; • Article 4.2 of the Agreement on Agriculture; and • Article 1.2 and 1.6 of the Agreement on Import Licensing Procedures.	Settled or terminated (withdrawn, mutually agreed solution) on 23 January 2006	Korea, Republic of	Japan	China; European Communities; New Zealand; United States

Case N.	RoC	Short title	Summary	Current status	Complaiant	Respondent	Third Parties
DS336	14 March 2006	Japan — DRAMs (Korea)	Japan — Countervailing Duties on Dynamic Random Access Memories from Korea Complaint by Korea. On 14 March 2006, Korea requested consultations with Japan concerning countervailing duties imposed by Japan on certain Dynamic Random Access Memories (DRAMs) from Korea. According to Korea, notice of the imposition of such duties was provided by Japan in Cabinet Order No. 13 and Finance Notice 35, published respectively in Issue No. 4264 and Special Issue No. 17 of the Official Gazette dated 27 January 2006. The request for consultations also concerns certain aspects of the investigation and the determination that led to the imposition of such duties. Korea considers that the foregoing determinations are inconsistent with Japan's obligations under the GATT 1994 and under the SCM Agreement , "including, but not limited to", Articles VI:3 and X:3 of the GATT 1994 and Articles 1, 2, 10, 11, 12, 14, 15, 15.5, 19, 19.1, 21, 22 and 32.1 of the SCM Agreement.	Authority for panel lapsed on 5 March 2010	Korea, Republic of	Japan	China; European Communities; Chinese Taipei; United States

Sourse:
DS8: https://www.wto.org/english/tratop_e/dispu_e/cases_e/ds8_e.htm
DS10: https://www.wto.org/english/tratop_e/dispu_e/cases_e/ds10_e.htm
DS11: https://www.wto.org/english/tratop_e/dispu_e/cases_e/ds11_e.htm
DS15: https://www.wto.org/english/tratop_e/dispu_e/cases_e/ds15_e.htm
DS28: https://www.wto.org/english/tratop_e/dispu_e/cases_e/ds28_e.htm
DS42: https://www.wto.org/english/tratop_e/dispu_e/cases_e/ds42_e.htm
DS44: https://www.wto.org/english/tratop_e/dispu_e/cases_e/ds44_e.htm
DS45: https://www.wto.org/english/tratop_e/dispu_e/cases_e/ds45_e.htm

DS66: https://www.wto.org/english/tratop_e/dispu_e/cases_e/ds66_e.htm
DS73: https://www.wto.org/english/tratop_e/dispu_e/cases_e/ds73_e.htm
DS76: https://www.wto.org/english/tratop_e/dispu_e/cases_e/ds76_e.htm
DS147: https://www.wto.org/english/tratop_e/dispu_e/cases_e/ds147_e.htm
DS245: https://www.wto.org/english/tratop_e/dispu_e/cases_e/ds245_e.htm
DS323: https://www.wto.org/english/tratop_e/dispu_e/cases_e/ds323_e.htm
DS336: https://www.wto.org/english/tratop_e/dispu_e/cases_e/ds336_e.htm

2. Korea

2.1 Korea as complainant

Case N.	RoC	Short case Name	Summary	Current status	Complainant	Third Parties
DS89	1997	N/A	Complaint by Korea. Summary: Anti-Dumping issues. US imposition of Anti-Dumping duties on imports of colour television receivers. Later US revoked the Anti-Dumping duties.	Settled or terminated (15 September 1998)	Korea, Republic of	N/A
DS99	1997	US — DRAMS	Complaint by Korea. Summary: Anti-Dumping issues. US imposition of Anti-Dumping duties on Korean **DRAMS** imports.	Mutually acceptable solution on implementation notified on 20 October 2000	Korea, Republic of	EU
DS179	1999	US — Stainless Steel	Complaint by Korea. Summary: Anti-Dumping issues. US imposition of Anti-Dumping duties on Korean **Stainless steel** which was contended by Korea as erroneous.	Implementation notified by respondent on 10 September 2001	Korea, Republic of	EU, Japan
DS202	2000	US — Line Pipe	United States — Definitive Safeguard Measures on Imports of Circular Welded Carbon Quality Line Pipe from Korea Complaint by Korea. Summary: US implementation of definitive safeguard measure on imports of **circular welded carbon quality line pipe** which was contended by Korea as inconsistent with the Safeguards Agreement and the GATT 1994.	Implementation notified by respondent on 18 March 2003	Korea, Republic of	Australia; Canada; European Communities; Japan; Mexico

Case N.	RoC	Short case Name	Summary	Current status	Complainant	Third Parties
DS215	2000	N/A	Philippines — Anti-Dumping Measures Regarding Polypropylene Resins from Korea Complaint by Korea. Korea considered the Anti-Dumping margins on **Polypropylene Resins** incompatible with the obligations of the Philippines under the provisions of the Anti-Dumping Agreement.	In consultations on 15 December 2000	Korea, Republic of	Philippines
DS217	2000	US — Offset Act (Byrd Amendment)	United States — Continued Dumping and Subsidy Offset Act of 2000 Joint complaint by Australia, Brazil, Chile, European Communities, India, Indonesia, Japan, Korea and Thailand. According to complainants, the "Continued Dumping and Subsidy Offset Act of 2000" (the "Act") usually referred to as "the Byrd Amendment" is inconsistent with the obligations of the US under several provisions of the GATT, the Anti Dumping Agreement, the SCM Agreement, and the WTO Agreement.	Authorization to retaliate granted on 26 November 2004	Australia; Brazil; Chile; European Communities; India; Indonesia; Japan; Korea, Republic of; Thailand	Argentina; Canada; Costa Rica; Hong Kong, China; Israel; Mexico; Norway
DS251	2002	US — Steel Safeguards	United States — Definitive Safeguard Measures on **Imports of Certain Steel Products** Complaint by Korea.			

Case N.	RoC	Short case Name	Summary	Current status	Complainant	Third Parties
			On 7 March 2002, EC firstly requested consultation with the US regarding the definitive safeguard measures imposed by the US in the form of an increase in duties on imports of certain flat steel, hot-rolled bar, cold-finished bar, rebar, certain welded tubular products, carbon and alloy fittings, stainless steel bar, stainless steel rod, tin mill products and stainless steel wire and in the form of a tariff rate quota on imports of slabs effective as of 20 March 2002. On 20 March 2002, Korea then requested consultations with the US with regard to the definitive safeguard measures imposed by the US on the imports of certain steel products.	Report(s) adopted, no further action required on 10 December 2003	Korea, Republic of	Brazil; Canada; China; Chinese Taipei; European Communities; Japan; Mexico; New Zealand; Norway; Switzerland; Thailand; Turkey; Venezuela, Bolivarian Republic of
DS296	2003	US — Countervailing Duty Investigation on DRAMs	United States — Countervailing Duty Investigation on **Dynamic Random Access Memory Semiconductors (DRAMS)** from Korea Complaint by Korea US authorities' affirmative preliminary and final countervailing duty determinations, the preliminary injury determination and any subsequent determinations that may be made during the injury investigation, on **DRAMs** and **DRAM** modules from Korea	Implementation notified by respondent on 14 March 2006	Korea, Republic of	China; Chinese Taipei; European Communities; Japan

Case N.	RoC	Short case Name	Summary	Current status	Complainant	Third Parties
DS299	2003	EC — Countervailing Measures on DRAM Chips	EC — Countervailing Measures on **DRAM** Chips On 25 July 2003, Korea requested consultations with the European Communities concerning the **EC's provisional countervailing measures** and any final countervailing measures which may be finalized and implemented later this year against dynamic random access memory chips (**DRAMs**) from Korea.	Implementation notified by respondent on 21 April 2006	Korea, Republic of	China; Chinese Taipei; Japan; United States
DS301	2003	EC — Commercial Vessels	European Communities — Measures Affecting Trade in **Commercial Vessels** Complaint by Korea. On 3 September 2003, Korea requested consultations with the European Communities concerning certain measures by the EC and its member States in favour of their **shipbuilding industry** which, according to Korea, are inconsistent with their WTO obligations. *Grosso modo*, the dispute is against EU subsidies on its declining shipbuilding industry, MFN breaches and NT of Korean commercial vessels in EU.	Mutually acceptable solution on implementation notified on 20 July 2005	Korea, Republic of	China; Japan; United States
DS307	2004	N/A	European Communities — Aid for Commercial Vessels Complaint by Korea.	In consultations on 13 February 2004	Korea, Republic of	European Communities

Case N.	RoC	Short case Name	Summary	Current status	Complainant	Third Parties
DS323	2004	Japan — Quotas on Laver	Japan — Import Quotas on **Dried Laver and Seasoned Laver** Complaint by Korea. According to the request for consultations, Korea believes that Japan's extremely restrictive import quotas on dried laver and seasoned laver are inconsistent with GATT 1994: Art. X:3, XI, Article 4.2 of the Agreement on Agriculture; and Article 1.2 and 1.6 of the Agreement on Import Licensing Procedures. *Grosso modo*, the dispute concerns Japanese governmental measure against **Laver (seaweed)** imports via quotas, and various rules and regulations.	Settled or terminated (withdrawn, mutually agreed solution) on 23 January 2006	Korea, Republic of	China; European Communities; New Zealand; United States
DS336	2006	Japan — DRAMs (Korea)	Japan — Countervailing Duties on **Dynamic Random Access Memories (DRAMS)** from Korea Complaint by Korea. On 14 March 2006, Korea requested consultations with Japan concerning countervailing duties imposed by Japan on certain Dynamic Random Access Memories (DRAMs) from Korea. *Grosso modo*, the dispute concerns the Japanese imposition of countervailing duties on Korean **DRAMs** imports.	Authority for panel lapsed on 5 March 2010	Korea, Republic of	China; European Communities; Chinese Taipei; United States

Case N.	RoC	Short case Name	Summary	Current status	Complainant	Third Parties
DS402	2009	US — Zeroing (Korea)	United States — Use of Zeroing in Anti-Dumping Measures Involving Products from Korea Complaint by Korea. On 24 November 2009, Korea requested consultations with the United States regarding their use of zeroing in three anti-dumping cases involving certain products from Korea, namely, stainless steel plate in coils, stainless steel sheet and strip in coils, and diamond sawblades and parts thereof. *Grosso modo*, the dispute concerns the US Department of Commerce's use of zeroing technique which Korea deems inconsistent and illegitimate in light of Art. VI of GATT 1994 Articles 1, 2.1, 2.4, 2.4.2, and 5.8 of the Anti-Dumping Agreement.	Implementation notified by respondent on 19 December 2011	Korea, Republic of	China; European Union; Japan; Mexico; Thailand; Viet Nam
DS420	2011	US — Carbon Steel (Korea)	United States — Anti-Dumping measures on **corrosion-resistant carbon steel flat products** from Korea Complaint by Korea. On 31 January 2011, Korea requested consultations with the United States concerning a number of anti-dumping measures on corrosion-resistant carbon steel flat products from Korea.	Panel established, but not yet composed on 22 February 2012	Korea, Republic of	European Union; Japan; Mexico; China; Norway; Brazil; Thailand

Case N.	RoC	Short case Name	Summary	Current status	Complainant	Third Parties
			Grosso modo, the dispute concerns the US Department of Commerce's use of zeroing technique which Korea deems inconsistent and illegitimate in light of Art. VI of GATT 1994 Articles 1, 2.1, 2.4, 2.4.2, and 5.8 of the Anti-Dumping Agreement.			
DS464	2013	US — **Washing Machines**	United States — Anti-Dumping and Countervailing Measures on **large residential washers** from Korea Complaint by Korea. On 29 August 2013, Korea requested consultations with the United States concerning anti-dumping and countervailing measures relating to large residential washers from Korea. *Grosso modo*, the dispute concerns the US anti-dumping and countervailing measures against Korean home appliances (washer), which Korea contends inconsistent with AD Agreement, SCM agreement and GATT 1994.	Report(s) adopted, with recommendation to bring measure(s) into conformity on 26 September 2016	Korea, Republic of	Brazil; Canada; China; European Union; India; Japan; Norway; Thailand; Turkey; Saudi Arabia, Kingdom of; Viet Nam
DS488	2014	US — **OCTG (Korea)**	United States — Anti-Dumping Measures on Certain **Oil Country Tubular Goods** from Korea Complaint by Korea. On 22 December 2014, Korea requested consultations with the United States regarding certain anti-dumping measures on oil country tubular goods (OCTG) from Korea and the investigation methodology underlying such measures.	Panel composed	United States	Canada; China; European Union; India; Russian Federation; Turkey; Mexico

Case N.	RoC	Short case Name	Summary	Current status	Complainant	Third Parties
			Korea claims that these are inconsistent with: • Articles 2.2, 2.2.2, 2.2.1.1, 2.3, 2.4, 6.2, 6.4, 6.9, 6.10, including Articles 6.10.1 and 6.10.2, and 12.2.2 of the Anti-Dumping Agreement; and • Articles I and X:3 of the GATT 1994.			

Sourse:
DS89: https://www.wto.org/english/tratop_e/dispu_e/cases_e/ds89_e.htm
DS99: https://www.wto.org/english/tratop_e/dispu_e/cases_e/ds99_e.htm
DS179: https://www.wto.org/english/tratop_e/dispu_e/cases_e/ds179_e.htm
DS202: https://www.wto.org/english/tratop_e/dispu_e/cases_e/ds202_e.htm
DS215: https://www.wto.org/english/tratop_e/dispu_e/cases_e/ds215_e.htm
DS217: https://www.wto.org/english/tratop_e/dispu_e/cases_e/ds217_e.htm
DS251: https://www.wto.org/english/tratop_e/dispu_e/cases_e/ds251_e.htm
DS269: https://www.wto.org/english/tratop_e/dispu_e/cases_e/ds269_e.htm
DS299: https://www.wto.org/english/tratop_e/dispu_e/cases_e/ds299_e.htm
DS301: https://www.wto.org/english/tratop_e/dispu_e/cases_e/ds301_e.htm
DS3075: https://www.wto.org/english/tratop_e/dispu_e/cases_e/ds307_e.htm
DS323: https://www.wto.org/english/tratop_e/dispu_e/cases_e/ds323_e.htm
DS336: https://www.wto.org/english/tratop_e/dispu_e/cases_e/ds336_e.htm
DS402: https://www.wto.org/english/tratop_e/dispu_e/cases_e/ds402_e.htm
DS420: https://www.wto.org/english/tratop_e/dispu_e/cases_e/ds420_e.htm
DS464: https://www.wto.org/english/tratop_e/dispu_e/cases_e/ds464_e.htm
DS488: https://www.wto.org/english/tratop_e/dispu_e/cases_e/ds488_e.htm

2.2 Korea as respondent

Case N.	RoC	Short case Name	Summary	Current status	Complainant	Third Parties
DS3	1997	N/A	**Korea — Measures Concerning the Testing and Inspection of Agricultural Products** Complaint by the United States. On 6 April 1995, the US requested consultations with Korea involving testing and inspection requirements with respect to imports of agricultural products into Korea. The measures are alleged to be in violation of GATT Articles III or XI, Articles 2 and 5 of the Agreement on Sanitary and Phytosanitary Measures (SPS), TBT Articles 5 and 6 and Agriculture Article 4.	In consultations on 4 April 1995	US	N/A
DS5	1995	N/A	**Korea — Measures Concerning the Shelf-Life of Products** Complaint by the United States. On 3 May 1995, the US requested consultations with Korea in respect of requirements imposed by Korea on imports from the US which had the effect of restricting imports. The US alleged violations of Articles III and XI of GATT, Articles 2 and 5 of the SPS Agreement, Article 2 of the TBT Agreement, and Article 4 of the Agreement on Agriculture.	Settled or terminated (withdrawn, mutually agreed solution) on 20 July 1995	US	N/A

Case N.	RoC	Short case Name	Summary	Current status	Complainant	Third Parties
DS20	1995	N/A	**Korea — Measures concerning Bottled Water** Complaint by Canada. In this request for consultations dated 8 November 1995, Canada claimed that Korean regulations on the shelf-life and physical treatment (disinfection) of bottled water were inconsistent with GATT Articles III and XI, SPS Articles 2 and 5 and TBT Article 2.	Settled or terminated (withdrawn, mutually agreed solution) on 24 April 1996	Canada	N/A
DS40	1996	N/A	Korea — Laws, Regulations and Practices in the Telecommunications Procurement Sector Complaint by the European Communities. This request for consultations, dated 9 May 1996, concerns the laws, regulations and practices in the telecommunications sector. The EC claims that the procurement practices of the Korean telecommunications sector (Korea Telecom and Dacom) discriminate against foreign suppliers. The EC also claims that the Korean government has favoured US suppliers under two bilateral telecommunications agreements between Korea and the US. Violations of GATT Articles I, III and XVII are alleged.	Settled or terminated (withdrawn, mutually agreed solution) on 22 October 1997	European Communities	N/A
DS41	1996		**Korea — Measures concerning Inspection of Agricultural Products** Complaint by the United States.			

Case N.	RoC	Short case Name	Summary	Current status	Complainant	Third Parties
			On 24 May 1996, the US requested consultations with Korea concerning testing, inspection and other measures required for the importation of agricultural products into Korea. The US claimed that these measures restrict imports and appear to be inconsistent with the WTO Agreement. Violations of GATT Articles III and XI, SPS Articles 2, 5 and 8, TBT Articles 2, 5 and 6, and Article 4 of the Agreement on Agriculture are alleged. The US requested consultations with Korea on similar issues on 4 April 1995 (WT/DS3).	In consultations on 24 May 1996	US	N/A
DS75	1997	Korea — Alcoholic Beverages	**Korea — Taxes on Alcoholic Beverages** Complaints by the European Communities and the United States. On 4 April 1997, the EC requested consultations with Korea in respect of internal taxes imposed by Korea on certain alcoholic beverages pursuant to its Liquor Tax Law and Education Tax Law. The EC contended that the Korean Liquor Tax Law and Education Tax Law appear to be inconsistent with Korea's obligations under Article III:2 of GATT 1994. On 23 May 1997, the US requested consultations with Korea in respect of the same measures complained of by the EC. The US also alleged violations of Article III:2. On 10 September 1997, the EC and the US requested the establishment of a panel. At its meeting on 25 September 1997, the DSB deferred the establishment of a panel.	Implementation notified by respondent on 27 January 2000	European Communities	Canada; Mexico

Case N.	RoC	Short case Name	Summary	Current status	Complainant	Third Parties
DS84	1997	Korea — Alcoholic Beverages	**Korea — Taxes on Alcoholic Beverages** **Complaints by the European Communities and the United States.** On 4 April 1997, the EC requested consultations with Korea in respect of internal taxes imposed by Korea on certain alcoholic beverages pursuant to its Liquor Tax Law and Education Tax Law. The EC contended that the Korean Liquor Tax Law and Education Tax Law appear to be inconsistent with Korea's obligations under Article III:2 of GATT 1994. On 23 May 1997, the US requested consultations with Korea in respect of the same measures complained of by the EC. The US also alleged violations of Article III:2. On 10 September 1997, the EC and the US requested the establishment of a panel. At its meeting on 25 September 1997, the DSB deferred the establishment of a panel.	Implementation notified by respondent on 27 January 2000	US	Canada ; Mexico
DS98	1997	Korea — Dairy	**Korea — Definitive Safeguard Measure on Imports of Certain Dairy Products** Complaint by the European Communities. On 12 August 1997, the EC requested consultations with Korea in respect of a definitive safeguard measure imposed by Korea on imports of certain dairy products. The EC contended that under the provisions of different governmental measures, Korea has imposed a safeguard measure in the form of an import quota on imports of certain dairy	Implementation notified by respondent on 26 September 2000	European Communities	US

Case N.	RoC	Short case Name	Summary	Current status	Complainant	Third Parties
			products. The EC considered that this measure is in violation of Articles 2, 4, 5 and 12 of the Agreement on Safeguard Measures, as well as a violation of Article XIX of GATT 1994.			
DS161	1999	Korea — Various Measures on Beef	**Korea — Measures Affecting Imports of Fresh, Chilled and Frozen Beef** Complaint by the United States. On 1 February 1999, the US requested consultations with Korea in respect of a Korean regulatory scheme that allegedly discriminates against imported beef by *inter alia*, confining sales of imported beef to specialized stores (dual retail system), limiting the manner of its display, and otherwise constraining the opportunities for the sale of imported beef. The US alleged that Korea imposes a mark-up on sales of imported beef, limits import authority to certain so-called "super-groups" and the Livestock Producers Marketing Organization (LPMO), and provides domestic support to the cattle industry in Korea in amounts which cause Korea to exceed its aggregate measure of support as reflected in Korea's schedule. The US contended that these restrictions apply only to imported beef, thereby denying national treatment to beef imports, and that the support to the domestic industry amounts to domestic subsidies that contravene the Agreement on Agriculture. The US alleged violations of Articles II, III, XI, and XVII of GATT 1994; Articles 3, 4, 6, and 7	Implementation notified by respondent on 25 September 2001	US	Australia; Canada; New Zealand

Case N.	RoC	Short case Name	Summary	Current status	Complainant	Third Parties
			of the Agreement on Agriculture; and Articles 1 and 3 of the Import Licensing Agreement.			
DS163	1999	Korea — Procurement	**Korea — Measures Affecting Government Procurement** Complaint by the United States. On 16 February 1999, the US requested consultations with Korea in respect of certain procurement practices of the Korean Airport Construction Authority (KOACA), and other entities concerned with the procurement of airport construction in Korea. The US claimed that such practices were inconsistent with Korea's obligations under the Agreement on Government Procurement (GPA). These include practices relating to qualification for bidding as a prime contractor, domestic partnering, and the absence of access to challenge procedures that are in breach of the GPA. The US contended that KOACA and the other entities are within the scope of Korea's list of central government entities as specified in Annex 1 of Korea's obligations in Appendix I of the GPA, and pursuant to Article I(1) of the GPA, apply to the procurement of airport construction.	Report(s) adopted, no further action required on 19 June 2000	US	European Communities; Japan
DS169	1999	Korea — Various Measures on Beef	**Korea — Measures Affecting Imports of Fresh, Chilled and Frozen Beef** Complaint by Australia. On 1 February 1999, the US requested consultations	Implementation notified by respondent on 25 September 2001	Australia	Canada; New Zealand; United States

Case N.	RoC	Short case Name	Summary	Current status	Complainant	Third Parties
			with Korea in respect of a Korean regulatory scheme that allegedly discriminates against imported beef by *inter alia*, confining sales of imported beef to specialised stores (dual retail system), limiting the manner of its display, and otherwise constraining the opportunities for the sale of imported beef. The US alleged that Korea imposes a mark-up on sales of imported beef, limits import authority to certain so-called "super-groups" and the Livestock Producers Marketing Organization (LPMO), and provides domestic support to the cattle industry in Korea in amounts which cause Korea to exceed its aggregate measure of support as reflected in Korea's schedule. The US contended that these restrictions apply only to imported beef, thereby denying national treatment to beef imports, and that the support to the domestic industry amounts to domestic subsidies that contravene the Agreement on Agriculture. The US alleged violations of Articles II, III, XI, and XVII of GATT 1994; Articles 3, 4, 6, and 7 of the Agreement on Agriculture; and Articles 1 and 3 of the Import Licensing Agreement.			
DS273	2002	Korea — Commercial Vessels	Korea — Measures Affecting Trade in Commercial Vessels Complaint by the European Communities. On 21 October 2002, the European Communities requested consultations with Korea on certain measures establishing subsidies to its shipbuilding industry which, according to the European	Implementation notified by respondent on 11 April 2005	European Communities	China; Chinese Taipei; Japan; Mexico; Norway; United States

Case N.	RoC	Short case Name	Summary	Current status	Complainant	Third Parties
			Communities, are inconsistent with Korea's obligations under the SCM Agreement. These measures are as follows: • Corporate restructuring subsidies in the form of debt forgiveness, debt and interest relief and debt-to-equity swaps, provided through government-owned and government-controlled banks; • Special taxation on in-kind contribution and the special taxation on spin-off scheme provided in the Special Tax Treatment Control Law which establishes two tax programmes limited to companies under corporate restructuring and provided tax concessions to Daewoo; • Pre-shipment loans and advance payment refund guarantees provided by the state-owned Export-Import Bank of Korea (KEXIM) to all Korean shipyards. The EC indicated that the subsidies in question were granted with respect to the production of commercial vessels for international commerce, including: bulk carriers, container ships, oil tankers, product and chemical tankers, LNG/LPG carriers, passenger and RoRo ferries and other non-cargo vessels (including offshore units). The EC considered that the Korean measures are in breach of Korea's obligations under the provisions of			

Case N.	RoC	Short case Name	Summary	Current status	Complainant	Third Parties
			the SCM Agreement, in particular, but not necessarily exclusively of: Articles 1, 2, 3.1, 5(a), 5(c), 6.3 and 6.5 of the SCM Agreement			
DS312	2004	Korea — Certain Paper	**Korea — Anti-Dumping Duties on Imports of Certain Paper from Indonesia** Complaint by Indonesia. On 4 June 2004, Indonesia requested consultations with Korea concerning the imposition of definitive Anti-Dumping duties by Korea on imports of business information paper and uncoated wood-free printing paper from Indonesia and certain aspects of the investigation leading to the imposition of such duties. According to the request for consultations from Indonesia, Korea violates its WTO obligations in respect of the following aspects: • Korea's initiation of investigation, notwithstanding several deficiencies such as the applicants' failure to include in the application sufficient and adequate evidence of dumping, injury and causal link; • Korea's failure to provide in the Notice of Initiation any information regarding the factors on which the allegation of injury was based, • the way Korea granted confidential treatment to information contained in the application,	Compliance proceedings completed with finding(s) of non-compliance on 22 October 2007	Indonesia	Canada; China; European Communities; Japan; United States; Chinese Taipei

Case N.	RoC	Short case Name	Summary	Current status	Complainant	Third Parties
			• Korea's making of a request for information from a firm not subject to investigation, without having obtained the agreement of that firm and having notified the Indonesian Government of such request, • Korea's rejection of information related to the sales of a certain firm, without explaining the reason. • Korea's preliminary determination, in such respects as: like products, constructed value, best information available, denial of access to information, and the refusal to provide an opportunity to the exporters to present their views; • Korea's final determination, in such respects as: like products, individual dumping margins, constructed value, treating a certain firm and other firms as a single economic unit; the impact and effect of the dumped imports on the domestic industry and prices in the domestic market, failure to evaluate all relevant economic factors and indices, and denial of access to information. Indonesia considers that these Korean measures are inconsistent with: Article VI of GATT 1994, inter alia, Article VI:1, VI:2 and VI:6; Articles 1, 2.1, 2.2, 2.2.1.1, 2.2.2, 2.4, 2.6, 3.1, 3.2, 3.4, 3.5, 4.1(i), 5.2, 5.3, 5.4, 5.7, 6.1.2, 6.2, 6.4, 6.5, 6.5.1, 6.5.2, 6.7, 6.8. 6.10, 9.3, 12.1.1(iv), 12.2, 12.3, Annex I, and paragraphs 3, 6, and 7 of Annex II of the Anti-Dumping Agreement.			

Case N.	RoC	Short case Name	Summary	Current status	Complainant	Third Parties
DS391	2009	Korea — Bovine Meat (Canada)	**Korea — Measures Affecting the Importation of Bovine Meat and Meat Products from Canada** Complaint by Canada. On 9 April 2009, Canada requested consultations with Korea concerning measures affecting the importation of bovine meat and meat products from Canada. According to Canada, since May 2003 Korea prohibits the importation of Canadian bovine meat and meat products. The alleged objective of this prohibition would be that of protecting against risks arising from bovine spongiform encephalopathy (BSE). Canada challenges two measures: • Administrative Order No. 51584-476, which entered into force on 21 May 2003, and would prohibit the importation into Korea of bovine meat and meat products from Canada; and • Korean Act No. 9130, amending the Act on the Prevention of Contagious Animal Diseases (also known as the Livestock Epidemic Prevention Act), which entered into force on 11 September 2008, and would set out a number of conditions for lifting the import ban, including subjecting any import health requirements for the importation of Canadian bovine meat and meat products to the approval of the Korean National Assembly (Korea's national legislature). For each of these measures, Canada's request	Settled or terminated (withdrawn, mutually agreed solution) on 20 June 2012	Canada	Argentina; Brazil; India; China; European Communities; Japan; Chinese Taipei; United States

Case N.	RoC	Short case Name	Summary	Current status	Complainant	Third Parties
			would also cover any amendments, replacements, extensions, implementing measures or other related measures. Canada argues that the measures at issue are inconsistent with the SPS Agreement and the GATT 1994, including the following provisions: • Articles 2.2, 2.3, 3.1, 3.3, 5.1, 5.5, 5.6, 5.7, 6.1, 8 and Annex C of the SPS Agreement; and • Articles I:1, III:4 and XI:1 of the GATT 1994.			
DS495	2015	Korea — Radionuclides (Japan)	**Korea — Import Bans, and Testing and Certification Requirements for Radionuclides** Complaint by Japan. On 21 May 2015, Japan requested consultations with Korea regarding: (a) import bans on certain food products; (b) additional testing and certification requirements regarding the presence of certain radionuclides; and (c) a number of alleged omissions concerning transparency obligations under the SPS Agreement. Korea's measures were adopted subsequent to the accident at the Fukushima Daiichi nuclear power plant in March 2011. Japan claims that the measures are inconsistent with: • Articles 2.2, 2.3, 4, 5.1, 5.2, 5.5, 5.6, 5.7, 5.8, 7, and 8, paragraphs 1 and 3 of Annex B, and paragraphs 1(a), 1(c), 1(e) and 1(g) of Annex C, of the SPS Agreement; and • Articles I:1, III:4 and XI:1 of the GATT 1994.	Panel composed on 8 February 2016	Japan	United States; European Union; Norway; New Zealand; India; Russian Federation; Chinese Taipei; China; Guatemala; Canada; Brazil

Case N.	RoC	Short case Name	Summary	Current status	Complainant	Third Parties
DS504	2016	Korea — Pneumatic Valves	Korea — Anti-Dumping Duties on Pneumatic Valves from Japan Complaint by Japan On 15 March 2016, Japan requested consultations with Korea regarding measures imposing anti-dumping duties on valves for pneumatic transmission from Japan and the documents and factual information underlying the imposition of those duties. Japan claims that the measures are inconsistent with: • Articles 1, 3.1,3.2,3.4, 3.5, 4.1, 6.5, 6.5.1, 6.9, 12.2 and 12.2.2 of the Anti-Dumping Agreement; and • Article VI of the GATT 1994.	Panel composed on 29 August 2016	Japan	Brazil; China; Ecuador; European Union; Norway; Singapore; Turkey; United States; Viet Nam

Sourse:
DS3: https://www.wto.org/english/tratop_e/dispu_e/cases_e/ds3_e.htm
DS5: https://www.wto.org/english/tratop_e/dispu_e/cases_e/ds5_e.htm
DS20: https://www.wto.org/english/tratop_e/dispu_e/cases_e/ds20_e.htm
DS40: https://www.wto.org/english/tratop_e/dispu_e/cases_e/ds40_e.htm
DS41: https://www.wto.org/english/tratop_e/dispu_e/cases_e/ds41_e.htm
DS75: https://www.wto.org/english/tratop_e/dispu_e/cases_e/ds75_e.htm
DS84: https://www.wto.org/english/tratop_e/dispu_e/cases_e/ds84_e.htm
DS98: https://www.wto.org/english/tratop_e/dispu_e/cases_e/ds98_e.htm
DS161:https://www.wto.org/english/tratop_e/dispu_e/cases_e/ds161_e.htm
DS163: https://www.wto.org/english/tratop_e/dispu_e/cases_e/ds163_e.htm
DS169: https://www.wto.org/english/tratop_e/dispu_e/cases_e/ds169_e.htm
DS273: https://www.wto.org/english/tratop_e/dispu_e/cases_e/ds273_e.htm
DS312: https://www.wto.org/english/tratop_e/dispu_e/cases_e/ds312_e.htm
DS391: https://www.wto.org/english/tratop_e/dispu_e/cases_e/ds391_e.htm
DS495: https://www.wto.org/english/tratop_e/dispu_e/cases_e/ds495_e.htm

3. China

3.1 China as complainant

Case N.	RoC	Short title	Summary	Current status	Complaiant	Respondent	Third Parties
DS252	26 March 2002	US — Steel Safeguards	United States — Definitive Safeguard Measures on Imports of Certain Steel Products On 26 March 2002, China (WT/DS252) requested consultations with the United States also with regard to the definitive safeguard measures imposed by the US on imports of certain steel products and claimed violations of Articles 2.1, 2.2, 3.1, 3.2, 4.1, 4.2, 5.1, 5.2, 7.1, 8.1, 9.1 and 12 of the Agreement on Safeguards and Articles I:1, II, X:3, XIX:1 and XIX:2 of GATT 1994. On 4 April 2002, Japan requested to join the consultations. On 5 April 2002, New Zealand also requested to join the consultations. The US informed the DSB that it had accepted the requests of Japan and New Zealand to join the consultations.	Report(s) adopted, no further action required on 10 December 2003	China	US	Brazil; Canada; Chinese Taipei; Cuba; European Communities; Japan; Korea, Republic of; Mexico; New Zealand; Norway; Switzerland; Thailand; Turkey; Venezuela, Bolivarian Republic of
DS368	14 September 2007	N/A	United States — Preliminary Anti-Dumping and Countervailing Duty Determinations on Coated Free Sheet Paper from China Complaint by China. On 14 September 2007, China requested consultations with the United States on the preliminary Anti-Dumping and countervailing duty determinations made by the US Department of Commerce in respect of coated free sheet paper from China.	In consultations on 14 September 2007	China	US	N/A

Case N.	RoC	Short title	Summary	Current status	Complainant	Respondent	Third Parties
			China considers that the measures are inconsistent with the United States' obligations under, inter alia, • Article VI of the GATT 1994; • Articles 1, 2, 10, 14, 17 and 32 of the SCM Agreement; and • Articles 1, 2, 7, 9 and 18 of the Anti-Dumping Agreement.				
DS379	19 September 2008	US — Anti-Dumping and Counter-vailing Duties (China)	United States — Definitive Anti-Dumping and Countervailing Duties on Certain Products from China Complaint by China. On 19 September 2008, China requested consultations concerning the definitive anti-dumping and countervailing duties imposed by the United States pursuant to the final Anti-Dumping and countervailing duty determinations and orders issued by the US Department of Commerce in several investigations. China considers that these measures, which include the conduct of the underlying Anti-Dumping and countervailing duty investigations, are inconsistent with the obligations of the United States under, inter alia, Articles I and VI of the GATT 1994, Articles 1, 2, 10, 12, 13, 14, 19 and 32 of the SCM Agreement, Articles 1, 2, 6, 9 and 18 of the Anti-Dumping Agreement, and Article 15 of the Protocol on the Accession of the People's Republic of China (the Protocol of Accession).	Implementation notified by respondent on 31 August 2012	Chin	US	Argentina; Australia; Bahrain, Kingdom of; Brazil; Canada; European Communities; India; Japan; Kuwait, the State of; Mexico; Norway; Saudi Arabia, Kingdom of; Chinese Taipei; Turkey

Case N.	RoC	Short title	Summary	Current status	Complaiant	Respondent	Third Parties
DS392	17 April 2009	US — Poultry (China)	United States — Certain Measures Affecting Imports of Poultry from China Complaint by China. On 17 April 2009, China requested consultations with the United States concerning certain measures taken by the United States affecting the import of poultry products from China. The measure primarily at issue is Section 727 of the Omnibus Appropriations Act of 2009, which effectively prohibits the establishment or implementation of any measures that would allow Chinese poultry to be imported into the United States because it denies the use of any funding by USDA for this purpose. China considers that the United States, through Section 727 and any closely related measures, is in violation, at a minimum, of Articles I:1 and XI:1 of GATT 1994 and Article 4.2 of the Agriculture Agreement. In addition, China also specifies that, although it does not believe that the US measure or any closely related measures at issue constitute sanitary and phytosanitary measures within the meaning of the SPS Agreement, if it were demonstrated that any such measure is a SPS measure, China would consider such measure also to be in violation of US obligations under various provisions of the SPS Agreement.	Report(s) adopted, no further action required on 25 October 2010	China	US	Brazil; European Communities; Guatemala; Korea, Republic of; Chinese Taipei; Turkey

Case N.	RoC	Short title	Summary	Current status	Complaiant	Respondent	Third Parties
DS397	31 July 2009	EC — Fasteners (China)	European Communities — Definitive Anti-Dumping Measures on Certain Iron or Steel Fasteners from China Complaint by China. On 31 July 2009, China requested consultations with the European Communities concerning Article 9(5) of Council Regulation (EC) No. 384/96 (the EC's Basic Anti-Dumping Regulation) which provides that in case of imports from non-market economy countries, the duty shall be specified for the supplying country concerned and not for each supplier and that an individual duty will only be specified for exporters that demonstrate that they fulfil the criteria listed in that provision. According to China, Article 9(5) of the Basic Anti-Dumping Regulation is inconsistent, as such, with the European Communities' obligations under: • Article XVI:4 of the WTO Agreement; • Articles I:1, VI:1, and X:3(a) of the GATT 1994; and • Articles 6.10, 9.2, 9.3, 9.4, 12.2.2 and 18.4 of the Anti-Dumping Agreement. China also requests consultations regarding Council Regulation (EC) No 91/2009 imposing definitive anti-dumping duties on imports of certain iron or steel fasteners originating in the People's Republic of China.	Report(s) adopted, with recommendation to bring measure(s) into conformity on 12 February 2016	China	European Communities	Brazil; Canada; Chile; Colombia; India; Japan; Norway; Chinese Taipei; Thailand; Turkey; United States

Case N.	RoC	Short title	Summary	Current status	Complaiant	Respondent	Third Parties
			China considers that the imposition of definitive Anti-Dumping duties on imports of certain iron or steel fasteners originating in the People's Republic of China is inconsistent with the European Communities' obligations under: • Articles VI and X:3(a) of the GATT 1994; • Articles 1, 2.1, 2.2. 2.4, 2.6, 3.1, 3.2, 3.4, 3.5, 4.1, 5.4, 6.1, 6.2, 6.4, 6.5, 6.10, 9.2, 9.4 and 17.6(i) of the Anti-Dumping Agreement; as well as • Part I, paragraph 15 of China's Protocol of Accession. • In addition, China also refers to Articles 9.3 and 12.2.2 of the Anti-Dumping Agreement.				
DS399	14 September 2009	US — Tyres (China)	United States — Measures Affecting Imports of Certain Passenger Vehicle and Light Truck Tyres from China Complaint by China. On 14 September 2009, China requested consultations with the United States concerning increased tariffs on certain passenger vehicle and light truck tyres (subject tyres) from China. The decision was announced on 11 September 2009 following an investigation pursuant to section 421 of the Trade Act of 1974 (19 U.S.C. 2451 et seq.). The USITC determined that there was market disruption as a result of rapidly increasing imports of subject	Report(s) adopted, no further action required on 5 October 2011	China	US	European Union; Japan; Chinese Taipei; Turkey; Viet Nam

Case N.	RoC	Short title	Summary	Current status	Complaint	Respondent	Third Parties
			tyres from China that were a significant cause of material injury to the domestic industry. Following a Presidential decision additional duties were imposed on subject tyres imports for a three year period in the amount of 35 per cent ad valorem in the first year, 30 per cent ad valorem in the second year and 25 per cent ad valorem in the third year (the tyres measure). This measure took effect on 26 September 2009. According to China the higher tariffs are inconsistent with Article I:1 of the GATT 1994 and have not been properly justified pursuant to Article XIX of the GATT 1994 and the Agreement on Safeguards. China also maintains that these measures are not properly justified as China-specific restrictions under paragraph 16 of its Protocolof Accession. Specifically, China alleges that the US statute defines "significant cause" more narrowly than required by the ordinary meaning of that phrase as used in paragraph 16.4 of the Protocol of Accession. China also alleges that these measures are also inconsistent, as applied, with the United States' obligations under China's Protocol of Accession, specifically: • paragraphs 16.1 and 16.4 because (a) imports from China were not "in such increased quantities" and were not "increasing rapidly"; (b) imports from China were not a "significant cause" of material injury or threat thereof; and (c) the domestic tyre producers were not experiencing "market disruption" or "material injury";				

Case N.	RoC	Short title	Summary	Current status	Complainant	Respondent	Third Parties
			• paragraph 16.3 because the restrictions are being imposed beyond the "extent necessary to prevent or remedy" any alleged market disruption; and • paragraph 16.6 because the restrictions are being imposed for a period of time longer than "necessary to prevent or remedy" any alleged market disruption.				
DS405	4 February 2010	EU — Footwear (China)	European Union — Anti-Dumping Measures on Certain Footwear from China Complaint by China. On 4 February 2010, China requested consultations with the European Union concerning three EU measures in connection with the imposition of Anti-Dumping duties on imports of certain leather footwear from China. In particular, China is challenging as WTO-inconsistent Article 9(5) of the Basic EC Anti-Dumping Regulation, which provides that, in cases involving imports from NME countries, the anti-dumping duty shall be specified for the supplying country concerned and not for each individual supplier. According to China, applicable WTO rules require that an individual margin and duty be determined and specified for each known exporter and producer and not for the supplying country as a whole. China states that the Basic Regulation provides that an individual duty will only be specified for exporters that demonstrate that they fulfil the criteria set forth in Article 9(5), the Individual Treatment rules, and is therefore inconsistent with	Implementation notified by respondent on 17 December 2012	China	European Union	Australia; Brazil; Colombia; Japan; Turkey; United States; Viet Nam

Case N.	RoC	Short title	Summary	Current status	Complaiant	Respondent	Third Parties
			various provisions of the WTO Agreement, China's Protocol of Accession, the GATT 1994, and the Anti-Dumping Agreement. China is also challenging as WTO-inconsistent the Review and Definitive Regulations imposing Anti-Dumping duties on imports of certain footwear from China, and various aspects of the expiry and original determinations and investigations underlying those regulations.				
DS422	28 February 2011	US — Shrimp and Sawblades	United States — Anti-Dumping Measures on Shrimp and Diamond Sawblades from China Complaint by China. On 28 February 2011, China requested consultations with the United States regarding the latter's anti-dumping measures on certain frozen warmwater shrimp from China. China alleged that the US Department of Commerce's (USDOC) use of zeroing in the original investigation and several administrative reviews to calculate dumping margins for the subject imports is inconsistent with the United States' obligations under Article VI:1 and VI:2 of the GATT 1994 and Articles 1, 2.1, 2.4, 2.4.2, 5.8, 9.2, 9.3, and 9.4 of the Anti-Dumping Agreement. China further asserted that the USDOC's reliance, in the sunset review, on the dumping margins calculated in the original investigation and administrative reviews is inconsistent with the United States' obligations under Article 11.3 of the Anti-Dumping Agreement. On 11 March 2011, Japan requested to join the consultations.	Implementation notified by respondent on 26 March 2013	China	US	European Union; Honduras; Japan; Korea, Republic of; Thailand; Viet Nam

Case N.	RoC	Short title	Summary	Current status	Complaiant	Respondent	Third Parties
			On 22 July 2011, China requested complementary consultations with the United States with regard to the zeroing practice by the USDOC in its Anti-Dumping measures on diamond sawblades and parts thereof from China. China alleged that the USDOC's zeroing practice has artificially created or, at a minimum, inflated dumping margins for the individually investigated respondents. China considered that the zeroing practices in the cited measures are inconsistent with the United States' obligations under Article VI:1 and VI:2 of the GATT 1994 and Articles 1, 2.1, 2.4, 2.4.2, 5.8, 9.2, 9.3, and 9.4 of the Anti-Dumping Agreement.				
DS437	25 May 2012	US — Countervailing Measures (China)	DS437: United States — Countervailing Duty Measures on Certain Products from China Complaint by China. On 25 May 2012, China requested consultations with the United States concerning the imposition of countervailing duty measures by the United States on certain products from China. China challenges various aspects of certain identified countervailing duty investigations, including their opening, conduct and the preliminary and final determinations that led to the imposition of countervailing duties. China also challenges the "rebuttable presumption" allegedly established and applied by the US Department of Commerce that majority government ownership is sufficient to treat an enterprise as a "public body".	Compliance proceedings ongoing on 21 July 2016	China	US	Australia; Brazil; Canada; European Union; India; Japan; Korea, Republic of; Norway; Russian Federation; Turkey; Viet Nam; Saudi Arabia, Kingdom of

Case N.	RoC	Short title	Summary	Current status	Complaiant	Respondent	Third Parties
			China claims that the challenge measures are inconsistent with: • Article VI of the GATT 1994; • Articles 1.1, 2, 11.1, 11.2, 11.3, 12.7 and 14(d) of the SCM Agreement; and • Article 15 of the Protocol of Accession of China.				
DS449	17 September 2012	US — Countervailing and Anti-Dumping Measures (China)	United States — Countervailing and Anti-dumping Measures on Certain Products from China Complaint by China. On 17 September 2012, China requested consultations with the United States concerning the following measures: (i) a new piece of legislation (Public Law 112-99) that explicitly allows for the application of countervailing measures to non-market economy countries; (ii) countervailing duty determinations or actions made or performed by US authorities between 20 November 2006 and 13 March 2012 in respect of Chinese products; (iii) Anti-Dumping measures associated with the concerned countervailing duty measures as well as the combined effect of these Anti-Dumping measures and the parallel countervailing duty measures; and (iv) the United States' failure to provide the US Department of Commerce (USDOC) with legal authority to identify and avoid the double remedies in respect of investigations or reviews initiated on or	Report(s) adopted, with recommendation to bring measure(s) into conformity on 22 July 2014	China	US	Australia; Canada; European Union; Japan; Turkey; Viet Nam; India; Russian Federation

Case N.	RoC	Short title	Summary	Current status	Complaiant	Respondent	Third Parties
			between 20 November 2006 and 13 March 2012. China considers that these measures are inconsistent with: • Articles 10, 15, 19, 21 and 32 of the SCM Agreement; • Articles VI, X:1, X:2 and X:3 of the GATT 1994; and • Articles 9 and 11 of the Anti-Dumping Agreement.				
DS452	5 November 2012	N/A	European Union and certain Member States — Certain Measures Affecting the Renewable Energy Generation Sector Complaint by China. On 5 November 2012, China requested consultations with the European Union, Greece and Italy regarding certain measures, including domestic content restrictions, that affect the renewable energy generation sector relating to the feed-in tariff programs of EU member States, including but not limited to Italy and Greece. China claims that these measures are inconsistent with: • Articles I, III:1, III:4 and III:5 of the GATT 1994; • Articles 3.1(b) and 3.2 of the SCM Agreement; and • Articles 2.1 and 2.2 of the TRIMs Agreement	In consultations on 5 November 2012	China	European Union; Italy; Greece	N/A

Case N.	RoC	Short title	Summary	Current status	Complaiant	Respondent	Third Parties
DS471	3 December 2013	US — Anti-Dumping Methodologies (China)	DS471: United States — Certain Methodologies and their Application to Anti-Dumping Proceedings Involving China Complaint by China. On 3 December 2013, China requested consultations with the United States regarding the use of certain methodologies in Anti-Dumping investigations involving Chinese products. China claims that the measures mentioned in the request for consultations are inconsistent with: • Articles 2.4.2, 6.1, 6.8, 6.10, 9.2, 9.3, 9.4 and Annex II of the Anti-Dumping Agreement; and • Article VI:2 of the GATT 1994.	Panel report under appeal on 18 November 2016	China	US	Brazil; Canada; European Union; India; Japan; Korea, Republic of; Norway; Russian Federation; Saudi Arabia, Kingdom of; Ukraine; Viet Nam; Turkey; Chinese Taipei
DS492	8 April 2015	EU — Poultry Meat (China)	European Union — Measures Affecting Tariff Concessions on Certain Poultry Meat Products Complaint by China. On 8 April 2015, China requested consultations with the European Union regarding measures to modify the European Union tariff concessions on certain poultry meat products. China claims that the measures are inconsistent with Articles I, II, XIII and XXVIII of the GATT 1994.	Panel composed on 3 December 2015	China	European Union	Brazil; Russian Federation; United States; Argentina; Canada; India; Thailand
DS515	12 December 2016	N/A	United States — Measures Related to Price Comparison Methodologies Complaint by China	In consultations on 12 December 2016	China	US	N/A

Case N.	RoC	Short title	Summary	Current status	Complaiant	Respondent	Third Parties
			On 12 December 2016, China requested consultations with the United States concerning certain provisions of US law pertaining to the determination of normal value for "non-market economy" countries in Anti-Dumping proceedings involving products from China. China claimed that the measures appear to be inconsistent with: • Articles 2.1, 2.2, 9.2, 18.1, 18.4 of the Anti-Dumping Agreement; • Articles I:1, VI:1 and VI:2 of the GATT 1994; and • Article XVI:4 of the Marrakesh Agreement.				
DS516	12 December 2016	N/A	European Union — Measures Related to Price Comparison Methodologies Complaint by China On 12 December 2016, China requested consultations with the European Union concerning certain provisions of the EU regulation pertaining to the determination of normal value for "non-market economy" countries in Anti-Dumping proceedings involving products from China. China claimed that the measures appear to be inconsistent with: • Articles 2.1 and 2.2 of the Anti-Dumping Agreement; and • Articles I:1 and VI:1 of the GATT 1994.	In consultations on 12 December 2016	China	European Union	N/A

Sourse:
DS252: https://www.wto.org/english/tratop_e/dispu_e/cases_e/ds252_e.htm
DS368: https://www.wto.org/english/tratop_e/dispu_e/cases_e/ds368_e.htm
DS379: https://www.wto.org/english/tratop_e/dispu_e/cases_e/ds379_e.htm
DS392: https://www.wto.org/english/tratop_e/dispu_e/cases_e/ds392_e.htm
DS397: https://www.wto.org/english/tratop_e/dispu_e/cases_e/ds_e.htm
DS405: https://www.wto.org/english/tratop_e/dispu_e/cases_e/ds405_e.htm
DS422: https://www.wto.org/english/tratop_e/dispu_e/cases_e/ds422_e.htm
DS437: https://www.wto.org/english/tratop_e/dispu_e/cases_e/ds437_e.htm
DS449: https://www.wto.org/english/tratop_e/dispu_e/cases_e/ds449_e.htm
DS452: https://www.wto.org/english/tratop_e/dispu_e/cases_e/ds452_e.htm
DS471: https://www.wto.org/english/tratop_e/dispu_e/cases_e/ds471_e.htm
DS592: https://www.wto.org/english/tratop_e/dispu_e/cases_e/ds492_e.htm
DS515: https://www.wto.org/english/tratop_e/dispu_e/cases_e/ds515_e.htm
DS516: https://www.wto.org/english/tratop_e/dispu_e/cases_e/ds516_e.htm

3.2 China as respondent

Case N.	RoC	Short title	Summary	Current status	Respondent	Third Parties
DS309	2004	N/A	China — Value-Added Tax on Integrated Circuits Complaint by the United States. On 18 March 2004, the United States requested consultations with China concerning China's preferential value-added tax (VAT) for domestically-produced or designed integrated circuits (IC). The United States claims that, although China provides for a 17 percent VAT on ICs, enterprises in China are entitled to a partial refund of the VAT on ICs that they have produced, resulting in a lower VAT rate on their products. In the US view, China thus appears to be subjecting imported ICs to higher taxes than applied to domestically produced ICs and to be according less favourable treatment to imported ICs. In addition, the United States claims that China allows for a partial refund of VAT for domestically-designed ICs that, because of technological limitations, are manufactured outside of China. In the US view, China thus appears to be providing for more favourable treatment of imports from one Member than from others, and also is discriminating against services and service suppliers of other Members. The United States considers that these measures are inconsistent with the obligations of China under Articles I and III of the GATT 1994, the Protocol on the Accession of the People's Republic of China (WT/L/432), and Article XVII of the GATS.	Settled or terminated (withdrawn, mutually agreed solution) on 5 October 2005	US	N/A

Case N.	RoC	Short title	Summary	Current status	Respondent	Third Parties
DS339	2006	China — Auto Parts	China — Measures Affecting Imports of Automobile Parts Complaint by the European Communities (WT/DS339). On 30 March 2006, the European Communities and the United States, and on 13 April 2006, Canada, requested consultations with China regarding China's imposition of measures that adversely affect exports of automobile parts from the European Communities, the United States and Canada to China. The measures include the following: (a) Policy on Development of Automotive Industry (Order No. 8 of the National Development and Reform Commission, 21 May 2004); (b) Measures for the Administration of Importation of Automotive Parts and Components for Complete Vehicles (Decree No. 125), which entered into force on 1 April 2005); and, (c) Rules for Determining Whether Imported Automotive Parts and Components Constitute Complete Vehicles (General Administration of Customs Public Announcement No. 4, which entered into force on 1 April 2005; as well as any amendments, replacements, extensions, implementing measures or other measures related. The European Communities argues that, under the measures identified, imported automobile parts that are used in the manufacture of vehicles for sale in China are subject to charges equal to the tariffs for complete vehicles, if they are imported in excess of certain thresholds. The European Communities considers that the measures are inconsistent with:	Implementation notified by respondent on 31 August 2009	European Communities	Argentina; Australia; Brazil; Japan; Mexico; Chinese Taipei; Thailand

Case N.	RoC	Short title	Summary	Current status	Respondent	Third Parties
			• Articles II:1(a), II:1(b), III:2, III:4, III:5 of the GATT 1994, as well as with the principles contained in Article III:1. • Articles 2.1 and 2.2 of the TRIMs Agreement in conjunction with paragraphs 1(a) and 2(a) of the Illustrative List annexed to the Agreement. • Article 3 of the SCM Agreement. • China's obligations under its Access Protocol, in particular Part I, para. 7.3 of the Accession Protocol, and in para. 203 of the Working Party Report on the Accession of China (WP Report) in conjunction with Part I, para. 1.2 of the Accession Protocol, and para. 342 of the WP Report. The European Communities also considers that China had nullified or impaired the benefits accruing to the European Communities under the Accession Protocol, in particular para. 93 of the WP Report, in conjunction with Part I, para. 1.2 of the Accession Protocol, and para. 342 of the WP Report.			
DS340	2006	China — Auto Parts	China — Measures Affecting Imports of Automobile Parts Complaint by the United States (WT/DS340). On 30 March 2006, the European Communities and the United States, and on 13 April 2006, Canada, requested consultations with China regarding China's imposition of measures that adversely affect exports of automobile parts from the European	Implementation notified by respondent on 31 August 2009	US	Argentina; Australia; Brazil; Japan; Mexico; Chinese Taipei; Thailand

Case N.	RoC	Short title	Summary	Current status	Respondent	Third Parties
			Communities, the United States and Canada to China. The measures include the following: (a) Policy on Development of Automotive Industry (Order No. 8 of the National Development and Reform Commission, 21 May 2004); (b) Measures for the Administration of Importation of Automotive Parts and Components for Complete Vehicles (Decree No. 125), which entered into force on 1 April 2005); and, (c) Rules for Determining Whether Imported Automotive Parts and Components Constitute Complete Vehicles (General Administration of Customs Public Announcement No. 4, which entered into force on 1 April 2005; as well as any amendments, replacements, extensions, implementing measures or other measures related. The European Communities argues that, under the measures identified, imported automobile parts that are used in the manufacture of vehicles for sale in China are subject to charges equal to the tariffs for complete vehicles, if they are imported in excess of certain thresholds. The European Communities considers that the measures are inconsistent with: • Articles II:1(a), II:1(b), III:2, III:4, III:5 of the GATT 1994, as well as with the principles contained in Article III:1. • Articles 2.1 and 2.2 of the TRIMs Agreement in conjunction with paragraphs 1(a) and 2(a) of the Illustrative List annexed to the Agreement. • Article 3 of the SCM Agreement.			

Case N.	RoC	Short title	Summary	Current status	Respondent	Third Parties
			• China's obligations under its Access Protocol, in particular Part I, para. 7.3 of the Accession Protocol, and in para. 203 of the Working Party Report on the Accession of China (WP Report) in conjunction with Part I, para. 1.2 of the Accession Protocol, and para. 342 of the WP Report.			
DS342	2006	China — Auto Parts	China — Measures Affecting Imports of Automobile Parts Complaint by Canada (WT/DS342). On 30 March 2006, the European Communities and the United States, and on 13 April 2006, Canada, requested consultations with China regarding China's imposition of measures that adversely affect exports of automobile parts from the European Communities, the United States and Canada to China. The measures include the following: (a) Policy on Development of Automotive Industry (Order No. 8 of the National Development and Reform Commission, 21 May 2004); (b) Measures for the Administration of Importation of Automotive Parts and Components for Complete Vehicles (Decree No. 125), which entered into force on 1 April 2005); and, (c) Rules for Determining Whether Imported Automotive Parts and Components Constitute Complete Vehicles (General Administration of Customs Public Announcement No. 4, which entered into force on 1 April 2005; as well as any amendments, replacements, extensions, implementing measures or other measures related. Canada argues that the measures identified above	Implementation notified by respondent on 31 August 2009	Canada	Argentina; Australia; Brazil; Japan; Mexico; Chinese Taipei; Thailand

Case N.	RoC	Short title	Summary	Current status	Respondent	Third Parties
			impose different charges on vehicles manufactured in China depending on the domestic content of the automobile parts used in the manufacture, thus providing domestic manufacturers with an advantage if they use domestic parts. Canada also argues that the measure may also have an impact on foreign investments as they confer an advantage to enterprises, conditioned on the use in vehicle production of domestic instead of imported parts. Canada adds that the charges that may be assessed on automobile parts once a vehicle is complete appear to constitute a charge in excess of those set forth in China's schedule of concessions. China would also be applying the tariff for completed vehicles to completely-knocked down and semi-knocked down kits. The measures also seem to provide subsidies contingent upon export performance and upon the use of domestic over imported goods. Canada considers that the measures at issue are inconsistent with: • The Protocol of Accession (WT/L/432) (including Parts I.1.2 and I.7.3, and paras. 93 and 203 of the Working Party Report). • Articles II (including para. 1) and III (including paras. 2, 4 and 5) of the GATT 1994. • Article 2 of the TRIMs Agreement. • Article 2 of the Agreement on Rules of Origin, specifically paras. (b), (c) and (d).			

Case N.	RoC	Short title	Summary	Current status	Respondent	Third Parties
			• Article 3 of the SCM Agreement.			
DS358	2007	China — Taxes	China — Certain Measures Granting Refunds, Reductions or Exemptions from Taxes and Other Payments Complaint by the United States. (See also dispute DS359) On 2 February 2007, the United States requested consultations with China concerning measures granting refunds, reductions or exemptions from taxes and other payments owed to the Government by enterprises in China. The request for consultations identifies various measures, including any amendments and any related or implementing measures. The United States considers the measures in question to be inconsistent with Article 3 of the SCM Agreement in that they provide refunds, reductions or exemptions to enterprises in China on the condition that those enterprises purchase domestic over imported goods, or on the condition that those enterprises meet certain export performance criteria. Further, the United States claims that, to the extent the measures accord imported products treatment less favourable than that accorded "like" domestic products, they are inconsistent with Article III:4 of the GATT 1994 and Article 2 of the TRIMs Agreement. The United States also claims that the measures do not comply with China's obligations under paras. 7.2-7.3 and 10.3 of Part I of its Accession Protocol, as well as para. 1.2 (to	Settled or terminated (withdrawn, mutually agreed solution) on 19 December 2007	United States	Argentina; Australia; Canada; Chile; Colombia; Egypt; European Union; Japan; Chinese Taipei

Case N.	RoC	Short title	Summary	Current status	Respondent	Third Parties
			the extent that it incorporates paras. 167 and 203 of the Report of the Working Party on the Accession of China), which forms part of the terms of accession agreed between China and the WTO and is an integral part of the WTO Agreement.			
DS359	2007	China — Taxes	China — Certain Measures Granting Refunds, Reductions or Exemptions from Taxes and Other Payments Complaint by the United States. (See also dispute DS359) On 2 February 2007, the United States requested consultations with China concerning measures granting refunds, reductions or exemptions from taxes and other payments owed to the Government by enterprises in China. The request for consultations identifies various measures, including any amendments and any related or implementing measures. The United States considers the measures in question to be inconsistent with Article 3 of the SCM Agreement in that they provide refunds, reductions or exemptions to enterprises in China on the condition that those enterprises purchase domestic over imported goods, or on the condition that those enterprises meet certain export performance criteria. Further, the United States claims that, to the extent the measures accord imported products treatment less favourable than that accorded "like" domestic products, they are inconsistent with Article III:4 of the GATT 1994 and	Settled or terminated (withdrawn, mutually agreed solution) on 7 February 2008	Mexico	Argentina; Australia; Canada; Chile; Colombia; Egypt; European Union; Japan; Chinese Taipei

Case N.	RoC	Short title	Summary	Current status	Respondent	Third Parties
			Article 2 of the TRIMs Agreement. The United States also claims that the measures do not comply with China's obligations under paras. 7.2-7.3 and 10.3 of Part I of its Accession Protocol, as well as para. 1.2 (to the extent that it incorporates paras. 167 and 203 of the Report of the Working Party on the Accession of China), which forms part of the terms of accession agreed between China and the WTO and is an integral part of the WTO Agreement.			
DS362	2007	China — Intellectual Property Rights	China — Measures Affecting the Protection and Enforcement of Intellectual Property Rights Complaint by the United States. On 10 April 2007, the United States requested consultations with China concerning certain measures pertaining to the protection and enforcement of intellectual property rights in China. The four matters on which the United States requests consultations are: • the thresholds that must be met in order for certain acts of trademark counterfeiting and copyright piracy to be subject to criminal procedures and penalties; • goods that infringe intellectual property rights that are confiscated by Chinese customs authorities, in particular the disposal of such goods following removal of their infringing features;	Implementation notified by respondent on 19 March 2010	US	Argentina; Australia; Brazil; Canada; European Communities; India; Japan; Korea, Republic of; Mexico; Chinese Taipei; Thailand; Turkey

Case N.	RoC	Short title	Summary	Current status	Respondent	Third Parties
			• the scope of coverage of criminal procedures and penalties for unauthorized reproduction or unauthorized distribution of copyrighted works; and • the denial of copyright and related rights protection and enforcement to creative works of authorship, sound recordings and performances that have not been authorized for publication or distribution within China. The United States claims that in relation to the four above-mentioned matters possible inconsistencies with the TRIPS Agreement arise as follows: • The lack of criminal procedures and penalties for commercial scale counterfeiting and piracy in China as a result of the thresholds appears to be inconsistent with China's obligations under Articles 41.1 and 61 of the TRIPS Agreement. • The requirement that infringing goods be released into the channels of commerce under the circumstances set forth in the measures at issue appears to be inconsistent with China's obligations under Articles 46 and 59 of the TRIPS Agreement. • Authors of works whose publication or distribution has not been authorized (and whose publication or distribution is therefore prohibited) appear not to enjoy the minimum standards of protection specially granted by the Berne Convention in respect of those works (and may never enjoy such protection if the work is not authorized, or is not authorized for			

Case N.	RoC	Short title	Summary	Current status	Respondent	Third Parties
			distribution or publication in the form as submitted for review). In addition, the rights of authors of works whose publication or distribution is required to undergo pre-publication or pre-distribution review appear to be subject to the formality of successful conclusion of such review. The foregoing appears to be inconsistent with China's obligations under Article 9.1 of the TRIPS Agreement. In addition, to the extent that the Copyright Law also denies protection of so-called related rights to performers and producers of sound recordings during the period of any pre-publication or pre-distribution, the Copyright Law appears to be inconsistent with China's obligations under Article 14 of the TRIPS Agreement. Furthermore, to the extent that different pre-distribution and pre-authorization review processes for Chinese nationals' works, performances (or their fixations) and sound recordings than for foreign nationals' works, performances (or their fixations) and sound recordings result in earlier or otherwise more favourable protection or enforcement of copyright or related rights for Chinese authors' works, Chinese performers' performances (or their fixations) and Chinese producers' sound recordings, the measures at issue appear to be inconsistent with China's obligations under Article 3.1 of the TRIPS Agreement. Additionally, to the extent that Article 4 of the Copyright Law causes foreign authors of works whose publication or distribution has not been authorized not to enjoy the rights granted to Chinese authors, the measures at issue appear to be inconsistent with China's obligations under Article			

Case N.	RoC	Short title	Summary	Current status	Respondent	Third Parties
			9.1 of the TRIPS Agreement (with respect at least to China's obligations to comply with Articles 5(1) and 5(2) of the Berne Convention). In addition, to the extent that Article 4 of China's Copyright Law makes it impossible for rights holders to enforce their copyrights or related rights with respect to works, performances or sound recordings that have not been authorized for publication or distribution, China appears to act inconsistently with China's obligations under Article 41.1 of the TRIPS Agreement. • To the extent that wilful copyright piracy on a commercial scale that consists of unauthorized reproduction — but not unauthorized distribution — of copyrighted works, and vice versa, may not be subject to criminal procedures and penalties under the law of China, this would appear to be inconsistent with China's obligations under Articles 41.1 and 61 of the TRIPS Agreement.			
DS363	2007	China — Publications and Audiovisual Products	China — Measures Affecting Trading Rights and Distribution Services for Certain Publications and Audiovisual Entertainment Products Complaint by the United States. On 10 April 2007, the United States requested consultations with China concerning: (1) certain measures that restrict trading rights with respect to imported films for theatrical release, audiovisual home entertainment products (e.g. video cassettes and DVDs), sound recordings and publications (e.g. books, magazines, newspapers and electronic	Implementation notified by respondent on 24 May 2012	US	Australia; European Communities; Japan; Korea, Republic of; Chinese Taipei

Case N.	RoC	Short title	Summary	Current status	Respondent	Third Parties
			publications); and (2) certain measures that restrict market access for, or discriminate against, foreign suppliers of distribution services for publications and foreign suppliers of audiovisual services (including distribution services) for audiovisual home entertainment products. • Regarding trading rights, the United States seeks consultations on various Chinese measures that reserve, to certain Chinese state-designated and wholly or partially state-owned enterprises, the right to import films for theatrical release, audiovisual home entertainment products, sound recordings and publications; • Regarding distribution services, the United States seeks consultations on various Chinese measures that impose market access restrictions or discriminatory limitations on foreign service providers seeking to engage in the distribution of publications and certain audiovisual home entertainment products. The United States claims that in relation to the two above-mentioned categories of measures possible inconsistencies with the Protocol of Accession, the GATT 1994 or the GATS arise as follows: • Regarding trading rights, the measures at issue appear not to allow all Chinese enterprises and all foreign enterprises and individuals the right to import the products into the customs territory of China. It also appears that foreign individuals and enterprises, including those not invested or			

Case N.	RoC	Short title	Summary	Current status	Respondent	Third Parties
			registered in China, are accorded treatment less favourable than that accorded to enterprises in China with respect to the right to trade. Accordingly, the measures at issue appear to be inconsistent with China's obligations under the provisions of paragraphs 5.1 and 5.2 of Part I of the Protocol of Accession, as well as China's obligations under the provisions of paragraph 1.2 of Part I of the Protocol of Accession (to the extent that it incorporates commitments in paragraphs 83 and 84 of the Report of the Working Party on the Accession of China). Furthermore, to the extent that the measures at issue impose prohibitions or restrictions other than duties, taxes or other charges, on the importation into China of the Products, these measures appear to be inconsistent with China's obligations under Article XI:1 of the GATT 1994.			
			• Regarding the measures affecting distribution services for publications, these appear to accord less favourable treatment to foreign suppliers of distribution services for publications than that accorded to Chinese suppliers. Accordingly, the GATS. Similarly, the measures affecting distribution services for audiovisual home entertainment products appear to accord less favourable treatment to foreign suppliers of audiovisual distribution services than that accorded to Chinese suppliers, and to impose restrictions on market access on foreign suppliers of audiovisual distribution services for audiovisual home entertainment products. The measures at issue appear to be inconsistent with China's obligations under Articles XVI and XVII of the GATS.			

Case N.	RoC	Short title	Summary	Current status	Respondent	Third Parties
DS372	2008	N/A	China — Measures Affecting Financial Information Services and Foreign Financial Information Suppliers Complaint by the European Communities. On 3 March 2008, the European Communities requested consultations with China with respect to measures affecting financial information services and foreign financial information services suppliers in China. The European Communities claims that a number of Chinese measures are adversely affecting financial information services and foreign financial services suppliers in China. Such measures include no fewer than a dozen legal and administrative instruments which empower the "Xinhua News Agency", the State news agency in China, to act as the regulatory authority for foreign news agencies and for foreign financial information providers. The European Communities contends that Xinhua News Agency is responsible for the examination and approval procedure in respect of foreign financial information providers and that, as a result, these foreign suppliers can only operate in China through an agent designated by Xinhua. As such, they are not allowed to directly solicit subscriptions for their services in China. The European Communities claims that Xinhua News Agency has only designated the China Economic Information Service (CEIS), a branch of Xinhua, as an agent and it has made the renewal of foreign financial information suppliers licences conditional upon the signature of agent agreements with CEIS.	Settled or terminated (withdrawn, mutually agreed solution) on 4 December 2008	European Communities	N/A

Case N.	RoC	Short title	Summary	Current status	Respondent	Third Parties
			The European Communities considers that the measures at issue are inconsistent with China's obligations under various provisions of the GATS, the TRIPS Agreement and China's Protocol of Accession.			
DS373	2008	N/A	China — Measures Affecting Financial Information Services and Foreign Financial Information Suppliers Complaint by the United States. On 3 March 2008, the United States requested consultations with China with respect to certain measures pertaining to financial information services and service suppliers. The United States makes claims against a number of Chinese measures affecting financial information services and foreign financial services suppliers in China. Such measures include no fewer than a dozen legal and administrative instruments which require foreign financial information suppliers to supply their services through an entity designated by Xinhua News Agency (Xinhua). Xinhua has designated only one such agent, China Economic Information Service (CEIS), one of Xinhua's commercial enterprises. According to the United States, China prohibits foreign financial information suppliers from directly soliciting subscriptions for their services, requiring that solicitation of subscriptions be done through the Xinhua-designated entity. China likewise prohibits users of financial information services in China from directly subscribing to services supplied by foreign suppliers. Furthermore, in order to renew their licenses, China	Settled or terminated (withdrawn, mutually agreed solution) on 4 December 2008	US	N/A

Case N.	RoC	Short title	Summary	Current status	Respondent	Third Parties
			requires foreign financial information suppliers to provide the Foreign Information Administration Center (FIAC), a regulatory body within the Xinhua framework, detailed and confidential information concerning their financial information services, their customers and their foreign suppliers. The United States contends that these and other requirements and restrictions accord less favourable treatment to foreign information services and service suppliers than that accorded to Chinese financial information services and service suppliers which are not affected by these requirements and restrictions. The United States also claims that China is preventing foreign financial information service suppliers from establishing any commercial presence in China other than limited representative offices. The United States considers that the measures at issue are inconsistent with various provisions of the GATS, the horizontal standstill commitment contained in China's schedule of obligations under the GATS, and China's Protocol of Accession.			
DS378	2008	N/A	China — Measures Affecting Financial Information Services and Foreign Financial Information Suppliers Complaint by Canada. On 20 June 2008, Canada requested consultations with China with respect to measures affecting financial information services and foreign financial information service suppliers in China. Canada makes claims against a number of Chinese measures affecting financial information services and foreign financial information service suppliers in	Settled or terminated (withdrawn, mutually agreed solution) on 20 June 2008	Canada	N/A

Case N.	RoC	Short title	Summary	Current status	Respondent	Third Parties
			China. uch measures include no fewer than a dozen legal and administrative instruments which require foreign financial information suppliers to supply their services through an entity designated by Xinhua News Agency (Xinhua). inhua has designated only one such agent, China Economic Information Service (CEIS), one of Xinhua's commercial enterprises. ccording to Canada, China prohibits foreign financial information suppliers from directly soliciting subscriptions for their services, requiring that solicitation of subscriptions to be done through the Xinhua-designated entity. China likewise prohibits users of financial information services in China from directly subscribing to services supplied by foreign suppliers to provide the Foreign Information Administration Center (FIAC), a regulatory body within the Xinhua framework, detailed and confidential information concerning their financial information services, their customers and their foreign suppliers. Canada contends that these and other requirements and restrictions accord less favourable treatment to foreign financial information suppliers than that accorded to Chinese financial information services and service suppliers which are not affected by these requirements and restrictions. Canada also claims that China is preventing foreign financial information service suppliers from establishing any commercial presence in China other than limited representative offices. Canada therefore considers that the measures at issue are inconsistent with Articles XVI, XVII and XVIII of the GATS, the horizontal standstill commitment contained in China's Schedule of obligations under the GATS, and China's Accession Protocol.			

Case N.	RoC	Short title	Summary	Current status	Respondent	Third Parties
DS387	2008	N/A	China — Grants, Loans and Other Incentives Complaint by the United States. On 19 December 2008, the United States requested consultations with China with regard to certain measures offering grants, loans and other incentives to enterprises in China. The United States indicated that these grants, loans and other incentives are reflected in a number of measures, as well as in any amendments or any related or implementing measures, including measures relating to the China World Top Brand Programme and the Chinese Famous Export Brand Programme. The United States considers that these measures appear to provide grants, loans, and other incentives to enterprises in China on the condition that those enterprises meet certain export performance criteria. Accordingly, the measures appear to be inconsistent with Article 3 of the SCM Agreement. Additionally, to the extent that these measures provide subsidies for agricultural products, they appear to be inconsistent with Articles 3, 9, and 10 of the Agreement on Agriculture. The measures also appear to be inconsistent with China's obligations under paragraph 12.1 of Part I of its Accession Protocol, as well as paragraph 1.2 of Part I of its Accession Protocol (to the extent that it incorporates paragraph 234 of the Report of the Working Party on the Accession of China), which forms part of the terms of accession agreed between China and the WTO and is an integral part of the WTO Agreement.	In consultations on 19 December 2008	US	N/A

Case N.	RoC	Short title	Summary	Current status	Respondent	Third Parties
			Finally, the grants, loans, and other incentives appear to be inconsistent with Article III:4 of the GATT 1994 to the extent that the measures benefit Chinese-origin products but not imported products. under paragraph 12.1 of Part I of its Accession Protocol, as well as paragraph 1.2 of Part I of its Accession Protocol (to the extent that it incorporates paragraph 234 of the Report of the Working Party on the Accession of China), which forms part of the terms of accession agreed between the PRC and the WTO and is an integral part of the WTO Agreement. Finally, the grants, loans and other incentives appear to be inconsistent with Article III:4 of the GATT 1994 to the extent that the measures benefit Chinese-origin products and not imported products.			
DS388	2008	N/A	China — Grants, Loans and Other Incentives Complaint by Mexico. On 19 December 2008, Mexico requested consultations with China with regard to certain measures offering grants, loans and other incentives to enterprises in China. Mexico indicated that these grants, loans and other incentives are reflected in a number of measures, as well as in any amendments or any related or implementing measures including measures relating to the China World Top Brand Programme and the Chinese Famous Export Brand Programme. Mexico considers that these measures appear to provide enterprises in China with grants, loans and other incentives contingent upon export	In consultations on 19 December 2008	Mexico	N/A

Case N.	RoC	Short title	Summary	Current status	Respondent	Third Parties
			performance. Accordingly, the measures appear to be inconsistent with Article 3 of the SCM Agreement. Additionally, to the extent that these measures provide subsidies for agricultural products, they appear to be inconsistent with Articles 3, 9, and 10 of the Agreement on Agriculture. The measures also appear to be inconsistent with the PRC's obligations the extent that the measures benefit Chinese-origin products and not imported products.			
DS390	2008	N/A	China — Grants, Loans and Other Incentives Complaint by Guatemala. On 19 January 2009, Guatemala requested consultations with China with regard to certain measures offering grants, loans and other incentives to enterprises in China. Guatemala indicated that these grants, loans and other incentives are reflected in a number of measures, as well as in any amendments or any related or implementing measures, including measures relating to the China World Top Brand Programme and the Chinese Famous Export Brand Programme. Guatemala considers that these measures appear to provide grants, loans, and other incentives that are contingent upon export performance. Accordingly, the measures appear to be inconsistent with Article 3 of the SCM Agreement. Additionally, to the extent that these measures provide subsidies for agricultural products, they appear to be inconsistent with Articles 3, 8, 9, and 10 of the Agreement on Agriculture.	In consultations on 19 December 2008	Guatemala	N/A

Case N.	RoC	Short title	Summary	Current status	Respondent	Third Parties
			The measures also appear to be inconsistent with China's obligations under paragraph 12.1 of Part I of its Accession Protocol, as well as paragraph 1.2 of Part I of its Accession Protocol (to the extent that it incorporates paragraph 234 of the Report of the Working Party on the Accession of China), which forms part of the terms of accession agreed between China and the WTO and is an integral part of the WTO Agreement. Finally, the grants, loans, and other incentives appear to be inconsistent with Article III:4 of the GATT 1994 to the extent that the measures benefit products of Chinese origin but not imported products.			
DS394	2009	China — Raw Materials	China — Measures Related to the Exportation of Various Raw Materials Complaint by the United States. (See also DS395 and DS398) On 23 June 2009, the United States requested consultations with China with respect to China's restraints on the export from China of various forms of raw materials. The United States cites 32 measures through which China allegedly imposes restraints on the exports in question and note that there appear to be additional unpublished restrictive measures. The United States considers that China, through these measures as well as any amendments, replacements, related measures, and implementing measures, is in violation of:	Implementation notified by respondent on 28 January 2013	US	Argentina; Brazil; Canada; Chile; Colombia; Ecuador; European Union; India; Japan; Korea, Republic of; Mexico; Norway; Chinese Taipei; Turkey; Saudi Arabia, Kingdom of

Case N.	RoC	Short title	Summary	Current status	Respondent	Third Parties
			• Articles VIII, X, and XI of the GATT 1994; and • Paragraphs 5.1, 5.2, 8.2, and 11.3 of Part I of the Protocol on the Accession of the People's Republic of China (Accession Protocol), as well as China's obligations under the provisions of paragraph 1.2 of Part I of the Accession Protocol (which incorporates commitments in paragraphs 83, 84, 162, and 165 of the Report of the Working Party on the Accession of China). The United States considers that the measures also appear to nullify or impair the benefits accruing to the United States directly or indirectly under the cited agreements.			
DS395	2009	China — Raw Materials	China — Measures Related to the Exportation of Various Raw Materials Complaint by the European Communities. (See also DS394 and DS398) On 23 June 2009, the European Communities requested consultations with China with respect to China's restraints on the export from China of various forms of raw materials. The European Communities cites 32 measures through which China allegedly imposes restraints on the exports in question and note that there appear to be additional unpublished restrictive measures. The European Communities considers that China, through these measures as well as any amendments, replacements, related measures, and implementing measures, is in violation of:	Implementation notified by respondent on 28 January 2013	European Communities	Argentina; Brazil; Canada; Chile; Colombia; Ecuador; India; Japan; Korea, Republic of; Mexico; Norway; Chinese Taipei; Turkey; Saudi Arabia, Kingdom of; United States

Case N.	RoC	Short title	Summary	Current status	Respondent	Third Parties
			• Articles VIII, X, and XI of the GATT 1994, and • Paragraphs 5.1, 5.2, 8.2 and 11.3 of Part I of the Protocol on the Accession of the People's Republic of China (Accession Protocol), as well as China's obligations under the provisions of paragraph 1.2 of Part I of the Accession Protocol (which incorporates commitments in paragraphs 83, 84, 162 and 165 of the Report of the Working Party on the Accession of China) and its commitments referred to in paragraph 342 of the Working Party Report. The European Communities considers that the measures also appear to nullify or impair the benefits accruing to the European Communities directly or indirectly under the cited agreements.			
DS398	2009	China — Raw Materials	China — Measures Related to the Exportation of Various Raw Materials Complaint by Mexico. (See also DS394 and DS395) On 21 August 2009, Mexico requested consultations with China with respect to China's restraints on the export from China of various forms of raw materials. Mexico cites 32 measures through which China allegedly imposes restraints on the exports in question and note that there appear to be additional unpublished restrictive measures. Mexico considers that China, through these measures as well as any amendments, replacements, related measures, and implementing measures, is in violation of:	Implementation notified by respondent on 28 January 2013	Mexico	Argentina; Brazil; Canada; Chile; Colombia; Ecuador; European Union; India; Japan; Korea, Republic of; Norway; Chinese Taipei; Turkey; Saudi Arabia,

Case N.	RoC	Short title	Summary	Current status	Respondent	Third Parties
			• Articles VIII, X, and XI of the GATT 1994; and • Paragraphs 5.1, 5.2, 8.2, and 11.3 of Part I of the Protocol on the Accession of the People's Republic of China (Accession Protocol), as well as China's obligations under the provisions of paragraph 1.2 of Part I of the Accession Protocol (which incorporates commitments in paragraphs 83, 84, 162, and 165 of the Report of the Working Party on the Accession of China). Mexico considers that the measures also appear to nullify or impair the benefits accruing to Mexico directly or indirectly under the cited agreements.			Kingdom of; United States
DS407	2010	N/A	China — Provisional Anti-Dumping Duties on Certain Iron and Steel Fasteners from the European Union Complaint by the European Union. On 7 May 2010, the European Union requested consultations with China regarding China's provisional Anti-Dumping duties on certain iron or steel fasteners from the European Union. The European Union alleges that Notice 115 (2009) of the Ministry of Commerce imposing the provisional anti-dumping measures in question is inconsistent with a number of provisions of the WTO Anti-Dumping Agreement and GATT 1994. The European Union also considers that Article 56 of the Chinese Anti-Dumping Regulations is inconsistent with various provisions of the Anti-Dumping Agreement, the DSU, and GATT 1994. The request notes in particular that Article 56 provides, in part, "where a country (region) discriminatorily imposes	In consultations on 7 May 2010	European Union	N/A

Case N.	RoC	Short title	Summary	Current status	Respondent	Third Parties
			Anti-Dumping measures on the exports from the People's Republic of China, China may, on the basis of actual situations, take corresponding measures against that country (region)".			
DS413	2010	China — Electronic Payment Services	China — Certain Measures Affecting Electronic Payment Services Complaint by the United States. On 15 September 2010, the United States requested consultations with China with respect to "certain restrictions and requirements maintained by China pertaining to electronic payment services for payment card transactions and the suppliers of those services". The United States alleged that China permits only a Chinese entity (China UnionPay) to supply electronic payment services for payment card transactions denominated and paid in renminbi in China. Service suppliers of other Members can only supply these services for payment card transactions paid in foreign currency. China also requires all payment card processing devices to be compatible with that entity's system, and that payment cards must bear that company's logo. It further argued that the Chinese entity has guaranteed access to all merchants in China that accept payment cards, while services suppliers of other Members must negotiate for access to merchants. The United States alleged that China appears to be acting inconsistently with its obligations under Articles XVI and XVII of the GATS.	Implementation notified by respondent on 23 July 2013	US	Australia; Ecuador; European Union; Guatemala; Japan; Korea, Republic of; India

Case N.	RoC	Short title	Summary	Current status	Respondent	Third Parties
DS414	2010	China — GOES	China — Countervailing and Anti-Dumping Duties on Grain Oriented Flat-rolled Electrical Steel from the United States Complaint by the United States. On 15 September 2010, the United States requested consultations with China with respect to measures imposing countervailing duties and Anti-Dumping duties on grain oriented flat-rolled electrical steel (GOES) from the United States as set forth in Ministry of Commerce of the People's Republic of China (MOFCOM) Notice No. 21 [2010], including its annexes. The subsidy that China determined to confer a benefit are the "Buy America" provisions of the American Recovery and Reinvestment Act of 2009 and also State government procurement laws. The United States alleged that China appears to be acting inconsistently with its obligations under: • Articles 10, 11.2, 11.3, 12.3, 12.4.1, 12.7, 12.8, 15.1, 15.2, 15.5, 19, 22.2(iii), 22.3 and 22.5 of the SCM Agreement, • Articles 1, 3.1, 3.2, 3.5, 6.9 and 12.2 of the Anti-Dumping Agreement; and • Article VI of the GATT 1994.	Report(s) adopted, with recommendation to bring measure(s) into conformity on 31 August 2015	US	Argentina; European Union; Honduras; India; Japan; Korea, Republic of; Saudi Arabia, Kingdom of; Viet Nam; Russian Federation
DS419	2010	N/A	China — Measures concerning wind power equipment Complaint by the United States	In consultations on 22 December 2010	US	N/A

Case N.	RoC	Short title	Summary	Current status	Respondent	Third Parties
			On 22 December 2010, the United States requested consultations with China concerning certain measures providing grants, funds, or awards to enterprises manufacturing wind power equipment (including the overall unit, and parts thereof) in China. The United States indicated that the measures appear to provide grants, funds, or awards that are contingent on the use of domestic over imported goods and, consequently, they appear to be inconsistent with Article 3 of the SCM Agreement. In addition, the United States considered that, as China has not notified these measures, it appears to have failed to comply with Article XVI:1 of the GATT 1994 and Article 25.1, 25.2, 25.3 and 25.4 of the SCM Agreement. The United States also alleged that, as China has not made available a translation of these measures into one or more of the official languages of the WTO, it also appears to have failed to comply with its obligation under Part I, Paragraph 1.2, of its Protocol of Accession (to the extent that it incorporates paragraph 334 of the Report of the Working Party on the Accession of China).			
DS425	2011	China — X-Ray Equipment	China — Definitive Anti-Dumping Duties on X-Ray Security Inspection Equipment from the European Union Complaint by the European Union On 25 July 2011, the European Union requested consultations with China concerning the imposition of definitive Anti-Dumping duties on x-ray security	Implementation notified by respondent on 26 February 2014	European Union	Japan; United States; Thailand; Norway; India; Chile

Case N.	RoC	Short title	Summary	Current status	Respondent	Third Parties
			inspection equipment from the European Union, pursuant to China's Ministry of Commerce Notice No. 1(2011), including its Annex. The European Union claims that the measure is inconsistent with various provisions of the Anti-Dumping Agreement related to the process of the Anti-Dumping investigation (including failure to provide access to relevant information and insufficient explanation of the basis for the determinations) as well as the anti-dumping determination at issue (absence of objective examination of the effect of the dumped imports on prices in the domestic market and absence of objective determination of causality). The European Union considers that the measure is inconsistent with Articles 2.4, 3.1, 3.2, 3.4, 3.5, 6.1, 6.2. 6.4, 6.5, 6.9, 12.2.2 of the Anti-Dumping Agreement, and Articles VI:1 and VI:6(a) of the GATT 1994.			
DS427	2011	China — Broiler Products	China — Anti-Dumping and Countervailing Duty Measures on Broiler Products from the United States Complaint by the United States. On 20 September 2011, the United States requested consultations with China concerning China's measures imposing Anti-Dumping and countervailing duties on broiler products from the United States. The United States claimed that the measures appear to be inconsistent with various provisions of the Anti-Dumping Agreement related to the process of the anti-dumping investigation as well as the Anti-Dumping duty determination at issue (including	Compliance proceedings ongoing on 22 June 2016	US	European Union; Japan; Norway; Thailand; Saudi Arabia, Kingdom of; Chile; Mexico

Case N.	RoC	Short title	Summary	Current status	Respondent	Third Parties
			improper dumping and injury determination, improper reliance on the facts available, failure to provide access to relevant information, insufficient explanation of the basis for the determinations, absence of proper analysis of the effects of imports under investigation, and absence of objective determination of causality). The United States alleges violations of Articles 1, 2.2, 3.1, 3.2, 3.4, 3.5, 4.1, 5.1, 6.2, 6.4, 6.5, 6.8, 6.9, and 12.2 of the Anti-Dumping Agreement. The United States further claimed that the measures appear to be inconsistent with various provisions of the SCM Agreement related to the process of the subsidy investigation as well as the countervailing duty determination at issue (including improper reliance on the facts available, insufficient explanation of the basis for the determinations, and imposition of countervailing duties in excess of the subsidy found to exist). The United States alleges violations of Articles 10, 11.1, 12.3, 12.4, 12.7, 12.8, 15.1, 15.2, 15.4, 15.5, 16.1, 19.4, 22.3, 22.4, and 22.5 of the SCM Agreement. The United States considered that the measures are also inconsistent with Article VI of the GATT 1994 as a consequence of the alleged violations of the Anti-Dumping Agreement and SCM Agreement.			
DS431	2012	China — Rare Earths	China — Measures Related to the Exportation of Rare Earths, Tungsten and Molybdenum Complaint by the United States. (See also DS432 and DS433)	Implementation notified by respondent on 20 May 2015	US	Brazil; Canada; Colombia; European Union; India; Japan; Korea, Republic of; Norway; Oman; Saudi Arabia, Kingdom

Case N.	RoC	Short title	Summary	Current status	Respondent	Third Parties
			On 13 March 2012, the United States requested consultations with China with respect to China's restrictions on the export of various forms of rare earths, tungsten and molybdenum. The request refers to materials falling under but not limited to 212 eight-digit Chinese Customs Commodity Codes and over 30 measures. The request also refers to a number of Chinese published as well as unpublished measures that, operating separately or collectively, allegedly impose and administer export restrictions. These restrictions include export duties, export quotas, minimum export price requirements, export licensing requirements and additional requirements and procedures in connection with the administration of the quantitative restrictions. The United States claims that these measures are inconsistent with: • Articles VII, VIII, X and XI of the GATT 1994; and • paragraphs 2(A)2, 2(C)1, 5.1, 5.2, 7.2, 8.2 and 11.3 of Part I of China's Protocol of Accession, as well as China's obligations under paragraph 1.2 of Part I of the Protocol of Accession.			of; Chinese Taipei; Viet Nam; Argentina; Australia; Indonesia; Turkey; Peru; Russian Federation
DS432	2012	China — Rare Earths	China — Measures Related to the Exportation of Rare Earths, Tungsten and Molybdenum Complaint by the European Union. (See also DS431 and DS433)	Implementation notified by respondent on 20 May 2015	European Union	Brazil; Canada; Colombia; India; Japan; Korea, Republic of; Norway; Oman; Saudi Arabia, Kingdom of; Chinese

Case N.	RoC	Short title	Summary	Current status	Respondent	Third Parties
			On 13 March 2012, the European Union requested consultations with China with respect to China's restrictions on the export of various forms of rare earths, tungsten and molybdenum. The request refers to materials falling under but not limited to 212 eight-digit Chinese Customs Commodity Codes and over 30 measures. The request also refers to a number of Chinese published as well as unpublished measures that, operating separately or collectively, allegedly impose and administer export restrictions. These restrictions include export duties, export quotas, minimum export price requirements, export licensing requirements and additional requirements and procedures in connection with the administration of the quantitative restrictions. The European Union claims that these measures are inconsistent with: • Articles VII, VIII, X and XI of the GATT 1994; and • paragraphs 2(A)2, 2(C)1, 5.1, 5.2, 7.2, 8.2 and 11.3 of Part I of China's Protocol of Accession, as well as China's obligations under paragraph 1.2 of Part I of the Protocol of Accession.			Taipei; United States; Viet Nam; Argentina; Australia; Indonesia; Turkey; Peru; Russian Federation
DS433	2012	China — Rare Earths	China — Measures Related to the Exportation of Rare Earths, Tungsten and Molybdenum Complaint by Japan. (See also DS431 and DS432) On 13 March 2012, Japan requested consultations with China with respect to China's restrictions on the	Implementation notified by respondent on 20 May 2015	Japan	Brazil; Canada; Colombia; European Union; India; Korea, Republic of; Norway; Oman; Saudi Arabia, Kingdom of; Chinese Taipei; United States;

Case N.	RoC	Short title	Summary	Current status	Respondent	Third Parties
			export of various forms of rare earths, tungsten and molybdenum. The request refers to materials falling under but not limited to 212 eight-digit Chinese Customs Commodity Codes and over 30 measures. The request also refers to a number of Chinese published as well as unpublished measures that, operating separately or collectively, allegedly impose and administer export restrictions. These restrictions include export duties, export quotas, minimum export price requirements, export licensing requirements and additional requirements and procedures in connection with the administration of the quantitative restrictions. Japan claims that these measures are inconsistent with: • Articles VII, VIII, X and XI of the GATT 1994; and • paragraphs 2(A)2, 2(C)1, 5.1, 5.2, 7.2, 8.2 and 11.3 of Part I of China's Protocol of Accession, as well as China's obligations under paragraph 1.2 of Part I of the Protocol of Accession.			Viet Nam; Argentina; Australia; Indonesia; Turkey; Peru; Russian Federation
DS440	2012	China — Autos (US)	China — Anti-Dumping and Countervailing Duties on Certain Automobiles from the United States Complaint by the United States On 5 July 2012, the United States requested consultations with China with regard to Notice No. 20 [2011] and Notice No. 84 [2011] of the	Report(s) adopted, no further action required on 18 June 2014	US	Colombia; European Union; India; Japan; Korea, Republic of; Oman; Turkey; Saudi Arabia, Kingdom of

Case N.	RoC	Short title	Summary	Current status	Respondent	Third Parties
			Ministry of Commerce of the People's Republic of China (MOFCOM) imposing Anti-Dumping and countervailing duties on certain automobiles from the United States, including any and all annexes. The United States alleges that these measures appear to be inconsistent with: • Articles 1, 3.1, 3.2, 3.4, 3.5, 4.1, 5.3, 5.4, 6.2, 6.5.1, 6.8 (including Annex II, paragraph 1), 6.9, 12.2, and 12.2.2 of the Anti-Dumping Agreement; • Articles 10, 11.3, 11.4, 12.4.1, 12.7, 12.8, 15.1, 15.2, 15.4, 15.5, 16.1 22.3, and 22.5 of the SCM Agreement; and • Article VI of the GATT 1994.			
DS450	2012	N/A	China — Certain Measures Affecting the Automobile and Automobile-Parts Industries Complaint by the United States. On 17 September 2012, the United States requested consultations with China concerning certain measures providing subsidies in the form of grants, loans, forgone government revenue, the provision of goods and services, and other incentives contingent upon export performance to automobile and automobile-parts enterprises in China. The United States claims that the measures appear to be inconsistent with:	In consultations on 17 September 2012	US	N/A

Case N.	RoC	Short title	Summary	Current status	Respondent	Third Parties
			• Articles 3, 25.1, 25.2, 25.3 and 25.4 of the SCM Agreement; • Article XVI:1 of the GATT 1994; and • Paragraphs 1.2, 2(C)(1) and 2(C)(2) of Part I of China's Accession Protocol.			
DS451	2012	N/A	China — Measures Relating to the Production and Exportation of Apparel and Textile Products Complaint by Mexico. On 15 October 2012, Mexico requested consultations with China concerning measures that allegedly support producers and exporters of apparel and textile products. Mexico claims that China maintains a wide variety of measures that support producers and exporters of apparel and textile products, as well as suppliers in the cotton and chemical fibres industries. Measures cited include tax exemptions for certain enterprises, reduction of import duties and VAT for purchase of equipment by certain groups of enterprises and those located in certain regions, measures contingent on use of Chinese goods and contingent on export performance, low cost loans by state-owned banks to certain industries, preferential land use rights, discounted electricity rates, support for production, sale and transportation provided to cotton farmers and the Chinese petrochemical industry, and cash payments from government	In consultations on 15 October 2012	Mexico	N/A

Case N.	RoC	Short title	Summary	Current status	Respondent	Third Parties
			agencies. According to Mexico, these measures appear to involve both prohibited and actionable subsidies that are causing or threatening to cause serious prejudice through displacement and impedance of Mexican exports to the United States as well as through significant price undercutting, price suppression, price depression, and lost sales in the United States. Mexico claims that these measures are inconsistent with: • Articles 3.1(a) and (b), 5(c), 6.3(b) and (c), 6.4, and 6.5 of the SCM Agreement; • Article III:4 of the GATT 1994; • Articles 3, 9 and 10 of the Agreement on Agriculture; and • Paragraph 1.2 of Part I of China's Accession Protocol.			
DS454	2012	China — HP-SSST (Japan)	China — Measures Imposing Anti-Dumping Duties on High-Performance Stainless Steel Seamless Tubes (HP-SSST) from Japan Complaint by Japan. (See also DS460) On 20 December 2012, Japan requested consultations with China concerning measures imposing Anti-Dumping duties on high-performance stainless steel seamless tubes (HP-SSST) from Japan, as set forth in Ministry of Commerce of the People's Republic of China (MOFCOM) Notice No. 21 [2012] and Notice No. 72 [2012], including any	Report(s) adopted, with recommendation to bring measure(s) into conformity on 28 October 2015	Japan	European Union; India; Korea, Republic of; Russian Federation; United States; Turkey; Saudi Arabia, Kingdom of

Case N.	RoC	Short title	Summary	Current status	Respondent	Third Parties
			and all annexes and any amendments thereof. Japan claims that the measures are inconsistent with: • Articles 1, 3.1, 3.2, 3.4, 3.5, 5.3, 5.8, 6.5, 6.5.1, 6.8, 6.9, 7.4, 12.2 and 12.2.2 of the Anti-Dumping Agreement; and • Article VI of the GATT 1994.			
DS460	2012	China — HP-SSST (EU)	China — Measures Imposing Anti-Dumping Duties on High-Performance Stainless Steel Seamless Tubes (HP-SSST) from the European Union Complaint by the European Union. (See also DS454) On 13 June 2013, the European Union requested consultations with China concerning measures imposing Anti-Dumping duties on certain high-performance stainless steel seamless tubes (HP-SSST) from the European Union, as set forth in Ministry of Commerce of the People's Republic of China (MOFCOM) Notice No. 21 [2012] and Notice No. 72 [2012], including any and all annexes and any amendments thereof. The European Union claims that the measures are inconsistent with: • Articles 1, 2.2, 2.4, 2.4.2, 3.1, 3.2, 3.4, 3.5, 6.4, 6.5, 6.5.1, 6.7, 6.8, 6.9, 7.4, 12.2 and 12.2.2 of the Anti-Dumping Agreement; and • Article VI of the GATT 1994.	Report(s) adopted, with recommendation to bring measure(s) into conformity on 28 October 2015	European Union	Japan; Korea, Republic of; India; Turkey; United States

Case N.	RoC	Short title	Summary	Current status	Respondent	Third Parties
DS483	2014	China — Cellulose Pulp	China — Anti-Dumping Measures on Imports of Cellulose Pulp from Canada Complaint by Canada. On 15 October 2014, Canada requested consultations with China with respect to China's measures imposing Anti-Dumping duties on imports of cellulose pulp from Canada, as set forth in the Ministry of Commerce of China Notice No. 75 of 2013 (6 November 2013), including its annex (the Preliminary Determination), and Notice No. 18 of 2014 (4 April 2014), including its annex (the Final Determination). Canada claims that the measures are inconsistent with: • Articles 1, 2.1, 2.2, 2.2.1.1, 2.2.2, 2.4, 3.1, 3.2, 3.4, 3.5, 4.1, 6.1, 6.2, 6.8, 6.9, 6.10, 6.10.2, 8.1, 8.3, 9.4, 12.2 and 12.2.2, and Annex II of the Anti-Dumping Agreement; and • Article VI of the GATT 1994.	Panel composed on 27 April 2015	Canada	European Union; Chile; Japan; Korea, Republic of; Norway; United States; Brazil; Singapore; Uruguay
DS489	2015	China — Demonstration Bases	China — Measures Related to Demonstration Bases and common Service Platforms Programmes Complaint by the United States. On 11 February 2015, the United States requested consultations with China with regard to certain measures providing subsidies contingent upon export performance to enterprises in several industries in China.	Panel established, but not yet composed on 22 April 2015	US	European Union; Australia; Canada; India; Korea, Republic of; Brazil; Japan; Russian Federation; Colombia; Singapore; Chinese Taipei; Saudi Arabia, Kingdom of; Dominican Republic

Case N.	RoC	Short title	Summary	Current status	Respondent	Third Parties
			The United States claims that the measures are inconsistent with Articles 3.1(a) and 3.2 of the SCM Agreement.			
DS501	2015	N/A	China — Tax Measures Concerning Certain Domestically Produced Aircraft Complaint by the United States On 8 December 2015, the United States requested consultations with China regarding tax measures in relation to the sale of certain domestically produced aircraft in China. The United States claims that the measures are inconsistent with: • Articles III:2, III:4 and X:1 of the GATT 1994; and • Paragraphs 2(C)(1) and 2(C)2 of Part I of China's Protocol of Accession, as well as paragraph 1.2 of the Accession Protocol (to the extent that it incorporates paragraph 334 of the Report of the Working Party on the Accession of China).	In consultations on 8 December 2015	US	N/A
DS508	2016		China — Export Duties on Certain Raw Materials Complaint by the United States On 13 July 2016, the United States requested consultations with China regarding China's export duties on various forms of antimony, cobalt, copper, graphite, lead, magnesia, talc, tantalum, and tin. The United States claims that the measures appear	Panel established, but not yet composed on 8 November 2016	US	Brazil; Canada; European Union; India; Indonesia; Japan; Kazakhstan; Korea, Republic of; Mexico; Norway; Russian Federation; Singapore; Chinese Taipei; Viet Nam

Case N.	RoC	Short title	Summary	Current status	Respondent	Third Parties
			to be inconsistent with: • Paragraph 11.3 of Part I of China's Accession Protocol. The United States also considers that the measures appear to nullify or impair the benefits accruing to the United States directly or indirectly under China's Accession Protocol. On 19 July 2016, the United States requested supplementary consultations concerning alleged restrictions on the export of various forms of antimony, chromium, indium, magnesia, talc, and tin. The United States claims that the alleged restrictions appear to be inconsistent with Paragraphs 2(A)(2), 5.1, 11.3 of Part I of China's Accession Protocol, as well as paragraph 1.2 of the Accession Protocol (to the extent that it incorporates paragraphs 83, 84, 162 and 165 of the Report of the Working Party on the Accession of China), and Articles X:3(a) and XI:1 of the GATT 1994. The United States also considered that the alleged restrictions appear to nullify or impair the benefits accruing to the United States directly or indirectly under the cited agreements.			
DS509	2016	China — Raw Materials II (EU)	China — Duties and other Measures concerning the Exportation of Certain Raw Materials Complaint by the European Union On 19 July 2016, the European Union requested consultations with China regarding China's duties	Panel established, but not yet composed on 23 November 2016	European Union	Brazil; Canada; Chile; Colombia; India; Indonesia; Japan; Korea, Republic of; Mexico; Oman; Chinese Taipei; Viet Nam; United States;

Case N.	RoC	Short title	Summary	Current status	Respondent	Third Parties
			and other alleged restrictions on the export of various forms of antimony, chromium, cobalt, copper, graphite, indium, lead, magnesia, talc, tantalum and tin. The European Union claims that the measures appear to be inconsistent with: • Paragraphs 2(A)(2), 5.1, 5.2 and 11.3 of Part I of China's Accession Protocol, as well as paragraph 1.2 of the Accession Protocol (to the extent that it incorporates paragraphs 83, 84, 162 and 165 of the Report of the Working Party on the Accession of China); and • Articles X:3(a) and XI:1 of the GATT 1994. The European Union also considers that the measures also appear to nullify or impair the benefits accruing to the European Union directly or indirectly under the cited agreements.			Russian Federation; Norway; Kazakhstan; Singapore
DS511	2016	N/A	China — Domestic Support for Agricultural Producers Complaint by the United States On 13 September 2016, the United States requested consultations with China regarding certain measures through which China appears to provide domestic support in favour of agricultural producers, in particular, to those producing wheat, India rice, Japonica rice and corn. The United States claimed that the measures appear	Panel established, but not yet composed on 25 January 2017	US	Australia; Brazil; Canada; Colombia; Egypt; El Salvador; European Union; Guatemala; India; Indonesia; Israel; Japan; Kazakhstan; Korea, Republic of; Norway; Pakistan; Paraguay; Philippines; Russian Federation; Saudi Arabia, Kingdom

Case N.	RoC	Short title	Summary	Current status	Respondent	Third Parties
			to be inconsistent with: • Articles 3.2, 6.3 and 7.2(b) of the Agreement on Agriculture.			of; Singapore; Chinese Taipei; Thailand; Turkey; Ukraine; Viet Nam
DS517	2016	N/A	China — Tariff Rate Quotas for Certain Agricultural Products Complaint by the United States On 15 December 2016, the United States requested consultations with China concerning China's administration of its tariff rate quotas, including those for wheat, short- and medium-grain rice, long grain rice, and corn. The United States claimed that the measures appear to be inconsistent with: • Articles X:3(a), XI:1 and XIII:3(b) of the GATT 1994; and • Paragraph 1.2 of Part I of China's Protocol of Accession (to the extent that it incorporates paragraph 116 of the Report of the Working Party on the Accession of China).	In consultations on 15 December 2016	US	N/A
DS519	2017	N/A	China — Subsidies to Producers of Primary Aluminium Complaint by the United States On 12 January 2017, the United States requested	In consultations on 12 January 2017	US	N/A

Case N.	RoC	Short title	Summary	Current status	Respondent	Third Parties
			consultations with China concerning alleged subsidies that China provides to its producers of primary aluminium. The United States claimed that the measures appear to be inconsistent with: • Articles 5(c), 6.3(a), 6.3(b), 6.3(c) and 6.3(d) of the SCM Agreement; and • Article XVI:1 of the GATT 1994.			

Sourse:
DS309: https://www.wto.org/english/tratop_e/dispu_e/cases_e/ds309_e.htm
DS339: https://www.wto.org/english/tratop_e/dispu_e/cases_e/ds339_e.htm
DS340: https://www.wto.org/english/tratop_e/dispu_e/cases_e/ds340_e.htm
DS342: https://www.wto.org/english/tratop_e/dispu_e/cases_e/ds342_e.htm
DS358: https://www.wto.org/english/tratop_e/dispu_e/cases_e/ds358_e.htm
DS359: https://www.wto.org/english/tratop_e/dispu_e/cases_e/ds359_e.htm
DS372: https://www.wto.org/english/tratop_e/dispu_e/cases_e/ds372_e.htm
DS373: https://www.wto.org/english/tratop_e/dispu_e/cases_e/ds373_e.htm
DS378: https://www.wto.org/english/tratop_e/dispu_e/cases_e/ds378_e.htm
DS387: https://www.wto.org/english/tratop_e/dispu_e/cases_e/ds387_e.htm
DS388: https://www.wto.org/english/tratop_e/dispu_e/cases_e/ds388_e.htm
DS390: https://www.wto.org/english/tratop_e/dispu_e/cases_e/ds390_e.htm
DS394: https://www.wto.org/english/tratop_e/dispu_e/cases_e/ds394_e.htm
DS395: https://www.wto.org/english/tratop_e/dispu_e/cases_e/ds395_e.htm
DS398: https://www.wto.org/english/tratop_e/dispu_e/cases_e/ds398_e.htm
DS407: https://www.wto.org/english/tratop_e/dispu_e/cases_e/ds407_e.htm
DS413: https://www.wto.org/english/tratop_e/dispu_e/cases_e/ds413_e.htm
DS414: https://www.wto.org/english/tratop_e/dispu_e/cases_e/ds414_e.htm
DS419: https://www.wto.org/english/tratop_e/dispu_e/cases_e/ds419_e.htm
DS425: https://www.wto.org/english/tratop_e/dispu_e/cases_e/ds425_e.htm

DS427: https://www.wto.org/english/tratop_e/dispu_e/cases_e/ds427_e.htm
DS431: https://www.wto.org/english/tratop_e/dispu_e/cases_e/ds431_e.htm
DS432: https://www.wto.org/english/tratop_e/dispu_e/cases_e/ds432_e.htm
DS433: https://www.wto.org/english/tratop_e/dispu_e/cases_e/ds433_e.htm
DS440: https://www.wto.org/english/tratop_e/dispu_e/cases_e/ds440_e.htm
DS450: https://www.wto.org/english/tratop_e/dispu_e/cases_e/ds450_e.htm
DS451: https://www.wto.org/english/tratop_e/dispu_e/cases_e/ds451_e.htm
DS454: https://www.wto.org/english/tratop_e/dispu_e/cases_e/ds454_e.htm
DS460: https://www.wto.org/english/tratop_e/dispu_e/cases_e/ds460_e.htm
DS483: https://www.wto.org/english/tratop_e/dispu_e/cases_e/ds483_e.htm
DS489: https://www.wto.org/english/tratop_e/dispu_e/cases_e/ds489_e.htm
DS508: https://www.wto.org/english/tratop_e/dispu_e/cases_e/ds508_e.htm
DS509: https://www.wto.org/english/tratop_e/dispu_e/cases_e/ds509_e.htm
DS511: https://www.wto.org/english/tratop_e/dispu_e/cases_e/ds511_e.htm
DS517: https://www.wto.org/english/tratop_e/dispu_e/cases_e/ds517_e.htm
DS519: https://www.wto.org/english/tratop_e/dispu_e/cases_e/ds519_e.htm

Index

A

B

C

D

U

V

W

About the Author

Jaemin Lee is currently Professor of Law at School of Law, Seoul National University in Seoul, Korea. He obtained his LL.B., LL.M. and Ph.D. from Seoul National University; LL.M. from Georgetown University Law Center; and J.D. from Boston College Law School. His major areas of teaching and research are public international law, international economic law and international dispute settlement. Upon graduation from College of Law, Seoul National University in 1992, he joined the Korean Ministry of Foreign Affairs as a foreign service officer. His post in the ministry included deputy directorship of the Treaties Division and the North American Trade Division. Between 2000 and 2004, he also practiced law with Willkie Farr & Gallagher LLP (Washington, D.C. office) as an associate attorney of the firm's international trade group. From 2004 to 2013 he taught international law and international economic law at School of Law, Hanyang University in Seoul, Korea. He has published articles and books (including book chapters) on various topics of public international law, international trade law, international investment law, and trade policy. He regularly writes for Korean newspapers for matters of international law, and contributes columns to Straits Times of Singapore and South China Morning Post of Hong Kong. Since 2012, he has been participating in UNCITRAL Working Groups II and III as delegate of the Republic of Korea. He can be reached at 82-2-880-7572 (office) or via e-mail at jaemin@snu.ac.kr.